Second Edition

MARKETING MANAGEMENT

A RELATIONSHIP APPROACH

Svend Hollensen

**Financial Times
Prentice Hall**
is an imprint of

PEARSON

Harlow, England • London • New York • Boston • San Francisco • Toronto • Sydney • Singapore • Hong Kong
Tokyo • Seoul • Taipei • New Delhi • Cape Town • Madrid • Mexico City • Amsterdam • Munich • Paris • Milan

Pearson Education Limited
Edinburgh Gate
Harlow
Essex CM20 2JE
England

and Associated Companies throughout the world

Visit us on the World Wide Web at:
www.pearsoned.co.uk

First published 2003
Second Edition 2010

ISBN 978-0-273-70683-0

British Library Cataloguing-in-Publication Data
A catalogue record for this book is available from the British Library

Library of Congress Cataloging-in-Publication Data
Hollensen, Svend.
  Marketing management : a relationship approach / Svend Hollensen. – 2nd ed.
      p. cm.
  ISBN 978-0-273-70683-0 (pbk.)
  1. Relationship marketing. 2. Marketing–Management. 3. Relationship marketing–Case studies.
I. Title.
  HF5415.55.H65 2010
  658.8–dc22   2009050104

ARP impression 98

Typeset in 10/12 Minion by 73
Printed and bound in Great Britain by Ashford Colour Press Ltd.

BRIEF CONTENTS

BPP Professional Education
32-34 Colmore Circus
Birmingham B4 6BN
Phone: 0121 345 9843

MARKETING
MANAGEMENT

Visit the *Marketing Management, A Relationship Approach*,
Second Edition, Companion Website at **www.pearsoned.co.uk/
hollensen** to find valuable **student** learning material including:

- Full versions of the video case studies at the start of each
  part opener
- Multiple choice questions to test your learning
- Weblinks

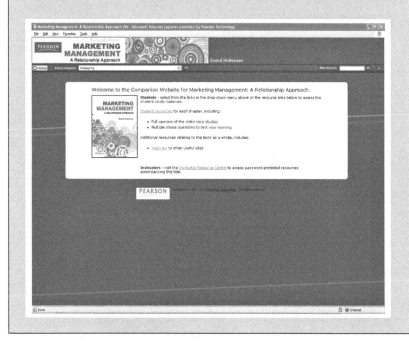

PEARSON

We work with leading authors to develop the
strongest educational materials in marketing
bringing cutting-edge thinking and best learning
practice to a global market.

Under a range of well-known imprints, including
Financial Times Prentice Hall, we craft high-quality
print and electronic publications which help readers to
understand and apply their content, whether studying
or at work.

To find out more about the complete range of our
publishing, please visit us on the World Wide Web at:
www.pearsoned.co.uk.

CONTENTS

Supporting resources

Visit **www.pearsoned.co.uk/hollensen** to find valuable online resources:

For students
- Full versions of the video case studies at the start of each part opener
- Multiple choice questions to test your learning
- Weblinks

For instructors
- A complete, downloadable Instructor's Manual
- PowerPoint slides that can be downloaded and used for presentations
- Extra online case material

For more information please contact your local Pearson Education sales representative or visit **www.pearsoned.co.uk/hollensen**.

GUIDED TOUR

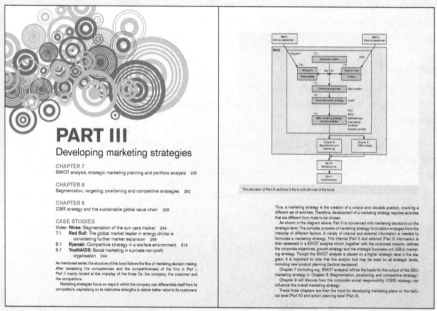

Each **Part Introduction** lists the chapters and case studies within the part and gives an overview of the topics covered. It also includes a structure map that allows you to get a clearer picture of how the part is set out and how it relates to the other sections in the book.

Following each part introduction, you will find a **Video Case Study** from a leading international company. Read the case study, watch the video, which is available on the Companion Website at: www.pearsoned.co.uk/hollensen, and then answer the questions.

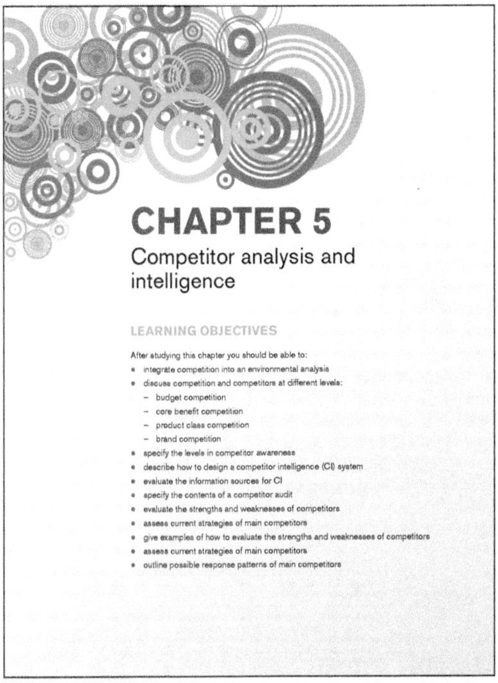

CHAPTER 5

Competitor analysis and intelligence

LEARNING OBJECTIVES

After studying this chapter you should be able to:

- integrate competition into an environmental analysis
- discuss competition and competitors at different levels:
  - budget competition
  - core benefit competition
  - product class competition
  - brand competition
- specify the levels in competitor awareness
- describe how to design a competitor intelligence (CI) system
- evaluate the information sources for CI
- specify the contents of a competitor audit
- evaluate the strengths and weaknesses of competitors
- assess current strategies of main competitors
- give examples of how to evaluate the strengths and weaknesses of competitors
- assess current strategies of main competitors
- outline possible response patterns of main competitors

156 PART II ASSESSING THE EXTERNAL MARKETING SITUATION

5.1 INTRODUCTION

Competitive intelligence Gathering, analysing and distributing information about products, customers, competitors and any aspect of the environment needed to support executives and managers in making strategic marketing decisions for an organization.

Competitor intelligence (CI) The process of identifying key competitors; assessing their objectives, strategies, strengths and weaknesses, and reaction patterns and selecting which competitors to attack or avoid. The analysis provides both an offensive and defensive strategic context through which to identify opportunities and threats.

Most often **competitive intelligence** is used to mean the action of gathering analysing and distributing information about products, customers, competitors and any aspect of the environment needed to support executives and managers in making strategic marketing decisions for an organisation. **Competitor intelligence (CI)** is a more narrow term, as it only focuses on the competitor aspect.

Except for a minor section dealing with interaction between competitors (section 5.3) this chapter is mainly about how to analyse competitors, their behaviour and their strategies. A more comprehensive analysis of competitor relationships is given in Chapter 6 (section 6.6).

Competitor intelligence is the publicly available information and other types of information on competitors, current and potential, that is an important input in formulating a marketing strategy. Managers at all levels in organisations should conduct competitive intelligence scanning to monitor market variables that are continuously shifting. To sustain competitive position, managers must prepare to respond quickly to changes in customer preferences, competitor strategies and technological advancements (Qiu, 2008; Dishman and Calof, 2008).

However, no general would order an army to march without first fully knowing the enemy's position and intentions. Similarly, before deciding which competitive moves to make, a firm must be aware of the perspectives of its competitors. CI includes information beyond industry statistics and trade gossip. It involves the close observation of competitors to learn what they do best and why and where they are weak.

In most Western countries the development has resulted in a major intensification of competitor intelligence. The reasons for increasing CI are:

- increasing competition between companies;
- deregulation;
- liberalisation;
- globalisation;
- periods of economic recession;
- reduced product and service differentiation.

Factors inhibiting the growth of CI include:

- data protection;
- different legislation from country to country;
- fear that competitive intelligence is unethical;
- fear of counter-intelligence;
- failure of competitive strategies to yield the expected gain.

The use of CI is increasing gradually. There is growing awareness of the need to have a competitor strategy, which is every bit as important as the customer strategies that are already commonplace (West, 1999).

In terms of their use of CI, companies seem to go through a series of stages (see Figure 5.1). At the first stage is competitor awareness. This stage is entered soon after a company is formed, or even before, when the start-up is being planned. Being competitor aware means that the key competitors are known and that there is some knowledge – usually incomplete and certainly unverified – about their products, their prices, the clients they have succeeded in winning business from, the market sectors they service and the staff they employ.

The organisation that is competitor aware rarely uses the data that it holds other than for occasional ad hoc tactical exercises, such as competitive pricing decisions, or as an input to a business plan that has to be submitted to an external organisation, such as a bank.

Each chapter begins with a set of **Learning Objectives** that will enable you to focus on what you should have achieved by the end of the chapter.

Short **Chapter Introductions** concisely introduce the themes and issues that are built upon within the chapter.

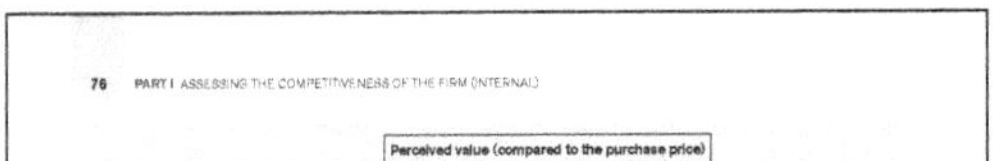

76 PART I ASSESSING THE COMPETITIVENESS OF THE FIRM (INTERNAL)

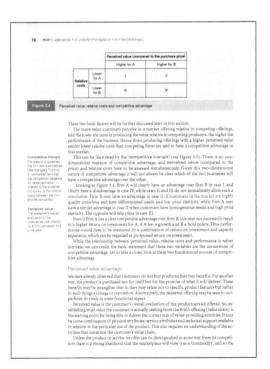

		Perceived value (compared to the purchase price)	
		Higher for A	Higher for B
Relative costs	Lower for A	I	II
	Lower for B	III	IV

Figure 3.4 Perceived value, relative costs and competitive advantage

Competitive triangle Consists of a customer, the firm and a competitor (the 'triangle'). The firm or competitor 'winning' the competition depends on perceived value offered to the customer compared to the relative costs between the firm and the competitor.

Perceived value The customer's overall evaluation of the product/service offered by a firm, compared to a price paid.

These two basic factors will be further discussed later in this section.

The more value customers perceive in a market offering relative to competing offerings, and the lower the costs in producing the value relative to competing producers, the higher the performance of the business. Hence firms producing offerings with a higher perceived value and/or lower relative costs than competing firms are said to have a competitive advantage in that market.

This can be illustrated by the '**competitive triangle**' (see Figure 3.3). There is no one-dimensional measure of competitive advantage, and **perceived value** (compared to the price) and relative costs have to be assessed simultaneously. Given this two-dimensional nature of competitive advantage it will not always be clear which of the two businesses will have a competitive advantage over the other.

Looking at Figure 3.4, firm A will clearly have an advantage over firm B in case I, and clearly have a disadvantage in case IV, while cases II and III do not immediately allow such a conclusion. Firm B may have an advantage in case II, if customers in the market are highly quality conscious and have differentiated needs and low price elasticity, while firm A may have a similar advantage in case II when customers have homogeneous needs and high price elasticity. The opposite will take place in case III.

Even if firm A has a clear competitive advantage over firm B, this may not necessarily result in a higher return on investment for A, if A has a growth and B a hold policy. Thus performance would have to be measured by a combination of return on investment and capacity expansion, which can be regarded as postponed return on investment.

While the relationship between perceived value, relative costs and performance is rather intricate, we can retain the basic statement that these two variables are the cornerstone of competitive advantage. Let us take a closer look at these two fundamental sources of competitive advantage.

Perceived value advantage

We have already observed that customers do not buy products; they buy benefits. Put another way, the product is purchased not for itself but for the promise of what it will 'deliver'. These benefits may be intangible; that is, they may relate not to specific product features but rather to such things as image or reputation. Alternatively, the delivered offering may be seen to outperform its rivals in some functional aspect.

Perceived value is the customer's overall evaluation of the product/service offered. So, establishing what value the customer is actually seeking from the firm's offering (value chain) is the starting point for being able to deliver the correct mix of value-providing activities. It may be some combination of physical attributes, service attributes and technical support available in relation to the particular use of the product. This also requires an understanding of the activities that constitute the customer's value chain.

Unless the product or service we offer can be distinguished in some way from its competitors there is a strong likelihood that the marketplace will view it as a 'commodity', and so the

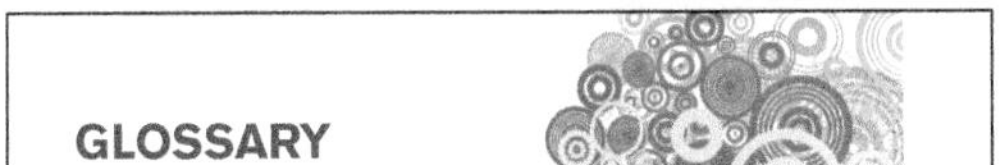

GLOSSARY

4 Ps The basic elements of the marketing mix: product, place (distribution), price and promotion; also called the controllable variables of marketing, because they can be controlled and manipulated by the marketer.

above-the-line advertising Advertising in the mass media, including press, radio, television and posters.

adoption process The mental and behavioural stages through which a consumer passes before making a purchase or placing an order. The stages are awareness, interest, evaluation, trial and adoption.

advertising Non-personal communication that is paid for by an identified sponsor, and involves either mass communication via newspapers, magazines, radio, television, and other media (e.g. billboards, bus stop signage) or direct-to-consumer communication via direct mail.

advertising agency A marketing services firm that assists companies in planning, preparing, implementing and evaluating all or portions of their advertising programmes.

advertising objective A specific communication task to be accomplished with a specific target audience during a specific period of time.

affordable approach Setting the promotion budget at the level management thinks the company can afford.

agent A marketing intermediary who does not take title to the products but develops a marketing strategy and establishes contacts abroad.

AIDA Awareness, interest, desire, action – the stages through which a consumer is believed to pass before purchasing a product.

allowance Promotional money paid by manufacturers to retailers in return for an agreement to feature the manufacturer's products in some way.

always-a-share customers Customers who have low switching costs and do not value long-term relationships with suppliers, making them more suited to transaction marketing.

baby boom The major increase in the annual birth rate following the Second World War and lasting until the early 1960s. The 'baby boomers', now moving into middle age, are a prime target for marketers.

below-the-line promotion Point-of-sale material, direct mail, exhibitions, i.e. any promotion which does not involve paid-for media channels.

benchmarking The process of comparing the company's products and processes to those of competitors or leading firms in other industries to find ways to improve quality and performance.

benefit segments Dividing the market into groups according to the different benefits that consumers seek from the product.

blue oceans The unserved market, where competitors are not yet structured and the market is relatively unknown. Here it is about avoiding head-to-head competition. See also *red oceans*.

bottom-up method A sales forecasting method that starts with small-scale estimates (e.g. product estimates) and works up to larger-scale ones. See also *top-down method*.

brand An identifying feature that distinguishes one product from another; more specifically, any name, term, symbol, sign or design, or a unifying combination of these.

brand equity The value of a brand, based on the extent to which it has high brand loyalty, name awareness, perceived quality, strong brand associations and other assets such as patents, trademarks and channel relationships.

brand extension Using a successful brand name to launch a new or modified product in a new category.

break-even analysis The calculation of the quantity needed to be sold to cover total costs.

break-even pricing Setting price to break even on the costs of making and marketing a product; or setting price to make a target profit.

bricks and mortar Physical retail stores.

broker A wholesaler who does not take title to goods and whose function is to bring buyers and sellers together and assist in negotiation.

business cycle Recurrent fluctuations in general economic activity. The four phases of the business cycle are prosperity, recession, depression and recovery.

business model The fundamental strategy underlying the way a business unit operates.

business-to-business (B2B) Marketing which involves exchange relationships between two or more business customers and suppliers.

business-to-consumer (B2C) Marketing which involves exchange relationships between a firm and its end customers, perhaps via retailers.

Key Terms are highlighted in the text with a brief explanation in the margin where they first appear. These terms are also included in the **Glossary** at the end of the book.

New and engaging **Exhibits** analyse and discuss specific companies to show how the theories in the chapter are used by well known brands in the business world.

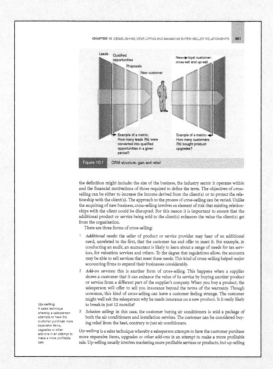

Colour **figures** and **photos** illustrate the key points and concepts and help clarify the topics discussed.

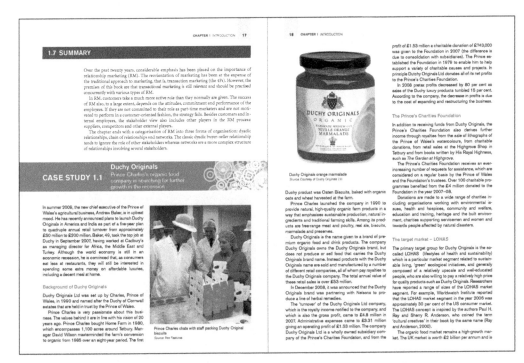

A **Case Study** concludes each chapter, providing a range of material for seminars and private study, by illustrating real-life applications and implications of the topics covered in the chapter. These also come with a set of questions to help you test your understanding of the case.

Chapter Summaries reflect on what the chapter has covered and will help you to consolidate your learning and provide an important revision tool.

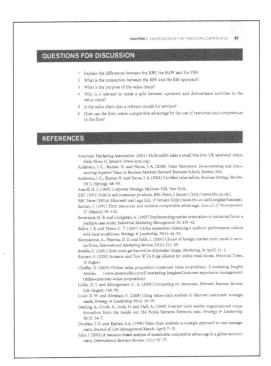

Questions for Discussion provide a useful assessment to test your knowledge and encourage you to review and/or critically discuss your understanding of the main topics and issues covered in each chapter.

An extensive list of **References** at the end of each chapter directs you to other books, journal articles and websites, which will help you develop your understanding and inspire independent learning.

PREFACE

The World Is Flat. This was the title of an international bestselling book by Thomas L. Friedman, published in first edition in 2005. It analyses globalisation, primarily in the early twenty-first century, and the picture has changed dramatically. The title is a metaphor for viewing the world as a level playing field in terms of commerce, where all players and competitors have an equal opportunity. We are entering a new phase of globalisation, in which there will be no single geographic centre, no ultimate model for success, no surefire strategy for innovation and growth. Companies from every part of the world will be competing – for customers, resources, talent and intellectual capital – with each other in every corner of the world's markets. Products and services will flow from many locations to many destinations. Friedman mentions that many companies in, for example, the Ukraine, India and China provide human-based sub-supplies for multinational companies, from typists and call centres to accountants and computer programmers. In this way these companies in emerging and developing countries are becoming integral parts of complex global supply chains for large multinational companies such as Dell, SAP, IBM and Microsoft.

As this new scene unfolds, the new global leaders will increasingly be forced to defend the ground they thought they had won and secured long ago. And their expansion into new markets will be challenged as never before. Their established processes and traditional business philosophies will be turned upside down by challengers whose experiences in new emerging markets cause them to see the world very differently and to do business in completely new ways. Many executives of developed-country companies are not prepared to deal with the massive wave of competition from skilled and determined new rivals.

As the world is becoming a flat playing field, there is also an increasing need in different industry supply chains for creating relationships between the involved companies in the industry value chains. This has important implications for the way that we look at the marketing discipline in the individual firm. The consequence is that the development of marketing theory and practice is undergoing a paradigm shift from a transactional to a relationship orientation. As many companies are still relying on the traditional marketing approach, this book will bridge the gap between **relationship marketing (RM)** and **traditional (transactional) marketing (TM)**.

In the traditional transactional approach, **marketing management** is about planning, coordinating and controlling marketing activities that are aimed at satisfying customer needs and desires – and receiving money from sales.

In recent years, marketing has been undergoing considerable self-examination and internal debate. The overriding emphasis in the 'traditional' marketing approach is on acquiring as many customers as possible. Evidence is mounting, however, that traditional marketing is becoming too expensive and is less effective.

Many leading marketing academics and practitioners have concluded that many of the long-standing practices and operating modes in marketing need to be evaluated, and we need to move towards a relationship approach that is based on repeated market transactions and mutual gain for buyers and sellers.

The 'new paradigm' is commonly referred to as relationship marketing (RM). Relationship marketing is not a new idea. Before the advent of mass production and mass media, relationship marketing was the norm; sellers usually had first-hand knowledge of buyers, and the successful ones used this knowledge to help keep customers for life.

Relationship marketing (RM)
The process of creating, maintaining and enhancing strong long-term relationships with customers and other stakeholders through mutual exchange and trust. RM seeks to build a chain of relationships between the firm and its main stakeholders.

Transactional marketing (TM)
The major focus of the marketing programme (the 4 Ps) is to make customers buy. Independence among marketing actors ('arm's length') is considered vital for marketing efficiency.

Marketing management
The process of planning, executing and controlling marketing activities to attain marketing goals and objectives effectively and efficiently.

Relationship marketing reflects a strategy and process that integrate customers, suppliers and other partners into the company's design, development, manufacturing and sales processes.

Fundamentally, relationship marketing draws from traditional marketing principles. Marketing can be defined as the process of identifying and satisfying customers' needs in a competitively superior manner in order to achieve the organisation's objectives. Relationship marketing builds on this.

The customer is still fundamental to a marketing relationship. Marketing exists to efficiently meet the satisfaction of customer needs, as well as those of the marketing organisation. There is a considerable body of knowledge in social sciences that sheds light on the many facets of human relationships. We draw from these sources to further our understanding of consumer relationships.

Marketing exchange seeks to achieve satisfaction for the consumer and the marketing organisation (or company). In this latter group we include employees, shareholders and managers. Other stakeholders (such as competitors, financial and governmental institutions) are also important. As we shall see later, relationships can cover a wide range of organisations in the environment, for example:

- governmental institutions
- industry associations
- European Union (EU) institutions
- religious groups.

However, the main focus of this book is still on the relationships between the firm and its closest external bodies, primarily the customers.

In the transactional approach, participants focus exclusively on the economic benefits of the exchange. Even though in relational exchange the focus widens, economic benefits remain important to all of the partners in marketing relationships.

With the relationship approach in mind, an integrated view of marketing management will be presented. To do this, the latest research findings in marketing management and related disciplines are summarised. Yet, marketing management is still a very practical discipline. People still have practical needs, firms still face practical problems, and solutions still have to work in real life. Most marketers cannot and should not hide in labs. Marketing is a social science based on theories and concepts, but it also requires that most marketers meet with people, observe them, talk to them, and understand their activities. In essence, marketing is a dialogue between sellers (marketers) and buyers (customers). This book reflects this applied approach. Together with important concepts and theories, my experience that has been obtained through work for many years with numerous companies – large and small, domestic and international – will be drawn on.

TARGET AUDIENCE

This book is written for people who want to know how the relationship and the traditional marketing approach (in combination) affect the development of effective and efficient marketing plans. This book is aimed primarily at students, MBA/graduate students and advanced undergraduates who wish to go into business. It will provide the information, perspectives and tools necessary to get the job done. My aim is to enable you to make better marketing decisions.

A second audience for this book is the large group of practitioners who want to build on the existing skills and knowledge already possessed. The book is of special interest to the manager who wishes to keep abreast of the most recent developments in the 'marketing management' field.

UNIQUE FEATURES OF THIS BOOK

This marketing text tries to integrate the 'new' relationship approach in the traditional process of developing effective marketing plans. Compared to other marketing management books this text will attach more importance to the following themes.

Buyer–seller relationships

The guiding principle of this textbook is that of building relationships between buyers and sellers. Relationships is a growing trend and for good reason. Dramatic changes in the marketing environment are presenting immense new opportunities for companies that really build and retain relationships with customers. Relationship marketing emphasises the tremendous importance of satisfied, loyal customers. Good customer relationships happen when all employees within the organisation develop the sensitivity and desire to satisfy customers' needs and wants. It may be argued that the traditional concept of marketing (as exemplified later in Chapter 1) does not adequately reflect the recognition of the long-term value of a customer. The argument is that many of the traditional definitions of marketing, although stressing the importance of customer needs and satisfaction, are essentially concerned with maximising the profitability of each transaction. Instead they should seek to develop long-term relationships with customers which cannot easily be duplicated by competitors.

Buyer–seller interaction on a global scale

Business-to-consumer (B2C)
Marketing which involves exchange relationships between a firm and its end customers, perhaps via retailers.

Today's companies are facing fierce and aggressive competition. Today most firms compete not only locally and nationally, but globally as well. Companies that have never given a thought to internationalisation now also face competition in their home market from international companies. Thinking globally also requires an understanding of the international diversity in buying behaviour and the importance of cross-cultural differences in both the **B2C** and **B2B** markets. This cross-cultural approach is centred on the study of the interaction between buyers and sellers (and their companies) who have different national and/or cultural backgrounds.

Business-to-business (B2B)
Marketing which involves exchange relationships between two or more business customers and suppliers.

Creating competitive advantage through relationships with other companies

Greater emphasis is given to the development of competitive advantage, and consequently to the development of resources and capabilities and competences within the organisation and with other companies. Relationship marketing seeks to build a *chain of relationships* (networks or value net) between the organisation and its main stakeholders, including customers, suppliers, distribution channel intermediaries and firms producing complementary products and services. Relationships to competitors are also considered.

Cross-functionalism

Cross-functional team
A team made up of individuals from various organisational departments who share a common purpose.

Marketing is not an isolated function. A marketer's ability to effectively implement a strategic marketing programme depends largely on the cooperation and competence of other functional areas within the organisation. Consequently, substantial attention is given to the interfunctional approach of marketing management. This includes: the concept of competitive advantages, **cross-functional teams** in the development of new products, **supply chain management**, internationalisation, quality management, and ethics.

Supply chain management
How products are moved from the producer to the ultimate consumer with a view to achieving the most effective and efficient delivery system.

What is new in the second edition?

- Completely new, four colour design with definitions of key concepts in the margin.
- The relationship approach is discussed further in Chapter 6, in the form of the firm's relationships and cooperation with customers, suppliers, complementors / partners and competitors (also called value net).

- New topics are covered: Long tail, customer-driven innovation, marketing in emerging markets, social marketing, lean business modelling, time-based marketing strategy, Blue Ocean strategy and new marketing metrics.

- New, comprehensive Chapter 9 on corporate social responsibility (CSR), including the sustainable Global Value Chain (SGVC), cause marketing and marketing to the bottom of the pyramid (BOP).

- Completely new cases: 16 comprehensive chapter case studies and five video part case studies. The author had personal contact and a dialogue with most of the companies involved.

- More e-marketing aspects are integrated throughout the book.

OUTLINE

The book is structured around the two main steps involved in marketing management, i.e. the decision-making process regarding formulating, implementing and controlling a marketing plan:

- Step 1: Analysis of the internal and external situation (Parts I and II)
- Step 2: Planning and implementation of marketing activities (Parts III, IV and V).

The schematic outline of the book in the diagram on page xxiii shows how the two main steps are divided into five parts. The book has a clear structure according to the *marketing planning process* of the firm. Based on an analysis of the competitive advantages of the firm (Part I) and the analysis of the external situation (Part II), the firm is able to develop marketing strategies (Part III) and marketing programmes (Part IV). Finally, the firm has to implement and control its activity in the market and if necessary make changes in the marketing strategy (Part V). Throughout the book this marketing planning process is seen in a relationship approach, as a supplement to the transactional approach.

The market research function gives a very important input to all five phases (parts) of this decision-making process, with a possible feedback to the marketing information system (MIS). Therefore, this section of the book is an Appendix, but a very important one, as the past marketing experiences are stored in the marketing information system, which may add important contributions to new marketing decision-making processes – i.e. for making better marketing decisions.

Pedagogical/learning AIDS

Many AIDS to student learning come with the book. These include:

- *Chapter learning objectives*: tell the reader what he/she should be able to do after completing each chapter.

- *Case studies*: there is a case study at the end of each chapter and each case study contains questions.

- *Video case studies*: each part starts with a video case study, which can be accessed on the book's website (**www.pearsoned.co.uk/hollensen**).

- *Exhibits*: examples from the real world to illustrate the text and the marketing models.

- *Summaries*: each chapter ends with a summary of the main concepts.

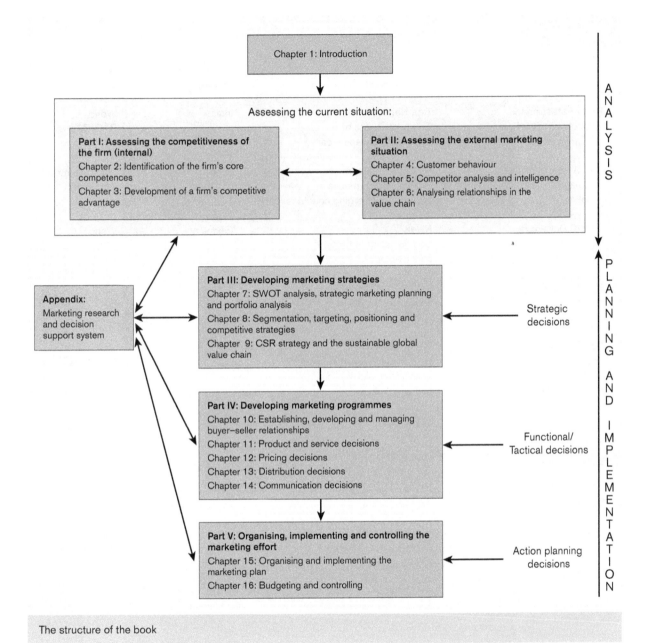

The structure of the book

- *Discussion questions*: at the end of each chapter the discussion issues are presented as questions.
- *Marginal definitions*: key concepts from the glossary are defined in the margins of the text.
- *Glossary*: a glossary on page 622 provides a quick reference to the key terms in the book.

Supplementary material to accompany the book can be downloaded by lecturers from **www.pearsoned.co.uk/hollensen**.

Tables 1 and 2 show the video case studies and the chapter case studies in this book.

Table 1	Video case studies in the book: overview		

Part	Video case study	Location of headquarters	Target market area and type
Part I Assessing the competitiveness of the firm (internal)	**Tata Nano** Competitiveness of the world's cheapest car	India	World B2C/B2B
Part II Assessing the external marketing situation	**Orascom Telecom** Developing the mobile business in emerging countries	Egypt	Emerging markets B2C/B2B
Part III Developing marketing strategies	**Nivea** Segmentation of the sun care market	Germany	World B2C
Part IV Developing marketing programmes	**Indian Tourist Board** Marketing of India in foreign countries	India	World B2C
Part V Organising, implementing and controlling the marketing effort	**Pret A Manger** How to control the expansion of an international restaurant chain	UK	UK/USA/World B2C/B2B

Table 2	Chapter case studies in the book: overview		

Chapter	Chapter case study	Location of headquarters	Target market area and type
1 Introduction	**1.1 Duchy Originals** Prince Charles's organic food company is searching for further growth in the recession	UK	World B2C/B2B
2 Identification of the firm's core competences	**2.1 Senseo** Competition is coming up in the coffee pod machine market	the Netherlands	World B2C
3 Development of the firm's competitive advantage	**3.1 Nintendo Wii** Taking the leadership in the games console market	Japan	World B2C
4 Customer behaviour	**4.1 Baxi** Trying to capture boiler market shares globally and in China	UK	World/China B2B
5 Competitor analysis and intelligence	**5.1 Cereal Partners Worldwide (CPW)** No. 2 world player is challenging the No. 1 – Kellogg	UK/ Switzerland	World B2C

Table 2	Chapter case studies in the book: overview (*continued*)		
6 Analysing relationships in the value chain	**6.1 Saipa** The Iranian car manufacturer seeks a drive to serve	Iran	World B2C/B2B
7 SWOT analysis, strategic marketing planning and portfolio analysis	**7.1 Red Bull** The global market leader in energy drinks is considering further market expansion	Austria	World/Japan B2C/B2B
8 Segmentation, targeting, positioning and competitive strategies	**8.1 Ryanair** Competitive strategy in a warfare environment	Ireland	Western Europe B2C
9 CSR strategy and the sustainable global value chain	**9.1 YouthAIDS** Social marketing in a private non-profit organisation	USA	World B2C/B2B
10 Establishing, developing and managing buyer–seller relationships	**10.1 Dassault Falcon** The private business jet, Falcon, is navigating in the global corporate business sector	France	World B2B
11 Product and service decisions	**11.1 Fisherman's Friend** Introducing chewing gum in some new markets	UK	Europe B2C
12 Pricing decisions	**12.1 Harley-Davidson** Is the image justifying the price level in a time of recession?	USA	World B2C
13 Distribution decisions	**13.1 Lindt & Sprüngli** The Swiss premium chocolate maker is considering an international chocolate café chain	Switzerland	World B2C/B2B
14 Communication decisions	**14.1 TAG Heuer** The famous Swiss watch maker is using celebrity endorsement as a worldwide communication strategy	Switzerland	World B2C
15 Organising and implementing the marketing plan	**15.1 Triumph** How to manoeuvre as a modern brand in the global underwear market	Switzerland/ Germany	World/Western Europe/USA B2C/B2B
16 Budgeting and controlling	**16.1 Jordan** Developing an international marketing control and budget system for toothbrushes	Norway	Europe B2C/B2B

ABOUT THE AUTHOR

Svend Hollensen is an Associate Professor of International Marketing at the University of Southern Denmark (Department of Border Region Studies). Furthermore he is a visiting professor at London Metropolitan University. He holds an MSc (Business Administration) from Aarhus Business School. He has practical experience from a job as International Marketing Coordinator in a large Danish multinational enterprise as well as from being International Marketing Manager in a company producing agricultural machinery.

After working in industry he received his PhD in 1992 from Copenhagen Business School.

He has published articles in journals and is the author of several marketing textbooks. Among others he is the author of *Global Marketing*, published by Financial Times-Prentice Hall and now in its fifth edition (published June 2010). It has been translated into Russian and Chinese. An Indian edition (co-authored with Madhumita Banerjee) came out in September 2009 and a Spanish edition (co-authored with Jesus Arteaga) is expected to come out in 2010.

The author may be contacted via:

University of Southern Denmark
Alsion 2
DK-6400 Sønderborg
Denmark
e-mail: **svend@sam.sdu.dk**

ACKNOWLEDGEMENTS

The successful completion of this book depended on the support and generosity of many people.

I wish to thank the many academics whose articles, books and other materials I have cited or quoted. It is not possible here to acknowledge everyone by name, but I thank you for all your help and contributions. I am particularly indebted to the following individuals and organisations:

University of Southern Denmark

- Management: the best possible environment for writing and completing this project.
- Colleagues: encouragement and support during the writing process.
- Janne Øe Hobson and Charlotte Lund Hansen: took care of the word processing of my drafts in a highly efficient manner.
- The Library team at the University of Southern Denmark: provided articles and books from sources worldwide.

Case study contributors

- Jon A. J. Wilson, Senior Lecturer in Advertising and Marketing Communications, University of Greenwich, London (contributed to Chapter 6 case study: Saipa).

In the development of this text a number of reviewers have been involved whom I would like to thank for their important and valuable contributions.

I am grateful to my publisher Pearson Education. During the writing process I had the pleasure of working with a team of editors, whom I thank for their encouragement and professionalism in transforming the manuscript into the final book. Especially, I would like to thank Editorial Director Matthew Smith for his encouraging comments during the last part of the process.

Throughout the writing period there has only been one constant in my life – my family. Without them, none of this would have been possible. Thus it is to my three girls – my wife, Jonna, and my two daughters, Nanna and Julie – that I dedicate this book.

Svend Hollensen
Sønderborg, Denmark

PUBLISHER'S ACKNOWLEDGEMENTS

We are grateful to the following for permission to reproduce copyright material:

Figures

Figure 1.2: After *Advances in Relationship Marketing*, Kogan Page, London (Payne, A. (ed) 1995), p. 31. Reproduced with permission from Kogan Page and A. Payne; Figure 1.3: Adapted from The evolution of relationship marketing, *International Business Review*, 4(4): 397–418 (Sheth, J. N. and Parvatiyar, A. 1995). Copyright © 1995 Elsevier. Reproduced with permission from Elsevier; Figure 2.6: Adapted from *Global Marketing: A Market Responsive Approach*, 2nd edition, Financial Times-Prentice Hall, Harlow (Hollensen, S. 2001), p. 16; Figure 2.8: Adapted from Internal marketing and supply chain management, *Journal of Services Marketing*, 14(1): 34 (Lings, I. N. 2000). Copyright © Emerald Group Publishing Limited. All rights reserved; Figure 2.9: Adapted from the journal article From market driven to market driving, *European Management Journal*, 18(2): 129–42 (Kumar, N., Scheer, L. and Kotler, P. 2000). Copyright © 2000 Elsevier. Reproduced with permission from Elsevier; Figure 3.1: Adapted from *Strategic Management: An Integrative Perspective*, 1st edition, Prentice Hall, Englewood Cliffs, NJ (Hax, A. C. and Majluf, N. S. 1984), p. 121. Copyright © 1984 Pearson Education, Inc. Reproduced with permission; Figure 3.7: Adapted from *Global Marketing: A Market Responsive Approach*, 2nd edition, Financial Times-Prentice Hall, Harlow (Hollensen, S. 2001), p. 95; Figure 3.8: Adapted from *Blue Ocean Strategy: How to Create Uncontested Market Space and Make the Competition Irrelevant*, Harvard Business School Publishing, Boston, MA (Kim, W. C. and Mauborgne, R. 2005). Copyright © 2005 by the Harvard Business School Publishing Corporation. All rights reserved. Reprinted by permission of Harvard Business School Press; Figure 3.11: Adapted from Outsourcing innovation: the new engine of growth, *MIT Sloan Management Review*, Summer, 20 (Quinn, J. B. 2000). Copyright © 2000 by Massachusetts Institute of Technology. All rights reserved. Distributed by Tribune Media Services; Figure 4.8: Adapted from *Relationship Marketing: Gaining Competitive Advantage Through Customer Satisfaction and Consumer Retention*, Springer-Verlag, Berlin-Heidelberg (Hennig-Thurau, T. and Hansen, U. 2000), p. 37; Figure 4.12: Adapted from *Marketing Management*, 3rd edition, McGraw-Hill, New York (Boyd, H. W., Walker, Jr, O. C., Mullins, J. W. and Larreche, J.-C. 1998), p. 133. Reproduced with permission from the McGraw-Hill Companies; Figure 4.16: Adapted from Customerization: the next revolution in customization, *Journal of Interactive Marketing*, 15(1): 18 (Wind, J. and Rangaswamy, A. 2001). Copyright © 2001 Elsevier. Reproduced with permission; Figure 5.1: After Competitive intelligence in Europe, *Business Information Review*, 16(3): 143–50 (West, C. 1999). Copyright © 1999 by Sage. Reprinted by permission of Sage Publications and C. West; Figure 5.4: Adapted from Competitor analysis and interfirm rivalry: toward a theoretical integration, *Academy of Management Review*, 21(1): 100–34 (Chen, M.-J. 1996). Copyright © 1996 by Academy of Management (NY). Reproduced with permission in the format Textbook via Copyright Clearance Center; Figure 6.6: Adapted from Developing buyer and seller relationships, *Journal of Marketing*, 51: 11–27 (Dwyer F. R., Schurr, P. H. and Oh, S. 1987). Reproduced with permission from the American Marketing Association; Figure 6.9: Adapted from Build customer relationships that last, *Harvard Business Review*, 63 (November–December): 120–8

(Jackson, B. B. 1985). Copyright © 1985 by the Harvard Business School Publishing Corporation. All rights reserved. Reprinted by permission of Harvard Business Review; Figure 6.11: Adapted from Buying loyalty or building commitment: an empirical study of customer loyalty programs, Research Report, Swedish School of Economics and Business Administration, Helsinki (Arantola, H. 2000). Reproduced with permission; Figure 6.12: Adapted from *Relationship Marketing: Gaining Competitive Advantage Through Customer Satisfaction and Consumer Retention*, Springer-Verlag, Berlin-Heidelberg (Hennig-Thurau, T. and Hansen, U. 2000), p. 283. Reproduced with permission; Figures 6.14 and 6.15: Adapted from *Global Marketing: A Market Responsive Approach*, 2nd edition, Financial Times-Prentice Hall, Harlow (Hollensen, S. 2001), pp. 274 and 421; Figure 7.4: Adapted from Strategies for diversification, *Harvard Business Review*, 35(5) (September–October): (Ansoff, H. I. 1957). Copyright © 1957 by the Harvard Business School Publishing Corporation, all rights reserved. Reprinted by permission of Harvard Business Review; Figure 7.12: Adapted from *Global Marketing: A Market Responsive Approach*, 2nd edition, Financial Times-Prentice Hall, Harlow (Hollensen, S. 2001), p. 209; Figure 7.13: Adapted from A portfolio approach to supplier relationships, *Industrial Marketing Management*, 26: 101–13 (Olsen, R. F. and Ellram, R. L. 1997). Copyright © 1997 Elsevier. Reproduced with permission; Figure 7.14: Adapted from Portfolio approaches to procurement: Analysing the missing link to specifications, *Long Range Planning*, 33: 245–67 (Nellore, R. and Söderquist, K. 2000). Copyright © 2000 Elsevier. Reproduced with permission; Figure 8.4: Adapted from Making segmentation work, *Marketing Management*, January–February: 24–28 (Barron, J. and Hollingshead, J. 2002), American Marketing Association. Reproduced with permission and courtesy of J. Barron, J. Hollingshead and the Monitor Group; Figure 8.5: Adapted from *Segmenting the Industrial Market*, D.C. Heath and Co., Lexington (Bonoma, T. V. and Shapiro, B. P. 1983). Reproduced with permission from Rowman and Littlefield Publishing Group (Lexington Books); Figure 8.7: Adapted from *Marketing: Strategic Foundations*, Richard D. Irwin (Busch, P. S. and Houston, M. J. 1985), p. 450. Reproduced with permission of The McGraw-Hill Companies; Figure 8.8: *Competitive Advantage: Creating and Sustaining Superior Performance*, The Free Press, New York (Porter, M. E. 1985) Copyright © 1985, 1998 by Michael E. Porter. All rights reserved. Reproduced with the permission of The Free Press, a Division of Simon & Schuster, Inc.; Figure 8.9: Adapted from *Marketing Management: Millennium Edition*, 10th edition, Upper Saddle River, NJ (Kotler, Philip), p. 241. Copyright © 2000 Pearson Education, Inc. Reproduced with permission; Figure 9.3: Adapted from The business case for corporate social responsibility: a company-level measurement approach for CSR, *European Management Journal*, 26: 247–61 (Weber, M. 2008). Copyright © 2008 Elsevier. Reproduced with permission; Figure 10.2: Adapted from Perceived Quality in Business Relationships, Hanken School of Economics, Helsinki/Helsingfros, Finland, CERS (Holmlund, M. 2000); Figure 10.3: Adapted from *Strategic Marketing and Marketing in the Service Sector*, Marketing Science Institute, Cambridge, MA (Grönroos, C. 1983), p. 75; Figures 10.4 and 10.6: Adapted from *Relationship Marketing: Gaining Competitive Advantage Through Customer Satisfaction and Consumer Retention*, Springer-Verlag, Berlin-Heidelberg (Hennig-Thurau, T. and Hansen, U. 2000), pp. 121 and 52; Figure 11.1: Adapted from How to design a service in J. Donnelly and W. George (eds) *Marketing of Services*, American Marketing Association, Chicago (Shostack, G. L. 1981), p. 22. Reproduced with permission from American Marketing Association; Figure 11.2: Adapted from *Global Marketing: A Market Responsive Approach*, 2nd edition, Financial Times-Prentice Hall, Harlow (Hollensen, S. 2001), p. 396; Figure 11.4: Adapted from The purchasing of full-service contracts, *Industrial Marketing Management*, 30 (Stremersch, S., Wuyts, S. and Frambach, R. T. 2001). Copyright © 2001 Elsevier Science. Reproduced with permission; Figure 11.5: *After Product Strategy and Management*, Prentice Hall, Harlow (Baker, M. and Hart, S. 1999), p. 175. Reproduced with permission of Pearson Education and M. Baker; Figures 11.8 and 11.9: Adapted from *Global Marketing: A Market Responsive Approach*, 2nd edition, Financial Times-Prentice Hall, Harlow (Hollensen, S. 2001), pp. 403 and 409; Figure 11.10: Adapted from The ACID Test™: a communications tool for leadership teams who want to interact with the whole organisation, *Journal of Brand Management*, 7(4) (Allen, D. 2000); Figure 11.11: Adapted from *International Marketing: Analysis and Strategy*, 2nd edition (Onkvisit, S. and Shaw, J. J. 1993), p. 534. Reproduced with permission of Sak Onkvisit and John J. Shaw; Figures 11.12 and 11.13: Adapted from *Global Marketing: A Market Responsive Approach*, 2nd edition, Financial Times-Prentice Hall, Harlow (Hollensen, S. 2001), pp. 417 and 428; Figure 11.14: Adapted from *The Long Tail: Why the Future of Business Is Selling Less of More* (Anderson, C. 2006). Published and reprinted by permission of Random House and Hyperion Books; Figure 12.2: Adapted from *Market-based Management: Strategies for Growing Customer Value and Profitability*, 2nd edition, Pearson, Upper Saddle River, NJ (Best, Roger J. 2000), p. 186. Copyright © 2000 Pearson Education, Inc. Reproduced with permission; Figure 12.5: Adapted from *Global Marketing: A Market Responsive Approach*, 2nd edition, Financial Times-Prentice Hall, Harlow (Hollensen, S. 2001), p. 450; Figure 12.7: Adapted from *Perspectives on Experience*, BCG (Boston Consulting Group 1970). Copyright © 1970 The Boston Consulting Group; Figure 12.8: Adapted from The European pricing bomb: and how to cope with it, *Marketing and Research Today*, February: 25–36 (Simon, H. and Kucher, E. 1993); Figure 13.2: Adapted from Distributor portfolio analysis and channel dependence matrix, *Journal of Marketing*, 47: 35–44 (Dickson, P. R. 1982). Reproduced with permission from the American Marketing Association; Figure 13.3: Adapted from US–Japan distribution channel cost structures: is there a significant difference?, *International Journal of Physical Distribution and Logistics Management*, 27(1): 57 (Pirog, S. F. and Lancioni, R. 1997). Copyright © Emerald Group Publishing Limited, all rights reserved. Reproduced with permission through Rightslink; Figures 13.4 and 13.5: Adapted from *Marketing Management: An Overview*, South-Western College Publishing (Lewison, D. M. 1996). Reprinted by permission of Dale M. Lewison; Figure 13.7: Adapted from *Global Marketing: A Market Responsive Approach*, 2nd edition, Financial Times-Prentice Hall, Harlow (Hollensen, S. 2001), p. 489; Figure 13.9: Adapted from Selecting foreign distributors: An expert systems approach, *Industrial Marketing Management*, 24: 297–304 (Cavusgil, S. T., Yeoh, P-L. and Mitri, M. 1995). Copyright © 1995 Elsevier. Reproduced with permission; Figure 13.10: Adapted from *International Marketing Management*, 5th edition, South-Western College Publishing (Jain, S. 1996), p. 523. Reprinted with permission of Subhash C. Jain; Figures 13.12 and 14.3: Adapted from *Global Marketing: A Market Responsive Approach*, 2nd edition, Financial Times-Prentice Hall, Harlow (Hollensen, S. 2001) pp. 507 and 516; Figure 14.5: Adapted from The false promise of mass customization, *McKinsey Quarterly*, 3: 62–71 (Agrawal, M., Kumaresh, T. V. and Mercer, G. A., 2001). Reproduced with permission from McKinsey and Company; Figure 14.6: Adapted from *Global Marketing: A Market Responsive Approach*, 2nd edition, Financial Times-Prentice Hall, Harlow (Hollensen, S. 2001) p. 520; Figure 14.8: Adapted from Visitor and exhibitor interaction at industrial trade fairs, *Journal of Business Research*, 32(1): 81–90 (Rosson, P. J. and Seringhaus, F. H. R. 1995) Reproduced with permission from Elsevier Science and P.J. Rosson; Figure 14.9 adapted from *Global Marketing: A Market Responsive Approach*, 2nd edition, Financial Times-Prentice Hall (Hollensen, S. 2001) p. 545; Figure 15.5: Adapted from Fundamental changes in marketing organization: the movement toward a customer-focused organizational structure, *Journal of the Academy of Marketing Science*, 28(4): 459–79 (Homburg, C., Workman, Jr., J.P. and Jensen, O. 2000). Reproduced with kind permission from Springer Science + Business Media; Figure 15.8: Adapted from *Market-led Strategic Change*, Butterworth-Heinemann (Piercy, N. F.), p. 371. Copyright © 1992 Elsevier. Reproduced with permission; Figure 15.10: Adapted from Selling supportive strategies, *Brand Strategy*, December 2008–January 2009: 37 (Hosea, M. 2009). Reproduced with permission; Figure 16.3: Adapted from Loyalty and the renaissance of marketing management, *Marketing Management*, 12(4): 17–25 (Reichheld, F. F. 1994). Published by and reproduced with permission from the American Marketing Association; Figure 16.5: Adapted from *International Marketing: Planning and Practice*, Macmillan, New York (Samli, A. C., Still, R. and Hill, J. S. 1993), p. 425. Reproduced with permission from A. Coskun Samli, the estate of Richard R. Still and John S. Hill; Figures 16.4 and 16.6: Adapted from *Global Marketing: A Market Responsive Approach*, 2nd edition, Financial Times-Prentice Hall, Harlow (Hollensen, S. 2001), pp. 600 and 605; Figure 16.7: After Supply chain metrics, *The International Journal of Logistics Management*, 12(1): 10 (Lambert, D. M. and Pohlen, T. L. 2001). Reproduced with permission from The Supply Chain Management Institute (www.scm-institute.org); Figures A.1, A.3 and A.4: Adapted from *Global Marketing: A Market Responsive Approach*, 2nd edition, Financial Times-Prentice Hall, Harlow (Hollensen, S. 2001), p. 629, 632 and 635; Figure A.5: Adapted from *Marketing Research Essentials*, 5th edition, John Wiley & Sons, New York (McDaniel Jr, S. and Gates, R. 2005), p. 228, Copyright © 2005 John Wiley & Sons, Inc. Reproduced with permission.

Tables

Table 2.2: After Configuring value for competitive advantage: on chains, shops and networks, *Strategic Management Journal*, 19: 413–37 (Stabell, C. B. and Fjeldstad, Ø. B. 1998). Reproduced with permission from John Wiley & Sons Ltd; Table 2.4: Adapted from Coffee machines: recommendations for policy design, Report, 7 August, Topten International Group (Nipkow, J. and Bush, E. 2008); Table 3.1: Adapted from Composite strategy: the combination of collaboration and competition, *Journal of General Management*, 21(1): 1–23 (Burton, J. 1995). Reproduced with permission from The Baybrooke Press Ltd; Tables 3.3 and 3.4: Adapted from Strategic assessment of outsourcing and downsizing in the service market, *Managing Service Quality*, 8(1): 7 (Blumberg, D. F. 1998). Copyright © 1998 Emerald Group Publishing Limited. All rights reserved. Reproduced with permission; Table P2.4: From the International Telecommunication Union (ITU) website (www.itu.in). Reproduced with the permission of the ITU; Tables 4.1 and 4.2: *Adapted from Relationship Marketing: Gaining Competitive Advantage Through Customer Satisfaction and Consumer Retention*, Springer-Verlag, Berlin-Heidelberg (Hennig-Thurau, T. and Hansen, U. (eds) 2000), p. 33 and 31; Table 5.1: Adapted from Managing competitive interactions, *Marketing Management*, 7(4): 8–20 (Clark, B. H. 1998). Reproduced with permission from the American Marketing Association; Table 6.1: Adapted from The outcome set of relationship marketing in consumer markets, *International Business Review*, 4(4): 447–69 (Gruen, T. W. 1995). Copyright © 1995 Elsevier. Reproduced with permission; Table 7.2: Adapted from *Marketing Planning: A Global Perspective* (Hollensen, S. 2006) Reproduced with permission from the McGraw-Hill Companies; Table 11.1: Adapted from *Global Marketing: A Market Responsive Approach*, 2nd edition, Financial Times-Prentice Hall, Harlow (Hollensen, S. 2001); Table 11.2: Adapted from *International Marketing: Analysis and Strategy*, 2nd edition, Macmillan (Onkvisit, S. and Shaw, J. J. 1993); Table 12.1: Adapted from *Global Marketing: A Market Responsive Approach*, 2nd edition, Financial Times-Prentice Hall, Harlow (Hollensen, S. 2001), p. 454; Table 12.2: Adapted from Prepare your company for global pricing, *MIT Sloan Management Review*, Fall: 61–70 (Narayandas, D., Quelch, J. and Swartz, G., 2000). Copyright © 2000 by Massachusetts Institute of Technology. All rights reserved. Distributed by Tribune Media Services; Table 14.1: Adapted from *Global Marketing: A Market Responsive Approach*, 2nd edition, Financial Times-Prentice Hall, Harlow (Hollensen, S. 2001), p. 519; Table 14.2: Adapted from *International Marketing Strategy: Analysis, Development and Implementation*, Routledge (Phillips, C., Poole, I. and Lowe, R. 1994). Copyright © 1994 Routledge. Reproduced by permission of Cengage Learning; Table 14.3: Adapted from *Marketing Management*, 3rd edition, McGraw-Hill (Boyd, H. W., Walker, Jr, O. C., Mullins, J. W. and Larreche, J-C. 1998), reproduced with permission of The McGraw-Hill Companies; Table 14.4: Adapted from *Global Marketing: A Market Responsive Approach*, 2nd edition, Financial Times-Prentice Hall (Hollensen, S. 2001) p. 538; Table 16.2: Adapted from Turning competitive advantage into customer equity, *Business Horizons*, 43(5): 11–18 (Pitt, L. F., Ewing, M. T. and Berthon, P. 2000), Copyright © 2000 Elsevier. Reproduced with permission; Table 16.4: Adapted from *International Marketing: Planning and Practice*, Macmillan, New York (Samli, A.C., Still, R. and Hill, J. S., 1993). Reproduced with permission of A. Coskun Samli, the estate of Richard R. Still and John S. Hill; Table 16.5: Adapted from *Marketing Management: Millennium Edition*, 10th edition, Prentice Hall, Upper Saddle River, NJ (Kotler, Philip), p. 698. Copyright © 2000 Pearson Education, Inc. Reproduced by permission; Table 16.6: Adapted from G*lobal Marketing: A Market Responsive Approach*, 2nd edition, Financial Times-Prentice Hall, Harlow (Hollensen, S. 2001), p. 605.

Text

Exhibit 9.2: From Grameen Telecom hears the call to take on poverty, *The Times*, 17 November 2008, p. 41 (Blakely, R.). Reproduced with permission from NI Syndication.

Photos

The publisher would like to thank the following for their kind permission to reproduce their photographs:

Page 17: Rex Features; 24: © P. Cox / Alamy; 25: B. O'Kane / Alamy; 31: © Lyroky / Alamy; 51: Courtesy of Philips Consumer Electronics; 94: © Lightly Salted / Alamy; 97: © epf model / Alamy; 105: Abdulqader Saadi / AFP / Getty; 144, 145 and 146: Courtesy of Baxi A/S; 162 (left): © Graham Oliver / Alamy; 162 (right): © Tracey Foster / Alamy; 177: Société des Produits Nestlé SA, trademark owners / The Nestlé name and images are reproduced with the kind permission of Société des Produits Nestlé SA; 192: iStockphoto: Aldomurillo (bottom left), grigphoto (top right), Neustockimages (top left) and Yuri Acurs (bottom right); 202: Courtesy of Speedo (www.speedo.com); 212: Courtesy of A.G. Barr plc; 224 (bottom): Jon Wilson; 225: Hassan Ammar / AFP / Getty Images; 234, 235 and 236: Courtesy of Beiersdorf AG; 305: Sergio Dionisio / Getty Images; 315: © Charles Polidano / Touch The Skies / Alamy; 320: Janerik Henriksson / Press Association Images; 336: Samantha Sin / AFP / Getty Images; 339: Sipa Press / Rex Features; 344: Reprinted with permission of Population Services International (PSI); all rights reserved (2009); 345: Courtesy of Darren Santos (2007); 346: Courtesy of Marshall Stowell (2007); 347: Reprinted with permission from Population Services International; all rights reserved (2009); 365: © David Osborn / Alamy; 371: © Todd Muskopf / Alamy; 381 and 382: Courtesy of Dassault Aviation; 416: © David Morgan / Alamy; 417: © frank'n'focus / Alamy; 423: Courtesy of Lofthouse of Fleetwood Ltd; 454: © Robert Convery / Alamy; 483 and 487: Lindt & Sprungli International AG; 505: © CarlssonInc. / Alamy; 523: Courtesy of TAG Heuer SA; 524 (left): © Rue des Archives / Collection CSFF; 524 (right): Courtesy of TAG Heuer SA; 531: © Cobie Martin / Alamy; 550: Courtesy of Triumph International textil a/s; 551: Courtesy of Triumph International textil a/s: Photographer: Olaf Wippefurth; 560: Courtesy of Triumph International textil a/s: Photographer: Stefan Noll; 586, 587, 589: Courtesy of Jordan AS.

Every effort has been made to trace the copyright holders and we apologise in advance for any unintentional omissions. We would be pleased to insert the appropriate acknowledgement in any subsequent edition of this publication.

CHAPTER 1
Introduction

LEARNING OBJECTIVES

After studying this chapter you should be able to:

- describe how marketing management is placed in the overall company strategy

- compare and discuss the differences and similarities between the traditional (transactional) marketing approach and the relationship marketing approach

- explain what implications the relationship marketing approach has on the traditional (transactional) marketing mix (the four Ps)

1.1 INTRODUCTION

Transactional marketing (TM)
The major focus of the marketing programme (the 4 Ps) is to make customers buy. Independence among marketing actors ('arm's length') is considered vital for marketing efficiency.

This chapter introduces marketing management in a relationship approach. The chapter contrasts the traditional **(transactional) marketing (TM)** concept with the **relationship marketing (RM)** approach. The marketing management process is introduced in the form of a hierarchical planning model.

This book will bridge the gap between the traditional **marketing planning** approach and the 'new' relational marketing (RM) approach.

This chapter will start by discussing where the marketing management strategy is placed in the overall company strategy. The book is structured (Figure 1.1) according to the hierarchical marketing management process.

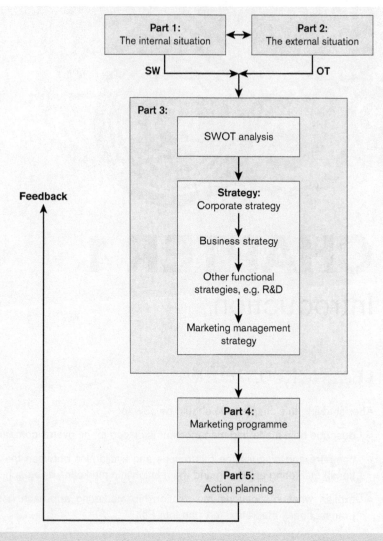

| Figure 1.1 | Structure of the book in relation to the hierarchical marketing management process |

1.2 THE MARKETING MANAGEMENT PROCESS

Marketing plan
A marketing plan is a written document that details the necessary actions to achieve the company's marketing objectives. It can be for a product or service, a brand or a product line. Basically a marketing plan describes the marketing activities of a company in order to produce sales at the customer level. Marketing plans cover between one and five years. A marketing plan may be part of an overall business plan.

Though it is not always the case, the starting point for the marketing management process and the **marketing plan** should be the corporate strategy.

Marketing strategy

Although marketing strategy first became a popular business buzzword during the 1960s, it continues to be the subject of widely differing definitions and interpretations. The following definition, however, captures the essence of the term:

> A marketing strategy is a fundamental pattern of present and planned objectives, resource deployments, and interactions of an organization with markets, competitors and other environmental factors.

This definition suggests that a strategy should specify what (objectives to be accomplished), where (on which industries and product markets to focus) and how (which resources and activities to allocate to each product/market to meet environmental opportunities and threats) in order to gain a competitive advantage.

Rather than a single comprehensive strategy, many organisations have a hierarchy of inter-related strategies, each formulated at a different level of the firm. The three major levels of strategy in most large, multi-product organisations are:

1 corporate strategy
2 business-level strategy
3 functional strategies, e.g. marketing strategy.

In small, single-product companies, corporate and business-level strategic issues merge.

Our primary focus is on the development of marketing strategies and programmes for individual product-market entries, but other functional departments – such as R&D and production – also have strategies and plans for each of the firm's product markets. Table 1.1 summarises the specific focus and issues dealt with at each strategy level.

The traditional strategy literature operates with a *hierarchical* definition of strategic marketing management. The terms mission and objectives all have specific meanings in this hierarchical definition of strategy and strategic management.

Mission and vision

The corporate mission can be considered as a brief statement of the purpose of the company: what the organisation is and what it does ('Who are we?').

The mission of Coca-Cola is:

Our Roadmap starts with our mission, which is enduring. It declares our purpose as a company and serves as the standard against which we weigh our actions and decisions.

- To refresh the world . . .
- To inspire moments of optimism and happiness . . .
- To create value and make a difference.

Source: www.thecoca-colacompany.com.

The mission statement may change if the company outlives the industry it started in, but it should still tie back to the core values. Example: 'Google's mission is to organize the world's information and make it universally accessible and useful.'

Ideally, the definition could cover Abell's three dimensions for defining the business: customer groups to be served, customer needs to be served, and technologies to be utilised (Abell, 1980).

A vision statement is what the enterprise wants to become ('Where do we wish to go?'). The vision is a description of the company's 'desired future state'. Thus the company may create a vision statement describing the organisation as it would be like in, say, ten or more years. Note the emphasis on the future; the vision statement is not true today. Rather, it describes the organisation as it could become – in the future.

A vision statement should build enthusiasm. It should provoke inspiration. It should stimulate people to care. It should 'rally the troops to action'. That is what President Kennedy accomplished with the vision statement he offered in early 1961. Kennedy said:

I believe that this nation should commit itself to achieving the goal, before this decade is out, of landing a man on the moon, and returning him safely to earth.

The vision of Coca-Cola is:

Our vision serves as the framework for our Roadmap and guides every aspect of our business by describing what we need to accomplish in order to continue achieving sustainable, quality growth.

- *People*: Be a great place to work where people are inspired to be the best they can be.
- *Portfolio*: Bring to the world a portfolio of quality beverage brands that anticipate and satisfy people's desires and needs.

Table 1.1	Different planning levels in the company		
Strategy components	**Corporate strategy**	**Business strategy**	**Marketing strategy**
Scope/mission	Corporate domain – which businesses should we be in?	Business domain – which product markets should we be in within this business or industry?	• Target market definition • Product-line depth and breadth • Branding policies
Strategy	Corporate development strategy • Conglomerate diversification (expansion into unrelated businesses) • Vertical integration • Acquisition and divestiture policies	Business development strategy Concentric (new products for existing customers or new customers for existing products)	• Product-market development plan • Line extension and product elimination plans
Goals and objectives	Overall corporate objectives aggregated across businesses • Revenue growth • Profitability • Return on investment (ROI) • Earnings per share • Contributions to other stakeholders	Constrained by corporate goals Objectives aggregated across product-market entries in the business unit • Sales growth • New product or market growth • Profitability • ROI • Cash flow • Strengthening bases of competitive advantage	Constrained by corporate and business goals Objectives for a specific product-market entry • Sales • Market share • Contribution margin • Customer satisfaction
Allocation of resources	• Allocation among businesses in the corporate portfolio • Allocation across functions shared by multiple businesses (corporate R&D, MIS)	• Allocation among product-market entries in the business unit • Allocation across functional departments within the business unit	Allocation across components of the marketing plan (elements of the marketing mix) for a specific product-market entry
Sources of competitive advantage	Primarily through superior corporate financial or human resources; more corporate R&D; better organisational processes or synergies relative to competitors across all industries in which the firm operates	Primarily through competitive strategy; business unit's competences relative to competitors in its industry	Primarily through effective product positioning; superiority on one or more components of the marketing mix relative to competitors within a specific product market
Sources of synergy	Shared resources, technologies, or functional competences across businesses within the firm	Shared resources (including favourable customer image) or functional competences across product markets within an industry	Shared marketing resources, competences, or activities across product-market entries

Diversification
The market and product development strategy that involves expansion to a relatively large number of markets and products.

Line extension
Using a successful brand name to introduce additional items in a given product category under the same brand name, such as new flavours, forms, colours, added ingredients or package sizes.

Return on investment (ROI)
A common measure of managerial effectiveness – the ratio of net profit to investment.

- *Partners*: Nurture a winning network of customers and suppliers, together we create mutual, enduring value.
- *Planet*: Be a responsible citizen that makes a difference by helping build and support sustainable communities.
- *Profit*: Maximize long-term return to shareowners while being mindful of our overall responsibilities.
- *Productivity*: Be a highly effective, lean and fast-moving organization.

Source: www.thecoca-colacompany.com.

McDonald's combine their mission with a vision statement:

Our vision is to be the world's best 'quick service restaurant'. This means opening and running great restaurants and providing exceptional quality, service, cleanliness and value.

Source: www.mcdonalds.com.

Objectives

Objectives in the hierarchical definition of strategy are the specific performance targets that firms aspire to in each of the areas included in a firm's mission statement. It is usually not enough for a firm just to assert that it wants to be a leader in its industry or that it wants to become a major diversified company. In addition, a firm needs to specify what it means to be a leader in its industry, what being a major diversified company means. Often, objectives are stated in financial or economic terms. Thus for one firm being a 'leader' in an industry may mean having the largest market share, but for other firms leadership might mean being the most profitable firm in the industry, having the highest-quality products, or being the most innovative. In the same way, being a major diversified company may mean unrelated diversification across a wide variety of industries for one firm and a relatively narrow product and industry focus for another. In this hierarchical definition of strategy, comparing actual behaviour with objectives is the way that managers can know whether they have fulfilled a firm's mission.

With a mission and objectives in place, a firm, according to the hierarchical definition of strategy, can then turn its attention to strategies. Strategies, here illustrated by the marketing strategy, thus become the means through which firms accomplish their objectives and mission.

Marketing plan

In most organisations strategic planning is an annual process, typically covering just the year ahead. Occasionally, a few organisations may look at a practical plan that stretches three or more years ahead. To be most effective, the plan must be formalised, usually in written form, as an identifiable marketing plan. The process of marketing management and the development of a marketing plan is no different from any other functional area of management in that it essentially comprises four key tasks.

Analysis

The starting point of marketing management decisions is analysis. Customers, competitors, trends and changes in the environment, and internal strengths and weaknesses must each be fully understood by the marketer before effective marketing plans can be established. Analysis in turn, requires information using systematic market research and **marketing information systems (MIS)**.

Marketing information system (MIS)
A system in which marketing information is formally gathered, stored, analysed and distributed to managers in accord with their informational needs on a regular, planned basis.

Planning

The second task of the manager is the planning process. The marketing manager must plan both long-term marketing direction for the organisation (strategic planning), including, for example, the selection of target markets, and the marketing programmes and tactics that will be used to support these strategic plans.

Implementation

Both strategic and tactical plans must, of course, be acted upon if they are to have any effect. The implementation tasks of marketing management involve such activities as staffing, allocating tasks and responsibilities, budgeting, and securing any financial and other resources needed to carry out the plans. Actions include activities such as placing an advert in the right media, delivering products, doing customer surveys, etc.

Control

Control
The process by which managers ensure that planned activities are completely and properly executed.

Effectiveness
Doing the right thing, making the correct strategic choice.

Marketing audit
An analysis and evaluation of the internal and external marketing environment of the company.

The fourth, and sometimes neglected, task of the manager is measuring and evaluating progress against objectives and targets established in plans. **Control** of marketing plans can be problematical, with difficulties associated with both measuring marketing performance and pinpointing cause and effect. For example, market share – a frequently used measure of marketing performance and hence a basis for marketing control – needs very careful analysis and interpretation if it is to provide a useful basis for controlling the **effectiveness** of marketing strategies and plans. Both qualitative and quantitative techniques of control should be used by the marketing manager and include budgetary control, control of marketing mix effectiveness and, from time to time, a full **marketing audit**.

In the following the strengths and weaknesses of the hierarchical approach to marketing planning will be highlighted.

Strengths of the hierarchical approach to marketing planning

The hierarchical approach has three important strengths. First, it emphasises the link between strategy and performance. Virtually all strategic management researchers, and most practising managers, are interested in the relationship between the actions taken by a firm and a firm's performance. The hierarchical definition provides explicit criteria for judging the performance quality of a firm's strategies – good strategies enable an organisation to reach its objectives and fulfil its mission; bad strategies make it more difficult for a firm to reach its objectives and fulfil its mission.

Second, this hierarchical definition focuses on the multiple levels of analysis that are important in formulating and implementing strategies. These levels of analysis vary in their degree of abstraction. Company missions are very abstract concepts. They specify what a firm wants to become but say little about how a firm will get to where it wants to go. Objectives translate missions into specific goals and targets and thus are less abstract. Strategies specify which actions firms will take to meet their objectives. Plans, the least abstract concept, focus on specific actions that need to be taken to implement strategies.

By emphasising the multiple levels of analysis in the strategic management process, hierarchical definitions appropriately emphasise the need in organisations to gather information, ideas and suggestions from all parts of the firm in order to formulate effective strategies. In this conception of strategy, each part of a firm plays an important role. Senior managers specialise in establishing missions and objectives, divisional managers specialise in strategy formulation, and functional managers focus their efforts on tactics. No one of these tasks is more important than any other. Missions and objectives will never be achieved without strategies and tactics. Strategies without missions and objectives will be unfocused. Strategies without tactics are usually not implemented. And plans without strategies or missions are not likely to improve a firm's performance.

A third strength of the hierarchical definition is that it emphasises that strategy, in order to have an impact on performance, cannot remain simply an idea in an organisation. Rather, it must be translated, through resource allocation, into action. An organisation's mission is often a statement of an idea, or a manifestation of the values, of top management. However, by itself, a mission statement is likely to have little impact on a firm's performance. Rather, this mission statement must be linked with objectives, strategies and tactics. In choosing objectives, strategies and tactics, managers must make tough decisions, set priorities and allocate resources. Firms that translate their mission into actions increase the probability that they will improve their performance.

Weaknesses of the hierarchical approach to marketing planning

The most important weaknesses of the hierarchical approach are as follows. First, it has a very underdeveloped notion of the external competitive environment's impact on strategy formulation and implementation. Mission statements summarise where the senior management want an organisation to be in the long run, but the development of these statements is encouraged to focus inward. In choosing a mission, senior managers are encouraged to look inward, evaluating their own personal priorities and values. Certainly, this kind of analysis is an important step in developing a firm's mission.

Indeed, part of this book is devoted to this kind of internal analysis. Such an analysis, however, must be linked with the external analysis (Part II) in order for firms to choose missions, objectives, strategies and thus marketing plans, that will add value to the firm.

A second weakness of the hierarchical definition is that it tends to focus, almost exclusively, on formal, routine, bureaucratic strategy-making processes. In this definition, strategic choices are made through systematic study and analysis. These analyses result in coherent, self-reinforcing sets of strategies that, taken together, lead a firm to reach its objectives and mission. There is little doubt that many organisations choose at least some of their strategies in this logical and systematic way. An enormous amount of research on formal strategic planning suggests that more and more firms are adopting explicit and formal planning systems to choose their strategies. The hierarchical definitions presented in Figure 1.1 tend to emphasise this formal, systematic aspect of choosing and implementing strategies.

SMEs
Small and medium-sized enterprises. In the EU, SMEs are characterised as having 250 employees or less. They comprise approximately 99 per cent of all firms.

Yet not all strategies are chosen in this way. Small and medium-sized enterprises (**SMEs**) choose strategies by discovering an unanticipated opportunity and exploiting that opportunity to improve performance resulting in 'emerging strategies' (Mintzberg, 1987; Mintzberg and Waters, 1985). Firms also choose strategies 'retroactively' – that is, they engage in certain kinds of behaviour over time, and then, only after that pattern of behaviour is in existence, senior managers label these actions as a coherent or consistent strategy. Some firms stumble into their strategy by chance. All these are ways that firms can choose strategies, yet none of them is consistent with the formal, systematic strategic management process presented in Figure 1.1.

A third weakness of hierarchical approaches to defining strategy and strategic management is that, despite their apparent rigour and clarity, they often fail to give significant guidance to managers when they are applied in real organisations. There are literally thousands of objectives that an organisation could choose to support any given mission statement. Which objectives a firm should choose, which should be given priority, and which should be ignored are questions that must be answered logically and with ideas that are not provided in the hierarchical definition. Moreover, there may be thousands of different strategies that firms could choose to support any given set of objectives. Which particular strategies a firm should choose goes beyond the hierarchical model.

1.3 THE TRADITIONAL (TRANSACTIONAL) MARKETING (TM) CONCEPT VERSUS THE RELATIONSHIP MARKETING (RM) CONCEPT

The American Marketing Association (AMA), an international organisation of practitioners and academicians, defines marketing as follows:

> Marketing is the process of planning and executing the conception, pricing, promotion, and distribution of ideas, goods, and services to create exchanges that satisfy individual and organizational objectives.

This definition describes what the traditional (transactional) marketing concept is: the conception, pricing, promotion and distribution of ideas, goods and services. Moreover, the definition implies a list of activities for the marketer to undertake: the planning and execution of these four elements of competition so that individual and organisational objectives are satisfied.

Another characteristic of transactional marketing is the belief that independence of choice among marketing players creates a more efficient system for creating and distributing marketing value. Maintaining an arm's length relationship is considered vital for marketing efficiency. Industrial organisations and government policy makers believe that independence of marketing players provides each player freedom to choose his/her transactional partners on the basis of preserving their own self-interests at each decision point. This results in the **efficiency** of lowest cost purchases through bargaining and bidding.

The so-called **4Ps** are the epitome of what should be done and are also known as the marketing mix. This transactional micro-economic and teacher-friendly marketing framework is straightforward to understand and use. Indeed, in the 1950s and 1960s the 4Ps approach proved very successful. In the USA this was the era of mass manufacturing and **mass marketing** of packaged consumer goods and, because of that, marketing was often more about attracting than retaining customers.

The model of transaction marketing (as in the 4Ps) rests on three assumptions:

1   there is a large number of potential customers;

2   the customers and their needs are fairly homogeneous;

3   it is rather easy to replace lost customers with new customers.

Looking at today's markets, and certainly when moving from consumer markets to industrial and service markets, this approach may not be appropriate.

The relationship marketing (RM) concept

According to the traditional (transactional) marketing concept the major focus of marketing programmes has been to make customers buy, regardless of whether they are existing or new customers. Often only a small part of the marketing budget has explicitly been allocated directly towards existing customers.

Since the 1980s academics have been questioning this approach to marketing (e.g. Grönroos, 1996 and 2006; Gummesson, 1999). They argue that this approach to marketing is no longer broad enough because of the importance of customer retention, the changes in the competitive environment and the limitations of transaction marketing.

In Europe, this new direction of marketing thought was mainly initiated by IMP (Industrial Marketing and Purchasing Group).

According to Gordon (1998), p. 9:

> Relationship marketing is the ongoing process of identifying and creating new value with individual customers and then sharing the benefits from this over a lifetime of association. It involves the understanding, focusing and management of ongoing collaboration between *suppliers* and *selected customers* for mutual value creation and sharing through interdependence and organizational alignment.

RM not only attempts to involve and integrate suppliers and customers. Besides a need for focusing on customer retention, Payne (1995) emphasises that RM indicates a shift towards the organisation of marketing activities around cross-functional activities. Payne (1995) presents a model (Figure 1.2) where six markets need to be considered if the customer is to be served satisfactorily.

Customers remain the prime focus in the centre of the model but, as shown in Figure 1.2, there are five other markets where a detailed marketing strategy may be needed.

Efficiency
A way of managing business processes to a high standard, usually concerned with cost reduction.

4Ps
The basic elements of the marketing mix: product, place (distribution), price and promotion; also called the controllable variables of marketing, because they can be controlled and manipulated by the marketer.

Mass marketing
One-to-many communications between a company and potential customers with limited tailoring of the message.

Figure 1.2	Relationship marketing's six-markets model

Source: After Payne, A. (ed) (1995) *Advances in Relationship Marketing*, Kogan Page, London, p. 31. Reproduced with permission from Kogan Page and A. Payne.

RM attempts to involve and integrate customers, suppliers, and other infrastructural partners into a firm's developmental and marketing activities. Such involvement results in close interactive relationships with suppliers, customers or other value chain partners of the firm.

Relationships are the fundamental asset of the company. More than anything else – even the physical plant, patents, products or markets – relationships determine the future of the firm. Relationships predict whether new value will continue to be created and shared with the company. If customers are amenable to a deepening bond, they will do more business with the company. If employees like to work there, they will continue along their **learning curve** and produce more and better. If investors and bankers are happy with their returns, they will continue to keep their funds in the company.

Thus, the development of relationship marketing points to a significant **paradigm** shift in marketing: competition and conflict to mutual cooperation, and independence and choice to mutual interdependence, as illustrated in Figure 1.3.

Today many companies realise the importance of the RM approach but most companies still operate with a mixture of the TM and RM approaches. Some firms are attaching more weight to RM than others, and vice versa.

RM emphasises cooperation rather than competition and consequent conflict among the parties. It also emphasises cooperation rather than competition and consequent conflict among the marketing players. The exchange-based transactional marketing approach is based on a notion of mass markets where individual customers are anonymous. The goal is to make customers choose one particular **brand** over competing brands. This easily creates a situation of competition between the marketer and the customer.

In transaction marketing situations, customers, as unidentified members of a segment, are exposed to a number of competing products, and they are supposed to make independent

Learning curves
Track the decreasing cost of production and distribution of products or services over time as a result of learning by doing, innovation and imitation.

Paradigm
A shared way of thinking, or meta-theory that provides a framework for theory.

Brand
An identifying feature that distinguishes one product from another; more specifically, any name, term, symbol, sign or design, or a unifying combination of these.

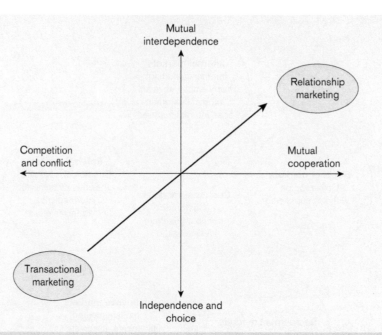

Figure 1.3	Transactional and relationship marketing

Source: Adapted from Sheth, J. N. and Parvatiyar, A. (1995) The evolution of relationship marketing, *International Business Review*, 4(4): 400. Copyright © 1995 Elsevier. Reproduced with permission.

choices from among the available options. The two parties have conflicting interests. The starting point is that the customer does not want to buy; he or she has to be persuaded to do so.

In RM, where interactions and cooperation exist at some level, the customer and the supplier or service provider are not totally isolated from each other. The relationship is based on value creation in interactions between the supplier or service provider and the customer. Cooperation is required to create the value that the customer is looking for. Of course, this does not mean that conflicts could not exist; however, cooperation is the driving force, not conflict.

In situations where there are a limited number of customers and/or where continuous interaction with customers occurs, a relationship approach is relatively easy to adopt, if this is considered profitable and appreciated by the customers. This is the case in many **business-to-business (B2B)** markets and in service markets. When a firm has mass markets with limited direct contact with its customers, a relationship approach is less obvious.

Business-to-business (B2B)
Marketing that involves exchange relationships between two or more business customers and suppliers.

Importance of customer retention

Recently, evidence has been provided about the value of long-term customer relationships and on how to improve performance by focusing on customer retention instead of single sales. It suggests that it can be up to ten times more expensive to win a customer than to retain a customer – and the cost of bringing a new customer to the same level of profitability as the lost one is up to 16 times more (Peppers and Rogers, 1993). Further evidence is provided by Lindgreen and Crawford (1999) who show that increasing customer retention from 80 per cent to 94 per cent in a food catering business quadrupled the value of its average customer. Moreover, existing satisfied customers can make up about two-thirds of the volume for an average business (Vavra, 1995).

Some important differences between the two marketing orientations are highlighted in Table 1.2.

It has been said that transaction marketing is too simplified a framework for today's businesses as they are confronted with many competitive challenges. Since the 1990s, markets have generally become mature and there is only little possibility for product differentiation. Therefore, customer retention is becoming more important.

Table 1.2	Transactional and relationship marketing	
Category	Transactional marketing	Relationship marketing
Focus	Economic transaction. Decision focus on product/ brand and 4Ps.	Decision focus on relationships between firms in a network and individuals.
The marketing environment	Marketing rules are very clear, defined and constant. Market is bound by countries and regions.	Marketing rules are relatively clear, defined and constant. Market is relatively bound by network and alliances. The boundaries between firms are blurred, if not completely eroded.
Parties involved	A firm and buyers are involved in a general market. Distant and impersonal contact.	Dyadic relationships: sellers, buyers, and other firms. Face-to-face, close interpersonal contacts based on commitment and trust.
Goals	Each party's goals and objectives, while similar, are geared to what is best for them.	Shared goals and objectives ensure common direction.
Managerial intent	Transaction/sales volume and creating new customers are considered a success. Customer attraction (to satisfy the customer at a profit).	Keeping the existing customers, retention, is considered to be a success. Satisfy the customer, increase profit, and attain other objectives such as increased loyalty, decreased customer risk, etc.
Production focus	Mass production.	Mass customisation.
Communication	Communications structured and guarded.	Open communication avoids misdirection and bolsters effective working relationships.
Customers	Low customer interactivity. Customers are less knowledgeable and informed.	High customer interactivity. Customers are aware and informed. Their feedback can be immediate.
Competitive advantage/differentiation	The quality of the product is important for differentiation. The marketing mix can be used for the differentiation.	Creativity is important for differentiation. Long-term and close relationships, adaptation, putting the customer at the centre of the organisation is a source of differentiation.
Balance of power/sharing	Active seller – less passive buyers. Suspicion and distrust. Each party wary of the motives and action by the other. Sharing limited by lack of trust and different objectives. Often opportunistic behaviour.	Seller and buyer mutually active and adaptive (interdependent and reciprocal). Mutual trust forms the basis for strong working relationships. Sharing of business plans and strategies.

Table 1.2	Transactional and relationship marketing cont.	
Category	Transactional marketing	Relationship marketing
Organisation/ managerial level	Functional marketers (e.g. sales manager, product development manager).	Managers from across functions and levels in the firm.
	Marketing is a concern of the marketing department.	Everyone in the organisation is a part-time marketer.
		Specialist marketers (e.g. key account managers).
Formality	Formal (yet personalised via technology).	Formal and informal (i.e. at both a business and social level).
Duration	Discrete (yet perhaps over time). Short-term.	Continuous (ongoing and mutually adaptive, may be short or long-term).
General advantages/ disadvantages	Advantage: independence of buyer and seller.	Advantage: intimate knowledge of needs and markets (developed over time), which has been likened to reading the minds of customers.
	Disadvantage: the firm is in a vulnerable situation if a competitor makes a better offer to the customer.	Disadvantage: the firm is in a vulnerable situation if its business supplier (customer) disappears.

Sources: Adapted from Payne (1995); Lindgreen *et al.* (2000); Zineldin (2000); Håkansson and Waluszewski (2005); Grönroos (2006).

Value chain
Chain of activities by which a company brings in materials, creates a good or service, markets it and provides service after a sale is made. Each step creates more value for the consumer.

RM suggests that the company should focus on the ultimate market segment and serve customers as individuals. Companies can give individual customers, or logical groups of customers (where serving the individual uniquely makes no sense to either customer or supplier), the value each wants by using technology appropriately throughout the **value chain**. Often this means taking apart existing business processes and inserting technology into them. For example, when the Internet is used for online ordering, the process for purchasing has been redesigned.

However, all this does not exclude transaction marketing. In a way transaction marketing and RM become part of the same fundamental paradigm: *focus on customer satisfaction*.

Although RM is a strong strategic concept, its implementation requires the use of powerful instruments. This instrumental dimension was largely neglected in the early academic discussion of the RM concept. Nevertheless, most companies and scholars do use the transactional paradigmatic framework when identifying adequate marketing instruments for building and maintaining relationships with customers.

1.4 BALANCING THE TRANSACTIONAL AND RELATIONSHIP CONCEPTS THROUGHOUT THE BOOK

This book links between the traditional marketing approach and the relationship marketing (RM) approach. Some chapters (Chapters 2–5) concentrate more on the traditional marketing approach, whereas Chapter 6 attempts to draw all the factors together into a true relationship approach (between-the-boxes approach)

in Figure 1.4 indicates that the actors (firm, customer and competitor) are treated more independently of the relationship approach. In other words, these four chapters do not focus so much on the relationships to other important players in the value chain.

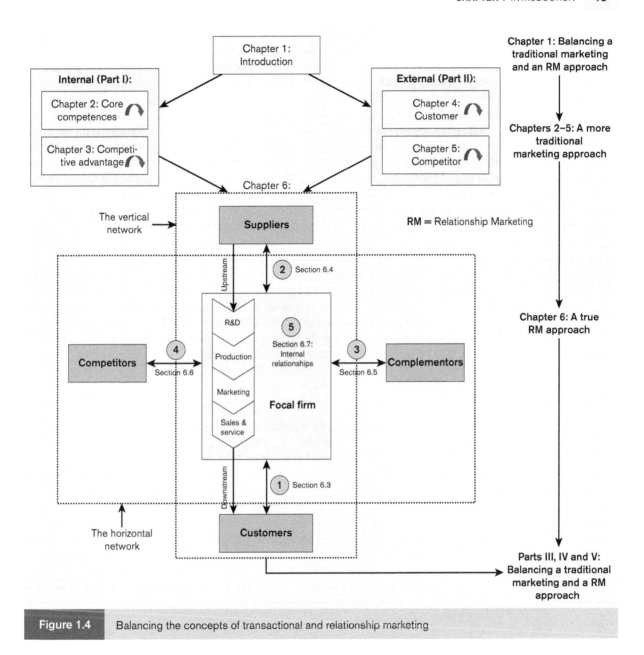

Figure 1.4   Balancing the concepts of transactional and relationship marketing

These relationships (double arrows between firm and the other actors) are then covered in Chapter 6, which also includes the firm's relations to suppliers and complementors. Hence, though there seems to be a paradigm shift going on from the transactional to the relationship marketing approach, most companies still are practising a mixture of both.

1.5 HOW THE RM CONCEPT INFLUENCES THE TRADITIONAL MARKETING CONCEPT

In the following, some of the consequences of a relationship orientation for the traditional four marketing parameters (4Ps) are given (Håkansson and Waluszewski, 2005).

Product

A key impact of RM on product policy is the integration of customised elements in what were previously standardised products for mass markets. Modern information technology allows firms to individualise their products and services according to the varying needs of their customers.

RM, when appropriately implemented, results in products being cooperatively designed, developed, tested, piloted, provided, installed and refined. Products are not developed in the historical way, with the company producing **product concepts**, researching these with customers, and then engaging in various research and development initiatives, leading to product introduction some time later. Rather, RM involves real-time interaction between the company and its priority customers as the company seeks to move more rapidly to meet customer requirements. The product is therefore the output of a process of collaboration that creates the value customers want for each component of the product and associated services. Products are not bundles of tangible and intangible benefits that the company assembles because it thinks this is what customers want to buy. Rather, products comprise an aggregation of individual benefits that customers have participated in selecting or designing. The customer thus participates in the assembly of an unbundled series of components or modules that together constitute the product or service. The product resulting from this collaboration may be unique or highly tailored to the requirements of the customer, with much more of the customer's knowledge content incorporated into the product than was previously the case.

Product concept
The end result of the marketing strategist's selection and blending of a product's primary and auxiliary components into a basic idea emphasising a particular set of consumer benefits; also called the product positioning concept.

Price

Traditional marketing sets a price for a product, perhaps discounting the price in accordance with competitive and other marketplace considerations. The price seeks to secure a fair return on the investment the company has made in its more or less static product.

Relationship-oriented pricing is centred on the application of price differentiation strategies. The pricing should correspond to **customer lifetime values (CLTV)**. This proposal represents an attempt to estimate the net present value of the current and future potential of various customers or customer segments.

In relationship marketing, the product varies according to the preference and dictates of the customer, with the value varying commensurately. So when customers specify that a product should have a specific feature and that certain services should be delivered before, during and after the sale, they naturally want to pay for each component of the package separately. Just as the product and services are secured in a process of collaboration, so too will the price need to reflect the choices made and the value created from these choices.

Customer lifetime value (CLTV)
It is the present value of the future cash flows attributed to the customer relationship or the amount by which revenue from a given customer over time will exceed the company's costs of attracting, selling and servicing that customer. Use of customer lifetime value as a marketing metric tends to place greater emphasis on customer service and long-term customer satisfaction, rather than on maximising short-term sales.

Business-to-business marketers, especially for larger capital goods and installations, have typically engineered the products and services to customer requirements and negotiated the prices of their services. But customers have not often been involved in all aspects of the value chain and the price/performance **trade-offs** that sellers have thought were necessary. RM invites customers into the pricing process, and all other value-related processes, giving customers an opportunity to make any trade-offs and to further develop trust in the relationship.

Trade-off
Balancing of two different options. If you have chosen a certain option, with certain advantages you also have to live with some disadvantages.

Distribution

The general message of RM for distribution is that it should get closer to the customer. Conventional marketing thinking sees distribution as the channel that takes the product from producer to consumer. In the case of the computer industry, Dell sees distribution as a direct sales approach, primarily using the Internet, telephone sales and order placement, whereas IBM uses many approaches to distribution, including its own stores, a direct sales force, and retailers that resell the firm's personal computers. RM instead considers distribution from the perspective of the customer, who decides where, how and when to buy the combination of products and services that constitute the vendor's total offering. Seen this way, distribution is not a channel but a process. The process allows customers to choose where and from whom they will obtain the value they want. Continuing the computer example just mentioned, the customer can choose whether to buy an off-the-shelf model from a reseller and take it home immediately, order one to be built to individual preferences at the factory and shipped within a week or so, or have one configured in-store that will be available within a few days. It thus may be more accurate to think of distribution as placement, giving customers choices with regard to the locations at which they will specify, purchase, receive, install, repair and return individual components of the products and services. That is, whereas traditional marketing considers a product as a bundled package of benefits, RM unbundles the product and service and allows the customer to initiate a placement decision for each element.

Communication (promotion)

Traditional marketing sends smoke signals for all within a specific market segment to see. 'Buy me', the signals say to all who can see them. RM instead gives individual customers an opportunity to decide how they wish to communicate with the enterprise, how often and with whom. Mass promotion becomes support to build equity in the firm or brand, rather than a means to influence purchase directly.

The RM approach indicates the need for integrated communication and the demand for interactive communication.

Technology can make promotion become communication because technology can help individuals and international-oriented companies to interact more frequently and more effectively across borders (Czinkota and Samli, 2007). For the producer in the B2B market this communication may involve opportunities for supplier and customer to interact at the strategic level – considering each other's plans, customers, strategies and initiatives – so that both can consider how best to be interdependent over the planning horizon. It may also tie into the customer's and supplier's information and communications systems, letting staff in each firm feel as though they work with the other in an integrated way. In this way, the lines between supplier and customer can be further blurred.

Producers in the B2C market could relate and communicate in much the same way with their channel intermediaries, such as the retailers. And now, with technology, customers can be interactively and uniquely engaged. Using technologies such as the Internet, computer–telephony integration at call centres, intelligence at point of sale, kiosks, smart cards and interactive voice response, companies can give consumers a host of options for communicating with the company and have information on hand to engage, inform and direct each customer with complete knowledge as to the customer's preferences and behaviours.

The introduction to Part IV discusses the extended version of the 4P mix – the so called 7P mix. Then Part IV of this book further develops the implications of the RM approach on the traditional 4P marketing mix (product, price, place, promotion).

1.6 DIFFERENT ORGANISATIONAL FORMS OF RM

It is important to understand the nature of relationship. The boundaries of RM have been discussed since RM was first investigated in the 1970s (Healy *et al.*, 2001).

It is possible to study relationships in different contexts. Figure 1.5 presents a context where it is possible to study relationships in three ways.

The dyadic relationship is the basic irreducible building block of inter-firm relationships. It can be used as the basis for studying a number of marketing phenomena ranging from

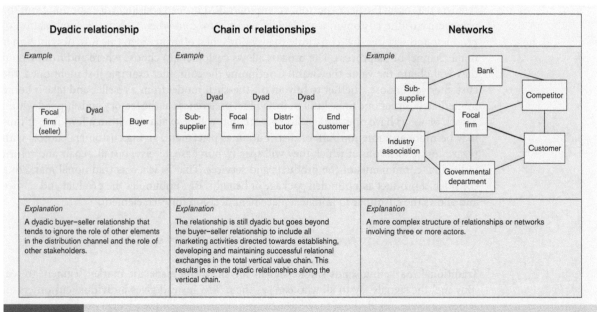

Dyadic relationship	Chain of relationships	Networks
Example	*Example*	*Example*
Explanation A dyadic buyer–seller relationship that tends to ignore the role of other elements in the distribution channel and the role of other stakeholders.	*Explanation* The relationship is still dyadic but goes beyond the buyer–seller relationship to include all marketing activities directed towards establishing, developing and maintaining successful relational exchanges in the total vertical value chain. This results in several dyadic relationships along the vertical chain.	*Explanation* A more complex structure of relationships or networks involving three or more actors.

Figure 1.5   Forms of relationships

Strategic alliances
Informal or formal arrangements between two or more companies with a common business objective.

Stakeholders
Individuals or groups having a stake in the organisation's well-being, e.g. shareholders, employees.

Guanxi
Describes a personal connection between two people in which one is able to prevail upon another to perform a favour or service, or be prevailed upon. It is based on a complex nature of personalised networks of influence and social relationships, and is a central concept in Chinese society.

buyer–seller relationships, salesperson–purchasing agent interactions to inter-firm relationships and **strategic alliances**.

Thus a chain of relationships' key distinction from RM is that although the unit of analysis is still dyadic, the dyad can be other than one buyer–seller relationship. Furthermore, more than one dyad can be involved in any given exchange.

From the relationship background, network theory evolved when researchers started looking beyond simple dyadic relationships and began to concentrate their research effort on the more complex structures of networks.

Network theory has been based on the players–activities–resources model which suggests that networks are dynamic entities exhibiting interdependence and connectedness between actor bonds, activity links and resource ties (Håkansson and Johanson, 1992; Håkansson and Snehota, 1995). Networks that involve three or more players place great emphasis on the role of marketing in building and managing relationships with a company's many **stakeholders**, which could include suppliers, competitors, governments and employees, as well as customers.

A related RM concept in the Chinese culture is the so-called **guanxi**. It is composed of two Chinese characters, 'guan' (gate) and 'xi' (connection). It is a special type of relationship that bonds the exchange partners through a continual cooperation and exchange of favours.

Western RM and Chinese guanxi share some basic characteristics such as mutual understanding, cooperative behaviour and long-term orientation. In the Western RM society, written contracts are necessary to bind the exchanging partners to follow the rules, even among long-term relationship partners. In contrast, Chinese network systems emerge from personal agreement, not written contracts. Chinese B2B relations are often based on contracts or bonds between specific individuals, not between organisations. While China (among other Asian countries) is often portrayed as a 'relational society', it is also a low-trust society in which relationship orientation is only applied to insiders of the guanxi networks, but not to outsiders of networks such as a foreign firm. Guanxi members are tied together through an invisible and unwritten code of reciprocity, and the underlying motive for reciprocal behaviours is face-saving (Wang, 2007).

1.7 SUMMARY

Over the past twenty years, considerable emphasis has been placed on the importance of relationship marketing (RM). The reorientation of marketing has been at the expense of the traditional approach to marketing, that is, transaction marketing (the 4Ps). However, the premises of this book are that transactional marketing is still relevant and should be practised concurrently with various types of RM.

In RM, customers take a much more active role than they normally are given. The success of RM also, to a large extent, depends on the attitudes, commitment and performance of the employees. If they are not committed to their role as part-time marketers and are not motivated to perform in a customer-oriented fashion, the strategy fails. Besides customers and internal employees, the stakeholder view also includes other players in the RM process: suppliers, competitors and other external players.

The chapter ends with a categorisation of RM into three forms of organisation: dyadic relationships, chain of relationships and networks. The classic dyadic buyer–seller relationship tends to ignore the role of other stakeholders whereas networks are a more complex structure of relationships involving several stakeholders.

CASE STUDY 1.1

Duchy Originals
Prince Charles's organic food company is searching for further growth in the recession

In summer 2009, the new chief executive of the Prince of Wales's agricultural business, Andrew Baker, is in upbeat mood. He has recently announced plans to launch Duchy Originals in America and India as part of a five-year plan to quadruple annual retail turnover from approximately £50 million to £200 million. Baker, 49, took the top job at Duchy in September 2007, having worked at Cadbury's as managing director for Africa, the Middle East and Turkey. Although the world economy is still in an economic recession, he is convinced that, as consumers eat less at restaurants, they will still be interested in spending some extra money on affordable luxuries, including a decent meal at home.

Background of Duchy Originals

Duchy Originals Ltd was set up by Charles, Prince of Wales, in 1990 and named after the Duchy of Cornwall estates that are held in trust by the Prince of Wales.

Prince Charles is very passionate about this business. The values behind it are in line with his vision of 20 years ago. Prince Charles bought Home Farm in 1980, which encompasses 1,100 acres around Tetbury. Manager David Wilson masterminded the farm's conversion to organic from 1985 over an eight-year period. The first

Prince Charles chats with staff packing Duchy Originals biscuits
Source: Rex Features

Duchy Originals orange marmalade
Source: Courtesy of Duchy Originals Ltd

Duchy product was Oaten Biscuits, baked with organic oats and wheat harvested at the farm.

Prince Charles launched the company in 1990 to provide natural, high-quality organic farm products in a way that emphasises sustainable production, natural ingredients and traditional farming skills. Among its products are free-range meat and poultry, real ale, biscuits, marmalade and preserves.

Duchy Originals is the name given to a brand of premium organic food and drink products. The company Duchy Originals owns the Duchy Originals brand, but does not produce or sell food that carries the Duchy Originals brand name. Instead products with the Duchy Originals name are sold and manufactured by a number of different retail companies, all of whom pay royalties to the Duchy Originals company. The total annual value of these retail sales is over £53 million.

In December 2008, it was announced that the Duchy Originals brand was partnering with Nelsons to produce a line of herbal remedies.

The 'turnover' of the Duchy Originals Ltd company, which is the royalty income notified to the company, and which is also the gross profit, came to £4.8 million in 2007. Administrative expenses came to £3.31 million giving an operating profit of £1.53 million. The company Duchy Originals Ltd is a wholly owned subsidiary company of the Prince's Charities Foundation, and from the

profit of £1.53 million a charitable donation of £743,000 was given to the Foundation in 2007 (the difference is due to consolidation with subsidiaries). The Prince established the Foundation in 1979 to enable him to help support a variety of charitable causes and projects. In principle Dutchy Originals Ltd donates all of its net profits to the Prince's Charities Foundation.

In 2008 pretax profits decreased by 80 per cent as sales of the Duchy luxury products tumbled 15 per cent. According to the company, the decrease in profits is due to the cost of expanding and restructuring the business.

The Prince's Charities Foundation

In addition to receiving funds from Duchy Originals, the Prince's Charities Foundation also derives further income through royalties from the sale of lithographs of the Prince of Wales's watercolours, from charitable donations, from retail sales at the Highgrove Shop in Tetbury and from books written by His Royal Highness, such as *The Garden at Highgrove*.

The Prince's Charities Foundation receives an ever-increasing number of requests for assistance, which are considered on a regular basis by the Prince of Wales and the Foundation's trustees. Over 100 charitable programmes benefited from the £4 million donated to the Foundation in the year 2007–08.

Donations are made to a wide range of charities including organisations working with environmental issues, health and hospices, community and welfare, education and training, heritage and the built environment, charities supporting servicemen and women and towards people affected by natural disasters.

The target market – LOHAS

The primary target group for Duchy Originals is the so-called LOHAS (lifestyles of health and sustainability) which is a particular market segment related to sustainable living, 'green' ecological initiatives, and generally composed of a relatively upscale and well-educated people, who are also willing to pay a relatively high price for quality products such as Duchy Originals. Researchers have reported a range of sizes of the LOHAS market segment. For example, Worldwatch Institute reported that the LOHAS market segment in the year 2006 was approximately 30 per cent of the US consumer market. The LOHAS concept is inspired by the authors Paul H. Ray and Sherry R. Anderson, who coined the term 'cultural creatives' in their book by the same name (Ray and Anderson, 2000).

The organic food market remains a high-growth market. The UK market is worth £2 billion per annum and is growing at 20 per cent a year. However, with recession, growth is expected to be more modest in 2009.

The current strategy

CEO Andrew Baker has a clear strategy to multiply sales, and market research revealed that Duchy consumers buy infrequently and rarely shop across the range. Andrew Baker was positively surprised that some 26 per cent of the respondents in the UK research said that their first criterion in any purchase was animal husbandry, meaning that the animals are treated well.

There are seven elements in the new Duchy Originals strategic plan:

1 Expand the business internationally to the United States and India.

2 Cut the existing range of 300 products by as much as a third. This will eliminate weaker lines and reverse the proliferation that has diluted earnings.

3 Promote the product range to consumers through new packaging. Baker wants the company to lead the way in a whole range of sustainability issues, including packaging. It has projects with Wrap (Waste Reduction Action Programme) and plans to cut the weight of packaging and use new materials.

4 The products should be affordable. As Andrew Baker explains: 'The problem was not that biscuit for biscuit we were more expensive, is was that we were the only ones in 250g packets.' Both Duchy's biscuits for cheese and its sweet biscuits will be reduced to 150g and its chocolate biscuits to 100g or 125g boxes. Other lines, including preserves, will be similarly reduced in weight and a very thin ham will be launched (Ford, 2009).

5 In order for Duchy organic products to be more available in the stores, the company has to make a communication plan together with the retailer. Better communication in the store would help shoppers to understand the true benefits of organic certified food products.

6 Relaunch of the website and offer online sales.

7 Move into new areas such as food service (tea shops and hotels) and travel retail.

United States

Duchy USA Inc. was formed in 2008 and the company's present finance director, Michael Bailey, moved to Washington in August 2008 to manage the project. Duchy Originals is undeterred by the failure of other British companies to break into the American market. It will have secured sufficient local financing in America to ensure it can develop a sound business. The market for organic food in United States is four times bigger than in the UK. As in Britain, the company's key aim is to protect local farming communities, encouraging them to grow food in a sustainable manner and then helping them sell their products under the Duchy brand.

It is much more than selling a quality English brand into America. Duchy Originals wants the Prince's original concept of a virtuous circle to be brought to life through its American products. In the United States, the Prince of Wales is also well respected as a spokesman on the environment and his views are well known and understood there, at least by the LOHAS segment.

The Prince hopes that Duchy Originals can capitalise on growing environmental and sustainability awareness in America, together with the cachet of the royal association. The success of the Oscar-winning film *The Queen* and the monarch's state visit have raised the royal family's profile there. The Prince also visited the USA in 2004, and in 2007 he received the Global Environmental Citizen Award, presented to him by last year's winner Al Gore.

India

Duchy Originals plans to set up a company in India by year-end 2009/10 and will help market organic produce of farms based in Punjab supported by the Prince's Bhumi Vardaan Foundation. Duchy's intention is to establish Duchy India as a commercial vehicle for the organic produce of farms supported by the Foundation.

In Andrew Baker's mind there is no doubt that the credit crunch has raised the stakes for the organic market. However, equally, Andrew has no doubt that Duchy Originals is ready to take on this challenge.

QUESTIONS

1 Who are the customers of Duchy Originals and how can the company develop its relationships with these?

2 The CEO, Andrew Baker, claims: 'Given the credit squeeze there is also an argument that consumers will eat less at restaurants and spend extra on a decent meal at home. This will help our business.' Discuss this statement

3 What do you think of Duchy Originals' expansion plans to the United States and India?

SOURCES

Duchy Originals (www.duchyoriginals.com); Ford, R. (2009) Duchy courage: interview with CEO Andrew Baker, *The Grocer*, 7 February, 38–9 (www.grocer.com); The Grocer (2009) Organic stands its ground, *The Grocer*, 7 February, 4–5 (www.grocer.com); Johncox, L. (2008) Prince Charles takes Duchy Originals into America, *The Sunday Times*, 22 June (http://business.timesonline.co.uk/tol/business/industry_sectors/retailing/article4186915.ece); LexisNexis; Ray. P. H. and Anderson, S. R. (2000) *The Cultural Creatives*, New York, Harmony Books; Steiner, R. (2009) Prince Charles' Duchy Originals down 80%, *Daily Mail*, 10 February (www.thisismoney.co.uk/markets/article.html?in_article_id=474138&in_page_id=3).

QUESTIONS FOR DISCUSSION

1   What are the similarities between relationship marketing (RM) and transactional marketing (TM)?

2   How does an RM strategy differ from a TM strategy?

3   Which kind of industries could benefit from the use of RM versus TM and vice versa?

4   In which situations would customers not be expected to be interested in RM?

REFERENCES

Abell, D. (1980) *Defining the Business: The Starting Point of Strategic Planning*, Prentice-Hall, Englewood Cliffs, NJ.

Barton, D. (2009) Asia's future and the financial crisis, *McKinsey Quarterly*, 1: 102–5.

Brown, S. (1999) Retro marketing: yesterday's tomorrows, today! *Market Intelligence and Planning*, 17(7): 363–76.

Czinkota, M. R. and Samli, A. C. (2007) The remarkable performance of international marketing in the second half of the twentieth century, *European Business Review*, 19(4): 316–31.

Deering, A., Cook, A., Jonk, G. and Hall, A. (2008) Internet tools enable organizational transformation from the inside out: the Nokia Siemens Network case, *Strategy & Leadership*, 36(5): 34–7.

Godin, S. (1999) *Permission Marketing*, Simon & Schuster, New York.

Gordon, I. H. (1998) *Relationship Marketing*, John Wiley & Sons, Canada Ltd.

Grönroos, C. (1996) Relationship marketing: strategic and tactical implications, *Management Decision*, 34(3): 5–14.

Grönroos, C. (2006) On defining marketing: finding a new roadmap for marketing, *Marketing Theory*, 6(4): 395–417.

Gummesson, E. (1999) *Total Relationship Marketing: Rethinking Marketing Management: From 4Ps to 30 Rs*, Butterworth-Heinemann, Oxford.

Håkansson, H. and Johanson, J. (1992) A model of industrial networks, in B. Axelsson and G. Easton (eds) *Industrial Networks: A New View of Reality*, Routledge, London, pp. 28–34.

Håkansson, H. and Snehota, I. (eds) (1995) *Developing Relationships in Business Networks*, Routledge, London.

Håkansson, H. and Waluszewski A. (2005) Developing a new understanding of markets: reinterpreting the 4Ps, *Journal of Business & Industrial Marketing*, 20(3): 110–17.

Healy, M., Hastings, K., Brown, L. and Gardiner, M. (2001) The old, the new, and the complicated: a trilogy of marketing relationships, *European Journal of Marketing*, 35(1/2): 182–93.

Kelly, S. (2001) Seeking permission for ultimate goal in true one-to-one marketing, *MAD*, 16 March.

Lindgreen, A. and Crawford, I. (1991) Implementing, monitoring and measuring a programme of relationship marketing, *Marketing Intelligence & Planning*, 17(5): 231–9.

Lindgreen, A., Davis, R., Brodie, R. J. and Buchanan-Oliver, M. (2000) Pluralism in contemporary marketing practices, *International Journal of Bank Marketing*, 18(6): 294–308.

Liu, B. (2001) Coca-Cola helps quench thirst during boycott of US goods, *Financial Times*, 26 October.

Mintzberg, H. (1987) The strategy concept 1: five Ps for strategy, *California Management Review*, Fall: 11–24.

Mintzberg, H. and Waters, A. (1985) On strategies, deliberate and emergent, *Strategic Management Journal*, 6: 257–72.

Payne, A. (ed) (1995) *Advances in Relationship Marketing*, Kogan Page, London.

Peppers, D. and Rogers, M. (1993) *One-to-One Future: Building Relationships One Customer at a Time*, Currency/Doubleday, New York.

Sheth, J. N. and Parvatiyar, A. (1995) The evolution of relationship marketing, *International Business Review*, 4(4): 397–418.

Vavra, T. G. (1995) *Aftermarketing: How to Keep Customers for Life Through Relationship Marketing*, Business One Irwin, Homewood, IL.

Voice Business (1997) No. 51–2, 21–8 December: 478–9.

Wang, C. L. (2007) Guanxi vs. relationship marketing: exploring underlying differences, *Industrial Marketing Management*, 36: 81–6.

Zineldin, M. (2000) Beyond relationship marketing: technologicalship marketing, *Marketing Intelligence Planning*, 18(1): 9–23.

PART I
Assessing the competitiveness of the firm (internal)

When the international economy was relatively static, competition was a 'war of position' in which firms occupied competitive space like squares on a chessboard. The key to competitive advantage was where a firm chose to compete. How it chose to compete was also important but secondary – a matter of execution. However, as markets fragment and product life cycles accelerate, dominating existing product segments becomes less

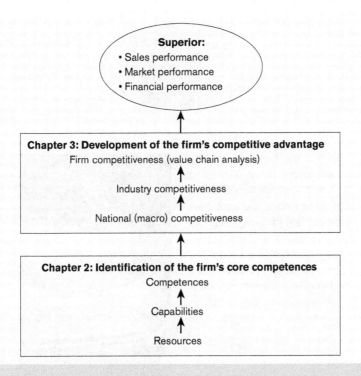

The structure of Part I

important. In today's dynamic business environment a firm's success depends on anticipation of market trends and quick response to changing customer needs. The essence of strategy is not the structure of a firm's products but the dynamics of its behaviour. In future the goal is to identify and develop the hard-to-imitate organisational capabilities that distinguish a firm from its competitors in the eyes of customers.

Part I covers the necessary internal analysis to assess the competitive advantages of the firm with regard to its customers and other stakeholders in the external environment, which is the focus of Part II.

The structure of Part I is shown in the diagram above.

Chapter 2 identifies the firm's core competences, based on the assessment of its resources and capabilities. Capabilities can be described as what an organisation does as opposed to what it has (resources or assets). Chapter 3 then continues with how the core competences might be used in the development of competitive advantages, from the macro-level (country-specific advantages) to the micro-level (value chain analysis).

The majority of growth in the global automobile industry in the coming decade will come from emerging economies such as India, China and Eastern Europe. And the largest contribution to growth of the auto market in these countries will be the fast-growing small car segment. The increasing disposable income of the middle-class population is the key driver of the small car market in developing nations. However, in developed regions such as the US and Western Europe, stringent environmental standards are increasing the need for more fuel-efficient cars.

Tata Nano European launch at a Motor Show 2008
Source: © P. Cox/Alamy

Tata motors

Indian conglomerate Tata Group (www.tata.com) employs nearly 300,000 people in 85 countries. Today the Tata Group is India's largest conglomerate company, with revenues in 2006–07 equivalent to US$28 billion (equal to 3.2 per cent of India's GDP), and a market capitalisation of US$73 billion at the end of 2007. The Tata Group comprises 98 companies in seven business sectors.

One of the companies in the Tata Group is Tata Motors. Tata Motors is gearing up for the global market. Tata Motors, one of India's largest automobile makers, manufactures buses, commercial trucks and tractor-trailers, passenger cars (Indica, Indigo, Safari, Sumo, and the ultra-cheap Nano), light commercial vehicles, and utility vehicles. The company sells its cars primarily in India, but about 20 per cent of sales comes from other Asian countries and Africa, Australia, Europe, the Middle East and South America. In 2008 Tata Motors bought the Jaguar and Land Rover brands from Ford for about $2.3 billion. Tata Motors has a workforce of 22,000 employees working in its three plants and other regional offices across the country.

Tata Motors has a lower than 20 per cent share of the Indian car market and has recently been suffering a sales slump. In 2007 Tata Motor produced 237,343 cars and more than 300,000 buses and trucks. Outside India Tata Motors is selling only a few cars so their international marketing experience is weak.

Tata Motors has some distinct advantages in comparison to other MNC competitors. There is a definite cost advantage as labour cost is 8–9 per cent of sales as against 30–35 per cent of sales in developed economies.

Tata Motors has extensive backward and forward linkages and it is strongly interwoven with machine tools and metals sectors from other parts of the Tata Group. There are favourable government polices and regulations to boost the auto industry, e.g. incentives for R&D.

The acquisitions of Jaguar and Land Rover created financial pressure for Tata Motors, with the company stating that it wanted to spend some $1.5 billion over the next four years to expand the facilities manufacturing the luxury brands. In addition to giving Tata a globally recognisable product, the Land Rover and Jaguar deal also gives Tata an entry into the US. Through a deal with Fiat, Tata is already distributing the Italian cars in India and may expand the offering into South America, a Fiat stronghold.

Development of Tata Nano

In 2008 Tata unveiled the Nano, the cheapest car in the world, at the Auto Expo in New Delhi. The car seats five people, gets up to 55 miles to the gallon, and sells for about $2,230. At first the Nano will be sold only in India, but Tata hopes to export them after a few initial years of production; the Nano might be exported to Europe as early as 2012. First shipments to Indian customers are expected in mid-2009.

The alternative for Tata Nano
Source: © B. O'Kane/Alamy

Tata Nano started with the vision of Ratan Tata, chairman of Tata Motors' parent, Tata Group, to create an ultra-low-cost car for a new category of Indian consumer: someone who couldn't afford the $5,000 sticker price of what was then the cheapest car on the market and instead drove his family around on a $1,000 motorcycle. Many drivers in India can only afford motorcycles and it is fairly common to see an Indian family of four on a motorcycle.

In India alone there are 50 million to 100 million people caught in that automotive chasm. Until now none of the Indian auto-makers have focused on that segment. In that respect, the Nano is a great example of the Blue Ocean Strategy.

The customer was ever-present in the development of the Nano. Tata didn't set the price of the Nano by calculating the cost of production and then adding a margin. Rather, it set $2,500 as the price that it thought customers could pay and then worked back, with the help of partners willing to take on a challenge, to build a $2,500 car that would reward all involved with a small profit.

The Nano engineers and partners didn't simply strip features out of an existing car, the tack Renault took with its Dacia Logan, which sells in India for roughly $10,000. Instead, they looked at their target customers' lives for cost-cutting ideas. So, for instance, the Nano has a smaller engine than other cars because more horsepower would be wasted in India's jam-packed cities, where the average speed is 10 to 20 miles per hour.

The Nano aims to bring the joys of motoring to millions of Indians, doing for the subcontinent what the Volkswagen Beetle did for Germany and the Mini for Britain. But the plan has horrified environmentalists, who fear that the demand for more cars from India's aspirational and increasingly middle-class population – now numbering 50 million in a country with a total 1.1 billion people – will add to pollution and global warming.

The global automotive industry and the current crises

In 2007, a total of 71.9 million new automobiles were sold worldwide: 22.9 million in Europe, 21.4 million in Asia-Pacific, 19.4 million in USA and Canada, 4.4 million in Latin America, 2.4 million in the Middle East and 1.4 million in Africa. The markets in North America and Japan were stagnant, while those in South America and Asia grew strongly. Of the major markets, Russia, Brazil, India and China saw the most rapid growth.

Since mid-2008 the sales from the world automotive industry has been developing negatively as a result of the current financial crises.

Two of the most promising markets for Tata Nano are characterised in the following:

India

India is likely to evolve into a global hub for small-car manufacturing. Currently, India is one of the largest producers of small cars with the small-car segment accounting for about three-quarters of the Indian car market. The fast-growing small-car market has encouraged several global auto companies (Renault, Nissan, Toyota, Hyundai) to announce plans for the launch of small cars in India. With the launch of Tata Nano, the stage is set for around a dozen new small and compact cars to be launched in India in the next two years. Currently, Maruti Suzuki India, the largest passenger car manufacturer in India, has more than a 60 per cent share of the domestic small-car segment.

China and Japan

In the long term the small car demand in China is expected to increase. However, the narrow price gap between the small-car segment and the medium-car segment has made medium segment cars a more attractive choice for consumers.

Mini-cars account for more than one-third of the total volume of sales in the Japanese auto market. Suzuki and Daihatsu are the market leaders in the small-car market in Japan. A large number of Japanese consumers are moving from luxury cars to mini-cars due to environmental standards and increasing gas prices.

Please watch the video before answering the questions.

QUESTIONS

1   What could be the main reasons for Tata Motors entering the global small-car market?

2   What are the competitive advantages that Tato Motors would enjoy with their Nano in emerging markets?

3   What are the barriers for entering Western markets with Tata Nano?

SOURCES

Tata Motors (www.tatamotors.com); http://tatanano.inservices.tatamotors.com/tatamotors; general public information.

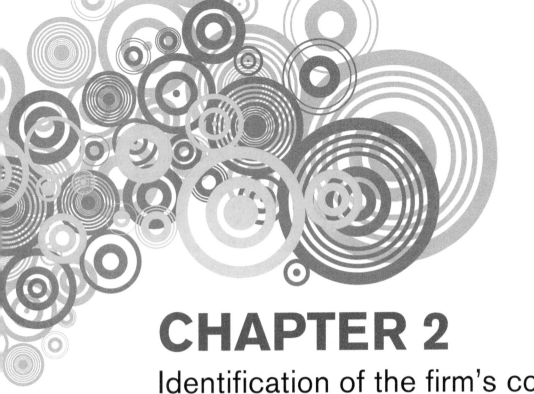

CHAPTER 2
Identification of the firm's core competences

LEARNING OBJECTIVES

After studying this chapter you should be able to:

- explain the difference between the resource-based view (RBV) and the market-orientation view (MOV)

- explain the connection between the RBV and RM

- describe and discuss the concept of the value chain

2.1 INTRODUCTION

Understanding competitive advantage is an ongoing challenge for decision makers. Historically, competitive advantage was thought of as a matter of position, where firms occupied a competitive space and built and defended market share. Competitive advantage depended on where the business was located, and where it chose to provide services. Stable environments allowed this strategy to be successful, particularly for large and dominant organisations in mature industries.

This ability to develop a sustained competitive advantage today is increasingly rare. A competitive advantage laboriously achieved can be quickly lost. Organisations sustain a competitive advantage only so long as the services they deliver and the manner in which they deliver them have attributes that correspond to the key buying criteria of a substantial number of customers. Sustained competitive advantage is the result of an enduring value differential between the products or services of one organisation and those of its competitors in the minds of customers. Therefore, organisations must consider more than the fit between the external environment and their present internal characteristics. They must anticipate what the rapidly changing environment will be like, and change their structures, cultures and other relevant factors so as to reap the benefits of changing times. Sustained competitive advantage has become more of a matter of movement and ability to change than of location or position.

The question of an enduring value differential raises the issue of why a firm is able to achieve a competitive advantage. To answer this, it is necessary to examine why and how organisations differ in a strategic sense. Identifying strengths and weaknesses requires introspection and self-examination. It also requires much more systematic analysis than has been done in the past.

From capability to advantage

How well a company assembles the capabilities that a new business requires determines how successful it is at gaining and keeping positional advantage. Some capabilities are more important than others, and combinations are generally harder to imitate than individual capabilities. The business builder's challenge begins with the need to assemble the capabilities that are most critical to making money in the business. Lasting competitive advantage comes only when companies assemble combinations of capabilities that are difficult to imitate.

Competitive advantage may not call for superior capabilities in every area of a business. But control of the most important capabilities can determine how much of the value of a growing business will flow to its owner. For every opportunity, it is important to distinguish the capabilities that influence competitive success from those that are merely necessary to stay in business. Capabilities that are less critical can be outsourced or controlled by others.

2.2 ROOTS OF COMPETITIVE ADVANTAGE

Market orientation view (MOV)
Outside-in perspective. Adapting the firm's resources to market conditions and the competitive environment.

Two theoretical perspectives are particularly relevant for understanding how firms deploy scarce resources to create competitive excellence. These are: the **market orientation view (MOV)** and the **resource-based view (RBV)**.

There is, however, a potential conflict between these two perspectives in the sense that one (MOV) advocates the advantages of outward-looking responsiveness in adapting to market conditions, while the other (RBV) is inward looking and emphasises the rent-earning

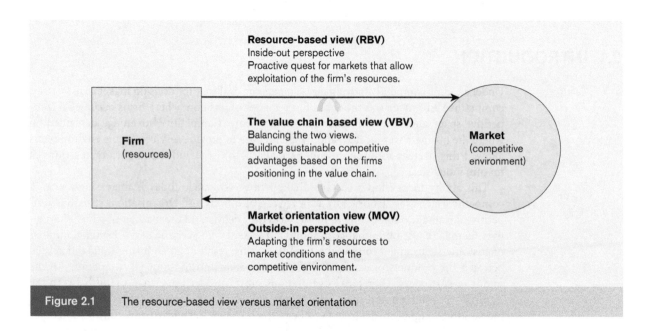

| Figure 2.1 | The resource-based view versus market orientation |

Resource-based view (RBV)
Inside-out perspective. Proactive quest for markets that allows exploitation of the firm's resources.

Value chain based view (VBV)
Building sustainable competitive advantages based on the firm's positioning in the value chain.

characteristics of corporate resources and the development of corporate resources and capabilities. Quite simply, from a marketing viewpoint, if strategy becomes too deeply embedded in corporate capabilities, it runs the risk of ignoring the demands of changing, turbulent marketing environments. Yet from a resource-based perspective, marketing strategies that do not exploit a company's distinctive competences are likely to be ineffective and unprofitable.

However, we argue that the **value chain based view (VBV)** provides a way of reconciling this potential conflict – it represents a balanced view of the RBV and the MOV – see Figure 2.1.

We will now look at the two theoretical perspectives.

2.3 THE RESOURCE-BASED VIEW (RBV)

Most firms that apply a relationship marketing approach are probably somewhere in this stage of the transition process. A true transition towards a relationship marketing strategy requires a focus on competences and resources in the relationship (because partners in the relationship use each other's resources (Grönroos, 1996)). This section focuses on identification of a single firm's competences from an RBV.

According to the resource-based theory, which has its roots in economic theory (e.g. Penrose, 1959) and early strategy theory (Selznick, 1957; Ansoff, 1965), the long-term competitiveness of a company depends on its resources that differentiate it from its competitors, that are durable, and that are difficult to imitate and substitute (e.g. Grant, 1991; Fahy, 2002). Each firm is unique and this uniqueness stems from the resources it possesses, their compatibility with one another, and/or the way they are deployed. Furthermore, this uniqueness is relatively long lasting, because the resources of the company are relative immobile (Barney, 1991; Sharma and Erramilli, 2004).

Various definitions and classifications for resources have been proposed in the literature. The most important in the current context are briefly described here.

Resources

The resources of the firm in the competence-based approach are typically classified into two types: tangible and intangible resources. Tangible resources are inputs into a firm that can be seen, touched and/or quantified. They include assets such as plant and equipment, access to raw materials and finance, a trained and skilled workforce and a firm's organisational structure. Intangible resources range from intellectual property rights such as patents, trademarks and copyrights to the know-how of personnel, informal networks, organisational culture and a firm's reputation for its products (Deering *et al.*, 2008). The dividing line between the tangible and intangible is often unclear, and how they are classified varies a little from one writer to another. Despite the problems with classification, proponents of the competence-based approach agree on the relative importance of the two types of resource. Although it is clear that both types of resource are required for any business to operate, competence-based theorists argue that intangible resources are the most likely source of competitive advantage. The reason for this, it is argued, is that, being less visible, they are more difficult to understand and imitate than tangible resources. As such they are therefore more likely to be a source of competitive advantage (Collis and Montgomery, 2008).

I use the word 'resource' as the most generic term to qualify the basic unit of asset, skill, ability, expertise, knowledge, etc. owned and controlled by one firm. Grant (1991) describes six types of resource: technological, financial, physical, human, organisational and reputation. Resources are extremely diverse, as shown in Figure 2.2 (examples are given in brackets).

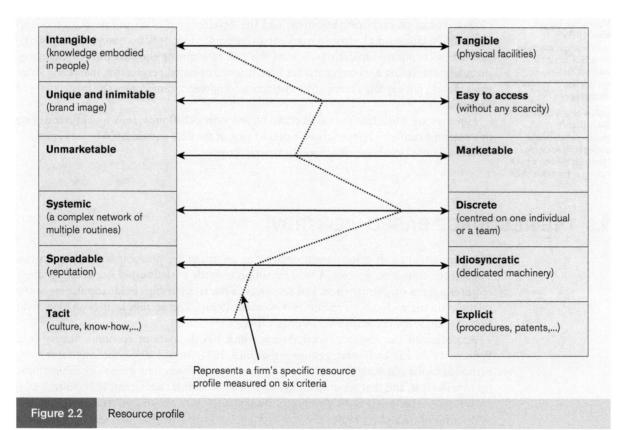

Intangible (knowledge embodied in people)	⟷	**Tangible** (physical facilities)
Unique and inimitable (brand image)	⟷	**Easy to access** (without any scarcity)
Unmarketable	⟷	**Marketable**
Systemic (a complex network of multiple routines)	⟷	**Discrete** (centred on one individual or a team)
Spreadable (reputation)	⟷	**Idiosyncratic** (dedicated machinery)
Tacit (culture, know-how,...)	⟷	**Explicit** (procedures, patents,...)

Represents a firm's specific resource profile measured on six criteria

Figure 2.2 Resource profile

The dotted line in Figure 2.2 represents a specific resource (e.g. technical) measured on six criteria. However, the resource-based theory does not consider all resources possessed by a company, but focuses only on critical (or strategic) resources, i.e. those that are the basis of the company's sustainable competitive advantage. To determine such resources, various authors have proposed a number of 'tests' (see also Grant, 1991; Prahalad and Hamel, 1994; Trott, Maddocks and Wheeler, 2009), the most important of which are:

- competitive superiority test, which evaluates if and to what extent the research contributes to differentiating the company from its competitors;
- imitation test, which analyses actual and potential competitors' difficulties in imitating the resource, due, for example, to its physical uniqueness, path dependency, casual ambiguity or economic deterrence;
- duration test, which measures if the resource's benefits will also be generated in the long term;
- appropriateness test, which verifies if the company owning the resource is able to exploit the advantages generated in the market;
- substitutability test, which assesses how difficult it is for competitors to replace the resource with an alternative that gives the same advantages.

The very basis of RBV is to increase the ability of the firm to act upon, shape and transform its environment. The objective is no longer to adapt to the environmental forces but to choose a strategy that allows the best exploitation (the best return) of resources and competences given the external opportunities. It means taking into account the external opportunities but with the objective of creating value beyond existing market standards. As a consequence, the strategic options for a firm are derived from its resource profile: the business portfolio is an output of the search of applications carried out for one competence.

Competence

One resource – such as a privileged access to raw material – may be a source of competitive edge. However, a greater competitive advantage should emerge from competences, i.e. the combination of different types of resources. It is the way in which the resources are assembled, or combined, for the execution of an activity that creates the difference between firms. This distinctive combination of resources emerges through organisational learning. Competence examples may be found in engineering knowledge, production expertise or marketing abilities.

Competence may be described by the following three attributes:

1 *Proprietariness*: a competence is a firm-specific set of resources.

2 *Learning*: a competence results from years of experience accumulated in a small number of fields (where the firm may dominate).

3 *Pervasiveness*: a competence is diffused pervasively throughout the entire firm and exists within several product lines (or strategic business units (SBUs)).

EXHIBIT 2.1
Honda's competences in small engines

A famous example of a business strategy that was clearly based on a focus on a core competency is Honda's application of small engine technology to a variety of products requiring small engines (motorcycles, jet skis, lawn mowers, etc.).

When Honda introduced motorcycles in the US market, it had focused most of its attention on selling its higher value (but problem-plagued) motorcycles through a dealer network. At the same time, it introduced a series of much smaller motorcycles with little fanfare through sporting goods stores. While their larger motorcycles floundered competing against the likes of firmly established Harley-Davidson, Honda's smaller engine motorcycles found a ready audience with a more utilitarian

A small Honda gasoline engine
Source: © Lyroky/Alamy

'nicest people' demographic group. This turned out to be Honda's beachhead into the US marketplace.

The ability to concentrate on customers and understand their changing needs is the first step in the value chain based view.

Although it is true that the small engines in both the motorcycles and the scooters were Honda's core competence, that core competence alone did not ensure success. Honda succeeded because it also looked to the other end of the value chain – it listened to what the customer wanted.

It turned out to be both a customer and a product very different from what Honda had envisioned. Honda quickly refocused its distribution channels and adjusted its product mix to meet the unexpected market demand. In the long term, Honda was able to refocus its efforts and eventually capture market share in the higher value motorcycle market.

Sources: Adapted from Prahalad and Hamel (1990); Webb and Gile (2001).

Core competences
The principal distinctive capabilities possessed by a company – what it is really good at.

A **core competence**, as articulated by Prahalad and Hamel (1990), has three traits: it makes a contribution to perceived customer benefits; it is difficult for competitors to imitate; and it can be leveraged to a wide variety of markets. Knowing a firm's core competence is important for developing strategy. By concentrating on their core competence and outsourcing other activities, managers can use their company's resources in four ways: they maximise returns by focusing on what they do best; they provide formidable barriers against the entry of competitors; they fully utilise external suppliers' strengths and investment that they would not be able to duplicate; and they reduce investment and risk, shorten cycle times, and increase customer responsiveness.

Figure 2.3 shows the connection between resources, core competences, sustainable competitive advantages and competitive excellence.

Resources alone are not a basis for competitive advantage. It is the way in which resources are integrated with each other to perform a task or an activity that provides the capability for

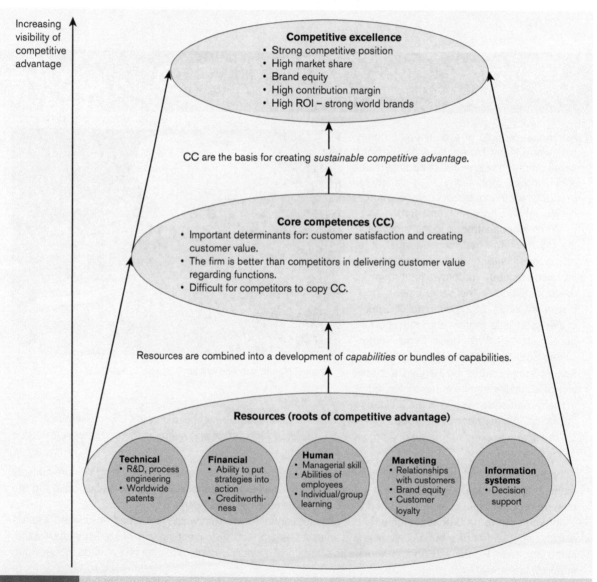

Figure 2.3	The roots of competition
	Source: Inspiration from Grant (1991).

an organisation to compete successfully in the marketplace. This being the case, the most important resource for any organisation is the skill and knowledge possessed by the organisation's employees. It is this skill and knowledge acquired over time and embedded in the firm's culture that influences how it operates and determines its success.

Whether or not resources and capabilities have the potential to become core competences depends on how difficult they are for competitors to acquire and how valuable they are to the firm as a basis for competitive advantage. When they are rare, difficult to imitate, non-substitutable and they allow a firm to exploit opportunities or neutralise threats, then they can be considered core competences and serve as the basis of an organisation's sustained competitive advantage.

A resource becomes a source of sustainable competitive advantage only if it passes several tests. First, it must be competitively superior and valuable in the product market. Second, it must be difficult to imitate. Third, it must not be easy to replace by an alternative capability. Fourth, it must be durable. Fifth, it must be difficult to move. If the capability can move with an employee, it is the employee, not the corporation that will acquire the value.

Some individual capabilities may pass the tests. A world-class brand, for example, will continue to confer advantage on its owner. But few individual capabilities are unassailable, and even a first-to-market advantage can fade away without proper support. The key to sustaining competitive advantage as a business grows is to assemble a bundle of distinctive capabilities that together satisfy the criteria.

The capabilities in the bundle can be built in-house, borrowed by means of alliances, or acquired out of house. As each new capability is added to the bundle, greater competitive advantage accrues because the combination becomes more difficult for competitors to imitate or substitute, and more difficult for employees to acquire from the company.

Cardy and Selvarajan (2006) classify competences into two broad categories: *personal* or *corporate*. Personal competences are possessed by individuals and include characteristics such as knowledge, skills, abilities, experience and personality. Corporate competences belong to the organisation and are embedded processes and structures that tend to reside within the organisation, even when individuals leave. These two categories are not entirely independent. The collection of personal competences can form a way of doing things or a culture that becomes embedded in the organisation. In addition, corporate characteristics can determine the type of personal competences that will best work or fit in the organisation.

2.4 MARKET ORIENTATION VIEW (MOV) COMPARED TO THE RESOURCE-BASED VIEW

Business model
The fundamental strategy underlying the way a business unit operates.

Customer value
The difference relation between the values the customer gains from owning and using a product and the costs of obtaining the product.

The MOV or fit model suggests that the firm adapts its assets to its environmental constraints in order to obtain a fit with the environment. Basically, MOV is about adapting to the market environment (Kohli and Jaworski, 1990). It can be understood as a culture, rather than a set of behaviours and espoused values (Beverland and Lindgreen, 2005). MOV can be defined as a culture in which all employees are committed to the continuous creation of superior value for the customers (Vesanen, 2007). However, adaptation to different customers in different countries can be an expensive **business model**. In this regard you get very satisfied customers but the costs involved in producing this **customer value**/satisfaction might also be very high.

Table 2.1 summarises the main differences between the RBV and the MOV.

As both views (models) have advantages and disadvantages, a way of bridging the gap between the RBV and the MOV will now be covered.

Table 2.1	Main differences between the resource-based view and the market orientation view	
	Market orientation view (MOV)	Resource-based view (RBV)
Basic principle	Adapt firm's resources to the requirements of its competitive environment, i.e. to key success factors	Pro-active quest for environments that allow the best exploitation of the firm's resources
Strategic analysis	Centred on industry structure and market attributes	Emphasis on internal diagnosis
Formulation process	Outside-in	Inside-out
Source for competitive edge	Market positioning in relation to local competitive environment	Firm's idiosyncratic set of resources and competences

2.5 THE VALUE CHAIN BASED VIEW (VBV)

The RBV focuses on what the firm has, whereas the VBV focuses on what the firm does. In addition, the VBV also integrates some elements of the MOV, but it does not ignore the costs of performing the activities.

Resources per se do not create value. Rather, value creation results from the activities in which the resources are applied.

The foundation of competitive advantage is a product and/or service that provides value to the business's customers (McPhee and Wheeler, 2006).

Perceived value is the *relation* between the benefits customers realise from using the product/ service and the costs (direct and indirect) they incur in finding, acquiring and using it (see Figure 2.4). The higher this relationship is, the better the perceived value for the customer.

Please do not think of Figure 2.4 as a mathematical formula for calculating and exact measure of Customer Perceived Value (CPV). Instead, think of it as what the customer *gets* compared to what the customer *gives* in order to be able to use or consume the product or service. After the product or service has been purchased and is used or consumed, the level of the customer's satisfaction can be evaluated. If the actual customer satisfaction with the purchase and quality exceeds initial expectations, then the customer will tend to buy the product or service again and the customer may become loyal towards the company's product or service (brand loyalty).

The components driving customer benefits include product values, service values, technical values and commitment value. The components driving costs fall into two categories: those that relate to the price paid, and those representing the internal costs incurred by the customer. These components can be unbundled into salient attributes. Commitment to value, for example, includes investment in personnel and customer relations. Internal costs might reflect set-up time and expense, maintenance, training and energy.

If the benefits exceed the costs then a customer will at least consider purchasing your product. For example, the value to an industrial customer may be represented by the rate of return earned on the purchase of a new piece of equipment. If the cost reductions or revenue enhancements generated by the equipment justify the purchase price and operating costs of the equipment through an acceptable return on investment, then value has been created.

Thus, the value of products is a function of buyer purchasing criteria (Porter, 1985, pp. 141–3). Variation in buyer purchasing criteria gives rise to selective adaptation of products or differentiation. Differentiated products can command a higher price if they provide a better match with buyer purchasing criteria. Customer value is defined either by the cost reductions that the product can provide in the customer's activities or by the performance

Product benefits for customer:

- Meeting customer requirements
- Flexibility to meet changing customer needs
- Fitness for use
- Improved efficiency in operation
- Better profitability
- Branding (trust in the brand, and that it provides 'safe' use)
- Technically superior product
- Sustainable product solution ('green' profile)
- Elimination of waste

Service benefits for customer:

- Product service and support
- Customer support
- BDA-service (before, during and after the actual buying of the product solution)
- Short lead time

$$\text{Customer perceived value (CPV)} = \frac{\text{'Get'}}{\text{'Give'}} = \frac{\text{Product benefits} + \text{Service benefits}}{\text{Direct costs} + \text{Indirect costs}}$$

Direct (monetary) costs for customer:

- Price of product (paid to the supplier)
- Lifetime costs (including financing)
- Quality assurance
- Spare part costs

Indirect costs for customer (customer participation in achieving the benefits):

- Conversation/negotiation with the supplier (transaction costs)
- Internal costs (administration etc. in order to get the product to work)
- Long lead time from suppliers resulting in necessary increased inventory of materials and final products
- Installation costs
- Service cuts

Figure 2.4	The concept of customer perceived value
	Sources: Adapted from Anderson *et al.* (2007; 2008); McGrath and Keil (2007); and Smith and Nagle (2005).

improvements that the customer can gain by using the product. Porter's generic strategies of cost or differentiation (1980) are aimed at improving either the cost or value of a product relative to the average of the industry.

Technology development is performed to either reduce the cost of a product, particularly through process improvements, or to raise the commendable price by improving the adaptation of the product to buyer purchasing criteria.

EXHIBIT 2.2
The value chain of Acme Axles, Inc.

Acme Axles, Inc. (a disguised name) makes custom-designed axles, wheels and related parts for trailers, tractors, generators, welders and other equipment requiring axle systems. Acme differentiates itself from competitors by providing fast on-time delivery of high-quality, custom-designed axles.

The value chain outline for Acme and the axle industry is shown in Figure 2.5.

There are three levels of value chain analysis:

- The industry value chain consists of the different firms in the vertical supply chain.

- The company's (Acme Axle, Inc.) internal value chain consists of the different functions in the company.

- Operational activities of a certain function (only the detailed description of operational activities is shown).

EXHIBIT 2.2
The value chain of Acme Axles, Inc. (*continued*)

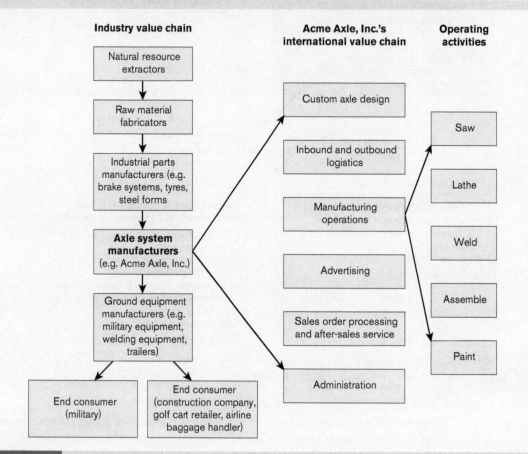

| Figure 2.5 | The value chain of Acme Axles, Inc. |

Natural resource extraction (i.e. ore mining and rubber plantations), raw material fabrication (i.e. steel foundries and tyre manufacturers), and industrial parts manufacturing are the supplier links in the value chain. Customer links include military and non-military ground equipment manufacturing. These downstream manufacturers use the axle systems as components of the equipment, such as welding trailers, airport baggage handling trailers, golf carts and tractors.

Source: Adapted from Donelan and Kaplan (1998).

Perception
The process by which people select, organise and interpret sensory stimulation into a meaningful picture of the world.

Understanding customers' **perceptions** of value is key to this part of the process and is one where many companies fall down. Too often, management determines what it believes the customer wants, develops and makes the product, then adds up the costs of production and puts a standard margin on top of that. The major problems with this approach are that the product may not effectively address changing customer needs and that the price may be too high for created customer value.

Value-driven companies spend enough time with customers to obtain a fundamental understanding of their customers' businesses and of their current and latent needs. They want to understand what product features really provide customer benefits, and which ones are merely going to add to the product cost without giving customers any additional reason to buy. They also determine the price that will deliver value to their customers early in the product development process. From that, they deduct their target profit and give their engineers and operations people firm targets for the cost of the final product or its components.

Superior value

Delivering value may not be enough to achieve competitive advantage though. Excellent quality is no advantage if your competitors all have similar offerings. Competitive advantage requires that the value of your product or service is superior to that of your competitors. The major challenge here is that your competitors are providing a moving target by continuously improving the value they provide.

Competitive advantage can be accomplished by providing the greatest level of benefits through a differentiation strategy. It can also be accomplished by enabling a customer to achieve the 'lowest life cycle cost' compared to comparable products. It is important to recognise that lowest life cycle cost does not require the lowest purchase price. Lowest life cycle cost can be achieved by helping the customer reduce start-up, training or maintenance costs.

The value chain

Porter's work (1985) is the key reference on value chains and value configuration analysis for competitive advantage.

Value chains are created by transforming a set of inputs into more refined outputs. The strategic challenges associated with managing a value chain are related to manufacturing products with the right quality at the lowest possible cost. The ways to reduce costs – or increase value – are primarily found through economies of scale, efficient capacity utilisation, learning effects, product and information flows, and quality measures. Critical drivers of value creation in chains also include the interrelationships between primary activities, on the one hand, and product development, marketing and service, i.e. support activities, on the other hand.

The firm's value chain as, for example, shown in Figure 2.5 provides a systematic means of displaying and categorising activities. The activities performed by a firm in any industry can be grouped into the nine generic categories.

At each stage of the value chain there exists an opportunity to contribute positively to the firm's competitive strategy by performing some activity or process in a way that is better than the competitors, and so providing some uniqueness or advantage. If a firm attains such a competitive advantage that is sustainable, defensible, profitable and valued by the market, then it may earn high rates of return, even though the industry may be unfavourable and the average profitability of the industry modest.

In competitive terms, value is the amount that buyers are *willing to pay for what a firm provides them (perceived value)* less the sacrifices that the customers offer to obtain access to the value (e.g. money, time). A firm is profitable if the value it commands exceeds the costs involved in creating the product. According to the 'formula' in Figure 2.4, it is implied that customer perceived value should be higher than 1. Creating value for buyers that exceeds the cost of doing so is the goal of any generic strategy. Value, instead of cost, must be used in analysing competitive position, since firms often deliberately raise their costs in order to command a premium price via differentiation. The concept of buyers' perceived value will be discussed further in this chapter.

The value chain displays total value and consists of value activities and margin. Value activities are the physically and technologically distinct activities that a firm performs. These are the building blocks by which a firm creates a product that is valuable to its buyers. Margin is the difference between total value (price) and the collective cost of performing the value activities.

Competitive advantage is a function of either providing comparable buyer value more efficiently than competitors (lower cost), or performing activities at comparable cost but in unique ways that create more customer value than the competitors are able to offer and, hence, command a premium price (differentiation). The firm might be able to identify elements of the value chain that are not worth the costs. These can then be unbundled and produced outside the firm (outsourced) at a lower price.

Value activities can be divided into two broad types: *primary activities* and *support activities*. Primary activities are the activities involved in the physical creation of the product, its sale and transfer to the buyer, and after-sales assistance. In any firm, primary activities can be divided into the five generic categories. Support activities support the primary activities and each other by providing purchased inputs, technology, human resources and various firm-wide functions.

Primary activities

The primary activities of the organisation are grouped into five main areas: inbound **logistics**, operations, outbound logistics, marketing and sales, and service.

1   Inbound logistics are the activities concerned with receiving, storing and distributing the inputs to the product/service. These include materials, handling, stock control, transport, etc.

2   Operations transform these various inputs into the final product or service: machining, packaging, assembly, testing, etc.

3   Outbound logistics collect, store and distribute the product to customers. For tangible products this would involve warehousing, material handling, transport, etc.; in the case of services it may be more concerned with arrangements for bringing customers to the service if it is in a fixed location (e.g. sports events).

4   Marketing and sales provide the means whereby consumers/**users** are made aware of the product or service and are able to purchase it. This would include sales administration, **advertising**, selling, etc. In public services, communication networks, which help users access a particular service, are often important.

5   Services cover all the activities that enhance or maintain the value of a product or service, such as installation, repair, training and spare parts.

Each of these groups of primary activities is linked to support activities.

Support activities

These can be divided into four areas.

1   *Procurement*: this refers to the process of acquiring the various resource inputs to the primary activities (not to the resources themselves). As such, it occurs in many parts of the organisation.

2   *Technology development*: all value activities have a 'technology', even if it is simply know-how. The key technologies may be concerned directly with the product (e.g. R&D, product design) or with processes (e.g. process development) or with a particular resource (e.g. raw material improvements).

3   *Human resource management*: this is a particularly important area that transcends all primary activities. It is concerned with the activities involved in recruiting, training, developing and rewarding people within the organisation.

4   *Infrastructure*: the systems of planning, finance, quality control, etc., are crucially important to an organisation's strategic capability in all primary activities. Infrastructure also consists of the structures and routines of the organisation that sustain its culture.

Having looked at Porter's complex value chain model, a simplified version will be used in most parts of this book (Figure 2.6). This simplified version of the value chain is characterised by the fact that it contains only the primary activities of the firm.

As indicated in Figure 2.6, a distinction is also made between the production-oriented 'upstream' activities and the more marketing-oriented 'downstream' activities.

Logistics
The activities involved in moving raw materials and parts into a firm, moving in-process inventory through the firm, and moving finished goods out of the firm.

User
The buying-centre role played by the organisational member who will actually use the product.

Advertising
Non-personal communication that is paid for by an identified sponsor, and involves either mass communication via newspapers, magazines, radio, television, and other media (e.g. billboards, bus stop signage) or direct-to-consumer communication via direct mail.

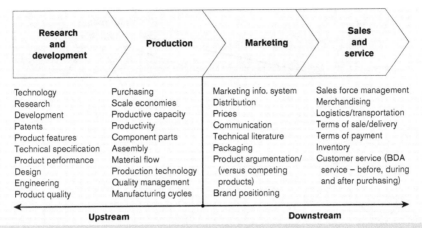

Research and development	Production	Marketing	Sales and service
Technology	Purchasing	Marketing info. system	Sales force management
Research	Scale economies	Distribution	Merchandising
Development	Productive capacity	Prices	Logistics/transportation
Patents	Productivity	Communication	Terms of sale/delivery
Product features	Component parts	Technical literature	Terms of payment
Technical specification	Assembly	Packaging	Inventory
Product performance	Material flow	Product argumentation/	Customer service (BDA
Design	Production technology	(versus competing	service – before, during
Engineering	Quality management	products)	and after purchasing)
Product quality	Manufacturing cycles	Brand positioning	

Upstream ←——————————————→ Downstream

Figure 2.6   A simplified version of the value chain
Source: Hollensen, S. (2001) *Global Marketing: A Market Reponsive Approach*, 2nd ed., Financial Times-Prentice Hall, Harlow, p. 16. Reproduced with permission.

EXHIBIT 2.3
Nike's value chain

In the 1980s, Nike learned that manufacturing had become a commodity that could be outsourced for less cost and better quality than it could achieve with its internal resources. Nike realised that its core competences were in product development and marketing, and so management grew the company around a strategy of designing innovative products that met evolving customer needs.

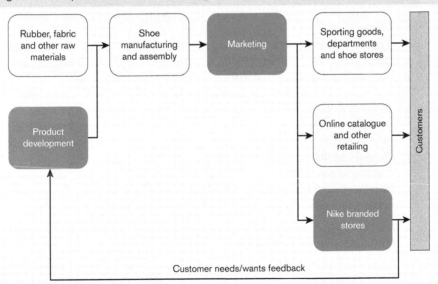

Figure 2.7   Nike's simplified value chain

The value chain in Figure 2.7 shows a simplified view of the athletic-shoe industry. Nike owns and controls just three elements: product development, marketing and its branded retail stores. Both serve Nike's strategic purpose: by owning and operating its branded stores the firm obtains valuable feedback directly from customers, which drives new product development. For B2B service providers seeking to do business with Nike, this suggests that some of the most lucrative opportunities are in supporting new-product development (shoe design and materials technologies), branded-store architecture and choosing store locations.

Sources: Adapted from Ramaswamy (2008); Crain and Abraham (2008), pp. 34–5.

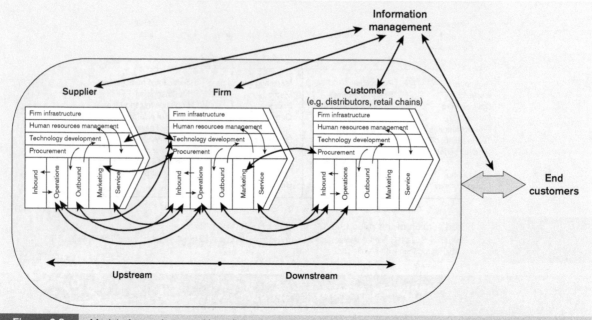

| Figure 2.8 | Model of some inter- and intra-firm relationships |

From value chain to value constellation

As markets are getting more complex the value chain of the single firm cannot be seen independently from the value chains of other actors in the market network (Prahalad and Ramaswamy, 2000).

Normann and Ramirez (1993) argue that strategic analysis should focus on the value-creating system itself within the different players – suppliers, business partners, customers and internal employees should work together to co-produce value.

Although value activities are the building blocks of competitive advantage, the value chain is not a collection of independent activities, but a system of interdependent activities. The value chains of different players are related to each other by linkages within the total industry (Jonk *et al.*, 2008). Linkages are relationships between the way in which one value activity is performed and the cost or performance of another.

In understanding the competitive advantage of an organisation, the strategic importance of the following types of linkage should be analysed in order to assess how they contribute to cost reduction or value added. There are two kinds of linkage (Figure 2.8):

- *Internal linkages* between activities within the same value chain, but perhaps on different planning levels within the firm.
- *External linkages* between different value chains 'owned' by the different players in the total value system.

Normann and Ramirez (1993) use the term value constellation to describe the 'chain' of different players' value chains and their relationships (see Figure 2.8). Figure 2.8 also stresses the importance of information management as a tool for coordinating information between the different players in the value chain.

The global furniture chain IKEA is used as an example of the new logic of value. IKEA's goal is not to create value for customers but to mobilise customers to create their own value from the company's various offerings (see Figure 2.9). IKEA's strategy is based on cost leadership (high volume production and standardised items) combined with turning consumers into **prosumers**, where IKEA's customers are expected to supply their time for assembly work after purchase.

Prosumer
A contraction of *producer* and con*sumer.* Prosumers are half consumers and half proactive producers of the value creation.

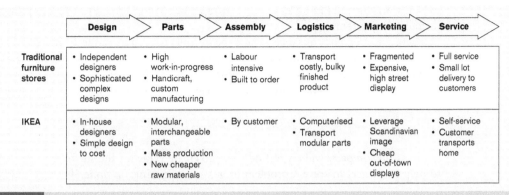

	Design	Parts	Assembly	Logistics	Marketing	Service
Traditional furniture stores	• Independent designers • Sophisticated complex designs	• High work-in-progress • Handicraft, custom manufacturing	• Labour intensive • Built to order	• Transport costly, bulky finished product	• Fragmented • Expensive, high street display	• Full service • Small lot delivery to customers
IKEA	• In-house designers • Simple design to cost	• Modular, interchangeable parts • Mass production • New cheaper raw materials	• By customer	• Computerised • Transport modular parts	• Leverage Scandinavian image • Cheap out-of-town displays	• Self-service • Customer transports home

Figure 2.9	The business system of IKEA

Source: From Kumar, N., Scheer L. and Kotler, P. (2000) From market driven to market driving, *European Management Journal*, 18(2). Copyright © 2000 Elsevier. Reproduced with permission.

Internal linkages

There may be important links between the primary activities. In particular, choices will have been made about these relationships and how they influence value creation and strategic capability. For example, a decision to hold high levels of finished stock might ease production scheduling problems and provide a faster response time to the customer. However, it will probably add to the overall cost of operations. An assessment needs to be made of whether the added value of extra stock is greater than the added cost. Sub-optimisation of the single value chain activities should be avoided. It is easy to miss this point in an analysis if, for example, the marketing activities and operations are assessed separately. The operations may look good because they are geared to high-volume, low-variety, low-unit-cost production. However, at the same time the marketing team may be selling quickness, flexibility and variety to the customers. When put together these two positions representing potential strengths are weaknesses, because they are not in harmony, which is what a value chain requires. The link between a primary activity and a support activity may be the basis of competitive advantage. For example, an organisation may have a unique system for procuring materials. Many international hotels and travel companies use their computer systems to provide immediate quotations and bookings worldwide from local access points.

External linkages

One of the key features of most industries is that a single organisation rarely undertakes all value activities from product design to distribution to the final consumer. There is usually a specialisation of roles, and any single organisation usually participates in the wider value system, which creates a product or service. In understanding how value is created, it is not enough to look at the firm's internal value chain alone. Much of the value creation will occur in the supply and distribution chains, and this whole process needs to be analysed and understood.

Suppliers have value chains (upstream value) that create and deliver the purchased inputs used in a firm's chain. Suppliers not only deliver a product, but also can influence a firm's performance in many other ways. For example, Benetton, the Italian fashion company, managed to sustain an elaborate network of suppliers, agents and independent retail outlets as the basis of its rapid and successful international development during the 1970s and 1980s.

In addition, products pass through the value chain channels (channel value) on their way to the buyer. Channels perform additional activities that affect the buyer and influence the firm's own activities. A firm's product eventually becomes part of its buyer's value chain. The ultimate basis for differentiation is a firm and its product's role in the buyer's value chain, which determine the buyer's needs. Gaining and sustaining competitive advantage depends on understanding not only a firm's value chain, but how the firm fits into the overall value system.

There are often circumstances where the overall cost can be reduced (or value increased) by collaborative arrangements between different organisations in the value system. It will be seen in Chapter 9 that this is often the rationale behind joint ventures (e.g. sharing technology in the international motor manufacture and electronics industries).

Customer value proposition (CVP)

A successful company will try to find a way to create value for the customers – that is, a way to help customers to solve a problem or get an important job done (Johnson *et al.*, 2008). Once we understand the 'job' and all its dimensions, including the full process for how to get it done, we can design the offering (= customer value proposition).

A conventional view of the value proposition is provided by Knox *et al.* (2003) in their review of approaches to customer relationship management. They say a value proposition is:

> an offer defined in terms of the target customers, the benefits offered to these customers, and the price charged relative to the competition.

However, some branding advocates believe that the value proposition is more than the sum of product features, prices and benefits. They argue that it also encompasses the totality of the experience that the customer has when selecting, purchasing and using the product. These customer experiences and also the service quality are very important elements in the process of designing the CVP. For example, Molineux (2002) states that:

> the value proposition describes the total customer experience with the firm and in its alliance partners over time, rather than [being limited to] that communicated at the point of sale.

2.6 VALUE SHOP AND THE 'SERVICE VALUE CHAIN'

Michael Porter's value chain model claims to identify the sequence of key generic activities that businesses perform in order to generate value for customers. Since its introduction in 1985, this model has dominated the thinking of business executives. Yet a growing number of services businesses, including banks, hospitals, insurance companies, business consulting services and telecommunications companies, have found that the traditional value chain model does not fit the reality of their service industry sectors. Stabell and Fjeldstad (1998) identified two new models of value creation – **value shops** and **value networks**. Fjeldstad and Stabell argue that the value chain is a model for making products, while the value shop is a model for solving customer or client problems in a service environment. The value network is a model for mediating exchanges between customers. Each model utilises a different set of core activities to create and deliver distinct forms of value to customers.

The main differences between the two types of value chains are illustrated in Table 2.2.

Value shops (as in workshops, not retail stores) create value by mobilising resources (e.g. people, knowledge and skills) and deploying them to solve specific problems such as curing an illness, delivering airline services to the passengers or delivering a solution to a business problem. Shops are organised around making and executing decisions – identifying and assessing problems or opportunities, developing alternative solutions or approaches, choosing one, executing it and evaluating the results. This model applies to most service-oriented organisations such as building contractors, consultancies and legal organisations. However, it also applies to organisations that are primarily configured to identify and exploit specific market opportunities, such as developing a new drug, drilling a potential oilfield or designing a new aircraft.

Value shop
A model for solving problems in a service environment. Similar to workshops. Value is created by mobilising resources and deploying them to solve a specific customer problem.

Value network
The formation of several firms' value chains into a network, where each company contributes a small part to the total value chain.

Table 2.2	The traditional value chain versus the service value chain

Traditional value chain model

Value creation through transformation of inputs (raw material and components) to products.

Service value chain ('value shop') model

Value creation through customer problem solving. Value is created by mobilising resources and activities to resolve a particular and unique customer problem. Customer value is not related to the solution itself but to the value of solving the problem.

Sequential process ('first we develop the product, then we produce it, and finally we sell it').

Cyclical and iterative process.

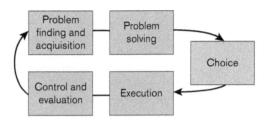

The traditional value chain consists of primary and support activities: *Primary activities* are directly involved in creating and bringing value to customers: upstream (product development and production) and downstream activities (marketing and sales and service). *Support activities* that enable and improve the performance of the primary activities are procurement, technology development, human resource management and firm infrastructure.

The primary activities of a value shop are:
1 *Problem finding*: activities associated with the recording, reviewing and formulating of the problem to be solved and choosing the overall approach to solving the problem.
2 *Problem solving*: activities associated with generating and evaluating alternative solutions.
3 *Choice*: activities associated with choosing among alternative problem solutions.
4 *Execution*: activities associated with communicating, organising and implementing the chosen solution.
5 *Control and evaluation*: activities associated with measuring and evaluating to what extent implementation has solved the initial situation.

Examples: Production and sale of furniture, consumer food products, electronic products and other mass products.

Examples: Banks, hospitals, insurance companies, business consulting services and telecommunications companies.

Source: After Stabell, C. B. and Fjeldstad, Ø. B. (1998) Configuring value for competitive advantage: on chains, shops and networks, *Strategic Management* 19: 413–37. Reproduced with permission from John Wiley & Sons.

Different parts of a typical business may exhibit characteristics of different configurations. For example, production and distribution may resemble a value chain, research and development a value shop.

Value shops make use of specialised knowledge-based systems to support the task of creating solutions to problems. However, the challenge is to provide an integrated set of applications that enable seamless execution across the entire problem-solving or opportunity-exploitation process. Several key technologies and applications are emerging in value shops – many focus on utilising people and knowledge better. Groupware, intranets, desktop videoconferencing and shared electronic workspaces enhance communication and collaboration between people, essential to mobilising people and knowledge across value shops. Integrating project planning with execution is proving crucial, for example, in pharmaceutical development, where bringing a new drug through the long, complex approval process a few months early can mean millions of dollars in revenue. Technologies such as inference engines and neural networks can help to make knowledge about problems and the process for solving them explicit and accessible.

The term 'value network' is widely used but imprecisely defined. It often refers to a group of companies, each specialising in one piece of the value chain, and linked together in some virtual way to create and deliver products and services. Stabell and Fjelstad (1998) define value networks quite differently – not as networks of affiliated companies, but as a business model for a single company that mediates interactions and exchanges across a network of its customers. This model clearly applies best to telecommunications companies, but also to insurance companies and banks, whose business, essentially, is mediating between customers with different financial needs – some saving, some borrowing, for example. Key activities include operating the customer-connecting infrastructure, promoting the network, managing contracts and relationships, and providing services.

Some of the most IT-intensive businesses in the world are value networks – banks, airlines and telecommunications companies, for instance. Most of their technology provides the basic infrastructure of the 'network' to mediate exchanges between customers. But the competitive landscape is now shifting beyond automation and efficient transaction processing to monitoring and exploiting information about customer behaviour.

The aim is to add more value to customer exchanges through better understanding of usage patterns, exchange opportunities, shared interests and so on. Data mining and visualisation tools, for example, can be used to identify both positive and negative connections between customers.

Competitive success often depends on more than simply performing your primary model well. It may also require the delivery of additional kinds of complementary value. Adopting attributes of a second value configuration model can be a powerful way to differentiate your value proposition or defend it against competitors pursuing a value model different to your own. It is essential, however, to pursue another model only in ways that leverage the primary model. For example, Harley-Davidson's primary model is the chain – it makes and sells products. Forming the Harley Owners Group (HOG) – a network of customers – added value to the primary model by reinforcing the brand identity, building loyalty and providing valuable information and feedback about customers' behaviours and preferences (see pages 454–9). Amazon.com is a value chain like other book distributors, and initially used technology to make the process vastly more efficient. Now, with its book recommendations and special interest groups, it is adding the characteristics of a value network. Our research suggests that the value network in particular offers opportunities for many existing businesses to add more value to their customers, and for new entrants to capture market share from those who offer less value to their customers.

Combining the 'product value chain' and the 'service value chain'

Blomstermo *et al.* (2006) make a distinction between *hard* and *soft services*. Hard services are those where production and consumption can be decoupled. For example software services can be transferred into a CD, or some other tangible medium, which can be mass-produced, making standardisation possible. With soft services, where production and consumption occur simultaneously, the customer acts as a coproducer, and decoupling is not viable. The soft-service provider must be present abroad from its first day of foreign operations. Figure 2.10 is mainly valid for soft services, but at the same time in more and more industries we see that physical products and services are combined.

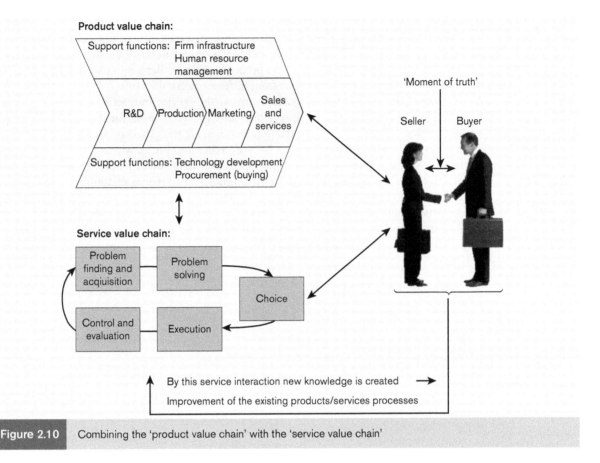

Figure 2.10   Combining the 'product value chain' with the 'service value chain'

Most product companies offer services to protect or enhance the value of their product businesses. Cisco, for instance, built its installation, maintenance and network-design service business to ensure high-quality product support and to strengthen relationships with enterprise and telecom customers. A company may also find itself drawn into services when it realises that competitors use its products to offer services of value. If it does nothing, it risks not only the commoditisation of its own products – something that is occurring in most product markets, irrespective of the services on offer – but also the loss of customer relationships. To make existing service groups profitable – or to succeed in launching a new embedded service business – executives of product companies must decide whether the primary focus of service units should be to support existing product businesses or to grow as a new and independent platform.

When a company chooses a business design for delivering embedded *services* to customers, it should remember that its strategic intent affects which elements of the delivery life cycle are most important. If the aim is to protect or enhance the *value* of a product, the company should integrate the system for delivering it and the associated *services* in order to promote the development of product designs that simplify the task of *service* (e.g. by using fewer subsystems or integrating diagnostic software). This approach involves minimising the footprint of *service* delivery and incorporating support into the product whenever possible. If the company wants the *service* business to be an independent growth platform, however, it should focus most of its delivery efforts on constantly reducing unit costs and making the *services* more productive (Auguste *et al.*, 2006).

In the 'moment of truth' (e.g. in a consultancy service situation), the seller represents all the functions of the focal company's 'product' and 'service' value chain – at the same time. The seller (the product and service provider) and the buyer create a service in an interaction process: 'The service is being created and consumed as it is produced.' Good representatives on the seller's side are vital to service brands' successes, being ultimately responsible for delivering the seller's promise. As such a shared understanding of the service brand's values needs to be anchored in their minds and hearts to encourage brand-supporting behaviour. This internal brand-building process becomes more challenging as service brands expand internationally drawing on workers from different global domains.

Figure 2.10 also shows the cyclic nature of the service interaction ('moment of truth') where the post-evaluation of the service value chain gives input for the possible redesign of the 'product value chain'. The interaction shown in Figure 2.10 could also be an illustration or a snapshot of a negotiation process between seller and buyer, where the seller represents a branded company, which is selling its projects as a combination of 'hardware' (physical products) and 'software' (services). Furthermore it is important to realise that buyers are increasingly active co-creators of value (Vargo & Lusch, 2008).

Anyway, one of the purposes with the 'learning nature' of the overall decision cycle in Figure 2.10 is to pick up the 'best practices' among different kinds of international buyer–seller interactions. This would lead to implications for a better set-up of:

- the 'service value chain' (value shop)
- the 'product value chain'
- the combination of the service and product value chains.

2.7 INTERNATIONALISING THE VALUE CHAIN

International configuration and coordination of activities

Glocalisation
The development and selling of products or services intended for the global market, but adapted to suit local culture and behaviour. (Think globally, act locally.)

All internationally oriented firms must consider an eventual internationalisation of the value chain's functions. The firm must decide whether the responsibility for the single value chain function is to be moved to the international markets or is best handled centrally from head office. Principally, the value chain function should be carried out where there is the highest competence (and the most cost effectiveness), and this is not necessarily at head office (Bellin and Pham, 2007).

The two extremes in 'global marketing' (globalisation and localisation) can be combined into the so-called 'glocalisation' framework, as shown in Figure 2.11.

| Figure 2.11 | The glocalisation frame work |

This global marketing strategy strives to achieve the slogan 'Think globally but act locally' (the so-called glocalisation framework), through dynamic interdependence between head-quarters and subsidiaries. Organisations following such a strategy coordinate their efforts, ensuring local flexibility while exploiting the benefits of global integration and efficiencies, as well as ensuring worldwide **diffusion** of innovation. A key element in knowledge manage-ment is the continuous learning from experiences. In practical terms, the aim of knowledge management as a learning-focused activity across borders is to keep track of valuable capabil-ities used in one market that could be used elsewhere (in other geographic markets), so that firms can continually update their knowledge. However, knowledge developed and used in one cultural context is not always easily transferred to another. The lack of personal relation-ships, the absence of trust and 'cultural distance' all conspire to create resistance, friction and misunderstandings in cross-cultural knowledge management.

With globalisation becoming a centerpiece in the business strategy of many firms – be they engaged in product development or providing services – the ability to manage the 'global knowledge engine' to achieve a competitive edge in today's knowledge-intensive economy is one of the keys to sustainable competitiveness. But in the context of global marketing the management of knowledge is *de facto* a cross-cultural activity, whose key task is to foster and continually upgrade collaborative cross-cultural learning. Of course, the kind and/or type of knowledge that is strategic for an organisation and which needs to be managed for competi-tiveness varies depending on the business context and the value of different types of knowledge associated with it.

A distinction immediately arises between the activities labelled downstream on Figure 2.6 and those labelled upstream activities. The location of downstream activities, those more related to the buyer, is usually tied to where the buyer is located. If a firm is going to sell in Australia, for example, it must usually provide service in Australia, and it must have sales-people stationed in Australia. In some industries it is possible to have a single salesforce that travels to the buyer's country and back again; other specific downstream activities, such as the production of advertising copy, can sometimes also be performed centrally. More typically, however, the firm must locate the capability to perform downstream activities in each of the countries in which it operates. In contrast, upstream activities and support activities are more independent of where the buyer is located (Figure 2.12). However, if the export markets are culturally close to the home market, it may be relevant to control the entire value chain from head office (home market).

Diffusion
The spread of a new product through society.

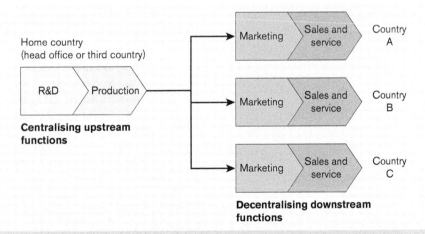

| Figure 2.12 | Centralising the upstream activities and decentralising the downstream activities |

This distinction carries some interesting implications. First, downstream activities create competitive advantages that are largely country specific: a firm's reputation, brand name and service network in a country grow largely out of its activities and create entry/mobility barriers largely in that country alone. Competitive advantage in upstream and support activities often grows more out of the entire system of countries in which a firm competes than from its position in any single country.

Second, in industries where downstream activities or other buyer-tied activities are vital to competitive advantage, there tends to be a more multidomestic pattern of international competition. In many service industries, for example, not only downstream activities but frequently upstream activities are tied to buyer location, and global strategies are comparatively less common. In industries where upstream and support activities such as technology development and operations are crucial to competitive advantage, global competition is more common. For example, there may be a large need in firms to centralise and coordinate the production function worldwide to be able to create rational production units that are able to exploit economies of scale.

Furthermore, as customers increasingly join regional cooperative buying organisations, it is becoming more and more difficult to sustain a price differentiation across markets. This will put pressure on the firm to coordinate a European price policy.

The distinctive issues of international strategies, in contrast to domestic, can be summarised in two key dimensions of how a firm competes internationally. The first is called the *configuration* of a firm's worldwide activities, or the location in the world where each activity in the value chain is performed, including the number of places. For example, a company can locate different parts of its value chain in different places – for instance, factories in China, call centres in India, and retail shops in Europe. IBM is an example of a company that exploits wage differentials by increasing the number of employees in India from 9,000 in 2004 to 50,000 by mid-2007 and by planning for massive additional growth. Most of these employees are in IBM Global Services, the part of the company that is growing fastest but has the lowest margins – which the Indian employees are supposed to improve, by reducing (wage) costs rather than raising the prices (Ghemawat, 2007).

The second dimension is called *coordination*, which refers to how identical or linked activities performed in different countries are coordinated with each other (Porter, 1986; Sanchez, 2007).

2.8 THE VIRTUAL VALUE CHAIN

By introducing the virtual value chain, Rayport and Sviokla (1996) have extended the conventional value chain model, which treats information as a supporting element in the value-adding process (see Figure 2.13).

Each of the physical value chain activities might make use of one or all four information processing stages of the virtual value chain, in order to create extra value for the customer. That is the reason for the horizontal double arrows (in Figure 2.13) between the different physical and virtual value chain activities.

In this way (in relation to Figure 2.13), information can be captured at all stages of the physical value chain. Obviously such information can be used to improve performance at each stage of the physical value chain and to coordinate across it. However, it can also be analysed and repackaged to build content-based products or to create a new line of business.

A company can use its information to reach out to other companies' customers or operations, thereby rearranging the value system of an industry. The result might be that traditional industry sector boundaries disappear. The CEO of Amazon.com, Jeffrey P. Bezos, clearly sees his business as not bookselling, but the information-broker business.

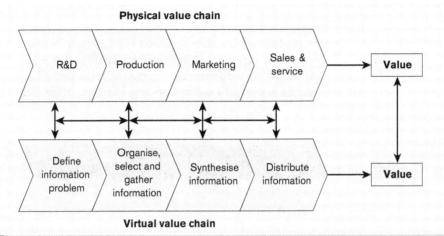

Physical value chain

| Figure 2.13 | The virtual value chain as a supplement to the physical value chain |

Online customer value proposition (OCVP)

Regarding the customer value proposition that can be created along the virtual value chain, it is very important to develop a profound understanding of the customer's online experience. Marketers must understand specific characteristics of online channels and the benefits they offer to customers. To help formulate the online customer value proposition (OCVP) we need to consider the special characteristics of the Internet and its online services as perceived by customers using them. Six criteria can be used to determine the sustainability of the formulated OCVP, in order to reach online customers (Chaffey, 2005):

1 *Content*: online content is rich, which means it provides something that other channels cannot. Often this means more detailed, in-depth information to support the buying process or product usage. However, often online product catalogues simply replicate what is in offline catalogues without adding extra information, images or example applications. Messaging through e-mail and SMS is also key to providing unique content – these media can be used to deliver timely, relevant media to individuals. As well as text-based content, which is king for business-to-business, there is also interactive content, which is king for consumer sites and particularly brands. FMCG brands now use the Web to deliver what they term as 'digital assets', which support offline branding campaigns.

Customisation
Making something (product/service) according to a customer's individual requirements.

2 **Customisation**: in this case mass customisation of content whether received as website pages or e-mail alerts and commonly known as personalisation. Of course, Amazon is quoted many times as an example of this, and it actually has a 'Director of Personalisation'. The ability for a subscriber to an online e-mail service to tailor their messages by selectively opting-in to particular types of message is a further example of customisation.

3 *Community*: these days this is also known as 'social networks'. Online channels such as the Internet are known as 'many-to-many' media, meaning that your audiences can contribute to the content.

4 *Convenience*: this is the ability to select and purchase, and in some cases use products, from your desktop at any time: the classic 24 $\times$ 7 $\times$ 365 availability of a service. Online usage of products is, of course, restricted to digital products such as music or other data services. Amazon has advertised offline using a creative showing a Christmas shopper battling in queues clutching several bags to reinforce the convenience message.

5 *Choice*: the Web gives a wider choice of products and suppliers than via conventional distribution channels. For example, Tesco.com provides Tesco with a platform to give

consumers a wider choice of products (financial, travel, white goods) with more detailed information than is physically available in store.

6   *Cost reduction*: the Internet is widely perceived as a relatively low-cost place of purchase. A key component of the low-cost airline carriers' OCVP is that it is cheaper than phone bookings. This simple price differential, together with the limited change behaviour required from phone booking to online booking, has been a key factor in, for example, Ryanair's online ticketing channel effectively replacing all other booking modes.

2.9 SUMMARY

Competences are the skills, knowledge and technologies that an organisation possesses on which its success depends. Although an organisation will need to reach a threshold level of competence in all its activities, it is likely that only some of these activities are core competences. These core competences underpin the ability of the organisation to outperform the competition and therefore must be defended and nurtured. Core competences concern those resources that are fundamental to a company's strategic position.

In the chapter, three basic perspectives on identification of core competences have been presented:

- resource-based view (RBV): an inside-out perspective;
- market orientation view (MOV): an outside-in perspective;
- value chain based view (VBV): between the RBV and the MOV.

The RBV emphasises the importance of firm-specific assets and knowledge. The underlying approach of the RBV is to see the firm as a bundle of tangible and intangible resources, and to see some of these resources as costly to copy and trade. A firm's resource position can lead to sustained competitive advantage.

Especially in knowledge-intensive firms, distinctive capabilities consist of intangible resources.

In contrast to the MOV, which takes the environment as the critical factor determining an organisation's strategy, the RBV assumes that the key factors for success lie within the firm itself in terms of its resources, capabilities and competences. The choice of the firm's strategy is not dictated by the constraints of the environment but is influenced more by calculations of how the organisation can best exploit its core competence relative to the opportunities in the external environment.

The MOV is basically about adapting to the market environment by concentrating mainly on customers and their needs.

The VBV integrates elements of both the RBV and the MOV, but it does so without ignoring the costs of performing the activities. The value chain provides a systematic means of displaying and categorising activities. Value activities can be divided in different ways:

- primary and support activities;
- upstream and downstream activities.

At each stage of the value chain the firm seeks to add value and thus compete with its rivals. The simplified version of the value chain used throughout the book contains only the primary activities of the firm. The value chain is not a collection of independent activities but a system of interdependent activities. The firm's value chain activities are also related to other actors' value chains. Competitive advantages are created if the firm can:

- offer better perceived value for customers;
- perform the value chain activities at a lower cost than competitors.

CASE STUDY 2.1

Senseo
Competition is coming up in the coffee pod machine market

A very brief history of coffee

Coffee was first consumed in the ninth century, when it was discovered in the highlands of Ethiopia. From there it spread to Egypt and Yemen, and by the fifteenth century had reached Azerbaijan, Persia, Turkey and northern Africa. From the Muslim world, coffee spread to Italy, then to the rest of Europe, to Indonesia, and to the Americas.

Coffee has played an important role in many societies throughout modern history. In Africa and Yemen, it was used in religious ceremonies. As a result, the Ethiopian Church banned its secular consumption. It was banned in Ottoman Turkey in the seventeenth century for political reasons, and was associated with rebellious political activities in Europe.

For many decades almost all coffee has been sold as filter coffee in package sizes of one pound (500 grams). However, during the last decade things have changed. New products and package sizes have been introduced. The present case deals with a few of these new innovations. Today coffee has become a popular drink around the world and comes in many variations, both in terms of roasting and of brewing.

Spurred by the strength of coffee bar culture in many developed markets, manufacturers have attempted to increase value sales by introducing a similar 'café experience' at home. The battle among coffee makers for at-home use has intensified, with leading coffee players, such as Procter & Gamble, Kraft Foods and Philips & Sara Lee (Senseo), launching single-service pod machines which can brew a high-quality cup of coffee in less than one minute.

The influence of specialist coffee shops with their speciality coffee products based on espresso fresh coffee beans has significantly influenced the consumption habits of younger people especially. These consumers have increasingly abandoned classic filter coffee and embraced the Italian-American varieties of espresso fresh coffee beans and coffee pods/capsules. The coffee produced by espresso/café crema grinders and pod/capsule machines have two things in common: less caffeine and a milder taste than traditional filter coffee, while providing the 'crema' effect enjoyed by many consumers.

The history and categorisation of the coffee maker

Before the coffee maker was invented, coffee was prepared in boiling water. The beans were roasted on an open fire and then added to boiling water for consumption. This process did not bring the desired taste and aroma, and hence coffee lovers started to devise ways to come up with a machine or a coffee maker that would prepare tasty coffee.

In 1912 Frau Benz invented the Melitta coffee filter, which is an efficient disposal method for coffee. Earlier, for the filtering purpose of coffee, linen or cloth was used.

Roughly, the coffee maker market can be categorised into three types:

- traditional filter machines
- espresso machines
- pod coffee machines (this is a sector that was actually pioneered by Nespresso, but the market leader now is Senseo; their growth is driven by their ease of use and affordable pricing – later described more in-depth).

These three categories are by no means complete; there are still so many categories that are not covered.

A new and innovative coffee maker was invented in the 1960s called the filter-type coffee maker, which has more advanced features than the earlier varieties. Developed more with the passage of time, this new design came to be manufactured by many companies and its demand rose in the market. The leading brands in this market have been Melitta and Mr Coffee brand, which was manufactured with an automatic drip process. Joe DiMaggio was its spokesperson from 1974. Today, Mr Coffee holds a major part of the market share in the world.

An espresso coffee drink gives more energy and is tastier than the other coffee drinks. The first espresso maker was invented by a manufacturing company owned by Lugia Bezzer in 1901 in Italy. Mr Bezzer was simply looking for a way to help speed up his employee's coffee breaks. He figured out that if pressure was applied in the brewing process, the drink could be made in a lot less time. Nicknamed 'the fast coffee

Table 2.3	The global market for coffee machines (2008)	
		Retail volume (million units)
Western Europe		17.8
Eastern Europe		0.6
North America		28.4
Latin America and Carribbean		4.1
Asia-Pacific (minus Australia and NZ)		2.9
Australia and NZ		0.3
Africa and Middle East		0.7
World total		54.8

Source: Adapted from Euromonitor International (www.euromonitor.com.).

machine', the espresso machine patent was sold in 1905. The new owner, Desidero Pavoni, developed an espresso machine that used a piston pump to force water through a tube and into the coffee.

The commercial espresso machine was invented in 1946. Since then, the espresso maker under different brands began to be produced by many companies. Some of the prominent brands include Juda, Mr Coffee, Kitchenaid and Braun. The modern espresso machines come with various features, styles, colours and prices.

The world market for coffee machines (coffee makers) is shown in Table 2.3.

As can be seen in Table 2.3 the market volumes vary a lot between the regions, but there are also huge differences within the different world regions. For example, in the Western European market the overall picture for the coffee machine market (divided into the three categories) is shown in Table 2.4.

The stock of coffee machines in Europe is estimated to be 100 million units. Traditional filter coffee machines still have the highest volume market share (55 per cent). There is a considerable trend towards espresso full-automatic and an extremely strong trend towards espresso-portioned machines. Low-comfort and low-quality machines (hand-operated espresso piston, pad-filters, combis) are losing market share.

Across the Western European region, the national markets are very different. There are countries such as Italy, Switzerland and Portugal with a huge market share of espresso machines (over 70 per cent). On the other

Table 2.4	The Western European coffee machine market			
Category	Typical brands	Sold units in millions, 2008	Typical price, (€), 2008	Value (€m), 2008
Traditional filter machines	Melitta, Mr Coffee	10.0	€30	€300m
Pod coffee machines	Nespresso, Senseo	3.5	€70	€245m
Espresso machines	De Longhi, Jura, Krups & Rowenta, Rotel	4.3	€200	€860m
Total		17.8		€1,405m

Source: Adapted from Nipkow, J. and Bush, E. (2008) Coffee machines: recommendations for policy design, 7 August, Topten International Group Report (www.topten.info). Reproduced with permission.

hand, some countries still have a very low market share of espresso machines, e.g. Belgium, Germany and the Netherlands (lower than 20 per cent). In Belgium or the Netherlands pad-filters are quite popular with a market share of about 40 per cent. Furthermore, it is interesting to have a look at the market values. Assuming roughly that typical prices are €30 for filter machines, €70 for single-serve coffee pod systems and €200 for espresso machines, there evolves an opposite picture. Espresso machines, are strongly dominating the market in value (see Table 2.4).

The remainder of this case deals with the single-serve coffee pod system.

The single-serve coffee pod system

While the single-serve brewing concept has proved successful in Western Europe, particularly in the Netherlands and France, the trend is still in its early stages in the US, and is yet to impact most developing markets, where disposable incomes have not reached levels that would sustain demand. However, manufacturers hope that the concept will take hold with American consumers because it allows coffee to be made quickly, cleanly and in small quantities. That said, product choice remains limited, and with 'closed' systems, consumers must stick to buying coffee pods compatible with their single-serve machine.

As consumers face growing choices of new-style coffee makers for home use, one of the deciding factors could be the availability of pods. After consumers have made their machine choice, probably based on price and the physical aspects of each machine, having easy access to the coffee pods themselves will be key. Flexibility may also turn out to be a competitive advantage. In addition to coffee, the Tassimo system allows consumers to make hot chocolate or tea, a feature rival Senseo offers only on upmarket models with specially purchased pods. On the other hand, Melitta One:One decided that the battle for pod control could only be won by revamping its pods to fit both its own system and those machines marketed by competitors.

Coffee pods and capsules largely imitate the benefits of freshly prepared espresso/café crema with the added benefit of convenience. They require less preparation time and offer standard one- or two-cup sizes, which appeal to single people. This segment has grown a lot to account (in e.g. Germany) for 10 per cent of retail value sales of fresh ground coffee in 2008. Due to the much higher unit prices of coffee pods, it accounted for only just over 5 per cent of retail volume sales of fresh ground coffee in the same year.

Senseo

The basis for the success of coffee pods was provided in 2001, when Philips introduced coffee pod machines under the Senseo brand. These machines are geared towards the use of coffee pods produced by Douwe Egberts.

So the Senseo coffee pod system is the result of a partnership between electronics expert Philips (supplier of the Senseo machine) and coffee roaster Douwe Egberts (supplier of the coffee pods) – both world-renowned companies from the Netherlands. Coffee pods are tiny packages weighing 5–10 grams. A traditional bag contains 25 pods – a pod is put into the machine and within 45 seconds or so it transforms into one cup of coffee (0.15–0.25 litres).

Philips Senso coffee machine, Latte Select
Source: Courtesy of Philips Consumer Electronics

A brief presentation of the two alliance partners

Philips

Royal Philips Electronics of the Netherlands is one of the world's biggest electronics companies and Europe's largest, with sales of €26.4 billion in 2008. With activities in the three interlocking domains of healthcare, lifestyle and technology and 121,400 employees in more than 60 countries, it has market leadership positions in medical diagnostic imaging and patient monitoring, colour television sets, electric shavers, lighting and silicon system solutions.

Sara Lee/Douwe Egberts (DE)

Douwe Egberts was founded in the middle of the eighteenth century by the Dutch entrepreneur Egbert Douwes and his wife Akke Thysses. The company's activities included coffee, tea and household and bodycare products. Soon they developed a reputation regionally by also supplying shop owners elsewhere, thereby spreading the Douwe Egberts brand around the country. Gradually, Douwes and his descendants built a company that grew to become the Dutch market leader for its core products, coffee and tea. Since 1978 Douwe Egberts has been allied to the Sara Lee Corporation, which opened new horizons worldwide. Today Douwe Egberts is the second largest coffee roaster in the world and the company employs over 26,000 people worldwide.

The company prospered, and continued to grow throughout the Netherlands, but it was not until the mid-twentieth century that it expanded beyond the borders of its homeland. In 1948, Douwe Egberts began selling coffee, tea and tobacco in Belgium. Over the next 20 years, the company added sales in Belgium, France and Spain. In 1978, the company was acquired by international food corporation Sara Lee. Since then, Sara Lee and Douwe Egberts has become familiarly known as Sara Lee/DE.

The Douwe Egberts brands include Pickwick tea, Douwe Egberts coffee, Piazza d'Oro espresso, Cafitesse, Pilao coffee and, of course, the Senseo system. Sara Lee sells products in nearly 200 countries. The Sara Lee brands include Sara Lee, Earth Grains, Hillshire Farm, Jimmy Dean, Ball Park, Bimbo, Kiwi, Ambi Pur, Sanex, and, of course, Douwe Egberts. Sara Lee/DE's part of the partnership is, of course, coffee. Douwe Egberts offers a wide variety of coffee blends to suit most tastes, as well as tea in pods to fit the Senseo machine. The current blends include Sumatra, Brazil, Kenya and Colombia, each of them with the characteristics common to the named region. In addition, there are selected speciality beverages, including espresso, cappuccino and Café Noir, a sweet, dark blend with a chocolate finish. There are also flavoured pods, which include Paris (vanilla caramel), Vienna (hazelnut, vanilla and mocha), and a number of limited edition varieties that are currently only available in select European locations. For tea lovers, Douwe Egberts offers Earl Grey and Minty Green T-pods for the Senseo.

In 1998, Sara Lee/DE filed a patent in Belgium to protect their use of the coffee pod system. The patent was challenged after the Senseo machine hit the market and competitors realised that the patent prevented them from manufacturing coffee pods. The patent was successfully challenged in the Belgian court. As of 2004, the year that the Senseo was introduced in the US, other companies have the legal right to make and sell coffee pods that fit the Senseo system. In addition, several pod makers on the market allow consumers to make their own coffee pods. This allows flexibility in making the coffee or tea of your choice, utilising the Senseo brewing system.

Working in tandem, the two companies developed every aspect of Senseo – from its patented coffee machine and the brewing process to its one-of-a-kind coffee pods. The machine uses single-portion Senseo coffee pods, containing the finest ground coffee, to guarantee a perfect cup every time it is used. Senseo has now been launched in more than a dozen countries worldwide. The biggest markets are Austria, Australia, Belgium, China, Denmark, France, Germany, the Netherlands, the UK and the USA.

Since Philips and Douwe Egberts introduced the coffee pod machine in spring 2001 it has sold more than 15 million units and more than 8 billion coffee pods in the first seven years of its lifetime. It is estimated that over 5 million coffee pod machines were sold in Germany by mid-2007. As coffee made from coffee pod machines is very expensive when consumed in large quantities, these machines are used as an additional coffee option rather than as a replacement for standard coffee machines. The typical owner of a coffee pod machine is young (40 years old and under), but owners include single people, couples and adults with small children.

When the Senseo coffee pod machine was introduced the end-user price was around €75; the current recommended price is €69, but in spring 2009 it was available for around €58.

It is reported that almost one-third of Dutch households own a Senseo machine, and the figure is expected to climb steadily in the years to come. Although most Dutch households continue to use both conventional filter coffee machines and single-serve coffee systems, unit sales of the latter in recent years have outperformed the former. Nevertheless, industry experts suggest that it will take a long time for conventional filter machines to disappear completely (just like it took many years for colour TV to supersede black and white TV or DVDs to oust VHS). Many Dutch households are expected to continue to use conventional machines when holding a party and the Senseo-type machines for everyday use. The consumption behaviour of Dutch households is suggested to be a rough model of the average household within the EU.

Competitive advantages of Senseo

Low-cost followers from China, used to selling cheaper filter coffee machines, have had problems catching up on this alliance, because they cannot easily copy the tight collaboration between Philips and Sara Lee's Douwe Egberts subsidiary that produces the coffee packets designed especially for the Senseo machine.

When big retail chains like Aldi and Wal-Mart see a product like this, they usually go to China and ask for something similar. But in the Senseo case it is not so easy, because the main profits from the Senseo concept come partly from coffee machines but mainly from coffee pods. It is very difficult for the Chinese competitors who have to recoup that money from machines alone.

Presently the market price for a traditional cup of filter coffee lies somewhere between 4 and 5 cents, whereas the price of a cup of pod coffee (7–10 grams) varies between 16 cents (Senseo) and 30–32 cents (Nespresso and Tchibo). Thus, for obvious reasons, coffee producers are very interested in the 'sky high' profit margins of the pods compared to the ruinous price levels of the traditional coffee package sizes (400 and 500 grams).[1]

Once the pods were introduced, no one had the slightest idea that this market niche would develop so fast and be so successful. While the competition in the ordinary coffee market continues to be as fierce as ever, the price competition in the pod market, while present, somehow appears to exist in a different world. It seems that many consumers do not mentally 'think' in unit or kilo prices.

As an industry executive recently remarked, 'Suddenly it has become possible to earn money by simply selling coffee.' For a generation or so coffee has been a typical discount product. In a lot of European markets, traditional coffee has been used by retailers (supermarkets, discount stores) as a promotional tool for generating store traffic. In TV ads and sales fliers specific brands are often on promotion. The retailer is losing money on the promoted coffee brand. However, once the consumer enters the store for buying the brand she/he will normally continue shopping in the same retail store and thus buy a lot of products that are not on promotion, thereby more than compensating for the loss generated by the promoted brand.

In 2004 the German market for pods was 2,750 tonnes (30 per cent up from 2003). Senseo alone sold 650 million pods. The same year Nestlé globally sold 1.3 billion pods (34 per cent up from 2003). During 2003 and 2004 Philips sold 2 million Senseo coffee machines. When Tchibo launched its Cafissimo machine the 60,000 units available were sold within two days! Because the machines are sold below production prices (€69–99), the producer of the machines is being compensated by the coffee producers. For instance, Philips obtains part of the profit generated by the sales of the Senseo pods.

Instead of bringing in two constituent brands (Philips and Sara Lee) to create a third brand (Senseo), the alliance team introduced a co-branding strategy, leveraging the equity in the Douwe Egberts brand to give credibility to the new composite brand, Senseo, forming a separate and unique product, thus ensuring single-minded focus.

Creating an overall identity that transparently links the coffee and appliance as part of one lock-and-key system, and building consumer intimacy around this, was a crucial building block to success, something from which our local equivalent can learn. Not only has this alliance brought an innovation to consumers, but it has also given Philips a chance to boost its brand by partnering with a reputable multinational; and Douwe Egberts has benefited from creating a new segment within coffee.

It is essential to ensure that both partners are aligned behind the collaboration, that the key people involved in managing the collaboration have the personal skills to make the collaboration a success, and that a sound co-branding strategy exists for the new product. In addition, there must be a commitment in funding that allows the partners to fully exploit the new product to the target market, creating demand and thus ensuring trade support. Creating a new category through shifting consumer behaviour requires a long-term commitment and an investment strategy to match. In the USA alone, for every dollar Procter & Gamble and Sara Lee have reaped selling coffee for their 'revolutionary' single-cup systems, they have spent three on marketing.

Invariably there will always be issues around the area of intellectual property, and financial arrangements. In the case of the Senseo collaboration, it was agreed that

---

[1] The strategy of developing mini-packages (where the kilo price is much higher) represents a current retail trend. For instance the German candy producer Haribo has for some time sold a unit package containing 10–25 mini-packages.

Philips would hold the intellectual property for the coffee machine, whilst Douwe Egberts would retain it for the coffee. And in order to ensure that Philips were aligned to view Senseo as a longer-term proposition, Douwe Egberts allowed Philips a share of royalties in the Senseo coffee brand.

A new model of the Senseo machine – the Senseo New Generation – was launched in selected markets in 2007. This updated version allows the user to adjust the height of the mechanism to accommodate larger cups or mugs, has an indicator light function which shows when there is insufficient water for two cups (as opposed to the previous model which only showed whether there was sufficient water left for one cup), features a larger water reservoir and has an option which allows the user to adjust the amount of hot water used per cup.

Competition is coming up

Following the success of Senseo, other branded manufacturers and the leading discounters copied Douwe Egberts's coffee pods and introduced their own for Senseo machines. The pod machines were also copied.

The battle among coffee makers for at-home use intensified in 2005. As a result of the growing competition from me-too products, Douwe Egberts started to seek legal protection for its coffee pods and it tried to prohibit the distribution of the me-too coffee pods. However, in 2006, the European patent covering the Senseo pods was completely revoked on appeal by the European Patent Office. Following the success of Senseo, the leading coffee companies jumped on the bandwagon and introduced not only their own coffee pods but also a similar system based on capsules. In 2005, Tchibo introduced a machine and capsules under Cafissimo, Kraft Foods/Braun introduced Tassimo and, in September 2006, Nestlé and the machine manufacturer Krups introduced Dolce Gusto to Germany.

Unlike the Nespresso system, which has been on the market for over ten years and is positioned as a top-end premium product, Dolce Gusto is a mass product and, like most products by Nestlé, it offers extra amounts of milk foam. All of these new systems are 'closed' systems, which means, for example, that consumers can only use capsules manufactured by Tchibo together with the 'Cafissimo' machine. However, most of the leading brands continue to offer coffee pods that can be used in the Senseo and similar machines.

The only temporary loser in this game was Melitta Unternehmensgruppe Bentz KG, which introduced the 'MyCup' coffee pod system in autumn 2004, as its differently shaped pods were not compatible with the coffee machines of other manufacturers. Consumers refused to buy these coffee pods and Melitta temporarily withdrew its coffee pod system. It launched universal coffee pods in the beginning of 2007 but also kept the differently shaped 'MyCup' pods in its range. At the same time, Melitta launched another product: empty pod sachets that can be filled with coffee of choice by the consumer, significantly reducing the cost per cup. However, as these sachets are awkward to handle, it is uncertain if they will catch on with consumers.

Private labelling – for example in Germany

In Europe, the private label plays an ever-increasing role in coffee pods, especially in Germany. Here the private labels accounted for over a 45 per cent share of retail volume sales in 2008, as many German consumers remain extremely price conscious. In the traditional fresh ground coffee category, private labels accounted for a 33 percent share of retail volume sales in 2008.

The discounter Aldi continues to play a major role in private labels in all coffee categories. In 2008, Aldi led in coffee pods (25 per cent share of retail volume sales) and whole coffee beans (18 per cent retail volume share). Only in traditional fresh ground coffee are the giant branded players Kraft Foods and Tchibo ahead of Aldi in terms of retail volume shares.

The continued success of Aldi is not simply due to low prices. In 2006, Aldi's fresh ground coffee and coffee pods were rated as 'very good' by the leading consumer magazine *Stiftung Warentest*. In fact, Aldi's coffee pods came out on top, ahead of more premium and more expensive branded products. Quality is very important to German consumers who are prepared to search for tasty products at low prices.

QUESTIONS

1   How do you define and explain Senseo's core competence?

2   Some experts think that consumer interest in coffee pods comprises a fad that will fade away within a few years. Others believe that pods over time will replace filter coffee. What do you think? Please present arguments on the basis of international lifestyle trends.

SOURCES

Senseo (www.senseo.com); Euromonitor International (www.euromonitor.com); Nipkow, J. and Bush, E. (2008) Coffee machines: recommendations for policy design, 7 August, Topten International Group Report (www.topten.info).

QUESTIONS FOR DISCUSSION

1 Explain the differences between the RBV, the MOV and the VBV.

2 What is the connection between the RBV and the RM approach?

3 What is the purpose of the value chain?

4 Why is it relevant to make a split between upstream and downstream activities in the value chain?

5 Is the value chain also a relevant model for services?

6 How can the firm create competitive advantage by the use of resources and competences in the firm?

REFERENCES

American Marketing Association (2001) McDonald's takes a small bite into UK sandwich chain, *Daily News*, 31 January (www.ama.org).

Anderson, J. C., Kumar, N. and Narus, J. A. (2007) *Value Merchants: Demonstrating and Documenting Superior Value in Business Markets*, Harvard Business School, Boston, MA.

Anderson, J. C., Kumar, N. and Narus, J. A. (2008) Certified value sellers, *Business Strategy Review*, 19(1) (Spring): 48–53.

Ansoff, H. I. (1965) *Corporate Strategy*, McGraw-Hill, New York.

BBC (2001) Intel to sell consumer products, *BBC News*, 2 January (http://news.bbc.co.uk).

BBC News (2001a) Microsoft and Lego link, 10 January (http://news.bbc.co.uk/hi/english/business).

Barney, J. (1991) Firm resources and sustains competitive advantage, *Journal of Management*, 17 (March): 99–120.

Beverland, M. B. and Lindgreen, A. (2007) Implementing market orientation in industrial firms: a multiple case study, *Industrial Marketing Management*, 36: 430–42.

Bellin, J. B. and Pham, C. T. (2007) Global expansion: balancing a uniform performance culture with local conditions, *Strategy & Leadership*, 35(6): 44–50.

Blomstermo, A., Sharma, D. D. and Sallis, J. (2006) Choice of foreign market entry mode in service firms, *International Marketing Review*, 23(2): 211–29.

Brabbs, C. (2001) Intel must get beyond its chipmaker image, *Marketing*, 26 April: 21–2.

Burnett, V. (2000) Amazon and Toys 'R' Us forge alliance for online retail stores, *Financial Times*, 10 August.

Chaffey, D. (2005) Online value proposition (customer value proposition) *E-marketing Insights Articles*, (www.davechaffey.com/E-marketing-Insights/Customer-experience-management/Online-customer-value-proposition).

Collis, D. J. and Montgomery C. A. (2008) Competing on resources, *Harvard Business Review*, July–August: 140–50.

Crain D. W. and Abraham S. (2008) Using value-chain analysis to discover customers' strategic needs, *Strategy & Leadership*, 36(4): 29–39.

Deering, A., Cook, A., Jonk, G. and Hall, A. (2008) Internet tools enable organizational transformation from the inside out: the Nokia Siemens Network case, *Strategy & Leadership*, 36(5): 34–7.

Donelan, J. G. and Kaplan, E.A. (1998) Value chain analysis: a strategic approach to cost management, *Journal of Cost Management*, March–April: 7–15.

Fahy, J. (2002) A resource-based analysis of sustainable competitive advantage in a global environment, *International Business Review*, 11(1): 57–77.

Farnham, J. (2001) Pret and McDonald's, *MAD*, 8 February.

Financial Times (2000) Amazon and Toys 'R' Us rewrite rules of the game: a shift from clicks and mortar to large-scale combinations of online and offline retailers may be about to become a trend in Jackson, *Financial Times*, 14 August.

Ghemawat, P. (2007) Managing differences, *Harvard Business Review*, March: 59–68.

Grant, R. M. (1991) The resource based theory of competitive advantage: implications for strategy formulation, *California Management Review*, Spring: 114–35.

Green, H. (2000) Double play, *Business Week*, 23 October.

Grönroos, C. (1996) Relationship marketing: strategic and tactical implications, *Management Decision*, 34(3): 5–14.

Hollensen, S. (2001) *Global Marketing: A Market Responsive Approach*, 2nd edn, Financial Times/Prentice Hall, Harlow.

Johnson, M. W., Christensen, C. M. and Kagermann, H. (2008) Reinventing your business model, *Harvard Business Review*, December: 50–9.

Jolly, D. (2000) Three generic resource-based strategies, *International Journal of Technology Management*, 19(718): 773–87.

Jonk, G., Handschuh, M. and Niewiem S. (2008) The battle of the value chains: new specialized versus old hybrids, *Strategy & Leadership*, 36(2): 24–9.

Knox, S., Maklan, S., Payne, A., Peppard, J. and Ryals, L. (2003) Customer relationship management: perspectives from the marketplace, Butterworth Heineman, Oxford, UK.

Kohli, A. K. and Jaworski, B. J. (1990) Market orientation: the construct, research propositions, and managerial implications, *Journal of Marketing*, 54(2): 1–18.

Kong, D. (2000) Amazon, Toys 'R' Us team for online toy store: complementary skills unite rivals, *USA Today*, 11 August.

Kumar, N., Scheer, L. and Kotter, P. (2000) From market driven to market driving, *European Management Journal*, 18(2) (April): 129–42.

Lego (2001) Lego Company and Microsoft Corp. announce a shared dream, press release, 10 January, Redmond, WA and Billund, Denmark (http://www.lego.com/info).

Lings, I. N. (2000) Internal marketing and supply chain management, *Journal of Services Marketing*, 14(1): 27–43.

Lipparini, A. and Fratocchi, L. (1999) The capabilities of the transnational firm, *European Management Journal*, 17(6): 655–67.

McGrath, R. G. and Keil, T. (2007) The value captor's process: getting the most out of your new business ventures, *Harvard Business Review*, May: 128–136.

McPhee W. and Wheeler, D. (2006) Making the case for the added-value chain, *Strategy & Leadership*, 34(4): 39–46.

Marchand, D. A. (1999) Hard IM choices for senior managers: part 10 of your guide to mastering information management, *Financial Times*, 5 April.

Marketing Week (2001) A brick too far, *Marketing Week*, 15 March.

Martinez, M. J. (2000) Amazon.com teams with Toys 'R' Us, *Washington Post*, 10 August.

Mascarenhas, B., Beveja, A. and Jamil, M. (1998) Dynamics of core competencies in leading multinational companies, *California Management Review*, 40(4) (Summer): 117–32.

Molineux, P. (2002) *Exploiting CRM: Connecting with Customers*. Hodder & Stoughton, London.

Normann, R. and Ramirez, R. (1993) From value chain to value constellation: designing interactive strategy, *Harvard Business Review*, July–August: 65–77.

Penrose, E. (1959) *The Theory of the Growth of the Firm*, John Wiley & Sons, New York.

Porter, M. (1980) *Competitive Strategy: Techniques for Analyzing Industries and Competitors*, Free Press, New York.

Porter, M. (1985) *Competitive Advantage: Creating and Sustaining Superior Performance*, Free Press, New York.

Porter, M. E. (1986) Competition in global industries: a conceptual framework, in M. E. Porter (ed), *Competition in Global Industries*, Harvard Business School Press, Boston.

Porter, M. (1990) *The Competitive Advantage of Nations*, Free Press, New York.

Prahalad, C. K. and Hamel, G. (1990) The core competence of the corporation, *Harvard Business Review*, May–June: 79–91.

Prahalad, C. K. and Hamel, G. (1994) Strategy as a field of study: why search for a new paradigm? *Strategic Management Journal*, 15: 5–16.

Prahalad, C. K. and Ramaswamy, V. (2000) Co-opting customer competence, *Harvard Business Review*, January–February: 79–87.

Quelin, B. (2000) Core competencies, R&D management and partnerships, *European Management Journal*, 18(5) (October): 476–87.

Ramaswamy, V. (2008) Co-creating value through customers' experiences: the Nike case, *Strategy & Leadership*, 36(5): 9–14.

Rangone, A. (1999) A resource-based approach to strategy analysis in small–medium sized enterprises, *Small Business Economics*, 12: 233–48.

Rayport, J. and Jaworski, B. (2004) *Introduction to E-commerce*, 2nd edn, McGraw-Hill, New York.

Rayport, J. F. and Sviokla, J. J. (1996) Exploiting the virtual value chain, *McKinsey Quarterly*, 1: 21–36.

Sanchez, F. (2007) Principles of global integration, *Industrial Management*, September–October: 8–13.

Schwartz, E. (2000) Amazon, Toys 'R' Us in e-commerce tie-up, *Infoworld*, 14 August.

Selznick, P. (1957) *Leadership in Administration*, Row, Peterson & Co., Evanston, IL.

Sharma, V. M. and Erramilli, M. K. (2004) Resource-based explanation of entry mode choice, *Journal of Marketing Theory & Practice*, Winter: 1–18.

Smith, G. E. and Nagle, T. T. (2005) A question of value, *Marketing Management*, July–August: 38–43.

Stabell, C. B. and Fjeldstad, Ø. B. (1998) Configuring value for competitive advantage: on chains, shops, and networks, *Strategic Management Journal*, 19: 413–37.

Trott, P., Maddocks, T. and Wheeler, C. (2009) Core competencies for diversifying: case study of a small business, *Strategic Change*, 18: 27–43.

Vargo, S. L. and Lusch, R. E. (2008), Service-dominant logic: continuing the evolution, *Journal of Academy Marketing Science*, Vol. 36, pp. 1–10.

Vesanen, J. (2007) What is personalization? A conceptual framework, *European Journal of Marketing*, 41(5/6): 409–18.

Walters, D. and Lancaster, G. (2000) Implementing value strategy through the value chain, *Management Decision*, 38(3): 160–78.

Webb, J. and Gile, C. (2001) Reversing the value chain, *Journal of Business Strategy*, March–April: 13–17.

Wernerfelt, B. (1984) A resource-based view of the firm, *Strategic Management Journal*, 5(2): 171–80.

Wingfield, N. and Bulkeley, W. M. (2000) Amazon.com, Toys 'R' Us agree to combine online toy stores, *Wall Street Journal*, 11 August.

CHAPTER 3
Development of the firm's competitive advantage

LEARNING OBJECTIVES

After studying this chapter you should be able to:

- define the concept 'international competitiveness' in a broader perspective from a macro level to a micro level
- discuss the basic sources of competitive advantages
- explain how 'economies of speed' can be used as a competitive advantage
- explain how Porter's traditional competitive-based five forces can be extended to a relationship (five sources) model
- define the steps in competitive benchmarking and explain how these steps are related to the outsourcing decision process
- explain the purposes and motives for outsourcing activities
- discuss the advantages and disadvantages of outsourcing

3.1 INTRODUCTION

Competitiveness is how effective and efficient a firm is, relative to its rivals, at serving customers and resellers. Effectiveness has to do with the quality of products, market share and profitability; efficiency has to do with response speed and low costs. Both effectiveness and efficiency ultimately depend on competitive rationality – the strength of the firm's competitive drives and its decision-making skills.

The topic of this chapter is how a firm creates and develops competitive advantage in the international market. The development of a firm's international competitiveness takes place interactively with the business environment. The firm must be able to adjust to customers, competitors and public authorities. To be able to participate in the international arena, the firm must have established a competitive basis consisting of resources, competences and relations to others in the international arena.

3.2 GENERAL SOURCES OF COMPETITIVE ADVANTAGE

Depending on the degree of internationalisation of its business, a company has access to different general sources of competitive advantage. A globally operating company may derive competitive advantage from qualities that are perhaps not available to firms with a regional or domestic focus, such as:

- economies of scale;
- economies of scope;
- strategic thinking as a core competence;
- exploitation of local advantages;
- ability to provide global services;
- company-specific competitive advantages;
- the ability to use human resources in developing competitive advantage.

Each factor will now be discussed in detail.

Economies of scale (efficiencies of global scale and volume)

Economies of scale are often the main feature of a market. The theory is that the greater the economies of scale, the greater the benefits accruing to those with a high sales volume. As a result, the competition to achieve larger market share is intense. Economies of scale can come about because larger plants are more efficient to run, and their cost per unit of output may be relatively less. There may be overhead costs that cannot be avoided – even by the smaller organisations – but can be spread over larger volumes by the bigger firms. Economies of scale may also be the result of learning. With increasing cumulative production the manufacturer learns more and finds more efficient methods of production. All of these effects tend to increase competition by offering incentives to buy market share in order to become the lowest-cost producer. By the same token economies of scale also produce significant barriers against new entrants to the market. The higher the initial investment, the more difficult it is to justify the investment for a new entry. But such economies of scale do not always last forever.

Hence, where economies through large-scale operations are substantial, a firm will do all it can to achieve scale economies. Attempts to capture scale economies may lead a firm to compete for market share aggressively, escalating pressures on other firms. A similar situation occurs when a business's fixed costs are high and the firm must spread them over a large volume. If capacity can only be added in large increments, the resulting excess capacity will also intensify competition.

Experience effects are based on size over time, rather than size at a particular point in time. The experience effect reflects the improvements (usually resulting in lower costs) that result from economies of scale, learning and improved productivity over time.

For example, capital costs do not increase in direct proportion to capacity. Higher capacity results in lower depreciation charges per unit of output, lower operating cost in the form of the number of operatives, lower marketing, sales, administration, and research and development

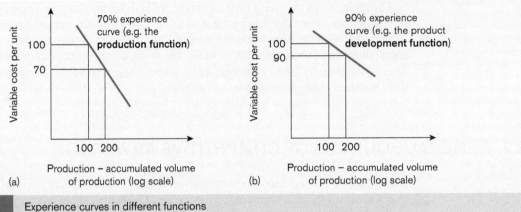

Figure 3.1	Experience curves in different functions

Source: Hax, A. C. and Majluf, N. S. (1984) *Strategic Management: An Integrative Perspective*, 1st ed., Prentice Hall, Englewood Cliffs, NJ, p. 121. Copyright © 1984. Reproduced with permission from Pearson Education, Inc.

Experience curve (learning curve)
The drop in the average per-unit production cost that comes with accumulated production experience.

Variable cost
A cost that varies directly with an organisation's production or sales. Variable costs are a function of volume.

costs, and lower raw materials and shipping costs. It is generally recognised, however, that cost reductions apply more to the value-added elements than to bought-in supplies. In fact, the Boston Consulting Group discovered that costs decrease by up to 30 per cent for every cumulative doubling of output. This phenomenon (a so-called 70 per cent **experience curve**: every time production output doubles, the unit cost falls to 70 per cent of the former cost) is shown in Figure 3.1(a). This experience curve would be typical for the production function, whereas the experience curve is less sensitive for value functions like marketing and product development (Figure 3.1(b)). The reason is that these functions are more innovative in nature. While there are many implications for marketing strategy, particularly in relation to pricing policy, discussion will be confined to the product/market implications.

Large economies of scale exist when there are high fixed versus **variable costs** in the predominant business model. Large organisations can amortise the fixed costs over greater volumes, which gives them a big advantage over small competitors.

However, Toyota taught the Western world that many fixed costs can be reduced. By reducing in-process inventories, set-up times for machinery, and the overhead costs inherent in an inventory-intensive batch-manufacturing process, Toyota flattened the scale economics of assembling a car. CAD (computer-aided-design) systems had a similar effect on reducing the fixed cost of designing a new model. As a result, there is no relationship between a car producer's market share and its profitability. Analogous innovations have flattened scale economics in steel, electric-power generation and computers – and rendered transitory what were once thought to be sustainable advantages (Kalpič, 2008).

Strategists in industries that today see leading companies enjoying scale-based competitive advantage ought to ask themselves if the fundamental trade-offs that create today's high fixed costs might change. Consider Intel. A barrier to potential competitors is the US$700 million cost to design a new family of microprocessors and the US$3 billion needed to build a new fabrication facility. However, disruptive technologies such as Tensilica's modular microprocessor architecture are flattening the scale economics of design. And small fabrication facilities, or mini-fabs, could reduce the fixed costs of production. Such technologies take root at the bottom end of the market first, but their capabilities are improving all the time (Christensen, 2001).

Economies of scope (transfer of resources, experience, ideas and successful concepts across products and markets)

A second source of competitive advantage, intertwined with scale economics, has been breadth of product range. For example, through the 1970s, Caterpillar's scope gave the company an unassailable advantage in construction equipment against smaller competitors such as Komatsu. Only Caterpillar was large enough to absorb the complexity-driven overhead costs of developing, manufacturing and distributing a full product range. Caterpillar's dealers did not need to carry equipment from other manufacturers in order to offer customers what they needed. Caterpillar's huge installed base of equipment in the field meant its dealers, who were the largest dealers in each market, could afford to stock the part necessary to offer 24-hour delivery of any spare part to any Caterpillar owner. No competitor could match this at that time.

Scope economies are also derived from activities in interrelated geographical markets. If they are strong, a sustainable advantage in one market can be used to build sustainability in another. The term scope economy is not just a new name for synergy; it actually defines the conditions under which synergy works. To achieve economies of scope, a company must be able to share resources across markets, while making sure that the cost of those resources remains largely fixed. Only then can economies be effected by spreading assets over a greater number of markets.

Global companies can transfer resources between business units in different parts of the world. These resources may include personnel (such as experienced production managers), funds (global organisations usually have a lower capital cost than domestic firms), and superior market information. Firms such as Kraft-Jacobs-Suchard, the Swiss chocolate and coffee manufacturer owned by Philip Morris, transfer their managers to operations where they need their specific know-how, for example in the growing markets of Eastern Europe, and profit from the capital transfer capacity of their company to respond quickly to market opportunities wherever they occur.

A global company is also able to transfer experience, ideas and successful concepts from one country to another. McDonald's country managers in Europe, for example, meet regularly to compare notes on products and promotional ideas, but also how to avoid waste, and to discuss whether such ideas might be appropriate in other markets. Faster knowledge transfer and learning result in superior customer benefits through lower prices and improved product and service features.

Finally, global companies often have a stronger brand reputation than can be achieved by domestic companies. As travel and communication across national boundaries increase, this potential for transfer of brand reputation is likely to grow.

Time-based competition (TBC)

Competitive advantage is a constantly moving target. The most successful firms know how to keep moving, always staying alert and pro-active. Today, time represents a powerful source of competitive advantage and includes managing time in production and service delivery, in new product development and introduction, and in sales distribution.

Time can be expressed in a variety of ways: cycle time, **time to market**, new product development time, time elapsed between order placement and payment, and real-time customer responsiveness. Time-based competitors focus on both activity and system delivery times as measures in all phases of their operations.

All **time-based competition** (TBC) uses process strategies to reduce one or more of the various types of **lead times** faced by the company. They are implemented using such tactics as team building, organisational flattening, flexible manufacturing systems and simultaneous engineering. The key challenge facing any company attempting to implement TBC is to ensure that there is a proper fit between how the company competes in the marketplace, the specific TBC process strategies selected, and the specific implementation tactics used.

By competing on time, a company enjoys first-entrant advantages that include higher pricing, higher market share, improved customer service, and productivity improvement. The goal of TBC, like just-in-time, is to eliminate all wasted time from activities in the value chain. Such time-reduction methods can be seen in overlapping product development activities through simultaneous engineering, improving communication channels between

Time to market
The time it takes for a company to develop a new product and turn it into a product which people can buy.

Time-based competition
Competition based on providing time utility by delivering a product when the consumer wants it.

Lead time
The time from the moment the customer places an order to the moment it is received by the customer.

various functions (including customers and suppliers), through set-up times, and smoothing production flow. The underlying premise of TBC is that the company fastest at responding to market needs will lead the rest.

The time-based competitor is able to use customer feedback to offer new products in less time, quickly discontinuing products that do not sell well. In an early example of TBC, Yamaha was overwhelmed when Honda responded to its challenge in motorcycles. Honda launched many of new motorcycle models in just a few months. Yamaha was forced to admit defeat and retreat from its position as market leader. Honda's gain of market share and its market dominance were a direct result of time-based strategies.

A strategy built on leadership alone or flexible manufacturing alone would not have been sufficient for Honda because Yamaha could have matched it on each score. Honda's competitive advantage came from optimising synergies between time-based characteristics of lower prices, flexible processes, top quality and heightened awareness of consumers via consumer service programmes.

However, that TBC is not everything is shown by the VCR industry where success in controlling the industry standard perhaps can indicate all competitive advantages in other areas.

Sony, as the first-to-market initially had many competitive advantages over JVC, e.g. innovation and differentiation. Yet losing in the industry standard war to JVC's VHS format, due to a lack of network building, diminished Sony's many competitive advantages in the VCR business. Sony had to abide by the standard set by JVC and reduce its own Betamax system to a niche product, hurting its performance in the business (Ma, 2000a).

The first-generation approach to speed has been radical in many ways. Managers in North America and Europe changed forever how they thought about manufacturing, for example. Borrowing from the Japanese, they introduced methodologies that helped to boost production speed and to match supply and demand more accurately. As the speed of manufacturing and service delivery increased, attention shifted upstream toward the much longer, less tangible product-development process. By breaking down functional barriers and introducing concurrent design processes, companies cut product development time by 30 per cent or more.

Today the focus is also on strategy. The companies that can make decisions fast, change direction nimbly, and figure out when to enter and exit markets will enjoy competitive advantage.

Speed plays an increasingly important role in more traditional strategic moves, such as mergers and acquisitions. Traditionally, acquisitions were used to buy earnings and remove competitors in mature markets. Now, innovation and access to capabilities drive many mergers and aquisitions. In those cases, senior managers must identify, execute and assimilate acquisitions very quickly or they will lose the deal. Partnerships can substantially enhance a company's ability to move swiftly by enabling it to focus on what it does best and fastest.

3.3 INTRODUCTION OF A HOLISTIC MODEL OF COMPETITIVENESS: FROM MACRO TO MICRO LEVEL

The theory of firm competitiveness implicitly assumes that the 'competitiveness of nations' is not simply based on country-specific factors but heavily influenced by firm-specific factors, as the latter is deeply ingrained in and shapes the former.

On the other hand, the competitive advantage developed by a firm in its home market is determined to a significant extent by the national business environment, with benefits being derived from access to resources and skills and competitive pressures derived from other national firms creating the need to invest and innovate.

The need to understand the advantages gained by firms in industries in these countries is valuable for the individual firm in seeing what it is about its own location that can determine its ability to gain competitive advantage.

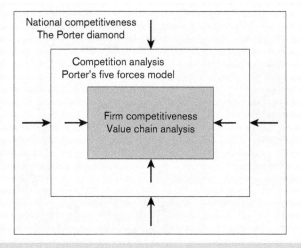

| Figure 3.2 | Three levels of international competitiveness |

It is relevant to look at why a nation becomes the base for successful international competition in an industry or how it is that firms in an industry from a particular country can create competitive advantage, and then sustain it over time.

This section focuses on the three levels of analysis – nation, industry and firm (see Figure 3.2).

To enable an understanding of the development of a firm's international competitiveness in a broader perspective, a model in three stages (see Figure 3.3) will be presented:

1 analysis of national competitiveness (the Porter diamond) – macro level;

2 competition analysis in an industry (Porter's five forces) – meso level;

3 value chain analysis – micro level:
   (a) competitive triangle;
   (b) **benchmarking**.

The analysis starts at the macro level and then moves into the firm's competitive arena through **Porter's five forces model**. Based on the firm's value chain, the analysis is concluded with a discussion of which activities/functions in the value chain are the firm's core competences (and must be developed internally in the firm) and which competences must be placed with others through alliances and market relations.

The graphical system used in Figure 3.3 (which will be referred to throughout this chapter) places the models after each other in a hierarchical windows logic, where you get from stage 1 to stage 2 by clicking on the icon box: 'Firm strategy, structure and rivalry'. Here Porter's five forces model appears. From stage 2 to 3 we click the middle box labelled 'Market competitors/Intensity of rivalry' and the model for a value chain analysis/competitive triangle appears.

Individual competitiveness and time-based competition

In this chapter the analysis ends at the firm level but it is possible to go a step further by analysing individual competitiveness (Veliyath and Zahra, 2000). The factors influencing the capacity of an individual to become competitive would include intrinsic abilities, skills, motivation levels and the amount of effort involved. Traditional decision-making perspectives maintain that uncertainty leads executives to search for more additional information with which to increase certainty. However, Kedia *et al.* (2002) showed that some executives increase competitiveness by using tactics to accelerate analysis of information and alternatives

Benchmarking
The process of comparing the company's products and processes to those of competitors or leading firms in other industries to find ways to improve quality and performance.

Porter's five forces model
The state of competition and profit potential in an industry depends on five basic competitive forces: new entrants, suppliers, buyers, substitutes and market competitors.

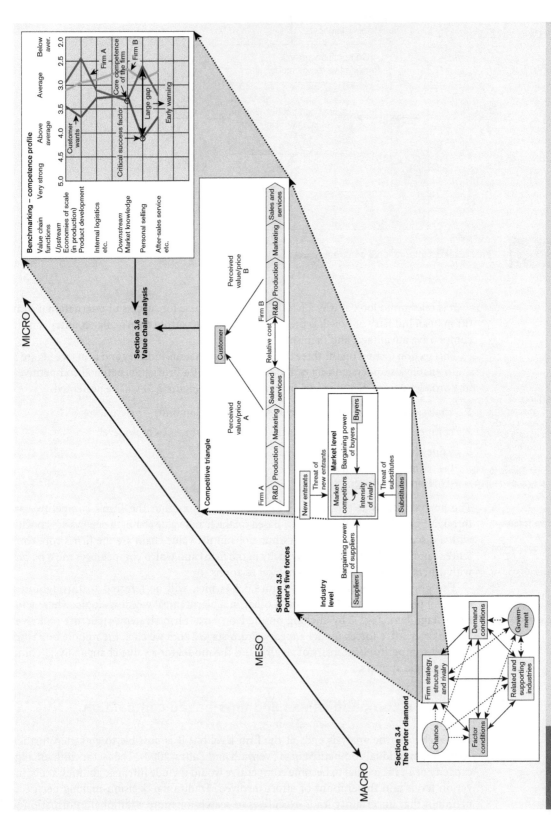

MICRO

MESO

MACRO

Benchmarking – competence profile

| Value chain functions | Very strong 5.0 | Above average 4.5 | 4.0 | 3.5 | Average 3.0 | 2.5 | Below aver. 2.0 |

Upstream
Economies of scale (in production)
Product development
Internal logistics
etc.

Downstream
Market knowledge
Personal selling
After-sales service
etc.

Firm A
Firm B
Core competence of the firm
Customer wants
Critical success factor
Large gap
Early warning

Section 3.6
Value chain analysis

Competitive triangle

Perceived value/price A

Firm A | R&D > Production > Marketing > Sales and services

Customer

Firm B | R&D > Production > Marketing > Sales and services

Perceived value/price B

Relative cost

Section 3.5
Porter's five forces

Industry level

Suppliers
Bargaining power of suppliers

New entrants
Threat of new entrants

Market level

Market competitors
Intensity of rivalry

Bargaining power of buyers
Buyers

Threat of substitutes
Substitutes

Section 3.4
The Porter diamond

Firm strategy, structure, and rivalry

Demand conditions

Govern-ment

Related and supporting industries

Factor conditions

Chance

Figure 3.3 Development of a firm's international competitiveness

during the decision-making process. For example, these executives examine several alternatives simultaneously. The comparison process speeds their analysis of the strengths and weaknesses of options.

3.4 ANALYSIS OF NATIONAL COMPETITIVENESS (THE PORTER DIAMOND)

Analysis of national competitiveness represents the highest level in the entire model (Figure 3.3). Michael E. Porter called his work *The Competitive Advantage of Nations* (1990), but as a starting point it is important to say that it is firms which are competing in the international arena, not nations. Yet the characteristics of the home nation play a central role in a firm's international success. The home base shapes a company's capacity to innovate rapidly in technology and methods, and to do so in the proper directions. It is the place from which competitive advantage ultimately emanates and from which it must be sustained. Competitive advantage ultimately results from an effective combination of national circumstances and company strategy. Conditions in a nation may create an environment in which firms can attain international competitive advantage, but it is up to a company to seize the opportunity. The national diamond becomes central to choosing the industries to compete with, as well as the appropriate strategy. The home base is an important determinant of a firm's strengths and weaknesses relative to foreign rivals.

Understanding the home base of foreign competitors is essential in analysing them. Their home nation yields them advantages and disadvantages. It also shapes their likely future strategies.

Porter (1990) describes a concentration of firms within a certain industry as industrial clusters. Within such industrial clusters firms have a network of relations to other firms in the industry: customers (including firms that work on semi-manufactured goods), suppliers and competitors. These industrial clusters may go worldwide, but they will usually have their starting point and location in a certain country or region of a country.

A firm gains important competitive advantages from the presence in its home nation of world-class buyers, suppliers and related industries. They provide insight into future market needs and technological developments. They contribute to a climate for change and improvement, and become partners and allies in the innovation process. Having a strong cluster at home unblocks the flow of information and allows deeper and more open contact than is possible when dealing with foreign firms. Being part of a cluster localised in a small geographic area can be even more valuable, so the central question we can ask is: what accounts for the national location of a particular global industry? The answer begins, as does all classical trade theory, with the match between the factor endowments of the country and the needs of the industry.

Porter's diamond
The characteristics of the 'home base' play a central role in explaining the international competitiveness of the firm – the explaining elements consist of factor conditions, demand conditions, related and supporting industries, firm strategy, structure and rivalry, chance and government.

Let us now take a closer look at the different elements in **Porter's diamond**. Throughout the analysis the Indian IT/software industry (especially illustrated by the Bangalore area) will be used as an example (Nair *et al.*, 2007).

Factor conditions

We can make a distinction between 'basic and advanced' factors. Basic factors include natural resources (climate, minerals, oil), where the mobility of the factors is low. These factors can also create the ground for international competitiveness, but they can never turn into real value creation without the advanced factors, like sophisticated human resources (skills) and research capabilities. Such advanced factors also tend to be specific to the industry.

In the Indian software industry, Bangalore has several engineering- and science-oriented educational institutions. Also the Indian Institute of Science (a research-oriented graduate school) can be identified as essential in the development of the software industry in the region. The presence of the public sector engineering firms and the private engineering colleges has attracted young people from the country to Bangalore and it has created a diverse, multilingual, tolerant and cosmopolitan culture. One of the most critical success factors of the industry was the availability of advanced and highly educated human resources, but with generalised skills. These generalists (not specialists in software or programming) could be trained into problem solvers in specific areas based on industry needs.

Demand conditions

These factors are represented in the right-hand box of Porter's diamond (Figure 3.3). The characteristics of this element that drive industry success include the presence of early home demand, market size, its rate of growth, and sophistication.

There exists an interaction between scale economies, transportation costs and the size of the home market. Given sufficiently strong economies of scale, each producer wants to serve a geographically extensive market from a single location. To minimise transportation costs the producer chooses a location with large local demand. When scale economies limit the number of production locations the size of a market will be an important determinant of its attractiveness. Large home markets will also ensure that firms located at that site develop a cost advantage based on scale and often on experience as well.

An interesting pattern is that an early large home market that has become saturated forces efficient firms to look abroad for new business. For example, the Japanese motorcycle industry with its large home market used its scale advantages in the global marketplace after an early start in Japan. The composition of demand also plays an important role.

A product's fundamental or core design nearly always reflects home market needs. In electrical transmission equipment, for example, Sweden dominates the world in the high-voltage distribution market. In Sweden there is a relatively large demand for transporting high voltage over long distances, as a consequence of the location of population and industry clusters. Here the needs of the home market shaped the industry that was later able to respond to global markets (with ABB as one of the leading producers in the world market).

The sophistication of the buyer is also important. The US government was the first buyer of chips and remained the only customer for many years. The price inelasticity of government encouraged firms to develop technically advanced products without worrying too much about costs. Under these conditions the technological frontier was clearly pushed much further and much faster than it would have been had the buyer been either less sophisticated or more price sensitive.

The Indian software industry was kick-started in connection with the Y2K problem (a problem caused due to a coding convention in older systems that assigned only two digits for the year count, thereby creating a potential disruption as the calendar year turned 2000), where US firms contracted with Indian software firms that had employees who were skilled in older programming languages such as Cobol and Fortran. As their experience with US firms increased and the Y2K problems were solved, India-based software firms began diversifying and offering more value-added products and services. Serving demanding US customers forced the Indian software firms to develop high-quality products and services. Later on this experience helped to address the needs of IT customers in Germany, Japan and other markets.

Related and supporting industries

The success of an industry is associated with the presence of suppliers and related industries within a region (Chen and Hsieh, 2008).

In many cases competitive advantages come from being able to use labour that is attracted to an area to serve the core industry, but which is available and skilled for supporting this industry. Coordination of technology is also eased by geographic proximity. Porter argues that Italian world leadership in gold and silver jewellery has been sustained in part by the local presence of manufacturers of jewellery-making machinery. Here the advantage of clustering is not so much transportation cost reductions but technical and marketing cooperation. In the semiconductor industry, the strength of the electronics industry in Japan (which buys the semiconductors) is a strong incentive to the location of semiconductors in the same area. It should be noted that clustering is not independent of scale economies. If there were no scale economies in the production of intermediate inputs, then the small-scale centres of production could rival the large-scale centres. It is the fact that there are scale economies in both semiconductors and electronics, coupled with the technological and marketing connections between the two, that give rise to clustering advantages.

In the beginning, Bangalore's lack of reliable supporting industries, such as telecommunication and power supply, was a problem, but many software firms installed their own generators and satellite communication equipment. Recently, firms that provide venture capital, recruitment assistance, network, hardware maintenance and marketing/accounting support have emerged in the Bangalore area to support the software firms. Also, the presence of consulting firms such as KPMG, PriceWaterhouseCoopers and Ernst & Young can assist incoming multinational companies with entering the Indian market by solving, for example, their currency and location problems. Consequently, a whole system of support has now evolved around the software industry.

Firm strategy, structure and rivalry

This fairly broad element includes how companies are organised and managed, their objectives, and the nature of domestic rivalry.

One of the most compelling results of Porter's study of successful industries in ten different nations is the powerful and positive effect that domestic competition has on the ability to compete in the global marketplace. In Germany, the fierce domestic rivalry among BASF, Hoechst and Bayer in the pharmaceutical industry is well known. Furthermore, the process of competition weeds out inferior technologies, products and management practices, and leaves as survivors only the most efficient firms. When domestic competition is vigorous firms are forced to become more efficient, adopt new cost-saving technologies, reduce product development time, and learn to motivate and control workers more effectively. Domestic rivalry is especially important in stimulating technological developments among **global firms**.

Global firm
A firm that by operating in more than one country gains marketing, production, R&D and financial advantages in its costs and reputation that are not available to purely domestic competitors.

The small country of Denmark has three producers of hearing-aids (William Demant, Widex and GN Resound/Danavox), which are all among the top ten of the world's largest producers of hearing-aids. In 1996 Oticon (the earlier William Demant) and Widex fought a violent technological battle to be the first in the world to launch a 100 per cent digitalised hearing-aid. Widex (the smaller of the two producers) won, but forced Oticon at the same time to keep a leading edge in technological development.

In relation to the Indian software industry, most firms in the Bangalore area experience fierce competition. The competition about future customers is not just with local firms, but also with firms outside Bangalore and multinational companies such as IBM and Accenture. It has resulted in a pressure on firms not only to deliver quality products and services, but also to be cost-effective. This competition has encouraged firms to seek international certifications, with a rating in software development. Today the Bangalore area has the world's highest concentration of companies with the so-called CMM-SEI (Carnegie Mellon University's Software Engineering Institute) Level 5 certification (the highest quality rating).

Government

According to Porter's diamond model, government can influence and be influenced by each of the four main factors.

Governments can play a powerful role in encouraging the development of industries within their own borders that will assume global positions. Governments finance and construct infrastructure, providing roads, airports, education and healthcare, and can support use of alternative energy (e.g. wind turbines) or other environmental systems that affect factors of production.

In relation to the Indian software industry, the federal government in Delhi had already targeted software as a growth area in the 1970s, because of its high skill requirements and labour intensity. Though the 1970s and 1980s the industry was mainly dominated by public sector companies, such as CMC. In 1984 the government started liberalising industrial and investment policies, which gave access to IT companies from abroad, e.g. Texas Instruments. One of the new initiatives was also setting up 'Technology Parks', e.g. the Software Technology Parks (STP) in Bangalore. The liberation policy continued throughout the 1980s and 1990s. In 1988 NASSCOM (National Association of Software and Service Companies) was formed. NASSCOMM is an association of IT firms that acts as a catalyst for the industry growth by supporting IT research and education in India. In 1999 the Ministry of Information Technology was set up to coordinate the IT initiatives at government, academic and business levels.

Thus Bangalore's success in becoming a software hub can be attributed to the state government's active role in the early and later stages of the industry's evolution.

Chance

According to Porter's diamond, national/regional competitiveness may also be triggered by random events.

When we look at the history of most industries we also see the role played by chance. Perhaps the most important instance of chance involves the question of who comes up with a major new idea first. For reasons having little to do with economics, entrepreneurs will typically start their new operations in their home countries. Once the industry begins in a given country, scale and clustering effects can cement the industry's position in that country.

In relation to the development of competitiveness of the Indian software industry (especially in Bangalore), two essential events can be identified:

1 The Y2K problems (described earlier), which created the increased demand for services of Indian software firms.
2 The collapse of the dot-com boom in 2001 in the USA and Europe, which created the search for ways to cut costs by outsourcing software functions to India.

From the firm's point of view the last two variables, chance and government, can be regarded as exogenous variables which the firm must adjust to. Alternatively, the government may be considered susceptible through lobbying, interest organisations and mass media.

In summary, we have identified six factors that influence the location of global industries: factors of production, home demand, the location of supporting industries, the internal structure of the domestic industry, government and chance. We have also suggested that these factors are interconnected. As industries evolve their dependence on particular locations may also change. For example, the shift in users of semiconductors from the military to the electronics industry has had a profound effect on the shape of the national diamond in that industry. To the extent that governments and firms recognise the source of any locational advantages that they have, they will be better able to both exploit those differences and anticipate their shifts.

In relation to the software industry in India (Bangalore), which was used throughout the diamond model, the following conclusions may be given (Nair *et al.*, 2007).

The software industry in Bangalore started off by serving not its domestic customers but the demanding North American customers. Also, the rivals for the software firms tend not to be so much local but more global.

The support needed for software services is much less sophisticated than for manufacturing. For the manufacturing sector it is also important to have access to a well-functioning physical infrastructure (transport, logistics, etc.), which is not necessary for the software industry, where most of the logistics can be done over the Internet. That is one of the reasons why Bangalore's software industry created international competitiveness but the manufacturing sector did not.

The software industry is very much dependent on advanced and well-educated human resources as the key factor input.

While the Bangalore-based firms started off at the low end of the value chain (performing coding work for the Y2K problem) they have continuously moved in the direction of delivering more value-added service in emerging areas.

3.5 COMPETITION ANALYSIS IN AN INDUSTRY

The next step in understanding the firm's competitiveness is to look at the competitive arena in an industry, which is the top box in the diamond model (see Figure 3.3).

One of the most useful frameworks for analysing the competitive structure has been developed by Porter. Porter (1980) suggests that competition in an industry is rooted in its underlying economic structure and goes beyond the behaviour of current competitors. The state of competition depends upon five basic competitive forces, as shown in Figure 3.3. Together these factors determine the ultimate profit potential in an industry, where profit is measured in terms of long-run return on invested capital. The profit potential will differ from industry to industry (Brookfield *et al.*, 2008).

To make things clearer we need to define a number of key terms. An *industry* is a group of firms that offer a product or class of products which are close substitutes for each other. Examples are the car industry and the pharmaceutical industry (Kotler, 1997, p. 230). A *market* is a set of actual and potential buyers of a product and sellers. A distinction will be made between industry and market level, as we assume that the industry may contain several different markets. This is why the outer box in Figure 3.3 is designated 'industry level' and the inner box 'market level'.

Thus the *industry level* (Porter's five forces model) consists of all types of actors (new entrants, suppliers, substitutes, buyers and market competitors) that have a potential or current interest in the industry.

The *market level* consists of actors with a current interest in the market; that is, buyers and sellers (market competitors). In section 3.6 (value chain analysis) this market level will be further elaborated on as the buyers' perceived value of different competitor offerings will be discussed.

Marketing myopia
The failure of a company to define its organisational purpose from a broad consumer orientation.

Although division into the above-mentioned two levels is appropriate for this approach, Levitt (1960) pointed out the danger of 'marketing myopia', where the seller defines the competition field (i.e. the market) too narrowly (Brookfield *et al.*, 2008). For example, European luxury car manufacturers showed this myopia with their focus on each other rather than on the Japanese mass manufacturers, who were new entrants into the luxury car market.

The goal of competition analysis is to find a position in industry where the company can best defend itself against the five forces, or can influence them in its favour. Knowledge of these underlying pressures highlights the critical strengths and weaknesses of the company, shows its position in the industry, and clarifies areas where strategy changes yield the greatest pay-off. Structure analysis is fundamental for formulating competitive strategy.

Each of the five forces in the Porter model in turn comprises a number of elements that combine to determine the strength of each force, and its effect on the degree of competition. Each force is now discussed.

Market competitors

The intensity of rivalry between existing competitors in the market depends on a number of factors:

- *Concentration of the industry*: numerous competitors of equal size will lead to more intense rivalry. There will be less rivalry when a clear leader (at least 50 per cent larger than the second) exists with a large cost advantage.
- *Rate of market growth*: slow growth will tend towards greater rivalry.
- *Structure of costs*: high fixed costs encourage price cutting to fill capacity.
- *Degree of differentiation*: commodity products encourage rivalry, while highly differentiated products, which are hard to copy, are associated with less intense rivalry.
- *Switching costs*: when switching costs are high, because the product is specialised, the customer has invested a lot of resources in learning how to use the product or has made tailor-made investments that are worthless with other products and suppliers (high asset specificity), rivalry is reduced.
- **Exit barriers:** when barriers to leaving a market are high, due to such factors as lack of opportunities elsewhere, high vertical integration, emotional barriers or the high cost of closing down plant, rivalry will be more intense than when exit barriers are low.

Exit barrier
The barriers to leaving an industry, e.g. cost of closing down plant.

Firms need to be careful not to spoil a situation of competitive stability. They need to balance their own position against the well-being of the industry as a whole. For example, an intense price or promotional war may gain a few percentage points in market share but lead to an overall fall in long-run industry profitability as competitors respond to these moves. It is sometimes better to protect industry structure than to follow short-term self-interest.

Suppliers

The cost of raw materials and components can have a major bearing on a firm's profitability. The higher the bargaining power of suppliers, the higher the costs. The bargaining power of suppliers will be higher in the following circumstances:

- Supply is dominated by few companies and they are more concentrated than the industry they sell to.
- Their products are unique or differentiated, or they have built up switching costs.
- They are not obliged to contend with other products for sale to the industry.
- They pose a credible threat of integrating forwards into the industry's business.
- Buyers do not threaten to integrate backwards into supply.
- The market is not an important customer to the supplier group.

A firm can reduce the bargaining power of suppliers by seeking new sources of supply, threatening to integrate backwards into supply, and designing standardised components so that many suppliers are capable of producing them.

Buyers

The bargaining power of buyers is higher in the following circumstances:

- Buyers are concentrated and/or purchase in large volumes.
- Buyers pose a credible threat of integrating backwards to manufacture the industry's product.
- Products they purchase are standard or undifferentiated.
- There are many suppliers (sellers) of the product.
- Buyers earn low profits, which create a great incentive to lower purchasing costs.
- The industry's product is unimportant to the quality of the buyer's products, but price is very important.

Firms in the industry can attempt to lower buyer power by increasing the number of buyers they sell to, threatening to integrate forward into the buyer's industry, and producing highly valued, differentiated products. In supermarket retailing, the brand leader normally achieves the highest profitability, partially because being number one means that supermarkets need to stock the brand, thereby reducing buyer power in price negotiations.

Customers who purchase the product but are not the end user (such as OEMs or distributors) can be analysed in the same way as other buyers. Non-end customers can gain significant bargaining power when they can influence the purchase decision of customers downstream (Porter, 2008). Over the years ingredient supplier DuPont has created enormous clout by advertising its 'Teflon' brand not only to the manufacturers of cooking equipment, but also to downstream end-customers (households). See also the section on ingredient branding in Chapter 11.

Substitutes

The presence of substitute products can reduce industry attractiveness and profitability because they put a constraint on price levels.

If the industry is successful and earning high profits it is more likely that competitors will enter the market via substitute products in order to obtain a share of the potential profits available. The threat of substitute products depends on the following factors:

- the buyer's willingness to substitute;
- the relative price and performance of substitutes;
- the costs of switching to substitutes.

The threat of substitute products can be lowered by building up switching costs. These costs may be psychological. Examples are the creation of strong, distinctive brand personalities, and maintaining a price differential commensurate with perceived customer values.

New entrants

New entrants can serve to increase the degree of competition in an industry. In turn, the threat of new entrants is largely a function of the extent to which barriers to entry exist in the market. Some key factors affecting these entry barriers include the following:

- economies of scale;
- product differentiation and brand identity, which give existing firms customer loyalty;
- capital requirements in production;
- switching costs – the cost of switching from one supplier to another;
- access to distribution channels.

Because high barriers to entry can make even a potentially lucrative market unattractive (or even impossible) to enter for new competitors, the marketing planner should not take a passive approach but should actively pursue ways of raising barriers to new competitors.

High promotional and R&D expenditures and clearly communicated retaliatory actions to entry are some methods of raising barriers. Some managerial actions can unwittingly lower barriers. For example, new product designs that dramatically lower manufacturing costs can make entry by newcomers easier.

The collaborative 'five sources' model

Porter's original model is based on the hypothesis that the competitive advantage of the firm is best developed in a very competitive market with intense rivalry relations.

The five forces framework thus provides an analysis for considering how to squeeze the maximum competitive gain out of the context in which the business is located – or how to minimise the prospect of being squeezed by it – on the five competitive dimensions that it confronts.

Over the past two decades, however, an alternative school (e.g. Reve, 1990; Kanter, 1994; Burton, 1995) has emerged which emphasises the positive role of cooperative (rather than competitive) arrangements between industry participants, and the consequent importance of what Kanter (1994) has termed 'collaborative advantage' as a foundation of superior business performance.

An all-or-nothing choice between a single-minded striving for either competitive or collaborative advantage would, however, be a false one. The real strategic choice problem that all businesses face is where (and how much) to collaborate, and where (and how intensely) to act competitively.

Put another way, the basic questions that firms must deal with in respect of these matters are as follows:

- choosing the combination of competitive and collaborative strategies that are appropriate in the various dimensions of the industry environment of the firm;
- blending the two elements together so that they interact in a mutually consistent and reinforcing, and not counterproductive, manner;
- in this way, optimising the firm's overall position, drawing upon the foundation and utilisation of both collaborative and competitive advantage.

This points to the imperative in the contemporary context of complementing the competitive strategy model with a sister framework that focuses on the assessment of collaborative advantage and strategy. Such a complementary analysis, which is called the *five sources framework* (Burton, 1995), is outlined below.

Five sources model
Corresponding to Porter's five competitive forces there are also five potential sources for building collaborative advantages together with the firm's surrounding actors.

Corresponding to the array of five competitive forces that surround a company – as elaborated in Porter's treatment – there are also five potential sources for the building of collaborative advantage in the industrial environments of the firm (the **five sources model**). These sources are listed in Table 3.1.

In order to forge an effective and coherent business strategy, a firm must evaluate and formulate its collaborative and competitive policies side by side. It should do this for two purposes:

- to achieve the appropriate balance between collaboration and competition in each dimension of its industry environment (e.g. relations with suppliers, policies towards customers/channels);
- to integrate them in a way that avoids potential clashes and possibly destructive inconsistencies between them.

This is the terrain of composite strategy, which concerns the bringing together of competitive and collaborative endeavours.

Table 3.1	The five sources model and the corresponding five forces in the Porter model
Porter's five forces model	**The five sources model**
Market competitors	Horizontal collaborations with other enterprises operating at the same stage of the production process/producing the same group of closely related products (e.g. contemporary global partnering arrangements among car manufacturers).
Suppliers	Vertical collaborations with suppliers of components or services to the firm – sometimes termed vertical quasi-integration arrangements (e.g. the *keiretsu* formations between suppliers and assemblers that typify the car, electronics and other industries in Japan).
Buyers	Selective partnering arrangements with specific channels or customers (e.g. lead users) that involve collaboration (value co-creation) extending beyond standard, purely transactional relationships (Vargo *et al.*, 2008).
Substitutes	Related diversification alliances with producers of both complements and substitutes. Producers of substitutes are not natural allies but such alliances are not inconceivable (e.g. collaborations between fixed-wire and mobile telephone firms in order to grow their joint network size).
New entrants	Diversification alliances with firms based in previously unrelated sectors, but between which a blurring of industry borders is potentially occurring, or a process (commonly due to new technological possibilities) that opens up the prospect of cross-industry fertilisation of technologies/business that did not exist before (e.g. the collaborations in the emerging multimedia field).

Source: Burton, J. (1995) Composite strategy: the combination of collaboration and competition, *Journal of General Management*, 21(1): 1–23. Reproduced with permission from The Baybrooke Press Ltd.

3.6 VALUE CHAIN ANALYSIS

Until now we have discussed the firm's international competitiveness from a strategic point of view. To get closer to the firm's core competences we will now look at the market-level box in Porter's five-forces model, which treats buyers and sellers (market competitors). Here we will look more closely at what creates a competitive advantage among market competitors towards customers at the same competitive level.

The competitive triangle

Success in the marketplace is dependent not only upon identifying and responding to customer needs, but also upon our ability to ensure that our response is judged by customers to be superior to that of competitors (i.e. high perceived value). Several writers (e.g. Porter, 1980; Day and Wensley, 1988) have argued that causes of difference in performance within a market can be analysed at various levels. The immediate causes of differences in the performance of different firms, these writers argue, can be reduced to two basic factors (D'Aveni, 2007):

1   The *perceived value* of the product/services offered, compared to the perceived sacrifice. The *perceived sacrifice* includes all the 'costs' the buyer faces when making a purchase, primarily the *purchase price*, but also acquisition costs, transportation, installation, handling, repairs and maintenance (Ravald and Grönroos, 1996). In the models presented the (purchase) price will be used as a representative of the perceived sacrifice. D'Aveni (2007) presents a strategic tool for evaluating how much a customer is willing to pay for a perceived benefit of a product/service.

2   The firm-related *costs* incurred in creating this perceived value.

		Perceived value (compared to the purchase price)	
		Higher for A	Higher for B
Relative costs	Lower for A	I	II
	Lower for B	III	IV

Figure 3.4	Perceived value, relative costs and competitive advantage

These two basic factors will be further discussed later in this section.

The more value customers perceive in a market offering relative to competing offerings, and the lower the costs in producing the value relative to competing producers, the higher the performance of the business. Hence firms producing offerings with a higher perceived value and/or lower relative costs than competing firms are said to have a competitive advantage in that market.

Competitive triangle
Consists of a customer, the firm and a competitor (the 'triangle'). The firm or competitor 'winning' the competition depends on perceived value offered to the customer compared to the relative costs between the firm and the competitor.

This can be illustrated by the '**competitive triangle**' (see Figure 3.3). There is no one-dimensional measure of competitive advantage, and **perceived value** (compared to the price) and relative costs have to be assessed simultaneously. Given this two-dimensional nature of competitive advantage it will not always be clear which of the two businesses will have a competitive advantage over the other.

Looking at Figure 3.4, firm A will clearly have an advantage over firm B in case I, and clearly have a disadvantage in case IV, while cases II and III do not immediately allow such a conclusion. Firm B may have an advantage in case II, if customers in the market are highly quality conscious and have differentiated needs and low price elasticity, while firm A may have a similar advantage in case II when customers have homogeneous needs and high price elasticity. The opposite will take place in case III.

Perceived value
The customer's overall evaluation of the product/service offered by a firm, compared to a price paid.

Even if firm A has a clear competitive advantage over firm B, this may not necessarily result in a higher return on investment for A, if A has a growth and B a hold policy. Thus performance would have to be measured by a combination of return on investment and capacity expansion, which can be regarded as postponed return on investment.

While the relationship between perceived value, relative costs and performance is rather intricate, we can retain the basic statement that these two variables are the cornerstone of competitive advantage. Let us take a closer look at these two fundamental sources of competitive advantage.

Perceived value advantage

We have already observed that customers do not buy products; they buy benefits. Put another way, the product is purchased not for itself but for the promise of what it will 'deliver'. These benefits may be intangible; that is, they may relate not to specific product features but rather to such things as image or reputation. Alternatively, the delivered offering may be seen to outperform its rivals in some functional aspect.

Perceived value is the customer's overall evaluation of the product/service offered. So, establishing what value the customer is actually seeking from the firm's offering (value chain) is the starting point for being able to deliver the correct mix of value-providing activities. It may be some combination of physical attributes, service attributes and technical support available in relation to the particular use of the product. This also requires an understanding of the activities that constitute the customer's value chain.

Unless the product or service we offer can be distinguished in some way from its competitors there is a strong likelihood that the marketplace will view it as a 'commodity', and so the sale will tend to go to the cheapest supplier. Hence the importance of seeking to attach additional values to our offering to mark it out from the competition.

What are the means by which such value differentiation may be gained? If we start in the value chain perspective (see section 2.5), we can say that each activity in the business system adds perceived value to the product or service. Value, for the customer, is the perceived stream of benefits that accrue from obtaining the product or service. Price is what the customer is willing to pay for that stream of benefits. If the price of a good or service is high, it must provide high value, otherwise it is driven out of the market. If the value of a good or service is low, its price must be low, otherwise it is also driven out of the market. Hence, in a competitive situation, and over a period of time, the price that customers are willing to pay for a good or service is a good proxy measure of its value.

If we look especially at the downstream functions of the value chain, a differential advantage can be created with any aspect of the traditional 4P marketing mix: product, distribution, promotion and price are all capable of creating added customer perceived value. The key to whether improving an aspect of marketing is worthwhile is to know if the potential benefit provides value to the customer.

If we extend this model, particular emphasis must be placed upon the following (see Booms and Bitner, 1981; Magrath, 1986; Rafiq and Ahmed, 1995):

* *People*: these include both consumers, who must be educated to participate in the service, and employees (personnel), who must be motivated and well trained in order to ensure that high standards of service are maintained. Customers identify and associate the traits of service personnel with the firms they work for.

* *Physical aspects*: these include the appearance of the delivery location and the elements provided to make the service more tangible. For example, visitors experience Disneyland by what they see, but the hidden, below-ground support machinery is essential for the park's fantasy fulfilment.

* *Process*: the service is dependent on a well-designed method of delivery. Process management assures service availability and consistent quality in the face of simultaneous consumption and production of the service offered. Without sound process management balancing service demand with service supply is extremely difficult.

Of these three additional Ps, the firm's *personnel* occupy a key position in influencing customer perception of product quality. As a consequence the *image* of the firm is very much influenced by the personnel. It is therefore important to pay particular attention to the quality of employees and to monitor their performance. Marketing managers need to manage not only the service provider – customer interface – but also the actions of other customers; for example, the number, type and behaviour of other people will influence a meal at a restaurant.

Relative cost advantage

Each activity in the value chain is performed at a cost. Getting the stream of benefits that accrue from the good or service to the customer is thus done at a certain 'delivered cost', which sets a lower limit to the price of the good or service if the business system is to remain profitable. Decreasing the price will thus imply that the delivered cost be first decreased by adjusting the business system. As mentioned earlier, the rules of the game may be described as *providing the highest possible perceived value to the final customer, at the lowest possible delivered cost.*

Relative cost advantage
A firm's cost position depends on the configuration of the activities in its value chain versus that of the competitors.

A firm's cost position depends on the configuration of the activities in its value chain versus that of competitors and its relative location on the cost drivers of each activity. A cost advantage is gained when the cumulative cost of performing all the activities is lower than competitors' costs. This evaluation of the **relative cost position** requires an identification of each important competitor's value chain. In practice, this step is extremely difficult because the firm does not have direct information on the costs of competitors' value activities. However, some costs can be estimated from public data or interviews with suppliers and distributors.

Creating a **relative cost advantage** requires an understanding of the factors that affect costs. It is often said that 'big is beautiful'. This is partly due to economies of scale, which enable fixed costs to be spread over a greater output, but more particularly it is due to the impact of the *experience curve.*

The experience curve is a phenomenon that has its roots in the earlier notion of the learning curve. The effects of learning on costs were seen in the manufacture of fighter planes for the Second World War. The time taken to produce each plane gradually fell as learning took place. The combined effect of economies of scale and learning on cumulative output has been termed the experience curve. The Boston Consulting Group estimated that costs reduced on average by approximately 15–20 per cent each time cumulative output doubled.

Subsequent work by Bruce Henderson, founder of the Boston Consulting Group, extended this concept by demonstrating that all costs, not just production costs, would decline at a given rate as volume increased. In fact, to be precise, the relationship that the experience curve describes is between real unit costs and cumulative volume.

This suggests that firms with greater market share will have a cost advantage through the experience curve effect, assuming that all companies are operating on the same curve. However, a move towards a new manufacturing technology can lower the experience curve for adopting companies, allowing them to leapfrog over more traditional firms and thereby gain a cost advantage even though cumulative output may be lower.

The general form of the experience curve and the above-mentioned leapfrogging to another curve are shown in Figure 3.5.

Leapfrogging the experience curve by investing in new technology is a special opportunity for SMEs and newcomers to a market, since they will (as a starting point) have only a small market share and thereby a small cumulative output.

The implications of the experience curve for the pricing strategy will be discussed further in Chapter 12. According to Porter (1980) there are other cost drivers that determine the costs in value chains:

- *Capacity utilisation*: underutilisation incurs costs.
- *Linkages*: costs of activities are affected by how other activities are performed. For example, improving quality assurance can reduce after-sales service costs.
- *Interrelationships*: for example, different SBUs sharing R&D, purchasing and marketing will lower costs.

Relative cost advantage
A firm's cost position depends on the configuration of the activities in its value chain versus that of the competitors.

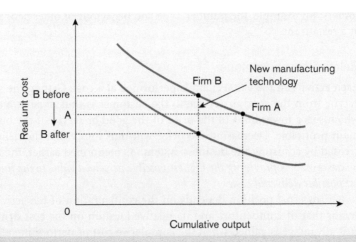

| Figure 3.5 | Leapfrogging the experience curve |

- *Integration*: for example, deintegration (outsourcing) of activities to subsuppliers can lower costs and raise flexibility.
- *Timing*: for example, first movers in a market can gain cost advantage. It is cheaper to establish a brand name in the minds of the customers if there are no competitors.
- *Policy decisions*: product width, level of service and channel decisions are examples of policy decisions that affect costs.
- *Location*: locating near suppliers reduces in-bound distribution costs. Locating near customers can lower out-bound distribution costs. Some producers locate their production activities in Eastern Europe or the Far East to take advantage of low wage costs.
- *Institutional factors*: government regulations, tariffs, local content rules, etc., will affect costs.

Competitive benchmarking

The ultimate test of the efficiency of any marketing strategy has to be in terms of profit. Those companies that strive for market share, but measure market share in terms of volume sales, may be deluding themselves to the extent that volume is bought at the expense of profit.

Because market share is an 'after the event' measure, we need to utilise continuing indicators of competitive performance. This will highlight areas where improvements in the marketing mix can be made.

Competitive benchmarking
A technique for assessing relative marketplace performance compared with main competitors.

In recent years a number of companies have developed a technique for assessing relative marketplace performance, which has come to be known as **competitive benchmarking**. Originally the idea of competitive benchmarking was literally to take apart a competitor's product, component by component, and compare its performance in a value engineering sense with your own product (Kolar and Toporisic, 2007). This approach has often been attributed to the Japanese, but many Western companies have also found the value of such detailed comparisons.

The concept of competitive benchmarking is similar to what Porter (1996) calls operational effectiveness (OE), meaning performing similar activities better than competitors perform them. However, Porter (1996) also thinks that OE is a necessary but not a sufficient condition for outperforming rivals. Firms also have to consider strategic (or market) positioning, meaning the performance of *different* activities from rivals or performing similar activities in different ways. Only a few firms have competed successfully on the basis of OE over a long period. The main reason is the rapid diffusion of best practices. Competitors can rapidly imitate management techniques and new technologies with support from consultants.

However, the idea of benchmarking is capable of extension beyond this simple comparison of technology and cost effectiveness. Because the battle in the marketplace is for 'share of mind', it is customers' perceptions that we must measure.

The measures that can be used in this type of benchmarking programme include delivery reliability, ease of ordering, after-sales service, the quality of sales representation and the accuracy of invoices and other documentation. These measures are not chosen at random, but are selected because of their importance to the customer. Market research, often based on in-depth interviews, would typically be employed to identify what these 'key success factors' are. The elements that customers identify as being the most important (see Figure 3.6) then form the basis for the benchmark questionnaire. This questionnaire is administered to a sample of customers on a regular basis: for example, German Telecom carries out a daily telephone survey of a random sample of its domestic and business customers to measure customers' perceptions of service. For most companies an annual survey might suffice; in other cases, perhaps a quarterly survey, particularly if market conditions are dynamic. The output of these surveys might typically be presented in the form of a competitive profile, as in the example in Figure 3.6.

Most of the criteria mentioned above relate to downstream functions in the value chain. Concurrently with closer relations between buyers and suppliers, especially in the industrial market, there will be more focus on the supplier's competences in the upstream functions.

Examples of value chain functions (mainly downstream functions)	Customer Importance to customer (key success factors)					Own firm (Firm A) How do customers rate performance of our firm?					Key competitor (Firm B) How do customers rate performance of key competitor?				
	High importance			Low importance		Good				Bad	Good				Bad
	5	4	3	2	1	5	4	3	2	1	5	4	3	2	1
Uses new technology															
High technical quality and competence															
Uses proven technology															
Easy to buy from															
Understands what customers want															
Low price															
Delivery on schedule															
Accessible for enquiries															
Takes full responsibility															
Flexible and quick															
Known contact person															
Provides customer training															
Take account of future requirements															
Courteous and helpful															
Specified invoices															
Gives guarantees															
ISO 9000 certified															
Right first time															
Can give references															
Environment conscious															

Figure 3.6   Competitive benchmarking (example with only a few criteria)

Development of a dynamic benchmarking model

On the basis of the value chain's functions, we will suggest a model for the development of a firm's competitiveness in a defined market (Collis and Rukstad, 2008). The model will be based on a specific market as the market demands are assumed to differ from market to market, and from country to country.

Before presenting the basic model for development of international competitiveness we will first define two key terms:

1   *Critical success factors*: those value chain functions where the customer demands/expects the supplier (firm X) to have a strong competence.

2   *Core competences*: those value chain functions where firm X has a strong competitive position.

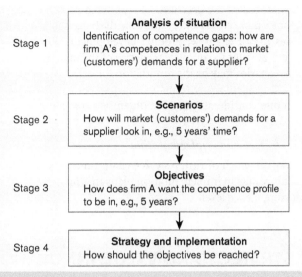

Figure 3.7	Model for development of core competences
	Source: Hollensen, S. (2001) *Global Marketing: A Market Responsive Approach*, 2nd ed., Financial Times-Prentice Hall, Harlow, p. 95. Reproduced with permission.

The strategy process

The model for the strategy process is shown in Figure 3.7.

Stage 1: Analysis of situation (identification of competence gaps)

We will not go into detail here about the problems there have been in measuring the value chain functions. The measurements cannot be objective in the traditional way of thinking, but must rely on internal assessments from firm representatives (interviews with relevant managers) supplemented by external experts ('key informants') who are able to judge the market's (customers') demand now and in the future.

The competence profile for firm A in Figure 3.3 (top-right diagram) is an example of how a firm is not in accordance with the market (= customer) demand. The company has its core competences in parts of the value chain's functions where customers place little importance (market knowledge in Figure 3.3).

If there is a generally good match between the critical success factors and firm A's initial position, it is important to concentrate resources and improve this core competence to create sustainable competitive advantages.

If, on the other hand, there is a large gap between customers' demands and the firm's initial position in critical success factors in Figure 3.3 (as with the personal selling functions), it may give rise to the following alternatives:

- improve the position of the critical success factor(s);
- find business areas where firm A's competence profile better suits the market demand and expectations.

As a new business area involves risk, it is often important to identify an eventual gap in a critical success factor as early as possible (Allen *et al.*, 2005). In other words, an 'early warning' system must be established that continuously monitors the critical competitive factors so that it is possible to start initiatives that limit an eventual gap as early as possible.

In Figure 3.3 the competence profile of firm B is also shown.

Stages 2 and 3: Scenarios and objectives

To be able to estimate future market demand different scenarios are made of the possible future development. These trends are first described generally, then the effect of the market's future demand/expectations on a supplier's value chain function is concretised.

By this procedure the described 'gap' between market expectations and firm A's initial position becomes more clear. At the same time the biggest gap for firm A may have moved from personal sales to, for example, product development. From knowledge of the market leader's strategy it is possible to complete scenarios of the market leader's future competence profile.

These scenarios may be the foundation for a discussion of objectives and of which competence profile the company wants in, say, five years' time. Objectives must be set realistically and with due consideration of the organisation's resources (the scenarios are not shown in Figure 3.3).

Stage 4: Strategy and implementation

Depending on which of firm A's value chain functions are to be developed, a strategy is prepared. This results in implementation plans that include the adjustment of the organisation's current competence level.

3.7 BLUE OCEAN STRATEGY AND VALUE INNOVATION

Red oceans
Tough head-to-head competition in mature industries often results in nothing but a bloody red ocean of rivals fighting over a shrinking profit pool.

Blue oceans
The unserved market, where competitors are not yet structured and the market is relatively unknown. Here it is about avoiding head-to-head competition.

Kim and Mauborgne (2005a, b, c) use the ocean as a metaphor to describe the competitive space in which an organisation chooses to swim. **Red oceans** refer to the frequently accessed marketspaces where the products are well-defined, competitors are known and competition is based on price, product quality and service. In other words, red oceans are an old paradigm that represents all the industries in existence today.

In contrast, the **blue oceans** denote an environment where products are not yet well-defined, competitors are not structured and the market is relatively unknown. Companies that sail in the blue oceans are those beating the competition by focusing on developing compelling value innovations that create uncontested marketspace. Adopters of blue ocean strategy believe that it is no longer valid for companies to engage in head-to-head competition in search of sustained, profitable growth.

In Michael Porter's models (1980, 1985), companies are fighting for competitive advantage, battling for market share and struggling for differentiation; blue ocean strategists argue that cut-throat competition results in nothing but a bloody red ocean of rivals fighting over a shrinking profit pool.

A blue ocean is a marketspace that is created by identifying an unserved set of customers, then delivering to them a compelling new value proposition. This is done by reconfiguring what is on offer to better balance customer needs with the economic costs of doing so. This is as opposed to a red ocean, where the market is well defined and heavily populated by the competition.

Blue ocean strategy should not be a static process but a dynamic one. Consider The Body Shop. In the 1980s, The Body Shop was highly successful, and rather than compete head on with large cosmetics companies, it invented a whole new marketspace for natural beauty products. During the 1990s The Body Shop also struggled, but that does not diminish the excellence of its original strategic move. Its genius lay in creating a new marketspace in an intensely competitive industry that historically competed on glamour (Kim and Mauborgne, 2005b).

Kim and Mauborgne (2005a) is based on a study of 150 strategic moves that spanned more than 100 years (1880–2000) and 30 industries. Kim and Mauborgne's first point in distinguishing this strategy from the traditional strategic frameworks is that in the traditional business literature the company forms the basic unit of analysis, and the industry analysis is the means of positioning the company. Their hypothesis is that since markets are constantly changing in their levels of attractiveness, and companies over time vary in their level of performance, it is the particular *strategic move of the company*, and not the company itself or the industry, which is the correct criterion for evaluating the difference between red and blue ocean strategies.

Value innovation

Value innovation
A strategic approach to business growth, involving a shift away from a focus on the existing competition to one of trying to create entirely new markets. Value innovation can be achieved by implementing a focus on innovation and creation of new marketspace.

Kim and Mauborgne (2005a) argue that tomorrow's leading companies will succeed not by battling competitors but by making strategic moves, which they call **value innovation.**

The combination of value with innovation is not just marketing and taxonomic positioning. It has consequences. Value without innovation tends to focus on value creation on an incremental scale, and innovation without value tends to be technology driven, market pioneering or futuristic, often overshooting what buyers are ready to accept and pay for. Conventional Porter logic (1980, 1985) leads companies only to compete at the margin for incremental share. The logic of value innovation starts with an ambition to dominate the market by offering a tremendous leap in value. Many companies seek growth by retaining and expanding their customer base. This often leads to finer segmentation and greater customisation of offerings to meet specialised needs. Instead of focusing on the differences between customers, value innovators build on the powerful commonalities in the features that customers value (Kim and Mauborgne, 1997).

Value innovation is intensely customer focused, but not exclusively so (Abraham, 2007). Like value chain analysis it balances costs of delivering the value proposition with what the buyer values are, and then resolves the trade-off dilemma between the value delivered and the costs involved. Instead of compromising the value wanted by the customer because of the high costs associated with delivering it, costs are eliminated or reduced if there is no or less value placed on the offering by the customer. This is a real win–win resolution that creates the compelling proposition. Customers get what they really want for less, and sellers get a higher rate of return on invested capital by reducing start-up and/or operational delivery costs. The combination of these two is the catalyst of blue ocean market creation (Sheehan and Vaidyanathan, 2009). Exhibit 3.1 illustrates this by using the case of Formule 1.

The output of the value innovation analysis is the value curves of the different marketers in the industry (also called 'strategy canvas' in Kim and Mauborgne, 2005 – see Exhibit 3.1). These different value curves raise four basic questions for the focal firm:

1 Which factors should be reduced well below the industry standard?
2 Which of the factors that the industry takes for granted should be eliminated?
3 Which factors should be raised well above the industry standard?
4 Which factors should be created that the industry has never offered?

The resulting new value curve should then determine if the firm is on its way into the 'blue ocean'.

EXHIBIT 3.1
Value innovation at hotel chain Formule 1

When Accor launched Formule 1 (a line of French budget hotels) in 1985, the budget hotel industry was suffering from stagnation and overcapacity. The top management urged the managers to forget everything they knew of the existing rules, practices and traditions of the industry. There were two distinct market segments in the industry. One segment consisted of no-star and one-star hotels (very cheap, around €20 per room per night) and the other segment comprised two-star hotels, with an average price €40 per room. These more expensive two-star hotels attracted customers by offering better sleeping facilities than the cheap segment. Accor's management undertook market research and found out what most customers of all budget hotels wanted: a good night's sleep at a low price. Then they asked themselves (and answered) the four fundamental questions:

→

EXHIBIT 3.1
Value innovation at hotel chain Formule 1 (*continued*)

1 Which of the factors that the budget hotel industry took for granted should be eliminated?

The Accor management eliminated such standard hotel features as costly restaurants and appealing lounges. Accor reckoned that they might lose some customers by this, but they also knew that most customers could live without these features.

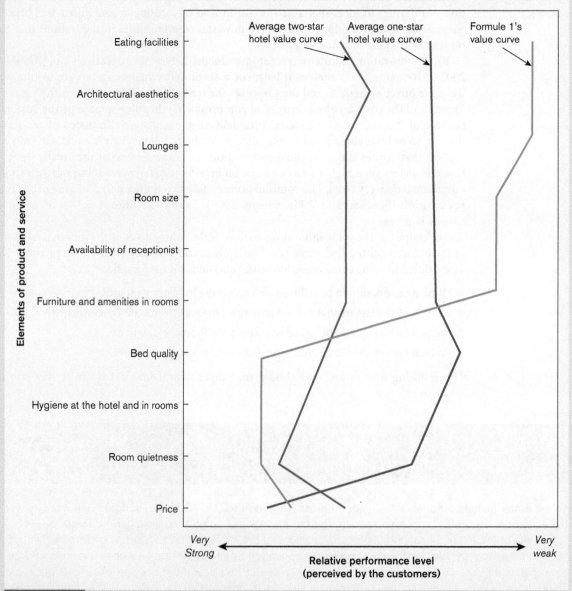

Figure 3.8	Formule 1's value curve

2 Which factors should be reduced well below the industry standard?

Accor also believed that budget hotels were overperforming along other dimensions. For example, at Formule 1 receptionists are on hand only during peak check-in and check-out hours. At all other times, customers use an automated teller. The rooms at Formule 1 are small and equipped only with a bed and bare necessities – no desks or decorations. Instead of closets there are a few shelves for clothing.

3 Which factors should be raised well above the industry standard?

As seen in Formule 1's value curve (Figure 3.8), the following factors:

- the bed quality
- hygiene
- room quietness

were raised above the relative level of the low-budget hotels (the one-star and two-star hotels). The price-performance was perceived as being at the same level as the average one-star hotels.

4 Which new factors (that the industry had never offered) should be developed?

These covered cost-minimising factors such as the availability of room keys via an automated teller. The rooms themselves are modular blocks manufactured in a factory. That is a method which may not result in the nicest architectural aesthetics but gives economies of scale in production and considerable cost advantages. Formule 1 has cut in half the average cost of building a room and its staff costs (in relation to total sales) dropped below the industry average (approximately 30 per cent) to between 20 per cent and 23 per cent. These cost savings have allowed Accor to improve the features that customers value most ('a good night's sleep at a low price').

Note that in Figure 3.8 if the price is perceived as relatively low, it is regarded as a strong performance.

WHAT HAS HAPPENED WITH ACCOR AND FORMULE 1?

Today Accor is owner of several hotel chains (besides Formule 1), for example Mercure, Sofitel, Novotel, Ibis and Motel 6. In 2005 the sales of Accor Group were €7.6 billion. As of 1 January 2006 Formule 1 has the following number of hotels in the following regions of the world (Table 3.2).

Table 3.2	Number of Formule 1 hotels worldwide

Region	Number
France	284
Rest of Europe	44
North America	–
South America	5
Africa (South Africa)	24
Asia-Pacific	20
Total	377

Formule 1 is represented in 12 countries: France, Germany, Sweden, the UK, the Netherlands, Switzerland, Spain, Belgium, South Africa, Japan, Australia and Brazil. In France, Formule 1's market share in the budget hotel segment is approximately 50 per cent.

Sources: Accor (www.accor.com); Hotel Formule 1 (www.hotelformule1.com); Kim and Mauborgne (1997).

3.8 OUTSOURCING – A STRATEGIC DECISION FRAMEWORK BASED ON CUSTOMERS' EVALUATION

After the dynamic benchmarking process the firm might have an idea about whether it should perform a certain value chain activity itself or if it should consider letting somebody else do it, e.g. outsource the activity.

It is important for a firm to decide which competences to keep in-house and which to outsource. The underlying assumption is that a firm should outsource non-core activities to be able to focus more on the core competence.

Outsourcing
Using another firm for the manufacture of needed components or products or delivery of a service.

Over the last number of years, **outsourcing** has become an important issue for many organisations. The potential for outsourcing has moved from peripheral activities such as cleaning and catering to critical activities such as design, product development, IT, manufacturing, logistics and marketing/advertising.

What is outsourcing? The word outsourcing defines the process of transferring the responsibility for a specific business function from an internal employee group to an external partner. An example of outsourcing (and how the boundary of the firm is 'reduced') is shown in Figure 3.9.

Though there might be differences, in- or outsourcing and make or buy analysis will be regarded as synonyms in this book.

Outsourcing is a contractual agreement between the firm and one or more suppliers to provide services or processes that the firm is currently providing internally. The fundamental difference between outsourcing and any other purchasing agreement is that the firm contracts-out part of its existing internal activity. There are many reasons why a company may choose to outsource and it will rarely be for one single reason.

The three most obvious reasons are listed in Table 3.3.

The hybrid situations enable the two organisations supporting the same market to share resources and increase revenue through synergistic relationships.

As indicated, one of the reasons why firms have outsourced a number of their primary supply chain activities is that the costs of remaining up to date in a multitude of value chain activities has become financially onerous. Where technology moves the fastest, the problem is the most serious. It would not be a surprise to learn, therefore, that a number of the pioneering outsourcers have been in the IT sector.

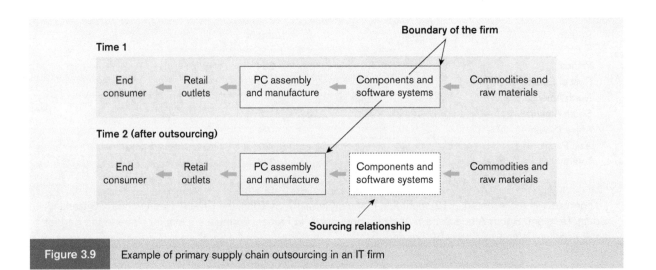

Figure 3.9   Example of primary supply chain outsourcing in an IT firm

Table 3.3	Reasons why companies outsource	
Rationale	Description	Benefits
Cost reduction	Outsourcing to another party to reduce cost of operations.	• Improve efficiency • Increase return on assets • Improve profitability
Revenue generation	Contracting with another party to provide products or services which the outsourcing firm cannot offer on its own.	• Increase revenue (new products to existing and/or new customers) • Reduce risk • Improve efficiency
Hybrid situations	Collaborations, alliances, partnerships, etc. with two or more like parties in the same business line to offer complementary products or services.	• Improve return on investment • Increase capability utilisation • Create economies of scope by offering a broader product concept to customers

Source: Adapted from Blumberg, D. F. (1998) Strategic assessment of outsourcing and downsizing in the service market, *Managing Service Quality*, 8(1): 7. Copyright © 1998 Emerald Group Publishing Limited. All rights reserved. Reproduced with permission.

An outsourcing/insourcing framework

The stages involved in the outsourcing framework are illustrated in Figure 3.10. The stages will now be described.

Stage 1: Analysis

Stage 1a: Evaluating customer value (KSF)

Key success factors (KSF)
Those factors in a market which determine competitive success or failure in that market.

Activities with high customer value are often **key success factors (KSF)**, which are central to the firm successfully serving the need of potential customers in each market. To point out KSFs, customers are asked if the firm's value chain activities are adding value for them. This is done by asking about the importance of activities (see also the questionnaire in Figure 3.6).

Stage 1b: Evaluating the firm's relative competence strengths

Focusing attention on customer needs and competitive advantage will involve applying the firm's distinctive capabilities to meet these needs. Here, each selected activity must be benchmarked against the capabilities of all potential external providers of that activity. This will enable the company to identify its *relative* performance for each activity (also illustrated in Figure 3.6 questionnaire).

The depth of evaluation of the organisation's value chain can take place at the activity (such as logistics) or sub-activity (materials handling) level depending on the particular circumstances of the organisation.

Stage 2: Decision about in/outsourcing

Stages 1a and 1b identify the disparity between the sourcing company and potential external providers of the core activities. It allows companies to focus on whether it will be detrimental to their competitive position to outsource activities such as research and development, design, engineering, manufacturing, marketing and service, both in the short and long term.

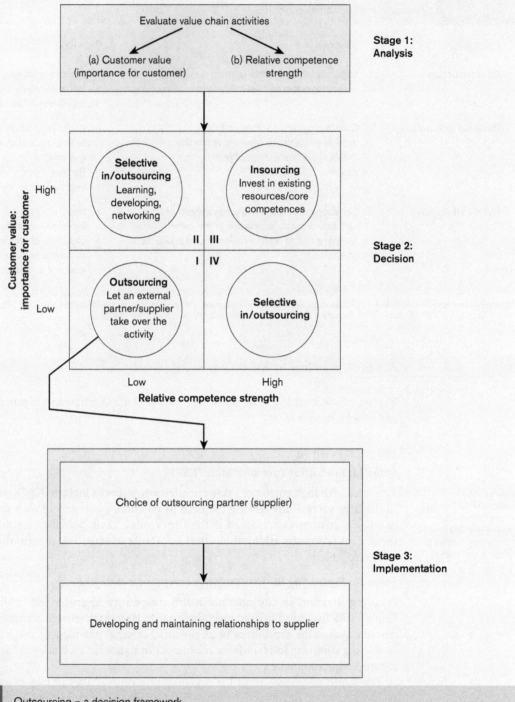

Figure 3.10   Outsourcing – a decision framework

Before the final decision the firm must identify and measure the costs associated with either retaining the activity in-house or outsourcing the activity.

In Box I in Figure 3.10 the firm faces one of its value chain activities, which only delivers low customer value, and the firm is also relatively poor in performing the activity (low relative competence strength). In this situation it is more appropriate for the company to outsource the activity to external suppliers that are more competent and have a lower cost base.

Unlike Box I, Box III is a situation where the company can focus resources on the activities where it can achieve pre-eminence and provide high customer perceived value. For example, if a company has leadership in a core activity then this activity should be held and further developed within the company in order to maintain and build this core competence.

In Boxes II and IV the outcome can be either keeping the activity in-house or outsourcing depending on the specific situation. The situation in Box II is very similar to the evaluation of the activity of '**personal selling**' in Figure 3.3. In this situation the firm could outsource the activity (because it is not good at performing the activity) or it could try to develop its competence level and move it from Box II to Box III, because the activity is very important for the customer.

The outcome of Box IV could also be a selective in/outsourcing depending on the situation. Perhaps this firm is able to transfer its high relative strength in these activities to another industry or a new customer group who would value it more. This would be a reverse situation where the firm itself would function as a sub-supplier to another outsourcing company.

Personal selling
Person-to-person inter-action between a buyer and a seller wherein the seller's purpose is to persuade the buyer to accept a point of view, to convince the buyer to take a course of action, or to develop a customer relationship.

Stage 3: Implementation

If the outcome of stage 2 is outsourcing (Box I), the firm believes it can be more flexible by outsourcing activities than performing activities internally by being in a better position to react rapidly to market changes and be more responsive to customer change. This strategy will result in the company gradually becoming a 'systems integrator' in which it manages and coordinates a network of best production and service providers. Such a strategy is based on the premise that the company should outsource those activities (both production and service) where it can develop no strategic advantage itself.

From this analysis of potential suppliers, the company will filter out any potential suppliers that are unsuitable (see also screening of potential suppliers in Figure 4.11). If it is found that there are no suppliers suitable with which to initiate a relationship, then the company may pursue an 'Invest to perform internally' strategy. However, if the company has found a suitable supplier then it should form a relationship while leveraging its own capabilities by focusing resources on high value-added activities.

A number of issues have to be addressed before the actual outsourcing to the chosen supplier can take place. The company may wish to maintain the knowledge (design skills, management skills, manufacturing, etc.) that enable the technology of the activity to be exploited, even when it is being provided by another partner. Therefore, it is important that the company controls the new product development and design process, as these are the activities that will drive future growth. The company may establish a partnership relationship or strategic alliance with a supplier in order to exploit their capabilities. This involves an intensive collaborative working relationship with the prospective partner.

If the company has succeeded in developing a best-in-world core competence, it would never outsource it. The company may even prefer to build defensive rings of essential competences that customers insist it have or that protect its core competence – as Sony has done (Exhibit 3.2).

EXHIBIT 3.2
Sony, an outsourcing company

Sony, as one of the largest electronics manufacturers in the world, certainly enjoys market power because of its strong market position globally, e.g. its dominant position in the personal stereo segment of the personal electronics market. Its efficient manufacturing capability and outsourcing expertise provide operating advantages. Sony is a firm that is known to be a pioneer, not a follower. Innovation lies at the heart of the whole corporation. It constantly launches new products and models to overwhelm the me-too competitors. And Sony is a company that is willing to make commitments, for good or bad, even when a technology's commercial viability is uncertain. Its commitment to the Betamax format in the VCR industry caused it to lose out in that lucrative

→

EXHIBIT 3.2
Sony, an outsourcing company (*continued*)

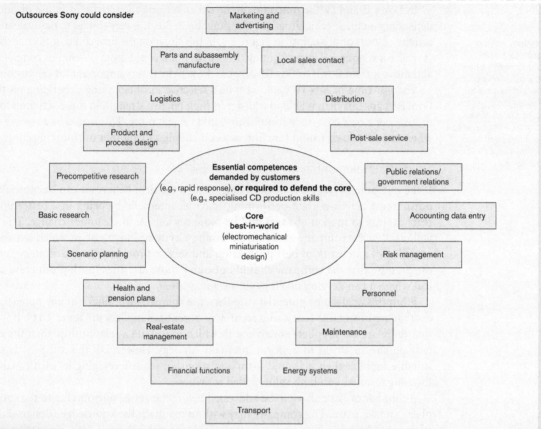

Figure 3.11	The structure of Sony, an outsourcing company
	Source: Adapted from Quinn, J. B. (2000) Outsourcing innovation: the new engine of growth, *MIT Sloan Management Review*, Summer: 20. Copyright © 2000 by the Massachusetts Institute of Technology. All rights reserved. Distributed by Tribune Media Service. Reproduced with permission.

market because it failed to become the industry standard. Sony failed to establish its leadership position in its business system of fellow VCR producers. The same can be said about its stubbornness in going alone on Mini-Disc and Digital Audio Tape (DAT), and not sharing its format through network alliances.

Nonetheless, one has to appreciate Sony's remarkable consistency and discipline in implementing its strategy: it is both a pioneer and the proprietary beneficiary of its new technology. Sony's miniaturisation skills have often been cited as a classical example of corporate core competence (Figure 3.11) which enables it to enjoy a commanding lead in portable and pocket-size electronics (Prahalad and Hamel, 1990).

Its unique capability lies in quickly adopting new knowledge and technology. In this sense, Sony is definitely a leading company in time-based competition.

Although it favours proprietary technology, Sony is also no stranger to cooperation and learning-inspired collaborative arrangement. To tackle technical challenges and share risks in R&D, in the late 1970s and early 1980s, Sony jointly developed the CD format with Philips. Once it learned enough from its partner and ironed out major technical obstacles, it decided to make a greater commitment to manufacturing facilities faster than Philips did and pre-empt the worldwide market for CD players. Philips saw the CD format as essentially a high-end consumer product, whereas Sony treated it as the future industry standard and a potential blockbuster for the firm, which would succeed its colour TV and Walkman as the next star product and help sustain its growth.

Sources: After Ma (2000b); Quinn (2000).

Table 3.4	Advantages and disadvantages of outsourcing

Advantages	Disadvantages
• Offers significant cost savings across a wide range of low-margin, non-differentiated services as well as additional income opportunities. • Outsourcing non-critical functions permits a company to increase its financial resources. • Eliminates investments in fixed infrastructure. • Allows for greater quality and efficiency. • Permits increased access to functional expertise. • Outsourcing provides a competitive advantage and creates new revenue streams by allowing suppliers to offer services that would otherwise require considerable expense and commitment of personnel. • Using an outside provider allows suppliers to test market demand for a product or service in a less risky, more cost-effective way than creating the service internally with service resources.	• Requires a change in management mind set. • Requires a new and more complicated level of communication. • Introduces a host of new outlooks, personalities and demands that can produce new problems. • Introduces insecurity to the workforce and unions. • Monitoring and evaluating the performance of suppliers is a difficult task. • Outsourcing functions that have customer contact risks alienating customers. • Outsourcing benefits may not be realised in the short term. • Long-term contracts which feature short-term savings may prove expensive later (resulting in high transaction costs).

Source: Adapted from Blumberg, D. F. (1998) Strategic assessment of outsourcing and downsizing in the service market, *Managing Service Quality*, 8(1): 7. Copyright © 1998 Emerald Group Publishing Limited. All rights reserved. Reproduced with permission.

Advantages and disadvantages of outsourcing

Outsourcing can create a number of economic advantages. However, there are also a number of risks in outsourcing, which may create perceived disadvantages (see Table 3.4).

These disadvantages are mostly of a psychological nature and if managed effectively do not lead to financial losses. For example, partnering with a third party introduces a host of new outlooks, personalities and demands that can produce new problems. These challenges include a more complicated level of communication, insecurity in the workforce, and the risk of high **transaction costs**.

Transaction costs
The total of all costs incurred by a buyer and seller as they gather information and negotiate a transaction.

The biggest barrier to outsourcing is that it requires a change in management mind set. Many managers fear the loss of control or conflict of interest and fail to compare the cost and benefit of using internal support organisations. Managers faced with an outsourcing decision often construe the financial cost and loss of control over individuals as their justification for not outsourcing, but fail to consider the long-and short-term savings to the organisation.

Motivating employees for the change towards outsourcing is not an easy task. However, the risk associated with outsourcing can be offset and controlled if managed properly.

3.9 SUMMARY

The main issue of this section is how the firm develops competitive advantage in the international marketplace. The sources of competitive advantage are:

• economies of scale (scale efficiencies);

• economies of scope (transfer of resources across products and markets);

• economies of speed (time-based competition advantages);

• exploitation of local advantages;

• ability to provide global services;

• ability to use 'human resources' (HR) (HR are especially important for RM and internal marketing).

A three-stage model allows us to understand the development of a firm's international competitiveness in a broader perspective.

Analysis of national/regional competitiveness

The Porter diamond indicates that the home base plays a central role in the firm's international success.

Competition analysis

Here the firm itself is the unit of analysis. Porter's five forces model suggests that competition in an industry is rooted in its underlying industry structure. The state of competition depends on five basic competitive forces, which determine profit potential in an industry.

Value chain analysis

According to the competitive triangle it can be concluded that firms have competitive advantage in a market if they offer products or services with the following characteristics:

- a higher perceived value to the customers;
- lower relative costs than the competing firms.

Influenced by core competency thinking, many companies have been attempting to reorganise their value chains and focus on a number of core activities in which they can achieve and maintain a long-term competitive advantage and outsource all other activities where they do not have high relative competence strength.

While the motives for outsourcing are normally specific to the particular situation, some commonly cited reasons are to:

- reduce cost;
- improve quality, service and delivery;
- improve organisational focus;
- increase flexibility;
- facilitate change.

The biggest obstacle to outsourcing is that the management may fear that they would lose control. However, the risks associated with outsourcing can be offset and controlled if managed properly.

CASE STUDY 3.1

Nintendo Wii
Taking the leadership in the games console market

A few years ago, very few analysts would have predicted that Nintendo Wii would become market leader in the games console market against the established PlayStation 3 (PS3) and Xbox 360 brands. But analysts can be in error: in the week ending 23 August 2007 data from VGChartz (www.vgchartz.com), which is based on sample data from retailers all over the world, indicated that Nintendo's Wii (which was released in November 2006 – one year after the Xbox 360) passed Xbox 360 lifetime units sales, making Nintendo the new world market leader in both the games console businesses.

This will have a large impact on third party publishers and will undoubtedly influence the decisions that the three major players (Microsft, Sony and Nintendo) will make in the future.

One factor that has no doubt helped Nintendo's Wii to gain so quickly is the console's broad appeal across all age groups, demographics and countries.

Nintendo – key facts and financial data

Nintendo Co. was founded in 1889 as the Marufuku Company to make and sell 'hanafuda', Japanese game cards. It became the Nintendo Playing Card Company in 1951 and began making theme cards under a licensing agreement with Disney in 1959.

During the 1980s Nintendo sought new products, releasing Game Boy in 1989 and the Super Family Computer game system (Super NES in the US) in 1991. The company broke with tradition in 1994 by making design alliances with companies such as Silicon Graphics. After creating a 32-bit product in 1995, Nintendo launched the much-touted N64 game system in 1996. It also teamed with Microsoft and Nomura Research Institute on a satellite-delivered Internet system for Japan. Price wars between the top contenders continued in the US and Japan.

In 1998 Nintendo released Pokémon, which involves trading and training virtual monsters (it had been popular in Japan since 1996), in the US. The company also launched the video game 'The Legend of Zelda: Ocarina of Time', which sold 2.5 million units in about six weeks. Nintendo issued 50 new games for 1998, compared to Sony's 131.

Nintendo announced in 1999 that its next-generation game system, Dolphin (later renamed GameCube), would use IBM's PowerPC microprocessor and Matsushita's DVD players.

In September 2001 Nintendo launched its long-awaited GameCube console system (which retailed at $100 less than its console rivals, Sony's PlayStation 2 and Microsoft's XBox); the system debuted in North America in November. In addition, the company came out with Game Boy Advance, its newest handheld model with a bigger screen and faster chip.

In 2003 Nintendo bought a stake (about 3 per cent) in game developer and toy-maker Bandai, a move expected to solidify cooperation between the two companies in marketing game software.

Today Nintendo (www.nintendo.co.jp) is engaged in the creation of interactive entertainment products. It manufactures and markets hardware and software for its home video game systems. The company primarily operates in Japan, Europe and America. It is headquartered in Kyoto, Japan, and employs about 3,400 people.

In the fiscal year 2007 Nintendo's recorded revenue was $8,189.4 million, an increase of 90 per cent over 2006. The operating profit of the company was $1,916.2 million during fiscal year 2007, compared to $773.7 million in 2006. Approximately 67 per cent of the company's revenue is generated from regions outside Japan. The net profit was $1,478.2 million in fiscal year 2007, an increase of 77.2 per cent over 2006. Nintendo has managed to achieve higher returns on its investments, assets and equity as compared to the industry average.

Nintendo has not raised any capital through debt in the past few years. The company's total debt to equity ratio at the beginning of 2007 is zero, compared to the industry average of 12 per cent. Debt-free status indicates the company's ability to finance its operations efficiently. Additionally, no debt obligation provides the company with significant liquidity and financial flexibility.

The video game console industry

The interactive entertainment software market is characterised by short product life cycles and frequent introductions of new products.

The game consoles are relative expensive in the beginning of the product life cycle. Hard-core game freaks pay dearly to have a console early, but sales really jump in years two and three, as Moore's law and economies of scale drive prices down and third-party developers release must-have games. By year four the buzz has begun about the next generation and, at that time, the game consoles can be found at the local grocery store at discount prices.

Nintendo has been operating in the video game console market since 1977 with colour television games, and is considered the oldest company in this market. It is one of the largest console manufacturers in the world, and a leader in the handheld console market. The company has released four generations of consoles over the past two decades, which include Nintendo Entertainment System; Super Nintendo Entertainment System; Nintendo 64; and GameCube. Nintendo has dominated the handheld games market since its release of the original Game Boy handheld system in 1989. In fiscal year 2007, Nintendo sold 79.5 million units of Game Boy Advance (GBA). Nintendo DS, another handheld console of Nintendo, sold 40.3 million units in fiscal year 2007.

Nintendo launches Wii

The company's latest console, Wii, was launched in November 2006.

Nintendo's arguments for using this brandname were:

Nintendo Wii console and remote
Source: © Lightly Salted / Alamy

- Wii sounds like 'we', which emphasises this console is for everyone.
- Wii can easily be remembered by people around the world, no matter what language they speak.
- Wii has a distinctive 'ii' spelling that symbolises both the unique controllers and the image of people gathering to play.

The Wii's success has done little to convince Microsoft executives they're on the wrong course. The company is positioning itself for a world where people play multiplayer games, download movies and control their TVs through one box. 'Nintendo has created a unique and innovative experience,' says Peter Moore, who runs Microsoft's Xbox business. 'I love the experience, the price point, and Nintendo content.' But Microsoft, Moore adds, 'provides experiences that Nintendo cannot provide' (O'Brien, 2007).

Of course, Microsoft has little more to lose than money, and there's plenty of that to go around. Sony is another matter. Gaming has been the company's profit centre for years. Suddenly, when everyone thought the PS3 would solidify Sony's dominance, along came the Wii. With an unheard-of price and few quality games to choose from, the PS3 has produced disappointing sales; the father of the PlayStation, Ken Kutaragi, was recently forced to resign his post as chairman of Sony Computer Entertainment (O'Brian, 2007).

But while he acknowledges a slow start, Jack Tretton, the president and CEO of Sony Computer Entertainment America, thinks it's too early to start talking winners. 'You have to give Nintendo credit for what they've accomplished,' says Tretton, who's quick to point out that Sony has come out with some innovative controllers too. 'But if you look at the industry, any industry, it doesn't typically go backwards technologically. The controller is innovative, but the Wii is basically a re-purposed GameCube. If you've built your console on an innovative controller, you have to ask yourself, Is that long term?' (O'Brien, 2007).

Wii's blue ocean strategy

Nintendo is attempting to create a blue ocean by creating a unique gaming experience and keeping the cost of its system lower than Sony's and Microsoft's.

In a recent Forbes.com interview, Perrin Kaplan, vice president of marketing and corporate affairs for Nintendo of America, discusses its implementation of Blue Ocean:

Inside Nintendo, we call our strategy 'Blue Ocean'. This is in contrast to a 'Red Ocean'. Seeing a Blue Ocean is the notion of creating a market where there initially was none – going out where nobody has yet gone. Red Ocean is what our competitors do – heated competition where sales are finite and the product is fairly predictable. We re making games that are expanding our base of consumers in Japan and America. Yes, those who've always played games are still playing, but we've got people who've never played to start loving it with titles like Nintendogs, Animal Crossing and Brain Games. These games are Blue Ocean in action (Forbes, 2006).

Part of blue ocean strategy involves creating a strategy canvas that depicts the current market space and relative offering level for major attributes that companies compete on. It helps visualise which offerings cost more to compete on. It also helps companies identify which values to eliminate, reduce and/or raise. And, finally, it helps identify new values that aren't currently competed on.

Here's a strategy canvas for the new Nintendo Wii when compared to Microsoft's Xbox 360 and Sony's PlayStation 3 (Figure 3.12). Nintendo's value curve is in blue.

The bottom of the graph lists the primary sources of competitive advantages:

- *Price*: Wii is 30–40 per cent cheaper than Xbox 360 and Sony Playstation 3.

- *CPU power*: Wii has comparatively low processor speed; it has no Dolby 5.1 (sound system). Both PS3 and Xbox 360 have processors that are far more powerful than you'll find in most PCs.

- *Storage (hard disk)*: In the basic model Wii has no hard disk.

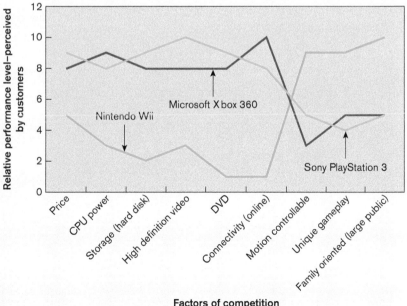

| Figure 3.12 | Value curves (strategy canvas) – Wii vs. Xbox and PS3 |

- *High definition video*: Both PS3 and Xbox 360 use high-end graphics chips that support high-definition games and are prepared for HD TV. Wii's graphics are marginally better than the PS2 and the original Xbox, but Wii pale next to the PS3 and Xbox 360.
- *DVD*: Both Sony and Microsoft provide the DVD opportunity. Sony even includes a Blu-Ray DVD drive.
- *Connectivity (online)*: Xbox has especially positioned itself as the online games console with multiplayer functions
- *Motion controllable*: With its innovative motion control stick, Wii adds new value to game playing. The stick integrates the movements of a player directly into the video game (tennis, golf, sword fights, etc.)
- *Unique gameplay*: The new Wii gaming console senses depth and motion from players, thus adding a whole new element to the play experience.
- *Family oriented (large public)*: With the motion control stick Nintendo opens up the console world to a completely new public of untapped non-gamers from the age of approximately 30. Parents to teens and even grandparents are getting easily into game fun on the Wii.

Wii's market shares compared to Microsoft (Xbox) and Sony (PS3)

Table 3.5 shows the worldwide sales of games consoles from 2005 to 2008, together with the corresponding market share.

Current Wii sales are pretty evenly split between the three major markets – 30 per cent have been sold in Japan, the American market (including Canada and South America) accounts for 40 per cent and other markets (including Europe and Australia and a few niche markets) for 30 per cent of units sold. The sales of Sony (PS2 and PS3) and Microsoft (Xbox and Xbox 360) have been more unequally distributed: Microsoft sells most Xbox and Xbox 360 in North America, whereas Sony's biggest markets for PS2 and PS3 are Japan, China and the rest of Asia.

At the retail level, games consoles are sold through a variety of electronic and audio/video retailers, supermarkets, discount stores, department stores and Internet retail stores.

Nintendo's strategy

Wii has managed to become a market leader by emphasising its simplicity and lower price (than Sony and Microsoft) to break down barriers for new customers.

Nintendo has attracted non-traditional users, such as women and those over 60 years old, with easy-to-play titles such as Brain Training and Wii Fit (launched in April/May 2008). The Brain Training software is sold among middle-aged people who seek to stimulate their memories and learning processes. The £70 Wii Fit game comes with a balance board, which links to the Wii console wirelessly. Players can stand, sit or lie on the board and undertake a range of exercises such as yoga and press-ups, as well as simulate slalom skiing or

Table 3.5	World sales of games consoles (units)							
	2005		2006		2007		2008	
	Mill. units	%	Mill. units	%	Mill. units	%	Mill. units	%
Sony:								
PS2	16.8		11.7		8.6		7.4	
PS3	–		1.2		7.2		10.3	
Total	16.8	69	12.9	53	15.8	40	17.7	33
Microsoft:								
Xbox	3.6		0.7		–		–	
Xbox 360	1.2		6.8		7.8		11.2	
Total	4.8	20	7.5	31	7.8	20	11.2	21
Nintendo:								
GameCube	2.7		1.0		–		–	
Wii	–		3.0		15.5		24.8	
Total	2.7	11	4.0	16	15.5	40	24.8	46
Total	24.3	100	24.4	100	39.1	100	53.7	100

Source: VGChartz (www.vgchartz.com and http://vgchartz.com/hwcomps.php?weekly=1).

Nintendo Wii Fit Trainer with balance board
Source: © epf model / Alamy

hula hooping – all with the guidance of an on-screen fitness expert. Experts think that this game can help people lose weight. Playing the Nintendo Wii Fit can also improve balance and help avoid falls among older people. Researchers ultimately hope to determine the effectiveness of computer games in developing muscle strength and coordination and reducing the risk of falls for people with Parkinson's disease.

Nintendo is highly dependent on sub-suppliers, for both hardware and software. The company commissions a number of sub-suppliers and contract manufacturers to produce the key components of game consoles or assemble finished products. The company was not able to meet the growing demand for its new Wii console, which was launched in November 2006, as its suppliers were not able to ramp up their production to meet the demand. A shortage of key components or the finished products had a negative effect on the company's revenues.

Nintendo is also very much dependent on its software suppliers, who are all developing new games based on a licensing agreement with Nintendo.

While the hardware (consoles) market is dominated by three players, the software market is more open and fragmented with several regional players and local developers. However, the games software industry is undergoing a period of consolidation. At the end of 2007, French company Vivendi Games acquired a 52 per cent stake in Activision and created a new entity, Activision Blizzard, which in size is close to that of the market leader, Electronic Arts. For example, Activision Blizzard launched 'Guitar Hero World Tour' for all three platforms in December 2007, at the same time as the announcement of Vivendi Games' acquisition of Activision.

The competitors' strategy

Sony PlayStation

In 2008, cumulative sales of PlayStation 2 (PS2) reached 130 million units, making it the world's best-selling game platform. However, the 2006–07 launch of Sony's new-generation PS3 did not translate into the immediate success that the company had hoped for; PS3 was not as successful as the Nintendo Wii. As a consequence Sony's game segment incurred losses of over US$1.2 billion in financial year 2007. However, it is possible that, in coming years, the profitability trend could be reversed. Because of the scale economies, the company's production costs have fallen over the years. At the same time, Blu-Ray has become the industry standard for high-definition DVD, as HD DVD development has ceased. The PS3 is one of the cheapest Blu-Ray DVD players on the market, and some consumers are likely to purchase the console to access its DVD player functions.

Sony will continue to promote the PS2 to the emerging markets of Africa, Asia and Latin America.

In 2009/10 the company is set to release PlayStation Portable 3000 which will have a built-in microphone and a new screen with more colours suitable for use outdoors. It also plans to launch a version of its flagship PS3 console with a 160 gigabyte hard drive to store more downloaded content and video.

Microsoft Xbox 360

Microsoft continues to target the 'serious' gamer segment with the Xbox 360. The Xbox graphics, games and Xbox live Internet gaming has been popular with the core user segment, primarily young males. The US market remains the most important so far, accounting for nearly 50 per cent of the overall Xbox sales.

Xbox is the console with the highest 'game attach' rate. This is defined as the average number of games each console owner buys. For the Xbox 360, Microsoft managed in 2008 a 'games per console' average of 8 to 1, the highest in the industry. This was good news for third-party game developers, and it is likely to encourage more games to be developed for this platform.

The strength of Microsoft's software distribution network has also kept the company alive in the business, allowing Microsoft to have a presence in more worldwide markets than Nintendo. Microsoft is strongly positioned in countries such as China, India, Malaysia and South Africa, all of which are growth markets, and this is promising for future sales of Xbox.

QUESTIONS

1 What were Microsoft's motives in entering the games console market with Xbox?

2 What are the competitive advantages of Microsoft Xbox and Sony PlayStation 3?

3 What are the competitive advantages in the business model of Wii?

4 What do you think are Nintendo's chances of creating a long-term blue ocean with Wii?

SOURCES

BBC News (2002) Price cut boosts Xbox sales, *BBC News*, 24 July; BBC News (2002) Works starts on new Xbox, *BBC News*, 26 June; CNN News (2002) Console wars: round two, *CNN News*, 22 May; Financial Times (2000) Companies and Markets: Microsoft to take on video game leaders, *Financial Times*, 10 March; Gamespot (2006) Microsoft to ship 13–15 million 360s by June 2007, *Gamespot*, 21 July (www.gamespot.com); New Media Age (2000) Let the games begin, *New Age Media*, 8 March; O'Brien, J. M. (2007) Wii will rock you, *Fortune*, 4 June (http://money.cnn.com/magazines/fortune/fortune_archive/2007/06/11/100083454/index.ht; Rosmarin, R. (2006) Nintendo's new look, *Forbes*, 6 July (www.forbes.com/technology/cionetwork/2006/02/07/xbox-ps3-revolution-cx_rr_0207nintendo.html); Smith, G. (2009) Seniors may benefit from Wii game system, *MyPractice Online*, 16 April (www.hpodemo.com/common/news/news_results.asp?task=Headline&id=11597&StoreID=A340488DBE514E6AAAA2480FC2404258); VGChartz (www.vgchartz.com).

QUESTIONS FOR DISCUSSION

1 Which sources of competitive advantage are the most important?

2 How can analysis of national competitiveness explain the competitive advantage of a single firm?

3 Is it possible to identify not only national competitiveness, but also regional competitiveness? (A region is here defined as more than one country.)

4 In which situations should a firm consider outsourcing its activities?

5 What are the advantages and disadvantages of outsourcing?

REFERENCES

Abraham, S. (2006) Blue oceans, temporary monopolies, and lessons from practice, *Strategy & Leadership*, 34(5): 52–7.

Allen, J., Reichheld, F. F., Hamilton, B. and Markey, R. (1998) On becoming a strategic partner: the role of human resources in gaining competitive advantage, *Human Resource Management*, 37(1): 31–46.

Allen, J., Reichheld, F. F., Hamilton, B. and Markey, R. (2005) Closing the delivery gap: how to achieve true customer-led growth, *Bain Briefs*, 10 May (www.bain.com/bainweb/pdfs/cms/hotTopics/closingdeliverygap.pdf).

Blumberg, D. F. (1998) Strategic assessment of outsourcing and downsizing in the service market, *Managing Service Quality*, 8(1): 5–18.

Bonn, I. (2001) Developing strategic thinking as a core competency, *Management Decision*, 39(1): 63–70.

Bonoma, T. V. and Shapiro, B. (1984) How to segment industrial markets, *Harvard Business Review*, May–June: 104–10.

Booms, B. H. and Bitner, M. J. (1981) Marketing strategies and organization structures for service firms, in J. H. Donelly and W. R. George (eds) *Marketing of Services*, American Marketing Association, Chicago.

Brookfield, J., Liu R.-J. and MacDuffie, J. P. (2008) Taiwan's bicycle industry A-team battles Chinese competition with innovation and cooperation, *Strategy & Leadership*, 36(1): 14–19.

Brownlie, D. (2000) Benchmarking your marketing process, *Long Range Planning*, 32(1): 88–95.

Burton, J. (1995) Composite strategy: the combination of collaboration and competition, *Journal of General Management*, 21(1): 1–23.

Cardy, R. L. and Selvarajan, T. T. (2006) Competencies: alternative frameworks for competitive advantage, *Business Horizons*, 49: 235–45.

Chen, Y. G. and Hsieh, P.-F. (2008) A service-based view of Porter's model of competitive advantage, *International Journal of Management*, 25(1): 38–53.

Chesbrough, H. and Teece, D. (1996) When is virtual virtuous? Organizing for innovation, *Harvard Business Review*, January–February: 68–70.

Cho, D. S. (1998) From national competitiveness to bloc and global competitiveness, *Competitive Review*, 8(1): 11–23.

Christensen, C. M. (2001) The past and future of competitive advantage, *MIT Sloan Management Review*, Winter: 105–9.

Collis, D. J. and Rukstad, M. G. (2008) Can you say what your strategy is? *Harvard Business Review*, April: 81–90.

Czepiel, J. A. (1992) *Competitive Marketing Strategy*, Prentice-Hall, Englewood Cliffs, NJ.

D'Aveni, R. A. (2007) Mapping your competitive position, *Harvard Business Review*, November: 110–20.

Day, G. S. (1984) *Analysis for Strategic Marketing*, West Publishing, New York.

Day, G. S. and Wensley, R. (1988) Assessing advantage: a framework for diagnosing competitive superiority, *Journal of Marketing*, 52(2): 1–20.

Flagestad, A. and Hope, C. A. (2001) *Tourism Management*, 22: 445–61.

Furner, O. and Thomas, H. (2000) The rivalry matrix: understanding rivalry and competitive dynamics, *European Management Journal*, 18(6): 619–37.

Grunert, K. G. and Ellegaard, C. (1992) The concept of key success factors, in *Marketing for Europe: Marketing for the Future*, Proceedings of the 21st Annual Conference of the European Marketing Academy, EMAC, pp. 505–24.

Haanes, K. and Fjeldstad (2000) Linking intangible resources and competition, *European Management Journal*, 18(1) (February): 52–62.

Hamholtz, E. and Lacey, J. (1981) *Personnel Management: Human Capital Theory and Human Resource Accounting*, Institute of Industrial Relations, UCLA, Los Angeles.

Harvard Business School (1998) Crown Cork & Seal in 1989. Sheila M. Cavanaugh, 1993, Rev. 29 May Harvard Business School, Case 9–793–035.

Heracleous, L. (1998) Strategic thinking or strategic planning? *Long Range Planning*, 31(3): 481–7.

Hollensen, S. (2001) *Global Marketing: A Market Responsive Approach*, 2nd edn, Financial Times/Prentice Hall, Harlow.

Kalpič, B. (2008) Why bigger is not always better: the strategic logic of value creation through M&As, *Journal of Business Strategy*, 29(6): 4–13.

Kanter, R. M. (1994) Collaborative advantage: the art of alliances, *Harvard Business Review*, July–August: 96–108.

Keiningham, T. L., Goddard, M. K. M., Vavra, T. G. and Iaci, A. J. (1999) Customer delight and the bottom line, *Marketing Management*, 8(3) (Fall): 57–63.

Ketelhöhn, W. (1998) What is a key success factor? *European Management Journal*, 16(3) (June): 335–40.

Kim, W. C. and Mauborgne, R. (2005) Blue ocean strategy: from theory to practice, *California Management Review*, 47(3): 105–21.

Kolar, T. and Toporišič, A. (2007) Marketing as warfare, revisited, *Marketing Intelligence & Planning*, 25(3): 203–16.

Kotler, P. (1997) *Marketing Management*, Prentice-Hall, Englewood Cliffs, NJ.

Krutten, J. (1999) Benchmarking in the pharmaceutical industry, *Marketing Health Services*, 19(3): 14–22.

Lepak, D. P. and Snell, S. A (1999) The human resource architecture: toward a theory of human capital allocation and development, *The Academy of Management Review*, 24(1): 31–48.

Levitt, T. (1960) Marketing myopia, *Harvard Business Review*, July–August: 45–56.

Lonsdale, C. and Cox, A. (2000) The historical development of outsourcing: the latest fad? *Industrial Management & Data Systems*, 100(9): 444–50.

Ma, H. (2000a) Competitive advantage and firm advantage, *Competitiveness Review*, 10(2): 15–32.

Ma, H. (2000b) Towards an advantage-based view of the firm, *Advances in Competitive Research (ACR)*, 8(1): 34–59.

Magrath, A. J. (1986) When marketing service's 4 Ps are not enough, *Business Horizons*, May–June: 44–50.

Meyer, C. (2001) The second generation of speed, *Harvard Business Review*, 24–5.

Nair, A., Ahlstrom, D. and Filer, L. (2007) Localized advantage in a global economy: the case of Bangalore, *Thunderbird International Business Review*, September–October: 591–618.

Olian, J. D., Durham, C. C. and Kristof, A. L. (1998) Designing management training and development for competitive advantage: lessons for the best, *HR – Human Resource Planning*, 21(1): 20–31.

Porter, M. E. (1980). *Competitive Strategy*, The Free Press, New York.

Porter, M. E. (1985) *Competitive Advantage*, The Free Press, New York.

Porter, M. E. (1990) *The Competitive Advantage of Nations*, The Free Press, New York.

Porter, M. E (1996) What is strategy? *Harvard Business Review*, November–December: 61–78.

Porter, M. E. (2008) The five competitive forces that shape strategy, *Harvard Business Review*, January: 78–93.

Prahalad, C. K. and Hamel, G. (1990) The core competence of the corporation, *Harvard Business Review*, May–June: 79–91.

Proff, H. (2002) Business unit strategies between regionalisation and globalisation, *International Business Review*, 11(2): 231–50.

Quinn, J. B. (2000) Outsourcing innovation: the new engine of growth, *MIT Sloan Management Review*, Summer: 13–27.

Rafiq, M. and Ahmed, P. K. (1995) Using the 7 Ps as a generic marketing mix, *Marketing Intelligence and Planning*, 13(9): 4–15.

Ravald, A. and Grönroos, C. (1996) The value concept and relationship marketing, *European Journal of Marketing*, 30(2): 19–30.

Rayport, J. F. and Sviokla, J. J. (1996) Exploiting the virtual value chain, *McKinsey Quarterly*, 1: 21–36.

Reve, T. (1990) The firm as a nexus of internal and external contracts, in M. Aoki, M. Gustafsson and O. E. Williamson (eds) *The Firm as a Nexus of Treaties*, Sage, London.

Rugman, A. and D'Cruz, J. (1993) The double diamond model of international competitiveness: the Canadian experience, *Management International Review*, 33 (special issue): 17–39.

Sheehan N. T. and Vaidyanathan, G. (2009) Using a value creation compass to discover 'Blue Oceans', *Strategy & Leadership*, 37(2): 13–20.

Senge, P. (1990) *The Fifth Discipline*, Doubleday, New York.

Sheth, J. N. and Sharma, A. (1997) Supplier relationships: emerging issues and challenges, *Industrial Marketing Management*, 26: 91–100.

Tampoe, M. (1994) Exploiting the core competences or your organization, *Long Range Planning*, 27(4): 66–77.

Vargo, S. L., Maglio, P. P. and Akaka M. A. (2008) On value and value co-creation: A service systems and service logic perspective, *European Management Journal*, 26(3): 145–52.

Webster, F. and Wind, Y. (1972) *Organizational Buying Behavior*, Prentice-Hall, New York.

Zairi, M. and Ahmed, P. Z. (1999) Benchmarking maturity as we approach the millennium? *Total Quality Management*, 4/5 (July): 810–16.

PART II
Assessing the external marketing situation

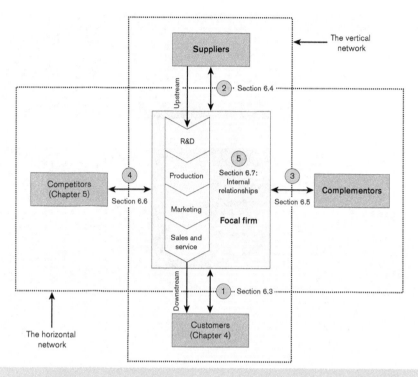

The structure of Part II

Part II looks at the environment in which marketing operates. The marketing environment consists of a *micro-environment* and a *macro-environment*.

The macro-environment consists of the larger societal forces which effect the whole micro-environment:

- *Demographic environment*: population size and growth trends, age structure of population, changes in family structure.
- *Economic environment*: income distribution, purchasing power, etc.
- *Political environment*: laws, government agencies, growth of public interest groups.

The ethical, social and environmental aspects and how they affect and shape the marketing plan will be analysed in Chapter 9.

The micro-environment consists of forces and players close to the firm such as customers, suppliers, complementors and competitors. The structure of Part II (see diagram above) shows how these players (via Chapter 6) are connected in a value net approach.

The focus of this part is on the micro-environmental factors and the relationships between the central players.

Chapters 4 and 5 start by analysing the most important issues of two of the most important players shown in above diagram:

- the customer 'box'
- the competitor 'box'.

Customers and competitors have been chosen for further analysis because they receive the most attention among managers in firms. These two types of player are also represented in the model labelled 'the competitive triangle' (see Figure 3.3).

Chapter 6 tries to analyse the relationships between the most important players in the value net.

The analysis in Chapters 4 and 5 contains the more traditional approach to customer and competitor behaviour and analysis. This forms the basis for the analysis of the relationships between the important players in the micro-environment.

Part I (assessment of the internal conditions) and Part II constitute the input for the later development of marketing strategies (Part III) and the marketing plan (Part IV) and its implementation (Part V).

PART II VIDEO CASE STUDY
Orascom Telecom
Developing the mobile business in emerging countries

Naguib O. Sawiris, Chairman and Chief Executive Officer of Orascom Telecom
Source: Abdulqader Saadi/AFP/Getty Images

Orascom Telecom Holding (OTH) provides wireless communications services in the Middle East and beyond. Its serves more than 70 million subscribers with GSM-based networks in Egypt (Mobinil), Tunisia (Tunisiana), Algeria (Djezzy), Pakistan (Mobilink), Bangladesh (Banglalink), and Zimbabwe (Telecel). Orascom's mobile service operations account for the majority of its revenues, but the company also provides Internet services, as well as network installation and support, procurement and distribution services under the Link brand. The family of founder Naguib Sawiris owns a controlling stake in Orascom.

Sawiris founded the company to take advantage of developing market opportunities in the Middle East, Africa and South Asia. The company's 2000 listing on the Cairo and Alexandria Stock Exchange set a record at the time as Egypt's largest IPO.

While northern Africa remains Orascom's largest market (it accounted for about 43 per cent of the company's revenues in 2007), the company continues to look outside its home region for growth. Orascom was granted a licence to operate mobile network services in North Korea in 2008.

The company is restructuring by divesting business lines that fall outside its core mobile communications operations. In 2008, Orascom sold its OrasInvest subsidiary, which built and maintained mobile phone transmission towers, to Abu Dhabi Investment for $180 million. The following year it sold subsidiary M-Link to Italy-based Wind Telecomunicazioni and later agreed to sell its IT service subsidiaries, LINKdotNet and Link Egypt, to Egyptian Company for Mobile Services.

Table PII.1   Orascom Telecom: financial data

	2007	2006	2005
Revenue (US$m)	$4,747	$3,904	$3,226
Net income (US$m)	$2,021	$721	$667
Net profit	43%	19%	21%
Employees	20,000	20,000	15,000

Table PII.2   Orascom Telecom: geographical segmentation of 2007 Revenue

	% of total
North Africa	43
South Asia	31
Middle East	22
Other regions	4
Total	100

Table PII.3   Orascom Telecom: product segmentation of 2007 revenue

	% of total
Cellular operations	88
Telecommunication service	11
Internet and fixed-line service	1
Total	100

Table PII.4   Africa: ICT (Information and Communication Technologies) Indicators, 2007

	Population 000s	Main telephone lines 000s	Main telephone lines per 100 persons	Mobile subscribers 000s	Mobile subscribers per 100 persons	Internet users 000s	Internet users per 100 persons
Algeria	33,860	2,922.7	8.63	21,446.0	63.34	3,500.0	10.34
Egypt	75,500	11,228.8	14.87	30,047.0	39.80	8,620.0	11.42
Libya	6,160	852.3	14.56	4,500.0	73.05	260.0	4.36
Morocco	31,220	2,393.8	7.67	20,029.0	64.15	7,300.0	23.38
Tunisia	10,330	1,273.3	12.33	7,842.0	75.94	1,722.2	16.68
North Africa	**157,070**	**18,670.9**	**11.91**	**83,865.0**	**53.39**	**21,402.2**	**13.64**
South Africa	48,580	4,642.0	9.56	42,300.0	87.08	5,100.0	10.75
South Africa	**48,580**	**4,642.0**	**9.56**	**42,300.0**	**87.08**	**5,100.0**	**10.75**
Angola	17,020	98.2	0.62	3,307.0	19.43	95.0	0.60
Benin	9,030	110.3	1.22	1,895.0	20.98	150.0	1.66
Botswana	1,880	136.9	7.78	1,427.0	75.84	80.0	4.55
Burkina Faso	14,780	94.8	0.70	1,611.0	10.90	80.0	0.59
Burundi	8,510	35.0	0.45	250.0	2.94	60.0	0.77
Cameroon	18,550	130.7	0.79	4,536.0	24.45	370.0	2.23
Cape Verde	530	71.6	13.80	148.0	27.90	33.0	6.36
Central African Rep.	4,340	12.0	0.29	130.0	2.99	13.0	0.32
Chad	10,780	13.0	0.13	918.0	8.52	60.0	0.60
Comoros	840	19.1	2.33	40.0	4.77	21.0	2.56
Congo	3,770	15.9	0.40	1,334.0	35.40	70.0	1.70
Côte d'Ivoire	19,260	260.9	1.41	7,050.0	36.60	300.0	1.63
D.R. Congo	62,640	9.7	0.02	6,592.0	10.52	230.4	0.37
Djibouti	830	10.8	1.56	45.0	5.40	11.0	1.36

Equatorial Guinea	510	10.0	1.99	220.0	43.35	8.0	1.55
Eritrea	4,850	37.5	0.82	70.0	1.44	100.0	2.19
Ethiopia	83,100	880.1	1.06	1,208.0	1.45	291.0	0.35
Gabon	1,330	36.5	2.59	1,169.0	87.86	81.0	5.76
Gambia	1,710	76.4	4.47	796.0	46.58	100.2	5.87
Ghana	23,480	376.5	1.60	7,604.0	32.39	650.0	2.77
Guinea	9,370	26.3	0.33	189.0	2.36	50.0	0.52
Guinea-Bissau	1,700	4.6	0.27	296.0	17.48	37.0	2.26
Kenya	37,540	264.8	0.71	11,440.0	30.48	2,770.3	7.89
Lesotho	2,010	53.1	2.97	456.0	22.71	51.5	2.87
Liberia	3,750	–	–	563.0	15.01	–	–
Madagascar	19,680	133.9	0.68	2,218.0	11.27	110.0	0.58
Malawi	13,930	175.2	1.26	1,051.0	7.55	139.5	1.00
Mali	12,340	85.0	0.69	2,483.0	20.13	100.0	0.81
Mauritania	3,120	34.9	1.10	1,300.0	41.62	30.0	0.95
Mauritius	1,260	357.3	28.45	936.0	74.19	320.0	25.48
Mozambique	21,400	67.0	0.33	3,300.0	15.42	178.0	0.90
Namibia	2,070	138.1	6.66	800.0	38.58	101.0	4.87
Niger	14,230	24.0	0.17	900.0	6.33	40.0	0.28
Nigeria	148,090	6,578.3	4.44	40,396.0	27.28	10,000.0	6.75
Rwanda	9,720	16.5	0.18	679.0	6.98	100.0	1.08
S. Tomé & Principe	160	7.7	4.86	30.0	19.09	23.0	14.59
Senegal	12,380	269.1	2.17	4,123.0	33.31	820.0	6.62
Seychelles	90	20.6	23.79	77.0	89.23	29.0	35.67
Sierra Leone	5,870	–	–	776.0	13.23	10.0	0.19
Somalia	8,700	100.0	1.15	600.0	6.90	94.0	1.11
Sudan	38,560	345.2	0.90	7,464.0	19.36	1,500.0	3.89
Swaziland	1,140	44.0	4.27	380.0	33.29	42.0	4.08
Tanzania	40,450	236.5	0.58	8,252.0	20.40	384.3	1.00
Togo	6,590	82.1	1.30	1,190.0	18.08	320.0	5.07
Uganda	30,880.0	162.3	0.53	4,195.0	13.58	2,000.0	6.48
Zambia	11,920	91.8	0.77	2,639.0	22.14	500.0	4.19
Zimbabwe	13,350	344.5	2.58	1,226.0	9.18	1,351.0	10.12
Sub-Saharan Africa	**757,880**	**12,098.3**	**1.65**	**138,310.0**	**18.28**	**23,904.2**	**3.23**
AFRICA	963,530	35,411.2	3.77	264,475.0	27.48	50,406.4	5.34

Source: Adapted from the International Telecommunication Union (ITU) website (www.itu.in). Reproduced with permission of ITU.

Please watch some of these YouTube videos:

- http://www.youtube.com/watch?v=BcUN1RDoHgQ
- http://www.youtube.com/watch?v= 7O29LTTJRVo&feature=related (interview with Chairman Naguib Sawiris – very good for describing Orascom's strategy)
- http://www.youtube.com/watch?v=kFMYaRFAh28&feature=related
- http://www.youtube.com/watch?v=QHj-acaQ8y4 (a commercial)

QUESTIONS

1 Which external factors are mainly influencing Orascom Telecom's business?

2 What are the main reasons for the success of Orascom Telecom in emergent markets?

3 Which markets would you suggest for the further international expansion in Africa? (Please use Table PII.4.)

SOURCES

Orascom Telecom (www.orascomtelecom.com); International Telecommunication Union (ITU) (www.itu.in).

CHAPTER 4
Customer behaviour

LEARNING OBJECTIVES

After studying this chapter you should be able to:

- understand why consumers make purchase decisions
- identify and discuss the main motives behind buying behaviour in the B2C market
- understand how customers make purchase decisions
- identify the various types of buyer in organisational markets and determine their distinct needs, wants and motivations
- identify different organisational buying situations
- describe and discuss the organisational buying process
- identify and understand the factors influencing the organisational buying process
- evaluate the roles of members of the buying centre
- understand the link between consumer demand and B2B marketing
- understand what is meant by customisation

4.1 INTRODUCTION

This chapter deals mainly with the behaviour of customers in the B2C and the B2B markets. This analysis is then used as an input for Chapter 6 (especially Section 6.3) where the firm's relationships with the customers are analysed.

To a producer or service provider a market is where the product or service is sold or delivered and the profits generated. The seller or marketer defines the market in types of customer. Thus, a market consists of all the potential customers sharing particular wants and needs who might be willing to engage in change to satisfy wants or needs. Once the potential customers' wants and needs are backed by their purchasing power, an actual market is formed.

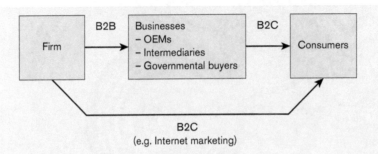

B2B markets:
- Customised products and services, highly complex products
- Personal relationships between buyer and the selling firm/salesperson – reliance on personal selling
- Sophisticated buyers
- More rational buying; more customer emphasis on risk-reduction; less customer emphasis on self-expressive benefits of brands

B2C markets:
- Standardised products, relatively unsophisticated products
- Impersonal relationships between buyer and the selling firm – more reliance on mass market advertising
- Buyers growing in sophistication
- Often more emotional buying – customer perception of functional, emotional and self-expressive benefits of brands

Figure 4.1   Customers in B2C and B2B markets

Not-for-profit organisation
An organisation which attempts to achieve an objective other than profit, for example relief of famine, animal rights or public service.

The market concept applies equally to service. The term market can even represent a powerful concept in the not-for-profit sectors. Although **not-for-profit organisations** do not refer to the target population they serve as a market, every not-for-profit organisation has clients or customers. Hence, in the long run, it is the customers – with their purchasing power – who will decide what the market really is. They set the boundaries and their purchases decide what products or services will remain in the market. Thus, to understand the market, the firm must understand the customer.

There are different types of customer depending on whether the firm is approaching the business-to-consumer market (B2C) or business-to-business market (B2B).

The firm (producer) may not sell directly to the consumers (end users). Instead, many firms sell to the B2B market (see Figure 4.1). Here, the firm may serve as a sub-supplier to other businesses (larger original equipment manufacturers (OEMs)) which may use a firm's component in its final product. The differences and similarities between B2B and B2C markets have long been debated, especially given the dynamic nature of the business environment in both markets (Mudambi, forthcoming). Figure 4.1 summarises some relevant comparisons and the main characteristics of B2B and B2C.

The firm may also have governmental organisations or intermediaries as buyers. Lately, many Internet firms (e.g. Amazon and Dell) have begun to cut the distribution chain by selling directly to consumers.

The outline and structure of this chapter can be illustrated, as shown in Figure 4.2.

In both B2C and B2B markets, the customer decision-making process forms the basis for the segmentation of the two markets.

Customer decision making is essentially a problem-solving process. Most customers – whether individual consumers or organisational buyers – go through similar mental processes in deciding which products and brands to buy. Obviously, though, various customers often end up buying very different things because of differences in their *personal characteristics*

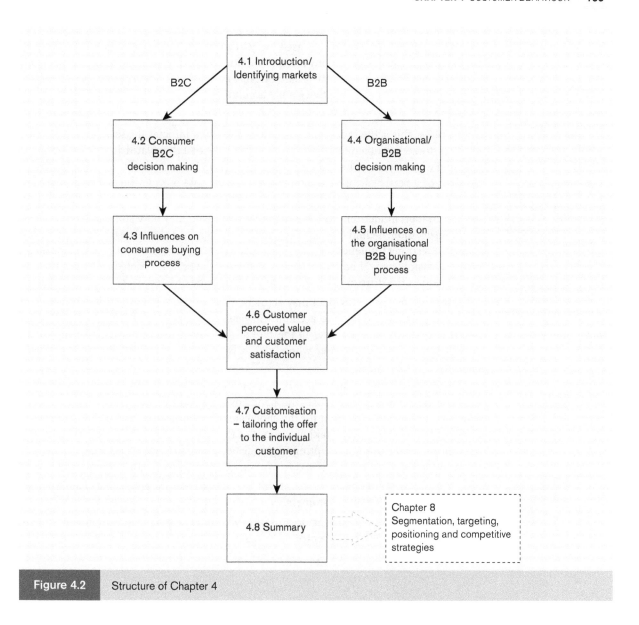

Figure 4.2   Structure of Chapter 4

Reference group
A group of people that
influences an individual's
attitude or behaviour.

(needs, benefits sought, attitudes, values, past experiences and lifestyles) and *social influences* (different social classes, **reference groups** or family situations).

Market segmentation is as important in business markets as it is in the marketing of consumer goods and services. Segmenting the market may, for example, enable the salesforce to emphasise different sales arguments in different segments and the firm can tailor its operations and marketing mix to each segment.

Thus, the more marketers know about the factors affecting their customers' buying behaviour, the greater their ability to design strategic marketing programmes to fit the specific concerns and desires of these segments. This chapter examines the mental processes that individual consumers go through when making purchase decisions – and the individual and environmental factors affecting these decisions. Our discussion provides a useful framework for choosing, organising and analysing information about current and potential customers for a particular product or service.

Irrespective of whether the firm is in the B2B or B2C market, the starting point is to define who the current customers are. The answer is not always obvious as there may be many people involved in the purchase and use of a particular product or service. Customers are not necessarily the same as consumers. A useful way to approach customer definition is to recognise six main roles that exist in many purchasing situations. Often several, or even all, of these roles may be held by the same individuals, but recognising each role separately can be a useful step in targeting marketing activity more accurately.

The roles in this **buying centre** are as follows.

Buying centre
A group involved in the buying decision for purchasing an item or system solution for a company. Also known as a decision-making unit (DMU). Members of such a group are normally: initiator, influencer, decider, purchaser, user and gatekeeper.

Influencer
The buying-centre role played by organisational members (or outsiders) who affect the purchase decision by supplying advice or information.

Decider
The buying-centre role played by the organisational member who makes the actual purchasing decision.

- *The initiator*: this is the individual (or individuals) who initiates the search for a solution to the customer's problem. In the case of the purchase of a chocolate bar it could be a hungry child who recognises her own need for sustenance. In the case of a supermarket the re-ordering of a particular product line which is nearly sold out may be initiated by a stock controller, or even an automatic order processing system.

- *The influencer*: influencers are all those individuals who may have some influence on the purchase decision. A child may have initiated the search for a chocolate bar, but the parents may have a strong influence on which product is actually bought. In the supermarket the ultimate customers will have a strong influence on the brands ordered – the brands they buy or request the store to stock will be most likely to be ordered.

- *The decider*: another individual may actually make the decision as to which product or service to purchase, taking into account the views of initiators and influencers. This may be the initiator or the influencer in the case of the chocolate bar. In the supermarket the decider may be a merchandiser whose task it is to specify which brands to stock, what quantity to order, and so on.

- *The purchaser*: the purchaser is the individual who actually buys the product or service. He or she is, in effect, the individual who hands over the cash in exchange for the benefits. This may be the child or parent for the chocolate bar. In industrial purchasing it is often a professional buyer who, after taking account of the various influences on the decision, ultimately places the order, attempting to get the best value for money possible.

- *The user*: finally comes the end user of the product or service, the individual who consumes the offer. For the chocolate bar it will be the child. For the goods in the supermarket it will be the supermarket's customers.

- *The gatekeeper*: people within the organisation who can control the flow of information to other members of the buying centre.

What is important in any buying situation is to have a clear idea of the various people who are likely to have an impact on the purchase and consumption decision. Where the various roles are undertaken by different individuals it may be necessary to adopt a different marketing approach to each. Each may be looking for different benefits in the purchase and consumption process. Where different roles are undertaken by the same individuals, different approaches may be suitable depending on what stage in the buy/consume process the individual is at the time.

Decision-making unit (DMU)
The initiator, the decider, the influencers, the purchaser, the gatekeeper and the users. Often identical with the buying centre in B2B.

A central theme of this book is that most markets are segmented; in other words, different identifiable groups of customers require different benefits when buying or using essentially similar products or services. Identifying who the various customers are and what role they play then leads to the question of what gives them value. For each of the above members of a **decision-making unit (DMU)**, different aspects of purchase and use may give value.

4.2 CONSUMER B2C DECISION MAKING

Approaches to understanding consumer buying behaviour draw heavily on the other social sciences.

The company also has a strong role to play in designing and providing appropriate stimulation to the purchase decisions. The process is dynamic as there is an interaction between the

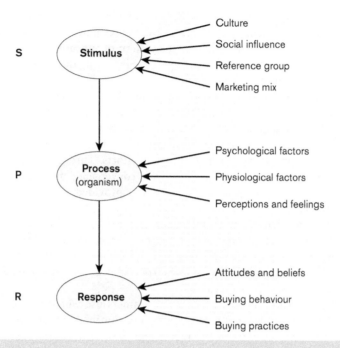

Figure 4.3   The SPR (SOR) model

buyer and the environment. The consumer actively participates in the process by searching for information on the alternatives available, by providing evaluations of products and services, and by expressions of risk. In this process the company also plays an active role by manipulating the variables that are under its control. The company modifies the marketing mix to accommodate the demands expressed by consumers. The more successful it is in matching its marketing mix with expressed and latent demands in the market, the greater the possibility is that consumers will buy the company's products now and in the future. Consumer behaviour is determined by a host of variables studied in different disciplines. Consumer behaviour may be described as a relationship between a stimulus of some kind, such as a new product, the way information about the innovation is processed by the consumer, and the response the consumer makes having evaluated the alternatives (Figure 4.3).

The stimulus is captured by the range of elements in the marketing mix which the company can manipulate to achieve its corporate objectives. These stimuli derive from the product or service itself, or from the marketing programme developed by the company to support its products and services. A number of symbolic stimuli derive from the use of media such as television. Stimuli also include many of the conditioning variables discussed above. Chief among these are the cultural and social influences on consumer behaviour and the role of reference groups.

Process refers to the sequence of stages used in the internal process of these influences by the consumer. This sequence highlights the cause-and-effect relationships involved in making decisions. The processes include the perceptual, physiological and inner feelings and dispositions of consumers towards the product or service being evaluated.

The third component refers to the consumer's response in terms of changes in behaviour, awareness and attention, brand comprehension, attitudes, intentions and actual purchase. This response may indicate a change in the consumer's psychological reaction to the product or service. As a result of some change in a stimulus, the consumer may be better disposed to the product, have formed a better attitude towards it, or believe it can solve a particular consumption-related problem. Alternatively, the response may be in the form of an actual change in purchasing activity. The consumer may switch from one brand to another or from one product category to another. Consumer responses may also take the form of a change in consumption practices, whereby the pattern of consumer behaviour is changed. Supermarkets frequently offer incentives to get people to shop during slack periods of the week, which involves a change in shopping practice.

Generally speaking, a great deal of interest is focused on responses that involve buying or the disposition to buy. Manufacturers spend considerable sums of money in developing and promoting their products, creating brands and otherwise designing marketing effort to influence consumer behaviour in a particular way. At the same time, consumers may be more or less disposed to these efforts. Through the influence of external stimuli and internal processing mechanisms, a convergence may occur between consumer wants and needs, and the products and services provided. On other occasions, no such convergence occurs.

It is known, however, that the same degree of interest may not be displayed for all products and services. For some products and services, consumers like to be heavily involved. Some purchases are planned, while others are unplanned and may even arise as a result of impulse. These are among the various outcomes or responses that arise in the stimulus–process–response model of consumer behaviour.

The decision-making processes consumers use when making purchases vary. Different buyers may engage in different types of decision-making processes depending on how highly involved they are with the product. A high-involvement product for one buyer may be a low-involvement product for another.

The decision processes involved in purchasing high- and low-involvement products are quite different (Figure 4.4). The following sections examine the mental steps involved in each decision process in more detail.

Determinants of consumer involvement

Consumer involvement is frequently measured by the degree of importance the product has to the buyer. Laurent and Kapferer (1985), for example, indicate a number of factors that influence the degree to which consumers become involved in a particular purchase. The most important factors are:

- perceived importance of the product;
- **perceived risk** associated with its use.

Perceived risk
Consumers' uncertainty about the consequences of their purchase decisions; the consumer's perception that a product may not do what it is expected to do.

The level of involvement with any product depends on its perceived importance to the consumer's self-image. High-involvement products tend to be tied to self-image, whereas low-involvement products are not. A middle-aged consumer who feels (and wants to look) youthful may invest a great deal of time in her decision to buy a sport-utility vehicle instead of an estate car. When purchasing an ordinary light bulb, however, she buys almost without thinking, because the purchase has nothing to do with self-image. The more visible, risky, or costly the product, the higher the level of involvement.

Involvement also influences the relationship between product evaluation and purchasing behaviours. With low-involvement products, consumers generally will try them first and then form an evaluation. With high-involvement products, they first form an evaluation (expectation), then purchase. One reason for this behaviour is that consumers do not actively search for information about low-involvement products. Instead, they acquire it while engaged in some other activity, such as watching television or chatting with a friend. This is called *passive learning*, which characterises the passive decision-making process. Only when they try the product do they learn more about it. In contrast, high-involvement products are investigated through *active learning* – part of an active decision-making process – in order to form an opinion about which product to purchase.

- Low perceived importance of product
- Lower risk of visibility
- Not related to self-image

- High perceived importance of product
- Higher risk of visibility
- Related to self-image

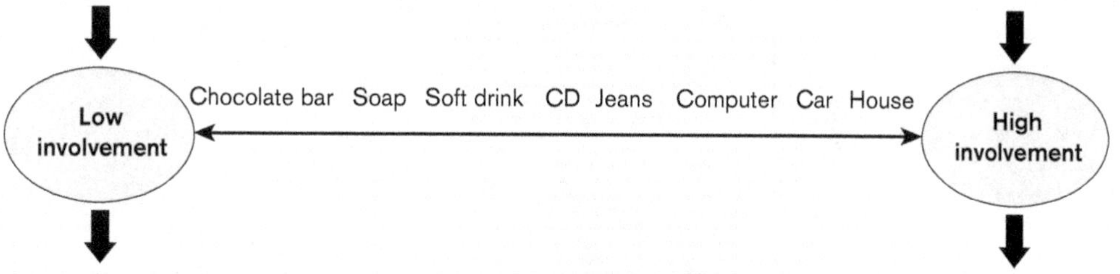

Low involvement — Chocolate bar Soap Soft drink CD Jeans Computer Car House — **High involvement**

- Passive/routine decision making.
- Passive learning.
- Consumers seek an acceptable level of satisfaction. They buy the brand least likely to give them problems and buy based on a few attributes. Familarity is the key.
- Personality and lifestyle are not related to consumer behaviour because the product is not closely tied to the personss self-ide ntity and beliefs.
- Reference groups exert little influence on consumer behaviour because products are not strongly related to their norms and values.
- Consumers buy first. If they do evaluate brands, it is done after the purchase.

- Active/complex decision making.
- Active learning.
- Consumers seek to maximize expected satisfaction. They compare brands to see which provides the most benefits related to their needs and buy based on a multi-attribute comparison of brands.
- Personality and lifestyle characteristics are related to consumer behaviour because the product is closely tied to the person's self-identity and belief system
- Reference groups influence consumer behaviour because of the importance of the product to group norms and values.
- Consumers evaluate brands before buying.

Managerial implications
- Consumers represent a passive audience for product information.
- Build up brand loyalty (the consumer just chooses the brand that he/she has good experiences with).

- Consumers represent an active audience for product information.
- Focus on product development/product quality.

Figure 4.4 Customer involvement in the buying decision

The consumer buying process

For a better understanding of consumer buying behaviour, marketers have broken the decision-making process into the five steps described below. These are shown in Figure 4.5, along with a description of how one consumer made a high-involvement purchase. For low-involvement purchases, the first three steps may be skipped. As involvement increases, each step takes on greater importance, and more active learning occurs.

Step 1: Problem identification

Consumers' purchase decision processes are triggered by unsatisfied wants or needs. Individuals perceive differences between ideal and actual states on some physical or sociopsychological dimension. This motivates them to seek products or services to help bring their current state more into balance with the ideal.

We human beings are insatiable – at least with respect to our sociopsychological needs – but we are limited by time and financial resources. It is impossible for us to satisfy all our needs at once. We tend instead to try to satisfy the needs that are strongest at a given time. The

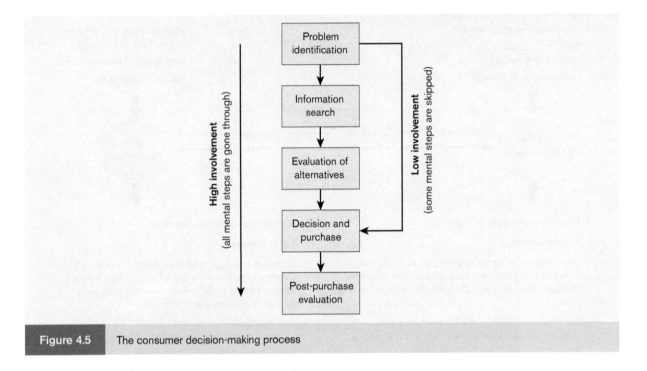

Figure 4.5	The consumer decision-making process

size of the gap between our current and our desired state largely determines the strength of a particular need.

If you are thirsty, you may simply run out and buy a soft drink. In a high-involvement purchase the recognition of a need may arise long before it is acted upon. In the case of a house, the cost may prevent you from acting on your need for several years.

Step 2: Information search

Having recognised that a problem exists and might be satisfied by the purchase and consumption of a product or service, the consumer's next step is to refer to information gained from past experience and stored in memory for possible later use.

The information search consists of thinking through the situation, calling up experiences stored in memory (internal search), and probably seeking information from the following:

- Personal sources include family members, friends and members of the consumer's reference group.
- Commercial sources refer to information disseminated by service providers, marketers, and manufacturers and their dealers. They include media advertising, promotional brochures, package and label information, salespersons, and various in-store information, such as price markings and displays.
- Public sources include non-commercial and professional organisations and individuals who provide advice for consumers, such as doctors, lawyers, government agencies, travel agencies and consumer-interest groups. Consumers are usually exposed to more information from commercial sources than from personal or public sources. Consumers do, however, use information from different sources for different purposes and at different stages within the decision-making process. In general, commercial sources perform an informing function for consumers. Personal and public sources serve an evaluation and legitimising function.

Each source has its benefits and drawbacks. Because services are tangible, difficult to standardise, and their production and consumption inseparable, they are more difficult to evaluate than products. Thus, most services are hard to assess until they are being consumed after purchase (e.g. cruises and restaurant meals). Indeed, some services are difficult to assess even after they have been consumed. Even when products are very expensive and ego-involving, some consumers are unlikely to conduct an exhaustive search for information before making a decision. Why? Because of the costs involved. Perhaps the biggest cost for most people is the opportunity cost of the time involved in seeking information. They give up the opportunity to use that time for other, more important or interesting activities, like work.

Another information-search cost is the possible negative consequence of delaying the decision too long. For example, a consumer has only a limited time to decide whether to take advantage of a special deal offered on a specific cruise. Finally, there are psychological costs involved in searching for information. Collecting information can be a frustrating task, often involving crowded stores and rude salespeople. Also, some consumers become frustrated and confused when they have a lot of complex information to evaluate before making a choice. Consequently they cut their information search short.

Step 3: Evaluation of alternatives

Consumers differ in their approach to evaluation, but a number of aspects are common. Products or services are viewed by individuals as bundles of attributes. Consumers find it difficult to make overall comparisons of many alternative brands because each brand might be better in some ways but worse in others. Instead, consumers simplify their evaluation task in several ways. First, they seldom consider all possible brands; rather, they focus on their invoked set – a limited number they are familiar with that are likely to satisfy their needs.

Second, consumers evaluate each of the brands in the invoked set on a limited number of product factors or attributes (Figure 4.6). They also judge the relative importance of these attributes, or the minimum acceptable performance of each. The set of attributes used by a particular consumer and the relative importance of each represent the consumer's choice criteria.

Category	Specific attributes
Cost attributes	Purchase price, operating costs, repair costs, cost of extras or options, cost of installation, trade-in allowance, likely resale value
Performance attributes	Durability, quality of materials, construction, dependability, functional performance (e.g. acceleration, nutrition, taste), efficiency, safety, styling
Social attributes	Reputation of brand, status image, popularity with friends, popularity with family members, style, fashion
Availability attributes	Carried by local stores, credit terms, quality of service available from local dealer, delivery time

Figure 4.6   Selected attributes consumers use to evaluate alternative products or services

Cars are seen as transport, safety, prestige, speed and carrying capacity. Some attributes are more important than others, so consumers allocate different levels of importance weights to each attribute identified. Some buyers will view safety as more important than speed. The company can divide the market into segments according to the attributes which are important to different groups.

Consumers tend to develop a set of beliefs about where each product or brand is in regard to each attribute. This set of beliefs about a particular brand is referred to as the brand image. For a particular consumer, the brand image of a BMW may be that it is expensive, reliable and fast, while the brand image of a Lada may be that it is cheap, plain and slow.

Step 4: The purchase decision

The purchase decision emerges from the evaluation of alternatives. The consumer may decide not to buy and save the money or spend it on a different item altogether. Or he or she may want to play safe by deciding to purchase a small amount for trial purposes, or by leasing rather than buying. The decision to buy often occurs some time before the actual purchase. The purchase is a financial commitment to make the acquisition. It may take time to secure a mortgage or car loan.

Consumers shopping in a retail store intent on purchasing one brand sometimes end up buying something different. This happens because the consumer's ultimate purchase can be influenced by such factors as being out of stock (no outside cabins on a particular cruise), a special display, or a message from a salesperson ('I can get you a better deal on a similar cruise if you can go two weeks later').

Step 5: The post-purchase evaluation

The purchase evaluation stage results in satisfaction or dissatisfaction. Buyers often seek assurance from others that their choice was correct. Positive assurance reinforces the consumer's decision, making it more likely that such a purchase will be made again. Positive feedback confirms the buyer's expectation.

Consumers are more likely to develop brand loyalty to services than to products because of the difficulty of obtaining and evaluating information about alternative services as well as, in some cases, the extra costs involved. Also, in some cases repeated patronage brings additional benefits such as preferential treatment (getting an appointment with your doctor) and the service provider getting better insights into the consumer's tastes/preferences.

Cognitive dissonance
Buyer discomfort caused by post-purchase conflict.

Even when a product performs as expected, consumers may doubt whether they made the best possible choice. Such doubts are called **cognitive dissonance**.

Doubts about whether the best possible purchase has been made can be reduced in two ways. First, they can simply withdraw from their decision – take the product back and ask for a refund (difficult to do with a service). A second way to reduce dissonance is for consumers to be convinced they really did make the best choice. Many people, thus, continue to seek information about their chosen brand *after* a purchase. Marketers play an active role in dissonance reduction by reinforcing consumers' purchase decisions via, for example, follow-up letters assuring customers they made a wise decision and that the firm stands behind the product should anything go wrong (Gurley *et al.*, 2005).

4.3 INFLUENCES ON CONSUMERS' DECISION MAKING

Demographics
Measures such as age, gender, race, occupation and income that are often used as a basis for selecting focus group members and market segments.

Even if some consumers have a similar involvement, they buy different brands for different reasons. Some of the important psychological variables that affect a consumer's decision-making process include needs, perception, memory and attitudes. The consumer's personal characteristics, such as **demographic** and **lifestyle** variables etc. influence these psychological factors – see Figure 4.7.

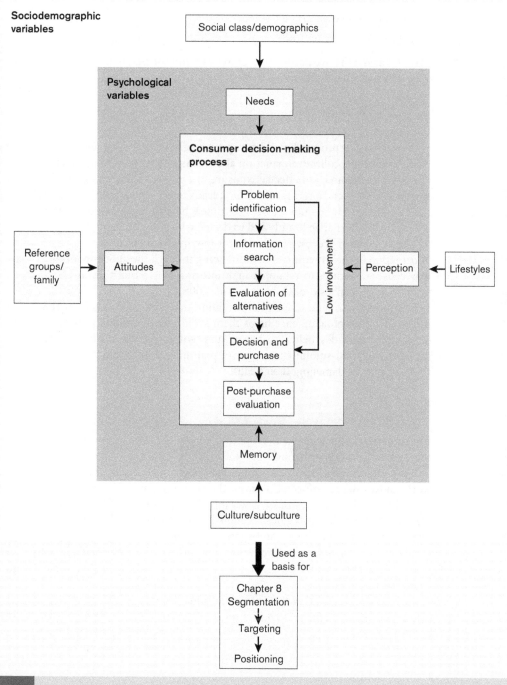

Figure 4.7 Hierarchy of variables affecting individual consumer behaviour

Needs

Lifestyle
An individual's activities, interests, opinions and values as they affect his or her mode of living.

Abraham Maslow's famous classification (1970) is often used by marketers to help categorise consumer desires. According to Maslow, five basic needs underlie most human goals:

1 *Physiological*: food, water, warmth, sleep;

2 *Safety*: security, protection;

3   *Love and belonging*: family, friendship and acceptance;

4   *Esteem*: prestige, status, self-respect;

5   *Self-actualisation*: self-fulfilment and personal enrichment.

Maslow ranked the five needs in a hierarchy to indicate that higher level needs tend to emerge only after lower level needs are satisfied.

Perception

Perception is the process by which a person selects, organises and interprets information. When consumers collect information about a high-involvement product they follow a series of steps, or a hierarchy of effects. Exposure to a piece of information, such as a new product, an advert or a friend's recommendation, leads to attention, then to comprehension, and finally to retention in memory. Once consumers have fully perceived the information, they use it to evaluate alternative brands and to decide which to purchase.

The perception process is different for low-involvement products. Here, consumers store information in their memories without going through the above-mentioned steps. Exposure may cause consumers to retain enough information so that they are familiar with a brand when they see it in a store (Goldstein *et al.*, 2008).

Consumers also tend to avoid information that contradicts their current beliefs and attitudes. This perceptual defence helps them avoid the psychological discomfort of reassessing or changing attitudes, beliefs or behaviours central to their self-images. For example, many smokers avoid anti-smoking messages, or play down their importance, rather than admit that smoking may be damaging their health.

Memory

Consumers are also selective in what they remember. Thus, they tend to retain information that supports what they believe.

There are different theories of how the human memory operates, but most agree that it works in two stages. Information from the environment is first processed by the short-term memory, which forgets most of it within 30 seconds or less because of inattention or displacement by new incoming information. Some information, however, is transferred to long-term memory, from where it can be retrieved later.

In long-term memory, a vast amount of information may be held for years or even indefinitely. It remains there until replacement by contradictory information through a process called interference.

Consumers are bombarded with promotional messages. Marketers hope that the more often their brand name is seen, the more likely consumers will be to process information about it.

Attitudes

An attitude is a positive or negative feeling about an object (say, a brand) that predisposes a person to behave in a particular way toward that object.

Attitudes are often described as consumer preferences – a like or dislike for products or their characteristics. Marketers usually think of attitudes as having three components: cognitive, affective and behavioural. The cognitive aspect refers to knowledge about product attributes that are not influenced by emotion. The affective component relates to the emotional feelings of like or dislike. The behavioural element reflects the tendency to act positively or negatively. In other words, attitudes toward purchasing a product are a composite of what consumers know about its attributes.

Generally, marketers use their knowledge of consumer attitudes to make sure that strategies are consistent with consumer tastes and preferences. From time to time, marketers attempt to change consumer attitudes, usually by influencing one of the three components.

Sociodemographic variables

Age/social class/demographics

The consumer's age category has a major impact on spending behaviour. For example, older consumers choose more products related to medical care and travel, and choose fewer products in home furnishings and clothing than do younger age groups; the presence of young children obviously affects the purchasing of a variety of goods and services. Teenagers spend a great deal of money on films, soft drinks and fast foods, for example.

Baby boom
The major increase in the annual birth rate following the Second World War and lasting until the early 1960s. The 'baby boomers', now moving into middle age, are a prime target for marketers.

The world population will continue to grow. The trend has occurred for two reasons. One is the lowering of the death rate, and the other is ageing 'baby boomers'. The **baby boom** is the name for the tremendous increase in births that occurred in most Western countries between 1946 and 1965, the 20 years following the Second World War. The generation born between 1965 and 1976 is often called Generation X. Generation X is smaller than the baby boom generation, but they are expected to overtake baby boomers as a primary market for many product categories at the beginning of this millennium. Another group of consumers came into being between 1977 and 1995, when adult baby boomers began having children, creating an 'echo' of the baby boom. The oldest members of this group are in their early thirties. We will use the term Generation Y for this group. They are growing up very accustomed to computers and the Internet.

Marketers increasingly look at social class from a global perspective. In some societies – such as India and Brazil – class distinctions are clear, and status differences are great. In others – such as Denmark and Canada – differences are less extreme. In countries with strong class differences, where people live, the cars they drive, the types of clothing they wear, how much they travel and where they go to college are largely determined by social class.

In a country with a more homogeneous class structure, such as Sweden or Denmark, it is not uncommon for executives from all levels to work as a team so, for example, Americans of various ranks are accepted as well.

Lifestyles

Two people of similar age, income, education, and even occupations do not necessarily live their lives in the same way. They may have different opinions, interests and activities. As a result, they are likely to exhibit different patterns of behaviour – including buying different products and brands and using them in different ways for different purposes. These broad patterns of activities, interests and opinions – and the behaviours that result – are referred to as lifestyles. To obtain lifestyle data, consumers are asked to indicate the extent to which they agree or disagree with a series of statements having to do with such things as price consciousness, family activities, spectator sports, traditional values, adventurousness and fashion. Lifestyle topologies have been developed by researchers in other countries.

Culture/subculture

Culture has perhaps the most important influence on how individual consumers make buying decisions. Culture is the set of beliefs, attitudes and behaviour patterns shared by members of a society and passed on from one generation to the next. Cultural values and beliefs tend to be relatively stable over time, but they can change from one generation to the next in response to changing conditions in society.

Cultural differences create both problems and opportunities for international marketers, particularly for such products as food and clothes. By taking cultural values into account, companies adjust to the particular customs of people in different countries. Values are the shared norms about what it is right to think and do. They reflect what society considers to be worthy and desirable. Marketers need to understand values so their actions are not counter to what consumers in a given market consider to be acceptable.

A **subculture** is a group of people with shared values within a culture. There are many groups of people in the USA (e.g. Hispanics and Jews) who share common geographic, ethnic, racial or religious backgrounds. They continue to hold some values, attitudes and behaviour patterns that are uniquely their own.

Subculture
A group within a dominant culture that is distinct from the culture. Members of a subculture typically display some values or norms that differ from those of the overall culture.

Reference groups/family

All consumers live with, depend on and are nurtured by other people. We influence and are influenced by those with whom we have frequent contact – friends, colleagues and family members. We are also influenced by people we know only indirectly through the mass media.

Reference groups are people whose norms and values influence a consumer's behaviour (Kotler, 2000).

The family

The family is especially important to marketers because it forms a household, which is the standard purchase and consumption unit.

How does the family make buying decisions? Here the marketers generally look at three important aspects.

1 How do families make decisions as a group?

2 What roles can various members play in a purchase decision?

3 How does family purchase behaviour change over time?

In research on families of European descent Lee and Collins (2000) found that several coalitions emerged in family decisions.

In particular, fathers and daughters appeared to work together, especially older daughters (aged between 12 and 19). However, this coalition was weakened when there were two daughters in the family, as the daughters seemed to side with their mother against the only male in the family. Also mothers and sons seemed to work best together, particularly when there were two sons in the family. There is also evidence that this coalition was strong where it was a son who was the oldest child. It seemed to be the older daughters who were the key players in this family interaction.

The marketing implications of Lee and Collins (2000) are as follows. In order to increase the effectiveness of promotional campaigns towards families, marketers must examine the relative influence of family members at each stage of the decision-making process for each product category under consideration. It is suggested that segmentation of some family markets on the basis of the type of household structure and demographics may also be useful. Further, during the development of promotional campaigns, marketers may wish to direct messages regarding decision making to family members who dominate particular stages of the decision process.

The influence of various family members varies substantially across countries. Generally speaking, the more traditional the society, the more men hold the power. In the more egalitarian countries – such as the Scandinavian countries – decisions are more likely to be made jointly. As women become better educated and have more buying power in Europe and Japan, more **joint decisions** will happen.

Joint decisions
Decisions made that are shared by all or some members of a group. Often, one decision maker dominates the process.

Not all families consist of a mother, a father and children. Some households consist of only one person, or several non-relatives, or a single parent with children (see Exhibit 4.1).

EXHIBIT 4.1
Example of loyalty: store loyalty versus brand loyalty

The following data is based on a household panel survey by GfK Nürnberg.

Many consumers describe themselves as more store loyal than brand loyal. Figure 4.8 shows both. Brand loyalty is drawn on the x-axis and is measured as the share of all purchases within a product group taken by the most preferred brand. Store loyalty is measured similarly, as the number of visits to the most preferred outlet expressed as a proportion of all shopping trips undertaken for any one product category.

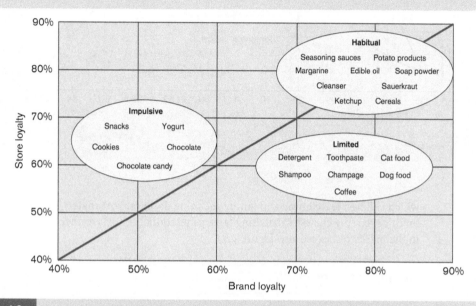

Figure 4.8	Intensity of brand and store loyalty for fast moving consumer goods

Source: Hennig-Thurau, T. and Hansen, U. (2000) *Relationship Marketing: Gaining Competitive Advantage Through Customer Satisfaction and Consumer Retention,* Springer Verlag, Berlin-Heidelberg, p. 37. Reproduced with permission.

Above the bisecting line, store loyalty is higher than brand loyalty, and this case applies above all to product categories where impulse buying is very common: sweets, snack products, yoghurts, chocolates etc. Nevertheless, brand loyalty in these product categories is still relatively high, at around 50 per cent. Very high rates for brand loyalty can be seen for products like cereals, soups, potato products, sauces, dog food, coffee and other products typically purchased repeatedly; loyalty rates reach 80 per cent and higher. Brand loyalty for these products is generally a little bit higher than store loyalty, but all in all we have to conclude that loyalty is a widespread phenomenon.

Source: Adapted from Hennig-Thurau and Hansen (2000), p. 37.

Family life cycle (FLC)

Family life cycle
A series of time stages through which most families pass.

The **family life cycle** describes the progress a household makes as it proceeds from its beginning to its end. Each stage reflects changes in a unit's purchasing needs and, hence, the difference in expenditure patterns – for instance, young married couples without children (DINKs = double income no kids) are often very affluent because both spouses work. They are a major market for luxury goods, furniture, cars and vacations (Weiss, 2000).

Dent (1999) describes how every generation of consumers makes predictable purchases over the course of their lifetime. At age 47, consumers finally reach their spending peak, after

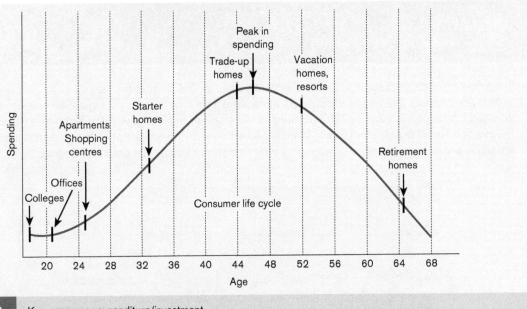

| Figure 4.9 | Key consumer expenditure/investment |

which children leave home and family spending declines. Fortunately, investors can capitalise on this spending curve by matching large generational cohorts to their anticipated behaviour in the marketplace (see also Figure 4.9).

Social networks

A social network is a collection of interconnected people.

Social networks comprise points (people and potential customers) and connections between those points. These connections may be manifested in many different forms. Examples include

- e-mail exchange
- SMS exchange
- purchases
- telephone calls.

Today online social network services are very popular. They focus on building online communities of people who share interests and/or activities, or who are interested in exploring the interests and activities of others. Most social network services are Web based and provide a variety of ways for users to interact, such as e-mail and instant messaging services.

Social networking has encouraged new ways to communicate and share information. Social networking websites are being used regularly by millions of people.

The main types of social networking services are those which contain category divisions (such as former school-year or classmates), means to connect with friends (usually with self-description pages) and a recommendation system linked to trust. Popular methods now combine many of these, with Facebook, MySpace, Twitter and LinkedIn widely used worldwide.

So now that we have identified the possible social network models, what is the next step?

The second step is isolating those network members worth investing our marketing efforts in. In other words, out of the potential customer base, we need to determine who the opinion leaders are.

Identifying opinion leaders

Opinion leaders are network members regarded as having relevant knowledge, and who are probably the first ones to be consulted in regards to purchasing decisions.

Usually, most opinion leaders possess one or more of the following characteristics:

Early adopter
A member of the group of consumers who purchase a product soon after it has been introduced, but after the innovators have purchased it.

- part of a social network
- good communicators
- usually **early adopters** of products or services
- information hungry.

There are different technological tools that can help identify the opinion leaders among our customers.

Now that we have identified the opinion leaders and their connections within the social network, we can divert all of our marketing efforts to focus on those specific customers, assuming that they, in turn, will spread the word to other network members. This way, we can reduce marketing costs and refocus our resources more effectively.

Once we fully understand the social networks surrounding us and learn to identify the opinion leaders within those networks, we will be able to establish suitable marketing strategies that will spontaneously produce word-of-mouth marketing.

Additionally, we will also be able to allocate our financial resources towards strengthening connections with opinion leaders and recruit them as advocates for our business (Doyle, 2007).

EXHIBIT 4.2
Brand-switching strategy in times of recession – the case of Skoda Superb

In a tough economic climate, consumers are less willing to spend on expensive items such as cars and homes. But Volkswagen-built brand Skoda is hoping that the 'switch' strategy for its new model, the Superb, will encourage consumers who would normally buy more pricey car brands to try a Skoda instead. The first generation of Skoda Superbs dates back to another global period of economic depression – the 1930s. They initially sold well, although the poor reputation of the Skoda brand in many countries, where it was seen as unreliable, persisted – until an ad campaign in the late 1990s persuaded consumers to laugh at their own preconceptions about the brand. Today, Skoda is the type of car brand that will fit well with consumer desires for cheaper products in a depressed economic environment. It has a well-established value proposition because it is competently built with good technology, thanks to its association with Volkswagen. A Skoda is a car that is great value for money, a recession may not affect its sales as badly as more upper to middle mass-market brands. It is aiming to get consumers switching from brands such as Ford or Honda.

Source: Adapted from Hosea (2008).

4.4 ORGANISATIONAL B2B DECISION MAKING

The marketing of goods and services to other businesses, governments and institutions is known as business-to-business marketing. It includes everything but direct sales to consumers. The products are marketed from one organisation to another, until the one at the end of the chain sells to the final consumer.

Derived demand
Demand for a product that depends on demand for another product.

Organisational markets consist of all individuals and organisations that acquire products and services which are used in the production of products and services demanded by others. The demand for most products and services arises because of a **derived demand** for the finished products and services that the company produces. About half of all manufactured goods in most countries are sold to organisational buyers.

The market behaviour, which affects the demand for industrial products and services, is generally quite different from that experienced in consumer markets. The differences arise mainly in regard to the behaviour of industrial buyers, the types of product and service purchased, and the purposes for which they are purchased.

Buying is performed by all organisations: manufacturing firms, service firms and not-for-profit organisations in the public and private sectors. Organisational buying is a complex process, which may be divided into a number of stages taking place over time. People with different functional responsibilities are usually involved in the industrial buying process. Their influence varies at the different stages, depending on the product or service being purchased. In broad terms, organisational buying is influenced by factors in the environment, by the nature and structure of the organisation itself and by the way the buying centre in the company operates.

There is a strong correlation between the level of a country's economic development and its demand for industrial goods and services. Thus, countries with a basically agrarian economy demand mainly farm equipment and supplies plus public sector purchases including military equipment and supplies. This is in contrast with highly developed countries, which are strong markets for high-technology products.

Identifying buyers in organisational markets

Buyers in organisational markets are typically manufacturers, intermediaries or customers in the public sector. To identify them it may be necessary to segment the market.

Manufacturers as customers

Manufacturers buy raw materials, components and semi-finished and finished items to be used in the manufacture of final goods. Manufacturers tend to be concentrated in particular areas of a country, and hence may more easily be served than consumer markets where the population is dispersed. Furthermore, buying power for certain products tends to be concentrated in a few hands, since a few manufacturers frequently account for most of the production of specific industrial products.

Intermediate customers (resellers)

Wholesaler
An organisation or individual that serves as a marketing intermediary by facilitating transfer of products and title to them. Wholesalers do not produce the product, consume it or sell it to ultimate consumers.

Intermediate customers are organisations which buy and sell to make a profit. They are sometimes referred to as resellers. Normally they make very few changes to the products handled. **Wholesalers** and retailers are the largest intermediaries in this market, but other specialised distributors also exist, which may also provide additional services.

Intermediate customers are also concerned with the derived demand further down the distribution channel for the products they carry. They are particularly concerned about product obsolescence, **packaging** and inventory requirements, since all three variables are important considerations in their financial well-being.

Public sector markets

Packaging
An auxiliary product component that includes labels, inserts, instructions, graphic design, shipping cartons, and sizes and types of containers.

The public sector market is in reality myriad markets. It consists of institutional markets such as schools, hospitals, prisons and other similar public bodies. It also consists of direct sales to government departments such as the health service and education departments. In most countries with an active public sector, the annual budgets of many of these institutions can be larger than the expenditure of organisations in the private sector.

Public sector tendering procedures

Many different purchasing terms are used in public sector purchasing, but it is possible to establish two broad categories of these. The first category contains terms refer to the extent of the publicity given to a particular public sector tender or contract, while the second category contains terms based on the discretion available to the awarding authority within the public service itself.

Where it is judged that many suitable qualified suppliers exist, the publicity given to a particular tender notice is widespread. The opposite is the case where the number of potentially suitable suppliers is limited. Three tendering procedures, each implying a different level of publicity, may be identified:

- open tendering
- selective tendering
- private contracting.

Open tendering procedures arise when an invitation to tender is given the widest publicity. In this situation, an unlimited number of suppliers have the opportunity of submitting bids. *Selective tendering procedures* occur when the invitation to tender is restricted to a predetermined list of suppliers. In this case, the invitation to tender normally takes the form of invitations sent to these suppliers. *Private contracting procedures* refer to the situation where the awarding authority contacts suppliers individually, usually a single supplier.

Buying situations

B2B buying behaviour is influenced by two overall organisational considerations. Organisations that have significant experience in purchasing a particular product will approach the decision quite differently from first-time buyers. Therefore, attention must centre on buying situations rather than on products. One firm may see the purchase of a new computer as a new task because of the firm's lack of experience in this area, whereas another firm may see the same situation as a **modified rebuy**. Therefore, a marketing strategy must begin with identifying the type of buying situation the buying firm is facing.

Three types of buying situations have been delineated: new task, modified rebuy and **straight rebuy**.

New-task buying

This occurs when an organisation faces a new and unique need or problem – one in which buying centre members have little or no experience in buying and, thus, must expend a great deal of effort to define purchasing specifications and to collect information about alternative products and vendors. Each stage of the decision-making process is likely to be extensive, involving many technical experts and administrators. The supplier's reputation for meeting delivery deadlines, providing adequate service and meeting specifications is often a critical factor in selling a product or service to an organisation for the first time. Because the buying centre members have limited knowledge of the product or service involved, they may choose a well-known and respected supplier to reduce the risk of making a poor decision.

When confronting new task buying, organisational buyers operate in a stage of decision making referred to as extensive problem solving. The buyers and decision makers lack well-defined criteria for comparing alternative products and suppliers, but they also lack strong predispositions towards a particular solution.

A modified rebuy

This occurs when the organisation's needs remain unchanged, but buying centre members are not satisfied with the product or the supplier they have been using. They may desire a higher-quality product, a better price or a better service. Here buyers need information about alternative products and suppliers to compare with their current product and vendor. Modified rebuys present good opportunities for new suppliers to win an organisation's business if they can offer something better than the firm's current vendor.

Modified rebuy
A purchase where the buyers have experience in satisfying the need, but feel the situation warrants re-evaluation of a limited set of alternatives before making a decision.

Straight rebuy
A type of organisational buying characterised by automatic and regular purchases of familiar products from regular suppliers.

Limited problem solving
An intermediate level of decision making between routine response behaviour and extensive problem solving, in which the consumer has some purchasing experience, but is unfamiliar with stores, brands or price options.

Limited problem solving best describes the decision-making process for the modified rebuy. Decision makers have well-defined criteria, but are uncertain about which suppliers can best fit their needs. In the consumer market, college students buying their second computer might follow a limited problem-solving approach.

A straight rebuy

This involves purchasing a common product or service the organisation has bought many times before. Such purchases are often handled routinely by the purchasing department with little participation by other departments. Such purchases are almost automatic, with the firm continuing to purchase proven products from reliable, established vendors. In straight rebuy situations, all phases of the buying process tend to be short and routine. Even so, when large quantities are involved, the need for quality assurance, parity pricing and on-time delivery to minimise inventory requires a competent salesforce to help the supplier maintain a continually satisfying relationship with the buyer over time. Indeed, the rapid spread of computerised reordering systems, logistical alliances and the like have made the development and maintenance of long-term relationships between suppliers and their customers increasingly important in the purchase of familiar goods and services.

For routine purchases or straight rebuys, the Internet is being used to streamline the purchasing process. To this end, firms are adopting electronic (e) procurement systems, joining trading communities or turning to electronic marketplaces that have been designed specifically for their industry (for example, buying steel in the car industry).

Routine problem solving is the decision process organisational buyers employ in a straight rebuy. Organisational buyers have well-developed choice criteria to apply to the purchase decision. The criteria have been refined over time as the buyers have developed predispositions toward the offerings of one or a few carefully screened suppliers.

The buy grid model

Buy grid model
The organisational buying process – consisting of eight buying stages – can be mapped like a grid, where the other dimension is the complexity of the buying (new task, modified rebuy and straight rebuy).

The buying process always begins when someone in the organisation recognises a problem that can be solved by a purchased product or service (Figure 4.10: the extended **buy grid model**). Sometimes the problem is nothing more than the company running out of regularly purchased items, in which case the purchasing professional determines the quantity needed and reorders the product or service. This would be a straight rebuy situation. Recognising the problem (stage 1), determining the product and quantity (stage 3), and evaluating the performance of the product or service (stage 8) are found in all three types of buying situation. Therefore, a minimum of three stages is found in all organisational purchases.

The new task situation is the most complex buying situation and therefore involves all eight buying stages. As we go to the right of Figure 4.10 some of the buying stages are left out because of the reduced complexity of the buying situation. We find the least number of buying stages in straight rebuy.

Figure 4.10 also suggests that some activities at each stage and their execution differ. More people are involved in organisational purchase decisions; the capability of potential suppliers is more critical; and the post-purchase evaluation process is more formalised. We will examine other unique features of each stage of the organisational purchase decision process next.

1 Recognition of a problem or need

The organisational purchasing process starts when someone in the firm recognises a need that can be satisfied by buying some product or service. Thus, while consumers may buy things impulsively to satisfy psychological or social needs, most organisational purchases are motivated by the needs of the firm's production processes and its day-to-day operations.

An organisation's demand for goods and services is a derived demand, which, as we noted earlier, comes from its customers' demands for the goods and services it produces. Fluctuations in economic conditions can produce change in the sales of an organisation's

	Buying situation		
Characteristics	New task	Modified rebuy	Straight rebuy
Buying stages			
1 Recognition of a problem/need	Always	Always	Always
2 Determination of characteristics and quantity of needed products/services	Always	Sometimes	Never
3 Determination of the product/service desired and quantities needed	Always	Always	Always
4 Search for potential suppliers and preliminary evaluation of their suitability	Always	Sometimes	Never
5 Acquisition and initial analysis of proposals (samples) from suppliers	Always	Sometimes	Never
6 Evaluation of proposals and selection of supplier(s)	Always	Sometimes	Never
7 Selection of an order routine	Always	Sometimes	Never
8 Performance, review, feedback and evaluation	Always	Always	Always
Importance of buying decision	High ←——————→ Low		
Degree of interaction between buyer and seller	High ←——————→ Low		
Number of criteria used in supplier selection	Many ←——————→ Few		

Figure 4.10 The extended buy grid model
Sources: Adapted from De Boer, *et al.* (2001) and Robinson, *et al.* (1967).

goods or services, which in turn can result in rapid changes in production schedules and in accumulations or depletions in the firm's materials and parts inventories. As a result, the organisation's purchase requirements for materials and parts can change dramatically in a short time.

In some cases, need recognition may be almost automatic, as when a computerised inventory control system reports that an item has fallen below the reorder level or when a piece of equipment wears out. In other cases, a need arises when someone identifies a better way of carrying out day-to-day operations. For example, a production engineer might recommend the purchase of a new machine that would increase production and thus reduce costs.

Changes in the company's strategy, resulting in a need for producing a new product line, may also result in a 'new-task' buying situation. Needs then may be recognised by many people within the organisation, including users, technical personnel, top management and purchasing agents.

Instead of simply monitoring inventories and reordering when they run low, some firms attempt to forecast future requirements so as to plan their purchases in advance.

Requirements planning governs the purchase of raw materials and fabricating components as well as supplies and major installations. One result of such planning is the signing of long-term purchase contracts, particularly for products projected to be in short supply or to a projected increase in price. Requirements planning can also lead to lower costs and better relations between a buyer and their suppliers.

2 Determination of characteristics and quantity of needed product or service

The need for particular goods and services is usually derived from a firm's production or operation requirements and, therefore, must meet specific technical requirements. Technical experts from the firm's R&D, engineering and production departments are thus often involved early in the purchase decision. When the firm needs a unique component or piece of equipment, it might even seek help from potential suppliers in setting the appropriate specifications. For example, car manufacturers consult their parts suppliers before finalising other specifications for a new model. Indeed, as we have seen, B2B marketers increasingly involve major customers in the process of developing new products and product improvements to help ensure that those items will meet the needs and specifications of potential buyers.

3 Determination of the product or service desired and quantities needed

When specifications for the desired product or service are to be determined, purchasing (and possibly other departments) may perform a value analysis. This systematic appraisal of an item's design, quality and performance requirements helps to minimise procurement costs. It includes an analysis of the extent to which the product might be redesigned, standardised or processed using cheaper production methods. A cost analysis that attempts to determine what the product costs a supplier to produce is also a part of a value analysis. Such information helps the purchasing agent better evaluate alternative bids or negotiate favourable prices with suppliers.

Sometimes a firm has the option of making some components or performing some services internally ('make'), or buying them from outside suppliers (outsourcing). See also section 3.8 for a further discussion of outsourcing.

Economic considerations typically dominate such decisions, although in the long term other factors may be important (for instance, overdependence on a single supplier).

4 Search for potential suppliers and preliminary evaluation of their suitability and qualifications

Once the specifications and workable solutions have been determined and precisely described, the buying organisation searches for alternative sources of supply. Here the purchasing department can exercise much influence as it provides most of the data for possible vendor sources. Figure 4.11 illustrates a process for screening potential suppliers.

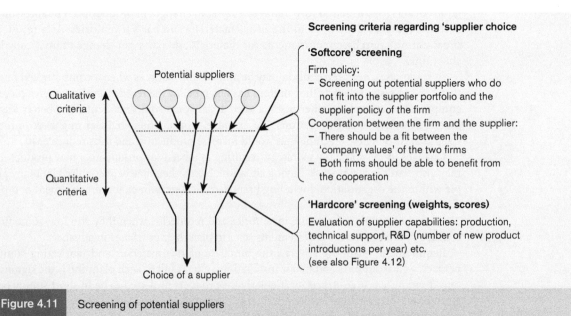

Figure 4.11 Screening of potential suppliers

If new potential suppliers are involved, the purchasing department typically engages in an in-depth investigation before qualifying that firm as a potential supplier. Such an investigation would include information such as the firm's finances, reputation for reliability and the ability to meet quality standards, information that can be obtained from personal sources (such as salespeople, **trade shows**, other firms and consultants) and non-personal sources including catalogues, advertising and trade literature.

For existing suppliers the firm may evaluate the performance quite frequently, and there is often considerable information about that supplier's quality of performance on file.

Trade show
A meeting or convention of members of a particular industry where business-to-business contacts are routinely made.

5 Acquisition and initial analysis of proposals (samples) from suppliers

Requests for specific proposals are made to qualified vendors in this phase. In a straight rebuy situation, the buyer may simply contact the chosen vendor to obtain up-to-date information about prices, delivery times and mode of shipment, so phases 4 and 5 may be skipped. For modified rebuys, more time might be spent on the analysis of the proposals submitted. New-task buys probably would take the most time and months may go by before a final decision is made.

6 Evaluation of proposals and selection of supplier(s)

Like individual consumers, organisational buyers evaluate alternative suppliers and their offerings by using a set of choice criteria reflecting the desired benefits. The criteria used and the relative importance of each attribute vary according to the goods and services being purchased and the buyer's needs. Always important is the supplier's ability to meet quality standards and delivery schedules. Price is critical for standard items such as steel desks and chairs, but for more technically complex items, such as computers, a broader range of criteria enters the evaluation process and price is relatively less important.

The various potential suppliers and their proposals are then analysed to determine which vendor or vendors can best match the product or service specifications and the desired price and delivery requirements. Subsequent negotiations may be needed to produce the desired results relative to prices, delivery and long-term commitment or other aspect of the vendor's proposal. Personal tastes and personalities cannot be ruled out, but the company that is well liked and can give the customer the best overall product and service will generally win the order, plus the strong possibility of a long-term partnering relationship.

Another factor that can influence the selection of suppliers is reciprocity, which occurs when an organisation favours a supplier that is a customer or potential customer for the organisation's own products or services. Although this situation sometimes causes inappropriate bonds between buyer and supplier, it can also develop into a rewarding long-term partner relationship. An example of Chrysler's supplier evaluation is given in Figure 4.12.

7 Selection of an order routine

After the selection of supplier, orders are forwarded to the vendor, and status reports are sent to the user department. The inventory levels will be established, and the just-in-time routines will be determined, if such a possibility exists. The user department views this phase as just the beginning. Delivery, set-up and training, if necessary, will then happen.

A good proportion of all industrial buying involves a purchasing contract. This streamlines the buying decision, making it a straight rebuy situation.

Contracts such as these enable a firm to standardise its purchasing activities across many locations. They can also introduce cost savings through scale economies (quantity discounts) and a reduction in paperwork. One problem with long-term legal contracts, though, is that they must specify precisely all the details of a purchase agreement, including product specifications, prices, credit terms, etc. But, in today's rapidly changing economic and technical environments, it can be difficult for the parties to foresee accurately what their needs and market conditions will be like months or years into the future. And it can be difficult to adjust

Supplier name_____ Shipping location_____	Type of product_____ Annual sales dollars_____					
	5 Excellent	4 Good	3 Satisfactory	2 Fair	1 Poor	0 N/A
Quality (45%)						
Defect rates	___	___	___	___	___	___
Quality of sample	___	___	___	___	___	___
Conformance with quality programme	___	___	___	___	___	___
Responsiveness to quality problems	___	___	___	___	___	___
Overall quality	___	___	___	___	___	___
Delivery (25%)						
Avoidance of late shipments	___	___	___	___	___	___
Ability to expand production capacity	___	___	___	___	___	___
Performance in sample delivery	___	___	___	___	___	___
Response to changes in order size	___	___	___	___	___	___
Overall delivery	___	___	___	___	___	___
Price (20%)						
Price competitiveness	___	___	___	___	___	___
Payment terms	___	___	___	___	___	___
Absorption of costs	___	___	___	___	___	___
Submission of cost savings plans	___	___	___	___	___	___
Overall price	___	___	___	___	___	___
Technology (10%)						
State-of-the-art-components	___	___	___	___	___	___
Sharing R&D capability	___	___	___	___	___	___
Ability and willingness to help with design	___	___	___	___	___	___
Responsiveness to engineering problems	___	___	___	___	___	___
Overall technology	___	___	___	___	___	___
Buyer _____ Date _____ Comments _____						

Figure 4.12 An example of supplier evaluation (Chrysler Corporation)
Source: Boyd, H. W., Walker, Jr, O. C., Mullins, J. W. and Larreche, J.-C. (1998) *Marketing Management*, 3rd ed., McGraw-Hill, New York, p. 133. Reproduced with permission from The McGraw-Hill Companies.

the terms of a contract in response to unforeseen product improvements, market conditions or cost improvements. Such inflexibility is one reason for the recent popularity of more informal relationships and alliances between suppliers and their major customers – relationships based more on flexibility and trust between the parties than on detailed legal contracts.

8 Performance review, feedback and evaluation

When a purchase is made and the goods delivered, the buyer's evaluation of both product and supplier begins. The buyer inspects the goods on receipt to determine whether they meet the required specifications. Later, the department using the product judges whether it performs to expectations. Similarly, the buyer evaluates the supplier's performance on promptness of delivery and post-sales service.

In this phase the user department determines whether the purchased item has solved the original problem. Because this time can be a difficult phase for the vendor (since some of the variables are not completely controlled by the vendor), it behoves the buying organisation to analyse the performance and provide feedback to all the interested parties for further evaluation. Feedback that is critical of the chosen vendor can cause the various members of the decision-making unit to re-examine their views. When this re-examination occurs, views regarding previously rejected alternatives become more favourable.

In some organisations this process is done formally, with written reports being submitted by the user department and other persons involved in the purchase. This information is used to evaluate proposals and select suppliers the next time a similar purchase is made. This formal evaluation and feedback process enables organisations to benefit from their purchasing mistakes and successes.

In other organisations (especially in SMEs with limited personnel resources) step 8 is done more informally.

The steps in the buying process described above apply primarily to 'new task' purchases, where an organisational customer is buying a relatively complex and expensive product or service for the first time. At the other extreme is the 'straight rebuy', where a customer is re-ordering an item it has purchased many times before (office supplies, bulk chemicals). Such repeat purchases tend to be much more routine. Straight rebuys are often carried out by members of the purchasing department with little participation by other employees, and many of the activities involved with searching for and evaluating alternative suppliers are dropped. Instead, the buyer typically chooses from among suppliers on an 'approved' list, giving weight to the company's past satisfaction with those suppliers and their products and services.

From the seller's viewpoint, being an approved supplier can provide a significant competitive advantage, and policies and procedures should be developed to help maintain and develop such favoured positions with current customers. Many firms have developed key account management programmes (see p. 373) and cross-functional customer service teams to help preserve the long-term satisfaction of their largest customers. Also, suppliers are offering new technologies – such as Internet-based reordering systems – and forming alliances with their customers to help them make their reordering process more efficient while simultaneously increasing the likelihood they will continue to reorder from the same supplier.

For potential suppliers not on a buyer's approved list, the strategic marketing problem is more difficult. A non-approved supplier's objective must be to move the customer away from the automatic reordering procedures of a straight rebuy towards a situation where the buyer is willing to consider new suppliers.

Kraljic's purchasing model

The purchasing function has a substantial impact on the total cost to a firm and thereby on the potential profit. Choosing the right suppliers has become increasingly important as they account for a large part of the value creation related to the buying firm's products and services. Thus, managing the firm's supplier base is becoming an essential strategic issue. Kraljic's (1983) model aims at matching external resources provided by suppliers with the internal needs of the buying firm.

In this portfolio, the perceived importance and complexity of a purchasing situation is identified in terms of two factors: profit impact and supply risk (Figure 4.13). Profit impact includes such elements as the (expected) monetary volume involved with the goods and/or services to be purchased and the impact on (future) product quality. Indicators of supply risk may include the availability of the goods or services under consideration and the number of potential suppliers. Depending on the values of these factors, purchases (and therefore the related supplier selection decisions) can be grouped according to Kraljic's classification into strategic, bottleneck, leverage and routine purchases.

Let us try to relate the buying situation in the buy grid model (Figure 4.10) to the four categories in Kraljic's model (Figure 4.13).

	Low supply risk/low complexity	High supply risk/high complexity
Low profit impact/low value added	**Routine items** Many suppliers Rationalise purchasing procedures Systems contracting Automate/delegate	**Bottleneck items** Monopolistic supply market Long-term contracts Develop alternatives (internally) Contingency planning
High profit impact/high value added	**Leverage items** Many suppliers available Competitive bidding Short-term contracts Active sourcing	**Strategic items** Few (difficult to switch) suppliers Medium/long-term contracts Supplier development/partnership (develop alternatives externally) Continous review

Figure 4.13 Supplier selection model
Sources: Adapted from De Boer, *et al.* (2001) and Kraljic (1983).

Leverage items typically involve modified rebuy situations. There are many suppliers to choose from while the high value (and saving potential) of the items justifies a proactive search and frequent selection of suppliers. However, the execution of the first steps in the process (problem definition, formulation of criteria and prequalification) is often decoupled from the final choice. The first three steps result in the so-called approved vendor lists. Final (frequent) choices are made from these approved vendor lists.

In case of a routine item, there are many suppliers that could supply the item. However, because of the low value of the item, it will not pay off for the firm to search frequently for and select suppliers. Moreover, usually a whole set of related routine items (e.g. stationery) is assigned to one (or two) suppliers in order to achieve a highly efficient ordering and administration procedure. The choice of the supplier is fixed for a reasonable period of time. Intermediate changes in the desired or required items are dealt with by the current supplier. Irrespective of such specific changes in the items requested and/or actually purchased, the appropriateness of the supplier is typically reconsidered periodically and if necessary a new (adaptive) selection will take place.

In case of bottleneck and strategic items, the choice of the supplier is also more or less fixed. Small changes in the specification of the items are automatically dealt with by the existing supplier. However, the reason for this is very different from that in the routine case. In these cases with a high supply risk, there are virtually no suppliers to choose from immediately, either because of a unique specification (i.e. a very strong resource tie between the buying company and the supplier) or because of the scarcity of the material. As a result, the choice set is often much smaller. Decision models are primarily used as means for periodic evaluation (monitoring) of the existing supplier.

The framework implicitly also addresses the impact of (inter-firm) relationships between the buyer and the seller on the selection process and the use of decision models. Depending on the substance and the strength of the relationship, the nature of the decision alternatives may differ. For example, in new task situations, where it is unlikely that the buying company has ever been in contact with the suppliers, the decision alternatives are primarily shaped by the offerings of these suppliers, i.e. the products or services they produce. In modified rebuys and especially in straight rebuys for strategic and bottleneck items, however, the interaction between buyer and supplier is likely to be more intense and relationships may have been going on for a long time.

4.5 INFLUENCES ON THE BUYING PROCESS

In this chapter we have already seen how the buying situation influences the B2B buying process.

The eight-stage model of the organisational buying process (Figure 4.14) provides the foundation for explaining other forces that influence a particular buying decision of an organisation. Figure 4.14 shows how **organisational buying behaviour** is influenced by four major categories of forces. The four major forces are:

Organisational buying behaviour
The decision-making activities of organizational buyers that lead to purchases of products.

1 environmental forces (e.g. growth rate of the economy)

2 organisational forces (e.g. the size of the buying)

3 group forces (e.g. the influence of the buying centre)

4 individual forces (e.g. personal preferences).

Environmental forces

A projected change in business conditions, a technological development or a new piece of legislation can drastically alter organisational buying plans. Such environmental influences define the boundaries within which buyer–seller relationships develop in the business market.

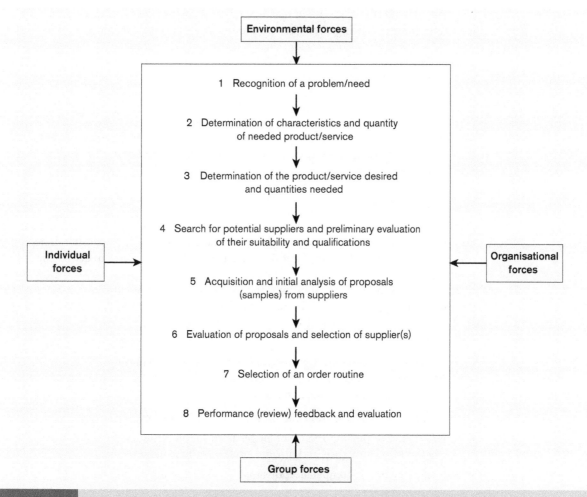

| **Figure 4.14** | Forces influencing the organisational buying process |

Economic influences

Because of the derived nature of industrial demand, the marketer must also be sensitive to the strength of demand in the ultimate consumer market. The demand for many industrial products fluctuates more widely than the general economy. Firms that operate on a global scale must be sensitive to the economic conditions that prevail across regions. A wealth of political and economic forces dictate the vitality and growth of an economy.

The economic environment influences an organisation's ability and, to a degree, its willingness to buy. However, shifts in general economic conditions do not affect all sectors of the market evenly. For example, a rise in interest rates may damage the housing industry but may have minimal effects on industries such as paper, hospital supplies and soft drinks. Marketers that serve broad sectors of the organisational market must be particularly sensitive to the differential impact of selective economic shifts on buying behaviour.

Technological influences

Internet
A worldwide network of interconnected computer networks that carry data and make information exchange possible.

Rapidly changing technology can restructure an industry and dramatically alter organisational buying plans. Notably, the **Internet** and **e-commerce** have changed the way firms and customers (whether they be consumers or organisations) buy and sell to each other, learn about each other and communicate.

The marketer must also actively monitor signs of technological change and be prepared to adapt the marketing strategy to deal with new technological environments.

e-commerce
Electronic commerce or business dealings using electronic media, such as the Internet.

Because the most recent wave of technological change is as dramatic as any in history, the implications for marketing strategists are profound and involve changing definitions of industries, new sources of competition, changing **product life cycles** and the increased globalisation of markets.

Product lifecycle (PLC)
The course of a product's sales and profits over its lifetime. It involves five distinct stages: product development, introduction, growth, maturity and decline.

Organisational forces

An understanding of the buying organisation is based on the strategic priorities of the firm, the role that purchasing occupies in the organisation, and the competitive challenges that the firm confronts.

Strategic solutions

Organisational buying decisions are made to facilitate organisational activities and to support the firm's mission and strategies. A business marketer who understands the strategic priorities and concerns that occupy key decision makers is better equipped to deliver the desired solution.

To provide such customer solutions, the business marketer requires an intimate understanding of the opportunities and threats that the customer is confronted with.

Strategic role of purchasing

In many firms, purchasing strategy is becoming more closely tied to corporate strategy (Nellore and Söderquist, 2000). Compared to traditional buyers, recent research suggests that more strategically oriented purchasing managers are:

- more receptive to information and draw it from a wide variety of sources;
- more sensitive to the importance of longer-term supplier relationships, questions of price in relation to performance, and broader environmental issues;
- more focused on the competences of suppliers in evaluating alternative firms.

Moreover, these purchasing managers are evaluated on performance criteria that are more tightly linked to strategic performance.

Given rising competitive pressures, purchasing managers are increasingly using rigorous cost modelling approaches to identify the factors that drive the cost of purchased goods and services.

To secure competitive advantage, purchasing managers are also tying purchasing strategies more directly to corporate goals to increase product quality, accelerate product development, capitalise on new technologies, or respond more quickly to changing customer expectations. Indeed, leading purchasing organisations have learned that these results can only be achieved by building close relationships with suppliers and by using B2B Internet-based marketplaces.

As purchasing assumes a more strategic role in the firm, the business marketer must understand the competitive realities of the customer's business and develop/produce better value for customers – in the form of products, services and ideas that improve the performance goals of the customer organisation.

An organisation that centralises buying decisions will approach purchasing differently from a company where purchasing decisions are made at individual user locations. When purchasing is centralised, a separate organisational unit is given authority for purchases at a regional, divisional or headquarters level. There seems to be a trend towards centralised purchasing. Why? First, through centralisation, purchasing strategy can be better integrated with corporate strategy. Second, an organisation with multiple plant locations can often achieve cost savings by pooling common requirements. Third, the nature of the supply environment can also determine whether purchasing is centralised. If the supply environment is dominated by a few large sellers, centralised buying may be particularly useful in securing favourable terms and proper service. If the supply industry consists of many small firms, each covering limited geographical areas, decentralised purchasing may achieve better support.

Finally, the location of purchasing in the organisation often hinges on the location of key buying influencers. If engineering plays an active role in the purchasing process, the purchasing function must be close organisationally and physically.

The organisation of the marketer's selling strategy should parallel the organisation of the purchasing function of key accounts. To avoid disjointed selling activities and internal conflict in the sales organisations, and to serve the special needs of important customers, many business marketers have appointed key account managers to take care of coordinating a key account's centralised and dispersed requirements, often on a global level (Pardo, 1999; Holt, 2000).

Group forces

Multiple buying influencers and group forces are critical in organisational buying decisions. The organisational buying process typically involves a complex set of smaller decisions made or influenced by several individuals. The degree of involvement of group members in the procurement process varies from routine rebuys, in which the purchasing agent simply takes into account the preferences of others, to complex **new task buying** situations, in which a group plays an active role throughout the decision process.

New task buying
An organisational buying situation in which a buyer is seeking to fill a need never before addressed. Uncertainty and lack of information about products and suppliers characterise this situation.

The business marketer address three questions:

- Which organisational members take part in the buying process?
- What is each member's relative influence in the decision?
- What criteria are important to each member in evaluating a prospective supplier?

The salesperson who can correctly answer these questions is ideally prepared to meet the needs of a buying organisation and has a high probability of becoming the chosen supplier.

The buying centre

A group of people in the organisation who make a purchase decision are said to form the buying centre, sometimes referred to as the decision-making unit (DMU).

The concept of the buying centre provides rich insights into the role of group forces in organisational buying behaviour. The buying centre consists of those individuals who participate in the purchasing decision and who share the goals and risks arising from the decision (Bonoma, 2006).

Roles for members of the buying centre have been classified as: users, influencers, buyers, deciders and **gatekeepers** (Webster and Wind, 1972). The importance of different organisational roles varies according to the phase of the buying process. The make-up of a buying centre in terms of members and the roles fulfilled changes depending on organisational factors, the organisation size and the buying situation (Ghingold and Wilson, 1998; Farrell and Schroder, 1999).

Roles can be conceived fairly easily for purchasing products such as production materials. It is more difficult to specify roles for services.

Determining who within the company is the user of transportation for inbound materials or outbound products, who is the gatekeeper or who has the decider role is a difficult task. It is quite likely that several individuals occupy the same role within the buying centre.

Gatekeeper
Those who control the flow of information, e.g. secretaries who may allow or prevent access to a DMU member, or a buyer whose agreement must be sought before a supplier can contact other members of the DMU.

Users

Users are those within the buying centre who will actually use the product being purchased. In manufacturing firms, for example, they are the employees who operate or service production equipment. When components are purchased, the users assemble the parts. In hospitals and other healthcare facilities, users may be nurses, physicians or the technicians who operate medical equipment. Users with a high degree of expertise may help develop product specifications. They are especially important in the last phase of the buying process, follow-through. They can provide valuable feedback to sales representatives about how well the product performs. Users can influence the buying decision in a positive way by suggesting the need for purchased materials and by defining standards of product quality, or in a negative way by refusing to work with the materials of certain suppliers for any of several reasons.

Influencers

Influencers are members of the firm who directly or indirectly influence buying or usage decisions. They exert their influence by defining criteria which constrain the choices that can be considered in the purchase decision, or by providing information with which to evaluate alternative buying actions. Technical personnel are significant influencers, especially in the purchase of equipment or the development of new products or processes.

Buyers

Buyers have formal authority for selecting the supplier and managing the terms of the purchase. Depending upon the nature of the organisation and its size, buyers may have such titles as purchasing manager, purchasing agent or buyer, or this responsibility and authority may reside with people other than those designated specifically as buyers – the production manager, for instance.

Deciders

Deciders are those members of the buying organisation who have either formal or informal power to determine the final selection of suppliers. The buyer may be the decider, but it is also possible that the buying decision is made by somebody else and that the buyer is expected to ensure proper implementation of the decision.

In practice, it is not always easy to determine when the decision is actually made and who makes it. An engineer may develop a specification that can only be met by one supplier. Thus, although purchasing agents may be the only people with formal authority to sign a buying contract, they may not be the actual deciders.

Often the selling organisation solidifies its relationship with the buying centre over time, which is called creeping commitment. The seller gradually wins enough support to obtain the order. In competitive bidding situations, the decision to purchase occurs when the envelopes are opened. In these cases, however, much depends on how the specifications are drawn up in the first place. Some salespeople work closely with the buying organisation at that stage to change the specifications and influence the decision in their favour.

Gatekeepers

Gatekeepers control the flow of commercial (outside) information into the buying organisation. Purchasing agents have been referred to as gatekeepers because they are often the first people that sales representatives contact. They are responsible for screening all potential sellers and allowing only the most qualified to gain access to key decision makers.

The control of information may be accomplished by disseminating printed information, such as advertisements, or by controlling which salesperson will speak to which individuals in the buying centre. For example, the purchasing agent might perform this screening role by opening the gate to the buying centre for some sales personnel and closing it to others.

As mentioned earlier, the buying process is seldom the same from one firm to the next, or even from one purchase to the next within a given firm. In each case, the decision-making process of the buying organisation is affected by a number of factors.

The background of the buying centre members affects the buying process. Purchasing agents, engineers, users and others in the organisation have expectations that are formed largely by their experience.

Exhibition
An event which brings buyers and sellers together in a commercial setting.

Organisational buying is influenced by sources of information such as sales people, **exhibitions** and trade shows, direct mail, press releases, journal advertising, professional and technical conferences, trade news and word-of-mouth.

So far, much of our discussion has focused on the buying centre. A more formalised buying centre, the buying committee, is used extensively in the resellers' market and by many business organisations, particularly when purchasing is centralised. In the resellers' market, organisations such as food chain retailers form buying committees that meet on a regular basis to decide on new product purchases.

Individual forces

Individuals, not organisations, make buying decisions. Each member of the buying centre has a unique personality, a particular set of experiences, a specified organisational function, and a perception of how best to achieve both personal and organisational goals. Importantly, research confirms that organisational members who perceive that they have an important personal stake and commitment in the buying decision will participate more forcefully in the decision process than their colleagues. To understand the organisational buyer, the marketer should be aware of individual perceptions of the buying situation.

4.6 CUSTOMER PERCEIVED VALUE AND CUSTOMER SATISFACTION

In this book, customer satisfaction and customer value are closely linked together though assessing customer perceived value sometimes goes beyond tracking customer satisfaction.

Delivering superior value to customers is an ongoing concern of management in many business markets. Knowing where value resides from the standpoint of the customer has become critical for suppliers because greater levels of customer satisfaction lead to greater levels of customer loyalty and repeat buying. This again leads to a higher degree of commitment and, ultimately, higher market share and higher profit (see Figure 4.15). In fact, delivering superior value to customers is key to creating and sustaining long-term industrial relationships.

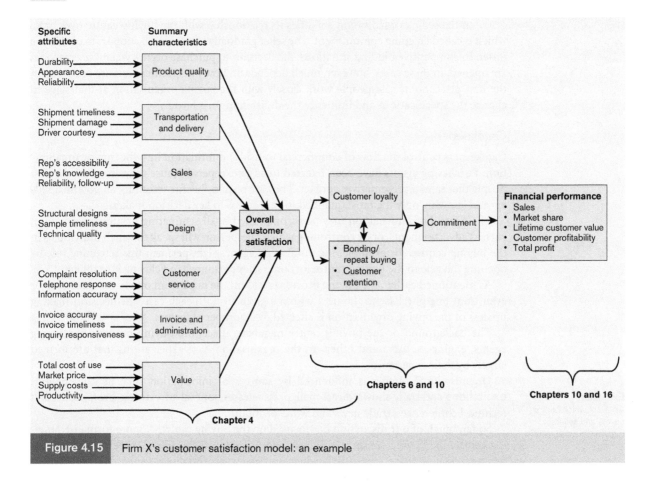

| Figure 4.15 | Firm X's customer satisfaction model: an example |

As seen in Figure 4.15, we will concentrate on the measurement of customer satisfaction in this section. Later on we will discuss the implications of customer satisfaction on other key measures.

Measuring customer satisfaction/customer value

Value is perceived subjectively by customers. Customers are not homogeneous; therefore, different customer segments perceive different values for the same product. Different people in the customer organisation are involved in the purchasing process. Whereas in some cases, firms may have established a formal buying centre, in other cases the people may be part of an informal group. Also, the number of people involved in the purchasing process and their positions may vary across customer organisations.

These members of a buyer's organisation have different perceptions of a supplier's value delivery. Therefore, in a customer value audit, it is necessary to identify and assess the value perceptions of all key people involved in the purchasing process. Such a multiple-person approach is considered to be more reliable by far than single-person studies.

In addition, within the supplier's organisation, opinions of how customers view the company's products differ among functional areas, i.e. general management, marketing and sales management, salespeople or customer service personnel. With value perceptions differing between customers and suppliers, and even within these organisations, identifying and bridging perceptual gaps become critical steps in value delivery.

Table 4.1	Customer satisfaction loyalty and bonding	
	Low satisfaction	High satisfaction
High customer penetration	Weak loyalty	Well-founded loyalty
Low customer penetration	No loyalty	Potential loyalty

Source: Hennig-Thurau, T. and Hansen, U. (2000) *Relationship Marketing: Gaining Competitive Advantage Through Customer Satisfaction and Consumer Retention*, Springer Verlag, Berlin-Heidelberg, p. 33. Reproduced with permission From T. Hennig-Thurau and U. Hansen.

Customer satisfaction, loyalty and bonding

The first qualitative criterion is customer satisfaction. Satisfaction arises if the customer's experience fulfils or exceeds expectations. When satisfaction and customer penetration are cross-referenced as in Table 4.1, the upper left corner is the most interesting, where **penetration** is high, but satisfaction low. This situation may arise when satisfaction and loyalty are changing at different rates.

Penetration
Entering a new market of customer.

With weak loyalty, customer recommendations or friendly customer feedback cannot be expected. Well-founded loyalty (upper right corner of Table 4.1), where there is high quantitative loyalty and satisfaction, should be the aim, if all the benefits of loyalty are to be enjoyed.

On the other hand, loyalty may be missing even though there is customer satisfaction, for example where there is some kind of barrier to a more intensive relationship. If this is the case, then these barriers have to be broken down if RM is to be successful.

Customer bonding may be seen as a process which influences customers, and customer loyalty as the result of this process. We can take three different perspectives in defining customer bonding and loyalty. These perspectives are described in more detail below (see also the summary in Table 4.2).

Suppliers will define customer bonding as a bundle of activities which builds up intensive relationships with customers, including contact opportunities, barriers to a change of supplier or creation of customer preferences for the supplier (which may be based on technology, materials, staff, etc.).

Table 4.2	Customer bonding: three different perspectives	
Supplier	Supplier–customer relationship	Customer
Customer bonding activities	Purchase behaviour	Attitudes and intentions
Building up contact centres, barriers to change, customer preferences etc.	Interaction between supplier and customer, atmosphere in supplier–customer relationship	Satisfaction, preferences, willingness to repurchase from, or contact, supplier
Customer bonding = bundle of activities which achieve a closer customer relationship	Customer loyalty = consecutive transactions (exchange of information, goods or money) between supplier and customer within a certain time period, good atmosphere in the relationship	Customer loyalty = positive attitude towards supplier combined with a willingness to perform further transaction

Source: Hennig-Thurau, T. and Hansen, U. (2000) *Relationship Marketing: Gaining Competitive Advantage Through Customer Satisfaction and Consumer Retention*, Springer Verlag, Berlin-Heidelberg, p. 31. Reproduced with permission From T. Hennig-Thurau and U. Hansen.

Looking at the relationships between supplier and customer, customer loyalty can be defined and measured in terms of the amount and the quality of transactions between both parties. Transactions cover, for example, the number of contacts or shopping visits, or the degree of customer penetration (the proportion of a customer's total buying volume accounted for by one supplier). The qualitative side of transactions refers to the atmosphere in which they take place, i.e. the climate of the relationship during the contact between both sides.

Customers will declare themselves loyal to a supplier through feelings and perceptions of (high) satisfaction, through positive attitudes and through certain preferences for the supplier, meaning that customers will be willing to repurchase from this supplier (Mouzas *et al.*, 2007; Illert and Emmerich, 2008).

Increasing customer skills through investments in customers

One effective way in which manufacturers might increase customer retention could be to increase customers' post-purchase skills through targeted investments in the customers themselves. Such a strategy is based on an interpretation of the *customer as a co-producer* in the value-creation process. If such a strategy is to succeed, a significant amount of product value must be initially inaccessible to the customer (e.g. the customer should be unable to use certain product features). At the same time, it must be possible to give the consumer access to this additional value by increasing his or her skills. Such an increase in customer skills should produce a higher level of customer satisfaction and also have positive effects on other dimensions of the quality of the customer–company relationship. Hence, an investment in customers aims to improve their post-purchase skills, for example by increasing their ability to use the full range of product features or to maintain the product adequately (Thurau and Hansen, 2000).

4.7 CUSTOMISATION – TAILORING THE OFFER TO THE INDIVIDUAL CUSTOMER

Customisation
Making something (product/service) according to a customer's individual requirements.

Traditional marketing often views the customer as a passive participant in the exchange process until the time of the sale. Customisation sees the customer as an active participant at every stage of the product development, purchase and consumption process, and as the co-producer of the product and service offering (Miceli, 2007).

Instead of accepting off-the-shelf products, customers are creating their own products, from configuring computers to building their own CDs. New products no longer come fully formed out of the laboratories, but arise through an interactive process of working directly with the market. Each customised product is a result of a co-design and production process of the customers and the firm. When this process is repeated across a number of customers, new insights emerge about customer preferences. Attributes and offerings that are not attractive can be dropped and those that are frequently requested can be enhanced.

By combining customer configuration with a mass production strategy, companies can also use the insights from the customised products to shape their mass-produced line. Customer design choices may catch emerging trends.

Database marketing
An interactive approach to marketing which uses individually addressable marketing media and channels to provide information to a target audience, stimulate demand and stay close to customers.

Early customisation efforts were in the form of 'made to order' products and services (e.g. furniture or tailored suits), which, however, had long lead times and were not tied to flexible manufacturing systems. The recent advances in flexible manufacturing coupled with the collection of detailed information about customers, and advances in database marketing and its associated analyses, enable firms to offer products tailored to customers' needs (customisation), but at costs that are almost the same as that of standardised production and mass marketing. This shift is illustrated in Figure 4.16.

As shown in Figure 4.16, mass customisation changed the centuries-old trade-off between tailoring a product to the needs of specific customers and the costs or time associated with

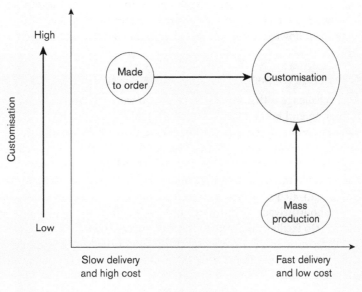

Figure 4.16 The process towards customisation
Source: Adapted from Wind, J. and Rangaswamy, A. (2001) Customerisation: the next revolution in customisation, *Journal of interactive Marketing,* 15(1) (Winter): 18. Copyright © 2001 Elsevier. Reproduced with permission.

delivering the desired product. Continuing innovations in flexible manufacturing, inventory management, and integration of global supply chains have provided further impetus in favour of delivering customised products quickly and at reasonable costs.

Individually and collectively, customers now have the means to directly influence a company's policies and strategies. For example, the growth of online product communities is profoundly altering the power structure in the exchange process.

Database marketing offers alternative approaches by which firms can tailor individual offerings and products to increase customer loyalty, volume of purchases and repeat purchases. First, companies that have made a commitment to one-to-one marketing are good at managing this information and communications process. In this way, companies can actually offer customers fewer options than mass marketers, because only the relevant options are visible. Second, firms can use innovative software to offer creative recommendations to a purchaser of music, movies, books, etc. based on related products purchased by other customers who purchase the same product(s). Third, companies can ask customers to provide them information about their preferences, and then design products and services to conform to the stated preferences.

While traditional marketing environments (mass-produced products sold through mass markets to target segments) will continue to play an important role in the economy, and while an increasing number of companies experiment with mass customisation and personalisation, the new type of marketing characterised by customisation represents a growing and increasingly important segment of the business. In the online environment, marketers are able to better identify customer preferences and either focus their messages and products and services on meeting the needs of each individual, or allow the customer to customise the message and products and services they desire.

The challenges of customisation

Customisation also raises a number of challenges including issues related to obtaining information from customers, the identification of the intangible factors that can make or break an offering, enhanced customer expectations, the need for limiting the complexity of options, and the required changes to the entire marketing and business strategy of the firm.

In the following, some of these challenging factors are discussed (Wind and Rangaswamy, 2001).

Knowledge exchange with customers

A key challenge is that for customisation to work effectively there needs to be exchange of information and knowledge between companies and customers. This requires the company to 'open up' some of its internal processes and structures to its customers. It also requires customers to be willing to share their attitudes, preferences and purchase patterns with the company on an ongoing basis. Currently, the knowledge transfer occurs because of the novelty of the new medium, and because both the customers and the company become better off to some extent with such a knowledge transfer. However, with increasing online competition and concerns about privacy, companies need to design privacy guidelines and incentive structures carefully to facilitate the knowledge exchange between themselves and their customers.

First, consider the privacy aspects. It is important to recognise that companies can obtain and provide information useful for customisation without having to know the identity of the customer.

Second, consider the incentive aspects. Customers must feel that they benefit in some measurable way by providing information to the company. This is more likely to happen if the company puts in place a structure in which it brings in its own knowledge in the service of its customers.

Real-time conjoint analysis studies that allow the company to assess consumers' preferences while offering the consumers the results, as an aid in their decision process, have great potential to offer value to both the company and the consumers.

Decision support system
A computer system that stores custom data and transforms them into accessible information. It includes databases and software.

In general, as consumers become more empowered, one can also see the further development of search engines and **decision support systems** to help consumers make better decisions including the customisation of the product and services they design and the associated information they seek.

Higher customer expectations

The customisation process creates higher expectations on the part of customers. They expect the product they receive to match their wants and needs perfectly. If it fails to meet these higher expectations, they are likely to be far more disappointed and dissatisfied than if they had bought a standard product.

Companies need to have the marketing and manufacturing capabilities to maintain a one-to-one relationship and to deliver what the customer wants efficiently. At the core of Dell's customised computer sales is an assembly process that can rapidly deliver exactly what the customers request. Yet these technological solutions have to be augmented with a marketing communication programme aimed at managing customer expectations.

Limiting the options offered to customers

The temptation in the customisation process is to give customers too many options, but this may lead to psychological shutdown. The key is to offer just the right amount of variety so customers are presented with the right choices without being overwhelmed.

The decision of how much customisation to offer depends not only on consumers' preferences and ability to handle the choices, but also on the nature of the product and its requirements to assure quality performance, capabilities of the available technology, the competitive offerings, and the implications of the target positioning and value proposition.

One way to limit the options to the feasible set is to present standardised option packages, as is common in the car industry. This gives customers a starting point in developing more customised products. The car industry uses these options very effectively, but does not do as good a job at inviting customers to use these options packages. The manufacturers generally offer many options, but customers typically buy the cars that are on display.

4.8 SUMMARY

Consumers' decision-making processes are classified largely on the basis of high and low involvement with the product and the extensiveness of the search for information. High-involvement products or services are psychologically important to the consumer. To reduce the psychological and financial risks associated with buying a high-involvement item, consumers engage in a complex decision-making process. The five major steps in the process are problem identification, information search, evaluation of alternatives, purchase and post-purchase evaluation. The way in which these steps are carried out differs between products and services.

Most purchase decisions have low consumer involvement. Therefore, consumers do not engage in an extensive search for information or make a detailed evaluation of alternative brands. Such search-and-evaluation behaviour is more likely to occur with products than with services. Buying behaviour is strongly influenced by psychological and personal characteristics that vary across individual consumers and countries. Information and social pressures received from other people influence consumers' wants, needs, evaluations and preferences for various products and brand names.

By definition, organisational customers can be grouped into three main categories:

- good and services producers (raw materials, components, software, office supplies);
- intermediates (resellers);
- public organisations/government.

Organisational buyers purchase goods and services for further production for use in operations, or for resale to other customers. In contrast, individuals and households buy for their own use and consumption. These two types of market also differ in numerous other ways, including their demand characteristics, their market demographics and their buyer–supplier relationships.

The buying task is determined by three interrelated factors:

- the newness of the problem to the decision makers;
- the information needs of the people in the buying centre;
- the number of new alternative products and/or suppliers to be considered.

Based on these factors, there are three buying situations: straight rebuy, modified rebuy and new-task buying. Organisational purchasing often involves people from various departments.

The individuals involved in the buying process form what is called a buying centre and share information relevant to the purchase of a particular product or service. One of the marketer's most important tasks is to identify which individuals in the buying centre are responsible for a particular product, determine the relative influence of each, identify the decision criteria of each, and understand how each group member perceives the firm and its products.

These participants in the buying process can be grouped as users, influencers, gatekeepers, deciders and buyers, and they buy in larger quantities – and purchase more complex and expensive goods and services – than consumers do. Differences between the business and consumer markets are summarised in Table 4.3.

The Internet is playing an increasing role in both B2B and B2C markets. Websites enable organisations to promote brand values, reduce printing costs, attract and qualify prospects and leads, and foster customer loyalty. Sites can also expand the customer database, provide customer service, and showcase and sell products.

The interactive age is providing businesses with the potential to strengthen RM and generate new customers. Consumers benefit from the Internet through better possibilities of providing relevant information (quality, prices, etc.) when comparing and evaluating product or brand alternatives in the buying process.

Table 4.3	Differences between the business and consumer markets	
	B2B market	**B2C market**
Market structure	Geographically concentrated Relatively few buyers Oligopolistic competition	Geographically dispersed Mass markets (often millions) Pure competition
Size of purchase	Often extremely large	Usually small
Buyer behaviour	Functional involvement Rational/task motives prevail Stable relationships Professionalism, expertise	Family involvement Social/emotional motives prevail Less buyer–seller loyalty Less trained, often inexperienced
Buying influences	Committees, technical experts, and management are all involved in decision making (buying centre)	The individual, household members, friends and relatives
Decision making	Distinct, observable stages Often group decisions	Vague, mental stages Usually individual decisions
Supplier relationship	Long-term contracts and supplier involvement	Many single purchases

CASE STUDY 4.1

Baxi
Trying to capture boiler market shares globally and in China

In Autumn 2008 CEO of Baxi, Martyn Coffey, is on his yearly trip to China. Since 1995, the annual growth of the Chinese domestic boiler market has been around 15%. In volume the Chinese market is still limited, compared to the main European markets such as the UK and Germany, but Martyn wonders if it is time for Baxi to do more in China, even in a recession period . . .

Source: Courtesy of Baxi AS

Introduction

Baxi traces its roots to Richard Baxendale, an English iron moulder, who began the Baxendale company in 1866. Today Baxi is best known for its heating systems. It started out selling solid-fuel fires, then launched gas boilers in the early 1960s. Today it has 1,400 staff in the UK and the group's turnover is approximately €1.2 billion (£850 million), with an EBITDA of £94 million in 2007. Its headquarters are in Preston, but it has manufacturing sites in Germany, Italy, France, Denmark, Spain and Turkey to cover the commercial, industrial and residential markets.

Globally it employs more than 4,200 people throughout Europe with a turnover exceeding €1.2 billion. The Group has significant market shares across all major Continental territories and in the UK. It is also expanding into new markets such as Romania and Argentina and already has a direct presence in Russia, China and the Czech Republic, and joint venture partnerships in developing locations such as Turkey.

Today, Baxi Group owns and sells some of the leading brands in the European market for heating products.

These include a portfolio of some of the best known and most respected brands in the heating industry: Baxi, Potterton, Main, Heatrae Sadia, Valor, Andrews Water Heaters, Santon and Potterton Commercial.

The Baxi brand is recognised in the UK, Italy, Turkey, Russia and a number of East European markets, Potterton is established the UK, Chappée and Ideal Standard in France, Roca in Spain and Broetje in Germany.

Baxi International, a division of Baxi Group, was formed in 2002 to manage the Group's international sales, marketing and after-sales activities in more than 70 countries all over the world. Baxi International has direct subsidiaries in Russia, China and the Czech Republic, and is represented in Romania and Argentina.

Here are some of the main characteristics of Baxi:

- leading market position in the UK gas boiler market (Europe's largest);

- solid brand recognition profile with UK installers;

- experienced management team, many of whom presided over the group's first LBO (leveraged buyout, where a significant percentage of the purchase price is financed through leverage – borrowing) in 2000;

- solid ability to generate free cash flow, which should allow the group to rapidly deleverage;

- highly leveraged financial profile;

- significant reliance on UK boiler market, which is undergoing major changes and which could thus weaken the group's market position; however, overall the UK market is quite healthy. There are about 26 million households in the UK and it is estimated that 1.5 million have to replace their heating system every year;

- committed to new heating technologies that will play a role in tackling climate change. They have launched a solar package, where they provide the solar panel, control system and other products, which mean installers don't have to get each part from different manufacturers and make sure they match. Baxi has also launched systems that use biomass and heat pumps. Lately, Baxi has also launched a microCHP (combined heat and power), powered by a fuel cell and which generates both heat and electricity;

- relatively weak positions in some European and Asian markets.

The current main shareholders of the Baxi Group are BC Partners and Electra.

Different types of domestic boiler

Floor-standing boilers

These floor-standing boilers are usually fairly 'slim' for fitting between kitchen units, although they may be installed in any suitable location. They are available as room sealed, fanned flue or conventional flue versions.

Wall-mounted boilers

The vast majority of boilers these days are wall mounted. These boilers have lighter, more compact heat exchangers, constructed from materials such as copper, aluminium, stainless steel or lightweight cast iron.

Combination boilers

A combination boiler (usually referred to as a 'combi') heats water for the taps from within the unit and combines this with central heating. A combi (storage) boiler is a variant, designed to give better hot water performance. Dependent upon the make and model, the improvement in hot water delivery will depend upon the size of hot water store, and this can vary considerably. Combination boilers dominate the European market (in the UK they account for 70 per cent of total sales). They have displaced the traditional floor-standing boiler.

Condensing boilers

A condensing boiler makes better use of the heat that it generates from burning fuels such as gas or oil. In a conventional boiler some of this heat is wasted because

A Baxi wall-mounted boiler (to the left)
Source: Courtesy of Baxi AS

the boiler releases very hot waste gases from its flue. A condensing boiler uses some of the heat from these waste gases to heat water returning from your central heating system, so it requires less heat from the burner. This makes your condensing boiler more efficient. The efficiency of a boiler is normally expressed as a percentage – some new condensing boilers can be up to 92 per cent efficient compared to new non-condensing ones that are around 78 per cent efficient and older boilers that are only 55 to 65 per cent efficient.

General trend in the use of different domestic boilers

Condensing boilers have been around for many years. Condensing types are more expensive, but users report reductions in fuel costs. This is possible because this type of boiler has a much more effective 'heat exchanger' allowing more heat to be removed from what goes up the flue. Condensing domestic boilers are now largely replacing 'conventional' central heating systems, especially in Europe. Condensing boilers can be wall mounted or floor standing, but the trend is towards the wall-mounted type.

Wall-hung boilers are getting more and more popular. Combis are not appropriate to every insulation application, however. They are best suited for small properties because of the limited amount of water available. The problem is, people use them in applications where separate boilers are more suitable.

The world market for domestic boilers

In 2007, the total world heating market was valued at US$31.1 billion with many European heating markets in decline. The total world heating market consists of many different products, such as domestic boilers, commercial boilers, water heaters, radiators and underfloor heating.

The total world domestic boiler market was estimated at 10.6 million units (2007) – see Table 4.4. The market is expected to grow at a moderate rate over the next few years. The UK is still the biggest market in both value and volume terms (1.7 million units in 2007), followed by South Korea and Italy.

Germany showed a large decline in the domestic boiler market in 2007, where it experienced a drop of 37 per cent, in which all boiler groups were affected, but in particular the floor-standing types, which saw a reduction of between 30 and 40 per cent. A similar situation was also reflected in France, Italy and other European countries.

Wall-hung boilers dominate the European market with nearly 6.2 million units in 2007. The UK is the biggest

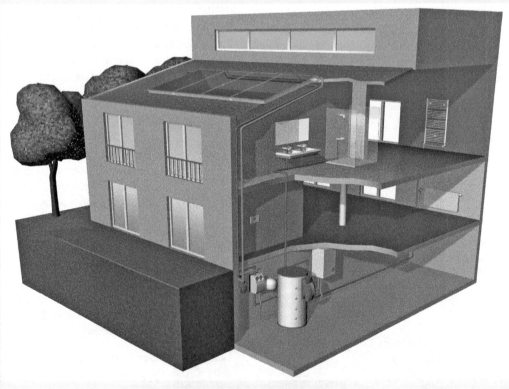

A total heating system with a Baxi wall-mounted boiler in the basement
Source: Courtesy of Baxi AS

| Table 4.4 | The world market for domestic boilers |

Region	Sold units 2007 (million)	Region market shares (%)	Main competitors in the region and their market shares (%)	
Europe (main markets are UK, Germany, Italy and France)	8.1	76	Bosch / Buderus Vaillant Baxi	18 18 10
Asia-Pacific (main market is South Korea)	2.2	21	Rinnai Kiturani Kyung Dong	10 10 10
Other markets (Americas, Middle East, Africa)	0.3	3		
Total World	10.6	100		

Sources: BSRIA reports, *Baxi Financial Report 2007* and author's estimates.

condensing boiler market in the world, accounting for nearly half the total world volume.

The total value of the world market for domestic boilers is approximately £11 billion (measured in manufacturers' selling prices). The average value (price ex factory) per unit sold in Europe is higher than in Asia.

In 2007 the total Baxi sale of boilers was 938,000 units, resulting in a worldwide market share of 8.8 per cent. Baxi is the market leader in the UK with around 50 per cent market share.

Competition within the boiler industry is based on the quality and functionality of products and services together with price and product range. As a consequence, the industry is characterised by new boiler product launches, together with promotional activity and aggressive pricing policies. Recently the growth in alternative technologies, such as heat pumps and solar panels, has been rapid.

An ongoing consolidation process is taking place in the industry. The main players in the industry continuously try to drive down costs, by making strategic acquisitions of complementary businesses.

The relationship of the individual market segments is going to change over the next years. Wall-hung non-condensing boilers, which represent about 50 per cent of the total market in volume, are expected to show decline over the next years. Condensing boilers, on the other hand, are going to grow rapidly. They are growing at a rate of over 15 per cent per year. The share of condensing boilers on the total European boiler market will rise from about 20 per cent to 27 per cent until 2010.

The wall-hung condensing boiler market is highly concentrated. The UK represents close to 50 per cent

of the total market, followed by the Netherlands and Germany, which account for 16 and 15 per cent respectively. Thus, around 80 per cent of the total condensing market is accounted for by just three countries. The next biggest markets are Japan, South Korea and Italy.

Seven major players dominate the European domestic boiler market, which include Bosch, Vaillant, Baxi, Viessmann, MTS Group, Riello and Ferroli. Often these firms have several brands under their umbrella and use them in individual countries.

Although the large domestic boiler manufacturers in the Asia-Pacific region have a significant share of the world market, they are only strong in their home country, with the exception of Rinnai and Kiturami for non-condensing wall-hung boilers. In Asia-Pacific, mainly local manufacturers and distributors supply boilers. North American boiler manufacturers are also confined to their own region, finding it difficult for existing products to conform to European regulations.

THE BAXI STRATEGY IN CHINA

A steady increase of production and profit in the Chinese construction industry is expected in coming years as both domestic and commercial demands are growing. With a population of 1.3 billion, plus an annual population increase of 20 million, the Chinese construction market will continuously increase in the future.

Heating requirements due to climate conditions

Heating is essential in the colder northern regions of China and some heating is desirable at certain times in

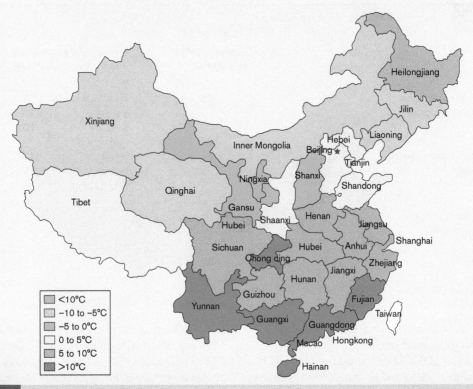

Figure 4.17	Average temperature by region (°C), November to December

Source: Based on data from 2006 *China Statistical Yearbook*.

Note: Average temperatures relate to largest city or cities in Province. Although inland provinces in the south have relatively high daytime temperatures, in winter there is still some need for heating at night. Many use individual heaters or air conditioning.

the south. These practices are also regulated by the government. For the northern regions (see Figure 4.17), heating is required for any new-build residential buildings, whereas in the south, heating is not required by regulation. Hence, currently the domestic boiler business is mainly focused on northern China.

In northern China, government policy is to increase the number of buildings, particularly housing, heated by collective and/or district heating. This particularly applies in the cold north-east region.

The use of different heating systems – the growth of individual heating

Chinese households use different types of heating, e.g. air conditioning, district heating and room heaters. Collective heating is still the most favourable heating system due to the tradition, living habit and the outlet of houses.

Individual central heating systems (domestic boilers) in homes have been a recent innovation in China since 1995 and currently account for a very small share of existing housing (1.5 per cent) and a little more in new housing (5 per cent) – see Table 4.5. Most individual domestic boilers are in small new developments of high-quality residences.

Many people may become dissatisfied with district heating systems and the price of heat may increase to approach real market levels as the result of the withdrawing of heating subsidised welfare from local government. This will result in further growth in usage of small domestic boilers.

Decision-making system

Residential market

In the residential market, end users play a less important role in decision making in both product and brand decision than house contractors. It is usually referred to collectively as the project market. The decision is normally based on price, brand image, design, function, after-sales services and, last but not least, guanxi.

Due to the lack of product awareness and knowledge, brand image and design are not the particularly important criteria to ordinary Chinese households at the moment.

Typically, in China, families own their own apartment.

For installation of domestic boilers in new buildings, the building developer/contractor plays the most important role.

Table 4.5	Type of heating in existing and new housing in China (2008)	
	Existing housing sector	New housing sector
% with individual central heating (domestic boilers)	1.5%	5%
Total number of dwellings (millions)	150	12
Number of domestic boilers (millions)	2.25	0.6 (new domestic boilers per year)

Sources: *China Statistical Yearbook* and BSRIA (World Heating 2007).

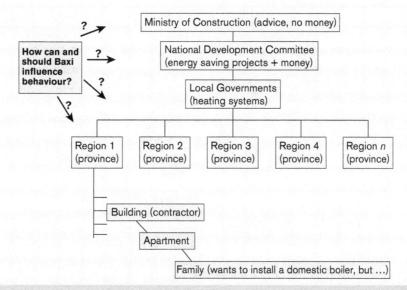

Figure 4.18 Decision-making system for domestic boilers (residential) in China

For installation of domestic boilers in existing buildings, service companies also play an important role, e.g. property services.

Non-residential market

For non-residential buildings, the decision is still mainly in the hands of end users or property owners, but architects and contractors will have some influence.

There are hardly any private consulting firms in China and the design institutes in various government departments employ all architects and consultants. The Ministry of Construction manages the design institutes. Each region has its own design institutes and they are divided into different grades and work on projects appropriate to their grade. For example, a design institute of a municipal grade is not allowed to work on provincial-level projects.

Architects (from the design institute) and contractors will play a role by suggesting certain product types and brands. The end users/property owners select a brand based on their own analysis and preference, consideration about price or, in some cases, personal relationship. For some extra large projects, it is possible for the contractors to be the decision makers; however, this is comparatively rare.

One of the major problems in motivating installation of the domestic boilers in China is that the consumption of energy for heating is not measured at the level of final consumption (in the apartments) and consumers are consequently not paying for their actual consumption. The implications of this are that there are no direct financial incentives for the individual consumer to invest in a new domestic boiler and to be environmentally conscious and save energy. Installation of heating meters is a necessary condition for families to be motivated to invest in new domestic boilers.

Environmental concern

With the rapid expansion of the economy and the development of urbanisation, China is challenged with the serious task of controlling urban atmospheric pollution.

The rapid development of urban transportation makes vehicle exhaust emissions the most serious problem concerning urban air pollution control. Moreover, acid rain and the production of greenhouse gases and ozone layer-depleting substances are of great concern to the Chinese government.

Market development

The Chinese market for individual central heating boilers was virtually non-existent up to the mid-1990s due to the strong domestic district/collective heating industry with China's heating park made up of district heating in urban areas and mostly solid fuel stoves, or no heating, in rural areas.

The market for low output (<50kW) domestic heating boilers began in 1995, with the first large-scale imports from Korea. After that, the markets for floor-standing and wall-hung gas boilers, based on European and Korean designs, expanded in the northern region.

In the past few years, several factors have contributed to the continuous growth of the low output domestic boiler market:

- increasing household income and improvement in living conditions with larger dwellings;
- the construction boom of recent years, which has created a huge demand from both new apartment blocks built outside the district heating network, and elite individual houses (villas);
- reform in the residential housing sector: private house ownership from state-owned housing;
- enhanced quality, designs and the reduction of prices of boilers;
- the Chinese government's environmental policy of reducing pollution from coal combustion;
- completion of the national west–east gas pipeline project by the end of 2003, which has mostly benefited eastern China.

The market has seen some changes in the product type and industry structure. Due to the environmental policy, alternatives have been provided to district heating which is run on coal. There is growing acceptance that European and Korean-style individual central heating systems are both more environmentally friendly and more efficient.

Until 2007 the Chinese domestic boiler market had been growing at nearly 15 per cent per year. This was also caused by the ever-increasing growth in new buildings and the improvements in the gas network.

The increase in sales is mostly being driven by wall-hung boilers. The main reason for this trend is that house developers prefer individual heating solutions to collective ones to reduce their property maintenance services. In Beijing, where wall-hung boilers account for around 55 per cent of national sales, there has been a trend where newly built apartments have been fitted with wall-hung boilers since 1996.

The Chinese domestic boiler market is forecast an average annual growth of 12 per cent in volume terms for the next five years. There are a few reasons for purchasing domestic boilers, as follows:

- the sustained increase of family income; more families can afford a domestic boiler;
- the need for some newly built high-grade villas, which are not connected to a collective district heating system, to have their own individual heating systems;
- the inefficiency of many collective heating systems due to distribution losses, etc. In some areas the price of heat has been increased to a higher level than the cost of individual heating;
- the improved quality and design of products;
- the growing recognition and reputation of the products.

However, the selling price will be under pressure, dropping 2–3 per cent p.a. depending on brands. Cheap labour and raw materials will allow lower product prices. Also, the replacement of the first-generation domestic boilers (installed from the mid-1990s with an average lifespan of 15 years) in turn will stimulate the market.

The domestic boiler market

The total domestic boiler market in China was estimated at 600,000 boilers in 2008 ($500 million), up from 345,000 boilers in 2003. This strong growth of around 15 per cent per year has been driven by new construction, a strong economy and new gas connections in the gasification programme. But domestic boilers remain a small part of the overall heating park, accounting for just 1.5 per cent of all heating and 5 per cent of heating installed in new buildings in 2007. District and collective heating remains the norm in cities while rural areas have either stoves or no heating in the south of China.

However, individual central heating is becoming more popular and is forecast to experience double-digit growth in the next 5 years.

The Chinese market mainly consists of gas boilers (including wall hung and floor standing), accounting for 54 per cent by volume in 2003. This is primarily due to the average Chinese home being satisfied by a boiler no larger than 30kW, and the desire to have a unit small enough to easily fit in the kitchen. Floor-standing boilers are only nec-essary if power outputs above 24kW are required.

The wall-hung boiler market has been created by European imports since the early 1990s, Apart from imports of many established European suppliers, there are also several joint ventures with local production, such as Saunier Duval with Yandi and Beretta with Devotion. Immergas (Italian producer) was the market leader in 2003 with over 20 per cent share, assisted by good connections of their Beijing importer in the project market. Kyung Dong was the leading Korean supplier, accounting for around 10 per cent share.

The market is still dominated by wall-hung (non-condensing) gas boilers. It will take several years for Chinese customers to gain knowledge and awareness of condensing boilers. Sales of condensing boilers will remain negligible in the next 5 years.

Competition

Sales of domestic boilers in 2003 may be divided by European imports and joint ventures (about 50 per cent of the total), Korean brands (20 per cent of the total) and domestic Chinese brands (30 per cent of the total).

Immergas is the leading European brand, as well as the leading supplier of the wall-hung boiler sector with over 20 per cent market share. Kyung Dong is the lead-ing Korean supplier, accounting for around 10 per cent share in the wall-hung gas boiler sector.

Of the domestic brands Devotion (Squirrel) is the most popular brand, accounting for around 6 per cent market share. There are also around 30 Chinese local domestic boiler producers – these are all very price competitive. Products of inferior quality or fake brands produced by some of the small and medium-sized Chinese enterprises occupy a considerably large mar-ket share in small cities because of cheaper prices.

China is an 'economy' market with European imports creating the 'upper' price segment, with the German manufacturers supplying the most expensive brands (Viessmann and Bosch). Korean import and local assembled brands represent the middle-price segment, and domestic Chinese offerings represent the low-price segment.

Competitors

Immergas (Italy) is the leading supplier of wall-hung gas boilers in China. The Italian company dominates the market by taking nearly 20 per cent market share by volume in 2007. The company only sell their products in Beijing, the biggest wall-hung boiler market in China, by using their sole distributor, Beijing H.T. Technology. The distributor plays a significant role in sales.

Riello Burners (Italy) entered China in 1996; Beretta boilers started to sell in 1998. The two companies moved into one sales operation office in 2001 and pro-duce products under the brand 'Riello' for burners and 'Beretta' for domestic boilers. They focus their

Table 4.6 The domestic boiler market in China (2008)

Total domestic boiler market (2007)	Units 600,000
Supplier (nationality)	%
Immergas (Italy)	20
Kyung Dong (South Korea)	10
Kiturami (South Korea)	6
Devotion (China)	6
Riello/Beretta (Italy)	6
Ocean/Baxi (UK)	4
Others (Viessmann, Bosch, Vaillant, Ferroli, Chinese and Italian brands)	48
Total	100%
Application	
Wall-hung domestic boilers (mainly gas)	80
Floor-standing domestic boilers (oil/gas)	20
Total	100%

Source: The figures are estimates made by the author and they are not necessarily according to real market data.

operations on the Beijing, Shangdong province and the north-west market. In 2002, Riello Group set up a joint venture with the leading Chinese domestic boiler manufacturer Devotion for local assembly of wall-hung combi boilers.

Baxi supplies a full range of space and water heating products for both residential and commercial applications. Baxi International manages the Baxi Group's international sales, marketing and after-sales activities in over 70 countries, including China. Baxi set up a sales subsidiary in Beijing in 2002, with the main responsibility of selling Italian manufactured boilers (from Baxi SpA) in China. The company used to sell wall-hung boilers through its Beijing importer, Beijing Zhong Ke Electric Corporation.

Distribution

It is important for European and Korean companies to have closed Chinese partners to achieve a permanent position in the market. In particular the Chinese partners' 'guanxi', or relationship with the authorities, is seen as essential for success in bidding for contracts in the project market. Guanxi is also a prerequisite for satisfying the government boiler inspection bodies of the Ministry of Labour and the Quality and Technology Investigation Bureau.

In the domestic boiler market, imported products and appliances manufactured by joint ventures and wholly foreign-owned enterprises are mainly sold via agents; nearly 70 per cent of the products are sold through this channel. Manufacturers sell the other 30 per cent direct to end customers (building contractors).

Main challenge for Baxi in China

One of the big challenges that Baxi faces in China is to get the governmental organisations (at different levels) involved and motivated in the economic and environmental requirements for more efficient boilers.

QUESTIONS

1 Who are the most important B2B decision makers for Baxi in the Chinese domestic boiler market? Please explain their buying behaviour.

2 Which global marketing strategy would you propose Baxi adopts in order to increase its global market share of domestic boilers?

3 How should Baxi proceed in China in order to increase its market share there?

SOURCES

Baxi AS (www.baxi.com); Baxi Group (2008) *Baxi Group Financial Report 2007*; Building Services Research and Information Association (BSRIA) reports; *2006 China Statistical Yearbook*.

QUESTIONS FOR DISCUSSION

1 What specific factors at the time of purchase may affect the buying decision in the B2C market?

2 What is the difference between Generations X and Y?

3 How does the demand for industrial products differ from the demand for consumer products?

4 What are the major differences between consumer and industrial buying behaviour?

5 How does the buying situation by class of purchase affect the organisational buying process?

6 What are the differences between the traditional 'buy grid' model and the 'extended buy grid' model?

7 Describe government buying procedures. Why is market orientation less important when selling to governments?

8 What is the buying centre in a company? Describe its functions and the implications for the selling organisation.

REFERENCES

Adage Global (2001) McDonald's taps DDB German shop for pork burger launch, *Adage Global*, 24 April (www.adageglobal.com).

BBC (2001) Defeat hits Man Utd shares, *BBC News*, 19 April (http://news.bbc.co.uk).

Boleslav, M. (2001) Slav Motown, *The Economist*, 4 January.

Bonoma, V. (2006) Major sales: who really does the buying? *Harvard Business Review*, July-August: 172–81.

Boyd, H. W., Walther O. C., Larréché, J. C. (1998) *Marketing Management*, 3rd edn., Irwin/McGraw-Hill.

Brown and Walsch (2000) Formulators outsource to make up lost margins, *Chemical Week*, 6 December: 51–62.

Customer Loyalty Today (2000) 'Unattractive' Skoda builds database for 2001 push, *Customer Loyalty Today*, 25 August.

De Boer, L., Labro, E. and Morlacchi, P. (2001) A review of methods supporting supplier selection, *European Journal of Purchasing & Supply Management*, 7: 75–89.

Dent, H. S. (1999) *The Roaring 2000s Investor*, Simon & Schuster, New York.

Doyle, S. (2007) The role of social networks in marketing, *Journal of Database Marketing & Customer Strategy Management*, 15(1): 60–4.

Farrell, M. and Schroder, B. (1999) Power and influence in the buying centre, *European Journal of Marketing*, 33(11/12): 1161–70.

Friedrich, S. A (2000) Was ist 'Core' und was ist 'Non-core'? *IO Management*, 4: 18–23.

Ghingold, M. and Wilson, D. T. (1998) Buying center research and business marketing practice: meeting the challenge of dynamic marketing, *Journal of Business & Industrial Marketing*, 13(2): 96–108.

Goldstein, D. G., Johnson, E. J., Herrmann, A. and Heitmann, M. (2008) Nudge your customers toward better choices, *Harvard Business Review*, December: 99–105.

Gurley, T., Lin, S. and Ballou, S. (2005) Consumer decision process modeling: how leaders can better understand buyers' choices, *Strategy & Leadership*, 33(3): 30–40.

Holt, S. (2000) Managing global networks: the role of the global account manager, IMP Conference 2000, Bath (CD-ROM article).

Hosea, M. (2008) The six secret strategies of shopkeepers, *Brand Strategy*, November: 26–32.

Illert, G. and Emmerich, R. (2008) The need for new promotional models, *Journal of Medical Marketing*, 8(1): 23–30.

Kotler, P. (2000) *Marketing Management*, Prentice Hall, Englewood Cliffs, NJ.

Kraljic, P. (1983) Purchasing must become supply management, *Harvard Business Review*, 61(5): 109–17.

Laurent, G. and Kapferer, J. (1985) Measuring consumer involvement profiles, *Journal of Marketing Research*, 22(2): 41–53.

Lee, C. K.-C. and Collins, B. A. (2000) Family decision making and coalition patterns, *European Journal of Marketing*, 34(9): 1181–98.

MAP (2001) United look to conquer America, *MAP*, 13 March.

Maslow, A. H. (1970) *Motivation and Personality*, 2nd edn., Harper & Row Publishers Inc., New York.

Micelli, G. N., Ricotta, F. and Costabile, M. (2007) Customizing customization: a conceptual framework for interactive personalization, *Journal of Interactive Marketing*, 21(2) (Spring): 6–25.

Mouzas, S., Henneberg, S. and Naudè, P. (2007) Trust and reliance in business relationships, *European Journal of Marketing*, 41(9/10): 1016–32.

Mudambi, S. (forthcoming) Branding importance in business-to-business markets: three buyer clusters, *Industrial Marketing Management*.

Naumann, E., Jackson, D. W. and Rosenbaum, M. S. (2001) How to implement a customer satisfaction program, *Business Horizons*, January–February: 37–46.

Nellore, R. and Söderquist, K. (2000) Portfolio approaches to procurement: analysing the missing link to specifications, *Long Range Planning*, 33: 245–67.

Osborne, J. (2000) Bootstrap marketing: taking on Procter & Gamble, *Inc. Magazine*, 1 October: 20–2.

Pardo, C. (1999) Key account management in the business-to-business field: a French overview, *Journal of Business & Industrial Marketing*, 14(4): 276–90.

Robinson, P. J., Faris, C. W. and Wind, Y. (1967) *Industrial Buying and Creative Marketing*, Allyn & Bacon, Boston, MA.

Thurau, T. H. and Hansen, U. (2000) *Relationship Marketing: Gaining Competitive Advantage Through Customer Satisfaction and Customer Retention*, Springer Verlag, Berlin/Heidelberg.

Webster, Jr, F. E. and Wind, Y. (1972) A general model for understanding organizational buying behaviour, *Journal of Marketing*, 36 (April): 12–19.

Weiss, M. J. (2000) The demographic investor, *American Demographics*, December (www.demographics.com).

Wind, J. and Rangaswamy, A. (2001) Customerization: the next revolution in customization, *Journal of Interactive Marketing*, 15(1) (Winter): 13–32.

CHAPTER 5
Competitor analysis and intelligence

LEARNING OBJECTIVES

After studying this chapter you should be able to:

- integrate competition into an environmental analysis
- discuss competition and competitors at different levels:
  - budget competition
  - core benefit competition
  - product class competition
  - brand competition
- specify the levels in competitor awareness
- describe how to design a competitor intelligence (CI) system
- evaluate the information sources for CI
- specify the contents of a competitor audit
- evaluate the strengths and weaknesses of competitors
- assess current strategies of main competitors
- give examples of how to evaluate the strengths and weaknesses of competitors
- assess current strategies of main competitors
- outline possible response patterns of main competitors

5.1 INTRODUCTION

Competitive intelligence

Gathering, analysing and distributing information about products, customers, competitors and any aspect of the environment needed to support executives and managers in making strategic marketing decisions for an organization

Competitor intelligence (CI)

The process of identifying key competitors; assessing their objectives, strategies, strengths and weaknesses, and reaction patterns; and selecting which competitors to attack or avoid. This analysis provides both an offensive and defensive strategic context through which to identify opportunities and threats.

Most often **competitive intelligence** is used to mean the action of gathering analysing and distributing information about products, customers, competitors and any aspect of the environment needed to support executives and managers in making strategic marketing decisions for an organisation. **Competitor intelligence (CI)** is a more narrow term, as it only focuses on the competitor aspect.

Except for a minor section dealing with interaction between competitors (section 5.3) this chapter is mainly about how to analyse competitors, their behaviour and their strategies. A more comprehensive analysis of competitor relationships is given in Chapter 6 (section 6.6).

Competitor intelligence is the publicly available information and other types of information on competitors, current and potential, that is an important input in formulating a marketing strategy. Managers at all levels in organisations should conduct competitive intelligence scanning to monitor market variables that are continuously shifting. To sustain competitive position, managers must prepare to respond quickly to changes in customer preferences, competitor strategies and technological advancements (Qiu, 2008; Dishman and Calof, 2008).

However, no general would order an army to march without first fully knowing the enemy's position and intentions. Similarly, before deciding which competitive moves to make, a firm must be aware of the perspectives of its competitors. CI includes information beyond industry statistics and trade gossip. It involves the close observation of competitors to learn what they do best and why and where they are weak.

In most Western countries the development has resulted in a major intensification of competitor intelligence. The reasons for increasing CI are:

- increasing competition between companies;
- deregulation;
- liberalisation;
- globalisation;
- periods of economic recession;
- reduced product and service differentiation.

Factors inhibiting the growth of CI include:

- data protection;
- different legislation from country to country;
- fear that competitive intelligence is unethical;
- fear of counter-intelligence;
- failure of competitive strategies to yield the expected gain.

The use of CI is increasing gradually. There is growing awareness of the need to have a competitor strategy, which is every bit as important as the customer strategies that are already commonplace (West, 1999).

In terms of their use of CI, companies seem to go through a series of stages (see Figure 5.1). At the first stage is competitor awareness. This stage is entered soon after a company is formed, or even before, when the start-up is being planned. Being competitor aware means that the key competitors are known and that there is some knowledge – usually incomplete and certainly unverified – about their products, their prices, the clients they have succeeded in winning business from, the market sectors they service and the staff they employ.

The organisation that is competitor aware rarely uses the data that it holds other than for occasional ad hoc tactical exercises, such as competitive pricing decisions, or as an input to a business plan that has to be submitted to an external organisation, such as a bank.

Stages of competitive development   **Characteristics of the three stages of competitive development**

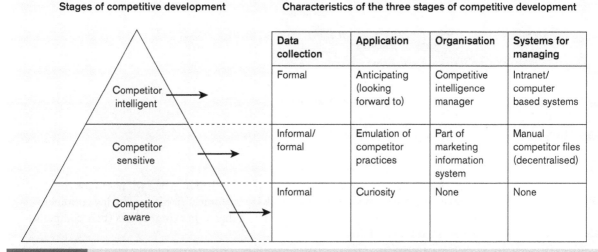

	Data collection	Application	Organisation	Systems for managing
Competitor intelligent	Formal	Anticipating (looking forward to)	Competitive intelligence manager	Intranet/ computer based systems
Competitor sensitive	Informal/ formal	Emulation of competitor practices	Part of marketing information system	Manual competitor files (decentralised)
Competitor aware	Informal	Curiosity	None	None

Figure 5.1	Development of competitive intelligence

Source: Adapted from West, C. (1999) Competitive intelligence in Europe, *Business Information Review*, 16(3) (September): 143–50. Copyright © 1999 Sage. Reproduced with permission of Sage Publications and C. West.

As companies grow they tend to become competitor sensitive, both in terms of their awareness of the damage competitors can inflict on their business and the need to win orders by competing more effectively. Unfortunately, being competitor sensitive does not always increase the demand for information on competitors. An alarming proportion of competitor sensitive companies continue to rely exclusively on informal information flows from their salesforces, business contacts and the trade press, rather than from a structured intelligence programme. When they do use sources other than the informal information channels the prime motive is usually emulation. They seek to copy what they perceive to be the best of their competitors' practices. There is nothing wrong with emulation as a business process, providing it is factually driven using such techniques as reverse engineering and competitor benchmarking, but it represents a very limited source of data that can be derived about competitors' activities.

The organisation that is competitor intelligent is one that devotes serious resources to studying its competitors and anticipating their actions. This includes identifying competitors' physical and intangible resources; studying their organisations and their methods in as much detail as possible; and developing knowledge of their strategies and potential plans. The competitor intelligent organisation is continuously aware of the threats posed by competitors, the nature and seriousness of those threats and what needs to be done to counteract them. They recognise the need to look forward to anticipate competitive actions and to predict the likely responses to actions they are proposing to take themselves. They are also aware that the most serious threats may arise from companies that are not yet active in their business sector.

Competitor analysis
The process of identifying key competitors; assessing their objectives, strategies, strengths and weaknesses, and reaction patterns; and selecting which competitors to attack or avoid. This analysis provides both an offensive and defensive strategic context through which to identify opportunities and threats.

There is a close parallel between the growth in **competitor analysis**, and the development of customer analysis. There was a time when organisations were only customer aware. Interest in competitive strategy was nurtured by the publication of books such as Michael Porter's *Competitive Advantage* and *Competitive Strategy* in the 1980s. This was accompanied by a short flirtation with marketing warfare that focused on beating the competition by adopting military tactics.

Competition is good for customers as it means that companies have to try harder or lose their customer base. In many markets competition is the driving force of change. Without competition, companies only satisfy: they provide satisfactory levels of customer value (satisfaction) but fail to excel. The conflict between improving customer value and costs is illustrated by the competitive triangle (Figure 5.2).

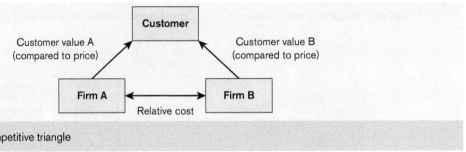

| Figure 5.2 | The competitive triangle |

This framework recognises that for example, for firm A to be a winner in the competition, it is no longer sufficient to be good at satisfying customers' needs (producing customer value). Companies also have to produce at a lower cost than other competitors (here competitor B). This is called lower relative costs.

When developing a marketing strategy (Chapter 7), companies need to be aware of their own strengths (S) and weaknesses (W), customer needs (O, opportunities) and the competitors (T, threats). Altogether these four elements represent the SWOT analysis, which in Chapter 7 will be used as a basis for developing the firm's marketing strategy. The focus of this chapter will be on analysing competitors at the strategic and tactical level.

Strategic intelligence looks to the future and allows an organisation to make informed decisions concerning future conditions in the marketplace and/or industry. *Tactical intelligence* looks at the present. This level of intelligence provides decision makers with the information necessary to monitor changes in the company's current environment and helps them search for new opportunities. To maximise the potential benefit of CI, the strategic and tactical levels must be coordinated. Because all the partner companies identified coordination as a high priority, these businesses create, continuously improve and use CI systems, processes and products that enable this to happen. Moreover, all of these companies believe that coordinating strategic and tactical intelligence with sales and marketing has led to a strengthening in competitive positions as well as increases in customer satisfaction and retention.

Competitive analysis flows out of customer analysis. To truly know how you compare with your competitors, you first need to understand your customers' wants and needs. Then you must identify both current and potential competitors in both your served and unserved markets. Industry analysis is also important. You need to know about the suppliers to your industry as well as the channels which serve as intermediaries between you and your competitors and the end users. These players have an impact on your competitive position. Once you have identified your competitors, it may be possible to group them by factors, such as degree of specialisation or degree of globalisation, to make it easier to discern patterns of competitive behaviour. Now you should be in a position to do an in-depth analysis of competitors' strategies. You must be careful not to focus simply on what your competitors are doing now. You must consider where your competitors are going.

This chapter focuses on eight issues.

1 Who are our competitors? (section 5.2)

2 How are the competitors interacting? (section 5.3)

3 How do we learn about our competitors? (section 5.4)

4 What are the strengths and weaknesses of our competitors (competitor audit)? (section 5.5)

5 Market commonality and resource commonality. (section 5.6)

6 What are the objectives and strategies of our competitors? (section 5.7)

7 What are the response patterns of our competitors? (section 5.8)

8 How can we set up an organisation for CI? (section 5.9)

5.2 WHO ARE OUR COMPETITORS?

The danger when identifying competitors is that competitive myopia prevails (Levitt, 1960). According to Levitt's thesis, the mission of a business should be defined broadly: an airline might consider itself in the holiday business; a railway company should not consider other railway companies as competitors but rather consider themselves as in the transport business, competing with other transport methods such as roads and air.

Later on Levitt's proposition was contradicted by some practical examples: among them was Coca-Cola, which in the early 1980s extended its business from being a soft drinks marketer to being a beverage company. Subsequently, the company bought three wine companies.

Competition for a certain product can be defined clearly at every level of the hierarchy shown in the examples of Figure 5.3.

The number of competitors grows as you go outwards from the centre. However, the terms industry and product class do not get to the heart of competition or market definition.

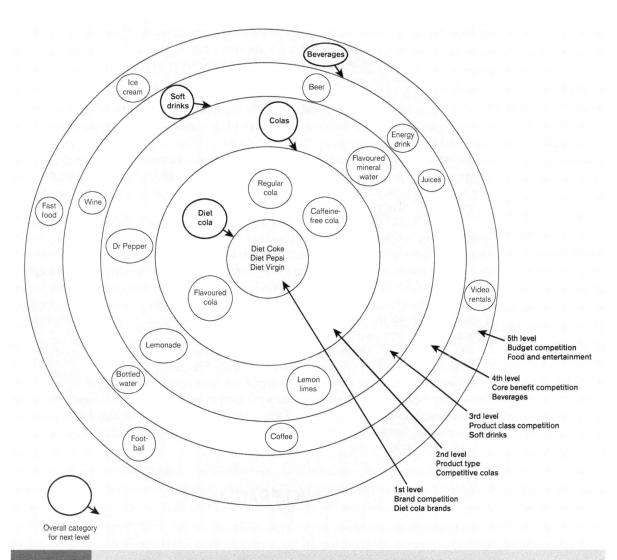

| Figure 5.3 | Examples of competition against colas |

A good definition of an industry is the following:

An industry should be recognisable as a group of products that are close substitutes to buyers, are available to a common group of buyers, and are distant substitutes for all products not included in the industry.

The key part of this definition is the fact that competition is defined by the customer, not by the marketing manager; after all, it is the customer who determines whether two products or services compete against each other.

An alternative way to define the competition that better incorporates the customer's perspective is also shown in Figure 5.3. The narrowest definition of competition that results in the fewest competitors would include only products or services of the same product types or brands. For a diet cola brand the narrowest way to define competition would be to include only the other diet cola brands.

Although there may be some product variations such as capacity, the most direct competitors are the brands that look like yours (first level of competition).

This narrow definition might be useful in the short term because these brands are your most serious competitors on a day-to-day basis. It is also a convenient definition of competition because it mimics the way commercial data services (e.g. A. C. Nielsen) often measure market shares. However, this narrow definition may set an industry standard for looking at competition and market shares in a way that does not represent the true underlying competitive dynamics. Thus, the product type level, though perhaps providing the set of the closest competitors, is too narrow for a longer-term view of competition.

The second level of competition is based on products that have similar features and provide the same basic function. In this type of competition, called product type competition, more brands are considered to be competitors such as Coca-Cola classic, Pepsi One, Caffeine Free Diet Pepsi.

At the third level (product class competition), other competitors are considered to be other soft drink brands such as Sprite, Dr Pepper and 7-Up. At the fourth level the products are competing generically because they satisfy the same need. In Figure 5.3 it is the need of thirst or the need of enjoying a beverage together with others.

The point is that there is a critical difference between generically defined competitors and product form or product category competition. The latter two are inward oriented, whereas generic competition is outward oriented. Product type and product class competitors are defined by products that look like yours. Generic competitors are defined by looking outside the firm to the customers. After all, the customer determines what products and services solve the problem at hand. Although in some cases there may be a limited number of ways to solve the same problem or provide the same benefit, in most instances focusing on the physical product alone ignores viable competitors.

The final level of competition (level 5) is the most general level, as many products and services are discretionary items purchased from the same general budget.

A person shopping in a department store in the housewares area faces many other discretionary items for the home that are unrelated to making coffee or quenching thirst. Products such as pots and pans and knives may find their way into the shopping basket and could be viewed as substitutable in the budget. This kind of competition is called budget competition.

5.3 HOW ARE THE COMPETITORS INTERACTING?

A competitive interaction occurs when a set of firms engages in a series of behaviours that affect each other's outcomes and/or behaviours over time. In this situation, the competitors are 'at war'; in other situations the interaction might be peaceful.

Table 5.1	Types of competitive interaction

		Firm A	
		Aware	Unaware
		Explicit	*Asymmetric*
Firm B	Aware	Relationship behaviours (benign or hostile)	Firm A – Ignorance Firm B – Stealth
		Asymmetric	*Implicit*
	Unaware	Firm A – Stealth B – Ignorance	Market behaviours (customer-mediated)

Source: From Clark, B. H. (1998) Managing competitive interactions, *Marketing Management*, 7(4): 8–20. Reproduced with permission from the American Marketing Association.

At a more general level, one can think of an interaction as consisting of a sequence of events, occurring as follows. Our firm and the competitor firm engage in a set of actions (e.g. marketing mix) that provoke a particular customer response.

While no interaction can be completely controlled, research and experience suggest that companies can influence competitive interactions to their advantage. To do so, though, they must know how to identify competitors, recognise their behaviours and the consequences, and then design effective actions and reactions.

Between two firms A and B, three types of interaction are possible (see Table 5.1): each competitor is aware of the other's effect on it. When neither competitor is aware of the other, the interaction is an implicit one. When one firm is aware of the interaction but the other is not, the interaction is asymmetric. Each type of interaction is characterised by a typical pattern of behaviours.

In an *explicit interaction*, each firm is aware of its relationship with the other and attempts to manage that relationship to its advantage. The relationship behaviours may be benign or hostile. In a benign situation, the two firms work to maximise the profits of both partners in the interaction by engaging in positive behaviours such as joint marketing or product development, or at least by avoiding negative behaviours such as price cuts. In this connection, openness regarding one's own marketing strategy (e.g. Firm's A) may be advantageous because if the competitor (Firm B) realises that the Firm A wants to focus on a special market then Firm B may search for other attractive markets. In a hostile situation, each firm tries to gain a sustainable advantage over the other, maximising its own gains. Explicit interactions are what we usually think of when we consider competitor interactions, such as Coca-Cola and Pepsi.

In an *implicit interaction*, the relationship is characterised by market behaviours alone. Customer response to the two competitors' actions creates certain outcomes for both organisations, but each firm is ignorant of the other's effect on its business. This is most common in markets with a large number of small competitors. For example, all restaurants in a given city compete with each other to some degree. This also occurs when different companies meet the same needs in very different ways.

In an *asymmetric interaction*, the aware firm has the opportunity to exercise stealth, taking actions that the ignorant competitor will not see. Stealth may allow a firm to steal business from competitors without their knowledge. Asymmetry often arises from differences in firm size: the small firm knows well that it is in an interaction with the large firm, but for the large firm the small firm is inconsequential.

In the fast-food industry, two leading players, McDonald's and Burger King, face the same market trends but have responded in markedly different ways to the obesity backlash. McDonald's has rolled out a variety of foods it promotes as healthy. Burger King has introduced high-fat, high-calorie sandwiches supported by in-your-face, politically incorrect ads. As the dominant player, McDonald's is the lightning rod for the consumer and government backlash on obesity. It cannot afford to ignore these concerns. Smaller players like Burger King, realising this, see an opportunity to cherry-pick share in the less health-conscious fast-food segment. Burger King competes asymmetrically.

Source: Adapted from Courtney *et al.* (2009).

Fast food's leading players: McDonald's and Burger King
Source: © Graham Oliver/Alamy (top); © Tracey Foster/Alamy (bottom)

5.4 HOW DO WE LEARN ABOUT OUR COMPETITORS?

CI activities can theoretically be performed by any person or department in an organisation, not just by marketing or corporate strategy personnel. Traditional CI activities, unlike acts of corporate espionage, include obtaining publicly disseminated or publicly accessible information (such as analysing annual reports) and engaging in routine transactions in open product markets (such as buying and testing a competitor's newest product). These activities are generally viewed as being both legal and ethical (Calof and Wright, 2008).

Once a firm has decided to engage in CI, it can choose from the following classifications of CI (Hannon, 1997).

Proactive or reactive CI

By definition, a proactive approach involves conscious, premeditated acts to avoid being surprised. Proactive tactics include periodic surveillance, continuous monitoring and targeted studies. These acts are more offensive, since they target and investigate identifiable and realistic threats. On the other hand, reactive, more defensive, approaches are more likely to be undertaken in response to competitive threats, whether they are actually realised or merely expected. Of course, there are numerous cost/benefits trade-offs that affect how proactive or reactive a company can be at any given time.

Formal or informal CI

Strategic business unit (SBU)
A unit of the company that has a separate mission, strategy and objectives and that can be planned independently from other company businesses. An SBU can be a company division, a product line within a division, or sometimes a single product or brand.

Formal acquisition is usually much quicker, better organised and more responsive. As might be imagined, it is usually also more expensive. Practically speaking, most formal corporate intelligence systems have at their core a staff that is charged with responsibility for CI operating procedures such as developing a modus operandi for the routine submission of competitor reports. Alternatively, informal intelligence activities, which are the norm for many Western organisations, are often uncoordinated, unfocused and shallow. Not surprisingly, they are usually less expensive. When companies adopt a reactive approach, whether by design or default, individual employees, departments and **strategic business units (SBUs)** may all be engaged in intelligence activities. Unfortunately, these efforts, more often than not, are disjointed, ineffective and inefficient.

No matter how formally or informally the competition is to be monitored, it is imperative for firms to a least identify those competitors who merit surveillance and determine if there are appropriate information sources for finding out more about these companies.

Essentially, three sources of CI can be distinguished: what competitors say about themselves, what others say about them, and what employees of the firm engaged in competitive analysis have observed and learned about competitors. Much information can be obtained at low cost.

As far as information from its own sources is concerned, the company should develop a structured programme to gather competitive information. First, a detailed information gathering programme must be developed. Second, salespeople may be trained to carefully gather and provide information on the competition, using such sources as customers, distributors, dealers and former salespeople. Third, senior marketing people should be encouraged to call on customers and speak to them in-depth. These contacts should provide valuable information on competitors' products and services. Fourth, other people in the company who happen to have some knowledge of competitors should be encouraged to channel this information to an appropriate office (Fleisher, 2008).

Information gathering on the competition has grown dramatically in recent years. Almost all large companies designate someone specially to seek CI. SMEs will normally not have the resources for that.

The information gathering techniques, summarised below, are all legal, although some may involve questionable ethics. A responsible company should carefully review each technique before using it to avoid practices that might be considered illegal or unethical.

Gathering information from internal employees and employees of competing companies

Firms can collect data about their competitors through interviews with new recruits or by speaking with employees of competing companies.

When firms interview, for example, students for jobs, they may pay special attention to those who have worked for competitors, even temporarily. Job seekers are eager to impress and often have not been warned about what they can and cannot divulge.

Companies send engineers to conferences and trade shows to question competitors' technical people.

Probably the oldest tactic in corporate intelligence gathering, companies hire key executives from competitors to find out what they know (Herstein and Mitki, 2008).

Gathering information from competitors' customers

Some customers may give out information on competitors' products. The close cooperative relationship that engineers cultivate with the customer's staff often enables them to learn what new products competitors are offering.

Gathering information from competitors' suppliers

A firm and its main competitor are sometimes supplied by the same subcontractor. As many firms today have close relations with their suppliers, some information exchange may be possible.

Gathering information by observing competitors or by analysing physical evidence

Companies can get to know competitors better by buying their products or by examining other physical evidence. Companies increasingly buy competitors' products and take them apart to determine costs of production and even manufacturing methods.

Gathering information from published materials and public documents

This type of material could be:

- financial reports of the firm
- government reports
- company presentation brochures
- company portraits in industry journals.

Most of this information can be found on the Internet.

Why the Internet is a good source of CI

Internet resources will provide an array of basic information. To paraphrase the old saying, 'All that glitters is not gold', one should be reminded that just because it is on the Internet does not mean it is accurate. WWW is not the source of data, it is the contact connect symbol. The analyst must document the author, method of data collection, date, publisher location and purpose of printing the data.

Reliability
If the same phenomenon is measured repeatedly with the same measurement device and the results are similar then the method is reliable (the 'how' dimension).

All too frequently, novices think they have an authoritative report if a portion of a report is dotted with Internet footnotes. Experienced researchers question the authenticity of data until there has been an opportunity to assess the **reliability** of the Internet (or any) data source. Although sales exaggerations affect few people, the same practice on the Internet could lead to vastly different conclusions unless the information and source credibility are questioned by those who use information in making important strategic decisions.

Falsifying data on the Internet is rare. However, the inability to police the Internet could lead to inaccurate if not intentionally false data inputs. Always keep in mind the fact that it is up to the data collector to verify the quality of the information taken from the Internet.

Types of CI available

In the broadest sense, data sources are either free or available for a fee. Paid-for services are of three types:

1 a database that charges a monthly fee for access to the data provided;
2 services that provide data to subscribers on a per-inquiry basis;
3 research reports which one can acquire from research firms.

Subscription services

There are many online data links that will give subscribers access to special databases. A subscription to Lexis-Nexis is one possibility. Subscribers can get up-to-date information direct from Lexis-Nexis (www.lexisnexis.com). Lexis contains legal materials, whereas Nexis is not focused on legal issues, but is concerned about future interaction.

Lexis-Nexis is one of the leading business intelligence providers. Over 30,000 sources are covered; 3 billion searchable documents make up their service. Over a million new documents are added every week.

Nexis will provide reports on a regular basis (such as *Lexis Monthly*). Each of these Lexis-Nexis monthly updates provides a list of any new articles on a selected subject that have been published in the past month.

5.5 WHAT ARE THE STRENGTHS AND WEAKNESSES OF OUR COMPETITORS?

Having identified our competitors and described how to collect CI the next stage is to complete a competitor audit in order to assess their relative strengths and weaknesses.

Whether competitors can carry out their strategies and reach their goals depends on their resources, capabilities and their resulting strengths and weaknesses. A precise understanding of competitor strengths and weaknesses is an important prerequisite for developing competitor strategy.

This information will enable predictions to be made about the competitor's future behaviour and reactions. It is not sufficient to describe how the competitor is performing in terms of market share and profits. A competitive analysis must diagnose how the competitor has managed to generate such performance outcomes, be they good or bad. In particular, it locates areas of competitive vulnerability. Military strategy suggests that success is most often achieved when strength is concentrated against the enemy's greatest weakness.

The process of assessing a competitor's strengths and weaknesses may take place as part of a marketing audit. As much internal, market and customer information as possible should be gathered. For example, financial data concerning profitability, profit margins, sales and investment levels, market data relating to price levels, market share and distribution channels used, and customer data concerning awareness of brand names, perceptions of brand and company image, product and service quality, and selling ability may be relevant.

Not all of this information will be accessible, and some may not be relevant. The management needs to decide the extent to which each piece of information is relevant. For example, the management must decide how much to spend on measuring customer awareness and perceptions through market research. This process of data gathering needs to be managed so that information is available to compare our company with its chief competitors on the key factors for success in the industry.

A four-stage model, as represented by a competitive benchmarking, can then be used as follows (the result of the competitive benchmarking can be seen in the upper right corner of Figure 3.3):

1 Identify the major attributes that customers value. Ask customers what features and performance levels they look for in choosing a supplier or a product. Different customers will mention different features and benefits (value chain functions). Assess the importance of different attributes. Rate or rank the importance of different functions to customers. The highest ranked functions are called key success factors (KSFs).

2 Assess the company's and the competitors' performance on different value functions.

3   Examine how customers rate the company's performance against a specific major competitor on an attribute-by-attribute basis. The key to gaining competitive advantage is to take each customer segment and examine how the company's offer compares to that of its major competitor. If the company's offer exceeds the competitor's offer on all important attributes, the company can charge a higher price and earn higher profits, or it can charge the same price and gain more market share. However, if the company is seen as performing at a lower level than its major competitors on some important attributes, it must invest in strengthening those attributes or finding other important attributes where it can gain an edge on the competitor.

4   Monitor customer values regularly. The company must review customer values and competitors' standings periodically if it wants to remain strategically effective.

The competence profile for firm A in Figure 3.3 is an example of how a firm is not in accordance with the market (customer) demand in the form of key success factors. The company has its core competences in parts of the value chain's functions where customers place little importance (e.g. market knowledge).

If there is a generally good match between key success factors and firm A's initial position, it is important to concentrate resources and improve this core competence to create sustainable competitive advantages.

If, on the other hand, there is a large gap between customers' demands and the firm's initial position in key success factors as shown in Figure 3.3 (as with the personal selling functions), it may give rise to the following alternatives:

*   improve the firm's initial position;
*   find business areas where firm A's competence profile better suits the market demand and expectations.

As a new business area involves risk, it is often important to identify an eventual gap in a critical success factor as early as possible. In other words, an early warning system must be established that continuously monitors the critical competitive factors so that it is possible to start initiatives that limit the size of an eventual gap as early as possible.

In Figure 3.3, the competence profile of firm B is also shown.

Assessing a competitor's strengths and weaknesses begins with identifying relevant techniques and assets in the industry. Weaknesses might include resource limitations or lack of capital investment. Ways of attacking competitors' strengths and weaknesses include the following:

*   attack geographic regions where a rival has a weak market share or is exerting less competitive effort;
*   attack buyer segments that a rival is neglecting or is poorly equipped to serve;
*   attack rivals that lag on quality, features or product performance; in such cases, a challenger with a better product can often convince the most performance-conscious customers of lagging rivals to switch to its brand;
*   attack rivals that have done a poor job of servicing customers; in such cases, a service-oriented challenger can win a rival's disenchanted customers;
*   attack rivals with weak advertising and brand recognition; a challenger with strong marketing skills and a good image can often take sales from lesser-known rivals.

5.6 MARKET COMMONALITY AND RESOURCE COMMONALITY

Chen (1996) proposed a model where both market commonality (market overlap) and resource similarity (resource overlap) affect the awareness and motivation to take actions and await competitive responses (see Figure 5.4). In this model, a competitor's likelihood of response is influenced by both market commonality and resource similarity.

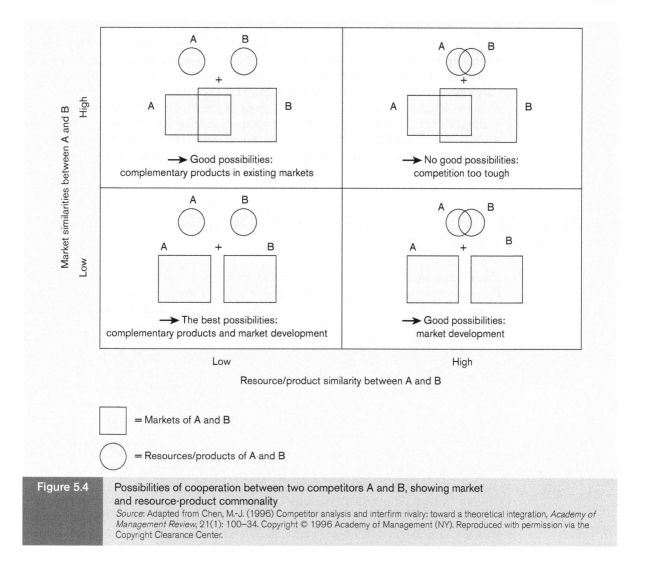

Figure 5.4 | Possibilities of cooperation between two competitors A and B, showing market and resource-product commonality
Source: Adapted from Chen, M.-J. (1996) Competitor analysis and interfirm rivalry: toward a theoretical integration, *Academy of Management Review*, 21(1): 100–34. Copyright © 1996 Academy of Management (NY). Reproduced with permission via the Copyright Clearance Center.

The *high market commonality* between Amazon.com and Barnes & Noble explains the fierce competition between these two companies. Amazon.com became, in a few years, the leading online bookseller in the USA. Barnes & Noble was the largest bookstore chain in the world. It sold books only in the USA and owned at least one store in every major US city. At the end of 1996, it operated 11.5 million square feet of selling space and had more than 20,000 employees. This market commonality explains the 1997 entry of Barnes & Noble into the online market and the subsequent moves and counter-moves of the two companies. On 28 January 1997, Barnes & Noble publicly announced that it planned to become the exclusive bookseller on America Online's (AOL's) Marketplace and to launch its own website later in the spring. On 10 March, Barnes & Noble announced that its website would feature a person-alised book recommendation service that the company had been working on since 1996. On 18 March, Barnes & Noble went online at AOL with a deep discount policy. Barnes & Noble launched its own website (bn.com) on 13 May 1997. Amazon reacted by reducing its prices, once on 10 June 1997 and again on 21 November 1997. Later, on 17 September 1999, Amazon launched Shop to sell rare and out-of-print books matching a service that had been offered by bn.com since November 1998.

The *high resource commonality* between Amazon and eBay also explains the fierce rivalry between these two companies. The two firms are both pure online businesses with few tangible resources. Their main resources are their customer bases. eBay runs the largest person-to-person auction website, connecting some 3.8 million buyers and sellers world-wide. It helps people buy and sell collectibles and antiques as well as many other goods normally sold through flea markets, antique stores and classified advertisements. The success of eBay's dynamic pricing system has been considered as a threat to Amazon's dominance of the online retail industry. So, on 30 March, 1999, Amazon's president Jeff Bezos launched Amazon's auctions in direct competition with eBay. As a reaction, eBay recently polled members on whether they would like to see fixed-price auctions (many said yes) and dealer storefronts. This was a direct counter-attack against Amazon's fixed-price business model.

5.7 WHAT ARE THE OBJECTIVES AND STRATEGIES OF OUR COMPETITORS?

Knowing a competitor's objectives is crucial to predicting how it will respond to changes in the environment, and if strategic changes are likely. Also, a company's strategies are driven by its goals and objectives. For example, in the USA K-Mart was alarmed by Wal-Mart's entry and expansion efforts into areas promising high growth potential.

Understanding the objectives of competitors can give guidance to strategy development on three levels (Fahey, 2007). Goals can indicate where the company is intending to develop and in which markets, either by industry or internationally, major initiatives can be expected. The areas of expansion could indicate markets that are to be particularly competitive but may also signify that companies are not so committed. Where the intention is profitable coexistence, it is often better to compete in areas that are deemed of secondary interest to major companies rather than to compete directly.

Percentage of sales
Setting the promotion budget at a certain percentage of current or forecasted sales or as a percentage of the unit sales price.

Reward structures for staff can also indicate objectives. Where sales staff, for example, are rewarded on a **percentage of sales** commission, that practice suggests that sales volume (rather than profitability) is a key objective.

When competing against a diversified company, ambitious goals in one sector may indicate that commitment to another is diminishing. Equally, very large and diversified companies may often not be able to take advantage of their enormous financial strengths because of their unwillingness to make strategic shifts in their resources. There is also a chance that financially driven companies may be unwilling to take the risks of new ventures, preferring instead to pick the bones of those who were damaged in taking the risk.

Also indicative of future goals can be the *ownership structure* of the competitor. Competitors owned by employees and/or managers may set a higher priority on providing continuity of employment than those owned by conventional shareholders. Likewise, competitors in the public sector may set higher priorities on social goals than profitability. Competitors owned as part of diversified conglomerates may be managed for short-term cash rather than long-term market position objectives.

Assessing competitors' current strategies

Assessing the current strategy involves asking the basic question: 'What exactly is the competitor doing at the moment?' This requires making as full a statement as possible of what competitors are trying to do, and how they are trying to achieve it.

Three main sets of issues need to be addressed with regard to understanding current competitor strategies, as follows:

1 *identification of the market* or markets they have chosen to operate in: their selection of target markets;

2   identification of the way in which they have chosen to operate in those markets: the *strategic focus* they are adopting with regard to the type of competitive advantage they are trying to convey;

3   the supporting *marketing mix* that is being adopted to enable the positioning aimed for to be achieved.

Beyond these three core elements of strategy it can also be helpful to assess the organisation of the marketing effort – the structures adopted – to facilitate implementation of the strategy.

Identification of competitors' chosen markets

Prices

Competitors' prices will often be an indicator of the target market. In grocery retailing, for example, Aldi and Netto have consistently pursued a minimum-range, low-price strategy in attempts to attract price-sensitive, bulk grocery purchasers rather than compete directly with industry leaders such as Tesco and J. Sainsbury on quality and service.

Product features

The features built into products and the type and extent of service offered will be good indicators of the types of customer the competitor is seeking to serve. In the car industry, for example, the products made by Jaguar, a **subsidiary** of Ford, indicate clearly the types of customer being pursued. Skoda, on the other hand, now owned by Volkswagen, offers very different cars to the market, suggesting a completely different target market.

> **Subsidiary**
> A company which is owned by another.

Advertisements and other promotional materials can also give clues as to what the target markets are. The wording of advertisements indicates the values the advertiser is attempting to convey and imbue in the product or service offered. Traditional Volvo advertising has clearly focused on safety, which appeals to safety-conscious, middle-class families. BMW advertising concentrates on technical quality and the pleasures of driving, suggesting a younger target market. The media in which the advertisements appear, or the scheduling adopted, will also give indications of the target market aimed for. Similarly, the distribution channels the competitor chooses to use to link the customer with offerings may give clues as to the targets it is aiming for.

Competitors' strategic focus

As discussed in the competitive triangle model, there are two main routes to creating a competitive advantage. The first is through low costs relative to competitors. The second is through providing valued uniqueness, differentiated products and services that customers will be willing to pay for.

Competitors may be focusing on cost reducing measures rather than expensive product development and promotional strategies. If competitors are following this strategy it is more likely that they will be focusing research and development expenditure on process rather than product development in a bid to reduce manufacturing costs.

Information about a competitor's cost structure is valuable, particularly when considering a low-cost strategy. Such cost structure information should include the competitor's overhead, all costs, investments in assets, and size of labour force.

The most effective competitors compete on the basis of value, offering superior quality, price and reliability. A company with exclusive access to specific raw materials establishes a differential advantage over its competitors. Strategically manoeuvring the variables of the marketing mix can give the company a special edge over competitors. The **cost leadership** route is a tough one for any firm to follow successfully and requires close, relentless attention to all cost drivers. As noted above, in the UK grocery market Aldi and Netto

> **Cost leadership**
> The achievement of the lowest cost position in an industry, serving many segments

have adopted this rigorous approach, restricting product lines and providing a 'no-frills' service.

Providing something different, but of value to customers, is a route to creating competitive advantage that all players in a market can adopt. The creative aspect of this strategy is to identify those differentiating features on which the firm has, or can build, a defensible edge. Signals of differentiation will be as varied as the means of differentiation. All are highly visible to competitors and show the ground on which a given supplier has chosen to compete.

Strategies can also be defined in terms of competitive scope. For example, are competitors attempting to service the whole market, a few segments or a particular niche? If the competitor is a niche player, is it likely that it will be content to stay in that segment or use it as a beachhead to move into other segments in the future? Japanese companies are renowned for their use of small niche markets as springboards for market segment expansion (e.g. the small car segments in the USA and Europe).

Knowing the strategic thrust of competitors can help our strategic decision making. For example, knowing that our competitors are considering expansion in North America but not Europe will make expansion into Europe a more attractive strategic option for our company.

Competitors' supporting marketing mix

Analysis of the marketing mix adopted by competitors can give useful clues as to the target markets at which they are aiming and the competitive advantage they are seeking to build with those targets. Analysis of the mix can also show areas where the competitor is vulnerable to attack.

The four Ps

Product

At the product level, competitor analysis will attempt to deduce positioning strategy. This involves assessing a competitor product's target market and differential advantage. The marketing mix strategies (e.g. price levels, media used for promotion, distribution channels) may indicate the target market, and market research into customer perceptions can be used to assess relative differential advantages.

Companies and products need to be continuously monitored for changes in positioning strategy. For example, Volvo's traditional positioning strategy based on safety has been modified to give more emphasis to performance.

Price

Analysis of competitor pricing strategies may identify gaps in the market. For example, a firm marketing vodka in the USA noted that the leader offered products at a number of relatively high price points but had left others vacant. This enabled the firm to position its own offerings in a different market sector.

Place

Understanding the distribution strengths and weaknesses of competitors can also identify opportunities. Dell, for example, decided to market their PCs direct to businesses rather than distribute them through office retail stores where their established competitors were already strong.

Promotion

Both the message and the media being used by competitors warrant close analysis. Some competitors may be better than others at exploiting new media such as satellite or cable. Others may be good in using public relations. Again, analysis will show where competitors are strong, and where they are vulnerable.

EXHIBIT 5.2
Predicting competitors in the video game
console industry

In the video game console business, the strategies of Microsoft and Sony, which are attempting to dominate next-generation systems, are largely predictable – based on each company's tangible and intangible assets and current market position. Although the core businesses of the two competitors will be affected by video game consoles differently, both sides see them as potential digital hubs replacing some current stand-alone consumer electronic devices, such as DVD players, and interconnecting with high-definition televisions, personal computers, MP3 players, digital cameras, and so forth.

For **Sony**, which has valuable resources and assets in consumer electronics – and in audio and video content (hardware) – it is important to establish the PlayStation as the living-room hub, so that any cannibalisation of the company's consumer electronics businesses comes from within. After the victory of Sony's Blu-ray standard over Toshiba's HD-DVD, Sony stands to realise a huge pay-off in future licensing revenues. The PlayStation, which plays only Blu-ray disks, is thus one of the company's most important vehicles in driving demand for Blu-ray gaming, video and audio content.

Microsoft has limited hardware and content businesses but dominates personal computers and network software. Establishing the Xbox as the living-room hub would therefore help to protect and extend its software businesses. For Microsoft, it is crucial that the 'digital living room' of the future should run on Microsoft software. If Apple products occupy future 'iHome' living rooms, the Microsoft's software business might suffer.

Sony and Microsoft therefore have different motives for fighting this console battle. It is predicted that they will produce consoles which, so far, have been far superior technologically to previous systems and interconnect easily with the Internet, computers and a wide variety of consumer electronics devices. It is also predicted that both companies would price their consoles below cost to establish an installed base in the world's living rooms quickly. For Microsoft and Sony, the resource-based view of strategy helps us to understand that this battle is about far more than dominance in the video game industry – it is about '*occupying the living room*'.

Nintendo, in contrast, is largely a pure-play video game company and thus an asymmetric competitor to Microsoft and Sony. Nintendo launched its Wii in November 2006. The resource-based view of strategy explains why Nintendo's latest console, the Wii, focuses primarily on the game-playing experience and isn't positioned as a digital hub for living rooms. The Wii's most innovative feature is a new, easy-to-use controller appealing to new and hardcore gamers alike. The Wii has few of the expensive digital-hub features built into the rival consoles and thus made its debut with a lower retail price.

The sales results in the world market indicates that the Wii's easy-to-play concept is about to be the winner – at least short term (until summer 2009).

Source: Adapted from Courtney *et al.* (2009).

5.8 WHAT ARE THE RESPONSE PATTERNS OF OUR COMPETITORS?

The ultimate aim of competitor analysis is to determine competitors' response profiles – that is, how a competitor might behave when faced with various environmental and competitive changes.

To succeed in predicting a competitor's next move, the marketing manager has to have a good feel for the rival's situation, how its managers think, and what its options are. Doing the necessary research can be time consuming since the information comes in bits and pieces from many sources. But scouting competitors well enough to anticipate their next moves allows managers to prepare effective countermoves and to take rivals' probable actions into account in designing the best course of action.

In evaluating the response patterns of our competitors the following questions are important:

- Is the competitor satisfied with the current position? If yes, this competitor may allow indirect competitors to exploit new markets without being perturbed. Alternatively, if this competitor is trying to improve its current position, it may be quick in chasing market changes or be obsessed by improving its own short-term profits performance. Knowledge of a company's future goals will clearly play an important part in answering this question.

- What likely moves or strategy shifts will the competitor make? History can provide some guide as to the way that companies behave. Goals, assumptions and capabilities will also give some guidance to how the company can effectively respond to market changes. After looking at these a company may be able to judge which of its own alternative strategies is likely to result in the most favourable reaction on the part of the competitors.

- Where is the competitor vulnerable? In a competitive market success is best achieved by concentrating strength against weakness. It is foolish for a firm to attack a market leader in areas where it is strongest.

The complacency of leaders in markets can provide major opportunities. The competitor's own feeling of invulnerability may be the weakness that could lead them to a downfall. What will provoke the greatest and most effective retaliation by the competitor?

Whereas market leaders may accept some peripheral activity, because of the low margins they perceive, or the low market volume involved, other actions are likely to provoke intense retaliation. This is often the case in price sensitive markets, where one competitor reduces the price (e.g. reducing petrol prices) in the hope of gaining market share. Sometimes the market leader may even go to the business press and claim that every price cut would be matched. Sometimes this step prevents a fierce price war.

EXHIBIT 5.3
Role play in CI as a predictor of competitive behaviour

At last, it's time to pull all of this together and come to something you can really use. Here are the vital sub-steps:

- Write a 'competitive novel'. If the competitor were a novel, what would be going on inside the heads of its key characters (including how they think about you)? Try this as an actual written exercise.

- Role play possible sequels to the story so far. Given what you've learned of the goals and assumptions that drive the competitor (and those that drive your own company), how would they respond to actions you have planned? How would you then respond? Play two or more rounds against your plans, not in an effort to absolutely predict what the competitor's actions will be, but to understand what kind of moves they would consider, and to make sure that you are prepared to deal with the consequences.

- Assess results and identify new questions. Nothing is static in the competitive world. As you assess the results of your effort, new questions will arise. Given the possible response scenarios you've developed, it may now be important to know, for instance, whether they could launch their new product in 7 months, or whether it has to be 18. These critical questions become worthy of further research, analysis and monitoring.

Source: Adapted from House (2000).

A result of the above is that most competitors fall into one of four categories:

1 *The laid-back competitor*: a competitor that does not react quickly or strongly to a rival's move. Reasons for a slow response vary. Laid-back competitors may feel their customers are loyal; they may be milking the business; they may be slow in noticing the move; they may lack the funds to react. Rivals must try to assess the reasons for the behaviour.

2 *The selective competitor*: a competitor that reacts only to certain types of attack. It might respond to price cuts, but not to advertising expenditure increases. Shell and Q8 are selective competitors, responding only to price cuts but not to promotions. Knowing what a key competitor reacts to gives its rivals a clue as to the most feasible lines of attack.

3 *The tiger competitor*: a competitor that reacts swiftly and strongly to any assault. Procter & Gamble does not let a new detergent come easily into the market.

4 *The stochastic competitor*: a competitor that does not exhibit a predictable reaction pattern. There is no way of predicting the competitor's action on the basis of its economic situation, history or anything else. Many SMEs are stochastic competitors, competing on miscellaneous fronts when they can afford to.

The aim of this step is to force a company to look beyond its own moves and towards those of its competitors and, like a great player of chess, think several moves ahead. It involves a firm thinking of its moves in a broad, strategic framework rather than the incremental manner in which strategies often emerge. Or, by following a series of seemingly small incremental shifts in pricing and promotion, a firm may be perceived to be making a major play in the marketplace and incur the wrath of major players.

5.9 HOW CAN WE SET UP AN ORGANISATION FOR CI?

Competitive, or business, intelligence is a powerful new management tool that enhances a firm's ability to succeed in today's highly competitive global markets. It provides early warning intelligence and a framework for better understanding and countering competitors' initiatives. Competitive activities can be monitored in-house or assigned to an outside firm.

Within the organisation, competitive information should be acquired both at the corporate level and at the SBU level. At the corporate level, competitive intelligence is concerned with competitors' investment strengths and priorities. At the SBU level, the major interest is in marketing strategy, that is, product, pricing, distribution and promotion strategies that a competitor is likely to pursue. The true pay-off of CI comes from the SBU review.

The CI task can be assigned to a SBU strategic planner, to a marketing person within the SBU who may be a market researcher or a product/market manager, or to a member of staff. Whoever is given the task of gathering CI should be allowed adequate time and money to do a thorough job.

International CI structures

When establishing an international CI structure, there are several ways of constructing the responsibilities based on geographic information needs, resources available and anticipated demand. When anticipated demand is low, the assignment of international responsibilities should probably fall to the initial project analyst. When anticipated demand is high or moderate, more formal structures are beneficial.

Limited human resources/additional responsibilities

When staffing is limited, a single individual may need to be assigned to cover the entire world. A better format though is to divide the world's regions among the CI team. If only a single

EXHIBIT 5.4
Shadow teams in CI

Shadow teams provide a way of integrating the firm's internal knowledge with external competitive intelligence. Shadow team members should represent a cross-functional composite, drawn from the organisation's best and brightest people. Each team's mission is to 'shadow' a chosen key competitor and to learn everything possible about the rival from published data, firm personnel, network connections, etc. As information is collected and analysed, the shadow team becomes a knowledge base that may soon operate as a think tank.

SHADOW TEAM CASE STUDY: PHARMACEUTICAL FIRM

A medium-size US pharmaceutical firm structured shadow teams around ailment classifications. During scanning activities, a shadow member heard a rumour from a US Food and Drug Administration contact, which was corroborated by a field sales person, that a new drug positioned to rival the firm's market leader was close to receiving approval. An upcoming conference gave the shadow team an opportunity to gather intelligence and validate – or refute – the rumour. Network connections identified the academic institution that was conducting the competitor product trials. During an evening cocktail party, shadow team members independently engaged scientists in discussions about chemistry and related topics. In time, they learned about the trials (although the product or sponsor was never noted by name), confirmed the rumour and, just as important, identified new procedures employed in clinical testing.

At the same time, the shadow team was charged with finding out why competitors were constantly beating the firm to market with new categories of drugs. Their experience with competitor scientists at the conference influenced the team's decision to launch a counter-intelligence investigation of their own firm. They learned that their own scientists, both in-house and those contracted to run clinical trials, behaved in the same way as the scientists at the conference, by discussing chemical issues close to the trials.

This firm obtained two results from this:

- It launched a campaign to bolster its product's market share.

- A programme was created to enhance awareness of protecting intellectual property and competitive information throughout the organisation. The shadow team drove home the importance not only of learning, but also of guarding knowledge.

Source: Adapted from Rothberg (1999).

region is of interest, such as Latin America, and the CI team has two full-time analysts, then assign each one half of the region; one would have South America, while the other would focus on, say, Central America, Mexico and the Caribbean. This division allows familiarity with and understanding of the culture, people, governments and commercial structures to grow. If only specific countries are being examined, then split them equally among the analysts.

Expanded human resources/single responsibility

In the event that budget or staffing can allow for specialists in specific international regions, based on demand, assign those responsibilities accordingly. A critical component of a single responsibility focus is the ability to maintain perspective within the scope of the organisation as a whole. The danger of confusing significant and insignificant information can be a problem when analysts are not able to maintain size and scope perspectives.

Should the CI team be able to hire someone specifically for an internationally focused intelligence assignment, background and experience in that culture may be preferable, but education and international orientation are the primary objectives. Specific requirements include active reading and listening skills to break down artificial or secondary barriers caused by translation; interest and enjoyment in working with people from other socio-economic backgrounds and cultural upbringing, and awareness of the home culture's biases, expectations and beliefs. In other words, hire someone who understands and is sensitive to these facts.

For example, US citizens typically prefer space between themselves and those around them and tend to depend on schedules and set times. Latin Americans tend to interact when physically closer, and are patient when the meeting scheduled at 1 pm takes place at 4 pm.

5.10 SUMMARY

This chapter has explored the key issues in analysing competitors and creating competitive advantage. Firms need to understand their competitors because corporate success results from providing more value to customers than the competition (competitive triangle). To prepare an effective marketing strategy, a company must study its competitors as well as its actual and potential customers.

Competitor analysis and CI focus on competitor identification, an audit of competitor capabilities (strengths and weaknesses), their objectives and strategies and prediction of response patterns. The aim is to provide a basis for creating a competitive advantage, anticipating future actions, and estimating how they will react to future actions our company may take.

There is no doubt that competitive pressure will continue to intensify in all markets. The forces that are active now are unlikely to diminish in the near future. Increasing numbers of companies will start to collect CI from internal and external sources and the number of specialists from whom they can outsource will grow.

As important as a competitive orientation is in today's global market, companies should not overdo the emphasis on competitors. Companies should manage a good balance of consumer and competitor monitoring.

In the next chapter we shall see that it might be beneficial to enter into relationships with former competitors.

CASE STUDY 5.1

Cereal Partners Worldwide (CPW)
No. 2 world player is challenging the No. 1 – Kellogg

On a lovely spring morning in April 2007, while giving her kids some Cheerios, the CEO of Cereal Partners Worldwide S.A. (CPW), Carol Smith, thinks about how CPW might expand international sales and/or capture further market shares in the saturated breakfast cereals market. Right now, CPW is the clear No. 2 in the world market for breakfast cereals, but it is a tough competition, primarily with the Kellogg Company, which is the world market leader.

Maybe there would be other ways of gaining new sales in this competitive market? Carol has just read the business bestseller *Blue Ocean Strategy* and she is fascinated by the thought of moving competition in the cereals breakfast market from the 'red ocean' to the 'blue ocean'. The question is, how?

Maybe it would be better just to take the 'head-on' battle with Kellogg Company. After all, CPW has managed to beat Kellogg in several minor international markets (e.g. in the Middle and Far East).

The children have finished their Cheerios and it is time to drive them to the kindergarten in Lausanne, Switzerland, where CPW has its HQ.

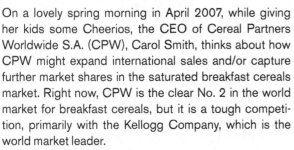

Later that day, Carol has to present the long-term global strategy for CPW, so she hurries to her office and starts preparing the presentation. One of her marketing managers has prepared a background report about CPW and its position in the world breakfast cereals market. The following shows some important parts of the report.

History of breakfast cereals

Ready-to-eat cereals first appeared during the late 1800s. According to one account, John Kellogg, a doctor who belonged to a vegetarian group, developed wheat and corn flakes to extend the group's dietary choices. John's brother, Will Kellogg, saw potential in the innovative grain products and initiated commercial production and marketing. Patients at a Battle Creek, Michigan, sanitarium were among Kellogg's first customers.

Another cereal producer with roots in the nineteenth century was the Quaker Oats Company. In 1873, the North Star Oatmeal Mill built an oatmeal plant in Cedar Rapids, Iowa. North Star reorganised with other enterprises and together they formed Quaker Oats in 1901.

The Washburn Crosby Company, a predecessor to General Mills, entered the market during the 1920s. The company's first ready-to-eat cereal, Wheaties, was introduced to the American public in 1924. According to General Mills, Wheaties was developed when a Minneapolis clinician spilled a mixture of gruel that he was making for his patients on a hot stove.

Cereal Partners Worldwide (CPW)

Cereal Partners Worldwide (CPW) was formed in 1990 as a 50:50 joint venture between Nestlé and General Mills (see Figure 5.5).

General Mills (USA)

General Mills, a leading global manufacturer of consumer food products, operates in more than 30 global markets and exports to over 100 countries. General Mills has 66 production facilities: 34 are located in the United States; 15 in the Asia/Pacific region; 6 in Canada; 5 in Europe; 5 in Latin America and Mexico; and 1 in South Africa. The company is headquartered in Minneapolis, Minnesota. In financial year 2008 the total net sales were US $13.6 billion of which 17 per cent came from outside the United States.

In October 2001 General Mills completed the largest acquisition in its history when it purchased the Pillsbury Company from Diageo. The US $10.4 billion deal almost doubled the size of the company, and consequently boosted General Mills's worldwide ranking, making General Mills one of the world's largest food companies. However, the company is heavily debt-laden following its Pillsbury acquisition, which will continue to eat into operating and net profits for the next few years.

The company now has more than 100 US consumer brands, including Betty Crocker, Cheerios, Yoplait, Pillsbury Doughboy, Green Giant and Old El Paso.

Integral to the successes of General Mills has been its ability to build and sustain huge brand names and maintain continued net growth. Betty Crocker, originally a pen name invented in 1921 by an employee in the consumer response department, has become an umbrella brand for products as diverse as cookie mixes to ready meals. The Cheerios cereal brand, which grew rapidly in the US post-war generation, remains one of the top cereal brands worldwide.

However, heavy domestic dependence leaves the company vulnerable to variations in that market, such as

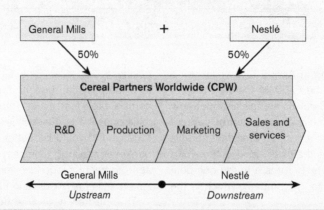

| Figure 5.5 | The CPW joint venture |

Source: The Nestlé name and images are reproduced with kind permission of Société des Produits Nestlé SA.

supermarket price-cutting or sluggish sales in prominent product types such as breakfast cereals.

Internationally, General Mills uses its 50 per cent stake in Cereal Partners Worldwide (CPW) to sell its breakfast cereals abroad. Cereal sales have faced tough competition recently leading to significant drops in sales and particularly tough competition from private labels.

Nestlé (Switzerland)

Founded in 1866, Nestlé is the world's largest food and beverage company in terms of sales. The company began in the field of dairy-based products and later diversified to food and beverages in the 1930s. Nestlé is headquartered in Vevey, Switzerland, and the company has 500 factories in 83 countries. It has about 406 subsidiaries located across the world. The company employs 247,000 people around the world, of which 131,000 employees work in factories, while the remaining employees work in administration and sales.

Nestlé's businesses are classified into six divisions based on product groups, which include Beverages; Milk Products, Nutrition and Ice Cream; Prepared Dishes and Cooking Aids; Chocolate, Confectionery and Biscuits; PetCare; and Pharmaceutical Products. Nestlé's global brands include Nescafé, Taster's Choice, Nestlé Pure Life, Perrier, Nestea, Nesquik, Milo, Carnation, Nido, Nestlé, Milkmaid, Sveltesse, Yoco, Mövenpick, Lactogen, Beba, Nestogen, Cerelac, Nestum, PowerBar, Pria, Nutren, Maggi, Buitoni, Toll House, Crunch, Kit-Kat, Polo, Chef, Purina, Alcon, and L'Oréal (equity stake).

Nestlé reported net sales of $110 billion for the fiscal year 2008.

CPW (HQ in Switzerland)

CPW markets cereals in more than 130 countries, except for the United States and Canada, where the two companies market themselves seperately. The joint venture was established in 1990 and the agreement also extends to the production of private label cereals in the UK. Volume growth for CPW was 4 per cent in 2008. The company's cereals are sold under the Nestlé brand, although many originated from General Mills. Brand names manufactured (primarily by General Mills) under the Nestlé name under this agreement include Corn Flakes, Crunch, Fitness, Cheerios and Nesquik. Shredded Wheat and Shreddies were once made by Nabisco, but are now marketed by CPW.

Headquartered in Lausanne, Switzerland, CPW has 14 factories and employs over 3,500 people all over the world. The CPW turnover in 2008 was a little less than US $2 billion.

When CPW was established in 1990 each partner brought distinctive competences into the joint venture:

General Mills:
- proven cereal marketing expertise;
- technical excellence in products and production processes;
- broad portfolio of successful brand.

Nestlé:
- world's largest food company;
- strong worldwide organisation;
- deep marketing and distribution knowledge.

CPW is No. 2 in most international markets, but it is also market leader in some of the smaller breakfast cereal markets such as China (50 per cent market share), Poland (40 per cent market share), Turkey (50 per cent market share), East/Central Europe (50 per cent market share) and South-East Asia (50 per cent market share).

Cereal Partners Worldwide has performed best in developing markets such as Russia and China, where market leader Kellogg has not yet established a strong presence. Although the Russian and Chinese markets are still relatively small in global terms (with US $263 million and US $71 million of sales in a US $20 billion global industry), they are growing rapidly. Moreover, per capita consumption rates are still very low (particularly in China), leaving considerable scope for future growth.

The world market for breakfast cereals

In the early 2000s breakfast cereal makers were facing stagnant, if not declining, sales. Gone are the days of the family breakfast, of which a bowl of cereal was standard fare. The fast-paced American lifestyle has more and more consumers eating breakfast on the go. Quick-serve restaurants like McDonald's, ready-to-eat breakfast bars, bagels and muffins offer consumers less labour-intensive alternatives to cereal. Although the value of product shipped by cereal manufacturers has grown in absolute figures, increased revenues came primarily from price hikes rather than market growth.

English-speaking nations represented the largest cereal markets. Consumption in non-English markets was estimated at only one-fourth the amount consumed by English speakers (see Table 5.2), where the breakfast cereal consumption per capita is 6 kg in UK, but only 1.5 kg in south-west Europe (France, Spain and Portugal). On the European continent, consumption per capita averaged 1.5 kg per year.

Growth in the cereal industry has been slow to non-existent in this century. The question at hand for the

Table 5.2	Breakfast cereal consumption per capita per year – 2008

Region	Per capita consumption per year (kg)
Sweden	9.0
Canada	7.0
UK	6.0
Australia	6.0
USA	5.0
South-west Europe (France, Spain)	1.5
South-east Asia	0.1
Russia	0.1

industry is how to remake cereal's image in light of the new culture. Tinkering with flavourings and offerings, such as the recent trend toward the addition of dried fresh fruit, proves some relief, but with over 150 different choices on store shelves and 20 new offerings added annually, variety has done more to overwhelm than excite consumers. In addition, cereal companies are committing fewer dollars to their marketing budgets.

Development in geographical regions

As seen in Table 5.3, the United States is by far the largest breakfast cereals market in the world. In total North America accounts for 50 per cent of the global sales of $20 billion in 2008. The United States accounts for about 90 per cent of the North American market.

The European region accounts for 30 per cent of global sales, at US $6 billion in 2008. By far the largest market is the UK, contributing nearly 30 per cent of the regional total, with France and Germany other key, if notably smaller, players. Eastern Europe is a minor breakfast cereal market, reflecting the product's generally new status in the region. It contributed just 6 per cent of world sales in 2008. However, the market is vibrant as new lifestyles born from growing urbanisation and westernisation – key themes in emerging market development – have fuelled steady sales growth. Despite its low level of per capita spending, Russia is the largest market in Eastern Europe, accounting for over 40 per

cent of regional sales in 2008. The continued steady growth of this market underpinned overall regional development over the review period. Cereals remain a niche market in Russia, as they do across the region, with the product benefiting from a perception of novelty. A key target for manufacturers has been children and young women, at which advertising has been aimed.

The Australasian breakfast cereals sector, like Western Europe and North America dominated by a single nation, Australia, is becoming increasingly polarised. In common with the key US and UK markets, breakfast cereals in Australia are suffering from a high degree of maturity, with annual growth at a low single-digit level.

The Latin American breakfast cereals sector is the third largest in the world, but at US $2 billion in 2008, it is notably overshadowed by the vastly larger North American and Western European markets. However, in common with these developed regions, one country plays a dominant role in the regional make-up, Mexico, accounting for nearly 60 per cent of the overall breakfast cereal markets in Latin America.

In common with Eastern Europe, breakfast cereal sales, whilst small in Africa and the Middle East, have displayed marked growth in recent years as a direct result of greater urbanisation and a growing trend (in some areas) towards westernisation. Given the overriding influence of this factor on market development, sales are largely concentrated in the more developed regional markets, such as Israel and South Africa,

Table 5.3	World market for breakfast cereals by region – 2008

Region	Billion US$	%
North America	10	50
Europe	6	30
Rest of the world	4	20
Total	20	100

where the investment by multinationals has been at its highest.

In Asia the concept of breakfast cereals is relatively new, with the growing influence of Western culture fostering a notable increase in consumption in major urban cities. Market development has been rapid in China, reflecting the overall rate of industry expansion in the country, with breakfast cereals sales rising by 19 per cent in 2008. In the region's developed markets, in particular Japan, market performance is broadly similar, although the key growth driver is different, in that it is health. Overall, in both developed and developing markets, breakfast cereals are in their infancy.

Health trend

With regards to health, breakfast cereals have been hurt by the rise of fad diets such as Atkins and South Beach, which have heaped much scorn on carbohydrate-based products. The influence of these diets is on the wane but their footprint remains highly visible on national eating trends. In addition, the high sugar content of children's cereals has come under intense scrutiny, which has caused a downturn in this sector, although the industry is now coming back with a range of 'better for you' variants.

Regarding convenience, this trend, once a growth driver for breakfast cereals, has now become a threat, with an increasing number of consumers opting to skip breakfast. Portability has become a key facet of convenience, a development that has fed the emergence and expansion of breakfast bars at the expense of traditional foods, such as breakfast cereals. In an increasingly cash-rich, time-poor society, consumers are opting to abandon a formal breakfast meal and instead are relying on an 'on-the-go' solution, such as breakfast bars or pastries. These latter products, in particular breakfast bars, are taking share from cereals, a trend that looks set to gather pace in the short term.

Trends in product development

Consumer awareness of health and nutrition has also played a major part in shaping the industry in recent years. Cereal manufacturers began to tout the benefits of eating breakfast cereal on the package – vitamin-fortified, low in fat and a good source of fibre. Another trend, begun in the 1990s and picking up steam in the 2000s, is adding dehydrated whole fruits to cereal, which provides colour, flavour and nutritional value. Yet touting health benefits to adults and marketing film characters to children have not been sufficient to reinvigorate this mature industry.

Under the difficult market conditions, cereal packaging is receiving new attention. Packaging was a secondary consideration, other than throwing in special offers to tempt kids. But these days, with meal occasions boiled down to their bare essentials, packaging and delivery have emerged as key weapons in the cereal marketer's arsenal. New ideas circulating in the industry usually include doing away with the traditional cereal box, which has undergone little change in its lifetime. Alternatives range from clear plastic containers to a return of the small variety six-packs.

Trends in distribution

Supermarkets tend to be the dominant distribution format for breakfast cereals. The discounter format is dominated by mass merchandisers, the most famous example of which is Wal-Mart in the United States. This discounter format tends to favour shelf-stable, packaged products and as a result they are increasingly viewed as direct competitors to supermarkets.

Independent food stores have suffered a decline during the past years. They have been at a competitive disadvantage compared to their larger and better resourced chained competitors.

Trends in advertising

Advertising expenditures of most cereal companies were down in recent years due to decreases in consumer spending. However, there are still a lot of marketing activities going on.

General Mills has a comprehensive marketing programme for each of its core brands, from traditional television and print advertisements to in-store promotions, coupons and free gifts. In 2002, the company teamed up with US publisher Simon & Schuster to include books or audio CDs with the purchase of its Oatmeal Crisp Raisin and Basic 4 cereals.

Other promotions have included free Hasbro computer games included in boxes, promotion of new millennium pennies and golden dollars in 2000, and the inclusion of scale models of the Cheerios-sponsored NASCAR.

In response to Kellogg's 2001 launch of Special K Red Berries, General Mills countered with the introduction of freeze-dried fruit in Cheerios, with Berry Burst and Triple Berry Burst product extensions from February 2003. The introduction is a response to the need for the packaging to communicate the inclusion of real berries in the box and not just flavouring. Consequently, the chosen designs consisted of vibrant red and purple boxes, each featuring a spoonful of Cheerios and fruit splashing in milk. Since freeze-dried fruit tends to absorb moisture, the company was also compelled to develop a more moisture-resistant package liner.

The introduction of Berry Burst Cheerios was supported by a US$40 million advertising and promotional campaign that included TV advertising, consumer couponing, outdoor advertising, in-store sampling and merchandising.

Celebrity glamour

Celebrity endorsements continue to play a critical part of General Mills's marketing strategies, in particular its association with sporting personalities dating back to the 1930s with baseball sponsorship. One of the main lines of celebrity endorsement involves Wheaties boxes and a long line of sports people have appeared on the box since the 1930s. In 2001, Tiger Woods, spokesman for the Wheaties brand, appeared on special edition packaging for Wheaties to commemorate his victory of four Grand Slam golf titles.

Distribution

General Mills distributes the majority of its products directly through its own sales organisation to retailers, cooperatives and wholesalers. In Europe and Asia-Pacific the company licenses products for local production, but it also exports to over 100 different countries.

New products, new channels

New products and new product innovations have helped create new distribution channels for General Mills recently. The success of General Mills's snack products has helped create a large demand for products in convenience stores and the company has actively developed products to meet the demands of the convenience store consumer such as its healthy Chex Mex range. A new chocolate-flavoured Chex Mex was added to the product line in 2005.

The development of a cereal-in-a-bowl range has helped create new outlets for General Mills's products in college cafeterias and hotel restaurants. This may see the development of additional products to complement these channels.

Traditional channels

Traditional retailers such as supermarkets continue to play a major role in the distribution of General Mills's products, and the company has an extensive number of cereal, snack, meal and yoghurt brands to maintain shelf space in major retail outlets.

In the United States General Mills and Nestlé market each of their breakfast cereal products independently, because the CPW only covers international markets outside the United States.

Private label competition intensifies

Across many categories, rising costs have led to price increases in branded products which have not been matched by any pricing actions taken in private labels. As a result, the price gaps between branded and private label products have increased dramatically and in some cases can be as much as 30 per cent.

This creates intense competitive environments for branded products, particularly in categories such as cereals which is one of General Mills's biggest markets, as consumers have started to focus more on price than brand identity. This shift in focus is partly the result of private labels' increased quality as they compete for consumer loyalty and confidence in their label products.

Competitors

Kellogg's

The company that makes breakfast foods and snacks for millions began with only 25 employees in Battle Creek in 1906. Today, Kellogg Company employs more than 25,000 people, manufactures in 17 countries and sells its products in more than 180 countries.

Kellogg was the first American company to enter the foreign market for ready-to-eat breakfast cereals. Company founder Will Keith (W.K.) Kellogg was an early believer in the potential of international growth and began establishing Kellogg's as a global brand with the introduction of Kellogg's Corn Flakes® in Canada in 1914. As success followed and demand grew, Kellogg Company continued to build manufacturing facilities around the world, including Sydney, Australia (1924), Manchester, England (1938), Queretaro, Mexico (1951), Takasaki, Japan (1963), Bombay, India (1994) and Toluca, Mexico (2004).

Kellogg Company is the leader among global breakfast cereal manufacturers with 2005 sales revenue of $10.2 billion (net earnings were $980 million). Wal-Mart Stores, Inc. and its affiliates, accounted for approximately 17 per cent of consolidated net sales during 2005.

Kellogg Company was the world's market leader in ready-to-eat cereals throughout most of the twentieth century. In 2005, Kellogg had 30 per cent of the world market share for breakfast cereals (see Table 5.4). Canada, the United Kingdom, and Australia represented Kellogg's three largest overseas markets.

A few well-known Kellogg products are Corn Flakes, Frosted Mini-Wheats, Corn Pops and Fruit Loops.

Table 5.4				

The world market for breakfast cereals, by company – 2008

Manufacturer	Germany market share (%)	UK market share (%)	USA market share (%)	World market share (%)
Kellogg Company	25	30	30	30
CPW	13	14	26	20
(General Mills + Nestlé)				
PepsiCo (Quaker)	–	5	15	10
Weetabix	–	14	–	5
Private label	35	16	10	15
Others	27	21	19	20
Total	100	100	100	100

PepsiCo

In August 2001, PepsiCo merged with Quaker Foods, thereby expanding its existing portfolio. Quaker's family of brands includes Quaker Oatmeal, Cap'n Crunch and Life cereals, Rice-A-Roni and Near East side dishes, and Aunt Jemima pancake mixes and syrups.

The Quaker Food's first puffed product, 'Puffed Rice', was introduced in 1905. In 1992, Quaker Oats held an 8.9 per cent share of the ready-to-eat cereal market, and its principal product was Cap'n Crunch. Within the smaller hot cereal segment, however, the company held approximately 60 per cent of the market. In addition to cereal products, Quaker Oats produced Aunt Jemima pancake mix and Gatorade sports drinks.

The PepsiCo brands in the breakfast cereal sector include Cap'n Crunch, Puffed Wheat, Crunchy Bran, Frosted Mini Wheats and Quaker.

Despite recent moves to extend its presence into new markets, PepsiCo tends to focus on its North American operations.

Weetabix

Weetabix is a UK manufacturer, with a relatively high market share (10 per cent) in United Kingdom. The company is owned by a private investment group – Lion Capital. The company sells its cereals in over 80 countries and has a product line that includes Weetabix, Weetos and Alpen. Weetabix is headquartered in Northamptonshire, UK. In 2005 Weetabix had an estimated turnover of US$1 billion.

The following section describes one of CPW's successful entries into an emerging market (China).

CPW enters China

CPW entered the Chinese breakfast cereals market in 2004, when it opened a manufacturing facility in the city of Tianjin, and it has relied on a combination of strong branding and intensive marketing to gain market share, particularly in children's cereals, where its market share stood at 60 per cent in 2005.

With most indigenous players in breakfast cereals still evolving, they tend to have limited marketing budgets and find it very difficult to compete. All of CPW's breakfast cereals are marketed under the name 'Que Cao', which means bird's nest in Mandarin. This name, together with a universal visual identity/logo and the tagline 'Choose Quality, Choose Nestlé' are the cornerstones of its Chinese marketing strategy, appearing on packaging, point-of-sale materials and media advertising. In-store promotions and sampling are also utilised. Moreover, unlike many of its indigenous rivals, CPW spends heavily on television advertising.

Thus, the marketing of these breakfast cereals is integrated into a wider portfolio of products. The Nestlé brand has had a presence in the Chinese packaged food market since 1990, providing an excellent springboard for the launch of Cereal Partners Worldwide in the country. However, this approach is not without its dangers, as demonstrated in 2005 when Nestlé's reputation in China took a hit after its baby formula was found to be contaminated with iodine. In this case, the scandal did not seem to have a serious impact on CPW's Chinese operations.

Nestlé is segmenting the breakfast cereals market into two groups: urban and rural customers. It targets its latest and most innovative products at the wealthier urban population, which is forecast to become the majority in around 2010, emphasising issues relating to health and wellness. In terms of China's diminishing rural population, who have significantly less disposable income than their urban counterparts, it takes a lower-cost approach, adapting existing product lines and highlights such issues as basic nutrition and affordability, as well as quality and safety.

Children's cereals accounted for 29 per cent of all Chinese breakfast cereal sales by value in 2008, not significantly different from the global figure of 30 per cent. However, adult breakfast cereal consumption is growing at a faster rate than that of children, which may also put pressure on the overall market shares of CPW in China and globally.

In China, there are two contradictory forces at play. Although the country's birth rate fell significantly, mainly due to the government's 'One Child' policy, disposable income is rising rapidly, so families now have much more money to spend on each child. As a result, the current generation, dubbed China's 'Little Emperors' by some marketers, would appear to be a ripe market for premium and value-added products, which CPW will have to exploit if its leadership of this category is not to be overhauled.

Another risk for Cereal Partners Worldwide is that it is relatively weak in hot cereals, which accounted for almost 53 per cent of total breakfast cereals sales in 2005 and is forecast to grow to 57 per cent by 2011. In contrast, the share of children's cereals is predicted to decline from 29 per cent to 26 per cent over the same period.

CPW's initial market entry strategy into the Chinese market was heavily based on its corporate links with Nestlé, whose strong presence in the wider packaged food market provided it with an instant market profile, providing CPW with a competitive advantage over Kellogg, whose activities are confined to breakfast products.

QUESTIONS

Carol has heard that you are the new global marketing specialist, so you are called in as a 'last-minute' consultant before the presentation to the board of directors. You are confronted with the following questions, which you are supposed to answer as best you can.

1 How can General Mills and Nestlé create international competitiveness by joining forces in CPW?
2 Evaluate the international competitiveness of CPW compared to the Kellogg Company.
3 What kind of competitive intelligence would you recommend CPW to collect about Kellogg in order to be better in challenging the No. 1 position.
4 Where and how can CPW create further international sales growth?

SOURCES

Bowery, J. (2006) Kellogg broadens healthy cereals portfolio, *Marketing*, 8 February: 5; Datamonitor (www.datamonitor.com); Euromonitor International (www.euromonitor.com); General Mills, Inc. (www.generalmills.com); Hanson, P. (2005) Market focus breakfast cereals, *Brand Strategy*, March, 190: 50; MarketWatch (www.marketwatch.com); Nestlé SA (www.nestle.com); Nestlé Whole Grain Cereals (www.cerealpartners.co.uk); Pehanich, M. (2003) Cereals run sweet and healthy, *Prepared Foods*, March: 75–6; Reyes, S. (2006) Saving Private Label, *Brandweek*, 5 August, 47(19): 30–4; Sanders, T. (2006) Cereals spark debate, *Food Manufacture*, August, 81(8): 4; Vignali, C. (2001) Kellogg's: internationalisation versus globalisation of the marketing mix, *British Food Journal*, 103(2): 112–30.

QUESTIONS FOR DISCUSSION

1 Why is competitor analysis essential in today's turbulent business environment?
2 What are the major steps in conducting a competitor analysis?
3 How does an industry's structure affect the intensity of competition?
4 What are the major sources of competitor intelligence?
5 How would you design a CI system?
6 How far is it possible to predict a competitor's response to marketing actions?

REFERENCES

Business Week (2000) How Viagra revived after a cold shower, *Business Week*, 28 August 28.
Buxton, P. (2000) Bitter truth Virgin is loath to swallow, *Marketing Week*, 23(8) (23 March): 21–2.
Calof, J. L. and Wright, S. (2008) Competitive intelligence: a practitioner, academic and interdisciplinary perspective, *European Journal of Marketing*, 42(7/8): 717–30.

Chen, M.-J. (1996) Competitor analysis and interfirm rivalry: toward a theoretical integration, *Academy of Management Review*, 21(1): 100–34.

Clark, B. H. (1998) Managing competitive interactions, *Marketing Management*, 7(4): 8–20.

Competitive Intelligence Magazine (1999) Managing your CI career, *Competitive Intelligence Magazine*, 2(3) (July–September) (www.scip.org).

Courtney, H., Horn, J. T. and Kar, J. (2009) Getting into your competitor's head, *McKinsey Quarterly*, 1: 128–37.

Dana, L. P. (1999) International Beverage Company, *British Food Journal*, 101(5/6): 479–82.

Dishman, P. L. and Calof, J. L. (2008) Competitive intelligence: a multiphasic precedent to marketing strategy, *European Journal of Marketing*, 42(7/8): 766–85.

Drott, M. C. (2000) Personal knowledge, corporate information: the challenges for competitive intelligence, *Business Horizons*, April–May: 31–7.

Dyer, C. and Clark, A. (2000) Pfizer loses Viagra battle: competitors ready to move in after patent on impotence drug is ruled invalid, *Guardian*, 9 November.

Fahey, L. (2007) Connecting strategy and competitive intelligence: refocusing intelligence to produce critical strategy inputs, *Strategy & Leadership*, 36(1): 4–12.

Fleisher, C. S. (2008) Using open source data in developing competitive and marketing intelligence, *European Journal of Marketing*, 42(7/8): 852–66.

Furrer, O. and Thomas, H. (2000) The rivalry matrix: understanding rivalry and competitive dynamics, *European Management Journal*, 18(6): December.

Geroski, P. A. (1999) Early warning of new rivals, *Sloan Management Review*, Spring: 107–16.

Glitman, E. (2000) Comprehending 'irrational' competitor actions through futures-based analysis, *Competitive Intelligence Magazine*, 3(4) (October–December).

Griffith, V. (2000) New drug threatens Viagra's reign, *Financial Times, Companies & Finance International*, 29 November.

Hannon, J. M. (1997) Leveraging HRM to enrich competitive intelligence, *Human Resource Management*, 36(4) (Winter): 409–22.

Herstein, R. and Mitiki, Y. (2008) How El Al Airlines transformed its service strategy with employee participation, *Strategy & Leadership*, 36(3): 21–5.

House, D. (2000) Getting inside your competitor's head: a roadmap for understanding goals and assumptions, *Competitive Intelligence Magazine*, 3(4) (October–December) (www.scip.org)

Independent (2000) It gives me energy and puts me in the mood: Viagra is finding favour on the black market as an aphrodisiac for women. But does it work? And is it safe? *Independent* – Health, 26 October.

Irish Times (2000) Home news: Pfizer loses its exclusive patent in Viagra case, *Irish Times*, 9 November.

Kotler, P. (2000) *Marketing Management*, Prentice Hall, Englewood Cliffs, NJ.

Levitt, T. (1960) Marketing myopia, *Harvard Business Review*, July–August: 46.

Porter, M. E. (1980) *Competitive Strategy*, The Free Press, New York.

Porter, M. E. (1985) *Competitive Advantage*, The Free Press, New York.

Prescott, J. (1998) Leveraging information for action: a look into the competitive and business intelligence consortium benchmarking study, *Competitive Intelligence Review*, 9(1) (Spring).

Qiu, T. (2008) Scanning for competitive intelligence: a managerial perspective, *European Journal of Marketing*, 42(7/8): 814–35.

Rothberg, H. N. (1999) Fortifying strategic decisions with shadow teams: a glance at product development, *Competitive Intelligence Magazine*, 2(2) (April–June) (www.scip.com).

Theodore, S. (2000) Mainstream alternatives, *Beverage Industry*, 91(10): 42–3.

Vezmar, J. M. (1996) Competitive intelligence at Xerox, *Competitive Intelligence Review*, 7(3) (Fall).

Vignali, C. (2001) Virgin Cola, *British Food Journal*, 103(2): 131–45.

West, C. (1999) Competitive intelligence in Europe, *Business Information Review*, 16(3) (September): 143–50.

Witt, J. (2000) Preparing Virgin cola for the fight of its life, *Marketing*, 2 November: 23.

CHAPTER 6
Analysing relationships in the value chain

LEARNING OBJECTIVES

After studying this chapter you should be able to:

- discuss the reasons and motives why firms go into relationships
- describe and understand the concept of the 'value net' model
- explain and discuss how relationships with suppliers and customers can add value in the total vertical chain
- describe the phases in the development of a relationship
- show and explain which factors determine a possible termination of inter-firm relationships
- explain and discuss how horizontal relationships with competitors and complementors can add value to the customers
- explain the difference between B2C and B2B relationships
- explore how internal marketing relationships can add value to the relationships with customers

6.1 INTRODUCTION

It is impossible to make sense of what happens in a firm or how to manage it without taking a relationship view of a company. This means that it is not enough to discuss the activities that a single firm performs. We need to understand how these activities are linked to the activities of the company's suppliers, its customers and indeed to their competitors. Because a firm's activities evolve within its relationships with others, each may have to do things that they do not really like, or they may be unable to do the things that they want. Hence, companies are dependent for their success on their relationships with customers and suppliers and with others. Many of the strategic choices that a company makes will be in response to the actions of these other companies.

In turn, the outcome of a firm's strategy will always depend on the actions of others, and how they react to what the company does. In this way a firm's strategy may be thought of as a kind of game, because there is nothing predetermined about the consequences of the various choices a firm might take. In a market where relationships matter, these games of action and reaction are complex and their results are vital to the firms involved.

Relationships enable firms to develop competitive advantage by leveraging the skills and capabilities of their partners to improve the performance of the total value chain. Firms no longer compete as individual companies; they compete as groups of companies that cooperate to bring value to the ultimate consumer. Across virtually all sectors of the economy, relationships have reshaped the interactions of companies.

In his classic 'From 4Ps to 30Rs' work, Gummesson (1994, 1999) identified 30 types of relationships. The relationships are divided into four levels:

1 *Classic market relationships (R1–R3)* are the *supplier–customer dyad,* the *triad of supplier–customer–competitor,* and the *physical distribution network,* which are treated extensively in general marketing theory.

2 *Special market relationships (R4–R17)* represent certain aspects of the classic relationships, such as *the interaction in the service encounter* or the *customer as member of a loyalty programme.*

3 *Mega relationships (R18–R23)* exist above the market relationships. They provide a platform for market relationships and concern the economy and society in general. Among these are *mega marketing* (lobbying, public opinion and political power), *mega alliances* (such as the NAFTA, setting a new stage for marketing in North America), and *social relationships* (such as friendship and ethnic bonds).

4 **Nano-relationships** *(R24–R30)* are found below the market relationships, that is, relationships inside an organisation (*intra*-organisational relationships). All internal activities influence the externally bound relationships.

Nano-relationships
Relations between internal customers, internal markets, divisions and business areas within organisations.

Micro-environment
A company, its customers and the other economic actors that directly and regularly influence it marketing practices.

Compared to this comprehensive approach to RM, the following analysis of relationships (the value net) is mainly focused on the four closest players in the **micro-environment**, plus relationships to internal employees. (These are the classic market relationships and the nano relationships in the Gummesson terminology.)

The basis for this chapter is the value chain (Figure 6.1).

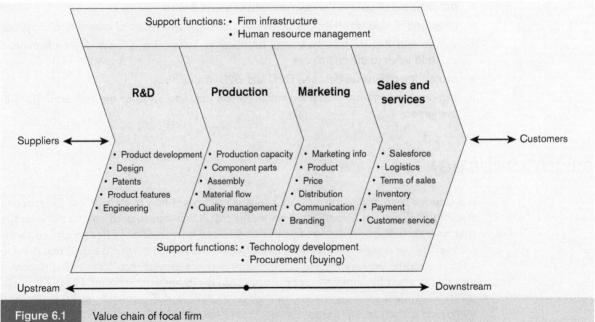

| | Figure 6.1 | Value chain of focal firm |

Value chain analysis implies a linear process, ignoring inputs from outside the chain – many firms may input into the process at various stages (Neves, 2007; Lorenzoni and Ferriani, 2008). The reality is, therefore, that the value chain becomes a value network, a group of interrelated entities, which contribute to the overall creation of value through a series of complex relationships, and the result is the so-called value net (see section 6.2).

EXHIBIT 6.1
Value chain of Braun (Oral-B electrical toothbrush)

Oral-B is the number three oral care brand in the world.

Within oral hygiene, the Oral-B strategy has always focused on the strongly established 'partnership' between the company and the dental profession. The brand highlights the fact that the products are developed using 'Clinical research conducted by leading dental professionals'.

Oral-B was originally only comprised of manual toothbrushes, but it now also encompasses a range of complementary offerings, including power products, electrical toothbrushes, floss and oral care products and toothpaste and mouth rinses. Gillette has further segmented sales with products for adults and a Stages product line to meet the changing and developing needs of a growing child. Its premium positioning of the Oral-B brand was enhanced by the development of the Advantage and Advantage Control Grip toothbrushes, and latterly the Cross Action brush in 1998.

The Oral-B brand has also experienced a relatively high level of new product development. This has included the launch of increasingly sophisticated and expensive toothbrushes, such as the Cross Action and Advantage.

Figure 6.2 illustrates the supply chain network, using Braun Oral-B as an example.

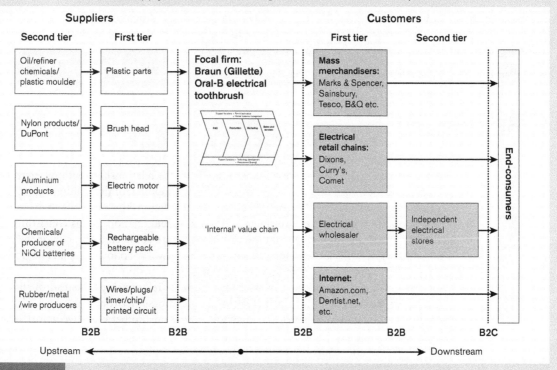

Figure 6.2 Illustration of the supply chain network, using Braun Oral-B as an example

The company has also focused on the children's market, with Gillette developing the Oral-B Stages line, which is designed for the four major phases of a child's development: infancy, pre-school, early school and pre-teen. A variety of toothpastes have been extended with sensitive, and tooth and gum care, and children's variants and in 2004 the company acquired Zooth, a manufacturer of manual and power toothbrushes for children, further expanding its presence in this sector.

EXHIBIT 6.1
Value chain of Braun (Oral-B) (*continued*)

GILLETTE EXTENDS POWER TOOTHBRUSH PORTFOLIO

The year 2001 marked the entry of Gillette into power portable toothbrushes. In 2003 the new Oral-B Cross Action Power battery toothbrush was claimed to be the most technologically advanced battery toothbrush available, combining CrissCross bristle technology (from manual products) with Oral-B's rotating Power Head.

In April 2004, Gillette extended its power toothbrushes range with the launch of the Oral-B Professional Care 8000 and the Oral-B Sonic Complete. Both products are rechargeable and the latter represents the company's entry into the sonic category. Gillette has further extended its range of power toothbrushes in 2005 with the launch of the Oral-B Professional Care 9000 in June 2005.

DOWNSTREAM ACTIVITIES OF THE SUPPLY CHAIN

The retail distribution of domestic electrical appliances, such as power toothbrushes, continued to be characterised by trends away from traditional formats, such as independent specialists and department stores, towards modern, large-format outlets such as hypermarkets, specialist electrical chains, DIY sheds and mass merchandisers.

Multiples increased their domination of retailing in developed markets. Major retailers pursued intensive expansion strategies, while consumer trends continued in the direction of one-stop shopping in the kind of large-scale outlets favoured by the major multiples. Moreover, major multiples' aggressive discounting policies, underpinned by significant economies of scale, have appealed to increasingly price-sensitive consumers in major markets experiencing economic difficulties, including the US, Germany and Japan.

Internet distribution (e-commerce) is still in its infancy regarding sales of domestic electrical appliances. Although sales are still relatively low, the Internet is critical to the domestic electrical appliances market as a marketing tool in countries where penetration of the Internet is high.

Source: Adapted from different sources, among others Oral-B (www.oralb.com).

6.2 THE VALUE NET

The value net shows how the firm can create value together with other partners in the vertical and horizontal network (Figure 6.3). Since the firm has relationships with different types of interdependence, with different objectives for the development of the relationship, it is important, organisationally, to differentiate between these relationships and how they are handled.

Suppose we regard the environment of the individual relationship as consisting of other relationships. Suppose further that the relationships are connected, directly or indirectly, to each other. Then we can envision the market as a network. Following a sociological definition, networks are sets of interconnected exchange relationships between actors. Exchange in one relationship is conditioned by exchange in other relationships. Instead of the concept 'markets-as-networks', 'industrial networks' and 'business networks' are used, signifying a somewhat different emphasis of the analyses. A relationship between two actors is 'embedded' in a network.

In particular, the relationships and interactions are typically established with the following actors (see Figure 6.3):

- customers (section 6.3)
- suppliers (section 6.4)
- complementors/partners (section 6.5)
- competitors (section 6.6)
- internal relationships (section 6.7).

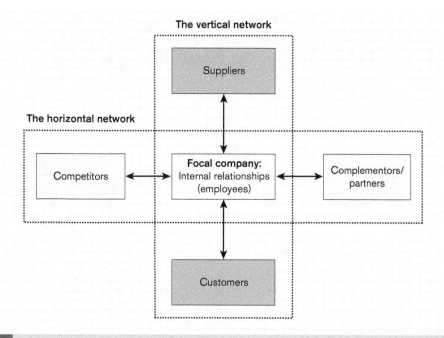

The vertical network

The horizontal network

Suppliers	
Competitors	Focal company: Internal relationships (employees)
Customers	Complementors/ partners

Figure 6.3	Relationships in the value net

Exhibit 6.2 shows Braun's (Oral-B) value net, especially its horizontal relationships.

The value net reveals two fundamental symmetries. Vertically, customers and suppliers are equal partners in creating value. Figure 6.2 shows the Oral-B example of the possible vertical network. The other symmetry is on the horizontal for competitors and complementors. The mirror image of competitors is complementors. A complement to one product or service is any other product or service that makes the first one more attractive, for example computer hardware and software, hot dogs and mustard, catalogues and overnight delivery service, red wine and dry cleaners. The value net helps you understand your competitors and complementors 'outside in'. Who are the players and what are their roles and the interdependences between them? Re-examine the conventional wisdom of 'Who are your friends and who are your enemies?' The suggestion is to know your business inside out and create a value net with the other players. Increase demand for whatever your customer sells.

The relationships in the value net are further discussed in the following.

EXHIBIT 6.2
Value net of Braun (Oral-B)

The value net of Braun (Oral-B) – the horizontal part – could look like Figure 6.4. The assumption here is that Braun Oral-B's product range only consists of electrical toothbrushes (it is, however, not quite true!) and that they can create further value by cooperating with complementors (such as a manufacturer of manual toothbrushes – Jordan – and a manufacturer of a complementary product – toothpaste – Colgate). Furthermore, Oral-B could also go into a technological cooperation with a company such as Philips. Such a cooperation could, for example, end up with a new technological platform, from which both Braun and Philips could develop new products based on the same basic technology.

Source: Adapted from different sources, among others, Oral-B (www.oralb.com).

→

EXHIBIT 6.2
Value net of Braun (Oral-B) (*continued*)

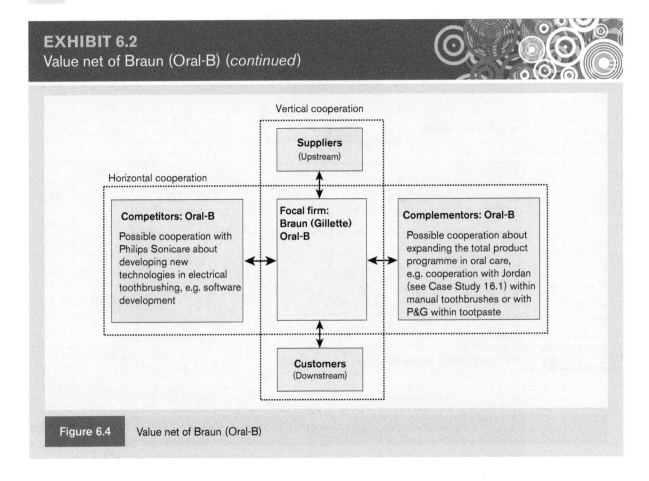

Figure 6.4   Value net of Braun (Oral-B)

6.3 RELATIONSHIPS WITH CUSTOMERS

In the relationship approach, a specific transaction between the focal company and a customer is not an isolated event but takes place within an exchange relationship characterised by mutual dependency and interaction over time between the two parties. An analysis could stop at the individual relationship. However, in the network approach such relationships are seen as interconnected. Thus, the various actors in a market are connected to each other, directly or indirectly. A specific market can then be described and analysed as one or more networks.

An exchange relationship implies that there is an individual specific dependency between the seller and the customer. The relationship develops through interaction over time and signifies a mutual orientation of the two parties towards each other. In the interaction the buyer is equally as active as the seller. The interaction consists of social, business and information exchange and an adaptation of products, processes and routines to better reach the economic objectives of the parties involved.

The simplest reason why firms seek to develop ongoing relationships with their customers is that it is generally much more profitable to retain existing customers than continually seek to recruit new customers to replace lost ones. There have been many exercises to calculate the effects on a company's profits of even a modest improvement in the rate at which customers defect to competitors.

RM signifies that the firm should seek to have close relationships with its customers. Please note that in this section, customers may cover both end buyers and distributors/resellers.

What is meant by a relationship, and how is it developed? As illustrated by the following quote, in essence this new approach means a focus on long-term interactions between a marketer and its customers, instead of a short-term transactional approach:

> Relationship marketing is the process of identifying and establishing, maintaining, enhancing, and when necessary terminating relationships with customers and other stakeholders. (Grönroos, 1996, p. 7)

In the development of relationships, managers have to realise that the customer is no longer interested in buying a product. The product, in fact, is no more than an artefact around which customers have experiences. What's more, customers are not prepared to accept experiences fabricated by companies. Increasingly, they want to shape those experiences themselves, both individually and with experts or other customers.

Prahalad and Ramaswamy (2000) distinguish between personalisation and customisation:

- *Customisation:* this assumes that the manufacturer will design a product to suit a customer's needs. It is particularly pronounced on the Internet, where consumers can customise a host of products and services such as business cards, computers and greeting cards.

- *Personalisation (co-creation):* this, on the other hand, is about the customer becoming a co-creator of the content of experiences. To provide personalised experiences, companies must create opportunities for customers to experiment with and then decide the level of involvement they want in creating a given experience with the company. Since the level of customer engagement cannot be predetermined, companies have to give consumers as much choice and flexibility as possible, both in the channels of distribution and communication and in the design of products. But companies can also help direct their customers' requirements and expectations by guiding public debate about the future technology and its impact on new products on the market (Ramaswamy, 2008; Morgado, 2008; Prahalad and Ramaswamy, 2004).

However, managing the variety of customer experiences is not the same as managing variety in products. It is about managing the interface between a company and its customers – the range of experience transcends the company's products (Sterling, 2008). Managers must develop a product that shapes itself to users' needs, not the other way around. But as noted, customers evolve over time through their experience with a product. The product has to evolve in a way that enables future modifications and extensions based both on a customer's changing needs and on the company's changing capabilities.

Developing buyer–seller relationships – the marriage metaphor

Over the past 15 years the analogy between building business relationships and personal relationships (marriage) has been utilised extensively (Schurr, 2007). Certainly there are some interesting parallels between them, and by considering the personal aspects of relationship development it is possible to arrive at a better understanding of the business issues. Sometimes human relationships and business relationships are quite 'blurring'. Figure 6.5 illustrates that the business relationship can develop from acquaintances.

A theoretical life cycle model of relationships proposed by Dwyer *et al.* (1987) identified five stages of relationship development – awareness, exploration, expansion, commitment and dissolution (see Figure 6.6).

The linking stages seem to be:

- meeting (awareness)
- dating (exploration)
- courting (expansion)
- marriage (commitment), and possibly
- divorce (dissolution of relationship).

Relationship types

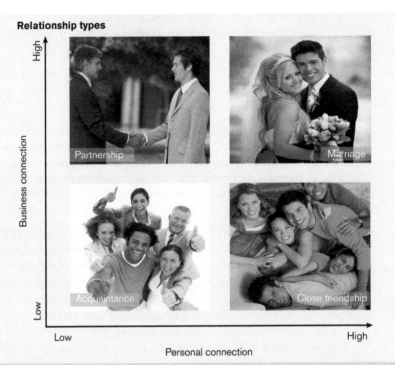

	Figure 6.5	Relationship types

Sources: Images from iStockphoto: Neustockimages (top left), grigphoto (top right), Aldomurillo (bottom left) and Yuri Acurs (bottom right).

Their model proposed that a relationship begins to develop significance in the exploration stage when it is characterised by the attempts of the seller to attract the attention of the other party. The exploration stage includes attempts by each party to bargain and to understand the nature of the power, norms and expectations held by the other. If this stage is satisfactorily concluded, an expansion phase follows. Exchange outcomes in the exploratory stage provide evidence as to the suitability of long-term exchange relationships. The commitment phase of

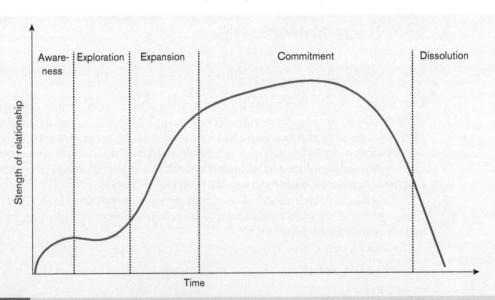

	Figure 6.6	Stages in buyer–seller relationship development

Source: Adapted from Dwyer F. R., Schurr, P. H. and Oh, S. (1987) Development buyer and seller relationships, *Journal of Marketing*, 51 (April): 11–27. Reproduced with permission from the American Marketing Association.

a relationship implies some degree of exclusivity between the parties and results in the information search for alternatives – if it occurs at all – being much reduced. The dissolution stage marks the point where buyer and seller recognise that they would be better able to achieve their respective aims outside the relationship.

Buyer–seller relationships in a cross-cultural perspective

International strategic alliances are being used with increasing frequency in order to keep up with rapidly changing technologies, gain access to specific foreign markets and distribution channels and create new products. Strategic alliances are becoming an essential feature of companies' overall organisational structure, and competitive advantage depends not only on the firm's internal capabilities, but also on its types of alliances with other companies.

Formation of international strategic alliances brings together managers from different organisations, different national origins, with differences in the partners' cultural bases. Nationality is the key personal attribute that shapes the interaction among managers. Managers with similar attributes, values and perceptions would be more likely to have strong ties with each other than managers with dissimilar attributes, values and perceptions. Thus a shared nationality is a basis for managers to establish and maintain strong network ties.

Capitalising on an effective understanding of this culture can be used by the seller to achieve a competitive advantage in developing and maintaining long-term buyer–seller relationships. The age of the person in the buyer's organisation with whom the seller interacts can play a major role in establishing relationships. The age factor has cultural consequences of its own. The older the buyer, the more his or her experience is integrated into the decision process.

Thus, it is interesting that companies which do business in an international context can handle the cultural complexity and heterogeneity. Good handling of cultural heterogeneity implies that the company can cope well in different cultural environments.

The success and the possibility of building both national and international cooperative relations depend on the interaction of the persons who want to establish the relation (Axelsson and Agndal, 2000; Mascarenhas and Koza, 2008).

Distance reduction in international strategic alliances

The formation of collaborative alliances among organisations is touted as a significant strategy that organisations can use to cope with the turbulence and complexity of their environments. An international strategic alliance is commonly defined as:

> Relatively enduring inter-firm cooperative agreements, involving cross-border flows and linkages that utilise resources and/or governance structures from autonomous organisations in two or more countries, for the joint accomplishment of individual goals linked to the corporate mission of each sponsoring firm. (Parkhe, 1991, p. 581)

The inter-firm distance is the degree to which the cultural norms, etc., in one country are different from those in another country. Inter-firm distance creates difficulties for managers when they adapt to the different cultures. Thus greater cultural distance may lead to misunderstandings, friction and conflict between managers. The distance is also often referred to as the psychic distance (Brewer, 2007). For international companies trying to use strategic alliances as a competitive weapon, it is crucial to identify the factors that reduce the distance between the partners. Figure 6.7 shows the possible factors that are believed to influence the distance reduction.

The dyadic relationship does not appear as an isolated entity, but as part of a larger context. Any company has to maintain relationships with several other players and some other relationships occur in the development of a certain relationship. Each relationship then appears to be embedded in or connected to some other relationships, and its development and functions cannot be properly understood if these connections are disregarded (Segil, 2005).

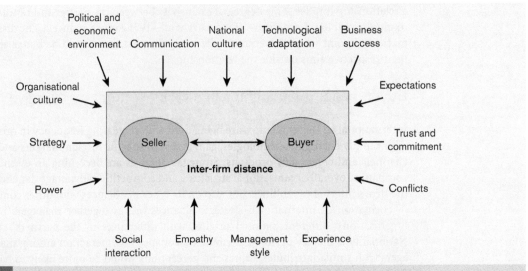

Figure 6.7	Factors influencing the inter-firm distance

Source: Preliminary work by Anna Marie Dyhr Ulrich, PhD Researcher at the University of Southern Denmark.

The interaction approach model takes four basic elements into consideration when assessing the importance and influence of interaction:

1 the *interaction process*, which expresses the exchanges between the two organisations along with their progress and evolution throughout time;

2 the *participants* in the interaction process, meaning the characteristics of the supplier and the customer involved in the interaction process;

3 the *environment* within which the interaction takes place;

4 the *atmosphere* affecting and being affected by the interaction.

The manipulation and control of these variables is of particular importance in international business and is a resource-intensive and time-consuming process. The interaction approach places the emphasis on processes and relationships; buyers and sellers are seen as active participants in long-term relationships that involve complex patterns of interaction (Bee and Kahle, 2006).

Since this section tries to explain the distance reduction by focusing on the atmosphere that has developed it seems relevant to define the concept of atmosphere. The concept of atmosphere is here defined as:

> the emotional setting, in which business is conducted. It constitutes the working environment for the individuals in their interaction with each other. (Hallén and Sandström, 1991, p. 113)

As a result of research on interaction processes five atmosphere criteria are suggested. These are cooperation/conflict, power/dependence, trustworthiness/commitment, expectations and closeness/distance (Håkansson 1982).

While focus in this section is on distance reduction, the following discusses distance in detail.

Psychic distance
Refers to the *perceived* degree of similarity or difference between the business partners in two different markets. Psychic distance is operationalised in terms of both cultural and business distance.

Psychic distance/closeness

Psychic distance is used here to denote the degree of familiarity with regard to mainly cultural, but also social, aspects.

Researchers of psychic distance are not very precise about the exact concept. These are factors that should hinder and hamper the information flow between a company and its market, e.g. differences in language, culture, political systems, level of education, level of development.

A problem with the psychic distance concept is that it relates to individuals' cognitive understanding instead of the whole company's behaviour. There is no objective goal, but a distance that exists in human thought, and the distance perceived depends on how the individual regards the world. The term 'psychic' refers to the individual perception.

In empirical studies, Hofstede (1983, 1992) introduced the concept of cultural distance as a measure of the distance between nations. Cultural distance is a potentially powerful determinant of the way relationships can develop.

The cultural distance is often used as a synonym for the psychic inter-firm distance. International business literature shows little consensus regarding an exact definition of the concept of distance. Here the perceived distance is considered as:

> The distance between the home market and a foreign market resulting from the perception and understanding of cultural, business, organisational and personal differences.

The inference is that distance is a consequence of a number of interrelated factors, of which perception is a major determinant. Perception is an interpretation of data and is, therefore, highly subjective in terms of an individual's personal experience and value systems; as value systems are largely a product of cultural background, it could be argued that culture has an influence on perception.

Cultural influence on the perceived distance and the interaction of the alliance partners

If perception is influenced by culture, and perception is used to interpret those factors, which constitute the distance, it is clear that culture has an influence on distance.

The concept of distance is multidimensional in connection with international buyer–seller relationship building. We suggest that the following cultural dimensions affect the distance:

- different understanding of the national and industrial culture;
- different understanding of the organisational culture;
- different personal behaviour because of different mental programming.

The national culture is only one level in the cultural hierarchy that influences the parties' behaviour and perception. The national culture must be seen as the basic, arranging structure for how to handle business activities. Throughout time, many researchers have defined the concept of culture. In this section the perception of culture will be based on Hofstede's definition. He defines culture as: 'The collective programming of the mind which distinguishes the members of one category of people from another' (Hofstede, 1994, p. 1). He has laid down five criteria, based on what the national, cultural differences are thought to be. The five criteria are: power distance, individualism versus collectivism, masculinity versus femininity, uncertainty avoidance and long-term versus short term-orientation (Hofstede, 1994).

A relationship between two firms begins, grows and develops – or fails – in ways similar to relationships between people. The development of a relationship has been mapped out in a five-phase model: awareness, exploration, expansion, commitment and dissolution. The five phases are shown in Figure 6.8.

Figure 6.8 shows, the initial psychic distance 1 between a buyer and a seller (both from different countries and cultures) and it is influenced by the psychological characteristics of the buyer and the seller, the firm's organisational culture, and the national and industrial culture to which the firm belongs. Figure 6.8 also shows that the initial psychic distance 1 at the beginning of the relationship is reduced to physical distance 2 through the interaction process of the two partners. However, relationships do not always last forever. The partners may 'move from each other' and the psychic distance may increase to distance 3. If the problems in the relationship are not solved, it may result in a 'divorce'.

Within such a framework one might easily characterise a marketing relationship as a marriage between a seller and a buyer (the dissolution phase being a 'divorce'). The use of the

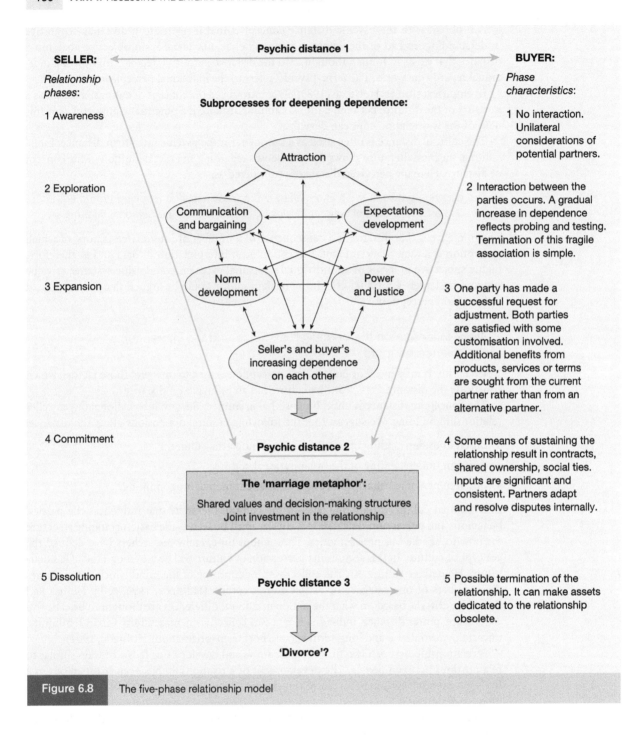

| Figure 6.8 | The five-phase relationship model |

Marriage metaphor
The process of reducing the psychic distance + increasing dependence between buyer and seller = shared values and joint investments in the relationship.

marriage metaphor emphasises the complexity as well as some affective determinants of the quality of the relationship. Dwyer *et al.* (1987) call the first phase in a relationship *awareness*, which means that the partners recognise each other as potential partners. In other words, in their model the decisions made about cooperating and choosing the partner are combined. Both types of decision making can exist at the beginning of cooperation, but it is difficult to state any definite chronological order between them.

In SMEs it is likely that the decision-making process is reactive, in the way that the SME probably first realises the existence of a potential partner (maybe 'love at first sight') and then decides to cooperate. The selection process may, however, be better if companies look for three key criteria (Kanter, 1994):

1 *Self-analysis:* relationships get off to a good start when partners know themselves and their industry, when they have assessed changing industry conditions and decided to seek an alliance. It also helps if executives have experience in evaluating potential partners. They will not be easily attracted by the first good-looking prospect that comes along.

2 *Chemistry:* to highlight the personal side of business relationships is not to deny the importance of sound financial and strategic analysis. But successful relations often depend on the creation and maintenance of a comfortable personal relationship between senior executives. This will include personal and social interests. Signs of managers' interests, commitment and respect are especially important in high-context countries. In China, as well as in Chinese-dominated businesses throughout Asia, the top manager of the Western company should show honour and respect to the potential partner's decision by investing his or her personal time.

3 *Compatibility:* the courtship period tests compatibility on broad historical, philosophical and strategic grounds: common experiences, values and principles, and hopes for the future. While analysts examine financial viability, managers can assess the less tangible aspects of compatibility. What starts out as personal rapport, philosophical and strategic compatibility, and shared vision between two companies' top executives must eventually be institutionalised and made public ('getting engaged'). Other stakeholders get involved, and the relationship begins to become depersonalised. But success in the engagement phase of a new alliance still depends on maintaining a careful balance between the personal and the institutional.

In the *exploration phase* (see Figure 6.8), trial purchases may take place and the exchange outcomes provide a test of the other's ability and willingness to deliver satisfaction. In addition, electronic data interchange can be used to reduce the costly paperwork associated with purchase orders, production schedule releases, invoices and so on.

At the end of the exploration phase it is time to 'meet the family'. The relations between a handful of leaders from the two firms must be supplemented with approval, formal or informal, by other people in the firms and by stakeholders. Each partner has other outside relationships that may need to approve the new relationship.

When a party (as is the case in the *expansion phase*) fulfils perceived exchange obligations in an exemplary fashion, the party's attractiveness to the other increases. Hence motivation to maintain the relationship increases, especially because high-level outcomes reduce the number of alternatives that an exchange partner might use as a replacement.

The romance or courtship quickly gives way to day-to-day reality as the partners begin to live together ('setting up house'). In the *commitment phase* the two partners can achieve a level of satisfaction from the exchange process that actually precludes other primary exchange partners (suppliers) that could provide similar benefits. The buyer has not ceased attending other alternative suppliers, but maintains awareness of alternatives without constant and frequent testing. In a buyer–seller relationship with a high conflict potential (e.g. caused by two very different partners) the partners tend to monitor the relationship more closely because each partner is afraid that its interests are not fully taken into account. However, the relationship is able to sustain its structure and remain an efficient mechanism for inter-firm transactions between buyer and seller, as long as partners' economic benefits exceed potential costs in managing the alliance (Wahyuni *et al.*, 2007).

During the description of the relationship development, the possibility of a withdrawal has been implicit. The **dissolution phase** may be caused by the following problems (Beloucif *et al.*, 2006; Pressey and Qiu, 2007):

Dissolution phase
'Divorce' is the termination of the relationship. It can make the assets dedicated to the relationship obsolete

● Operational and cultural differences emerge after collaboration is under way. They often come as a surprise to those who created the alliance. Differences in authority, reporting and decision-making styles become noticeable at this stage.

- People in other positions may not experience the same attraction as the chief executives. The executives spend a lot of time together both informally and formally. Other employees have not been in touch with one another, however, and in some cases have to be pushed to work with their overseas counterparts.

- Employees at other levels in the organisation may be less visionary and cosmopolitan than top managers and less experienced in working with people from different cultures. They may lack knowledge of the strategic context in which the relationship makes sense and see only the operational ways in which it does not.

- People just one or two tiers from the top might oppose the relationship and fight to undermine it. This is especially true in organisations that have strong independent business units.

- Termination of personal relationships, because managers leave their positions in the companies, is a potential danger to the partnership.

Firms have to be aware of these potential problems before they go into a relationship, because only in that way can they take action to prevent the dissolution phase. By jointly analysing the extent and importance of the attenuating factors, the partners will become more aware of the reasons for continuing the relationship, in spite of the trouble they are already in. Moreover, this awareness increases the parties' willingness to engage in restorative actions, thus trying to save the relationship from dissolution (Tähtinen and Vaaland, 2006)

Managerial implications

Managers may consider relationship termination as a strategic decision. Firms should evaluate which relationships to initiate, which to develop, which to continue to invest in and also which to discontinue (Mittal *et al.*, 2008). Once a firm has made the decision to discontinue or terminate a relationship, it should be aware that there is a range of termination strategies which may be employed. The firm could be looking for strategies that could be labelled 'beautiful exits' (Alajoutsijärvi *et al.*, 2000). A beautiful exit is achieved by a strategy that minimises damage occurring to the disengager, the other party and the connected network.

In fact there is a lot to learn from all types of personal relationships, not just marriage. After all, business relationships are not impersonal; they depend entirely on the people who represent the supplier and the customers. There are interesting parallels with the Chinese concept of guanxi, which involves different levels of personal commitment and connections (Pressey and Qiu, 2007).

The implications for business of the marriage metaphor are:

- choose your partner carefully;
- structure the partnership carefully;
- devote time to developing the relationship;
- maintain open, two-way communication;
- be entirely trustworthy.

It is important to point out that not all personal relationships progress to a marriage, monogamous or polygamous, and it is equally appropriate that not all marketing partnerships have to, or are even able to, develop beyond the friendship stage.

The nature of the customer and the behaviour spectrum

Always-a-share customers
Customers who have low switching costs and do not value long-term relationships with suppliers, making them more suited to transaction marketing.

Lost-for-good customers
Customers who have high switching costs and long-term horizons making them suitable for relationship marketing (RM).

The behaviours of buyers and sellers interact with fundamental characteristics of the exchange environment to define the nature of their relationship. This section will use some basic elements of each sphere to describe a continuum of trading relations.

Jackson (1985) suggests that business marketers should assess 'the time horizon within which a customer makes a commitment to a supplier and also the actual pattern the relationship follows over time'. Figure 6.9 highlights the typical characteristics of customers at the end points of the account behaviour spectrum: **always-a-share customers** (transactional exchange) and **lost-for-good customers** (collaborative exchange).

Always-a-share customer
Transaction focus

Lost-for-good customer
Relationship focus

←——————————————————————————————————→

Always-a-share customer (Transaction focus)	Lost-for-good customer (Relationship focus)
• Lower switching costs (suppliers are largely interchangeable)	• High switching costs
• Smaller investment actions	• Substantial investment actions, especially in procedures and lasting assets
• Single sale	• Customer retention
• Discontinuous customer contact	• Continuous contact
• Focus on product features	• Focus on product benefits and the technology behind
• Short-term scale	• Long-term scale
• Little emphasis on customer sevicer	• High emphasis on customer service
• Limited commitment to meeting customer expectations	• High commitment to meeting customer expectations
• Quality is the concern of production staff	• Quality is the concern of all staff
• Low transaction costs	• High transaction costs
• Lower importance	• Higher importance: strategic, operational and personal
Examples of products: Print services, office supplies, bulk chemicals, PC supplies	Examples of products: Telecommunication systems, franchises, computer systems (e.g. CRM systems)

Figure 6.9	The marketing relationship continuum

Source: Adapted from Jackson, B. B. (1985) Build customer relationships that last, *Harvard Business Review*, 63 (November–December): 120–8. Copyright © 1985 by the Harvard Business School Publishing. All rights reserved. Reproduced with permission.

Franchise
A contractual association between a manufacturer, wholesaler or service organisation (a franchiser) and independent business people (franchisees) who buy the right to own and operate one or more units in the franchise system.

Exit barrier
The barriers to leaving an industry, e.g. cost of closing down plant.

Always-a-share and lost-for-good represent different ends of a continuum of exchange situations. Sellers will retain customers by giving good service and responding to customer needs. Differentiating the offering on dimensions that forge structural ties and create **exit barriers** will tend to move the relationship toward the lost-for-good variety. For example, an always-a-share supplier might move from a fill-in role to become a major supplier by meeting customer criteria for becoming a preferred supplier. The standards for preferred supplier vary from firm to firm, but often include quality programmes, employee safety and training efforts, and delivery specifications.

The always-a-share customers

These customers can allocate their purchases to several vendors. A period of no purchases can be followed by a period of high purchases.

The always-a-share customer purchases repeatedly from some product category, displays less loyalty or commitment to a particular supplier, and can easily switch part or all of the purchases from one vendor to another. Because of low switching costs, these customers may share their patronage over time with multiple vendors and adopt short-term commitments with suppliers.

The lost-for-good customers

Relationships cemented by switching costs are called *lost-for-good relationships* because the prospects of a customer making a costly switch to a competitor followed by a costly return to the first are remote – probably weaker than a cold-call prospect. It is not likely that the customer would pay the switching costs again to return to the first firm.

Customers are tied to a system. They face significant switching costs which may include:

● specific investments

● cancellation penalties

- set-up costs for a new supplier
- retraining
- finding and evaluating a new supplier.

The lost-for-good customer makes a series of purchases over time, and views the commitment to a particular supplier as relatively permanent. Once won, this type of account is likely to remain loyal to a particular supplier for a long time. If lost, however, it is often lost for good.

The behaviour of many customers in the business market is somewhere between a pure transaction focus and a pure relationship focus. The particular position that a customer occupies depends on a host of factors: the characteristics of the product category, the customer's pattern of product usage, and the actions taken by both the supplier and the customer.

Implications for relationship marketing strategies

Business marketers often have a portfolio of customers who span the whole customer behaviour spectrum. Some emphasise low price and a transaction perspective while others place a premium on substantial service and desire a more collaborative relationship. Indeed, some customers fall somewhat in the middle of the account spectrum and represent accounts that might be effectively upgraded to a level that adds value to the relationship for both parties. To develop responsive and profitable relationship marketing strategies, special attention must be given to four areas: selecting accounts, developing account-specific product offerings, implementing relationship strategies, and evaluating relationship strategy outcomes.

A relationship with customers targeted on strong and lasting commitments is especially appropriate for lost-for-good accounts. Business marketers can sensibly invest resources in order to secure commitment and to aid customers with long-term planning. Given the long-term nature and the considerable stakes involved, customers are concerned both with marketers' long-term capabilities and with their immediate performance. Because the customers perceive significant risk, they demand competence and commitment from the selling organisation.

If we transfer this to Figure 6.10, the upper figure ('bow-tie') illustrates the always-a-share and the lower figure ('diamond') illustrates the lost-for-good. In the traditional 'bow-tie' relationship, the purchasing agent and the salesperson assume the primary roles in the exchange process.

Relational exchanges, in contrast, have a structure similar to the 'diamond' where the boundaries between the firms become more opaque. Interactive, cross-functional teams now openly exchange ideas for improving efficiency and effectiveness (see Figure 6.10). The goal is to create new value together (Jones *et al.*, 2005; Philipsen *et al.*, 2008).

Perhaps the most important prerequisite for the 'diamond' model is the need for a high level of 'connectivity' between the firm and its strategic suppliers. This implies not just the exchange of information on demand and inventory levels, but multiple, collaborative working relationships across the organisations at all levels. It is increasingly common today for companies to create supplier development teams that are cross-functional and, as such, are intended to communicate with the equivalent customer management team in the supplying organisation (Kothandaraman and Wilson, 2000).

Behavioural conditions in buyer–seller relationships

The key dimensions in the basic behavioural conditions for establishing and developing buyer–seller relationships are as follows.

Bonding/goal compatibility

Bonding is defined as the part of a business relationship that results in two parties (customer and supplier) acting in a unified manner toward a desired goal.

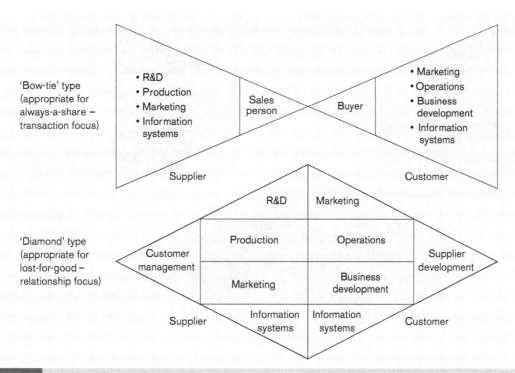

| Figure 6.10 | Organisation of buyer–seller relationship |

Partners in the relationship must share mutually achievable goals although the goals do not have to be the same. It would be unrealistic to expect that partners would share the same goals as each probably has different parts of the value chain, such as to source product exclusively from a certain key supplier. However, it is likely that both share the goal of better meeting the needs of the end customer. Given the economics of the different levels of the supply chain, one partner might focus on reducing the total cost of ownership, whereas the other partner might look at accessing a new market segment as its major goal.

EXHIBIT 6.3
Speedo's relations with its retailers

Speedo is a leading international brand company of professional swimwear, based in the UK. Like many companies today, Speedo has set up different, parallel structures for managing its diverse customer base.

Its current organisation comprises three distinct interface structures: first, a traditional sales organisation with a large and dispersed field salesforce who deal with the small independent sports stores. They have traditionally been the mainstay of the business and represented in the past the main channel of distribution. For Speedo, however, the sports stores are low-volume customers that are spread all over the country and therefore best dealt with by individual salespeople. The company's concern for these relationships is manifested in the strong emphasis they place on an experienced, well-qualified salesforce with a high level of employee retention.

The portion of the business accounted for by the second customer segment, major high street retailers and sports multiples, has gradually increased over the last few years to approximately 50 per cent, with the prospect of a further rise to 80 per cent in the near future. The shifting balance and the concentration within this channel of distribution leverages the relationship value, which in turn justifies the resource-intensive account structure Speedo maintains to deal with these customers. The work between the dedicated account managers and their counterparts on the retailer side is facilitated by the provision of back-up support from other functions within the company.

→

EXHIBIT 6.3
Speedo's relations with its retailers (*continued*)

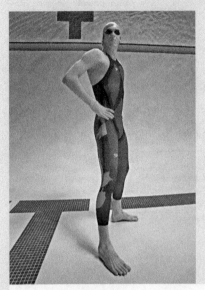

Source: Courtesy of Speedo (www.speedo.com)

Finally, Speedo started an even closer cooperation with two potentially high-growth customers in 1999. The relationship project and the corresponding interface structure are still in a trial phase but both parties' commitment is high. One of the clients is Sports Division, Europe's biggest independent sports retailer with approximately 120 high street stores, with additional in-store concessions, as well as a number of superstores. For Speedo, the relationship is crucial because, aside from the high economic relationship value, Sports Division shares its interest, stocking only leading brands and not own-label products. The initiative for the project came from the operations director who is still in charge of the implementation and who assigned an account development team to work exclusively on this one account. The team members have been selected to match the retailer's supply management team and both teams' target is to improve the effectiveness and efficiency of the supply chain.

Source: Adapted from Christopher and Jüttner (2000).

Trust

Trust is the belief that one's alliance partner will act in a predictable manner, will keep his or her word, and will not behave in a way that negatively affects the other. This last point is particularly salient under conditions where one partner might feel vulnerable due to a heightened dependence on the other.

In many alliances, partners are compelled to share information or knowledge that lies near, if not at, the core of their business. Trust diminishes the concern that this knowledge might be expropriated and used later to compete against the partner. This fear is very real among managers of small companies that seek alliances with larger companies. These managers fear that the larger firm is using the relationship to gain knowledge for its own benefit (Mendez *et al.*, 2006).

Empathy

Empathy is the dimension of a business relationship that enables the two parties to see the situation from the other's perspective. It is defined as seeking to understand somebody else's desires and goals. It involves the ability of individual parties to view the situation from the other party's perspective in a truly cognitive sense. The empathy dimension plays a major role in Chinese business relationships (guanxi framework) and is also apparent in Western business relationships (Buttery and Wong, 1999).

Reciprocity

Allowance
Promotional money paid by manufacturers to retailers in return for an agreement to feature the manufacturer's products in some way.

Reciprocity is the part of a business relationship that causes either party to provide favours or make **allowances** for the other in return for similar favours or allowances to be received at a later date. It covers the interdependence for mutual benefit and equality of exchanged values between two individuals.

These behavioural factors emphasise the importance of personal social ties in business relationships. Business relationships are built on friendships, and friendships are built upon a variety of social interactions. The individual's networks are also the enablers and driving forces of many firms' internationalisation. This is a phenomenon well known to marketing practitioners, but has received little attention among academics (Axelsson and Agndal, 2000).

Relationships in B2B markets versus B2C markets

For many years RM was conceived as an approach for the inter-organisational B2B markets. Recently, however, the domain of RM has been extended to incorporate innovative applications in mass consumer markets. Much has changed in a few years. Recent applications of RM in consumer markets have been facilitated by developments in direct and database marketing within an increasingly competitive and fragmented marketplace.

In Table 6.1 the major differences between B2B and B2C relationships are highlighted.

One-to-one marketing relationships

According to Peppers *et al.* (1999), one-to-one marketing means being willing and able to change your behaviour toward an individual customer based on what the customer tells you and what else you know about that customer.

One-to-one relationship marketing is often expressed as being synonymous with relationship marketing, but is treated here as an extension of the initial effort that results from the ever-increasing personalisation of promotional efforts in a variety of industries.

Telemarketing
Using the telephone as the primary means of communicating with prospective customers. Telemarketers often use computers for order taking.

The two obvious approaches are either segmentation or personalisation. Segmentation is information distributed to narrow, well-defined bands of target customers – an approach used for years. Conversely, personalisation is information distributed and designed to be one-to-one. The historical methods for collecting data for either segmented or personalised databases have been direct mail and **telemarketing**. One-to-one relationships can be enhanced today by most firms using the Internet, which gives the opportunity of personal addressed marketing communications. One-to-one marketing goes hand in hand with customisation. It is all about generating feedback so that marketers can learn more about customers' preferences with future offers being tailored to those preferences.

The intention of one-to-one marketing is to increase the value of a customer base by establishing a learning relationship with each customer. The customer tells you of some need, and you customise your product or service to meet it. The theory behind one-to-one marketing is simple, with implementation being another matter. Effectiveness will require differentiating customers and interacting with them.

The emphasis on the customisation of products and services to meet the very specific needs of individual customers is altering the manufacturing requirements of most firms. New technology has emerged that permits such emphasis on individualism in the final

Table 6.1	Comparison of B2C and B2B relationships	
Characteristic	Business-to-consumer (B2C)	Business-to-business (B2B)
1 Relationship form	Membership. The individual acknowledges some relationship (though informal affiliation with the organisation).	Working partnership, just-in-time exchange, co-marketing alliance, strategic alliance, distribution channels relationship.
2 Average sale size; potential lifetime value of the customer to the selling firm	Normally small sale size; relatively small and predictable lifetime value of the customer; limit on the amount of investment in relationship on any single customer.	Normally large and consequential; allows for large and idiosyncratic investments in a single relationship.
3 Number of customers	Large number; requires large overall investment in relationship management, but low investment per customer.	Relatively fewer customers to spread investment in relationships over.
4 Seller's ability and cost to replace lost customer	Normally can be replaced quickly at relatively low cost.	Large customers can be difficult and time consuming to replace.
5 Seller dependence on buyer	Low for any single customer.	Varies based on customer size; can be devastating.
6 Buyer dependence on seller	Normally has more alternatives, low switching costs, and switching can be made quickly.	Viable alternatives can take time to find, switching costs can be high, and changes impact on multiple people in the organisation.
7 Purchasing time frame, process, and buying centre complexity	Normally a short time frame, simple process, and simple buying centre where one or two individuals fill most buying roles.	Often a long time frame, complex process; may have multiple individuals for a single buying role; may be subject to organisational budget cycles.
8 Personal knowledge of other party	Relatively few contact points with seller even when loyal user; seller's knowledge of buyer often limited to database information.	Multiple personal relationships; multiple inter-organisational linkages.
9 Communication used to build and sustain relationships	Dependence on non-personal means of contact; seller's knowledge generally limited to database information of customers.	Emphasis on personal selling and personal contact; customer knowledge held in multiple forms and places.
10 Relative size	Seller normally larger than buyer.	Relative size may vary.
11 Legal	Consumer protection laws often favour consumers.	Relationships governed by prevailing contract law as well as industry standard regulations and ethics.

Source: Adapted from Gruen, T. W. (1995) The outcome set of relationship marketing in consumer markets, *International Business Review*, 4(4): 449–69. Copyright © 1995 Elsevier. Reproduced with permission.

Idiosyncratic investment
Specific investment in a single relationship.

product. Mass customisation is the term used to describe the ability of manufacturers to make almost instant changes in the production process to individualise output in quantities as small as one. This technology coupled with the emphasis on relationships has permitted the pursuit of relationship marketing on a one-to-one basis. Mass customisation will further drive relationship marketing with its associated demands for greater understanding of each customer within the seller's marketing umbrella. This additional emphasis will spur marketers to find new and better ways of gaining customer information and keeping it current.

Bonding in buyer–seller relationships

The following is mainly developed for the service sector, but the bonds described are applicable to the majority of B2B relationships. Liljander and Strandvik (1995) define bonds as 'exit barriers that tie the customer to the service provider and maintain the relationship'.

The authors propose ten different types of bond between the customer and the seller: legal, economic, technological, geographical, time, knowledge, social, cultural, ideological and psychological bonds. The authors point out that the first five bonds can be managed by a service firm while the remaining five are difficult for a firm to measure and manage:

1 A *legal bond* is a contract between a customer and a service provider. The present study views legal bonds as belonging to the legal factor group.

2 An *economic bond* refers to a situation in which price reductions are used as incentives towards the customers. The economic bond belongs to the economic factor group.

3 A *technological bond* refers to a situation in which the customer is required to use repair/maintenance facilities and/or original spare parts from a manufacturer. The technological bond belongs in the technological factor group.

4 A *geographical bond* describes the limited possibility to buy a service because of distance. The present study views the geographical bond as belonging to the contextual factor group.

5 A *time bond* illustrates the situation where a service provider may be used because of suitable business hours. The present study categorises the time bond as belonging to the procedural factor group.

6 A *knowledge bond* means that a customer gains knowledge about a service provider. The knowledge bond belongs in the information factor group.

7 A *social bond* exists when a customer and a service provider know each other well. Social bonds belong in the social factor group.

8 A *cultural bond* exists when a customer identifies with certain companies or products made in certain countries. The cultural bond belongs in the contextual factor group.

9 An *ideological bond* indicates personal values, for example a preference for 'green' or environmentally sound products. The ideological bond is part of the social factor group.

10 A *psychological bond* refers to a customer being convinced of the superiority of a certain service provider. The present study sees the psychological bond as belonging to the social factor group.

Figure 6.11 presents one suggestion for the relationship of the concepts of bonds and commitment over time. It illustrates the holistic view of bonds, i.e. that their combination dictates the state of commitment and no bond operates in isolation from others. Bond is proposed as a term to be used for ties, and the resulting state would be called 'commitment', i.e. a combination of interrelated bonds that evolve in the bonding process in the course of the relationship. Further, the state of commitment and the combination of bonds are perceived in their own way by both parties in the relationship.

Commitment may be positive or negative. In semantic terms the idea of a negative bond may seem odd – how could a tie be measured on the minus scale? However, the concept helps in assessing the negative situations when bonds act as exit barriers for a customer who wants

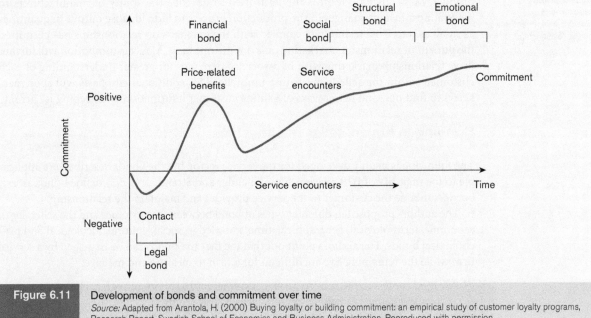

Figure 6.11	**Development of bonds and commitment over time**

Source: Adapted from Arantola, H. (2000) Buying loyalty or building commitment: an empirical study of customer loyalty programs, Research Report, Swedish School of Economics and Business Administration. Reproduced with permission.

to exit. The customer perceives ties and the situation is perceived as negative. This situation is illustrated in Figure 6.11 with the legal bond, where the customer is bound by a legal agreement that prevents an exit. In Figure 6.11, the financial bond results in positive commitment in the following ways. The customer perceives being tied to the supplier due to relationship investment or special pricing, and perceives the relationship as beneficial and positive. Financial bonds are usually rather short term (as seen in Figure 6.11), but a service encounter may immediately build a positive emotional bond, or it may take a couple of months for the first bonus voucher to arrive and build a positive economic bond. When positive bonds develop, elements of loyalty such as repeat experiences and positive attitude are also present.

The role of encounters in RM

Moments of truth
A critical or decisive time on which much depends; a crucial moment when seller's staff meets the customer.

Encounters can be considered to be the period of time during which a customer directly communicates with a specific product or service. We can see these encounters as 'moments of truth'. In this approach, an encounter is not limited to personal interaction, but includes customer contact with physical facilities and other tangibles.

Communication is defined as the process of *assigning meaning*. Each perception we have of our environment involves a transactional process between ourselves and the object(s) we perceive. Each participant's perception of the other in an encounter is a transaction between the qualities of this other and the participant's interpretation of these qualities. You form a *relationship* with the other participant in a dyadic encounter when you become aware that this other person is aware of you. Your participation in a specific encounter means that it will have an effect on you, irrespective of whether you are primarily creating or deciphering the message. In any transaction, each participant is simultaneously sending and receiving.

A person is aware that he or she is in a relationship when he or she is aware of being perceived by the other party. A relationship is therefore formed during a specific encounter when the following elements are present:

- you and another are interacting;
- you are aware of the other's behaviour;
- the other is aware of your behaviour;
- as a result, you are aware that the other is aware, and the other is aware that you are aware.

A relationship is formed when two people are aware both of each other and of the other's awareness. But this is only the beginning of a potential relationship. The key to building a relationship and sustaining communicative behaviour is in the way in which each participant adjusts to the other.

The awareness of being perceived by the other party at the start of a relationship is not limited to interpersonal encounters where customers have face-to-face contact with employees, although the potential for creating relationships in such encounters is rather high. The relationship might well be created and maintained during encounters with a mediated human contact, e.g. via phone, fax, e-mail or the Internet, or through encounters involving no human contact, e.g. interaction with a company through an ATM. The complexity of interaction decreases where there is no face-to-face human contact; responses are reduced to verbal or written expressions in the mediated human encounter, while interaction during an encounter with no human contact is limited to automatic predesigned response patterns performed by or through mechanical and electronic equipment.

In Figure 6.12, encounters have been categorised using two factors: *degree of human interaction* and *intensity of the relationship bond*. The latter describes the extent to which a single encounter contributes to relationship bonding. Figure 6.12 distinguishes seven types of encounter and positions them according to these two factors.

Internationalisation of encounter-based strategies

Companies that have been able to establish and maintain lasting relationships with customers in their home markets might be interested in exploring the potential for transferring encounter-based relationship strategies to other markets. Although the ground rules for establishing relationships might be the same all over the world, the prevailing (cultural) conditions underpinning the formation and consolidation of relationships with customers may be different in parts of the world.

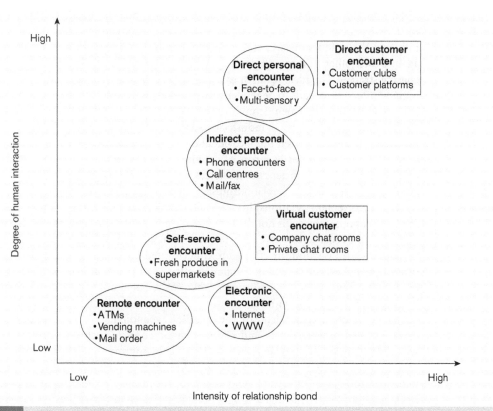

Figure 6.12   Typology of encounters based on the degree of human interaction and the intensity of the relationship bond
Source: Hennig-Thurau, T. and Hansen, U. (2000) *Relationship Marketing: Gaining Competitive Advantage Through Customer Satisfaction and Consumer Retention,* Springer Verlag, Berlin-Heidelberg, p. 283. Reproduced with permission.

The management has to be aware of the considerably higher complexity of the environment under consideration (compared to a purely domestic market) when a company takes and implements decisions concerning the standardisation of encounters with the aim of establishing customer relationships in foreign cultures. A careful assessment of the opportunities for encounter standardisation should provide an efficient and effective basis for establishing and maintaining relationships with customers, provided the product and/or service on offer is able to satisfy customer expectations.

6.4 RELATIONSHIPS WITH SUPPLIERS

There seem to be three major strategic issues related to purchasing management:

- decision whether to make an item in-house or to buy from external suppliers;
- development of appropriate relationships with suppliers;
- management of the supplier base in terms of size and relations between suppliers.

The first strategic issue is to decide what items to procure. This is defined by the scope of the operations that are undertaken in-house by the buying company. This determines the degree of vertical integration, which in purchasing terms has been addressed as the make-or-buy issue (Ghauri *et al.*, 2008; Freytag and Mikkelsen, 2007; Mclvor, 2008) .

What to produce internally and what to buy from external suppliers has been an issue in manufacturing firms for a very long time, despite the fact that it was apparently not identified as a matter of strategic importance until the 1980s. It is evident that buying firms over time have come to rely more on 'buy' than 'make'. Consequently, outsourcing to external suppliers has increased dramatically over time (Soroor *et al.*, 2009; Preston, 2004).

Having suppliers that compete with one another is one way of increasing efficiency in the purchasing operations. A buying company can switch from one supplier to the other and thus influence the vendors towards improving their efforts. The opportunity to play off suppliers against each other in terms of price conditions has been a particularly recommended purchasing strategy. The idea of this strategy is to avoid becoming too integrated with suppliers, because integration leads to dependence. Customer relationships based on this logic are characterised by low involvement from both parties.

The tendency in the overall industrial system towards increasing specialisation has called for more coordination between the individual companies. This in turn leads to more adaptation between buyer and seller in terms of activities and resources. These adaptations are made because they improve efficiency and effectiveness. They also create interdependencies between customer and supplier. Such relationships are characterised by a high involvement approach.

High-involvement relationships typically provide different types of benefits than low involvement ones, since it is not the individual transaction that is optimised. On the contrary, customers are eager to improve long-term efficiency and effectiveness. Instead of focusing on price in each transaction the efforts are concentrated on affecting long-term total costs. The purchasing behaviour of buying companies affects a number of costs, of which price is sometimes only minor in comparison with other costs. For example, product development has become increasingly common. Integrating resources with suppliers can reduce lead times in product development and decrease the total R&D spending.

The widely recognised *lean* and *agile* supply practices in such relationships have demonstrated that buyers and suppliers can work together to improve supply relationship, or even supply network, performance and consequently allow the supply chain to deliver better value to the ultimate customer. Lean supply techniques aim to eliminate waste in all areas of the business, from the shop-floor to manufacturing processes, and from new product development to supply chain management. Agile supply techniques, on the other band, are directed towards reducing the time it takes for a supply chain to deliver a good or service to the end customer and are aimed at supply chains that have to respond to volatile demand patterns. Both the 'lean' and 'agile' supply schools have provided a great deal of case evidence that demonstrates that collaboration, in the cause of lean or agile goals, can be effective in bringing down costs and/or increasing product functionality. For example, the lean school has often referred to the Japanese automobile industry, especially the Toyota Motor Corporation, as a good example of lean practice. The agile school has pointed to the production of the Smart Car, a car that offers total customisation, backed up by a service that offers responsiveness to customer demands.

However, the idea that collaboration constitutes 'best practice' ignores two key factors. First, not all transactions will justify the resources required for a collaborative relationship. Entering a collaborative relationship will only make economic sense if the expected financial and strategic rewards are deemed to be higher than the costs associated with the establishment of such a relationship. Second, not all the buyers that suppliers deal with will wish to allocate the resources required for a collaborative relationship to be developed. A supplier may have both the resources and the inclination to develop a collaborative relationship in a given situation. However, the buyer in question may have other priorities. The supplier may prefer to allocate its resources to other customers – those that it deems more relevant to the achievement of its business goals (Andersen and Christensen, 2004).

Furthermore, even where collaborative relationships are developed, there is by no means one form of collaboration. For example, in some power situations, getting buyers to collaborate will not be possible. In particular, such relationships will differ in both their conduct and outcome depending on the power-dependence relations concerned. As has long been argued in the social science literature, there are four generic buyer–supplier power structures: buyer dominance, interdependence independence and supplier dominance (see Figure 6.13).

		BUYER DOMINACE	INTERDEPENDENCE
ATTRIBUTES OF BUYER POWER RELATIVE TO SUPPLIER	HIGH	• Few buyers/many suppliers • Buyer has high % share of total market for supplier • Supplier is highly dependent on buyer for revenue with limited alternatives • Supplier switching costs are high • Buyer switching costs are low • Buyer account is attractive to supplier • Supplier offerings are customised • Buyer search costs are low • Supplier has no information asymmetry advantages over buyer	• Few buyers/few suppliers • Buyer has relatively high % share of total market for supplier • Supplier is highly dependent on buyer for revenue with few alternatives • Supplier switching costs are high • Buyer switching costs are high • Buyer account is attractive to supplier • Supplier offerings are not commoditised and standardised • Buyer search costs are high • Supplier has significant information asymmetry advantages over buyer
		INDEPENDENCE	SUPPLIER DOMINANCE
	LOW	• Few buyers/few suppliers • Buyer has relatively low % share of total market for supplier • Supplier is not dependent on buyer for revenue and has many alternatives • Supplier switching costs are low • Buyer switching costs are low • Buyer account is not particularly attractive to supplier • Supplier offerings are commoditised and standardised • Buyer search costs are relatively low • Supplier has only limited information asymmetry advantages over buyer	• Many buyers/few suppliers • Buyer has low % share of total market for supplier • Supplier is not at all dependent on the buyer for revenue and has many alternatives • Supplier switching costs are low • Buyer switching costs are high • Buyers account is not attractive to the supplier • Supplier offerings are not customised • Buyer search costs are very high • Supplier has high information asymmetry advantages over buyer

LOW   ATTRIBUTES OF SUPPLIER POWER RELATIVE TO BUYER   HIGH

Figure 6.13 The attributes of buyer and supplier power

The bonding between buyers and suppliers can also increase by investing in relationship-specific adaptations to processes, products or procedures (Hughes, 2008; Johnsen *et al.*, 2008). By relationship-specific adaptations, we mean those adaptations that are non-transferable to relationships with other buyers or suppliers. It could be adaptations of the following kind: adaptations of the product specification, adaptations to the product design, adaptations to the manufacturing process, adaptations to delivery procedures, adaptations to stockholding, adaptations to planning procedures, adaptations to administrative procedures and adaptations to financial procedures.

To understand the power relation the power resources of both sides need to be put together. When the buyer has high power resources and the supplier has low power resources, the buyer will be dominant. When the buyer has low power resources and the supplier has high power resources, the supplier will be dominant. When the power resources are high for both the buyer and the supplier, then they will be interdependent. When both parties have low power resources, then they will be independent from each other.

Figure 6.13 provides a description of some of the key attributes that one might expect to find if one were trying to position buyer and supplier relationships using the power matrix. The power matrix is explained in more detail elsewhere, but it is constructed around the idea that all buyer and supplier relationships are predicted on the relative value and the relative scarcity of the resources that are exchanged between the two parties.

In the buyer dominance box, the buyer has power attributes relative to the supplier that provide the basis for the buyer to leverage the supplier's performance on quality and/or cost improvement, and ensure that the supplier receives only normal returns.

In the interdependence box, both the buyer and the supplier possess resources that require the two parties to the exchange to work closely together, since neither party to the exchange can force the other to do what it does not wish to do. In this circumstance, the supplier may achieve above-normal returns but must also pass some value to the buyer in the form of less-than-ideal returns, as well as some degree of innovation.

In the independence box, neither the buyer nor the supplier has significant leverage opportunities over the other party, and the buyer and the supplier must accept the current prevailing price and quality levels. Fortunately for the buyer, this price and quality level is often not that advantageous for the supplier because the supplier has few leverage opportunities (other than buyer ignorance and incompetence) and may be forced to operate at only normal returns.

In the supplier dominance box, the supplier has all of the levers of power. It is in this box that one would expect the supplier to possess many of the isolating mechanisms that close markets to competitors and many of the barriers to market entry that allow above-normal returns to be sustained. In such an environment, the buyer is likely to be both a price and quality receiver.

As well as the possible buyer–supplier power structures to consider, there is huge potential in exploiting better the opportunities offered by coping with suppliers. However, potential benefits are not reaped automatically. The focus has shifted from buying well towards managing within relationships (Gadde and Snehota, 2000).

Reverse marketing

Reverse marketing
The buyer (and not the seller as in traditional marketing) takes the initiative of searching for a supplier that is able to fulfil the buyer's needs.

Firms increasingly realise that rapidly changing market conditions require significant changes in their purchasing function. In more and more firms, purchasing is becoming proactive and of strategic importance. This phenomenon has been referred to as **reverse marketing**. As the term implies, there are clear similarities with the marketing concept (Biemans and Brand, 1995). The phenomenon was described in Chapter 4, in the section about supplier selection in the B2B market.

Reverse marketing describes how purchasing actively identifies potential subcontractors and offers suitable partners a proposal for long-term cooperation. Similar terms are proactive procurement and buyer initiative (Ottesen, 1995). In recent years, the buyer–seller relationship has changed considerably. The traditional relationship, in which a seller takes the initiative by offering a product, is increasingly being replaced by one in which the buyer actively searches for a supplier that is able to fulfil its needs.

Implementing a reverse marketing strategy starts with fundamental market research and with an evaluation of reverse marketing options (i.e. possible suppliers). Before choosing suppliers the firm may include both present and potential suppliers in the analysis as well as current and desired activities.

Based on this analysis the firm may select a number of suitable partners as suppliers and rank them in order of preference.

6.5 RELATIONSHIPS WITH COMPLEMENTORS/PARTNERS

This kind of relationship is based on collaboration between manufacturers of complementary functions and or products/services. In such a collaboration, each partner has a strategic resource that the other needs and in this way each partner is motivated to develop some kind of exchange process.

For example, partners divide the value chain activities between themselves: one partner develops and manufactures a product while letting the other partner market it. Another example is a joint marketing agreement where complementary product lines of two firms are sold together through existing or new distribution channels, and thus broaden the market coverage of both firms.

In Figure 6.14, different types of coalition are shown in the value chain perspective. These are based on the possible collaboration pattern along the value chain. In Figure 6.14 two partners are shown, A and B, each having its own value chain. Three different types of value chain partnership appear:

- *upstream-based collaboration (1)*: A and B collaborate on R&D and/or production;
- *downstream-based collaboration (2)*: A and B collaborate on marketing, distribution, sales and/or service;
- *upstream/downstream-based collaboration (3)*: A and B have different but complementary competences at each end of the value chain.

In such collaboration, each partner has a strategic resource that the other needs and so they are prepared to develop some form of extended exchange mechanism in order to expedite the process. For example, it could involve the transfer of technology in exchange for knowledge and understanding of a market. The resources involved are, by definition, strategic in nature. They are the long-term, relatively stable bases upon which the organisations create value in the product offerings that they exchange.

Types 1 and 2 represent the so-called Y coalition and type 3 represents the so-called X coalition.

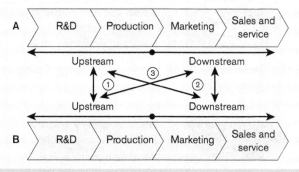

| Figure 6.14 | Collaboration possibilities for partners A and B in the value chain |

Source: Hollensen, S. (2001) *Global Marketing: A Market Responsive Approach*, 2nd ed., Financial Times-Prentice Hall, Harlow, p. 274. Reproduced with permission.

Y coalitions

Partners share the actual performance of one or more value chain activities. For example, joint production of models or components enables the attainment of scale economies that can provide lower production costs per unit. Another example is a joint marketing agreement where complementary product lines of two firms are sold together through existing or new distribution channels, and thus broaden the market coverage of both firms.

EXHIBIT 6.4
Irn-Bru's distributor alliance (Y coalition) with Pepsi Bottling Group (PBG) in Russia

A. G. Barr, the UK's leading independent branded soft drinks manufacturer was founded in Falkirk, Scotland, in 1875. The company expanded to Glasgow in 1887 and its headquarters are now in Cumbernauld just outside the city. A. G. Barr makes the renowned Irn-Bru soft drink, introduced in 1901, which, in 2008 had about 5 per cent of the UK carbonated soft drinks (CSD) market. Despite tough domestic competition, Irn-Bru is Scotland's largest selling single-flavoured CSD and is the third best selling soft drink in the UK, after Coca-Cola and Pepsi.

In 2008, A. G. Barr's turnover was £170 million (Annual Report and Accounts 2009) with an operating profit of £23.1 million. The formula for Irn-Bru is a closely guarded secret, known only by two of Barr's board members. Irn-Bru is most famous for its unique taste, maverick advertising and eccentric bright orange colour, making it easily recognisable even when not in its packaging.

Source: Courtesy of A. G. Barr plc

In the late 1980s, Barr actively began to look at expansion through international markets. It considered France, Germany and Benelux countries, among others, but found that Coca-Cola and Pepsi dominated these mature markets. Competition was fierce and margins tight. Consequently, it examined other emerging markets and was attracted to Russia. In the years following the break-up of the Soviet Union, Russia showed much potential with a large population, growing prosperity and standard of living, and a rising demand for consumer goods. Moreover, the Russians, like the Scots, have a 'sweet tooth', leading to high soft drinks consumption. As part of the international expansion strategy, in 1994, Barr began direct exports of its trademark Irn-Bru to Russia.

Barr eventually parted company with its initial franchisee but the Irn-Bru brand by that time was so well-established that, in 2002, Barr arranged a new manufacturing franchise contract with the Pepsi Bottling Group (PBG) of Russia to manufacture, distribute and sell Irn-Bru. PBG (Russia) has over 4,000 employees and distributes the PepsiCo brands throughout Russia. Since February 2002, the distribution network has been greatly enlarged, especially by using the PBG retail space and coolers in the retail outlets, improving brand availability to the trade, retailers, wholesalers and clubs. The brand is produced in 250 ml glass, 330 ml cans, 600 ml, 1.25 l and 2 l plastic bottles.

→

Value of the distribution alliance for both partners:

Irn-Bru:

- Irn-Bru in Russia has been a part of A. G. Barr's international expansion plan.
- Irn-Bru has provided extra turnover and profit for A.G. Barr.

PBG:

- In many Russian retail stores (with a broader PBG product range) the Irn-Bru has blocked the available shelf space for Pepsi's main competitor, Coca-Cola.
- Irn-Bru has provided extra turnover and profit for PBG.

Irn-Bru is now established as one of the leading soft drink brands in the country.

Sources: A. G. Barr plc (www.agbarr.co.uk) and Irn-Bru website (www.irn-bru.co.uk).

X coalitions

Partners divide the value chain activities between themselves. For example, one partner develops and manufactures a product while letting the other partner market it. Forming X coalitions involves identifying the value chain activities where the firm is well positioned and has its core competence. Take the case where A has its core competences in upstream functions, but is weak in downstream functions. A wants to enter a foreign market, but lacks local market knowledge and does not know how to get access to foreign distribution channels for its products. Therefore A seeks and finds a partner, B, which has its core competences in the downstream functions, but is weak in the upstream functions. In this way A and B can form a coalition where B can help A with distribution and selling in a foreign market, and A can help B with R&D or production.

In summary, X coalitions imply that the partners have asymmetric competences in the value chain activities: where one is strong, the other is weak and vice versa. In Y coalitions, on the other hand, partners tend to be more similar in the strengths and weaknesses of their value chain activities.

The so-called **co-branding** is closely connected to the downstream-based collaboration.

Co-branding
The practice of using the established brand of two different companies on the same product with a common marketing message.

Co-branding

The term co-branding is relatively new to the business vocabulary and is used to encompass a wide range of marketing activity involving the use of two or more brands. Thus co-branding could be considered to include:

- *Sponsorship*: where Marlboro sponsors the Ferrari team in Formula 1;
- *Licensing*: where Mattel has been granted the worldwide rights to manufacture a Ferrari-branded range of boys' and girls' toys including vehicles, dolls, soft toys, games and puzzles. Licensed products, especially with entertainment properties, can sometimes have a limited shelf life. Using a licence such as Hello Kitty could be very short term. Others, such as Disney's Mickey Mouse, could go on practically for ever;
- *Retailing*: where BP hosts Safeway mini-stores;
- *Retail co-promotion*: where McDonald's and Disney get together;
- *Manufacturing collaborations*: for example the Mercedes-Swatch car.

Motives for co-branding

The basis for any cooperative arrangement is the expectation of synergies, which create value for both participants, over and above the value they would expect to generate on their own.

Co-branding is a form of cooperation between two or more brands with significant customer recognition, in which all the participants' brand names are retained. It is of medium- to long-term duration and its net value creation potential is normally too small to justify setting up a new brand and/or legal joint venture. (The Mercedes-Swatch car is an exception here.)

Logic and experience confirm that the stronger the brands that form the co-brand, the more likely it is that their identities will be preserved, whatever the extent of cooperation. If the participants were to destroy significant value by abandoning very powerful brands and investing resources in another name instead, the net value creation potential would be severely reduced.

Duration

How long cooperative relationships last depends very much on the lifecycle of the products and/or the characteristics of the markets involved.

The relationship between McDonald's and Disney where McDonald's uses the latest Disney movie on its product range will typically last for three to four months and can best be defined as a co-promotion.

At the other extreme, Mercedes-Benz and Swatch are cooperating on the development, manufacture and launch of a new urban vehicle, a process likely to take five years. This cooperation is taking place in a joint venture.

Similarly, a number of airlines are cooperating on routes, flights and customer marketing in major global initiatives, such as the Star Alliance. These initiatives have no evident end-point at all, have new brand identities created for them, and are generally described as alliances.

In between these extremes lie a number of arrangements usually referred to as co-branding and/or ingredient branding, such as Intel with a variety of PC manufacturers to co-brand its machines with the 'Intel inside' logo. But these arrangements are also without fixed end-points.

It appears that the envisioned duration strongly influences the categorisation of many instances of co-branding, but it is not the only discriminating factor. Longer-term cooperations generally imply more extensive sharing of assets and expertise, with the potential to generate more shared value.

Values endorsement co-branding

This level of cooperation is specifically designed to include endorsement of one or other's brand values and positioning or both. In fact, it is often the principal reason for the tie-up.

In recent years many charities have launched co-branded 'affinity' credit cards with a bank or credit card company, in fact so many that the concept has been somewhat devalued, but the principle remains intact. This is a win–win situation for the bank, the charity and the customer. The charity benefits from extra revenue, the bank gets extra transaction volume along with the kudos of charitable associations and the customer feels that they are contributing to a worthwhile cause.

So the essence of value endorsement co-branding is that the two participants cooperate because they have, or want to achieve, alignment of their brand values in the customer's mind. This substantially decreases the pool of potential partners for any projected co-branding deal and increases the value creation potential.

Le Cordon Bleu's co-branding deal with Tefal offers a more conventional example of value endorsement co-branding. Le Cordon Bleu is a French culinary academy whose brand has become synonymous with the highest standards of cooking. Tefal, a leading French cookware manufacturer, was launching its new Integral range of high-quality cookware and negotiated for the endorsement of Le Cordon Bleu in its marketing campaign.

This helped to build brand awareness for Tefal Integral, and it endowed the Integral brand with strong associations of culinary quality, particularly as Le Cordon Bleu academy's chefs were shown to be using Integral cookware and endorsing its quality values. The chief executive officer of Le Cordon Bleu knowingly staked his brand's values and reputation on the co-branded products.

Both companies were able to reinforce their complementary brand reputations through the tie-up and stimulate increased sales revenues for the co-branded products. This highlights the importance of appropriate partner selection.

Ingredient branding

The rationale here is that a brand noted for the market-leading qualities of its product supplies that product as a component of another branded product. Despite the similarities between co-branding and ingredient branding there is also an important difference, as indicated in Figure 6.15.

Co-branding

In the case of co-branding, two powerful and complementary brands combine to produce a product that is more than the sum of their parts and relies on each partner committing a selection of its core skills and competences to that product on an ongoing basis (Erevelles *et al.* 2008).

This was the case some years ago when Bacardi Rum and Coca-Cola marketed a bottle with the finished mixed drink 'Rum-and-Coca-Cola'.

Ingredient branding

OEM
Original equipment manufacturer. In the OEM contract the customer is called the OEM or 'sourcer' whereas the parts suppliers are called manufacturers of OEM products.

Normally the marketer of the final product (**OEM**) creates all of the value in the consumer's eyes. But in the cases of Intel and NutraSweet, the ingredient supplier is seeking to build value in its products by branding and promoting the key component of an end product. When promotion (pull strategy: see Figure 6.15) of the key component brand is initiated by the ingredient supplier, the goal is to build awareness and preference among consumers for that ingredient brand. Simultaneously, it may be the manufacturer (OEM) that seeks to benefit from a recognised ingredient brand. Some computer manufacturers are benefiting from the quality image of using an Intel chip.

However, ingredient branding is not suitable for every supplier of components. An ingredient supplier should fulfil the following requirements:

- The ingredient supplier should be offering a product that has a substantial advantage over existing products. DuPont's Teflon, NutraSweet, Intel chips and the Dolby noise reduction system are all examples of major technological innovations, the result of large investment in R&D.

Co-branding

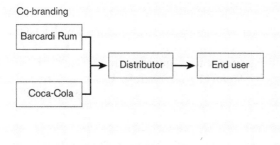

Ingredient branding

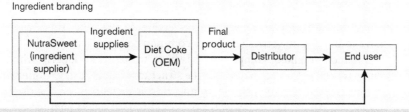

| Figure 6.15 | Illustration of co-branding and ingredient branding |

Source: Hollensen, S. (2001) *Global Marketing: A Market Responsive Approach*, 2nd ed, Financial Times-Prentice Hall, Harlow, p. 421. Reproduced with permission.

- The ingredient should be critical to the success of the final product. NutraSweet is not only a low-calorie sweetener, but has a taste that is nearly identical to that of sugar.

An important part of the value for IBM, Compaq or any other PC manufacturer of co-branding with Intel is the reputation that Intel enjoys in the PC marketplace for the manufactured quality and functional performance of its Pentium microprocessors. Quality and performance are core values for the Intel Pentium brand and they migrate through to the PC product.

The categorisation of ingredient branding as a value added tool is justified because there is an identifiable physical component – the chip – contained in the product as sold to the customer. Without it, the value of the product would be greatly diminished.

Cars provide a good illustration of the benefits of ingredient co-branding. They are the most expensive branded purchases that most consumers ever make, so the manufacturers want to attach strong emotional and intuitive values to them in addition to their rational benefits and values. Many of the car companies, particularly the global volume producers, have found that co-branding deals enable them cost-effectively to reinforce particular brand images and customise their products. Various premium car manufacturers use Bose audio products. The use of such a strongly branded item, associated in the consumer's mind with high quality, is heavily promoted with the car's advertising to reaffirm the premium positioning of the vehicle.

In summary, the essence of ingredient co-branding is that a manufacturer (OEM)/ ingredient supplier wishing to convey focused messages about the attributes and values of its product uses and promotes branded components whose own brand image reinforces the desired attributes and values.

The ingredient supplier benefits by guaranteeing sales volumes at the same time as reinforcing the attributes of its product brand. The manufacturer (OEM) benefits by confirming the attributes and image of its product while sharing the marketing costs.

6.6 RELATIONSHIPS WITH COMPETITORS

The relationships between competitors (horizontal network) have not been analysed to the same extent as vertical relationships. Cooperative relationships in the vertical network (Figure 2.3) are easier to grasp as they are built on a distribution of activities and resources among players in a supply chain. Horizontal networks, on the other hand, are more informal, invisible, and based more on social exchanges.

When competitors are involved in resource exchange alliances, competition introduces same problems. The dilemma is that in creating an alliance with a competitor, an organisation is, in fact making them more competitive.

For collaboration to succeed, each competitor must contribute something distinctive: basic research, product development skills, manufacturing capacity, access to distribution. In the network approach, the market includes both complementarities and substitutes, both cooperating and competing firms. Competitors also strive to develop their nets. Such competitive activity is a major force for change in the networks. Competitors are predominantly negatively connected to each other. They might compete for customers, suppliers or other partners. Competing firms also often have customers, distributors or suppliers in common. Sometimes this implies a negative connection, but at other times competing firms do not have conflicting objectives vis-à-vis a common counterpart.

Interaction among competitors has been treated traditionally within economic theory, and has been explained in terms of the structure of an industry within which it operates. It is further argued that intensity in competition is dependent on the degree of symmetry between companies, while the degree of concentration determines whether competitors act in collusion or competition with each other.

Variations in patterns of interaction are also viewed via a relational approach to competitive interaction.

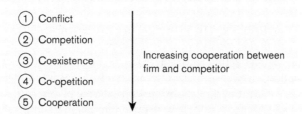

| Figure 6.16 | Five types of relationship between a firm and its competitor |

Based on the motives for interaction and the intensity of the relationship concerned, five types of interaction are distinguished: *conflict, competition, coexistence, co-opetition* and *cooperation* (see Figure 6.16).

Conflict between competitors occurs when the strategies they employ are largely directed at each other with the aim of destruction. The strongest version of conflict requires that an organisation has as its single overriding objective the effective destruction of a specific competitor.

In the early 1980s, a number of authors took upon themselves the task of transferring the principles of war and battle, as codified by generations of military strategists such as Von Clausewitz, into the business arena. Organisations cannot only seek to destroy existing competitors, but also to prevent the emergence of new ones. Pre-emptive strategies may be used to render it unlikely that a new competitor survives.

Competition is goal-oriented, directed towards achieving one's own goals even though this may have a negative effect on other competitors. Coexistent competition occurs when actors do not see one another as competitors, and therefore act independently of each other.

It may be argued that one single relationship can comprise both cooperation and competition, that two firms can compete and cooperate simultaneously. In any specific relationship, elements of both cooperation and competition can be found, but one or the other of these elements can in some cases be tacit. If both the elements of cooperation and competition are visible, the relationship between the competitors is named co-opetition. For example, two competitors can complement each other by creating new markets, but will compete when it comes to separating the markets. Hence, organisations may make the same products, but not compete in the same markets or segments or may not compete in the same way (Bengtsson and Kock, 2000). However, the two competitors have to be careful not to be seen to be engaging in anti-competitive behaviour.

Finally, in cooperation, the companies involved strive towards the same goals, for example by working together on a common technological platform in strategic alliances. The interaction between competitors is variable and can involve both cooperative and competitive interaction. Individuals moving from one competitor to another provide a potential link and a powerful means by which cooperation between them can be achieved. Such an individual brings with him or her the existing relationships from the organisation left behind. These relationships may reduce with time, but are unlikely to disappear.

The individual provides a potential communication mode. In many industries movement of employees between competitors is common, and the resultant network of personal relationships is an important input for the implementation of the firm's marketing strategy.

In summary, if the firm, on the other hand, needs resources held by the competitor and does not have a strong position, cooperation is the best option. The advantage of cooperation is related to development, but the function of cooperation is the access to resources rather than a driving force or pressure to develop. Through cooperation a company can gain competence, market knowledge, reputation, access to other products and other resources of importance for its business.

6.7 INTERNAL MARKETING (IM) RELATIONSHIPS

Parallel to relationships that curb the free market mechanism outside the company, there is an internal market consisting of groups communicating to other groups within the organisation. Internal marketing is considered to be the process of creating market conditions within the organisation to ensure that internal employees' wants and needs are met. This will be the best basis for creating a relationship with external players.

Rafiq and Ahmed (2000) have defined internal marketing as

a planned effort using a marketing-like approach to overcome organizational resistance to change and to align, motivate and inter-functionally co-ordinate and integrate employees towards the effective implementation of corporate and functional strategies in order to deliver customer satisfaction through a process of creating motivated and customer-orientated employees.

Internal marketing emerged from services marketing. Its purpose was to get the front-line personnel – who have interactive relationships with external customers – to handle the service encounter better and with more independence. The distinction between internal and external marketing becomes blurred.

For instance, the motivation of employees via marketing-like activities was implicit in the early stages of the evolutionary development of IM. Grönroos (1981) and others also recommend the marketing-like approach to improve the inter-functional coordination and hence customer orientation. Inter-functional coordination and integration are in later stages. In later stages of the evolutionary development of IM, the central reason for interest in IM was its contribution to effective implementation of strategy via increased inter-functional coordination and employee motivation.

At the centre of this framework is customer orientation, which is achieved through a marketing-like approach to the motivation of employees, and inter-functional coordination. The centrality of customer orientation reflects its importance in the marketing literature and its central role in achieving customer satisfaction and hence organisational goals.

The objective of internal marketing within RM is to create relationships between management and employees and between functions. The personnel can be viewed as an internal market, and this market must be reached efficiently in order to prepare the personnel for external contacts.

Making staff feel more valued motivates them to pull out all the stops and provide a better service to those outside.

Companies that fully embrace the concept of IM will therefore reflect their commitment in, for example, values, assumptions, behaviours, dress codes, reward schemes and office arrangements. In fact, an organisation's position relating to IM can be aptly communicated by the whole corporate brand.

Key components of IM include (Strategic Direction, 2009):

- *Trust*: employees who feel trusted are much more likely to collaborate and share information that will help the organisation satisfy customer demands. Highlighting similarities rather than differences can help cultivate trust and a community spirit. In contrast, too great an emphasis on rank or status can destroy any such ambitions.

- *Empowerment*: insightful management encourage employees to use discretion when dealing with the customer. Being allowed this flexibility on how to perform duties improves employee self-worth and helps nurture a 'can do' attitude that makes for greater adaptability and responsiveness. While potential issues lurk in the shape of overconfidence and role ambiguity, finding an optimal level of empowerment should prevent any serious problems. Likewise, clarifying performance expectations can avert confusion by helping employees strike the right balance between individuality and teamwork.

- *Behaviour-based evaluation*: the norm for many organisations is to use measurable outputs such as sales figures to gauge success. However, a focus on competences that include communication, personal qualities and service-related behaviours such as problem solving is deemed a more appropriate assessment of customer service encounters. That way, it is easier to identify where additional or enhanced employee input can improve the customer's experience.

- *Recognition and appreciation*: reward schemes provide a powerful means of encouraging enforcement and continuity. While the type of programme should be appropriate to organisational culture, it is worth remembering that a simple 'thank you' or 'well done' can also do wonders for morale.

An IM organisation can expect to reap rewards in the shape of customer loyalty, positive word-of-mouth (WOM), increased customer spending and cross-buying behaviour. But the benefits do not come cheap because the initiative demands significant capital investment in human resource capabilities.

Intranets
Connects the computers within a business together.

To a large extent, internal marketing must be interactive. An **intranet** can help, but the social event is also important. At the start of a sales season, large groups gather to learn, to be entertained and to mix socially for a day or two.

Training and education can be seen as tools for internal marketing. Disney has its own university, and McDonald's has its Hamburger University.

Internal marketing can be based on personal and interactive relationships as well as on a certain amount of mass marketing. Traditional activities to reach employees have often been routinely performed and have built more on bureaucratic principles and wishful thinking than on professional marketing and communications know-how (Mahnert and Torres, 2007).

6.8 SUMMARY

Relationships, rather than simple transactions, provide the central focus in marketing. It is not enough to discuss the activities that a single firm performs. RM includes relationships or networks among companies and their suppliers, lateral partnerships among competitors, government and not-for-profit organisations, internal partnerships with business units, employees and functional departments, and buyer partnerships with intermediate and ultimate customers.

Competitive advantage stems from the many discrete activities a firm performs in designing, producing, marketing, delivering and supporting its product. Each of these activities can contribute to a firm's relative cost position and create a basis for differentiation. The value chain disaggregates a firm into its strategically relevant activities in order to understand the behaviour of costs and the existing and potential sources of differentiation. *A firm gains competitive advantage by performing these strategically important activities more cheaply or better than its competitors.*

The focus in the value net is managing relationships – similar to the systems idea of positive synergistic effects created through linkages – rather than optimising individual components of the system. The systems approach focuses not only on the components (e.g. functions or activities), but also on how they are related.

In this chapter, we have limited our understanding and analysis to how the activities are linked to the activities of a company's customers, suppliers, competitors, complementors and employees (the value net). Furthermore the company has to have good relations (internally) and communication to its employees (internal marketing).

According to the value net a company's activities evolve within its relationships with these organisations.

Relationship with customers

The always-a-share customer and the lost-for-good customer represent opposite ends of a continuum of exchange situations. The always-a-share customer displays less loyalty to a particular supplier, whereas the lost-for-good customer remains loyal to a particular supplier for a long time.

Relationship with suppliers

The adversarial approach is derived from a transaction-based theory as it explains how firms try to minimise the total production costs by maintaining multiple sources in order to reduce the power of their suppliers with the cooperative relationships. On the other hand, the company develops a close relationship with a small number of selected suppliers.

Relationship with competitors

Four different types of relationship have been identified, taking the trade-off between cooperation and competition into account: competition, coexistence, co-opetiveness and cooperation.

Relationship with complementors

These are based on collaboration between manufacturers of complementary functions and/or products.

Relationship with internal employees

The employees can be viewed as an internal market. Internal marketing is considered to be the process of creating market conditions within the organisation to ensure that the internal employees' wants and needs are met. This will be the best basis for creating relationships with external organisations.

The development of a customer relationship can be explained by use of the marriage metaphor: awareness, exploration, expansion, commitment and termination (dissolution). The decision to terminate is considered to be due to the interaction of a trigger event and the existing state of the relationship. The factors that characterise an inter-firm relationship cannot only provide a cause for the termination, but impact greatly on the strategies firms utilise when ending a relationship. A model of inter-firm relationship termination was proposed and propositions regarding choice and use of relationship termination strategies were explored.

CASE STUDY 6.1

Saipa
The Iranian car manufacturer seeks a drive to serve

Background

Saipa (an acronym for Société Anonyme Iranienne de Production Automobile) was established in 1966 as an Iranian-based car company. Its focus lay initially in producing cars, to cater for a predominantly Iranian audience.

In 1990 Saipa decided to consolidate its activities by forming the Saipa Group, which has grown to house a mixture of 86 separate companies, sub-divisions and subsidiaries. With 48 per cent of the company being owned by the Iranian government, Saipa reached a local market share of 55 per cent in 2006. It has also now become the largest automotive group in the Middle East, with the production of more than 1 million cars per year.

A contributing factor to Saipa's success has been the adoption of more than one strategic approach to producing vehicles. Its vehicle portfolio is made up of:

- existing overseas designs, with their final assembly being completed by Saipa;

Saipa's range of cars
Source: Courtesy of Saipa

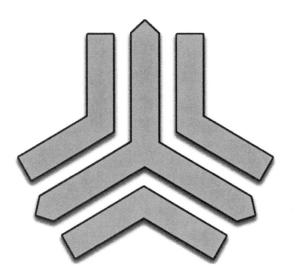

The Saipa logo
Source: Courtesy of Saipa

- the manufacture of licensed versions of existing designs;
- Saipa-designed and manufactured vehicles.

Partnerships and joint ventures that have been forged with Citroën (France), Renault (France), Nissan (Japan) and Kia Motors (Korea) have resulted in Saipa manufacturing or assembling selected lines from each of these companies. The vehicles which Saipa has completed have served both its own domestic market and other overseas markets – including France, the Middle East and North Africa.

The strategic decision to form partnerships and joint ventures in this way has allowed Saipa to develop its own manufacturing competences over time. The company has benefited from understanding the manufacturing process, from the component upwards, with the support of established manufacturers. Production growth has also been managed smoothly through, first, being able to utilise imported parts and, second, by becoming more self-reliant – moving towards taking control of these manufacturing duties. In addition, Saipa by externally co-branding its vehicles, has capitalised on

---

Sapia facts

- Established in 1966
- Heaquarters in Teheran, Iran
- 18,500 employees
- Second-largest car manufacturer in Iran after IKCO (Iran Khodro Company)
- Iranian government owns 48 per cent of Saipa

---

some of the existing brand equity and product values previously built up using its partners' resources.

Exports from the Saipa Group

Saipa's exporting activities are of increasing importance. The value of exports by Saipa and its affiliates surpassed US$150 million in the last Iranian calendar year ended 20 March 2009, showing a 30 per cent rise over its preceding year. Commercial vehicles and cars accounted for 50 per cent and 40 per cent of the exports respectively. Spare parts and technical-engineering services had a 10 per cent share in the value of exports.

The company has set a goal of $300 million exports for the current year through expanding its target markets to 40 countries.

Political positioning

In 2008 Saipa signed a memorandum of understanding with Malaysia's Proton, with the aim of encouraging a unified strategy looking to share resources and supply networks. An additional objective was to exert leverage on the ties that exist between Muslim countries, in the interests of then strengthening them. The aim of both companies, as stated, has been to encourage other Muslim counties to adopt this approach in order to better serve new markets collectively.

It appears that not only religion, but also global politics have afforded Saipa some successes in the face of the difficulties associated with conducting business under existing sanctions against Iran: Saipa has established automobile assembly lines in Venezuela and Syria, countries that have previously been termed by the US as 'axes of evil'. However, in the shadow of the economic downturn of 2009, references to axes seemed to have shifted away from politics and more towards the manufacture of vehicles. Saipa issued a press release

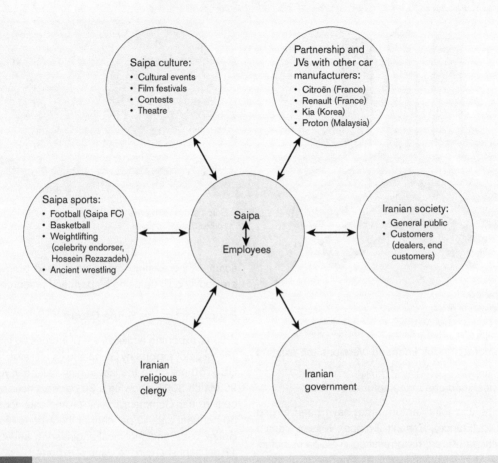

| Figure 6.17 | Saipa's diversified network of relationships |

indicating that 'big auto-makers' in the US have now invited them to participate in joint projects. Further to this, other (European) auto-makers, which have previously shown little interest in working with Saipa, have also considered selling shares to it.

The people factor

But perhaps the most significant and critical success factor in all of these activities lies in Saipa's ability to manage consumer and employee relationships with tact, diplomacy and compassion. The company has extended this underlying principle beyond car manufacture and reframed it – to secondarily encompass a desire to serve the generalist needs of society. A people-centred approach, driven by human resource management and relationship marketing principles, has led Saipa towards a course of action which would see it attempt to actively embed these values much further than just management and marketing communications activities.

Saipa formed a subsidiary company called the Saipa Culture and Sport Company, in the interests of promoting

Iranian culture, health, sport, well-being and family values. The company's focus has been to offer worthwhile 'other' initiatives for the general public, which have little to do with cars. As they all carry strong Saipa branding, this approach has in turn provided another platform, serving the expansion of both Saipa's brand proposition and core competences.

Culture counts

Activities have seen the company organise Saipa cultural events, film festivals and contests, and distribute CDs, books and magazines on a variety of topics. In addition, employees have enjoyed access to on-site courses held in lecture theatres (ranging from job-related technical subjects to English), a dedicated mosque, on-site healthcare, a pharmacist and sports facilities. The children of Saipa employees have also received presents delivered to them on their birthdays.

In a country with an ancient tradition of passionately celebrating the arts, romance, sports and Persian excellence, Saipa would argue that its approach is more than a strategic business decision. Instead, staff hold the view that, as individuals, it is both in their DNA and a social responsibility, and therefore has to be reflected in the activities of Saipa.

In the field of sports, Iran is proud of its national treasure, ancient wrestling. This, however, is being quickly replaced by many other activities including football, martial arts, basketball and other mainstream sports. This is perhaps a sign that despite much International press coverage, Iranians are no different than other nations and they are keen to compete and share experiences with people from other countries. In trying to cater for its consumers, these trends have meant that Saipa has had to keep a keen eye on consumer preferences, paying particular attention to emotional, behavioural and psychographic factors outside car consumption.

A thirst for knowledge

Iran holds a large, young and increasingly educated population. In contrast to other conservative Islamic societies such as Saudi Arabia, Iranian women are free to drive and make up approximately 60 per cent of the university student population. Also, interestingly, it was reported in 2006 that 70 per cent of the students in the applied physics department of Azad University were women. While women still need the permission of their families, or husband, to work, there has been strong encouragement from the government for them to do so.

With such large numbers of ambitious and educated Iranians, there have been consequential problems associated with increased economic migrancy. In 2006, the International Monetary Fund reported that of the 90 countries that it measured, Iran had the highest rate of brain drain. Saipa seems to have positioned itself well through its part-government ownership and strong intent to serve society. The company is attempting to address this issue through social inclusion, job creation and the championing of Iranian values.

By embedding itself into mainstream society and encouraging the consumption of at least one of its offerings, Saipa has been gifted a variety of touch-points with the consumer. Collectively, they afford it the opportunity to develop meaningful relationships and take advantage of a strong brand presence.

Sport becomes another vehicle

Saipa decided to branch into the field of sport, forming a portfolio of Saipa-branded clubs and teams. Sporting activities have included football, female futsal, volleyball and weightlifting, among others.

The company cites three underlying key strategic reasons for this approach:

1 to demonstrate that Saipa cares about personal health and well-being. Saipa wanted to address a possible concern, that in encouraging consumers to purchase its vehicles, this was not an excuse for them to become lazy or neglect personal fitness. In conjunction with this, Saipa has attempted to design more environmentally friendly vehicles. These safeguards are particularly necessary for those discerning consumers who perhaps scrutinise the activities of a partly owned government organisation more;

2 to take further advantage of the associated marketing communications and relationship marketing opportunities that sport affords;

3 to assist in the execution of Saipa's wider organisational objectives and its commitment towards serving people and Iranian culture.

Football – the chance to score brand extensions

It is possible that Saipa's relationships with French car manufacturers have had a more profound effect than simply producing cars. FC Sochaux is a French football club that was founded in 1928, as a works team for the Peugeot motor car factory. In 1929 they became France's first professional football club. In 1989, Saipa purchased a 4th division team, already playing in the Tehran league. They went one step further than Peugeot, however, in renaming their team Saipa FC.

Initially workers were encouraged to join the team, but they were eventually replaced by higher-profile professional players. A notable addition to the team was Iran's most famous footballer: player/manager Ali Daei. Daei's credentials and achievements remain unrivalled. He was the first Asian player to feature in a UEFA Champions League match and he currently holds the honour of being UEFA's all-time leading goal scorer in international matches, with 109 goals in 149 games for Iran. Daei also provided kit for the team, through his own sports manufacturing operation. While he no longer plays for or manages Saipa, his presence is still felt and he often appears at press events.

Saipa FC became league champions on three occasions: in 1994, 1995 and 2007. They also won the Hazfi cup in 1995. Despite these successes and a reputation for having the best youth training programme in Iran, Saipa FC's fan base has remained relatively small in comparison to teams such as Persepolis FC. This is perhaps due to football supporters' views of government – i.e. football is an activity that many involve themselves in

Saipa FC football team in action
Source: Courtesy of Saipa

to escape from politics. Having said this, Eastern bloc communist regimes have historically exploited football, especially during the Cold War, as a vehicle for their propaganda machines. This is not to say that Saipa and the Iranian government have attempted to do the same; nevertheless, this legacy remains and appears to still have some bearing on supporters' perceptions.

Lifting Saipa to a higher level

Another high-profile celebrity endorsement has come in the towering frame of Hossein Rezazadeh, nicknamed the 'Iranian Hercules'. A former Saipa weightlifting club member, but now retired due to injury, Rezazadeh still holds world records in weightlifting's super-heavy-weight class, in the snatch, clean and jerk and total weight categories. He became the first Iranian athlete to win two Olympic gold medals. In 2003 Saipa also grabbed the Asian Club Weightlifting title.

Rezazadeh was famously asked by Turkey's Weightlifting Federation to join them, by switching nationalities. In return it was suggested that he would receive a stipend

Hossein Rezazadeh as celebrity endorser or mineral water (truck advertisement in Teheran)
Source: Jon Wilson

Support for Hossein Rezazadeh at Asian Games, Doha, Qatar
Source: Hassan Ammar/AFP/Getty Images

for US$20,000 a month, a luxury villa and a further lump sum reward of US$10 million if he won a gold for Turkey at the 2004 Athens Olympics. To the delight of Saipa and Iranians alike, Rezazadeh rejected the offer, saying that 'I am an Iranian and I love my country and people.'

Supporting regulations and the battle for ideals

Saipa's relationships, however, have at times faced added challenges. The religious clergy plays a pivotal role in Iranian affairs. Its Supreme Leader, who is currently Ayatollah Ali Khomeini, also sits at the very top of Iran's power structure, ahead of the president. In 2006 Ayatollah Ali Khameini vetoed a ruling by President Mahmoud Ahmadinejad that would have allowed women to attend major sporting events.

The Iranian clergy and government go further than many other sporting nations in outlining what is allowed or deemed acceptable. This set of conditions is often seen as being quite complicated by outsiders, especially from non-Muslim countries. The general principle is one which aims to either segregate or control the interaction between the sexes in public places. For example, females are not allowed to attend male sporting stadium events,

but they can watch them on television, the rationale being that this is to avoid mixed socialising outside the family unit and female fans swooning or chasing after sportsmen. Females do have their own sporting activities, with all female staff and spectators, in dedicated closed venues. This is to allow them to take off garments, such as the chadar or hijab (headscarf and cloak), which they would normally have to wear in the presence of male non-family members. If there are occasions where females are participating in sporting events with a male presence, or photographs and footage is being taken for public consumption, then they have to cover their entire body – with the exception of their faces, hands and feet.

It is worth mentioning that this increase in perceived bureaucracy is not meant to deter people, but is in fact part of a genuine attempt by the Iranian Republic to balance adherence to religious beliefs with more generalist and globally held societal values. Comparably, conservative countries such as Saudi Arabia have tended to opt for simpler rules and regulations, as they see them, which instead suggest prohibiting women from engaging in many of these activities, full stop. The Iranian regulations also demand that supporters and athletes alike reflect on their moral conduct on and off the field, lest further restrictions be applied.

Women's futsal
Source: Maryam Majd/Shirzanan

Sensitivity when serving society

In light of these sensitivities, Saipa has had to pay particular attention to the way in which it promotes and organises its activities, for fear of being accused of encouraging what would be deemed inappropriate behaviour. As a result, marketing communications initiatives steer well away from using images, music and stories that are provocative, sexually explicit or erotic, encourage sexual promiscuity, or are seen to erode the ideals of marriage.

It could be said that this is in stark contrast to some of the approaches adopted by other car manufacturers outside Iran. There is instead an established tradition of drawing heavily from these aspects – positioning the car as an object connected to, and manifest in, its sexuality and evocation of lust. Having said this, it is unlikely that Iranian consumers remain unaware of these brand messages. It is in fact possible that they will still have their perceptions influenced, and in turn their value systems, in a more subversive fashion.

Future brand opportunities

Perhaps a greater limiting factor may occur if Saipa were to choose to extend their lines into the luxury car market. With government having such a large share of ownership,

Saipa may find it difficult to communicate the necessary associated brand values to Iranian consumers. The idea that government has a role in marketing extravagance, opulence and luxurious consumables may require some additional work; at its worst, it could even backfire, subject to future political affairs.

Research suggests that attaining qualifications can, in the long term, lead to increased economic wealth. In turn, the appetite of an individual to choose to spend their wealth on more goods and services, of a perceived higher value, may increase. With Iran's educated population growing, there is likely to be both this appetite and a potential for market growth, which Saipa may not currently be positioned to take full advantage of. There is a risk that government involvement could devalue the premium aspects of the Saipa brand, in the eyes of the consumer, which may lead to cravings for alternative brand offerings.

Following this, an additional threat may appear when competing with other car manufacturers' brand extensions and their associated emotional brand components. Porsche, for example, has branched into producing branded luxury goods, ranging from pens and watches to coffee-makers and audio systems, among other items. Through this diversity, they are both capitalising on a legacy of existing brand ideals and, in much the same way as Saipa, attempting to wean a new audience of consumers.

Global identity

While most other car manufacturers seek to develop a globally neutral identity, differences between Saipa and especially premium brands might centre on whether culture plays a pivotal role in intrinsic values demonstrating brand superiority. Further to this, premium luxury brands are often seen as being better positioned to offer line and brand extensions in high-involvement and price categories. This is possibly why Saipa has decided to focus on more experienced-based activities as they encourage a greater deal of participation from the consumer and, as a result, avoid many of these dilemmas. The reason being that, if a consumer is satisfied by the offering (in this case an event), they are more likely to transfuse their own intrinsically self-held perceptions of worth to Saipa. More emotionally driven communications, if executed well, are also seen to appeal more strongly to consumers. By the same token, sports offer Saipa an added mode by which they can compete both domestically and abroad. A triumph on the field can lead to successes on the parking lot.

QUESTIONS

1 How is Saipa's network of relationships different from the relationships of typical Western car manufacturers?

2 Explain the fundamentals of Saipa's market communication strategy.

3 In order to fulfil Saipa's export goals, which international markets would you recommend them to focus on?

SOURCES

Written by Jon A. J. Wilson (Senior Lecturer in Advertising and Marketing Communications, University of Greenwich, London) and Svend Hollensen (Associate Professor, University of Southern Denmark, Sønderborg), with support from Mehrdad Hashemi and Payman Bayat (Saipa Group); http://www.saipacorp.com/en; http://www.saipasport.com. Majd, M. (2009) Iranian women's national futsal team in pictures, *Shirzanan,* 24 February, Issue 91.

QUESTIONS FOR DISCUSSION

1 What are the main differences between B2C and B2B relationships?

2 What might be the advantages and disadvantages of creating relationships with consumers for a manufacturer?

3 Motorola and Hewlett-Packard compete in some markets, are supplier and customer respectively for each other in various markets, share suppliers in other markets, often have the same customers, and have relationships in yet other markets. What should be done by the firms to achieve joint goals, minimise conflicts and protect core assets?

4 Some consulting companies argue that by properly incorporating suppliers in the product development process, firms can cut the cost of purchased parts and materials by as much as 30 per cent. Discuss how a buyer–supplier relationship might create these costs savings.

5 Discuss the possibilities for a manufacturer who wants to integrate consumers into the product development process.

6 Explain how distance in cross-cultural buyer–seller negotiations can be reduced.

7 Dell has entered into a relationship with IBM's Global Service Division. Under this agreement, IBM will now provide the service support for Dell's big customers. Evaluate the benefits of the relationship to Dell and IBM.

8 Relationships often involve more than the salesperson and a purchasing agent ('bow-tie' model). Often, both a whole selling team and a whole buying team are involved. Describe the interactions between buyer and seller in the 'diamond' model.

REFERENCES

Alajoutsijärvi, K., Møller, K. and Tähtinen, J. (2000) Beautiful exit: how to leave your business partner, *European Journal of Marketing*, 34(11/12): 1270–89.

Andersen, P. H. and Christensen, P. R. (2005) Bridges over troubled water: suppliers as connective nodes in global supply networks, *Journal of Business Research*, 58(9): 1261–73.

Anderson, E. and Weitz, B. A. (1989) Determinants of continuity in conventional industrial channel dyads, *Marketing Science*, 8 (Fall): 310–23.

Arantola, H. (2000) Buying loyalty or building commitment: an empirical study of customer loyalty programs, research report, Swedish School of Economics and Business Administration, Helsinki.

Axelsson, B. and Agndal, H. (2000) Internationalization of the firm: a note on the crucial role of the individual's contact network, paper presented at the IMP Conference, Bath, 7–9 September.

Bee, C. C. and Kahle, L. R. (2006) Relationship marketing in sports: a functional approach, *Sport Marketing Quarterly*, 15(2): 102–10.

Beloucif, A., Donaldson, B. and Waddell, M. (2006) A systems view of relationship dissolution, *Journal of Financial Services Marketing*,11(1): 30–48.

Bengtsson, M. and Kock, S. (1999) Co-operation and competition in relationships between competitors in business networks, *Journal of Business and Industrial Marketing*, 14(3): 179–93.

Bengtsson, M. and Kock, S. (2000) 'Co-opetition' in business networks: to cooperate and compete simultaneously, *Industrial Marketing Management*, 29: 411–26.

Biemans, W. G. and Brand, M. J. (1995) Reverse marketing: a synergy of purchasing and relationship marketing, *International Journal of Purchasing and Materials Management*, Summer: 28–37.

Brewer, P. A. (2007) Operationalizing psychic distance: a revised approach, *Journal of International Marketing*, 15(1): 44–66.

Brown, P. J. (2000) Satellites: the next generation, *Broadcasting & Cable*, 31 July: 48–50.

Bullock, C. (2000) Alcatel Space cashes in on global joint ventures, *Interavia*, December: 45–7.

Burton, T. T. (1988) JIT/repetitive sourcing strategies: tying the knot with your suppliers, *Production and Inventory Management Journal*, 29(4): 38–41.

Buttery, A. A. and Wong, Y. H. (1999) The development of a Guanxi framework, *Market Intelligence & Planning*, A(3): 147–54.

Centaur Communications (1999) *Kids Marketing Report*, Centaur Communications, London, 28 October.

Chemist & Druggist (2001) More power to Aquafresh sales: GlaxoSmithKline launches battery-powered toothbrush, *Chemist & Druggist*, 25 September: 8.

Chen, M. J. (1996) Competitor analysis and interfirm rivalry: toward a theoretical integration, *Academy of Management Review*, 21(1): 100–34.

Christopher, M. and Jüttner, V. (2000) Developing strategic partnerships in the supply chain: a practioner's perspective, *European Journal of Purchasing & Supply Management*, 6: 117–27.

Conway, T. and Swift, J. S. (2000) International relationship marketing: the importance of psychic distance, *European Journal of Marketing*, 34(11/12): 1391–413.

Cordona, M. M. (2000) Colgate challenges Gillette dominance in electric brushes, *Advertising Age*, 71(14) (3 April): 10–11.

Cox, A. (2001) Understanding buyer and supplier: a framework for procurement and supply competence, *Journal of Supply Chain Management*, Spring: 8–15.

Dwyer F. R., Schurr, P. H. and Oh, S. (1987) Developing buyer and seller relationships, *Journal of Marketing*, 51 (April): 11–27.

Easton, G. (1992) Industrial networks: a review, in B. Axelsson and G. Easton (eds) *Industrial Networks: A New View of Reality*, Routledge, London, pp. 3–27.

Erevelles, S., Horton, V. and Fukawa, N. (2008) Understanding B2C brand alliances between manufacturers and suppliers, *Marketing Management Journal*, Fall: 32–46.

Ford, D. (1979) Developing buyer–seller relationships in export marketing, *Organisation, Marknad och Samhälle*, 16(5).

Ford, D. (1984) Buyer/seller relationships in international industrial markets, *Industrial Marketing Management*, 13(2).

Ford, D., Gadde, L. E. and Lundgren, A. (1998) *Managing Business Relationships*, John Wiley & Sons, Chichester.

Freytag, P. V. and Mikkelsen, O. S. (2007) Sourcing from outside: six managerial challenges, *Journal of Business & Industrial Marketing*, 22(3): 187–95.

Gadde, L.-E. and Snehota, I. (2000) Making the most of supplier relationships, *Industrial Marketing Management*, 29: 305–16.

Ghauri, P. N., Tarnovskaya, V. and Elg, U. (2008) Market driving multinationals and their global sourcing network, *International Marketing Review*, 25(5): 504–19.

Giller, C. and Matear, S. (2001) The termination of interfirm relationships, *Journal of Business & Industrial Marketing*, 16(2): 94–112.

Grönroos, C. (1981) Internal marketing: an integral part of marketing theory, in J. H. Donnelly and W. E. George (eds) *Marketing of Services*, American Marketing Association Proceedings Series, Chicago, pp. 236–8.

Grönroos, C. (1996) Relationship marketing: strategic and tactical implications, *Management Decision*, 34(3), pp. 5–14.

Gruen, T. W. (1995) The outcome set of relationship marketing in consumer markets, *International Business Review*, 4(4): 449–69.

Gummesson, E. (1994) Making relationship marketing operational, *International Journal of Service Industry Management*, 5(5): 5–20.

Gummesson, E. (1999) *Total Relationship Marketing*, Butterworth Heinemann, London.

Håkansson, H. (ed) (1982) *International Marketing and Purchasing of Industrial Goods*, John Wiley & Sons, Chichester.

Håkansson, H. and Johanson, J. (1987) *Industrial Technological Development: A Network Approach*, Croom Helm, London.

Håkansson, H. and Johanson, J. (1992) A model of industrial networks, in B. Axelsson and G. Easton (eds) *Industrial Networks: A View of Reality*, Routledge, London.

Håkansson, H. and Snehota, I. (1995) *Developing Relationships in Business Networks*, Thomson, London.

Hallén, L. and Sandström, M. (1991) Relationship atmosphere in international business, in S. J. Paliwoda (ed.) *New Perspectives on International Marketing*, Routledge, London.

Hallén, L. and Wiedersheim, P. F. (1979) Psychic distance and buyer–seller interaction, *Organisasjon, Marked og samfunn*, 16(5): 308–24.

Hallén, L. and Wiedersheim, P. F. (1984) The evolution of psychic distance in international business relationships, in I. Hagg and P. F. Wiedersheim (eds) *Between Market and Hierarchy*, University of Uppsala Press, Uppsala.

Hallén, L., Johanson, J. and Mohamed, N. S. (1987) Relationship strength and stability in international and domestic industrial marketing, *Industrial Marketing & Purchasing*, 2(3).

Hamel, G., Doz, Y. and Prahalad, C. K. (1989) Collaborate with your competitors – and win, *Harvard Business Review*, 67(1): 133–9.

Han, S. L., Wilson, D. T. and Dant, S. P. (1993) Buyer–supplier relationships today, *Industrial Marketing Management*, 22: 331–8.

Harbert, T. (2000) Beaming business abroad, *Electronic Business*, June: 76–84.

Harrigan, K. R. (1985) An application for clustering for strategic group analysis, *Strategic Management Journal*, 6: 55–73.

Hocutt, M. A. (1998) Relationship dissolution model: antecedents of relationship commitment and the likelihood of dissolving a relationship, *International Journal of Service Industry Management*, 9(2): 189–200.

Hofstede, G. (1983) National cultures in four dimensions: a research-based theory of cultural differences among nations, *International Studies of Management and Organization*, 13: 1–2.

Hofstede, G. (1992) *Kulturer og Organisationer: Overlevelse i en grænseoverskridende verden*, J. H. Schulz Grafisk A/S, Copenhagen.

Hofstede, G. (1994) The business of international business is culture, *International Business Review*, 3(1).

Hollensen, S. (2001) *Global Marketing: A Market Responsive Approach*, 2nd edn, Financial Times/Prentice Hall, Harlow.

Hörnell, E., Vahle, J.-E. and Wiedersheim, P. F. (1973) *Export och Utlandsetableringar*, Almqvist & Wiksell, Stockholm.

Hughes, J. (2008) From vendor to partner: why and how leading companies collaborate with suppliers for competitive advantage, *Global Business and Organizational Excellence*, March/April, 21–37.

Jackson, B. B. (1985) Build customer relationships that last, *Harvard Business Review*, 63 (November–December): 120–28.

Johanson, J. and Mattsson, L.-G. (1987) Interorganizational relations in industrial systems: a network approach compared with the transaction-cost approach, *International Studies of Management and Organization*, 17(1).

Johanson, J. and Vahle, J.-E. (1999) The internationalization process of the firm: a model of knowledge development and increasing foreign market commitments, in P. J. Buckley and P. N. Ghauri (eds) *The Internationalization of the Firm: A Reader*, 2nd edn, Thomson Business Press, London.

Johanson, J. and Wiedersheim, P. F. (1975) The internationalization of the firm: four Swedish cases, *Journal of Management Studies*, October.

Johanson, M., Polsa, P. E. and Törnroos, J. Å. (1999) Business network in different cultural contexts: Western – Russian – Chinese, paper presented at the 15th IMP Conference, Dublin.

Johnsen, T. E., Johnsen, R. E. and Lamming, R. C. (2008) Supply relationship evaluation: the relationship assessment process (RAP) and beyond, *European Management Journal*, 26 (4): 274–87.

Jones, E., Dixon, A. L., Chonko, L. B. and Cannon, J. P. (2005) Key accounts and team selling: a review, framework, and research agenda, *Journal of Personal Selling & Sales Management*, Spring: 181–98.

Kanter, R. M. (1994) Collaborative advantage, *Harvard Business Review*, July–August: 96–108.

Kiff, J. S. (2000) The lean dealership: a vision for the future: from hunting to farming, *Marketing Intelligence & Planning*, 18(3): 112–26.

Kothandaraman, P. and Wilson, D. T. (2000) Implementing relationship strategy, *Industrial Marketing Management*, 29: 339–49.

Kotler, P. (2000) *Marketing Management*, Prentice Hall, Englewood Cliffs, NJ.

Liljander, V. and Strandvik, T. (1995) The nature of customer relationship, in T. A. Swartz, D. E. Bowen and S. W. Brown (eds) *Advances in Services Marketing and Management: Research and Practice*, JAI Press, London, pp. 141–67.

Lorenzoni, G. and Ferriani, S. (2008) Searching for new units of analysis: firms, dyads and networks, *European Management Review*, 5(2): 125–33.

McCurry, J. W., Rozelle Jr. W. N., Isaacs, M., Owen, P. and Woodruff, C. (2000) Glen Raven: textiles' visionary global merchant, *Textile World*, June: 1–35.

McIvor, R. (2008) What is the right outsourcing strategy for your process? *European Management Journal*, 26(1): 24–34.

Mahnert, K. F. and Torres, A. M. (2007) The brand inside: the factors of failure and success in internal branding, *Irish Marketing Review*, 19(1/2): 54–63.

Mascarenhas, B. and Koza, M. P. (2008) Develop and nurture an international alliance capability, *Thunderbird International Business Review*, 50(2): 121–8.

Mazurkiewicz, G. and Hall, J. R. (1999) Honeywell–Blue Dot alliance partners contractors with profitable accessories, *Air Conditioning, Heating & Refrigeration News*, 27 December.

Méndez, J. L., Oubina, J. and Rubio, N. (2006) Explanatory factors regarding manufacturer brand price consistency, *Journal of Product & Brand Management*, 15(6): 402–11.

Michalczyk, I. (1999) P&G signs home Tupperware deal, *Marketing*, 4 November.

Mittal, V., Sarkees, M. and Murshed, F. (2008) The right way to manage unprofitable customers, *Harvard Business Review*, April: 95–102.

Morgado, A. (2008) Logoplaste: innovation in the global market, *Management Decision*, 46(2): 1414–36.

Morgan, R. M. and Hunt, S. D. (1994) The commitment-trust theory of relationship marketing, *Journal of Marketing*, 58 (July): 20–38.

Nelson, E. (2001) Colgate's net rose 10% in period: new products helped boost sales, *Wall Street Journal*, 2 February.

Neves, M. F. (2007) Strategic marketing plans and collaborative networks, *Marketing Intelligence & Planning*, 25(2): 175–92.

New York Times (2000) Corel and Microsoft form alliance, *New York Times*, 3 October: 12.

Nordström, K. A. and Vahle, J.-E. (1994) Is the globe shrinking? Psychic distance and the establisment of Swedish sales subsidiaries during the last 100 years, in M. Landeck (ed.) *International Trade: Regional and Global Issues*, St Martins Press.

O'Grady, S. and Lane, H. W. (1996) The psychic distance paradox, *Journal of International Business Studies*, Second Quarter.

Ottesen, O. (1995) *Buyer Initiative: Ignored, but Imperative for Marketing Management – Towards a New View of Market Communication*, Tidvise Skrifter, no. 15, adverlung for Okonomi, Kultur og Samfunnsfag, Stavanger College, Norway.

Parkhe, A. (1991) Interfirm diversity, organisational learning and longevity in global strategic alliances, *Journal of International Business Studies*, 22.

Peppers, D., Rogers, M. and Dorf, B. (1999) Is your company ready for one-to-one marketing? *Harvard Business Review*, 77 (January–February): 151–60.

Perks, H. and Easton, G. (2000) Strategic alliances: partner as customer, *Industrial Marketing Management*, 29(4) (July): 327–38.

Philips (1997) Philips and Jordan sink their teeth into oral toothbrush with new alliance, press release, 8 April.

Philips (2000) Philips to acquire Optiva Corporation, maker of the Sonicare® Sonic Toothbrush, press release, 22 August.

Philips (2001) Name change for Optiva, press release, 9 January.

Philipsen, K., Damgaard, T. and Johnsen, R. E. (2008) Suppliers' opportunity enactment through the development of valuable capabilities, *Journal of Business & Industrial Marketing*, 23(1): 23–34.

Porter, M. E. (1980) *Competitive Strategy*, The Free Press, New York.

Prahalad, C. K. and Ramaswamy, V. (2000) Co-opting customer competence, *Harvard Business Review*, January–February: 79–87.

Prahalad, C. K. and Ramaswamy, V. (2004) Co-creating unique value with customers, *Strategy & Leadership*, 32(3): 4–9.

Pressey, A. D. and Qiu, X. X. (2007) Buyer–supplier relationship dissolution: the Chinese context, *Journal of Business & Industrial Marketing*, 22(2): 107–17.

Preston, S. (2004) Lost in migration: offshore need not mean outsourced, *Strategy & Leadership*, 32(6): 32–6.

Rafiq, M. and Ahmed, P. K. (2000) Advances in the internal marketing concept: definition synthesis and extension, *Journal of Services Marketing*, 14(6): 449–62.

Ramaswamy, V. (2008) Co-creating value through customers' experiences: the Nike case, *Strategy & Leadership*, 36(5): 9–14.

Schurr, P. H. (2007) Buyer–seller relationship development episodes: theories and methods, *Journal of Business & Industrial Marketing*, 22(3): 161–70.

Segil, L. (2005) Metrics to successfully manage alliances, *Strategy & Leadership*, 33(5): 46–52.

Smith, B. A. (1999) New launchers seek commercial market share, *Aviation Week & Space Technology*, 13 December: 50–2.

Soroor, J., Tarokh, M. J. and Shemshadi, A. (2009) Theoretical and practical study of supply chain coordination, *Journal of Business & Industrial Marketing*, 24(2): 131–42.

Steinriede, K. (2000) Alliances provide marketing edge, *Beverage Industry*, February.

Sterling, J. (2008) A non-profit theater's strategy focuses on experiences, *Strategy & Leadership*, 36(5): 15–21.

Strategic Direction (2009) Improving customer service, *Strategic Direction*, 25(1): 5–9.

Svenson, G. (2002) The measurement and evaluation of mutual dependence in specific dyadic business relationships, *Journal of Business and Industrial Marketing*, 17(1): 56–74.

Tähtinen, J. and Vaaland, T. (2006) Business relationships facing the end: why restore them? *Journal of Business & Industrial Marketing*, 21(1): 14–23.

Thurau, T. H. and Hansen, U. (2000) *Relationship Marketing: Gaining Competitive Advantage Through Customer Satisfaction and Customer Retention*, Springer Verlag, Berlin–Heidelberg.

Wahyuni, S., Ghauri, P. and Karsten, L. (2007) Managing international strategic alliance relationships, 49(6) (November–December): 671–87.

Walker, C. (1999) Nescafé blends relations with new charity support, *Precision Marketing*, 8 November.

Wedin, T. (2000) Value creation in industrial networks, contribution to the IMP Conference, Bath, 7–9 September.

PART III
Developing marketing strategies

As mentioned earlier, the structure of this book follows the flow of marketing decision making. After assessing the competences and the competitiveness of the firm in Part I, Part II mainly looked at the interplay of the three Cs: the company, the customer and the competitors.

Marketing strategies focus on ways in which the company can differentiate itself from its competitors, capitalising on its distinctive strengths to deliver better value to its customers.

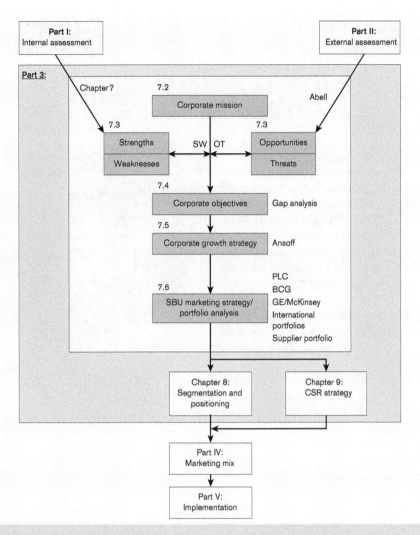

The structure of Part III and how it fits in with the rest of the book

Thus, a marketing strategy is the creation of a unique and valuable position, involving a different set of activities. Therefore, development of a marketing strategy requires activities that are different from rivals to be chosen.

As shown in the diagram above, Part III is concerned with marketing decisions on the strategic level. The complex process of marketing strategy formulation emerges from the interplay of different factors. A variety of internal and external information is needed to formulate a marketing strategy. This internal (Part I) and external (Part II) information is then assessed in a SWOT analysis which, together with the corporate mission, defines the corporate objectives, growth strategy and the strategic business unit (SBU) marketing strategy. Though the SWOT analysis is placed on a higher strategic level in the diagram, it is important to note that this analytic tool may be used on all strategic levels, including new product planning (tactical decisions).

Chapter 7 (including e.g. SWOT analysis) will be the basis for the output of the SBU marketing strategy in Chapter 8 (Segmentation, positioning and competitive strategy).

Chapter 9 will discuss how the corporate social responsibility (CSR) strategy can influence the overall marketing strategy.

These three chapters are then the input for developing marketing plans on the tactical level (Part IV) and action planning level (Part V).

Hamburg-based Beiersdorf AG can trace its origins back to a patent received for medical plasters in 1882 by the pharmacist Paul C. Beiersdorf. The business did not remain focused on this area alone: the first Labello lip care stick was sold almost 100 years ago. In 1911, Nivea Creme (which literally means 'snow white') – the first stable oil-and-water-based creme – was created. From early on, the company was looking abroad. Already in 1913 the company generated 42 per cent of its sales abroad.

The 1990s saw the start of Nivea's systematic expansion into an umbrella brand. Today, the process is regarded internationally as a classic example of successful brand development. Brand trust has been extended to a wide range of products: men's care, hair care, body care, face care, hand care, sun protection, bath and shower care, deodorants and make-up. Thanks to Nivea Sun, Beiersdorf is not just the European market leader for sun care products; it was also the catalyst for the introduction of a sun protection factor as a new global standard.

For a long time, Beiersdorf was active in four business areas: cosmetics, toiletries, and medicinal and pharmaceutical products. Since the 1990s, Beiersdorf has focused consistently on the growing market of skin and beauty care – a strategic decision that has now made Beiersdorf Germany's largest cosmetics company.

Today the company's skin care products are sold in more than 100 countries.

Sales of the first full-spectrum range of men care products for the mass market began in 1993. Today Nivea for Men has also a strong position on the global market and is consistently gaining market share.

The global market of cosmetics and toiletries totalled €200 billion in 2008. In the same year Beiersdorf had total sales of nearly €6 billion, and €480 million in net income. The company had 21,700 employees as of 31 December 2008.

Nivea sun care

The Nivea Sun brand portfolio has grown to over 40 products, which can be characterised in four different categories:

Source: Courtesy of Beiersdorf AG

1 Sun protection

It is vital that skin is adequately protected against the sun's harmful effects (although no sunscreen can provide total protection). Nivea Sun provides products that enable people to be as safe as possible. Nivea Sun also encourages the use of other forms of protection (e.g. wearing a sun hat and avoiding midday sun). Protection is the largest segment in the sun care market.

2 After-sun

Providing cooling and refreshing effects for the skin after a whole day in the sun.

3 Self-tan

In contrast to protection and after-sun, the self-tan category is concerned mostly with cosmetic appeal. Many adults use self-tan to have an all-year-round sun-kissed glow.

4 Whitening products

The popularity of whitening products in Asia is based on the old Asian belief that 'white skin conceals facial defects', a philosophy passed on for generations, and it reflects the traditional criteria for beauty.

The choice of product depends on *usage occasion (when)* – e.g. holiday, outdoor sports, gardening, working. This relates to the Sun Protection Factor (SPF) required, e.g. the SPF required for a holiday in Egypt differs greatly to outdoor work in the UK. This is one of the reasons why Nivea Sun includes a wide range of sun protection, from SPF 4 to 50+.

Sun protection is the primary benefit but the preference by which this is delivered will vary by segment, e.g. convenience is important to men (so they choose spray applicators). Parents want to provide maximum protection for children (high SPFs and coloured products are therefore important).

Women are the main purchasers of sun care for the family. This is reflected in above-the-line (advertising) communications, generally targeted towards a female audience.

Children are not purchasers of sun care. However, Nivea Sun recognises it can play an important part in

Source: Courtesy of Beiersdorf AG

educating children from a young age to be safer when in the sun.

In Asia, Nivea has considerable success with a combination of sun care and whitening products in face care. While there may be a market for bleaching products in these zones, Nivea sticks to gentle formulas. In 2005, Nivea was the world's first brand to introduce whitening products for men in Thailand.

QUESTIONS

1 Discuss and suggest segmentation criteria for the Nivea Sun Care business.

2 What degree of globalisation and/or localisation does Nivea Sun Care represent, based on the following videos?

The video clip featured on the book's online site: www.pearsoned.co.uk/hollensen

The following YouTube videos (TV commercials):
http://www.youtube.com/watch?v=J0c0BsdhxsU
http://www.youtube.com/watch?v=tJ0tq9KR3nQ &feature=PlayList&p=E10C6DB9BFDB4BFB& playnext=1&playnext_from=PL&index=30
http://www.youtube.com/watch?v=JaQ6Qjq4BpA
http://www.youtube.com/watch?v=fce3omjKRFE
http://www.youtube.com/watch?v=qnwzcjDSZok
http://www.youtube.com/watch?v=AeNkHpSyKAg& feature=related
http://www.youtube.com/watch?v=Cwz8Sn9sguk& feature=related

3 Discuss the target groups for the different TV commercials in question 2.

SOURCES

Hosea, M. (2006), Comfortably creme, *Brand Strategy,* October, pp. 20–23; Nivea website (www.nivea.com); Beiersdorf (www.beiersdorf.com); Hoover company records; other public sources; YouTube.

CHAPTER 7
SWOT analysis, strategic marketing planning and portfolio analysis

LEARNING OBJECTIVES

After studying this chapter you should be able to:

- describe the stages in strategic market planning
- understand the nature of corporate strategy and how it is connected to the SBU marketing strategy
- describe and understand the role of SWOT analysis in strategic marketing
- understand when and how to use different strategic tools in strategic market planning
- describe the two downstream portfolio models: the BCG and GE models
- discuss the advantages and disadvantages of these models
- explain the different levels of international portfolio analysis
- explain the purposes of integrating a supplier portfolio model in a marketing analysis
- understand how a supplier can be involved in product development with the manufacturer

7.1 INTRODUCTION

A strategic approach to marketing has a number of advantages. First, a strategic emphasis helps organisations orient themselves toward key external factors such as consumers and competition. Instead of just projecting past trends, the goal is to build market-driven strategies that reflect customer concerns. Strategic plans also tend to anticipate changes in the environment rather than just react to competition. Another reason strategic marketing is important is that it forces you to take a long-term view.

The structure of this chapter will follow the phases in the corporate marketing planning process.

7.2 CORPORATE MISSION

A formal organisation exists to serve a purpose. This purpose may take a variety of forms and may be classified in a number of ways according to the viewpoints of a particular organisation.

A well-defined organisation provides a sense of direction to employees and helps guide them towards the fulfilment of the firm's potential. Managers should ask, 'What is our business?' and 'What should it be?' The idea is to extract a purpose from a consideration of the firm's history, resources, distinctive abilities and environmental constraints. A mission statement should specify the business domains in which the organisation plans to operate, or more broadly, for example, 'we are an office productivity company'. The firm should try to find a purpose that fits its present needs and is neither too narrow nor too broad.

Determining a corporate mission that fulfils these requirements is by no means easy. Some companies spend two or three years redefining their corporate mission and still manage to produce a corporate mission statement that is not particularly useful or relevant. But what precisely is the nature of such a statement?

To be useful and relevant, a business definition should ideally fulfil a number of criteria. The following represents the more important of these criteria when thinking about how to define a business:

- The definition should be neither too broad nor too narrow. Definitions such as 'we are in the business of making profits' or 'we produce pens' are not really useful. Effective mission statements should cover product line definition, market scope and growth direction.

- Ideally, the definition should encompass the three dimensions of what Abell (1980) refers to as the 'business domain'. These three dimensions are customer groups to be served, customer needs to be served and technologies to be utilised.

7.3 SWOT ANALYSIS

SWOT (strengths, weaknesses, opportunities and threats) analysis is a technique specially designed to help identify suitable marketing strategies for the company to follow.

A SWOT analysis encompasses both the internal and external environments of the firm. Internally, the framework addresses a firm's strengths and weaknesses on key dimensions such as financial performance and resource; human resources; production facilities and capacity; market share; customer perceptions of product quality, price, and product availability; and organisational communication. The assessment of the external environment includes information on the market (customers and competition), economic conditions, social trends, technology and government regulation. When performed correctly, a SWOT analysis can drive the process of creating a sound marketing plan. SWOT analysis can be especially useful in discovering strategic advantages that can be exploited in the firm's marketing strategy. In this section, we will explore the benefits of a SWOT analysis and discuss guidelines for conducting a productive one.

The effective use of SWOT analysis provides the following four key benefits to the manager creating the marketing strategy.

- *Simplicity*: SWOT analysis requires no extensive training or technical skills to be used successfully. The analyst needs only a comprehensive understanding of the firm and the industry in which it operates. Because specialised training and skills are not necessary, the use of SWOT analysis can actually reduce the costs associated with strategic planning.

- *Collaboration*: because of its simplicity, SWOT analysis fosters collaboration and open information exchange between the managers of different functional areas. By learning what their colleagues do, what they know, what they think, and how they feel, the marketing manager can solve problems and fill voids in the analysis before the marketing strategy is finalised. The SWOT analysis framework provides a process that generates open information exchange in advance of the actual marketing strategy development process.

- *Flexibility*: also closely related to its simplicity is the flexibility of SWOT. It can enhance the quality of an organisation's strategic planning even without extensive marketing information systems. However, when comprehensive systems are present, they can be structured to feed information directly into a SWOT framework. In addition, the presence of a comprehensive marketing information system, even though it is not needed, can make repeated SWOT analyses run more smoothly and efficiently.

- *Integration*: SWOT analysis can also deal with a wide variety of information sources. SWOT analysis allows the planner to integrate and synthesise diverse information, both of a quantitative and qualitative nature. It organises information that is widely known, as well as information that has only recently been acquired or discovered.

SWOT analysis can help push the planning team toward agreement as it uncovers potentially harmful disagreements. All of these different forms of information are inherent to, and sometimes problematic for, the strategic planning process. SWOT analysis helps transform this information from a weakness of the planning process into one of its major strengths.

Conditions for an effective and productive SWOT analysis

The degree to which a firm receives the full benefits of a SWOT analysis will depend on the way the framework is used. If done correctly, SWOT can be a strong catalyst for the planning process. If done incorrectly, it can be a great waste of time and other valuable resources. To ensure that you receive the full benefits, you should:

- stay focused;
- collaborate with other functional areas;
- research issues from the customer's perspective;
- separate internal issues from external issues.

Stay focused

A major mistake planners often make in conducting a SWOT analysis is to complete only one generic SWOT analysis for the entire organisation (corporate SWOT).

Instead you have to decide which organisational level is being analysed and then start the SWOT analysis there. However, as shown in Figure 7.1, SWOT analyses at the different levels are interlinked.

So when we say SWOT analysis, we really mean SWOT analyses. In most firms there should be a series of analyses, each focusing on a specific organisational level and/or a specific product/market combination. Such a focus enables the marketing manager to focus on the specific marketing mix being used in a given market. This focus also allows the manager to analyse the specific issues that are relevant to the particular product/market. If needed, separate product/market analyses can be combined to examine the issues that are relevant for the entire strategic business unit, and business unit analyses can be combined to create a complete SWOT for the entire organisation. The only time a single SWOT would be appropriate is when an organisation has only one product/market combination.

Besides increased relevance, another major benefit of a focused SWOT analysis is its ability to identify knowledge gaps. The identification of such gaps depends on the firm's ability to gather market intelligence.

The requirement of staying focused is also true when we talk about competitors. Information on competitors and their activities is an important aspect of a well-focused SWOT analysis.

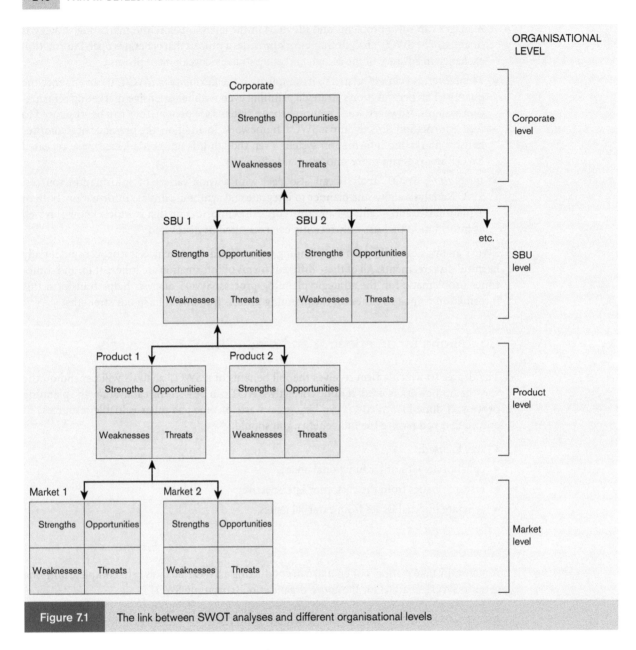

ORGANISATIONAL
LEVEL

| **Figure 7.1** | The link between SWOT analyses and different organisational levels |

The key is not to overlook any competitor, whether a current rival or one that is not yet a competitor. As we discussed in Chapter 5, the firm will focus most of its efforts on brand competition. As the SWOT analysis is conducted, the firm must watch for any current or potential direct substitutes for its products. Product and total budget competitors are important as well. Looking at all types of competition is important because many planners never look past brand competitors. Thus, although the SWOT analysis should be focused, it must not be myopic. Even industry giants can lose sight of their potential competitors by focusing exclusively on brand competition. Kodak, for example, had always taken steps to maintain its market dominance over rivals such as Fuji, Konica and Polaroid in the film industry. However, entering the market for digital cameras completely changed Kodak's set of competing firms. Kodak was forced to turn its attention to giants like Sony and Canon in the fast-growing market for digital cameras.

Collaborate with other functional areas

The SWOT analysis should be a powerful stimulus for communication outside normal channels. The final outcome of a properly conducted SWOT analysis should be an amalgamation of information from many areas. Managers in product development, production finance, inventory control, quality control, sales, advertising, customer service, and other areas should learn what other managers see as the firm's strengths, weaknesses, opportunities and threats. This allows the marketing planner to come to terms with multiple perspectives before actually creating the marketing strategy and the marketing plan.

As the SWOT analyses from individual areas are combined, the marketing manager can identify opportunities for joint projects and **cross-selling** of the firm's products. In a large organisation, the first time a SWOT analysis is undertaken is the first time that managers from some areas have formally communicated with each other. Such cross-collaborations can generate a very good environment for creativity and innovation. Moreover, research has shown that the success of introducing a new product, especially a radically new product, is extremely dependent on the ability of different functional areas to collaborate and integrate their differing perspectives. This collaboration must occur across divisions and between different organisational levels.

Cross-selling
Selling an additional product or service to an existing customer

Research issues from the customer's perspective

Every issue in a SWOT analysis must be examined from the customer's perspective. To do this, the analyst must constantly ask questions such as:

- What do our customers (and non-customers) believe about us as a company?
- What do our customers (and non-customers) think of our product quality, customer service, price and overall value, and promotional messages in comparison to our competitors?
- What is the relative importance of these issues, not as we see them, but as our customers see them?

Examining every issue from the customer's perspective also includes the firm's internal customers: its employees. Some employees, especially front-line employees, are closer to the customer and can offer a different perspective on what customers think and believe. Other types of stakeholders, such as investors who are involved in providing capital for the firm, should also be considered. The SWOT analysis forces managers to change their perceptions to the way customers and other important groups see things. The contrast between these two perspectives often leads to the identification of a gap between management's version of reality and customers' perception. It is like putting a mirror in front of the manager and saying: 'This is how customers look at you – is this also how you see yourself?'

Separate internal issues from external issues

As you conduct a SWOT analysis, it is important to keep the internal issues separate from the external ones. Internal issues are the firm's strengths and weaknesses, while external issues refer to opportunities and threats in the firm's external environments.

The failure to understand the difference between internal and external issues is one of the major reasons for a poorly conducted SWOT analysis. This happens because managers tend to get ahead of themselves by listing their existing marketing strategies and tactics as opportunities. Opportunities and threats exist independently of the firm. Strategies and tactics are what the firm intends to do about its opportunities and threats relative to its own strengths and weaknesses.

SWOT-driven strategic marketing planning

In the previous section we looked at the conditions for conducting an effective SWOT analysis.

Now, we will consider how a firm can use its set of strengths, weaknesses, opportunities and threats to drive the development of strategic plans that will allow the firm to change its current marketing strategy and achieve its goals and objectives. Remember that SWOT analysis should not be an academic exercise to classify information correctly. Rather, it should serve as a catalyst to facilitate and guide the creation of marketing strategies that will produce the desired results. The process of organising information within the SWOT analysis can help the firm see the difference between where it thinks it is, where others see it as being, and where it hopes to be.

To address these issues properly, the marketing manager should appraise every strength, weakness, opportunity and threat to determine its total impact on the firm's marketing efforts. This assessment will also give the manager an idea of the basic strategic options that might be available to emphasise the firm's capabilities or convert/minimise its weaknesses and threats. One method of conducting this SWOT assessment is to create and analyse the SWOT matrix. Let's look at how a marketing manager might conduct this assessment.

These are two main steps in a SWOT analysis (see Figure 7.2). In this process the assessment of the firm's strengths and weaknesses involves looking beyond the firm's current products. The manager should also assess the firm's business processes that are key to meeting customers' problems rather than specific products.

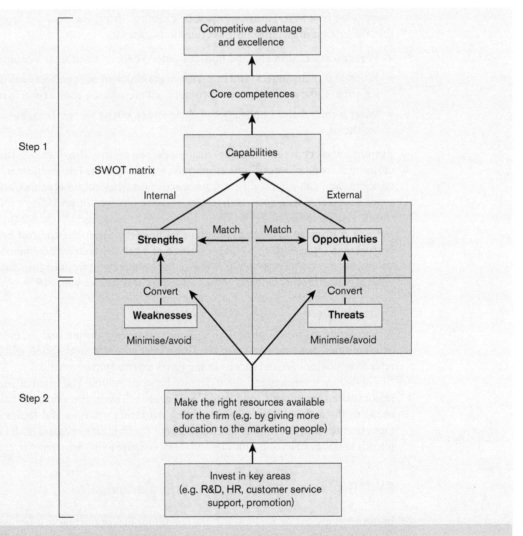

| Figure 7.2 | Turning the SWOT analysis into a strategic tool for gaining competitive advantage |

Step 1: The matching of strengths and opportunities

The key to the successful achievement of the firm's goals and objectives depends on the ability of the firm to transform key strengths into capabilities by matching them with opportunities in the marketing environment. Capabilities can become competitive advantages if they provide better value to customers than competitors' offerings.

When we refer to capabilities or competitive advantage, we usually speak in terms of real differences between competing firms. After all, capabilities and competitive advantage stem from real strengths possessed by the firm. However, the capabilities and competitive advantage that any firm possesses are often based more on perception than reality. Most customers make purchase decisions based on their own perceptions of the firm's capabilities and advantages. How customers see a company is how that firm is. Regardless of the facts about a company, if customers perceive the company as slow to react, impersonal, or having excessively high priced or out-of-date products, that is quite simply the way that firm is.

Effectively managing customers' perceptions has been a challenge for marketers for generations. The problem lies in developing and maintaining capabilities and competitive advantage that customers can easily understand, and that solve specific customers' needs. Capabilities or competitive advantage that do not translate into specific benefits for customers are of little use to a firm.

Successful firms attempt to get very close to their customers by seeking their input on how to make the firm's goods and services better or how to solve specific customer problems. These firms also attempt to create long-term relationships between themselves and their customers.

As outlined in Chapter 3, a firm must possess certain core competences to be able to implement a market strategy of competitive excellence. Before a competitive advantage can be translated into specific customer benefits, the firm's target market(s) must recognise that its competences give it an advantage over the competition.

Step 2: Converting weaknesses and threats

Firms can convert weaknesses into strengths, and even capabilities, by investing strategically in key areas (e.g. R&D, customer support, promotion, employee training) and by linking key areas more effectively (such as linking human resources to marketing). Likewise, threats can often be converted into opportunities if the right resources are available. Finding new markets for a firm's products could be a viable conversion strategy.

In some cases, weaknesses and threats cannot be successfully converted in the short or long term. When this occurs, the firm must adopt strategies that avoid these issues or minimise their repercussions. One such strategy is to become a niche marketer. Another strategy for minimising or avoiding weaknesses and threats is to reposition the product. Changes in demographics, declining sales or increasing competition are common reasons for product **repositioning**. Despite a company's best efforts, some weaknesses and threats simply cannot be minimised or avoided. When this situation occurs, the firm is said to have a limitation. Limitations occur most often when the firm possesses a weakness or faces a threat that coincides with one of its opportunities. Limitations can be particularly troublesome if they are obvious to consumers. How does a company deal with its limitations? One way is to diversify, thus reducing the risk of operating solely within a single business unit or market.

The manager has several potential marketing activities that can be used to take advantage of capabilities and convert weaknesses and threats. At this stage, however, there are likely to be many potential directions for the manager to pursue. Because most firms have limited resources, it is difficult to accomplish everything at once. The manager must prioritise all potential marketing activities and develop specific goals and objectives for the marketing plan.

Repositioning
A product strategy that involves changing the product design, formulation, brand image or brand name so as to alter the product's competitive position.

7.4 CORPORATE OBJECTIVES

Broadly, setting objectives involves a company in considering the following two questions:

- Where do we wish to go?
- When do we intend to arrive?

Without an answer to these questions, a company can be likened to a ship without a compass; it can move, but it lacks a clear sense of direction. More specifically, objectives:

- provide for a *sense of purpose* in a company; without objectives, companies lack the means to focus and organise their efforts;
- help a company to *achieve consistency* between the various levels of decision making, and between the different functions;
- help to *stimulate effort*; they provide a basis for motivating individuals to achieve them;
- provide the *basis for control* in a company; unless we know precisely what is required, it is difficult, if not impossible, to know the extent to which we have achieved it.

In order to fulfil these important functions, objectives must have certain characteristics. Objectives should be:

- *Quantified*: quantitative objectives with respect to both levels of performance and time reduce the risk of their being vague or ambiguous.
- *Acceptable* and *agreeable*: to those charged with the responsibility of attaining them. It is pointless setting objectives if they are not acted upon – or if the effort to achieve them is given grudgingly. A frequent reason for objectives being unacceptable is that they are felt to be too difficult or impossible to achieve.
- *Consistent*: as we shall see shortly, often companies have a variety of objectives as opposed to a single one. It is important that these multiple objectives do not conflict one with another in such a way that the achievement of an objective in one area is inconsistent with the achievement of objectives in others. For example, an objective of improved profitability may be inconsistent with an objective of maximum sales.

Having discussed the functions of objectives, and the characteristics that objectives ideally should possess if they are to serve these functions, we can now turn our attention to the variety of corporate objectives that a company might set.

In economic analysis it is often asserted that a firm has one, and only one, objective: namely, to maximise its total profits. In addition to profit objectives, it is now recognised that companies may have a variety of objectives encompassing a spread of activities. Some of the most frequently encountered objectives and their corresponding performance criteria/measures are shown in Table 7.1.

Whatever the mix of objectives, it must be remembered that the objectives themselves relate to some point in the future, hence the importance of specifying a timescale for their achievement. For an existing business there will also be a past. It is possible, therefore, to measure the past and current performance of the company with respect to those areas in which it has objectives for the future. Management can then compare where it wishes to be (objectives) with where it is likely to be on the basis of a projection from past performance. Any difference constitutes what is referred to as a planning gap, which would cause some kind of **gap analysis**. This notion of a planning gap is illustrated in Figure 7.3.

The gap stems from the difference between future desired profit objectives and a forecast of projected profit based on past performance and following existing strategy.

If there is a planning gap, a number of options are available; the intention, however, is to close the gap. For example, the gap could be closed by revising objectives downwards. Such a

Gap analysis
A technique which compares future likely company performance against desired performance outcomes in order to identify any gaps.

Table 7.1	Common objectives, their performance criteria and measures	
Objectives	**Performance criteria**	**Possible measure or indexes**
Profit and financial objectives	Profitability	• Profit • Profit as percentage of sales • Contribution margin • Return on investment (ROI)
	Contribution to owners	• Earnings per share • Price/earnings ratio
	Utilisation of fixed assets	• Capacity utilisation • Fixed assets as percentage of sales
Growth objectives/marketing objectives	Percentage yearly growth	• Sales • Unit sales • Profits
	Competitive strengths	• Market share • Brand awareness • Brand preference
	Contribution to customers	• Price relative to competitors • Product quality • Customer satisfaction • Customer retention • Customer loyalty
Social responsibility objectives	Contribution to employees	• Wage rates, benefits • Personnel development, promotions • Employment stability, turnover
	Contribution to society	• Contributions to charities or community institutions • Growth in employment

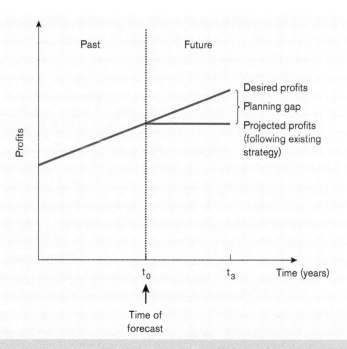

Figure 7.3	The planning gap

step might be taken where the initial objectives are unrealistic. Alternatively, or in addition, the gap could be closed by actions designed to move the company off the projected curve and towards the desired curve.

This next step in the process of corporate planning is the formulation of strategies.

7.5 CORPORATE GROWTH STRATEGY

Market penetration
A strategy for company growth by increasing sales of current products to current market segments without changing the product.

Market development
A strategy by which an organisation attempts to draw new customers to an existing product, most commonly by introducing the product in a new geographical area.

A strategy for reaching long-term objectives needs to be developed specifically for each SBU. **Market penetration**, product development, **market development** and diversification are the four basic product strategies (Figure 7.4) for closing the planning gap. Each cell in the Ansoff matrix presents distinct opportunities, threats, resource requirements, returns and risks, and will now be discussed.

Market penetration

The most frequently used strategy is to take the existing product in the existing market and try to obtain an increased share of that market. The two ways in which this can be achieved are by increasing sales to existing customers and by finding new customers in the same market. The first strategy means persuading users to use more of the product on more occasions, perhaps by replacing an indirect competitor. Alternatively, the strategy may be to use the product more often without any need to take business from competitors.

	Current products	**New products**
Current markets	Market penetration strategies • Increase market share • Increase product share • Increase frequency of use • Increase quantity used • New applications	Product development strategies • Product improvements • Product-line extensions • New products for same market
New markets	Market development strategies • Expand markets for existing products • Geographic expansion • Target new segments/ customer groups	Diversification strategies • Vertical integration • Forward integration • Backward integration • Diversification into related businesses (concentric diversification) • Diversification into unrelated businesses (conglomerate diversification)

Figure 7.4 The Ansoff product–market matrix
Source: Adapted from Ansoff, H. I. (1957) Strategies for diversification, *Harvard Business Review*, September–October: 113–24. Copyright © 1957 by Harvard Business School Publishing Corporation. All rights reserved. Reproduced with permission.

The second strategy takes business directly from competitors by increasing both penetration and market share. This can be achieved either by changing the product offering or by changing the positioning of the product offering.

With this option, product improvement is also an option. An example of a company following such a tactic is Japan-based Komatsu, Caterpillar's most important competitor in the market for earthmoving and construction equipment. They have taken a significant market share by continually raising the quality of their products, which has allowed an extension of warranties, and by extending the range of their products' application through improved technologies. A company may attempt to expand a market that they already serve by *converting non-users to users* of their product. This can be an attractive option in new markets when non-users form a sizeable segment and may be willing to try the product given suitable inducements. Thus when Carnation entered the powdered coffee whitening market with Coffeemate, a key success factor was its ability to persuade hitherto non-users of powdered whiteners to switch from milk. Former users can also be targeted. Kellogg has targeted former breakfast cereal users (fathers) who rediscover the pleasure of eating cornflakes when feeding their children. Market expansion can also be achieved by *increasing usage*. Colman attempted to increase the use of mustard by showing new combinations of mustard and food. Kellogg has also tried to increase the usage (eating) rate of its cornflakes by promoting eating them in the evening as well as at breakfast.

Market development

This entails the marketing of current products to new customer groups and new regions.

New customer groups

The promotion of nylon for new customer groups accounted for the growth in sales of nylon, which was first marketed as a replacement for silk in parachutes, but expanded into shirts, carpets, tyres, etc.

Geographic expansion

Geographic expansion is appropriate when important competitors are opening up new markets, or when opportunities in new markets will be available for only a short time. These characteristics are often found in high-tech industries such as computer technology and advanced circuit technology. The speed with which new computer chips, for example, can be matched by competitors means that they are marketed globally as quickly as possible to take advantage of product superiority for as long as possible.

Geographic expansion also becomes necessary when intense price competition in slow-growing markets leads to diminishing profit margins. To achieve higher sales volumes, the company introduces its products in markets where few product modifications are required. Eastman Kodak, for example, faced with strong competition from Japan's Fuji and Germany's Agfa-Gevaert (both penetrating growing US, European and Japanese markets), turned to China, where 35 mm film sales have quintupled since the early 1980s, to roughly 120 million rolls in 1995. Only one of the country's seven domestic makers, Lucky Film Corp., had a truly national brand in 1996. While just 12 per cent of China's 1.3 billion people owned a camera, picture taking is fast becoming as popular as it is in Japan. By the end of the decade, China is expected to overtake Japan, becoming the world's second-largest film market, behind the USA. But competition is unavoidable. With less than 30 per cent of the Chinese film market and an even smaller share of photographic paper in 1996, Kodak remains behind. Fuji leads in film and is fighting a price war with Agfa-Geveart for that company's leading share of the photographic paper market. (Jobber, 1998).

Product development

This strategy involves a major modification of the goods or service, such as quality, style, performance or variety.

A company follows its basic strategy of product market development, allocates resources to a limited number of markets and focuses its operations on the development of new products in these areas. This approach is appropriate if the company is well established in its markets and lacks the motivation, ability or knowledge to adapt to a new environment. Product market development is most appropriate when the current product market has matured and new product markets are growing fast in existing markets.

An offer of 'high performance' versions of existing car models can be used to extend the ranges to additional customers. Similarly, adding vitamins to orange juice will possibly cause some existing users to increase their usage but may also attract new users.

Diversification

This option concerns the development of *new products for new markets*. This is the most risky option, especially when the entry strategy is not based upon the core competences of the business. Firms must be aware of diversification simply because the grass looks greener in the new market.

One obvious example is the tobacco companies that have diversified – often at considerable cost – into areas as varied as cosmetics and engineering. However, diversification can also be a positive move to extend the application of existing expertise.

Honda's move from motorcycles to cars (based on its core competence in engines) and Sony's move into 8 mm camcorders (based on its core competences in miniaturisation and video technology) extended the application of existing expertise.

Disney Corporation diversified from cartoons to theme parks and television broadcasting. Heinz has steadily and successfully extended beyond its core ketchup business; its Weight Watchers brand is now worth hundreds of millions of dollars. But it should be noted that, like many other similarly successful diversifications, Heinz's strategy was built on a logical extension of the company's existing strengths.

Vertical integration
Seeking control of channel members at different levels of the channel, e.g. the manufacturer's acquition of the distributor (= forward integration).

Vertical integration is one way for corporations to diversify their operations. *Forward integration* occurs when a firm moves downstream in terms of the product flow – as when a manufacturer acquires a wholesaler or retail outlet. *Backward integration* occurs when a firm moves upstream by acquiring a supplier. For example, Compaq has strengthened its position in computer software markets by acquiring several software developers.

Concentric diversification occurs when a firm internally develops or acquires another business that does not have products or customers in common with its current business, but that might contribute to internal synergy through the sharing of production facilities, brand names, R&D know-how, or marketing and distribution skills. Thus, Sara Lee has made more than 60 acquisitions in recent years, most involving businesses that could benefit from the firm's well-respected brand and its distribution strengths in grocery stores.

Conglomerate diversification, the riskiest diversification of all, moves into completely new areas. For example, British Aerospace decided to apply the huge cash flow from its defence business to investments in cars, construction and property. The company never found the expected synergy and either divested the acquisitions or reported large losses (*Economist*, 1995).

Ansoff's product–market matrix is probably one of the best-known frameworks for delineating overall corporate strategies. A second and increasingly popular group of techniques aimed at the identification and selection of corporate strategies is also based on analysing appropriate marketing strategies. These are the so-called portfolio models and they will be discussed in the next section.

7.6 SBU MARKETING STRATEGY/PORTFOLIO ANALYSIS

Portfolio planning
Managing groups of
brands and product lines.

The definition of the unit of analysis for **portfolio planning** is a critical stage and one that is often poorly done in practice. The components of a firm involved in portfolio analysis or businesses are called strategic business units, or SBUs. Managers within each of these business units decide which objectives and strategies to pursue. Senior corporate managers typically reserve the right to grant final approval of such decisions to ensure their overall consistency with corporate objectives and resource allocations across SBUs in the company portfolio. Lower-level general managers, however, conduct much of the analysis on which such decisions are based. These managers are more familiar with a given SBU's products and customers, and ultimately they are responsible for implementing its strategy.

Ideally, strategic business units have the following characteristics:

- *homogeneous set of markets to serve with a limited number of related technologies*: minimising diversity across an SBU's product market entries enables the unit's manager to better formulate and implement a coherent and internally consistent business strategy;
- *unique set of product markets*: in the sense that no other SBU within the firm competes for the same customers with similar products. Thus, the firm avoids duplication of effort and maximises economies of scale within its SBUs;
- *control over those factors necessary for successful performance*: production, R&D and engineering, marketing and distribution, etc. This does not mean an SBU should not share resources – such as manufacturing plant or a salesforce – with one or more other business units. But the SBU should determine how its share of the joint resource is used effectively to carry out its strategy;
- *responsibility for their own profitability.*

As you might expect, firms do not always meet all of these ideals when creating business units. There are usually trade-offs between having many small homogeneous SBUs versus large but fewer SBUs that managers can more easily supervise.

Portfolio analysis was originally intended for use at the SBU level, where these are generally defined as subsidiaries which can operate independently as businesses in their own right. In reality, however, boundaries are seldom clear-cut and the problems of definition can be substantial.

Practitioners have often used the portfolio models (e.g. the BCG model) to look at products rather than business units or to provide a pictorial presentation of international markets. These applications do not conform strictly to those for which it was originally intended, but its value as a means of presenting much information still remains, providing the limitations of the matrix are kept in mind.

Where products are selected as the unit of analysis it is important that market shares and growth rates reflect the more specific market sectors in which they are operating.

Product life cycle (PLC)

In relation to portfolio models, the most important message the PLC can bring to management is that of cash flow. The model offers a clear reminder that the launch of a new brand requires significant investment that can last from its launch to the end of the growth phase, which can be a longer period than most organisations allow for. In addition, the more successful the new brand, the greater the investment needed.

This proposition suggests that products are born, grow to maturity and then decline, much like plants and animals. During the introductory period, sales grow rapidly but the high expenses mean that no profits are made. Near the end of the growth stage, the rate of expansion of sales begins to slow down and profits reach a peak. During the maturity phase, sales reach their peak and profits are slowly eroded by increasing competition. If nothing is done to revive declining products, they eventually have to be dropped. However, sometimes it is hard to know when a product is leaving one stage and entering the next. The life cycle concept helps managers think about their product line as a portfolio of investments.

Most organisations offer more than one product or service, and many operate in several markets. The advantage here is that the various products – the **product portfolio** – can be managed so that they are not all in the same phase in their life cycles. Having products evenly spread out across life cycles allows for the most efficient use of both cash and human resources. Figure 7.5 shows an example of such life cycle management and some of the corresponding strategies that follow the different stages of the product life cycle.

The current investment in C, which is in the growth phase, is covered by the profits being generated by the earlier product B, which is at maturity. This product had earlier been funded by A, the decline of which is now being balanced by the newer products. An organisation

Product portfolio
A collection of products balanced as a group. Product portfolio analysis focuses on the interrelationships of products within a product mix. The performance of the mix is emphasised rather than the performance of individual products.

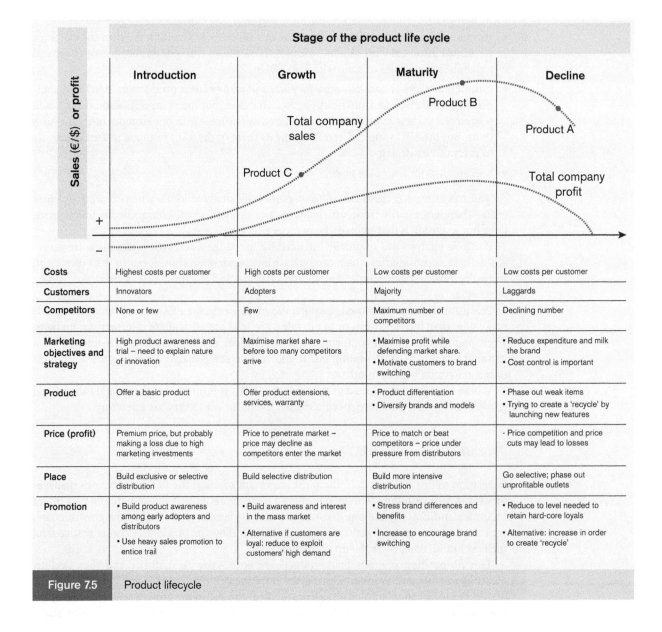

	Introduction	Growth	Maturity	Decline
Costs	Highest costs per customer	High costs per customer	Low costs per customer	Low costs per customer
Customers	Innovators	Adopters	Majority	Laggards
Competitors	None or few	Few	Maximum number of competitors	Declining number
Marketing objectives and strategy	High product awareness and trial – need to explain nature of innovation	Maximise market share – before too many competitors arrive	• Maximise profit while defending market share. • Motivate customers to brand switching	• Reduce expenditure and milk the brand • Cost control is important
Product	Offer a basic product	Offer product extensions, services, warranty	• Product differentiation • Diversify brands and models	• Phase out weak items • Trying to create a 'recycle' by launching new features
Price (profit)	Premium price, but probably making a loss due to high marketing investments	Price to penetrate market – price may decline as competitors enter the market	Price to match or beat competitors – price under pressure from distributors	- Price competition and price cuts may lead to losses
Place	Build exclusive or selective distribution	Build selective distribution	Build more intensive distribution	Go selective; phase out unprofitable outlets
Promotion	• Build product awareness among early adopters and distributors • Use heavy sales promotion to entice trail	• Build awareness and interest in the mass market • Alternative if customers are loyal: reduce to exploit customers' high demand	• Stress brand differences and benefits • Increase to encourage brand switching	• Reduce to level needed to retain hard-core loyals • Alternative: increase in order to create 'recycle'

Figure 7.5   Product lifecycle

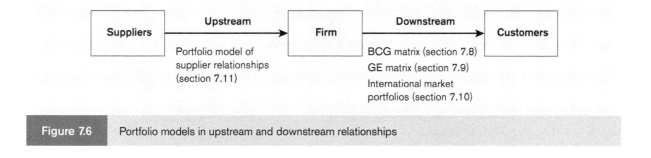

| Figure 7.6 | Portfolio models in upstream and downstream relationships |

looking for growth can introduce new goods or services that it hopes will be bigger sellers than those that they succeed. However, if this expansion is undertaken too rapidly, many of these brands will demand investment at the beginning of their life cycles, and even the earliest of them will be unlikely to generate profits fast enough to support the numbers of later launches. Therefore, the producer will have to find another source of funds until the investments pay off.

7.7 INTRODUCTION TO PORTFOLIO MODELS

Relationship marketing attempts to involve and integrate customers, suppliers and other partners into the firm's development of marketing actitivies.

Portfolio models have their foundation in Markowitz's (1952) pioneering portfolio theory for the management of equity investments. Since then, portfolio models have been widely used in strategic planning, essentially at the SBU level.

The portfolio models discussed in this chapter tend to focus on the downstream relationships to the customers (market). Portfolio models have been used in strategic planning and marketing, but their application to the field of purchasing has been limited. This seems, however, to be changing, as procurement management has become more strategic. This is why the dyadic aspect of interdependence between buyer and suppliers, the upstream aspects of relationships, are also included in this chapter (Figure 7.6).

We will start with the downstream-oriented portfolio models (sections 7.8, 7.9 and 7.10) and then look at an upstream-oriented portfolio model of supplier relationships in section 7.11.

7.8 THE BOSTON CONSULTING GROUP'S GROWTH–SHARE MATRIX – THE BCG MODEL

One of the first – and best known – of the portfolio models is the growth–share matrix developed by the Boston Consulting Group in the late 1960s. The Boston Matrix offers a useful map of an organisation's product strengths and weaknesses as well as the likely cash flows. It was reasoned that one of the main indicators of cash generation was relative market share, and market growth rate was indicative of cash usage. Figure 7.7 shows the Boston Matrix. It is well worth remembering that one of the key underlying assumptions of this matrix is the expectation that the position of products in their markets will change over time. This assumption is, of course, the incorporation of the product life cycle thinking discussed earlier.

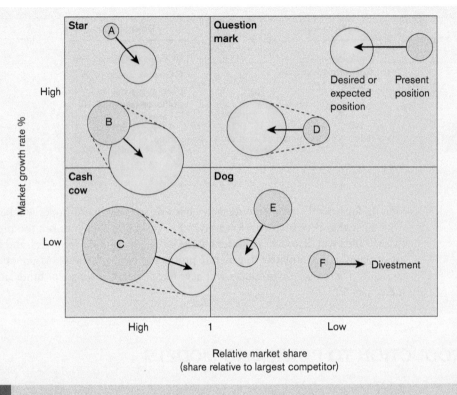

| Figure 7.7 | The BCG model |

Market growth rate
The theory behind the
BCG model assumes that
a higher growth rate is
indicative of accompany-
ing demands on invest-
ment. Inflation and/or
gross national product
have some impact on the
range and thus the verti-
cal axis can be modified
to represent an index
where the dividing hori-
zontal line between low
and high growth is at e.g.
5%. Industries expanding
faster than inflation or
GNP would show above
the line and those grow-
ing at less than inflation
or GNP would be classed
as low growth and show
below the line. The theory
behind the BCG model
assumes that a higher
growth rate is indicative
of accompanying de-
mands on investment.

Figure 7.7 presents an example of the share/growth matrix in which six product lines (A–F) make up the portfolio. A pink circle represents the current position, and a blue circle the forecast future position. The area of the circle is proportional to the product's contribution to company sales volume.

Figure 7.7 shows also the two factors which underlie the Boston Consulting Group's approach. Market share is used because it is an indicator of the product's ability to generate cash; market growth is used because it is an indicator of the product's cash requirements.

Market growth rate

The vertical axis recognises the impact of '**market growth rate**' on cash flow. This dimension acts as a proxy, or more easily measured substitute, for the more difficult to assess product life cycle and reflects the strategies and associated costs typical over the cycle. At product launch costs are likely to far outstrip revenues. R&D costs will need to be recouped, production capacity created and market beachheads established. Typically during the launch and introductory phases of the life cycle, cash flow will be negative and hence there will be a need to invest cash generated elsewhere (or borrowed from external sources) in the venture.

As the product becomes established in the market, revenues will pick up, but the venture is likely to remain cash hungry because of the need to make further capital investment.

Relative market shares

The horizontal axis of the BCG model depicts relative market share. The term '**relative market share**' is measured *relative* to the firm's largest competitor. This is important because it reflects

Relative market share
Comparing your market share with that of your biggest competitor. Having a relative market share of >1 means you are the market leader that outperforms the next biggest by this factor. A relative market share <1 shows how far away you are from being the market leader.

the degree of dominance enjoyed by the product in the market. For example, if company A has 20 per cent market share and its biggest competitor has 40 per cent, the relative market share is $1:2 = 0.5$. If company A has 20 per cent market share and its biggest competitor also has 20 per cent market share, this position is usually less favourable than if company A had 20 per cent market share and its biggest competitor had only 10 per cent market share. The relative ratios would be 1:1 compared with 2:1. It is this ratio, or measure of market dominance, that the horizontal axis measures.

While market growth rate has been found to be a useful indicator of cash use (or the need for investment), market share has been found to be related to cash generation. Higher market shares, relative to competitors, are associated with better cash generation because of economies of scale and experience curve effects. The experience curve concept, also developed by the Boston Consulting Group in the 1960s, forms the foundation for this relationship, but further supporting evidence comes from the influential **Profit Impact of Marketing Strategy (PIMS)** study of the 1970s and 1980s. Relative market share is in effect used as a proxy for profitability, the underlying premise being that dominant share leads to superior profitability.

Profit Impact of Marketing Strategy (PIMS)
An empirical study, which seeks to identify the key factors underlying profitability and strategic success in an industry.

Each of the four cells in the growth–share matrix represents a different type of business with different strategy and resource requirements. The implications of each are discussed below.

Question marks

Businesses in high-growth industries with low relative market shares are called question marks or problem children. Such businesses require large amounts of cash, not only for expansion to keep up with the rapidly growing market, but also for marketing activities (or reduced margins) to build market share and catch the industry leader. If management can successfully increase the share of a question mark business, it becomes a star. But if they fail, it eventually turns into a dog as the industry matures and the market growth rate slows.

Stars

Star
A high market share product in a high-growth market.

A **star** is the market leader in a high-growth industry. Stars are critical to the continued future success of the firm. As their industries mature, they move into the bottom-left quadrant and become cash cows. Paradoxically, while stars are critically important, they are often net users rather than suppliers of cash in the short term. This is because the firm must continue to invest in such businesses to keep up with rapid market growth and to support the R&D and marketing activities necessary to stave off competitors' attacks and maintain a leading market share. Indeed, share maintenance is crucial for star businesses to become cash cows rather than dogs as their industries mature.

Cash cows

Cash cow
A high market share product in a low-growth market.

Businesses with a high relative share of low-growth markets are called cash cows because they are the primary generators of profits and cash in a corporation. Such businesses do not require much additional capital investment. Their market shares are stable, and their share leadership position usually means they enjoy economies of scale and relatively high profit margins. Consequently, the corporation can use the cash from these businesses to support its question marks and stars (as shown in Figure 7.8). However, this does not mean the firm should necessarily maximise the business's short-term cash flow by cutting R&D and marketing expenditures to the bone – particularly not in industries where the business might continue to generate substantial future sales. When firms attempt to harvest too much cash from such businesses, they risk suffering a premature decline from cash cow to dog status, thus losing profits in the long term.

Dogs

Low-share businesses in low-growth markets are called dogs because, although they may generate some cash, they typically generate low profits, or losses. Divestiture is one option for such businesses, although it can be difficult to find an interested buyer. Another common

| Figure 7.8 | Cash generation in the BCG Matrix |

strategy is to harvest dog businesses. This involves maximising short-term cash flow by paring investments and expenditures while the business is gradually phased out.

Strategy implications of BCG

In a typical company, products could be scattered in all four quadrants of the portfolio matrix. The appropriate strategy for products in each cell is given briefly in Table 7.2.

Table 7.2	Characteristics and strategy implications of products in the matrix quadrants		
Quadrant	Investment characteristics	Cash flow characteristics	Strategy implication
Stars	Continual expenditures for capacity expansion Pipeline filling with cash	Negative cash flow (net cash user)	Continue to increase market share, if necessary at the expense of short-term earnings
Cash cows	Capacity maintenance expenditures	Positive cash flow (net cash contributor)	Maintain share and leadership until further investment becomes marginal
Question marks	Heavy initial capacity expenditures High research and development costs	Negative cash flow (net cash user)	Assess chances of dominating segment: if good, go after share; if bad, redefine business or withdraw
Dogs	Gradually deplete capacity	Positive cash flow (net cash contributor)	Plan an orderly withdrawal so as to maximise cash flow

Source: Adapted from Hollensen, S. (2006) *Marketing Planning: A Global Perspective*, McGraw-Hill Education, Maidenhead. Reproduced with permission from the McGraw-Hill Companies.

In summary, the portfolio matrix approach provides for the simultaneous comparison of different products. It also underlines the importance of cash flow as a strategic variable. Thus, when continuous long-term growth in earnings is the objective, it is necessary to identify high-growth product/market segments early, develop businesses, and pre-empt the growth in these segments. If necessary, short-term profitability in these segments may be forgone to ensure achievement of the dominant share. Costs must be managed to meet scale-effect standards. The appropriate point at which to shift from an earnings focus to a cash flow focus must be determined and a liquidation plan for cash flow maximisation established. A cash-balanced mix of businesses should be maintained.

The portfolio matrix approach, however, is not a panacea for strategy development. In reality, many difficulties limit the workability of this approach. Some potential mistakes associated with the portfolio matrix concept are:

1 over-investing in low-growth segments (lack of objectivity and 'hard' analysis);
2 under-investing in high-growth segments (lack of guts);
3 misjudging the segment growth rate (poor market research).

The relationship between the BCG model and the concept of PLC

The product portfolio matrix approach propounded by the Boston Consulting Group may be related to the product life cycle by putting the introduction stage in the question mark quadrant; growth starts toward the end of this quadrant and continues well into the star quadrant. Going down from the star to the cash cow quadrant, the maturity stage begins. Decline is positioned between the cash cow and the dog quadrants (see Figure 7.9). Ideally, a company should enter the product/market segment in its introduction stage, gain market share in the growth stage, attain a position of dominance when the product/market segment enters its

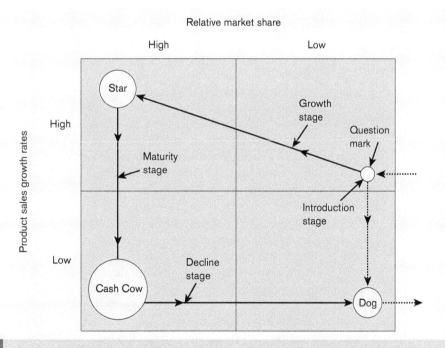

| Figure 7.9 | The BCG model and the product life cycle |

maturity stage, maintain this dominant position (with a generation of cash for new products) until the product/market segment enters its decline stage, and then determine the optimum point for removing the product.

This ideal PLC is often in contrast to the typical PLC flow which is represented by the dotted line in Figure 7.9.

The advantages of the BCG model

The advantages of the BCG model are as follows:

1   It fulfils a human desire for taxonomy, classifying a complex mix of different businesses. It is easy to grasp, has an attractive presentation and uses catch phrases and terms which are easy to memorise and have a clear link to strategy. These may be poor reasons for using a strategic tool, but they make it an effective means of communication in an area where little else is clear.

2   Research has provided some evidence to support the Boston Matrix. It embodies simple ideas with cash flow implications which are intuitively appealing to managers. The PIMS study has been a particularly fruitful source of support for the Boston Matrix.

3   Simplicity is probably the Boston Matrix's greatest virtue. It brings together a number of very important strategic issues and allows them to be presented and understood quickly. Fashion has led to the popularity of the Boston Matrix. This means it is an idea that is well understood and liked by many managers and therefore one which allows communication between headquarters and SBUs. It has become part of the common business vocabulary.

4   One of the most informative uses of the Boston Matrix is to plot competitors' positions along with the firm's own. This gives a valuable insight into their position (especially their cash position), indicates how they may behave in the future, and shows the relative strengths and weaknesses of the firm's own brands.

The disadvantages of the BCG model

The BCG model is not without problems and limitations. Some of the more frequent criticisms are as follows:

1   Defining the relevant industry and market served (i.e. the target market segments being pursued) can present problems. Market share varies depending on the definition of the corresponding product/market. Hence, a product may be classified in different cells, depending on the market boundaries used. For example, Coke Classic holds about a 24 per cent share of the US soft-drinks market, but less than 8 per cent of the market for all beverages. Given that consumers substitute other beverages – such as coffee, bottled water and fruit juice – for soft drinks to varying degrees, which is the most appropriate market definition to use?

2   Many critics have argued that the BCG growth share matrix is an oversimplification of product markets and can lead to insufficient management attention to the range of factors that is important in marketing strategy. For example, the matrix is based on only two key factors – market growth and relative market share. While the matrix specifies appropriate investment strategies for each business, it provides little guidance on how best to implement those strategies. While the model suggests that a firm should invest cash in its question mark businesses, it does not consider whether there are any potential sources of competitive advantage that the business can exploit to successfully increase its share. Simply providing a business with more money does not guarantee that it will be able to improve its position within the matrix.

3   Market growth rate is an inadequate description of overall industry attractiveness. For one thing, market growth is not always directly related to profitability or cash flow. Some high-growth industries have never been very profitable because low entry barriers and low capital requirements have enabled supply to grow even faster, resulting in intense price competition. Also, rapid growth in one year is no guarantee that growth will continue in the following year.

4   Relative market share is inadequate as a description of overall competitive strength. The assumption is that an experience curve resulting from a combination of scale economies and other efficiencies gained through learning and technological improvements over time leads to continuing reductions in unit costs as a business's relative market share increases. But a large market share within an industry does not always give a business a significant cost advantage – especially when the product is a low-value-added item.

5   The model implicitly assumes that all business units are independent of one another except for the flow of cash. If this assumption is inaccurate, the model can suggest some inappropriate resource allocation decisions. For instance, if other SBUs depend on a dog business as a source of supply, or if they share functional activities, such as a common salesforce, harvesting that dog might increase the costs or reduce the effectiveness of the other SBUs.

Screening
The stage in new product or market development in which a marketer analyses ideas to determine their appropriateness and reasonableness in relation to the organisation's goals and objectives.

6   The BCG portfolio framework was developed for balancing cash flows. It ignores the existence of capital markets. Cash balancing is not always an important consideration. Partly because of limitations and criticisms of the BCG growth share matrix, a number of product/market portfolio techniques now use several factors to analyse strategic business units instead of only the two found in BCG's approach. Working in conjunction with McKinsey & Co., General Electric USA (GE) has developed one of the more popular of these multiple-factor **screening** methods.

7.9 GENERAL ELECTRIC MARKET ATTRACTIVENESS – BUSINESS POSITION MATRIX (GE MATRIX)

In the GE matrix, SBUs are evaluated using the two factors of *market attractiveness* and *competitive position*. In contrast to the BCG approach, each of these two dimensions is, in turn, further analysed into a number of sub-factors that underpin each factor.

The market attractiveness–business position portfolio assessment model was developed by General Electric USA and designed to overcome some of the problems of models such as the BCG Matrix.

The classic analysis of attractiveness is contained in the nine-cell GE matrix, which also includes a study of the competitive strength of a supplier. Other similar matrices are the Shell directional policy matrix and the Arthur D. Little product–market evolution portfolio. Each is a logical refinement of the heavily criticised Boston Consulting Group (BCG) Matrix. The replacement of the single BCG factor of market growth with the more complex multidimensional market attractiveness on the vertical axis, and, on the horizontal, using measures of competitive strength instead of the single factor of relative market share makes the nine-cell alternative far stronger as an analytical tool.

Compiling the GE matrix

As shown in Figure 7.10, the process of compiling the GE matrix consists of the following three major steps:

- Step 1: determine the factors and the position of the SBU in the GE matrix;
- Step 2: prepare the GE matrix (estimate position of SBUs);
- Step 3: make strategic recommendations based on the GE matrix.

Step 1:
Determining the factors
(only shown for hydraulic pumps)

The SBU only, e.g. hydraulic pumps		Weight ×	Rating = (1–5)	Score/value
Market attractiveness	Overall market size	0.20	4	0.80
	Annual market growth rate	0.20	5	1.00
	Historical profit margin	0.15	4	0.60
	Competitive intensity	0.15	2	0.30
	Technological requirements	0.15	4	0.60
	Inflationary vulnerability	0.05	3	0.15
	Energy requirements	0.05	2	0.10
	Environmental impact	0.05	3	0.15
	Total	1.00		3.70

		Weight ×	Rating = (1–5)	Score/value
Business strength	Market share	0.10	4	0.40
	Share growth	0.15	2	0.30
	Product quality	0.10	4	0.40
	Brand reputation	0.10	5	0.50
	Distribution network	0.05	4	0.20
	Promotional effectiveness	0.05	3	0.15
	Productive capacity	0.05	3	0.15
	Productive efficiency	0.05	2	0.10
	Unit costs	0.15	3	0.45
	Material supplies	0.05	5	0.25
	R&D performance	0.10	3	0.30
	Managerial personnel	0.05	4	0.20
	Total	1.00		3.40

Step 2:
Estimate position of SBUs in the GE matrix

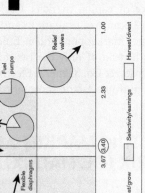

Business strength: High — Medium — Low
Market attractiveness: High — Medium — Low

SBUs plotted: Hydraulic pumps, Joints, Aerospace fittings, Fuel pumps, Relief valves, Clutches, Flexible diaphragms

Scale values: 5.00, 3.70, 3.67, 2.33, 1.00 / 3.67, 3.40

Legend:
- Invest/grow
- Selectivity/earnings
- Harvest/divest

Step 3:
Strategic implications of SBU positions

		Business strength		
		High	**Medium**	**Low**
Market attractiveness	**High**	Protect position • Invest to grow at maximum sustainable rate • Concentrate effort on maintaining strength	Invest to build • Challenge for leadership • Build selectively on strengths • Reinforce vulnerable areas	Build selectively • Specialise on limited strengths • Seek ways of overcoming weaknesses • Withdraw if indications of sustainable growth are lacking
	Medium	Build selectively • Invest heavily in most attractive segments • Build up ability to counter competition • Emphasize profitability by raising productivity	Selectivity/manage for earnings • Protect existing programme • Concentrate investments in segments where profitability is good and risk is relatively low	Limited expansion or harvest • Look for ways to expand without high risk; otherwise, minimise investment and rationalise operations
	Low	Protect and refocus • Manage for current earnings • Concentrate attractive segments • Defend strengths	Manage for earnings • Protect position in most profitable segments • Upgrade product line • Minimise investment	Divest • Sell at time that will maximise cash value • Meanwhile cut fixed costs and avoid investment

Figure 7.10 Compiling the GE matrix and making conclusions based on it

Sources: Adapted from Hosmer (1982), p. 310; Kotler (2000), pp. 71–2; and Day (1986), p. 204.

The five sub-steps in step 1 are:

- list the products and services that you intend to include in the analysis;
- determine factors contributing to market attractiveness;
- determine factors contributing to business position;
- establish ways of measuring market attractiveness and business position;
- rank each strategic business unit according to whether it is high, medium or low on business strength; and high, medium or low on market attractiveness.

Products and services

The list can consist of: countries, companies, subsidiaries, regions, products, markets, segments, customers, distributors or any other unit of analysis that is important. The GE matrix can be used at any level in an organisation and for any kind of SBU.

Factors

In order to use the GE matrix, the strategic planner must first determine the various factors contributing to market attractiveness and business position. The total list of possible factors to include could look like Table 7.3.

Ranking each SBU

After selecting some important factors from the list, the strategic planner should try to estimate the position of the single SBUs in the GE matrix. Within the matrix, the circle size represents the size of the market and the shaded part the share of the market held by the SBU.

The positions of these SBUs could then give implications for different strategies (step 3). The three cells in the upper-left corner indicate strong SBUs in which the company should invest or grow. The diagonal cells stretching from the lower left to the upper right indicate SBUs that are medium in overall attractiveness. The company should be selective and manage for earnings in these SBUs. The three cells in the lower-right corner indicate SBUs that have low overall attractiveness.

Advantages and disadvantages of the GE matrix

Advantages

- The GE matrix uses several factors to assess SBUs instead of only two, and is also based on return on investments rather than simply cash flow.
- The GE analysis is much richer than the BCG analysis because more factors are taken into account, and it is more flexible.
- Much of the value of such a tool lies in the discussion and debate necessary to identify and weight relevant factors.

Disadvantages

- The technique is much more complex than the BCG approach, and requires much more extensive data gathering and processing.
- Evaluation and scoring of SBUs is subjective. Subjectivity can be a problem, especially if planners are inexperienced in exercising the judgement required.

Table 7.3	Factors contributing to market attractiveness and competitive position

Attractiveness of your market	Competitive position of your business (business strengths)
Market factors	
Size (value, units or both)	Your share (in equivalent terms)
Size of key segments	Your share of key segments
Growth rate per year:	Your annual growth rate:
– total	– total
– segments	– segments
Diversity of market	Diversity of your participation
Sensitivity to price, service features and external factors	Your influence on the market
Cyclicality	Lags or leads in your sales
Seasonality	
Bargaining power of upstream suppliers	Bargaining power of your suppliers
Bargaining power of downstream suppliers	Bargaining power of your customers
Competition	
Types of competitor	Where you fit, how you compare in terms of products, marketing capability
Degree of concentration	
Changes in type and mix	Service, production strength, financial strength, management
Entries to and exits from market segment	Segments you have entered or left
Changes in share	Your relative share change
Substitution by new technology	Your vulnerability to new technology
Degrees and types of integration	Your own level of integration
Financial and economic factors	
Contribution margins	Your margins
Leveraging factors, such as economies of scale and experience	Your scale and experience
Barriers to entry or exit (both financial and non-financial)	Barriers to your entry or exit (both financial and non-financial)
Capacity utilisation	Your capacity utilisation
Technological factors	
Maturity and volatility	Your ability to cope with change
Complexity	How strong your skills are
Differentiation	Types of your technological skills
Patent and copyrights	Your patent protection
Manufacturing process technology required	Your manufacturing technology
Socio-political factors in your environment	
Social attitudes and trends	Your company's responsiveness and flexibility
Law and government agency regulations	Your company's ability to cope
Influence with pressure groups and government representatives	Your company's aggressiveness
Human factors, such as unionisation and community acceptance	Your company's relationships

● Another limitation is the unproven relationship between influencing factors and the overall factors (market attractiveness and business position) themselves. For instance, management recognises that its company's technological innovativeness gives it a strong status in the market, but the form and the direction of that relationship is not specified or easily quantifiable. Again, informed debate about the nature and form of such relationships can be highly beneficial.

Despite the limitations and practical difficulties in assessing future changes and strategic choices to deal with them, the technique has useful implications for marketing strategy. The limitations may be somewhat minimised if management uses informed judgement throughout the assessment. The model can be used to build up a qualitative picture of the product portfolios of its own or other companies, hence also providing a useful insight into competitors' market positions and business strengths.

7.10 INTERNATIONAL PORTFOLIO ANALYSIS

To decide which markets should be served, management must simultaneously examine the attractiveness of potential product and country markets and the firm's competitive position in the markets. On the one hand, management will try to focus the activities of the firm on the most attractive markets. On the other, it has to consider the firm's ability to build on or develop competitive advantages in those markets.

A potential method of simultaneously analysing the attractiveness of markets and the competitive position of the firm (its business units, product range or products) in those markets is portfolio analysis. The matrix used for international portfolio analysis is very similar to the GE matrix, but factors such as political and financial risk, transferability of funds, taxes and subsidies, or the potential for standardisation influence the portfolio structure. These factors have to be introduced to the comparison to increase the information level included in the analysis. A highly profitable market can be threatened by political unrest, religious upheavals or restrictive laws concerning business.

Figure 7.11 shows an example of how a country is positioned in an international portfolio. The principle behind the positioning process is the same as with the GE matrix.

The corporate portfolio analysis provides an important tool to assess how to allocate resources not only across geographic areas, but also across the different product businesses (Douglas and Craig, 1995). The global corporate portfolio represents the highest level of analysis and it might consist of operations by product businesses or geographic areas.

As illustrated in Figure 7.12 Unilever's highest level of analysis is its different product businesses. With this global corporate portfolio as a starting point, the further analysis of single corporate product businesses can go in a product factor, a geographic factor or a combination of the two factors.

It appears from the global corporate portfolio in Figure 7.12 that Unilever's foods business is characterised by high market attractiveness and high competitive strengths. However, a more distinct picture of the situation is obtained by analysing underlying levels. This more detailed analysis is often required to give an operational input to specific market planning decisions.

By combining the product and geographic dimensions it is possible to analyse the global corporate portfolio at the following levels (indicated by the arrows in Figure 7.12):

1 product category by region (or vice versa)
2 product category by country (or vice versa)
3 region by brand (or vice versa)
4 country by brand (or vice versa).

Of course, it is possible to make further detailed analysis of, for example, the country level by analysing different customer groups (e.g. food retailers) in certain countries. Thus, it may be important to assess the interconnectedness of various portfolio units across countries or regions. A customer (e.g. a large food retail chain) may have outlets in other countries, or the large retailers may have formed cross-border alliances in retailing with central purchasing from suppliers (e.g. Unilever) – see also section 13.11 on retailing.

Step 1:
Factors of country attractiveness and competitive strength

Market/country attractiveness	Competitive strength
Market size (total and segments)	Market share
Market growth (total and segments)	Marketing ability and capacity (country specific know-how)
Buying power of customers	Product fit to market demands
Market seasons and fluctuations	Price
Average industry margin	Contribution margin
Competitive conditions (concentration, intensity, entry barriers, etc.)	Image
Market prohibitive conditions (tariff/non-tariff barriers, import restrictions, etc.)	Technology position
Government regulations (price controls, local content, compensatory exports, etc.)	Product quality
Infrastructure	Market support
Economic and political stability	Quality of distributors and service
Psychic distance (from home base to foreign market)	Financial resources
	Access to distribution channels

Step 2:
Questionnaire for locating countries on a market attractiveness/competitive strength matrix

Time of analysis:
Analysis of product areas:
In country:

A. Market attractiveness

	1 Very poor	2 Poor	3 Medium	4 Good	5 Very good	% Weight factor	Result (grading × weight)
Market size							
Market growth							
Buying structure							
Prices							
Buying power							
Market access							
Competitive intensity							
Political/economical risks							
Other							
Total						100	

Market attractiveness = Result: 100 =

B. Relative competitive strength
With regard to the strongest competitor

	1 Very poor	2 Poor	3 Medium	4 Good	5 Very good	% Weight factor	Result (grading × weight)
Products fit to market demands							
Prices and conditions							
Market presence							
Marketing							
Communication							
Obtainable market							
Financial results							
Other							
Total						100	

Market attractiveness = Result: 100 =

Step 3:
Strategic implications of country positions

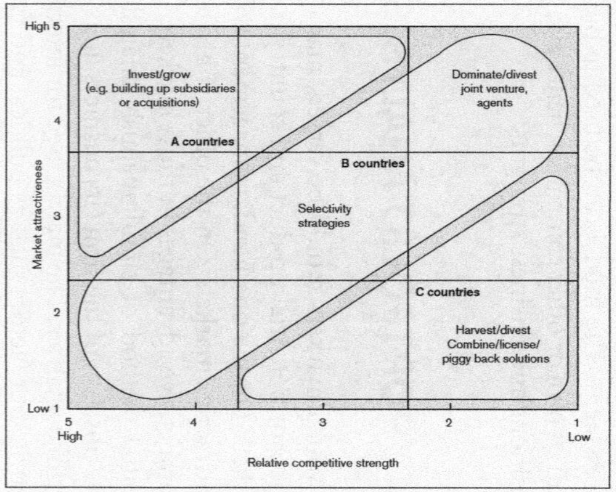

Figure 7.11   Country positioning in the international portfolio

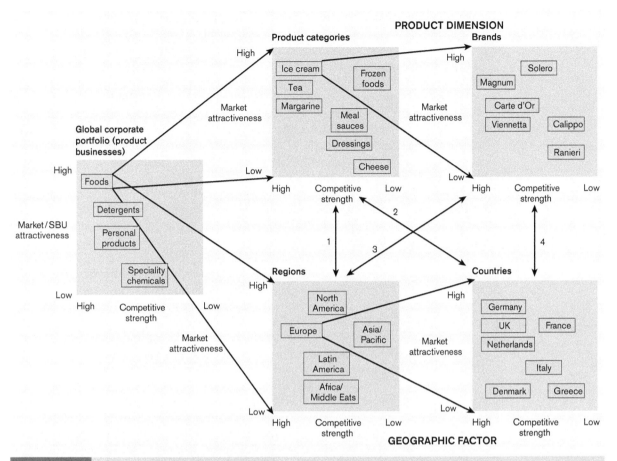

Figure 7.12	Unilevers global portfolio
	Source: Hollensen, S. (2001) *Global Marketing: A Market Responsive Approach*, 2nd ed., Financial Times-Prentice Hall, Harlow, p. 209. Reproduced with permission.

7.11 PORTFOLIO ANALYSIS OF SUPPLIER RELATIONSHIPS

During the past two decades, the strategic importance of firms' supply sides has increased considerably. These changes are commonly referred to as a shift from purchasing to supply management. According to this perspective, competitive advantage no longer resides with a firm's own capabilities, but rather with the relationship and linkages that the firm can establish with external organisations, including suppliers.

In particular, it has been emphasised that buying firms tend more and more to:

- outsource non-critical activities;
- establish close 'partnership' relationships with suppliers;
- reduce and trim their supplier base.

Why are there so many advocates of the relationship focus in marketing?

The transaction cost approach argues that every arm's-length transaction involves a transaction cost in search, negotiation and other associated activities. This leads to inefficiencies instead of efficiencies for the firms engaged in exchange transactions.

Relationship marketers, therefore, believe that interdependencies reduce transaction costs and generate higher quality while keeping management costs lower than exchange marketing. In short, better quality at a lower cost is achieved through interdependence and partnering among the value chain players.

The primary objective of this section is to describe some important considerations when analysing and developing a supplier portfolio. Based on the Kraljic (1983) supplier portfolio model, the approach in this study suggests that power and the risk of opportunistic behaviour are only two factors influencing the appropriate strategy when managing supplier relationships. Therefore, the portfolio of supplier relationships associated with purchases is categorised based on the relative supplier attractiveness and the strength of the relationship between the buyer and the supplier (Olsen and Ellram, 1997).

The portfolio model in Figure 7.13 illustrates an example of a firm by representing each relationship with a circle where the size of the circle illustrates the current allocation of resources to the relationship. This is often equivalent to the yearly value of purchase at that particular supplier. In Figure 7.13 the firm has 14 suppliers.

The relative supplier attractiveness describes the factors that make a company choose a specific supplier. It is necessary to use a contingency approach, because the factors and especially their importance will vary from company to company. Figure 7.13 contains some important factors that could be used to evaluate the relative supplier attractiveness. Therefore, it is important to emphasise that the company has to do this. The current supplier should be compared with alternative suppliers to determine the attractiveness. The list is not comprehensive, and firms may benefit from including other more specific factors. It is important that the company discusses which factors are important and allocates a weight to each relevant factor.

The financial and economic factors include an evaluation of the supplier's margins, financial stability, scale and experience, and the barriers to the supplier's entry and exit. An assessment of the economic factors also includes an evaluation of the slack, that is, a measure of the effect of the supplier's activities on the reduction of the buyer's internal economic process costs. The performance factors include a traditional evaluation of delivery, quality, price, etc. The technological factors include an assessment of the supplier's ability to cope with changes in the technology and an assessment of the current and future strength and types of the supplier's technological capabilities, the supplier's current and future capacity utilisation, the supplier's design capabilities, the speed in development, and the supplier's patent protection.

The organisational, cultural and strategic factors include an evaluation of the relationship's influence on the company's overall supply chain position. An evaluation of the possibility of opportunistic behaviour and other internal and external factors is also important. Finally, the group of other factors includes an assessment of the supplier's ability to cope with general changes in the environment. These changes could include changes in legislation, supply condition or the level of competition. Another important factor could be the safety record of the supplier.

The strength of the relationship describes the factors that create bonds between two companies. Figure 7.13 illustrates some factors that could be evaluated; it is not comprehensive.

The economic factors describing the strength of the relationship include the value of the purchase, the importance of the buyer in terms of the percentage of the supplier's sales being purchased by the buyer, and the cost of exiting that market. In this situation, the transaction-specific investments will create exit costs, because the investments cannot be transferred to other customers or suppliers.

The character of the exchange relationship describes characteristics of the exchange situation that creates stronger bonds between the companies.

Strategic implications of the suppliers' portfolio

The two 'extreme' situations (cells 3 and 7 in Figure 7.13) will be used as examples for the strategic implications.

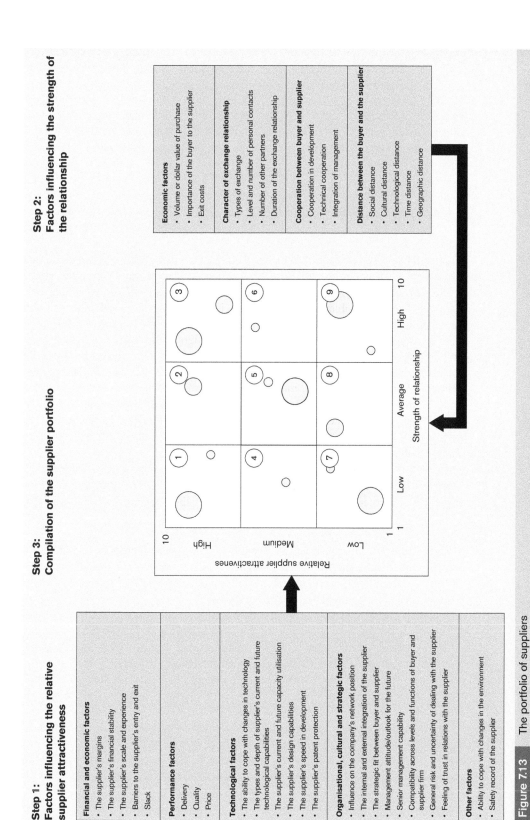

Step 1:
Factors influencing the relative supplier attractiveness

Financial and economic factors
- The supplier's margins
- The supplier's financial stability
- The supplier's scale and experience
- Barriers to the supplier's entry and exit
- Slack

Performance factors
- Delivery
- Quality
- Price

Technological factors
- The ability to cope with changes in technology
- The types and depth of supplier's current and future technological capabilities
- The supplier's current and future capacity utilisation
- The supplier's design capabilities
- The supplier's speed in development
- The supplier's patent protection

Organisational, cultural and strategic factors
- Influence on the company's network position
- The internal and external integration of the supplier
- The strategic fit between buyer and supplier
- Management attitude/outlook for the future
- Senior management capability
- Compatibility across levels and functions of buyer and supplier firm
- General risk and uncertainty of dealing with the supplier
- Feeling of trust in relations with the supplier

Other factors
- Ability to cope with changes in the environment
- Safety record of the supplier

Step 2:
Factors influencing the strength of the relationship

Economic factors
- Volume or dollar value of purchase
- Importance of the buyer to the supplier
- Exit costs

Character of exchange relationship
- Types of exchange
- Level and number of personal contacts
- Number of other partners
- Duration of the exchange relationship

Cooperation between buyer and supplier
- Cooperation in development
- Technical cooperation
- Integration of management

Distance between the buyer and the supplier
- Social distance
- Cultural distance
- Technological distance
- Time distance
- Geographic distance

Step 3:
Compilation of the supplier portfolio

Figure 7.13 The portfolio of suppliers
Source: Adapted from Olsen, R. F. and Ellram, R. L. (1997) A portfolio approach to supplier relationships, *Industrial Marketing Management*, 26: 106–7. Copyright © 1997 Elsevier. Reproduced with permission.

Cell 3 includes the supplier relationships where the supplier has a high relative attractiveness and the relationship is relatively strong. The strategy for these relationships could be to reallocate resources among different activities in order to maintain a strong relationship.

Strong relationships are costly because coordination, adaptation and interaction entail costs. Increasing involvement usually means a substantial increase in relationship and supply handling costs, but may, under certain circumstances, lead to lower direct procurement and transaction costs. However, the main rationale for strong relationships is to achieve cost benefits, for instance through taking advantage of supplier skills and developing capabilities to improve the quality of the customer's end product. Increased involvement makes sense only when the increased relationship costs are more than offset by relationship benefits. Reaping these benefits most often requires non-standardised solutions and customer-specific adaptations. High-involvement relationships are associated with investment logic.

Cell 7 includes relationships with low supplier attractiveness combined with a weak relationship. These relationships need attention because a reasonable strategy would be to change the supplier.

Weak relationships may lead to higher direct procurement costs and transaction costs. On the buyer side, there may be costs for adapting internal resources to fit with what suppliers have to offer. In the absence of good coordination, the buyer might be obliged to build up inventories as a buffer against possible risks. Furthermore, in order to enssure availability of supplies, the customer might tend to use many suppliers, resulting in increased supply handling costs.

At first sight it does not seem right that the firm offers so many resources to the relationship with the 'big size circle' supplier in cell 7. However, before changing the supplier, it is important to reconsider the supplier's influence on the company's network position. The supplier could be important in relation to other members of the network (other suppliers or customers). This could be an important reason to maintain the supplier. Other strategies include outsourcing the purchase or using systems contracting to enhance the supplier attractiveness.

Supplier types

Based on the assessment of the supplier portfolio model it is possible to develop a typology which breaks the suppliers into four categories (Figure 7.14). The following analyses the involvement of partner suppliers into one of the key activities of the firm, product development.

Involvement of partner suppliers in product development

In many industries, manufacturing companies give suppliers increasing responsibilities with regard to the design, development and engineering of products. The overall aims are to make better use of suppliers' technological capabilities and expertise and to improve (short-term) product development efficiency and effectiveness.

In terms of efficiency, supplier involvement can lead to the reduction of development costs and the reduction of development lead-time. This is mainly achieved by preventing, reducing or introducing design changes earlier by means of early and intensive communication with the supplier ('right first time' development).

In terms of effectiveness, supplier involvement may lead to the reduction of product cost and the increase of product value. This can be achieved by mobilising and leveraging supplier expertise.

Apart from improving (short-term) development project performance in terms of effectiveness and efficiency, manufacturers may have an interest in collaborating with suppliers in product development to achieve long-term benefits. One common long-term goal involves getting (long-term) access to the technological knowledge of suppliers. Ultimately, manufacturers may even have an interest in influencing supplier decisions with regard to the kind of technologies to invest in, in order to provide the best conditions for future technological collaboration (Wynstra *et al.*, 2001). However, it has been pointed out (ibid.) that not all efforts regarding supplier involvement in product development do result in the envisaged benefits; there are several problems to overcome.

Contractual suppliers
Obtain a product by simply specifying out of the supplier's catalogue. No need for any discussions concerning the product being bought.

Child suppliers
Involve the supplier after all the specifications have been cleared and simulated so that the supplier can deliver to OEM specifications.

Mature suppliers
Involve the supplier after the initial work of identifying overal l design and critical dimensions has generated the critical (or rough) specification. The critical (or rough) specifications contain functional data and rough envelopes of functionality. The supplier is entrusted to deliver the system within the quality and budget constraints as decided jointly.

Partner suppliers
Involve the supplier from the first instant and trust in his or her abilities to understand the interfaces and deliver a product that is compatible with all the necessary interfaces within the budget and quality levels decided jointly.

Increasing commitment/involvement in the activities of the firm

Figure 7.14	Four categories of suppliers

Source: Adapted from Nellore, R. and Söderquist, K. (2000) Portfolio approaches to procurement, *Long Range Planning*, 23: 253–4. Copyright © 2000 Elsevier. Reproduced with permission.

There may be problems that cannot be attributed only to the manufacturer or the supplier, but which are primarily connected to the relationship between the two. Problems such as a lack of communication and trust may lead to unclear agreements and diverging expectations, which hinder the collaboration's effectiveness and efficiency. Significant problems arise when the manufacturer fails to communicate clearly to suppliers what it expects from them, especially in terms of development responsibility for the products developed.

A lack of trust between the two parties may also hinder collaboration, as both parties will see large potential risks. Because of that, it may be especially difficult to collaborate with new suppliers, which may be necessary, for example, when the manufacturer needs a new type of component it has not used before.

Furthermore, manufacturers may end up selecting suppliers with little or limited experience in joint product development, for example due to supplier selection criteria only focusing on price. Weighting technological and innovative capabilities more heavily in supplier selection could improve the results of supplier involvement.

Despite the difficulties with supplier involvement, it can result in major benefits, both in the short and long term.

7.12 SUMMARY

Developing a successful marketing strategy requires activities to be chosen that are different from competitors'. The structure of this chapter has followed the main phases in the complex marketing planning process, where the end result emerges from the interplay of different factors.

A corporate mission is the reason why a firm exists. It can be considered as a definition of what the organisation is and what it does.

SWOT analysis structures the internal and external information into four categories:

- strengths and weaknesses (internal)
- opportunities and threats (external).

The SWOT analysis serves as a catalyst for structuring the creation of marketing strategies that will produce the desired result. It focuses on creating competitive advantage by matching company strengths to market opportunities. Furthermore, it provides guidance on how the firm might structure its marketing strategy to convert weaknesses and threats, and minimise or avoid those weaknesses and threats that cannot be converted.

Corporate objectives state where the firm intends to be at some specific time in the future. A corporate growth strategy describes how the long-term objectives will be achieved. According to the Ansoff product–market matrix there are four options: market penetration, market development, product development and diversification.

An SBU marketing strategy is concerned with how to create competitive advantage in each of the SBUs (combination of products/markets). The portfolio models (PLC, BCG, GE/McKinsey, etc.) guide the development of strategic alternatives for each of the company's SBUs and new business possibilities. In this way, this chapter has described the 'corporate' input to the later formulation of marketing plans.

In order to manage a firm's collection of SBUs, products or markets (countries), three downstream portfolio models were presented:

- The Boston Matrix (BCG model), where businesses are positioned in terms of market growth rate and relative market share, is certainly one of the best known.
- General Electric pioneered another matrix (GE model) which is more marketing oriented. In this portfolio model, each business is rated in terms of market attractiveness and competitive position.
- The international market portfolio is very similar to the GE model in its structure.

Furthermore, an upstream-oriented supplier portfolio was presented. This portfolio approach is a three-step approach to managing supplier relationships. The first step is to classify the components into the different factors of the portfolio model. The second step is to classify the suppliers based on their attractiveness to the firm (manufacturer) and the strength of the buyer–supplier relationship. Finally, strategies are drawn up to improve the supplier's strength and/or relationship with the buyer, in order to deliver the desired component optimally.

Portfolio models have been criticised both for their general structure, in which the different factors are only approximate estimations of the parameters that are supposed to be measured, and for their limited applicability in specific fields such as marketing and purchasing. This might be due to the fact that companies focus too much on developing very complex factors, in order to classify components, customers or suppliers, and become confused. The classification is not an end in itself, but a means to aid the development of appropriate action plans.

Involving suppliers in product development can result in major benefits in terms of money and time. Supplier involvement in product development holds great potential, both in the short and long term, but few companies seem to be able to realise these benefits. A large part of the unfulfilled potential is due to common problems such as lack of communication and trust, insufficient supplier abilities and internal resistance at the manufacturer. Also, it requires a great deal of thinking and effort. Primarily, it presupposes active management on behalf of the manufacturer, both in the short and long term, supported by adequate organisational and human resources.

CASE STUDY 7.1

Red Bull

The global market leader in energy drinks is considering further market expansion

The beginning

Energy drinks may well have come from Scotland in the form of Irn-Bru, first produced in the form of 'Iron Brew' in 1901. In Japan, the energy drink phenomenon dates at least as far back as the early 1960s, with the release of the Lipovitan. Most such products in Japan bear little resemblance to soft drinks, and are sold instead in small brown glass medicine bottles or cans styled to resemble such containers. These so-called 'genki drinks', which are also produced in South Korea, help employees to work long hours, or to stay awake on the late commute home.

In the UK, Lucozade Energy was originally introduced in 1929 as a hospital drink for 'aiding the recovery'; in the early 1980s, it was promoted as an energy drink for 'replenishing lost energy'.

Red Bull dates back to 1962 where the original formula was developed by Chaleo Yoovidhya, a Thai businessman, and sold under the name Krating Daeng by a local pharmaceutical company to treat jetlag and boost energy for truck drivers.

Dietrich Mateschitz grew up in a small village in Styria, Austria. When he turned 18, he went to the University of Vienna. It took Mateschitz 10 years to finally graduate with a degree in world trade. His friends said that Mateschitz liked to play, party and pursue pretty women. After graduation he decided to get serious and become a 'really good marketing man'. His natural charm helped him land a training position at Unilever, and soon he was promoting dishwashing detergents and soap all over Europe. Colleagues described him as 'funny, full of ambition and always filled with crazy ideas'.

Mateschitz had a natural talent for selling. He was creative and had a knack for getting things done. He soon got promoted to the position of marketing director for a leading international toothpaste brand called Blendax.

After years of travelling and selling toothpaste around the globe, Mateschitz became obsessed with the idea of creating his own business. In the summer of 1982 Mateschitz read a story about the top 10 taxpayers in Japan. He was surprised that a certain Mr Taisho, who had introduced a high-energy drink to Japan, made the top of the list. On the next stop of his sales trip – in Thailand – he learned from a local toothpaste distributor that energy

drinks were a hot item among tired drivers stopping at gas stations. The top brand was Krating Daeng, meaning water buffalo. The ingredients were clearly written on the can. Like the original Yellow Pages, there was no trademark or patent to protect the formula.

Dietrich Mateschitz met up with Chaleo Yoovidhya (owner of Krating Daeng) shortly after and they decided to start an energy drink company together. Each partner would contribute about half a million dollars in start-up capital. Chaleo Yoovidhya provided the beverage formula and his partner contributed with the marketing flair.

Red Bull was, then, founded in 1984 by Deitrich Mateschitz and Chaleo Yoovidhya, and was headquartered in Austria.

The start-up in Austria and the further international expansion

The optimistic 40-year-old Mateschitz quit his job and applied for a licence to sell the high-energy drink in Austria. However, the Austrian bureaucracy would not allow the drink to be sold without scientific tests. It took three years and many sales calls to get a licence to sell the product. While waiting for the official licence, Mateschitz asked his old school friend Johannes Kastner, who ran an advertising agency in Frankfurt, Germany, to design the can and logo. Mateschitz rejected dozens of samples before settling on a macho logo with two red bulls charging each other. Kastner worked diligently on a snappy slogan, but Mateschitz rejected one after the other, each time saying, 'Not good enough.'

Kastner told Mateschitz to find someone else to come up with a better slogan, but Mateschitz pleaded, 'Sleep on it, and give me one more tag line.' The next morning Kastner called and said, 'Red Bull – gives you wings.' The slogan turned into a prophecy for the Red Bull brand, which continues to soar around the globe.

Mateschitz still had to find a bottler to produce his drink. Every bottler he called told him that Red Bull had no chance of success. Finally, Mateschitz found a sympathetic ear in Roman Rauch, the leading soft-drink bottler in Austria, and soon the shiny silver cans rolled off the production line. Within two years, and after many creative promotions, sales began to grow, but so did his losses.

While a million-dollar loss in two years may scare an entrepreneur into closing the business, Mateschitz was undaunted. He financed everything without outside capital, and by 1990 Red Bull was in the black. He soon realised that Austria was not a big enough market, and in 1993 he expanded to neighbouring Hungary and then focused his energies on conquering the German market.

Once the news of Red Bull's advancing sales spread in Europe, dozens of copycat competitors came on the market. Red Bull's initial move into the German market was highly successful. However, after three months of increasing demand, Mateschitz could not get enough aluminum to produce the cans anywhere in Europe, and sales of Red Bull dropped fast. A competitor named Flying Horse became the market leader. It took Red Bull four years to reclaim the top spot in the German market.

In 1995, Red Bull hit Britain; in 1997, the United States, starting in California. There, in a marketing trick typical of his unusual style, he hired students to drive around in liveried Minis with a Red Bull can on the roof to promote the drink.

The rest is history. Red Bull has become extremely popular over recent years with almost 1 billion 250 ml cans sold in 2000 to more than 3 billion cans sold in 2006 in over 130 countries. In 2006, Red Bull generated over €2.6 billion throughout the world with the help of its 3,900 employees.

Red Bull is produced at a single facility in Austria and then distributed around the world via a network of local subsidiaries and distributors. By the end of 2007 Red Bull had subsidiaries in the following countries:

Europe:

Germany, Switzerland, Ireland, Italy, Netherlands, Finland, Greece, Portugal, Czech Republic and Slovakia.

Outside Europe:

Australia, New Zealand and United Arab Emirates.

Marketing orientation and consumers

Red Bull devised an innovative viral marketing approach to target mainly consumers seeking an energy boost: young adults (16–29), young urban professionals, post-secondary school students and club-goers.

The company also set about promoting the Red Bull brand directly to Generation Y, the so-called 'millennials', people born after 1981 who were believed to be cynical of traditional marketing strategies. Part of this idea involved recruiting 'student brand managers' who would be used to promote Red Bull on university campuses. These students would be encouraged to throw a party at which cases of Red Bull would be distributed. The brand managers would then report back to the company, giving the firm a low-cost form of market research data.

Red Bull tries to portray its products as drinks for energetic, physically active and health-conscious consumers, characterised by the sugar-free version. People in need of energy boosts include, but are not limited to, club-hoppers, truck drivers and students.

The Red Bull marketing strategy

Red Bull essentially threw the traditional marketing book out the window. Their highly acclaimed strategy has been variously described as: grassroots, guerilla, word-of-mouth, viral marketing, underground, buzz-marketing and, without a doubt, successful.

The first marketing trials of Red Bull failed miserably. The respondents didn't like the taste, colour or the 'stimulates mind and body' concept. At this point, many companies would have abandoned their plan or reformulated to make it more appealing to the consumer. However, Mateschitz rejected any suggestion that this testing of consumer taste should be the basis for their marketing strategy. Mateschitz's message was that Red Bull was not selling a beverage; rather, it was selling a 'way of life.' Red Bull will *give you wings* . . . Red Bull is an enabler for what you desire. Red Bull needed to be enjoyed in the right context – where an energy boost was needed.

One effective brand builder was not initiated by the company. Red Bull faced many obstacles in gaining regulatory approval in several countries because of their unique ingredients. During this time a rumour circulated that the taurine used came from bull's testicles and Red Bull was 'liquid Viagra', which made the drink even more mystic. Adding to the allure was the fact that the beverage has actually been banned in several countries such as France and Denmark.

The product

Red Bull is sold as an energy drink to combat mental and physical fatigue. Active ingredients include, but are not limited to, 27 g of sugar, B-complex vitamins, and 80 mg of caffeine – which is a little less than the amount of caffeine found in an average cup of coffee and about two times as much caffeine as many leading cola drinks. Besides water, sugar and caffeine the drink contains an ingredient named taurine, an amino acid that, according to Japanese studies, benefits the cardiovascular system.

A sugar-free version has been available since the beginning of 2003. The drink tastes of citrus and herbs, and is commonly used as a mixer in alcoholic drinks such as Red Bull Wings (Red Bull and Vodka) or a base ingredient in the famous Jägerbomb (a cocktail combining one shot of Jägermeister dropped into a glass of Red Bull).

Red Bull Original
Source: Red Bull GmbH

Red Bull Sugarfree
Source: Red Bull GmbH

Red Bull specialises in energy drinks. Red Bull is the company's main brand and with only two flavour varieties and one packaging size, this allows the company to focus its efforts and expand its footprint quickly while leveraging marketing and promotions used in other regions. In most countries and regions, Red Bull was the first energy drinks brand and, as a result, is the leading brand in almost all regions where it is sold.

Red Bull distinguishes itself from a lot of the beverage market by only offering its product in one size, 8.3 ounce (250 ml) cans, which is smaller than a typical soft drink. The cans are small, sleek vessels with distinctive printing, which have been described as more 'European' styling. With the exception of mandated warning labels, the can design does not vary by country. Furthermore, unlike soft drinks or vodka, Red Bull is only offered in two varieties: original and sugar-free. This recognisable packaging provides Red Bull an advantage, and the one size that is used worldwide creates production efficiencies.

On 24 March 2008 Red Bull introduced 'Simply Cola', or Red Bull Cola. The cola, which contains natural flavouring and caffeine, was introduced in several countries (as of 2008, Red Bull Cola is available in the Netherlands, Austria, Czech Republic, Egypt, Switzerland, Spain, Poland, Germany, Belgium, Italy, the United Kingdom, Ireland, Thailand, Romania, Hungary, Russia and the United States). Red Bull Cola is not manufactured by Red Bull itself, but in Switzerland by Rauch Trading AG for Red Bull GmbH. It is the company's own take on a cola beverage. The product was the first major brand extension since Red Bull Sugar-Free was introduced in 2003. It was available in both the original 250 ml cans and the newer 355 ml version. Red Bull Cola also has slightly more caffeine, at 45 milligrams per 355 ml (12-ounce) can, than Coca-Cola (34 mg) or Pepsi-Cola (37.5 mg), but less than Diet Coke (47 mg).

Price

This clear positioning has created a foothold in key markets such as the UK, Germany and the US. Sales in key markets help drive the global positioning of the company, as well as providing the opportunity to sell Red Bull at a premium price over other brands. A single can is generally around €2.00, which is up to five times the cost of other branded soft drinks.

Premium pricing is a feature of the energy drinks category. Since its inception the category has been positioned as providing products that not only refresh you, but give you the energy and related brain power to make the most of your time. While it could never be said that energy drinks position themselves as healthy, there is little doubt that they claim to provide a functional benefit to the consumer, which is the main reason why they can command a premium price. In 2006, the average price per litre for an energy drink across the world was US$5.78, almost four times the average price of a litre of carbonates (US$1.54), and similarly ahead of the average price per litre in the soft drinks category as a whole (US$1.50).

Distribution

A key growth strategy at Red Bull has been increased international distribution. It has consistently worked on growing international sales, first making moves outside its domestic market in 1992, only five years after the first cans of Red Bull appeared in Austria. Now available in over 100 countries worldwide, Red Bull has a well-developed network of local subsidiaries set up in key markets to oversee distribution in any given region. These subsidiaries are responsible for importing Red Bull from Red Bull GmbH in Austria and either setting up an independent distribution network or working with a partner, such as in Australia where Red Bull Australia uses Cadbury Schweppes's distribution network. In this case, Red Bull Australia imports and sells on to Cadbury Schweppes, which then sells to vendors in its network.

The typical Red Bull national distribution strategy for new markets is, like all else, atypical. Instead of targeting the largest distributors with the greatest reach, Red Bull targets small distributors who often become exclusively Red Bull distributors. They even went to the extreme of hiring teenagers/college students and giving them vans to distribute the product.

Small independent venues were the first targets. Red Bull would find the small bars, restaurants and stores and give them a small cooler to sell the beverage from. This was their preferred method rather than dealing with the demands of the larger stores, which eventually were begging to sell the product.

Promotion/advertising

Many product launches are coupled with large advertising campaigns, both in print and on TV, taste tests, give-aways and celebrity endorsements to get the brand and product out into the public. This is not a technique that is used by Red Bull.

Red Bull does not use traditional advertising to enter a market. Only after the product is in the market does advertising serve as a reminder. Furthermore, they never use print media since it is too dull and flat to express the product. Television ads are often cartoon drawings using the 'Red Bull gives you wings' slogan and are very

Red Bull Simply Cola
Source: Red Bull GmbH

carefully placed. Stations and programming are carefully selected to maximise exposure to the target audience such as late-night TV shows.

Red Bull does not hire celebrity endorsers, but they do enable celebrity endorsers. Some of the earliest deliveries of Red Bull in the US were to Hollywood movie sets for consumption during long days of filming, even before the beverage was readily available. This created a scheme where the celebrities were doing what they could to get Red Bull and instantly became endorsers for the brand to the masses. Celebrities are not the only ones who were enabled for endorsements. Again, before the product was widely available, the company made it available to bar tenders in New York's trendiest spots for their own consumption. This led to an unpaid endorsement to the club patrons by the bar tenders.

Every year the company sponsors dozens of extreme sporting events, like the climbing of iced-down silos in Iowa or kite sailing in Hawaii, as well as cultural events like break-dancing contests and rock music jam sessions. Red Bull also sponsors a DJ camp where some of the up-and-coming DJs get a chance to learn from some of the masters, courtesy of Red Bull. Red Bull also sponsors some 500 athletes around the world, the type who would surf in Nova Scotia in January or jump out of a plane to 'fly' across the English Channel.

Red Bull X Fighters
Source: © Balazsgardi.com/Red Bull Photo Files

It also hosts events such as the 'Red Bull Flugtag' (German for 'flight day' or 'flying day'), a competition where entrants launch themselves off a 30-foot ramp in homemade 'flying machines' into a body of water. It takes place in big cities such as London (here it is taking place in Hyde Park).

The local subsidiaries are also responsible for local marketing content such as buzz marketing, local sponsorships and arranging media including TV, billboards and radio. In addition to local marketing and advertising, local subsidiaries also acquire marketing material from Red Bull GmbH and its exclusive advertiser Kastner & Partner.

Red Bull X Fighters
Source: © Flohagena.com/Red Bull Photo Files

Red Bull is also involved with more popular sports, such as football and racing. Red Bull has extended its presence in sports to purchasing and entirely rebranding a number of sports teams.

On 6 April 2005, Red Bull bought the Austrian club SV Austria Salzburg and renamed it Red Bull Salzburg, a move which has been heavily criticised by supporter groups within Austria and across Europe.

Red Bull Racing is one of two Formula One teams owned by Red Bull (the other being Scuderia Toro

Red Bull Flugtag
Source: © Marcel Lammerhirt/Red Bull Photo Files

Rosso). The team is based in Milton Keynes in the UK but holds an Austrian licence. The team won its first Grand Prix as Red Bull at the 2009 Chinese Grand Prix in Shanghai, with young German driver Sebastian Vettel.

In addition to sports sponsorships, Red Bull has developed the Mobile Energy Team programme consisting mostly of outgoing college students who drive specially designed Red Bull Mini Coopers with the red can on the roof to promote the drink. They go to all types of events and arrange sampling of the energy drink. They are usually employed by Red Bull on a part-time basis and often have teams running on 24/7 formats.

All in all, Red Bull spends relatively little on traditional print and TV advertising, instead relying on sponsorships of sports or giving away samples at local events. Since its introduction, Red Bull has invested heavily in building the brand, spending around 40 per cent of revenue on marketing and promotion. As a comparison, Coca-Cola spends 9 per cent.

Competition

By definition, Red Bull operates within the functional drinks market, which is mostly made up of sales from energy drinks and sports drinks – Red Bull is only active in the energy drinks market. Sports drinks are not to be confused with energy drinks. Sports drinks are intended to replenish electrolytes, sugar, water and other nutrients, and are usually isotonic (containing the same proportions as found in the human body) and used after strenuous training or competition. Energy drinks, on the other hand, mainly provide sugar and caffeine in order to increase concentration or mental and physical capacities. The most well-known sports drink is Gatorade (Quaker Oats Co.), which was introduced in 1965.

Red Bull, despite being widely known as an energy drink, has other uses such as a coffee, tea and soda substitute, a vitamin/energy supplement, and a mixer for alcohol.

The majority of consumers use Red Bull as a vitamin supplement or energy stimulant in place of preferred stimulants such as ginseng. Red Bull, with its liquid

Red Bull Mini
Source: Red Bull GmbH

B-vitamin supplement, competes in the niche market for vitamins and is competing with the larger pharmaceutical companies. Red Bull also competes indirectly with various drink mixers such juice, sour mix and tonic. Red Bull initially marketed its energy drink mixed with alcohol to the average club-goers. However, due to various health concerns and fatal incidents associated with Red Bull when mixed with alcohol, explicit warnings have been placed on product labels discouraging improper use.

The market for energy drinks is characterised by the presence of specialised manufacturers as well as food and beverage powerhouses. Key players in the marketplace include Pepsi, Coca-Cola, Danone, Hansen Beverage Company, Monarch Beverage Co., Red Bull, Dark Dog, GlaxoSmithKline, Extreme Beverages, Taisho Pharmaceuticals and Otsuka Pharmaceuticals. In terms of market share, Gatorade and Red Bull lead the sports and energy drinks segments respectively. Most of the soft drink multinationals (e.g. Pepsi, Coca-Cola, Danone, GlaxoSmithKline) also cover the functional drinks market. For example, Coca-Cola added the Von Dutch and Tab Energy brands to its energy drinks portfolio in 2006. While smaller players have proven the most innovative, the production, distribution and marketing resources of the major multinationals represent a considerable threat to Red Bull.

The total market for functional drinks (including energy drinks)

Today's 24/7 lifestyle is driving the sales of functional drinks, with volume having increased by impressive figures. Functional drinks have now clearly moved from niche to mass market, having seen significant growth every year since their introduction. In order to get the most out of every day, consumers are increasingly looking at products with an extra kick, which is one reason why so many people are reaching for these kinds of drink.

In the overall functional drinks market, Red Bull is increasingly being challenged by new innovative brands.

With global sales of 3 billion cans in 2006, Red Bull reached a 45 per cent market share of the world market in energy drinks. This has made Red Bull a clear world market leader in this segment. Higher per litre revenue in 'energy drinks' has attracted brands from all the major players into the market, such as Coca-Cola's Burn and Pepsi's Adrenaline, but so far they have not come close to dislodging Red Bull from its position as global market leader.

In the overall global soft drink market the Red Bull market share is small: according to Euromonitor (2007) it is 0.8 per cent.

The overall Red Bull market shares in the 'functional drinks market' are shown in Table 7.4.

The market development in the 'global energy drinks' market

Asia dominates consumption of energy drinks, accounting for around 40 per cent of volume. However, at a per capita level it is North America and Australia/NZ that lead the way. In almost all regions, the concept of energy drinks has been established and accepted by the consumer. The only two regions that partly remain exceptions are Eastern Europe and Central and South America, where lower levels of disposable income remain a barrier.

Not surprisingly, the US is the largest country market, ahead of Japan, Indonesia and China. Three other Asian countries also appear in the top ten markets for energy drinks, namely Thailand, South Korea and Vietnam. While still accounting for nearly half of all energy drinks consumed worldwide, Asian dominance is starting to slowly slip as other regions begin to catch up. In fact, worldwide growth in consumption is beginning to slow. Following year-on-year growth of 31 per cent in 2004, and 24 per cent in 2005, growth slowed to 17 per cent in 2006.

In Western Europe, the UK leads the way in volume terms, accounting for nearly half of energy drinks consumed in the region. However, the Republic of Ireland and Austria have a far higher per capita consumption figure, with Irish consumers drinking an average of just under 8 litres of energy drinks per year, hugely more than the regional average of 1.6 litres per capita. Higher per capita figures in Austria can perhaps be explained by the fact that Red Bull and other energy drinks companies originated there.

In Western Europe, many energy drinks are banned from sale due to certain ingredients, including Red Bull, which is banned in France and Denmark. This obviously has a marked effect on the market when compared to other geographic regions.

On-trade and off-trade challenges

Red Bull was originally targeted at the on-trade (bars, discos, etc.), and still in Spain, for example, the popularity of Red Bull as a mixer underpins the fact that on-trade channels accounted for 59 per cent of energy drinks volume sales in 2007. The role of fashion in determining product choice in the on-trade channel presents

---

Table 7.4   Red Bull market shares (value) in the functional drinks market, 2006

Region	Red Bull market share in the functional drinks market %
Western Europe	26.8
Eastern Europe	31.4
North America	10.0
Latin America	11.7
Asia (excluding Aus/NZ)	2.8
Aus/NZ	13.6
Africa/Middle East	22.7
Total world	10.9
Total world market (functional drinks market)	US$24,250 million

Source: Euromonitor International (2008) Functional drinks: world market report, *Euromonitor*.

Red Bull with the opportunity to generate sales by developing new combinations with alcoholic drinks.

Off-trade (retail) has now become the principal channel for energy drinks, with approximately two-thirds of worldwide volume being sold through these channels. This picture is pretty consistent worldwide, other than in Central and South America where the split is far more even, and North America where the emphasis is far heavier on the retail channels (85 per cent). In many markets, the UK being a good example, the volume sold through on-trade channels is heavily impacted by energy drinks being sold as mixers with spirits, primarily vodka.

Overall, the energy drinks market has seemed to shift from impulse-dependent to planned purchases with the expansion through supermarkets/hypermarkets. The development of non-impulse-oriented off-trade distribution creates opportunities to develop new packaging formats, including larger cans, multipacks and bottles. Furthermore, the shift to supermarket/hypermarket distribution may further encourage Red Bull to engage in agreements with major multinationals which have strong relationships with large and powerful retailers. The expansion of a non-impulse off-trade presence carries a risk of undermining Red Bull's fashionable image, especially given the emergence of rival brands targeting cutting-edge niches.

Red Bull is challenged in the US market by Monster

When Monster and other brands launched a larger 16-ounce can, Red Bull reacted too slowly. It was costly: from 2001 to 2006 Red Bull's market share in dollar terms went from 91 per cent to well under 50 per cent, and much of that loss has been Monster's gain.

From 2006 to 2008 California-based Hansen Natural Corp.'s line of Monster energy drinks gained further market shares from Red Bull and Monster is now the top US energy drink in terms of both unit volume and value (dollars) in the important convenience store channel. Monster has strong momentum in the US across all channels. However, taken together (off-trade plus on-trade), Monster is still the nation's No. 2 selling energy drink (in value) behind Red Bull. Both companies had around 25 per cent market share in 2008. Rockstar is a distant third with approximately 14 per cent market share in 2008.

In October 2008 Monster and Coca-Cola Enterprises (Coca-Cola's bottler) made a 20-year deal to distribute Monster energy drinks in about 20 US states, Canada and in six Western Europe countries. This deal with Monster could give Coca-Cola a stronger position in the growing energy drink market. Conversely, it could help Monster by giving it access to Coca-Cola's distribution system in Europe. In January 2009 Coca-Cola began distributing the Monster line in France, Monaco, Belgium, Holland, Luxembourg and Canada (Much, 2009).

In February 2009, it was announced that the No. 3 brand in US energy drinks, Rockstar, had signed a 10-year distribution deal with PepsiCo Inc., which in future will distribute Rockstar to most parts (approximately 80 per cent) of the United States and Canada. Both companies hope the deal will give the brand more consistent coverage across the US and increase PepsiCo's presence in the energy drink category. (Rockstar had in fact signed a distribution agreement with Coca-Cola Enterprises in 2005, and renegotiated the deal in 2008 as Coke was in negotiations with Monster-parent Hansen Natural; Casey, 2009.)

In contrast to Monster and Rockstar, Red Bull still has full confidence in its own distribution model in the United States, by having its sales subsidiary Red Bull North America taking care of the overall distribution strategy and then relying on smaller distributors (often young committed entrepreneurs) in order to penetrate local markets.

Strategic options

In October 2008 Dietrich Mateschitz is preparing for the next top management meeting: he summarises some current strategic options for Red Bull in random order:

(a) *Expansion in emerging markets*: The top management team of Red Bull is considering placing the focus of its further expansion on new markets such as India, Turkey, Russia, Mexico, Japan, China or the Middle East. These markets are seeing demand for energy drinks grow strongly in urban areas thanks to rising purchasing power, accelerated lifestyles and improving distribution. Red Bull's prime consumers are in their 20s and the large youth population in the region can potentially become energy drinks consumers in the long term. India boasts the highest number of 20- to 24-year-olds (98 million), followed by China (82 million) and Indonesia (21 million). The liberalisation of the Chinese and Indian economies is set to raise living standards and improve levels of disposable incomes, which will benefit sales of highly valued consumer products. Along with total increases in the consumption of soft drinks, China, India and Indonesia will continue to see high sales growth of energy drinks in years to come, implying optimistic business prospects for Red Bull.

(b) *International production*: Expanding the Red Bull production infrastructure would help the company to diminish the negative impact of exchange rate fluctuations and provide greater flexibility on price in the context of international expansion.

(c) *Healthier product variants*: Rising consumer health-consciousness is creating opportunities to develop energy drinks with healthier ingredients and more specific functional properties.

(d) *Hybrid products*: As busy consumers look for quick energy boosts, there are growing opportunities to develop hybrid products which combine energy-giving properties with other drink categories, such as tea, fruit/vegetable juice and bottled water. Another example is the emergence of malt-based alcohol brands with already added energy components. In the USA in 2005, Anheuser-Busch launched 'B to the E', a beer with added ginseng and guarana. In 2006 Miller Brewing purchased Sparks, a malt beverage with added caffeine, ginseng and taurine. Such drinks pose a particular threat to Red Bull's position as a mixer for alcoholic beverages in on-trade establishments.

(e) *Strategic alliances*: Red Bull may consider engaging in more agreements with major multinational partners, such as Cadbury Schweppes in Australia, which would allow it to exploit established distribution networks and accelerate its penetration of new markets. This has also been the strategy of the main US competitor, Monster, which has allied itself with Coca-Cola Enterprises as its US and European distributor.

Dietrich Mateschitz is interested in your input for the following tasks/questions.

QUESTIONS

1 Prepare a SWOT analysis for Red Bull.

2 Was it a wise decision of Red Bull to:
- launch Red Bull Cola?
- launch Red Bull Cola in many markets at the same time?

3 Should Red Bull counteract US competitor Monster's new marketing initiatives? If yes, what should Red Bull do in response?

4 Which of the five strategic options would you recommend for Red Bull's future strategy? Present arguments in support of your suggested priority list.

Red Bull targets the Japanese market

After evaluating the different international options, Red Bull decided to conduct further analysis on the Japanese market. The following paragraphs contain key facts about the Japanese market for functional drinks (including energy drinks).

Energy drinks became popular in Asia long before they reached Europe or the United States. In 1962, Japanese pharmaceutical company, Taisho, released its Lipovitan D drink. It was designed to help employees work hard well into the night. Lipovitan D contains taurine, the same ingredient found in many of today's energy drinks.

Energy drinks in Japan are under intense competition from other beverages, namely over-the-counter (OTC) tonic drinks. Energy drinks are registered as shokuhin or food products in Japan, which means that they can be sold through all retail channels, including vending machines. In 1999, however, deregulation in Japanese OTC healthcare reclassified tonic drinks as 'newly designated quasi-drugs', allowing for their sale through the same retail channels as energy drinks. This resulted in intense competition, as consumers in need of a pick-me-up generally prefer to consume tonic drinks as these contain stronger ingredients.

At the same time, energy drinks suffered from shifting consumer trends towards healthier beverages. Energy drinks in Japan are often very sweet, containing high amounts of sugar in addition to caffeine, guarana and other energy-boosting ingredients. However, with growing consumer awareness about healthier lifestyles and the growing incidence of diabetes in Japan, Japanese consumers are becoming increasingly concerned about blood glucose levels. Many are therefore shifting towards soft drinks that contain no sugar or reduced levels of sweeteners.

As seen in Table 7.5, Coca-Cola (Japan) Co. Ltd continues to lead the Japanese functional drinks market, followed by strong domestic manufacturers.

With a per capita consumption of 1.7 litres, Japan has a highly concentrated energy drinks market, with Otsuka's brands and Coca-Cola's brands together accounting for over 70 per cent of the market. The two top brands have their own strong consumer base and it would be very costly for a new brand to fight for the shrinking consumer base in the face of declining birth rates and a rapidly ageing population. In fact, energy drinks players have failed to find new consumers and total consumption has declined consistently since the late 1990s, and this trend is expected to continue in years to come.

From 2000 to 2006 the functional drink sector has seen a decline of 5 per cent in volume and 4 per cent in value terms. The market sector is currently being squeezed by functional bottled water and OTC tonic drinks. A reason for decline in functional drinks is the limited consumer base for energy drinks. Energy drinks

Table 7.5	Red Bull market shares (value) in the Japanese functional drinks market, 2005	
Company	**Biggest brand**	**Market share %**
Coca-Cola (Japan) Co. Ltd	Real Gold, Aquarius	35.6
Otsuka Pharmaceutical Co. Ltd	Oronamin C, Pocari Sweat	34.3
Suntory Ltd	Suntory	3.0
Kirin Beverage Corp.	Gekiryuu	2.7
Asahi Soft Drinks Ltd	Super H2O	2.5
Dydo Drinco Inc.	Miu	2.2
Private label	–	0.6
Others	–	19.1
Total		**100.0**

Source: Euromonitor International (2006) **Functional drinks in Japan: market report**, *Euromonitor*, pp. 5–6.

mainly target male office workers, who consume such drinks as a pick-me-up during stressful work conditions. However, this consumer base will shrink over the forecast period, not only because of population decline, but also because the growing incidence of diabetes and other lifestyle diseases is generating rising awareness about foods containing high amounts of sugar, which include carbonates and energy drinks.

Red Bull is known for being aggressive in marketing terms but cautious in terms of product development. Its unwillingness to modify the product format and the taste of the drink may not be attractive to young Japanese consumers, who typically flirt with new products and are quick to change brands. In the competitive Japanese soft drinks market, even established brands need to be revamped regularly to cater for ever-changing preferences and fads. On top of this, the new consumer trend favouring natural ingredients may well work against Red Bull.

Nevertheless, Japan is a wealthy country and the ready ability to pay for premium drinks is in no doubt. Red Bull may stand a chance of winning over young Japanese consumers if it manages to carve itself a niche in the on-trade channel, which currently records negligible sales of energy drinks. Success may be more likely if Red Bull partners local players such as Suntory, which has experience in distributing international brands and operates a large number of vending machines across the country. Suntory's expertise and its connection with on-trade channels for both alcoholic and soft drinks would help Red Bull to quickly penetrate the market.

QUESTIONS

5 Would you recommend that Red Bull invests in the penetration of the Japanese market, or would you rather use the market resources elsewhere?

6 Suppose you choose to invest your marketing resources in the Japanese market. Which marketing planning process would you suggest for this market? Which parts of the marketing mix are the most critical?

7 Which changes would you suggest for Red Bull's future global marketing mix, in order to meet the future challenges?

SOURCES

Beverage World (2008) Energy drinks are on steady track, *Beverage World*, 15–17; Casey, M. (2009) PepsiCo signs deal to distribute Rockstar via Pepsi Bottlers, *Bevnet.com*, (www.bevnet.com/news/2009/2-19-2009-rockstar_pepsi); Datamonitor (2007) Red Bull GmbH, company profile, *Datamonitor*, 25 April; Euromonitor International (2006) Functional drinks: Japan, *Euromonitor*, October: 1–11; Euromonitor International (2007) Red Bull GmbH: softdrink – world, global company profile, *Euromonitor*, March: 1–15; Gschwandtner, G. (2004) The powerful sales strategy behind Red Bull, *Selling Power Magazine*, September; Hosea, M. (2007) Running with bulls, *Brand Strategy*, September: 20–3; Lerner, M. (2007) Running with 'Red Bull' and an arena of speciality drinks, *American Metal Market*, August: 20–2; Marketing Week (2006) Red Bull spreads its wings, *Marketing Week*, 6 January: 33; Much, M. (2009) Coke distribution deal could be a Monster boost for drink maker, Investers.com,(http://beta.investors.com/NewsAndAnalysis/Article.aspx?id=459831).

QUESTIONS FOR DISCUSSION

1 How can corporate objectives be derived from the corporate mission?

2 What is the purpose of a SWOT analysis?

3 How can a SWOT analysis be carried out? What are the critical issues?

4 What are the differences between marketing objectives and marketing strategies?

5 What purpose may a product portfolio serve in the context of a marketing strategy?

6 What is the meaning of relative market share in the BCG model?

7 The Ajax company has 4 SBUs, as shown in the table below:

SBU	Ajax SBU market share (%)	Largest competitor's market share (%)	Market growth rate (%)	Dollar sales ($ millions)
A	30	10	8	5.0
B	40	20	14	2.0
C	10	40	5	1.0
D	10	30	16	0.5

   (a) Prepare the BCG (Boston Consulting Group) Matrix for Ajax's SBUs.
   (b) What are the strategic implications of Ajax's BCG Matrix?
   (c) What are the general drawbacks of using the BCG Matrix in the strategic planning?
   (d) Is there a relevant alternative portfolio planning model to the BCG Matrix?

8 What are the advantages and disadvantages of using portfolio models in strategic marketing planning?

9 What is the purpose of integrating supplier portfolio models in marketing planning?

10 Why is it important to involve suppliers in product development?

REFERENCES

Abell, D. (1980) *Defining the Business: The Starting Point of Strategic Planning*, Prentice Hall, Englewood Cliffs, NJ.

Akan, O., Allen, R. S., Helms, M. M. and Spralls, III, S. A. (2006) Critical tactics for implementing Porter's generic strategies, *Journal of Business Strategy*, 27(1): 43–53.

Ansoff, H. I. (1957) Strategies for diversification, *Harvard Business Review*, September–October: 113–24.

BBC (2001) Microsoft's X-Box goes online, *BBC News*, 29 March (http://news.bbc.co.uk).

Byrne, B. (2007) Finally, a strategic way to cut unnecessary SKUs, *Strategy & Leadership*, 35(1): 30–5.

Day, G. S. (1986) *Analysis for Strategic Market Decisions*, West Publishing, St Paul, MN.

Douglas, S. P. and Craig, C. S. (1995) *Global Marketing Strategy*, McGraw-Hill, New York.

Duracell (1999) The Gillette company prevails in lawsuit against Ralson Purina, press release, 13 May (www.duracell.com).

Economist (1995) A tale of two conglomerates, *The Economist*, 18 November: 20.

Gadde, L. E. and Snehota, I. (2000) Making the most of supplier relationships, *Industrial Marketing Management*, 29: 305–16.

Hollensen, S. (2006) *Marketing Planning: A Global Perspective*, McGraw-Hill Education, Maidenhead.

Hollensen, S. (2007) *Global Marketing: A Market Responsive Approach*, 4th edn, Financial Times-Prentice Hall, Harlow.

Hosmer, La Rue T. (1982) *Strategic Management*, Prentice-Hall, Upper Saddle River, NJ.

Jobber, D. (1998) *Principles and Practice of Marketing*, 2nd edn, McGraw-Hill, New York.

Kaufmann, S. (2000) Ford introduces new golf car, *Golf Week*, 1 October: 10 (www.golfweek.com).

Kotler, P. (2000) *Marketing Management*, Prentice Hall, Englewood Cliffs, NJ.

Kraljic, P. (1983) Purchasing must become supply management, *Harvard Business Review*, 61: 109–17.

Lofton, L. (2000) Kellogg and Keebler: a tasty combo, www.tool.com (news), 27 October.

Maremont, M. (2001) Gillette plans to pour its energies into reviving Duracell: marketing strategy includes a coppertop label, but signals an avoidance of price cuts, *Wall Street Journal*, 28 March: 6.

Marketing Week (1998) Duracell combats new Energizer range with extra-strength launch, *Marketing Week*, 26 February: 10.

Markowitz, H. (1952) Portfolio selection, *Journal of Finance*, March: 7.

Nellore, R. and Söderquist, K. (2000) Portfolio approaches to procurement, *Long Range Planning*, 23: 245–67.

Olsen, R. F. and Ellram, R. L. (1997) A portfolio approach to supplier relationships, *Industrial Marketing Management*, 26: 101–13.

Progressive Grocer (2000) Batteries, *Progressive Grocer*, August: 26.

Rummell, J. (1999) What's new at Gillette? *Global Cosmetic Industry*, 4 (October): 16–18.

Woonghee, L. and Lee, N. S. (2007) Understanding Samsung's diversification strategy: the case of Samsung Motors, Inc., *Long Range Planning*, 40 (August): 488–504.

Wynstra, F., Van Weele, A. and Weggemann, M. (2001) Managing supplier involvement in product development: three critical issues, *European Management Journal*, 19(2): 157–67.

CHAPTER 8
Segmentation, targeting, positioning and competitive strategies

LEARNING OBJECTIVES

After studying this chapter you should be able to:

- understand the importance and meaning of market segmentation
- explain the principle of STP
- identify and discuss the various bases for segmenting B2C markets and B2B markets
- outline how firms select target segments
- explain the differences between various strategic approaches to target marketing, undifferentiated, differentiated and concentrated marketing
- comprehend what is involved in positioning a product or service against competitors
- explain the difference between positioning in the B2C market and B2B markets

8.1 INTRODUCTION

Market segmentation has long been considered one of the most fundamental concepts in marketing. Ever since Smith (1956) published his article in the *Journal of Marketing*, market segmentation has become a dominant concept both in marketing theory and in real-world applications. It not only provides one of the major ways of implementing the marketing concept but also directs a firm's marketing strategy and resource allocation among different markets and products.

Market segmentation is the process of dividing a market into distinct groups of buyers with similar requirements. It has become increasingly important in the development of marketing strategies for at least three reasons.

Brand extension
Using a successful brand name to launch a new or modified product in a new category.

Micro-segmentation
Segmentation according to choice criteria, decision-making unit structure, decision-making process, buying class, purchasing structure and organisational innovativeness.

STP-approach
Principle of segmentation, targeting and positioning in order to select a distinct group of consumers who require a special marketing mix.

1   Population growth has slowed, and more product markets are maturing. This, in turn, sparks more intense competition as firms seek growth via gains in market share as well as in an increase of **brand extensions**.

2   There is an important trend toward **micro-segmentation** (one-to-one marketing). This trend has been accelerated in some industries by new technology such as computer-aided design, which has enabled firms to mass customise many products such as designer jeans and cars. For example, many car companies are using a flexible production system that can produce different models on the same production line. This enables the company to make cars to order. More specialised media have also sprung up to appeal to narrow interest groups, e.g. special interest magazines, radio programmes, cable TV, Internet (Schmid *et al.*, 2008).

3   Expanding disposable incomes, higher educational levels, and more awareness of the world have produced customers with more varied and sophisticated needs, tastes and lifestyles than ever before. This has led to an increase in goods and services that compete with one another for the opportunity of satisfying some groups of consumers.

Generally, marketers cannot use averages. Instead, they use the **STP-approach** to define unique customer groups, select those they wish to serve, and then integrate the marketing mix to establish a unified image of the product relative to the competition (Jonk *et al.*, 2008).

Pitfalls with segmentation

Despite all the advantages with market segmentation there are also problems involved (Gibson, 2001).

Segmentation is descriptive not predictive

Segmentation and the research to implement it are designed to describe markets as they exist today. In contrast decisions are based on the expectation of a certain favourable future outcome, and the only information useful to the decision maker is information about the likelihood of that expected outcome. In short, a description of the market as it currently exists, before a decision is made, is irrelevant to making a decision about future events.

Segmentation assumes homogeneity

Segmentation asserts that customers are so different they cannot be averaged and therefore must be classified into segments. However, within defined segments, it assumes customers are not different and can be averaged.

In fact, the fundamental assumption of customer heterogeneity is true, radically true. Customers are different not only at the market level, but at the segment level. This heterogeneity is apparent to anyone looking at the individual respondents in any study. The fact that we seldom look prevents us from seeing and accepting this reality.

Segmentation assumes competition-free segments

Competitors are considered when choosing the target segment, and segments with strong competitors are disqualified. However, once the target segment is selected, competitors are ignored.

The consequences of ignoring competitors can be dangerous. For example, Coca-Cola found that cola drinkers preferred sweeter cola. Repeated paired product comparison tests showed the new sweeter Coca-Cola was preferred over regular Coke. Yet, the new sweeter Coca-Cola failed because the market already had a sweeter cola – Pepsi Cola.

Segmentation may define the wrong segment

The target segments finally selected in traditional segmentation research may exclude significant numbers of real prospects and include significant numbers of non-prospects.

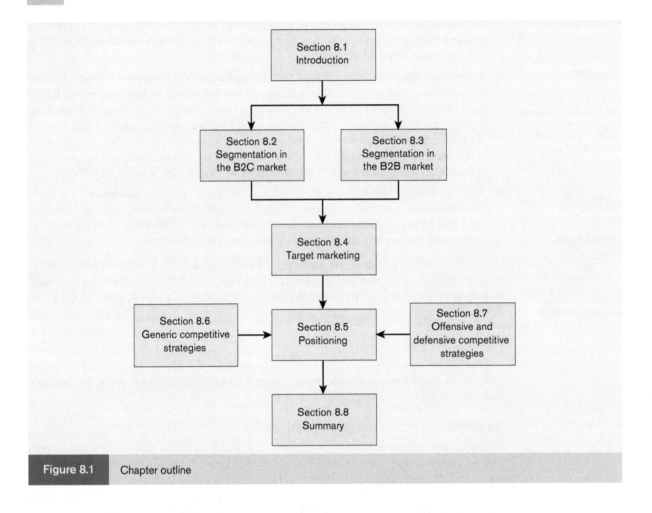

Figure 8.1   Chapter outline

It is a feature of segmentation that when any one segment is selected as a target, prospects in the other segments are excluded (Raynor and Weinberg, 2004).

Because of the segmentation, targeting and positioning are critical. You simply cannot be a leading-edge marketer without these three steps. The activities required to accomplish each stage are described in the following sections. The structure of Chapter 8 is shown in Figure 8.1.

A market segment is a homogeneous group of customers with similar needs, wants, values and buying behaviour. Each segment is an arena for competition.

Market segmentation is the process by which a market is divided into distinct customer subsets of people with similar needs and characteristics that lead them to respond in similar ways to a particular product offering and strategic marketing programme.

Each segment will vary in size and opportunity. Since it may be difficult to appeal successfully to each segment, companies select certain ones for emphasis and will try to satisfy them more than competitors – this is called target marketing.

Positioning means creating an image, reputation or perception in the minds of consumers about the organisation or its products relative to the competition. The company appeals to customers in the target segments by adjusting products, prices, promotional campaigns, service and distribution channels in a way consistent with its positioning strategy.

These three decision processes – market segmentation, market targeting and positioning – are closely linked and have strong interdependence (see Figure 8.2). All must be well considered and implemented if the firm is to be successful in managing a given product–market relationship.

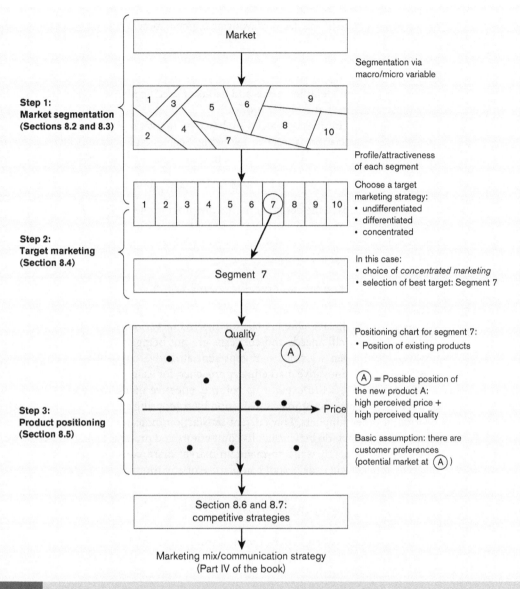

Figure 8.2   The three-step STP

It is important to keep the distinction between product differences and market segments in mind. Market segments should not be defined by product names or characteristics. Markets are made up of customers (people and organisations).

Factors favouring market segmentation

A firm has the option of adopting a market aggregation strategy or a segmentation strategy. Most companies adopt the latter. A market aggregation strategy is appropriate where the total market has few differences in customer needs or desires, especially when the product can be standardised. It is also appropriate where it is operationally difficult to develop distinct products or marketing programmes to reach different customer segments; that is, not all segmentation schemes can be used.

The benefits of segmentation more than offset the difficulties involved in identifying individual market segments. These factors favouring segmentation fall into three main categories.

Better strategic allocation of marketing resources

The strategic benefits of segmentation are sometimes overlooked. Targeted plans and programmes, based on identified needs and habits of specific markets, result in better allocation of company resources and higher profits.

Most successful business strategies are based on market segmentation and a concentration of resources in the more attractive segments. Segmentation should focus on subdividing markets into areas in which investments can gain a long-term competitive advantage.

Creation of more effective marketing programmes

Segmentation helps in the design of marketing programmes that are most effective for reaching homogeneous groups of customers. The seller can create separate marketing programmes aimed at more completely satisfying the needs of different buyers. This creates a competitive advantage (Ashton *et al.*, 2003).

Better opportunities for new product or market development

The seller is in a better position to spot and compare new product or market opportunities as well as potential threats. Often, a careful analysis of various segments reveals one or more groups whose specific needs and concerns are not being satisfied by existing competitive offerings. Such open segments may represent attractive opportunities for development of new products or innovative marketing approaches; for example, the laptop computer.

When a firm seeks to expand its volume, effective market segmentation analysis will uncover the degree of customer satisfaction by comparing each segment's needs against the offering of other suppliers. Low current satisfaction indicates a marketing opportunity, assuming the firm can do better than its competitors and produce an acceptable profit.

When a firm merely wants to maintain market share, constant surveillance of individual market segments will usually spot competitive or environmental threats.

Factors discouraging market segmentation

Special organisational and environmental problems may discourage market segmentation. Not every perceived opportunity becomes a profitable venture. Some of the specific instances in which segmentation in business markets is not useful are as follows:

1   Heavy users or buyers make up such a large proportion of the sales volume that they appear to be the only relevant target. Public utilities consume such large quantities of coal for generating electricity that they dwarf other users of coal.

2   The market is so small that marketing to a portion of it is not profitable. Therefore, a brand or product would have to appeal to all segments and level of users.

Requirements for effective market segmentation

An effective and useful segmentation scheme should define market segments according to five criteria.

Adequate size

Marketers evaluate the degree to which the segments are large or profitable enough to be worth considering for separate marketing cultivation. It involves a trade-off between customer homogeneity and scale effects.

Measurability

Marketers evaluate the degree to which information on particular buyer characteristics exists or can be obtained. There is often a need for a combination of specific (e.g. age) and abstract segmentation variables.

Accessibility

Marketers evaluate the degree to which the firm can effectively focus its marketing efforts on chosen segments. Segmentation variables must identify members in ways that facilitate their contact.

Responsiveness

Marketers assess the degree to which segments respond differently to different marketing mix elements, such as pricing or product features. Segmentation variables must maximise behavioural differences between segments.

Compatibility

Marketers evaluate the degree to which the firm's marketing and business strengths match the present and expected competitive and technological state of the market.

Thus, the art of market segmentation involves identifying groups of consumers that are sufficiently large, and sufficiently unique, to justify a separate marketing strategy. The competitive environment of the market segment is also a factor that must be analysed.

Business firms segment their markets primarily to allocate their resources more effectively and to maximise return on investment. Unfortunately, a segmentation strategy involves added costs in obtaining and analysing data, and in developing and implementing separate marketing and manufacturing plans to serve each segment effectively. The strategy must therefore result in additional sales volume and profits to justify its costs. Before implementing a segmentation strategy, the marketer should develop an estimate of the costs versus the benefits.

Two common segmenting methods

Segmentation can be quite complicated because most markets are complex. There are many different types of customers, and, as we have seen, literally thousands of variables can be used to segment them. Marketers typically use one of two approaches in selecting variables and grouping customers. The **top-down method** starts with all consumers and seeks meaningful variables for subdividing the entire market. The **bottom-up method** starts with a single potential customer and adds others with similar characteristics. Anyone without those characteristics is placed in a new segment, and the process continues. In other words, rather than the whole market, the focus is on one segment at a time. The following is based on the top-down method.

Top-down method
A forecasting/planning approach based on objectives and works down to product/market estimates.

Bottom-up method
A sales forecasting method that starts with small-scale estimates (e.g. product estimates) and works up to larger-scale ones.

Identifying segmentation variables

The total market is heterogeneous, meaning it has many types of buyer. Market segmentation divides the total market into homogeneous subgroups, or clusters with similar characteristics. We then can inspect each subgroup in greater detail. Without a well-focused picture of the market, it is virtually impossible to create a powerful marketing strategy.

How is segmentation done? First, the marketer must select a way of categorising potential customers into subgroups. A segmentation variable is any descriptive characteristic that helps separate all potential purchasers into groups. Examples include gender, age and income. Variables are then subdivided into categories. For example, within the gender variable, the two categories are male and female. Categories may be very broadly or very narrowly defined.

There are many ways of dividing a market into segments. These ways of dividing a market (segmentation variables) can vary from the B2C market to the B2B market. The next two sections deal with segmentation in:

● the B2C market
● the B2B market.

Once the segmentation scheme is developed, you need to describe, or profile, each group in more detail. The market segment profile compiles information about a market segment and the amount of opportunity it represents. The profile may include: the number of current and potential buyers; the potential number of products these buyers may purchase; the amount of revenue the segment may provide; and the expected growth rate. In addition to size and growth, other criteria used to select targets include competitive factors, cost and efficiency factors, the segment's leadership qualities, and the segment's compatibility with the company's vision, objectives, and resources.

8.2 SEGMENTATION IN THE B2C MARKET

Secondary data
Data which already exist but were collected in the first instance for another purpose.

Psychographics
The characteristics of individuals that describe them in terms of their psychological and behavioural make-up.

Primary data
Data collected for the first time for the specific purpose of a particular market research study.

Figure 8.3 lists the categories and variables commonly used for segmentation in the B2C market. The left side of Figure 8.3 shows the trade-off problem of using segmentation variables from the different categories of segmentation variables. The use of the sociodemographic variables results in a high degree of measurability (easy and cheap to use, often based on **secondary data** or desk research), but they would perhaps only have low relevance for marketing planning. As we move down the list in Figure 8.3 to **psychographic** and 'benefit sought' variables, the implications for the formulation of marketing strategies and plans become more relevant and meaningful.

But all the various variables are important and would be likely to be used to some extent in the segmentation of a given market. Thus, marketers might try to define segments using a combination of benefit, behavioural and physical factors, even though this requires the combination of **primary data** (field research) – see also the Appendix.

The sociodemographic variables

Variables like gender, age, family life cycle, household type and income are used in demographic segmentation. This type of information is readily available. Demographics are very useful in categorising different tastes and preferences. An added benefit is that it is relatively easy to measure and project the composition and size of demographic segments for the next 5, 10 or 15 years (high degree of measurability in Figure 8.3). Consequently, this kind of segmentation is an excellent tool for long-range strategic planning as well as short-term marketing.

Different locations vary in their sales potential, growth rates, customer needs, cultures, climates, service needs and competitive structures, as well as purchase rates for a variety of goods. Consequently, one of the most common ways to segment a market is by geography.

City

Segmentation by city is often used by global companies. Coca-Cola knows that soft drink consumption relates to population size. With the exception of New York City and Los Angeles, all metropolitan areas of more than 10 million are located outside the USA. So it is no mystery why Coca-Cola markets globally. A city's population size alone does not always provide enough segmentation information, so marketers think about other factors. Some metropolitan areas are known for their industry expertise: in Hollywood it is films; in Silicon Valley, computer software.

	Segmentation variables	Examples
High ↑	**Sociodemograhic variables**	
	Age	Under 2, 2–5, 6–11, 12–17, 18–24, 25–34, 35–49, 50–64, 65 and over
	Gender	Male, female
	Geography	Regions, countries, cities, metropolitan areas, counties and blocks
	Lifecycle family	Young, single; newly married, no children; couples with youngest child under 6; youngest child 6 or over; older couples with dependent children; older couples without dependent children; older retired couples; single
	Income	Under £15,000, £15,000–24,999, £25,000–74,999 etc.
	Occupation	Professional, manager, clerical, sales, supervisor, blue collar, homemaker, student, unemployed
	Education	Some high school, graduated high school, some college, graduated college
	Events	Birthdays, graduations, anniversaries, national holidays, sporting events
	Race and ethnic origin	Anglo-Saxon, African American, Italian, Jewish, Scandinavian, Hispanic, Asian
	Religion	Protestant, Catholic, Jewish, Muslim
	Social class	Lower-lower, upper-lower, lower-middle, middle, upper-middle, lower-upper, upper-upper
Degree of measurability	**Behaviouristic**	
	Readiness	Unaware, aware, interested, knowledgeable, desirous, intend to buy, trial
	Media and shopping habits	Magazine subscriber, cable user, mall, convenience stores, Internet-shopper
	Ability and experience	None, novice, expert, professional, non-user, first-time user, regular user, former user
	Loyalty	Switcher, moderate, high loyalty
	Usage frequency	Heavy (daily), weekly (medium), light (monthly)
	Innovativeness	Innovators, early adopters, early majority, late majority, laggards
	Psychographic	
	Lifestyle	Actualiser, fulfiller, achiever, experiencer, believer, striver, maker, struggler
	Personality	Compliant, aggressive, detached, sensory, intuitive, thinking, feeling
↓ **Low**	**Benefits sought**	
	Delivery	Convenience, speed, flexibility
	Product features	Safety, reliability, taste, packaging
	Price/service	Low, medium, high

Figure 8.3   Segmentation criteria for the B2C market

Events

These include a varied set of activities ranging from national holidays, sports and back-to-school week, to personal events such as birthdays, anniversaries and weddings. Each requires a specific marketing programme.

Race and ethnic origin

More and more companies are targeting three segments via specialised marketing programmes. Motorola has run separate advertising campaigns for its papers and mobile phones to African Americans, Asian Americans, and Hispanics. Spiegel and *Ebony* magazine have combined to produce a direct-mail catalogue designed to provide clothing that meets the style, colour and fit of African Americans. Efforts, so far, have been successful.

However, it is important to remember that ethnic segments are not homogeneous. There are demographic differences within ethnic groups. For many people, race has nothing to do with their buying behaviour. Consequently, other forms of segmentation may work much better.

Social class

Every social class has its status groupings based largely on similarities in income, education and occupation. Because researchers have long documented the values of the various classes, it is possible to infer certain behaviour concerning a given product. For example, the middle classes tend to place more value on education, family activities, cleanliness and being up to date than do lower-class families. In the international field, one has to be careful in using social class as a segmentation variable since the differences among classes can become blurred, as they do in the Scandinavian countries. In the USA, many of the criteria used to define class status seem to some to be no longer applicable as the nation becomes increasingly fragmented into dozens of distinct subcultures, each with its own unique tastes and ambitions.

Behaviouristic variables

These variables reflect the behaviour of customers towards a specific product. Behaviouristic segmentation categorises consumers based on people's awareness, product and media uses, and actions. Past behaviour is one of the best predictors of future behaviour, so these variables require an understanding of what consumers have previously done. The variables include purchase volume, purchase readiness, ability and experience, loyalty, media habits and shopping behaviours.

Segmentation by readiness

For many products, potential users go through a series of stages that describe their readiness to purchase. These stretch all the way from being unaware of a product, through trial, leading up to loyalty. Readiness is a useful segmentation variable, particularly for new products. This scheme is often used in adjusting the communications mix.

Segmentation by media and shopping habits

A broad range of media and shopping habits can be used to categorise shoppers. For example, some people subscribe to cable, others do not; some prefer shopping at department stores or on the Internet and so forth. These variables focus on accessibility of target customers. Those who shop only in malls are accessed differently from those who prefer Internet shopping or catalogue shopping at home.

Segmentation by ability and experience

The performance of products is determined by the ability and experience of its user. Consequently, ability is an excellent segmentation variable for almost any skill-based product. For example, the marketing of software games for PCs, skis, tennis rackets and golf equipment is targeted to ability segments. This is due in large part to the performance requirements of these products. As performance requirements increase, new technologies produce products with higher performance capabilities but which generally require more skill.

Segmentation by loyalty

As we have discussed, a key goal of firms is to create brand loyalty. Some consumers are naturally loyal to particular product categories. There are many ways to look at loyalty, but the most popular seems to be the most straightforward. It looks at switchers, moderately loyal and highly loyal categories. Switchers may select a different brand with nearly every purchase. They may actually seek variety or they simply do not care which brand they buy. Moderately loyal customers have a preference for a brand but will switch if it is convenient to do so. Loyal buyers have strong preferences. Not all buyers are loyal to a single brand within a product class. Some people have two or three that are equally acceptable.

Usage frequency

This is important because in many markets a small proportion of potential customers makes a high percentage of all purchases (the '80–20' rule, 20 per cent of buyers purchase 80 per cent of the volume of any product). It is amazing how true this is for many products. Heavy users can be extremely important to companies. Consequently, most marketers divide the market into heavy, moderate and light users, and then they look for characteristics that may explain why some people consume vastly greater amounts. Therefore, the marketing costs are lower per unit of sales.

Still, marketing strategists need to realise that competition for heavy users can be extreme. If medium or light users are being ignored, they may provide a marketing opportunity. For example, giants like Coca-Cola and Pepsi are always targeting students. They spend a great deal of money to be represented on campus in order to 'capture' students.

Innovativeness

Adoption process
The mental and behavioural stages through which a consumer passes before making a purchase or placing an order. The stages are awareness, interest, evaluation, trial and adoption.

This is concerned with how individuals and organisations vary in their capacity and desire to innovate. This is particularly true for the **adoption process** of new products. There are substantial differences between early and late adopters. Thus, each of the various adopter groups can be considered as a segment. All too frequently, current customers are not considered an important segment despite their value over time and their being easy to identify.

Psychographic variables

Segmentation by lifestyle, or personality, groups consumers on the basis of their activities, interests and opinions. From such information it is possible to infer what types of product and service appeal to a particular group, as well as how best to communicate with individuals in the group. Lifestyle has been used to describe, for example, the **benefit segments** for sportswear.

Benefit segments
Dividing the market into groups according to the different benefits that consumers seek from the product.

Psychographic and lifestyle segmentation links geographic and demographic descriptors with a consumer's behavioural and psychological decisions. Psychographic variables used alone are often not very useful to marketers; however, they can be quite useful when joined with demographic, geographic and other data. Lifestyle is a person's distinctive mode of living. It describes how time and money are spent and what aspects of life are important. The choice of products, patterns of usage, and the amount of enjoyment a person gains from being a consumer are all part of a lifestyle. Consider the difference between people who are physically fit from exercise and proper nutrition and those who are out of shape from high-fat diets and sedentary living. Since there are so many lifestyles, the trick is to identify them in the context of your company's marketing strategy.

Benefits sought variables

Customer needs are expressed in benefits sought from a particular product or service. Individual customers do not have identical needs and thus attach different degrees of importance to the benefits offered by different products. In the end, the product that provides the best bundle of benefits – given the customer's particular needs – is most likely to be purchased.

Since purchasing is a problem-solving process, consumers evaluate product or brand alternatives on the basis of desired characteristics and how valuable each characteristic is to the consumer – choice criteria. Marketers therefore can define segments according to these different choice criteria in terms of the presence or absence of certain characteristics and the importance attached to each. Firms typically single out a limited number of benefit segments to target. Thus, for example, different car manufacturers (such as Volvo) have emphasised different benefits over the years, such as reliability, safety and high mileage versus styling, speed and status.

Benefits sought must be linked to usage situations. There is ample evidence that usage often strongly affects product choice and substitutability. Thus, the appropriateness of product attributes varies across different usage environments. Any attempt to define viable segments must recognise this fact; for example, consumer needs vary in different usage situations for many products. For example, toothpaste consumers can be segmented into sensory, sociable, worrier and independent segments. Sociable consumers seek bright teeth; worriers seek healthy teeth. Aqua packaging could indicate fluoride for the worrier segment, and white (for a white smile) for the sociable segment (Kumar and Naspal, 2001).

Mittal and Katrichis (2000) found that the attributes important to newly acquired customers were not the same as the ones that were important to loyal customers.

A survey among credit card holders showed that the format of the statement and the performance of the customer service representative are more important for new rather than loyal customers. Conversely, the promotional benefits associated with the card and adequacy of credit limit were more important to loyal customers than to new ones.

Based on these insights, the credit card company redesigned its communication strategy for customer attraction. It started emphasising its attractive interest rate, the quality of its customer service department, and its statements' easy-to-read and user-friendly format. With regard to loyal customers, the firm undertook an internal campaign to reassess the credit limit of all customers, then made appropriate revisions. The company also launched a series of research studies to identify special benefits that customers desired, and then offered these benefits to customers. Finally, the company revised its customer satisfaction philosophy to a segmented focus on the different needs of the newly acquired and loyal customer (Mittal and Katrichis, 2000).

EXHIBIT 8.1
Segmentation in work ('salty snacks in the workplace')

Some time ago the consulting firm Monitor Group did a segmentation job for a client in the food and beverage sector. The scope of the segmentation was defined around the marketing objective – *selling more of the client's snacks in the setting of the workplace*. A team was established with members from both the client and Monitor Group.

Once the scope was established, the first step was to identify a number of proxy segmentation variables that were both actionable and meaningful. The team brainstormed a long list of segmentation variables, which were scored and then tested. One of the more interesting results here is how powerful relatively simple demographic variables turned out to be. After the brainstorming and quantitative testing it turned out that age, gender

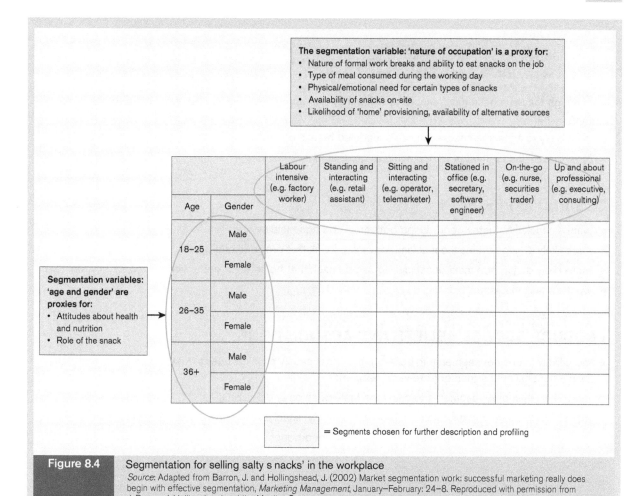

Figure 8.4 Segmentation for selling salty s nacks' in the workplace
Source: Adapted from Barron, J. and Hollingshead, J. (2002) Market segmentation work: successful marketing really does begin with effective segmentation, *Marketing Management*, January–February: 24–8. Reproduced with permission from J. Barron, J. Hollingshead and the Monitor Group.

and 'nature of occupation' were the most powerful segmentation variables. Figure 8.4 illustrates the frame for segmentation of 'salty snacks in the workplace'.

After setting up the segmentation frame the next step was to create profiles of each segment. The data for this came from multiple sources, ranging from existing quantitative and qualitative customer research to the experiences and latent knowledge of the team and the broader organisation.

After evaluating each segment (cell) the following segment turned out to be the most relevant target group: 'labour intensive' male consumers (18–35 years old) in manufacturing jobs. The team then created an in-depth profile (customer portrait) of this target group.

PURCHASE AND USAGE ENVIRONMENT

- predominantly men working in suburban or rural settings;
- find work physically demanding and repetitive – they are usually standing or moving around and constantly on their feet;
- work environment likely to be unpleasant – least likely to work in an environment with heating or air conditioning;
- break room without kitchen is primary facility where they can relax, socialise and consume snacks;
- the most commonly available snacks are chips, pretzels and sweets;

EXHIBIT 8.1
Segmentation in work ('salty snacks in the workplace') cont.

- although they purchase most snacks at work, they are more likely than any other segment to bring snacks from home;
- least likely to consume snacks outside scheduled breaks or mealtimes;
- have to walk the farthest of all segments to get their snack source.

DESIRED EXPERIENCE

- want a snack that tastes good during both meal and non-meal occasions;
- more likely during non-meal occasions to want a snack that provides energy;
- more likely during non-meal occasions to use a snack that helps them cope with their work environment;
- want a snack that is fun.

PRODUCT/SERVICE BELIEFS AND ASSOCIATIONS

- more likely than other segments to believe that snacks satisfy physical needs (taste and refreshment) rather than emotional needs (personal, reward, escape);
- more likely than other segments to enjoy the taste of chips and pretzels;
- more likely than other segments to believe that 'healthy' snacks will improve their work performance;
- only segment to prefer competitor product over client product.

RESULTING PURCHASE AND USAGE BEHAVIOR

- most likely to use vending machines as their source of snacks;
- chips and pretzels are their top choice of snack for both meal and non-meal occasions;
- client brands consumed more often during non-meal occasions, but at the same rate as competitor brands during meal occasions;
- medium bag is the package of choice;
- most likely segment to use a single-serving bag during meal times;
- more likely to consume a snack in social settings than other segments.

This in-depth target group profiling then formed the basis for the creation of targeted marketing plans.

Source: Adapted from Barron and Hollingshead (2002).

Multidimensional segmentation

In segmenting markets, most researchers use a single set of variables, such as demographics, psychographics, product category-related attitudes, product usage-related behaviours, derived importance from joint exercises or latent structures.

The acid test for successful market segmentation is to demonstrate that the derived segments respond differently to variations in the marketing mix. Unfortunately, many segmentation schemes fail this key test.

However, there is no reason to limit the basis for segmentation to only one type of variable when many criteria actually determine buyers' response to offerings in the category. These criteria are multidimensional, encompassing attitudes, needs, values, benefits, means, occasions and prior experience, depending on the product or service category and the buyer.

A segmentation scheme based on only one set of variables may have limited utility to the firm because various users of segmentation schemes have different needs. For example, product development managers may want the market segmented on perceived values and benefits sought; marketing communications managers may want it divided into groups of buyers with similar needs, desires or psychographic profiles; sales managers may prefer segmentation based on sales potential or profitability.

Market segmentation based on multiple dimensions, using separate segmentation schemes for each one, is often more useful and more flexible for planning marketing strategy and executing marketing tactics. Thus, researchers may consider different segmentation variables for buyers using different bases concerning product-user identity (e.g. performance needs, means and desires).

8.3 SEGMENTATION IN THE B2B MARKET

The concept of B2B segmentation has gained increasing attention among academic researchers (Goller *et al.*, 2002; Crittenden *et al.*, 2002; Powers and Sterling, 2008). Since B2B customers, like B2C consumers, differ in their needs, resources and buying attitudes, a practical approach to understanding these differences is to identify variables by which potential buyers can be segmented. Market segmentation attempts to identify groups of firms that are similar in their purchasing needs, product expectations and responses to marketing programmes. These firms do not have to be similar in company structure, size or end markets, although similarity in such factors can provide a basis for more finely tuned segmentation. We will discuss this point further later.

Business marketing managers attempt to find the best product–market match, that is, the most likely customers for each of their products.

Given the considerable difference between business customers, marketers find it difficult to determine which segmentation variables are the most or least likely to provide a desirable fit. Compounding the problem, Bonoma and Shapiro (1983) state that most business marketers use segmentation as a way to explain what has happened rather than as a means to plan and predict what will happen.

There is no magic formula for segmenting the business market. The marketer should try different variables, either alone (which may be sufficient in some cases) or in combination. For segmentation variables to be meaningful, however, they must involve characteristics that are easily identified, understood and discernible. B2C markets are typically segmented on the basis of demographic and psychographic variables. The B2B marketer typically segments organisations on the basis of size and end use, and organisational buyers on the basis of decision style and other criteria. Thus, the business or organisational market can be segmented on several bases, broadly classified into two major categories: macro-segmentation and micro-segmentation.

Macro-segmentation centres on the characteristics of the buying organisation and situation, thus dividing the market by such organisational characteristics as size and geographic location.

In contrast, micro-segmentation requires a higher degree of market knowledge, focusing on the characteristics of decision-making units within each macro-segment – including buying decision criteria, perceived importance of the purchase, and attitudes towards vendors. Wind and Cardozo (1974) recommend a two-stage approach to business market segmentation: identify meaningful macro-segments, and then divide the macro-segments into micro-segments.

Variables forming the macro-segments and micro-segments would include the following:

Macro-variables

- *Industry*: e.g. agriculture, mining, construction, manufacturing, reselling, finance, services.
- *Organisational characteristics*: e.g. size, plant characteristics, location, economic factors, customers' industry, competitive forces, purchasing factors.
- *End use markets*: e.g. manufacturers of end products, commercial contractors, wholesalers and retailers, banks and other financial institutions.
- *Product application*: e.g. components in specific end products, consumer home or recreational usage, resale, production line or office productivity.

Micro-variables

- *Organisational variables*: e.g. purchasing stage, customer experience stage, customer interaction needs, product innovativeness, organisational capabilities.
- *Purchase situation variables*: e.g. inventory requirements, purchase importance, purchasing policies, purchasing criteria, structure of the buying centre.
- *Individual variables*: e.g. personal characteristics, power structure.

One of the most famous and cited segmentation models for the B2B market will now be presented and discussed.

Bonoma and Shapiros (1983) macro/micro-segmentation process

Figure 8.5 shows the five nests advocated by Bonoma and Shapiro in their macro/micro approach to business market segmentation. Working from the outside to the inside, the analyst would start with the first nest, demographics.

Demographics

The variables in the demographic nest are the industry, company size and company location, all relating to the customer's needs and usage patterns. Industry provides a broad understanding of product and service needs. Company size affects the size of a potential order, which forces the seller's attention on to its own ability to produce and manage the delivery of the product. Customer location impacts on the seller's salesforce organisation, its territorial placement, and associated physical distribution factors.

Operating variables

The second nest, operating variables, contains three relatively stable components: company technology, user/non-user status and customer capabilities. Company technology, both product and manufacturing process, can determine buying needs. The technology used indicates the company's needs for tooling, test instruments, components and appropriate support systems. Product and brand-use status would help to isolate common experiences with a brand or product, thus enabling the seller to categorise similar buyers. Customer capabilities include organisational strengths and weaknesses that could help to classify a company's attractiveness and its 'fit' with the seller's abilities to provide satisfaction.

Purchasing approaches

The third nest, purchasing approach, investigates five components: the organisation of the purchasing function (decision-making unit (DMU)), power structures, buyer–seller relations, general purchasing policies and purchasing criteria. The organisation of the purchasing function helps to determine the size, location and levels of authority that exist in a customer's purchasing unit, which affects the size, location and cost of the seller's salesforce.

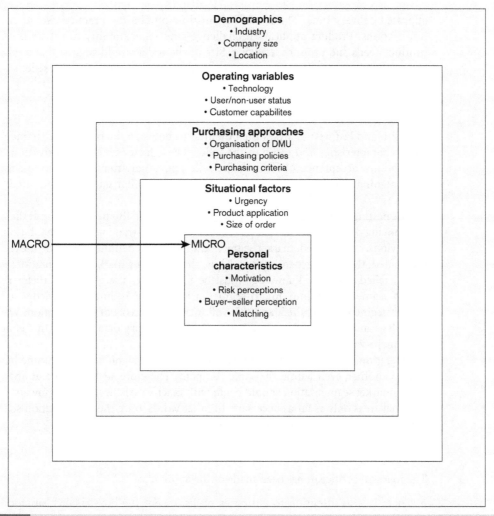

Figure 8.5	The 'nested' approach to segmentation

Source: Bonoma, T. V. and Shapiro, B. P. (1983) *Segmenting the Industrial Market*, D.C. Heath and Co., Lexington. Reproduced with permission from Rowman and Littlefield Publishing Group.

Power structures that exist within specific customers have an impact on the type of suppliers they would choose. As discussed earlier, the seller could pursue a firm with a powerful engineering unit that dominated purchasing, or the potential customer's power base could lie in the manufacturing department and/or the general manager. Either situation would help to determine required salesforce talents, product/service features to emphasise, and the broad outline for a successful selling strategy. These interrelations were discussed at length in Chapter 4. General purchasing policies, such as leasing, bidding and doing business with only well-established vendors, would dictate policy to those suppliers willing to do business within these constraints. Purchasing criteria are those product and organisational benefits deemed necessary for vendors to satisfy before a buyer–seller relationship can be established.

Situational factors

The fourth nest, situational factors, has three components: urgency of order fulfilment, product application and size of order. Urgency of order fulfilment would be a function of the customer's inventory on hand, and the availability of suppliers to meet their needs in the allocated delivery time. The use of just-in-time purchasing practices would carry further implications. Product application challenges the seller's ability to satisfy both technical product needs and product servicing. Size of the order would suggest that a seller concentrate on those customers whose normal orders would mesh with the seller's production economies of scale.

Personal characteristics

The fifth and last nest analyses the potential fit between the buying centre member's personal characteristics and those of the seller. These factors include motivation, individual perceptions, acceptance of risks by the seller, personal attention to buyer demands, and the matching of the buyer's personality traits with similar sales representatives' personality traits.

The nesting approach encourages the integration of all five nests starting at the macro level and moving down to the micro level for successful industrial market segmentation. However, as previously mentioned, market segmentation involves definite costs. The more a market is segmented, the more expensive it is. Thus, the degree of market segmentation depends on how detailed customer knowledge must be for effective use. As the marketer moves from macro-segmentation into micro-segmentation, more intimate knowledge of potential market segments is required, and this will increase the costs of segmentation. While macro-variables can be obtained easily from available secondary data sources, this is not the case with micro-variables.

Operational and personal attributes can also change significantly from one buying situation to another, even within the same company. Therefore, as Bonoma and Shapiro (1983) argue, market segmentation should begin with macro-variables, working inward to the more personal areas only as far as necessary. In other words, once the segmentation scheme seems 'good enough', further efforts should cease.

Criticism of Bonoma and Shapiro's nested approach

The following criticism has been made of the approach:

- There is little attention to customer needs, except the box labelled 'situational factors' (Mitchell and Wilson, 1998).

- There is little insight into which of these variables may be most useful and in what combination or sequence.

- When moving from outside into the nest, when should the marketer stop looking for relevant variables?

- Systematic methods (like Bonoma and Shapiro) have limited relevance when there are few customers and the market is concentrated. Then a single customer can change everything on the market due to its role or its weight. One single event can ruin instantaneously the most serious analysis. Furthermore, in industrial environments, data are rare, uncertain, changing and unreliable, which does not fit with rigorous methods. Consequently, industrial companies often have difficulty in segmenting their markets.

In such a case Millier (2000) suggests a combination of intuition and rationalization in segmentation.

A relationship approach to B2B segmentation

This section thus presents an alternative framework for the segmentation of industrial markets – one based on the nature of the buyer–seller relationship and which seeks to tap into the interests of both parties.

Segmenting in the marketing relationship case needs a deep understanding of the customers' characteristics, needs and future directions, whereas the same information would be too costly and time consuming to collect and too comprehensive to use when segmenting in the simple exchange.

Freytag and Clarke (2001) propose a two-step selection process. The first step is finding attractive future segments for further evaluation. The second step is the selection of the target segment and involves the company and the segments. The aim of this process is to find a perfect match between segment demands and an optimal use of the company's resources and capabilities.

In this way segments are developed in the interaction between the company and potential market segments. The demands that the relationship's development will require from the involved parties need to be identified and considered. The seller in particular will be required to make adaptations and commitments, but they may also be needed from the buyer. In many situations, the wants and needs of the customer will be developed in interaction between the parties.

A result of this two-step segmentation selection process may be that segments that seem attractive are not selected because they do not suit the resources and capabilities of the seller firm.

When evaluating to decide which segments the company should focus on, it is advantageous to find a synergy between the segments. The closer segments are to each other regarding customer needs and technology, the less they require of the company's resources.

The purpose of segmentation is to establish which value the customer wants and which solution the seller should provide. The degree to which the seller is able to fulfil the buyer's needs will depend on the degree to which the seller is able to adapt resources, activities and actors (Håkansson and Snehota, 1995). The seller will only have limited control over activities, resources and actors, which again will limit the firm's possibility to freely select its customers (Freytag and Clarke, 2008).

The proposed typology embraces the central concepts of customer relationships, customer value and customer loyalty and incorporates them into the important process of market segmentation in industrial markets.

The symmetry in the interest of buyers, customers and sellers (suppliers) is also reflected in a negotiable and bilateral 'fit-seeking' process where suppliers frame tentative segments (based on initial research) subject to exploration with well-placed key managers. This would encourage the development of evolutionary segmentation that focuses not only on consumer needs, but also on supplier needs, because these are mutually synergistic. The process would also help to develop the sort of long-term relationships between supplier and customer that help to ensure that supplier offerings are developed in line with customer expectations and needs.

Reverse segmentation

Reverse segmentation
The buyer (and not the seller, as in traditional marketing) takes the initiative for searching out a supplier that is able to fulfil the buyer's needs.

The notion of **reverse segmentation** is a convenient expression to highlight a process that parallels segmentation, a process whereby customers select suppliers that meet particular criteria (e.g. quality, financial stability, investors in relationships approaches, ethical stances, delivery reputation, collaborative product development strategies). By implication, a supplier able to exhibit appropriate 'reverse segmentation' criteria to a customer (and such criteria may well shift from customer to customer) can become significantly more attractive – not least through their evident customer understanding. Similarly, active seeking of particular reverse segmentation criteria could become a significant segmentation variable, especially for those organisations seeking to focus on long-term supplier–customer relationships (e.g. in the car components industry or in corporate sponsorship markets) (Mitchell and Wilson, 1998).

Thus, the reverse segmentation (supplier segmentation) is widespread in the car industry, where the success of Japanese firms has often been attributed to close supplier relationships, or a partner model of supplier management. Various studies suggest that, compared to arm's-length relationships, Japanese-style partnerships result in superior performance because partnering firms (Dyer *et al.*, 1998):

- share more information and are better at coordinating interdependent tasks;
- invest in dedicated or relation-specific assets which lower costs, improve quality and speed development;
- rely on trust to govern the relationship, which is a highly efficient mechanism that minimises transactions costs.

On the other hand, because suppliers only work primarily with one customer, they do not have opportunities to learn from multiple customers. Consequently, this impedes the supplier's abilities to learn and upgrade its technological capabilities.

Dyer *et al.* (1998) found that the Japanese car makers Nissan and Toyota were the most effective at strategically segmenting suppliers to realise the benefits of both the arm's-length and partner models. Independent Japanese suppliers such as Bridgestone (tyres) and Mitsubishi Belting Co. (belts, hoses) realised economies of scale by selling their relatively standardised products to all car makers. Moreover, these suppliers made fewer investments in assets dedicated to a particular car maker. Car makers provided less direct assistance to these suppliers mainly because the benefits of assistance to the supplier would more easily spill over to competitors. In contrast, more affiliated and smaller suppliers such as Nippondenso and Calsonic made substantial investments in relation-specific assets and coordinated activities closely with car makers through frequent face-to-face interactions. Toyota and Nissan provided significantly more assistance to affiliated suppliers to help them lower production costs, improve quality and minimise inventories. Toyota and Nissan had greater incentives to assist these suppliers since their own success (i.e. ability to differentiate their products) is closely tied to the success of these particular suppliers (a 'win–win' situation).

8.4 TARGET MARKETING

Market targeting is not the same as market segmentation. As discussed earlier, market segmentation is the process of dividing a market into groups of potential customers who are similar in needs, expectations and response to marketing stimuli. The seller selects variables that identify this market and develops a marketing mix that best fits the market's expectations and anticipated response.

Target marketing is the process of selecting one or more of these market segments and developing products and programmes that are tailored for each segment.

Once the segments have been identified, management must evaluate the opportunities each segment offers.

Large multinationals can operate in many market segments, but most new entrants into a given market have to select one or a few segments. Limited financial and managerial capacities prevent broader activity as it might spread their resources too thinly and set them up as a takeover target. The number of segments in which a company competes is determined by its shared goals, the flexibility of its manufacturing base, and the heterogeneity of the market's requirements.

In order to select the right segment as a target market, a manager can compare the future potential of different segments using the same set of criteria and then prioritise them to decide which segments to target and how resources and marketing efforts should be allocated. One useful analytical framework managers can use for this purpose is the market attractiveness/business position matrix. At the corporate level, managers use such models to allocate resources across businesses, or at the business-unit level to assign resources across products/markets. In principle, it is the McKinsey/GE model (Chapter 7).

A number of strategies can help guide a manager's choice of target markets. Three of the more common of these are undifferentiated, differentiated and concentrated marketing strategies. They are illustrated in Figure 8.6.

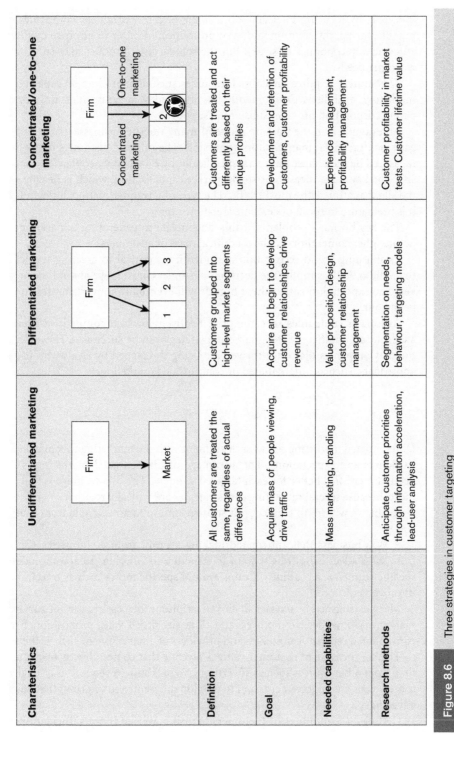

Charateristics	Undifferentiated marketing	Differentiated marketing	Concentrated/one-to-one marketing
Definition	All customers are treated the same, regardless of actual differences	Customers grouped into high-level market segments	Customers are treated and act differently based on their unique profiles
Goal	Acquire mass of people viewing, drive traffic	Acquire and begin to develop customer relationships, drive revenue	Development and retention of customers, customer profitability
Needed capabilities	Mass marketing, branding	Value proposition design, customer relationship management	Experience management, profitability management
Research methods	Anticipate customer priorities through information acceleration, lead-user analysis	Segmentation on needs, behaviour, targeting models	Customer profitability in market tests. Customer lifetime value

Figure 8.6 Three strategies in customer targeting

Undifferentiated (mass) marketing

Undifferentiated marketing
A marketing effort not targeted at a specific market segment, but designed to appeal to a broad range of customers. The approach is appropriate in a market that lacks diversity of interest.

Portal
A website that acts as a gateway to the information on the Internet by providing search engines, directories and other services such as personalised news or free e-mail.

Undifferentiated marketing treats all the customers the same. Companies look for desires that are common to most potential customers and then try to design products that appeal to everyone. By focusing internally on a single or a few products, companies can streamline manufacturing, distribution and even promotion in order to improve quality and gain cost efficiencies (economies of scale). But the standardised product may fail to meet individual customer needs.

This strategy requires substantial resources, including production capacity, and good mass marketing capabilities. Consequently, it is favoured by larger business units or by those whose parent corporation provides substantial support.

An example is in the start-up phase of many website businesses, such as **portals** that engage in attracting as many visitors as possible. The value of customers to the firm primarily is measured by their sheer numbers; specifically, by how many people view the advertising at a site. The key value measure is stock-market capitalisation, which is heavily skewed towards the site that attracts the most traffic. The type of customer matters little; in fact, at this stage it is premature to speak of customer relationships.

The key business problems at this stage relate to generating a market presence quickly before other competitors achieve a critical mass of customers.

Establishing brand recognition and identity is critical to creating traffic. Strong brands (e.g. Yahoo, AOL) simplify the decisions customers must make about how to access the market. The expectation is that these brands will eventually convert impression into purchase behaviour.

As long as companies keep the price relatively low and competitive alternatives are unavailable, an undifferentiated marketing strategy can be successful. However, competition is tough. Companies that once thrived are being threatened by rivals who use more targeted approaches, such as differentiated or concentrated marketing.

Differentiated marketing

Differentiated marketing serves each segment with the marketing mix matched specifically to its desires and expectations. The advantage of differentiated marketing is that wants and needs are satisfied better for each targeted segment. The disadvantage is that it may also cost more, because several marketing mix strategies are typically required.

Again, we will try to connect this strategy option to an example from e-business (Wyner, 2000).

A Web business that anticipated making a profit from e-commerce (rather than solely from mass advertising) might want to structure its offerings to accommodate the needs of specific segments, e.g. affinity groups around specific topics such as travel, sports and home improvement.

Many established businesses fit this description; they clearly cannot survive with a mass-market, customer-selection process and a 'one size fits all' value proposition. Examples include conventional retailers, car makers and providers of entertainment such as theme parks.

The key measure of customer value is revenue that comes directly from customers, rather than from other sources such as advertisers. To maximise revenue, it is critical to identify customer needs and requirements and to develop differentiated offerings that have a competitive advantage.

Getting large numbers of customers to visit a website is not sufficient; they must also be buyers. Customer relationship development becomes important, including cross-selling additional products to maximise revenues across the entire product and service portfolio. Increasing the depth of the relationship with customers has significant economic benefits, in some cases exceeding the value of new customer acquisition.

Concentrated (niche) marketing

This strategy involves serving one or more segments that, while not the largest, consist of substantial numbers of customers seeking somewhat specialised benefits from a supplier.

Such a strategy is designed to avoid direct competition with larger firms that are pursuing the bigger segments. For example, overall coffee consumption is down substantially, but the sales of gourmet coffees have boomed in recent years. Companies pursuing this strategy must make sure they have a great deal of knowledge about their major target segment.

Concentrated marketing has worked extremely well for new companies or companies entering new areas of the world. By gaining a foothold in a core market, a company can build the financial strength, experience and credibility needed for expansion to other similar segments.

Niche marketing is another strategy worth mentioning. A niche is a very small market that most companies ignore because they do not perceive adequate opportunity. The smallest possible niche is the individual. Marketing to one customer is called *one-to-one marketing* (also illustrated in Figure 8.6).

Niche marketing
The process of targeting a relatively small market segment with a specific, specialized marketing mix.

Peppers *et al.* (1999) use a questionnaire to identify a firm's readiness for using one-to-one marketing on a daily basis.

A business can achieve superior profitability if it can give each customer the best offer for him or her, provided there is an efficient and effective fulfilment capability. Issues of customer loyalty and retention have become increasingly important because it is often more profitable to keep an existing customer than to find new ones.

This customer selection process is possible in businesses with detailed individual customer level information, such as financial service companies that capture virtually all customer transactions in digital form. Customers can be grouped into categories based on their past use of products and services. There is no need to use higher-level groups (such as a high or low frequency transaction on credit cards) when customers can be identified with particular product features that suit them (such as specific interest rates, annual fees and reward programmes).

An emerging type of business design goes beyond selecting customers based on refined targeting to individuals and enables individual customers to build their own 'offer' (individualised self-selection). Customers select what they want to meet their own needs.

This Web-based technology is used to develop a digital customer interface enabling each individual to choose from potential products that are exactly what the customer wants. These 'choiceboards' are becoming more common, and as commerce becomes increasingly electronic, they promise to capture significant market shares.

In financial services, for example, a customer can select mutual funds from a vast selection of offerings through fund networks. Choiceboards in the PC business allow the customer to design completely a personal computer to incorporate the desired functionality.

Dell is an example of a company that has essentially become a customer-specific Web store, where customers can design their own computer.

8.5 POSITIONING

Once the segmentation process gives a clear picture of the market and the target marketing strategy has been selected, the positioning approach can be developed.

Success requires a sustainable strategy that is differentiated from competitors. A higher probability of success can be achieved if the marketing mix is arranged so that it is unmatched by competitors.

Positioning is the process of creating in the mind of consumers an image, reputation or perception of the company and/or its products relative to competitors. Positioning (or

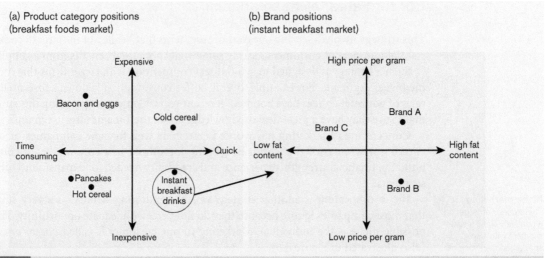

Figure 8.7	Positioning at product and brand level

Source: Adapted from Busch, P. S. and Houston, M. J. (1985), *Marketing Strategic Foundations*, Richard D. Irwin, Burr Ridge, IL, p. 450. Reproduced with permission from the McGraw-Hill Companies.

repositioning), then, is the perceived fit between a particular product and the needs of the target market. The positioning concept must be defined relative to competitive offerings and consumer needs.

Thus, the following critical question needs to be answered: 'How can a business position its offering so that customers in the target market perceive it as providing the desired benefits, thereby giving it an advantage over current and potential competitors?' The choice of market position is a strategic decision with implications not only for how the firm's product or service should be designed but also for detailing the other elements of the strategic marketing programme. Each of the marketing mix elements is capable of making a contribution to the positioning of a product.

A positioning analysis can take place at the company product category and at brand levels. At the product category level, the analysis examines customers' perceptions about types of product they might consider as substitutes to satisfy the same basic need. Suppose, for example, that a company is considering introducing a new instant breakfast drink. The new product would have to compete with other breakfast foods, such as bacon, eggs and breakfast cereals. To understand the new product's position in the market, a marketer could obtain customer perceptions of the new product concept relative to likely substitute products on various critical attributes. Figure 8.7(a) shows a product positioning map constructed from such information. The two attributes defining the product space are price and convenience of preparation. The proposed new drink occupies a distinctive position because customers perceive it as a comparatively low-cost, convenient breakfast food.

Once competitors introduce similar brands into the same product category, a marketer needs to find out how the brand is perceived compared with competitors. Thus, Figure 8.7(b) shows the result of a positioning analysis conducted at the brand level. It summarises customer perceptions concerning three existing brands of instant breakfast drinks. This brand level analysis is very useful for helping marketers understand a brand's competitive strengths and weaknesses and for determining whether the brand should be repositioned to differentiate it from competitive products.

Once the perceptions are plotted, most marketers want to know the consumer's ideal position. The ideal position is the one most preferred by each consumer.

Finally, what is the difference in positioning on the B2C market and B2B market? The principles in the two markets are the same. What matters is that the customer (and prospective customer) sees the merits in your positioning and that you link other strategies to this positioning in order to deliver the 'promise' implied by the positioning decision. If you claim to be a comprehensive supplier, you must be a comprehensive supplier to sustain customer support. And the same goes for other choices.

However, in the B2B market, company image considerations, rather than brand image building factors, are determinants of perceived positioning strategies. The brand-image-led positioning strategies that are prevalent in consumer goods marketing do not transfer well to business marketing (Kalafatis *et al.*, 2000).

EXHIBIT 8.2
Björn Borg's brand positioning and business modelling in the international apparel market

Back in the mid to late 1970s, a tennis player from Sweden captivated the crowds at Wimbledon, winning five straight titles and nearly a sixth in 1981. His name was Björn Borg. Today Björn Borg AB, formerly Worldwide Brand Management AB, is a Sweden-based company active within the fashion industry. In December 2006, the Björn Borg Group acquired the Björn Borg trademark and rights to the tennis legend's name from Björn Borg for US$18 million. Today Björn Borg himself has nothing to do with Björn Borg AB or its business activities. Björn Borg AB is headquartered in Stockholm, Sweden.

The Company's operations comprise five product areas: clothes, footwear, bags, eyewear and fragrances.

A majority of the company's sales are currently in the northern part of Europe, i.e. Sweden, the Netherlands and, to a lesser extent, Norway and Denmark. From 2007, the company has been developing new markets in the UK, Germany and Switzerland. In 2008–09 Björn Borg was launched in a number of new markets: Spain, Canada, the USA, Italy and Greece.

In 2008 the net sales of Björn Borg AB's activities was €48 million (80 per cent of this was clothing, primarily underwear), with total profits of €9 million. The Björn Borg turnover corresponds to €221 million turn-over in consumer prices. Björn Borg AB has 88 employees at its HQ in Stockholm.

Björn Borg today is a strong, well-known brand in its established markets thanks to consistent, long-term branding from a clearly defined platform and focused marketing. The brand has an especially strong position

Source: Sergio Dionisio/Getty

→

EXHIBIT 8.2
Björn Borg's brand positioning and business modelling in
the international apparel market (*continued*)

in men's underwear, where Björn Borg is considered a market leader in terms of quality and design in its established markets.

Based on its established position in underwear (especially for men), Björn Borg is working actively to strengthen its position in clothing as well as shoes and accessories. In its main product group, underwear, Björn Borg competes with well-known international brands such as Calvin Klein, Hugo Boss and Hom, in addition to local players. Competition is generally expected to grow as more major fashion brands such as Diesel and Puma introduce their own underwear collections and new companies enter the market.

Björn Borg's business model utilises a network of product companies and distributors which are either part of the Group or independent companies and have been granted licences to one or more product areas or geographical markets. The network also includes Björn Borg stores operated by the Group or as independent franchisees. By utilising its own network as well as independent companies, Björn Borg can be involved in every part of the value chain and develop the brand internationally with a compact organisation and minimal financial investment and risks. The business model requires little capital investment by the company, since the distributors in the network are responsible for marketing, including investments and inventory.

With the exception of production, which is handled outside the Group, Björn Borg is involved with all value chain activities from product development to distribution and consumer sales. This gives Björn Borg the best chances of ensuring the further development and correct future positioning of the brand.

Sources: Adapted from Björn Borg AB (www.bjornborg.com); O'Mahony, P. (2006) Björn Borg brand headed for stock exchange, *The Local: Swedish News in English*, 7 December (www.thelocal.se/5733/20061207/); Kullin, H. (2006) The brand 'Björn Borg' sold for 18 MUSD, *www.kullin.net* (www.kullin.net/2006/12/brand-bjrn-borg-sold-for-18-musd.html).

8.6 GENERIC COMPETITIVE STRATEGIES

Generic
The term generic means that the strategy can be applied to any organisation, regardless of size, industry sector, or product or service.

Porter (1985) states that there are only three potentially successful **generic** strategies to outperforming other firms in an industry: overall cost leadership, differentiation and focus. Figure 8.8 shows Porter's thoughts in a modified way.

Cost leadership

A cost leadership strategy focuses on gaining advantages by reducing economic costs below the costs of competitors. This alternative has come to prominence in recent years, as companies have invested vast sums to achieve economies of scale. Many segments in the industry (broad industry focus) are served and great importance is placed on minimising costs on all fronts (Morehouse *et al.*, 2008)

Markets have been expanded to entire continents to support massive new plant as in the European car industry. Here, Hyundai has implemented a cost-leadership strategy with its emphasis on low-priced cars for basic transportation.

Economies of scale and economies of scope
Obtained by spreading the costs of distribution over a large quantity of products (scale) or over a wide variety of products (scope).

There are many reasons why an individual firm may have a cost advantage over its competitors. The two most important sources of cost advantages are **economies of scale** and **economies of scope**.

Economies of scale

Economies of scale reflect the efficiencies that come with size. Fixed costs such as administration, facilities, equipment, staff and R&D can be spread over more units. Cost advantages arise where a producer derives economies of scale by having a large sales volume. Fixed costs

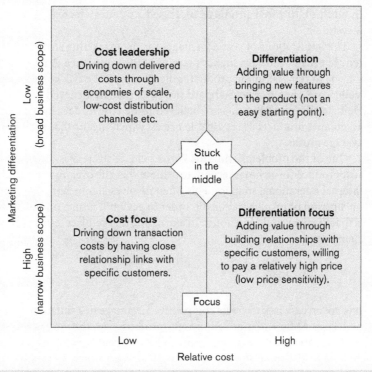

can then be spread over a greater output. In addition there are the added benefits of what is called the 'experience curve'. The experience curve is similar to the learning curve with which we are familiar as people. As we perform a task or job again and again, we develop our skills. In time we become more efficient at doing the task or job. The experience curve extends this concept to show that efficiency increases and value added costs decline as the volume of production increases. Where a firm has the predominant market share, it should be able to reap the benefits of experience and hence enjoy cost advantages. These same benefits do not apply, however, where a firm has deliberately sought to increase its market share by buying it through price reductions, increased marketing effort and product development at the expense of long-term profitability.

Economies of scope (synergy)

Economies of scope (synergy) is where a business enjoys an advantage because it is linked to another business within the same enterprise. Both enterprises may benefit from shared resources, and in so doing reduce costs or investment. They may also be able jointly to offer a combination of complementary products. Synergy often results from some commonality in two operations, such as:

- R&D
- operating costs
- plant usage
- company or brand image and its impact on the market
- distribution
- sales or advertising.

In addition, it often produces increased revenues, decreased operating costs or reduced investment.

The implications of cost advantages for the marketing strategy is that they can be used to reduce prices or to earn higher margins at the same price. A preferable alternative, however, may be to reinvest in the product rather than run the risk of initiating price wars. Thus cost leaders are often market standard products that are believed to be acceptable to customers. Heinz and United Biscuits are believed to be cost leaders in their industries. They market acceptable products at reasonable prices, which means that their low costs result in above-average profits.

One of the problems with this Porter generic strategy is that there can be only one lowest cost producer in any market and, to achieve this, the organisation tends to focus too much on internal operational matters. This often involves significant capital investment, which relies on a period of relative stability in order to get a full return on the investment. The major risk is that the firm could lose touch in a dynamic marketplace, especially one where technology is changing.

Differentiation

It is not an easy task to create competitive advantage in a situation where the firm has relatively high costs. Differentiation removes the product from the most direct elements of competition by differentiating the marketing mix to the different buyer groups in the industry.

Differentiation strategies are usually associated with a premium price, and higher than average costs for the industry as the extra value to customers (e.g. higher performance) often raises costs. The aim is to differentiate in a way that leads to a price premium which is greater than the cost of differentiating. Differentiation gives customers a reason to prefer one product over another.

An important way in which a firm can attempt to differentiate its products is through linking different functions within the firm. For example, in selling computers and IT solutions, IBM has been very successful in linking the sales and service function. When a customer purchases an IBM mainframe computer it is not just buying a big box with electronic components. Instead, it is buying a relationship with IBM – a relationship that includes high levels of service and technical support. At IBM, the relationship with the company does not end with the purchase of a computer; it begins with this purchase.

Differentiation focus

With this strategy a firm aims to differentiate within one or a small number of target market segments. Focusing on the special needs of the segment means that there is an opportunity to differentiate the product offering from competitors and also charge a higher price. This could still result in a profitable business, in spite of the relatively high costs.

An example of differentiation focus can be seen in Harley-Davidson's decision to stay in the heavyweight motorcycle segment, where it had distinctive styling. Other companies following this strategy are Rolex (watches) and Porsche (sports cars).

Cost focus

With this strategy a firm seeks a cost advantage with one or a small number of market segments or single customers. By dedicating itself to a specific segment or a specific customer the cost focuser can seek economies that may be ignored or missed by broadly targeted competitors. By creating a close relationship with a few important customers, the firm can drive down the transaction costs associated within the buyer–seller relationship.

Porter argues that failure to make the choice between cost leadership, differentiation and focus strategy means that a company is stuck in the middle with no competitive advantage, resulting in poor performance (Porter, 1985).

Some researchers have suggested that the most effective strategy for some situations is systematic oscillation between cost leadership and differentiation (Gilbert and Strebel, 1988).

EXHIBIT 8.3
Good-enough markets in China – the case of Duracell batteries

Historically, China's markets have had a fairly simple structure: at the top, a small premium segment served mainly by foreign companies, with solid margins and sometimes rapid growth. At the bottom, a large, low-end segment served by Chinese companies offering lower-quality, undifferentiated products that carry prices 40 per cent to 90 per cent below the premium products in that segment. These companies often lose money – if there's rigorous accounting. Between the two is the good-enough segment – where reliable-enough products at low-enough prices appeal to China's fast-growing mid-level consumers. Indeed, the good-enough segment is growing faster than either the premium or low-end segments.

In the early 1990s, foreign battery products such as Duracell (Gillette) and Energizer accounted for more than half of the Chinese mainland alkaline-battery market. However, by the end of the 1990s Gillette's Duracell division had been losing market share to lower-priced competitors throughout the decade. Nanfu and other domestic battery brands have grabbed market share from the foreign giants in recent years by offering similar-quality products at lower prices. By 2002, Duracell's share of the Chinese domestic battery market was just 6.5 per cent. By contrast, Nanfu accounted for more than 40 per cent of China's alkaline-battery market in terms of sales volume.

Founded in 1988, Nanfu (Fujian Nanping Nanfu Battery Co. Ltd) became a joint venture in 1999 by acquiring money from overseas investors based in the United States, Singapore and the Netherlands, among other countries.

Gillette's management recognised that its Duracell unit had a fundamental cost disadvantage compared with its rivals, and concluded that broadening the brand's own market penetration would be difficult. Facing such odds, Gillette decided to acquire a majority stake (70 per cent) in Nanfu.

Gillette was extremely careful to protect both Duracell's and Nanfu's brands – a crucial part of the strategy as Gillette continues to sell premium batteries under the Duracell brand and has maintained Nanfu as the leading national brand for the mass market. Dual branding, cost synergies, a broadened product portfolio, economies of scale and distribution to more than 3 million retail outlets in China have paid off for Gillette, which has seen significant increases in its operating margins in China.

Today, Gillette is the leading player in the Chinese battery market, and both Duracell and Nanfu have gained market share since 2003.

Sources: Adapted from Gadiesh *et al*. (2007); Bain & Company (www.bain.com); China Internet Information Center (2003) Battery giant Gillette obtains rival Nanfu, *www.china.org.cn*, 22 August (http://mdjnkj.china.com.cn/english/BAT/73007.htm).

Indeed, the strongest situation could be where a firm enjoys the benefits of both a cost advantage and a value advantage. Streamlined, automated production facilities coupled with active and effective product differentiation strategies have enabled many Japanese consumer goods manufacturers to achieve very strong competitive positions which are very difficult to dislodge.

Honda motorcycles have maintained their initial success in the USA by consistent action to sustain a competitive advantage based on distribution and brand image in addition to low cost realised through high-volume production.

8.7 OFFENSIVE AND DEFENSIVE COMPETITIVE STRATEGIES

If a market cannot be expanded through new users, new uses and increased frequency of purchase, a 'build market share' strategy may be a relevant alternative. This implies gaining marketing success at the expense of the competition.

A successful strategy amounts to combining attacking and defensive moves to build a stronger position in the chosen marketplace. In recent years several authors, most notably Kotler and Singh (1981) and Ries and Trout (1986), have drawn an analogy between military warfare and competitive battles in the marketplace. Their basic contention is that lessons for the conduct of business strategy can be learned by a study of warfare and the principles developed by military strategies.

Offensive strategies

As indicated, when a build objective is pursued in a market that cannot, for one reason or another, be expanded, success must, by definition, be at the expense of competitors.

In the battle with competitors, organisations must decide on what dimensions to attack or defend. This decision is based, in part, on the size of the firm relative to its competitors. It will also depend on the strategies that are viable in a particular industry.

Kotler and Singh have identified five competitor confrontation strategies (see Figure 8.9) designed to win sales and market share.

Frontal attack

A frontal attack means taking on a competitor head-on. This is one of the most difficult and dangerous of all marketing strategies. To be successful, the firm must have a substantial

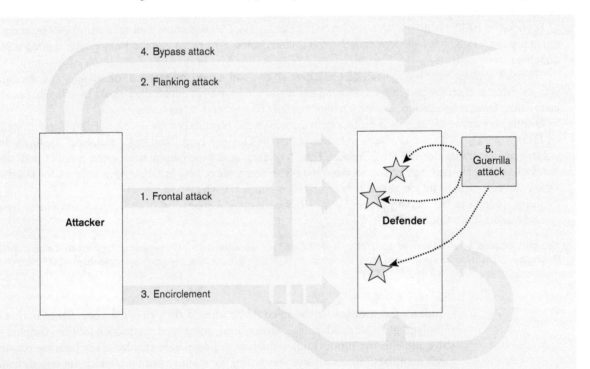

Figure 8.9	Attack strategies

Source: Adapted from Kotler, P. (2000) *Marketing Management: The Millennium Edition*, 10th ed., Prentice Hall, Upper Saddle River, NJ, p. 241. Copyright © 2000. Reproduced with permission of Pearson Education, Inc.

marketing advantage or considerable resources. For instance, the firm might have a similar product, but be able to sell it at a lower price.

The requirement of a similar 3:1 advantage to ensure success in a commercial frontal attack has been suggested (Kotler and Singh, 1981). Some question this 3:1 force, but all agree, however, that to defeat a well-entrenched competitor, who has built a solid market position, requires substantial superiority in at least one key area of the marketing programme.

IBM's attack on the PC market in the early 1980s is a classic example of the frontal attack. The market pioneer (Apple) was attacked partly as a defensive move by IBM as the company saw the likelihood that Apple's desktop machines would become executive workstations and hence threaten IBM's traditional dominance of the mainframe business market. There were several aspects to IBM's attack on the market. It was spearheaded by a technological improvement (16-bit processors gave increased power and speed over the competing 8-bit machines.)

At the same time IBM made the technical specification of its machines widely available to software houses and other peripheral equipment manufacturers so that software became readily available and soon established an industry standard ('IBM-compatible'). The creation of this standard was made possible by the use of that prime marketing asset – the IBM name and reputation. Finally, a massive promotional campaign was launched in the small business market. The results were not only a dominant share of the markets for IBM, but they also managed to encourage the further growth of the market as a whole.

Flanking attack

In contrast to the frontal attack the flanking attack seeks to concentrate the aggressor's strengths against the competitor's weaknesses. In warfare, a flanking attack would seek to shift the battleground away from the enemy's strength to the unguarded or less well-defended flanks. A flanking attack is appropriate for segments of the market where customer needs are not being fully met. This may simply mean fighting in geographical regions, where the competition is weak. More likely, it means bringing out new products for emerging segments of the market. Flanking addresses gaps in existing market coverage of the competition. This strategy has been used very effectively by Japanese corporations.

The entry of Japanese cars into Western car markets is a classic example of a flanking strategy. In cars especially, the Japanese took advantage of the OPEC-induced oil crisis of the early 1970s to cater to customer needs in the small car segment. The Japanese cars were cheap, reliable and offered good fuel consumption to the hard-hit motorist. Having established a toe-hold in the market, the Japanese car manufacturers have subsequently moved into other segments. Timing can be crucial to a successful flanking strategy. The Japanese entry into the US small car market was timed to take advantage of the recession and its power. The strategy requires the identification of competitor weaknesses, inability or unwillingness to serve particular sectors of the market. Another example of a flanking attack is Mercedes-Benz's introduction of the Smart car in 1997. With less space and lower gas mileage than many of its competitors, the primary marketing message of the Smart car is its ability to offer consumers an alternative fashion statement. By 2009, the Smart was available in 25 countries all over the world and has notched up over 800,000 sales.

Encirclement

This involves attacking the defender from all sides to spread its resources thinly by probing on many fronts at once. Again, superior resources are required. For this strategy to succeed, the attacker must possess not only a 3:1 power advantage, as with the in-your-face portion of the attack, but additional resources to achieve victory in the multiple change-the-field strategies. The encirclement strategy, therefore, is a viable alternative only for companies possessing resources vastly superior to those of the individual being attacked.

In business there are two approaches to the encirclement attack. The first is to attempt to isolate the competitor from the supply of raw materials on which it depends and/or the customers it seeks to sell to. The second approach is to seek to offer an all-round better product or service than the competitor. After their original flanking attack on the small car market, the Japanese used an encirclement attack aimed at many segments simultaneously with many different brands.

Bypass attack

Bypass attack
Circumventing the defender's position, usually through technological leap-frogging or diversification.

A **bypass attack** (or 'leapfrogging') is one of non-confrontation and instead focuses on another weaker competitor (Burns and Warren, 2008). When one's primary competitor possesses a significant resource base to defend against the frontal attack and possesses few weak points which can be used as a focus of a change-the-field attack, a leapfrogging strategy may be appropriate. The leapfrogging strategy involves changing the company's targets to other, weaker companies where the chance of success may be higher.

With this strategy the firm may also diversify into unrelated products or it diversifies into new markets for existing products, as Marks & Spencer has done with its move into financial services.

Bypass attacks are most prevalent in high-technology markets, where a challenger puts its efforts into bypassing existing technology and winning the battle for the next generation of technology to be brought to the market. Such a move needs significant funding, but it can put the winner in an almost impregnable position. Such a technological leapfrogging happened when Casio bypassed the Swiss analogue watches with digital technology.

Guerrilla attack

Guerrilla warfare entails small, intermittent attacks on a competitor. One goal might be to gain small amounts of market share while provoking minimal competitive reaction.

Guerrilla tactics may be the only feasible option for a small company facing a larger competitor. Such tactics allow the small company to make its presence felt without the dangers of a full frontal attack. By being unpredictable, guerrilla activity is difficult to defend.

One of the most long lasting guerrilla actions is Virgin Atlantic's campaign against British Airways (BA). Despite being in an alliance that carries more people across the Atlantic than BA, Virgin Atlantic still successfully positions itself as the little victim of BA's alliance with American Airlines.

Guerilla attacks can be a lucrative, though fickle market strategy. Businesses can appeal to this market by depicting their products as decidedly different from popular products. Newly introduced products and those that are relatively unknown are best suited for this appeal. Although it is unlikely that products targeted toward this market will have the potential to become top sellers, it can be a great market for 'niche' products which differ materially from top-selling products. Examples of products that have successfully employed this strategy include Dr Pepper and Apple.

Defensive strategies

Defensive strategies exist to counter each offensive strategy. In defending market share, the firm also has several alternatives: Kotler and Singh (1981) suggest six basic holding strategies.

Position defence

This involves erecting barriers around the company and its markets to shut out competition. The military analogy is the opposite side of the wall from the siege. The defender creates the largest walls and moats possible and sits tight until the aggressor gets weary, or finds other more pressing priorities, and withdraws. The main risk in this strategy is marketing myopia. Redesigning or reformulating your product can keep you one step ahead of the competition.

Flanking defence

This is the defending parallel to flanking attack. The aggressor seeks to concentrate strength against the weaknesses of the defender, often (especially in military warfare) using the element of surprise to gain the upper hand.

A flanking defence requires the company to strengthen the flanks, without providing a weaker and more vulnerable target elsewhere.

Pre-emptive defence

This follows the philosophy that the best form of defence is to attack first. The objective is to strike a physical or demoralising blow which will prevent the aggressor attacking in the first place.

Counter-offensive

Where deterrence of a potential attack before it occurs may be the ideal defence, a rapid counter-attack to 'stifle' the aggression can be equally effective. The essence of a counter-offensive is to identify the aggressor's vulnerable spots and to strike hard. The counter-offensive defence is most effective where the aggressor has become vulnerable through overstretching resources.

One example is where the defender attacks the competitor's home territory so that it has to divert its efforts into protecting its existing products. For example, some US firms have entered the Japanese market mainly to force Japanese firms that had entered the US market to reconcentrate their efforts back in their home market.

Mobile defence

This involves creating a flexible response capability to enable the defender to shift the ground which is being defended in response to environmental or competitive threats and opportunities. When a company's major market is under threat a mobile defence may make strategic sense. The two options are diversification and market broadening. A classic example of a company using diversification as a form of mobile defence was Philip Morris diversifying into the confectionery and food business when its cigarette market was threatened.

The mobile defence is an essential strategic weapon in markets where technology and/or customer wants and needs are changing rapidly. Failure to move with these changes can result in making the company vulnerable to a flanking or bypass attack.

Strategic withdrawal

A strategic withdrawal requires giving up untenable ground to reduce overstretching and allow concentration on the core business that can be defended against attack. The company has to define its strengths and weaknesses, and then to hold on to its strengths while divesting (or outsourcing) its weaknesses. This results in the company concentrating on its core business.

By the end of January 2001 the Swedish mobile telephone manufacturer Ericsson outsourced production of mobile telephones to a US partner, while keeping the value-adding R&D function within the Ericsson company.

Strategic withdrawal is usually necessary where the company has diversified too far away from its core skills and distinctive competences that gave it a competitive edge.

8.8 SUMMARY

This chapter has focused on two interrelated decisions that are involved in the formulation of a strategic marketing programme for a product–market entry – market segmentation, market targeting and positioning.

Market segmentation separates potential customers into several groups or segments with distinctive characteristics. Customers within a segment should have similar wants, needs and preferences; they should have similar media habits and buying patterns. The group should be large enough to justify attention, and data about individuals in each segment should be available.

Two common segmenting methods are the top-down method and the bottom-up method. The top-down method begins by selecting segmentation variables and assigning customers to the category they fit. The bottom-up method starts with the unique characteristics of one potential customer. Each time someone with unique characteristics is discovered, a new segment is added.

For the B2C market, typical segmentation variables are geographic and demographic factors, ethnic factors, psychographic and behaviouristic factors, and desired benefits.

In the B2B market two segmentation stages may be required. The first, macro-segmentation, divides the market according to the organisational characteristics of the customer, while micro-segmentation groups the customers by the characteristics of the individuals who influence the purchasing decision. Product usage and geographical locations are examples of macro-segmentation variables, while purchase influence, loyalty and area of expertise are micro-segmentation variables.

Micro-segmentation centres on key characteristics of the decision-making unit and requires a higher level of market knowledge.

Target marketing focuses on selecting groups of customers so marketers can more clearly understand their specific wants and needs and adjust accordingly.

Market targeting may use a market-attractiveness matrix as an analytical framework to help managers decide which market segments to target and how to allocate resources and marketing efforts.

The three basic target marketing strategies are undifferentiated, differentiated and concentrated marketing.

Undifferentiated marketing treats all customers alike and is similar to mass marketing. For this strategy to work, companies generally must have significant cost advantages. Differentiated marketing involves serving several segments but adjusting the marketing mix for each. It usually requires decentralised decision making. Concentrated marketing focuses on one segment or only a few. Because differentiated and concentrated strategies consider customer needs and wants within a certain group of customers, they are far superior to an undifferentiated strategy.

Positioning creates in the mind of consumers an image, reputation or perception of the company and/or its products relative to competitors. It helps customers understand what is unique about a company and its products.

Positioning seeks to maximise a product's performance relative to competitive offerings and to the needs (benefits sought) of one or more targeted market segments.

Marketers can use a positioning map to depict how customers perceive products according to certain characteristics. For business products, a commodity, differentiated or speciality positioning strategy can be used. Products are often positioned by benefit, by price and quality, by the time of use or application.

Positioning analysis can take place on different levels: company, product category and brand levels. The main difference between positioning in the B2C and B2B markets is that in business markets company image considerations rather than brand image building are determinants of positioning strategies.

Successful marketing strategies are often based on differentiation, market focus and lower costs. Firms must identify windows of opportunity and select appropriate attack and defence strategies to reach organisational goals.

Military analogies have been drawn upon to identify strategic options under the conditions of conflict and competition. The strategies of frontal, flank, encirclement, bypass and guerrilla attacks provide five options for companies wishing to build sales and/or market share. Position, flank, pre-emptive, counter-offensive and mobile defences and strategic withdrawal are options for companies defending sales and/or market share against aggressive competitors.

CASE STUDY 8.1

Ryanair
Competitive strategy in a warfare environment

Sources: © Charles Polidano/Touch the Skies/Alamy

As those who fly with Ryanair (www.ryanair.com) know, the great thing about the discount airline is: you get what you pay for and no more. There is no class structure, no snobbery, none of the pretence that you are a valued member of a club. They get you there, on a modern aircraft and usually on time, and that is it. But there is something else.

Ryanair has been a huge force for the opening up of Europe. The budget airline phenomenon is profoundly democratic for two reasons. People who could not afford to fly can now do so, and, more than this, regions and even countries that suffer disadvantages because of their location are now better able to compete with luckier places. That is why small little-known airports are so eager for airlines to open services.

Over the years Ryanair has been reporting strong revenue growth (see Table 8.1).

Table 8.1	Key financial figures for Ryanair Holding Plc (2005–2007) (€ m)			
	2008	2007	2006	2005
Revenue	2,714	2,237	1,692	1,319
Profits before tax	439	451	339	309

Source: Ryanair (www.ryanair.com).

One of the main reasons for the decline in profits (before tax) from 2007 to 2008 was the increase in the fuel and oil costs of nearly €100 million.

Ryanair has continued to develop its business by improving turnaround time for its aircraft and also generating cost efficiencies, which are at the heart of its business model. The airline has started to discourage passengers from checking in luggage by charging a fee for baggage that needs to go into the hold. The move is likely to create savings for Ryanair of around £170 million. The business model of Ryanair is:

Ryanair = Low costs (e.g. marketing budget is cost-effective) + **Low fares** (with an average of €44, compared to easyJet €66, Air Berlin €82 and AER Lingus €94) + **No Frills** (any additional service is paid for by passengers).

Ryanair aims to offer low basic ticket prices (in order to maximise the number of paid seats on each flight), and then charges extra for items such as checking in at the airport or for additional luggage. By the end of February 2009, Ryanair's chief executive, Michael O'Leary, received a lot of protests when he suggested that the airline may charge passengers £1 to use its toilets. He said that the carrier had been investigating fitting coin slots to the doors of aircraft toilets, similar to those installed at train stations.

History

Tony Ryan and his sons Declan and Cathal founded Ryanair in 1985. Ryan had made his fortune from airline leasing when he founded Guiness Peat Aviation in 1975 with the help of his former employer of 20 years, Aer Lingus. Despite his experience in the industry, however, his new enterprise got off to a slow start, with only one route running between Ireland's Waterford Airport and London Gatwick. Ryanair's fleet consisted of a single 15-seat Bandeirante turboprop, which could not make its scheduled flights if the clouds over Waterford were too low; passengers were often forced to get off in Cork or Dublin.

In 1986 the airline was approved for a Dublin–Luton route, and within six months it began offering unrestricted return tickets on its new route for less than half the price of the two state carriers, British Airways and Aer Lingus. The move effectively undercut their dominance, making air travel over the Irish Sea, which had been limited to more affluent travellers, accessible to the general public.

With an expanded fleet, Ryanair began offering low-fare services to 12 destinations in the British Isles in 1989. Despite the public's embrace of its low fares, the airline met with turbulence. The company's rapid growth,

combined with heavy competition from the state carriers, caused its losses to grow. It was spared bankruptcy with a £20 million infusion from the Ryan family.

It received another boost in 1989 from the Irish government when the state forced its own carrier, Aer Lingus, to give up three routes to the fledgling carrier for a three-year period. In return, Ryanair had to relinquish its Dublin–Paris route. The deal also made Ryanair the sole carrier from Ireland to Luton, Liverpool and Stansted, essentially eliminating competition between the two Irish carriers.

The real groundwork for the company's recovery, however, was laid in 1990 when Tony Ryan and personal adviser Michael O'Leary (a former tax consultant) went to Texas to meet Southwest Airlines founder and CEO Herb Kelleher. Upon his return, O'Leary began modelling Ryanair on Southwest's no-frills, low-fares model. The company reduced the airline's regular routes from 30 to 6 and made flight attendants and pilots take salary cuts. The changes worked, and by 1991 the airline had turned its first profit. O'Leary was appointed CEO (the airline's fifth) in 1993 and given a 25 per cent stake in the company.

By 1994 Ryanair had added low-fare service on four more UK routes and was carrying 1.5 million passengers a year. That year the airline boosted its fleet by ordering six Boeing 737s. Also in 1994 it began offering its first domestic UK service between Stansted and Prestwick, and in 1996 it was offering a service from Dublin to Leeds Bradford, Cardiff, and Bournemouth.

European airline deregulation in 1997 gave Ryanair a chance to move into continental Europe with flights from London to Stockholm and Oslo, and from Dublin to Paris and Brussels. That year it acquired six more Boeing 737s and went public, trading shares on both the Dublin Stock Exchange and Nasdaq.

In 1999 Ryanair added 11 new destinations in continental Europe, including Venice and Pisa, Frankfurt and St Etienne. The airline also received five new Boeing 737s. By 2000 Ryanair was serving 45 destinations throughout Europe and the British Isles and transporting nearly 6 million passengers.

The airline acquired buzz, the low-fare arm of KLM, for about $21 million in 2003. KLM was trying to take on low-fare carriers that had been sprouting up around Europe, including Ryanair, but it had struggled to make Buzz profitable.

In 2005 and 2006 Ryanair expanded its network to include destinations in Croatia, Latvia, Morocco, Poland and Slovakia.

Founder Tony Ryan died in 2007, aged 71, after a long illness.

International expansion of Ryanair

Just as Southwest expanded beyond its home region in the US, Ryanair has moved well beyond Ireland and the UK. Ryanair generated around 61 per cent of its revenues from the UK in 2001. However, in 2005 over 51 per cent of revenues came from outside the UK. This marks a distinct shift in focus for both Ryanair and easyJet as the wider aviation sector in Europe opens up opportunities.

However, future expansion eastward into Europe will provide the low-cost carriers such as Ryanair with challenges as well as opportunities. In Eastern Europe, low-cost airlines that wish to compete in this region will have to maintain even tighter cost controls, as margins will come under pressure. Ryanair has been adding destinations and increasing the frequency of routes within its network, and it has ordered more 737-800s to keep pace. The carrier flies to about 125 destinations, including some two dozen in Ireland and the UK; overall, it serves more than 20 countries throughout Europe, plus Morocco. Ryanair specialises in short-haul routes between secondary and regional airports. It operates from more than 20 bases, including airports in Belgium, France, Germany, Italy, Spain and Sweden, as well as Ireland and the UK. The carrier maintains a fleet of some 140 Boeing 737-800s.

In October 2006 Ryanair announced plans to buy rival Irish airline Aer Lingus, but the effort has been unsuccessful. Ryanair had gained a 16 per cent stake in Aer Lingus when it said it would try to buy the formerly state-owned carrier, which had begun trading publicly just a few days before. By October 2007, Ryanair had increased its stake in Aer Lingus to about 30 per cent. Buying Aer Lingus would give Ryanair long-haul routes and create a company that would approach the size of Europe's leading airlines. The proposed acquisition, news of which surprised many observers, would represent a departure from strategy for Ryanair.

The company has grown organically and has in many ways modelled itself on low-fare pioneer Southwest Airlines. Like Southwest, the carrier flies point-to-point rather than routing traffic through major hub airports, and it uses a single type of aircraft to reduce training and maintenance costs.

Ryanair augments its airline ticket revenue by enabling customers to arrange ground transportation and hotel accommodation through the company's website and by selling food and beverages in flight. It also collects commissions on travel-related products sold on sites linked to the Ryanair website.

Dark clouds coming up

The rise in fuel prices, coupled with wider environmental concerns, has inevitably cast a long shadow over the aviation industry.

That leads to the biggest issue facing air transport. Despite the work of Ryanair and the other budget airlines in Europe, and despite the growth of Southwest Airlines (the US pioneer of the genre), the main growth of global air travel in the world is not in Europe or North America, but Asia. India has benefited hugely from deregulation. A string of private sector carriers with pretty low fares and excellent service has opened up the country. In China they are building 97 new regional airports in the next 12 years. Air travel is rising by about 25 per cent a year compound. At some stage that growth will tail off; it has to. But meanwhile it may be seen as an engine of economic development, opening up parts of the country that have lagged in economic terms.

Most obviously, demand for aviation fuel will remain high, as will demand for all oil products. The world is close to a tipping point, where overall demand for oil from the emerging countries will exceed that from the developed world.

The world will probably go through that point in this downswing of the economic cycle. That in turn will make the world reserve oil for the applications where there are no obvious substitutes, one of which is air travel. It will be too valuable to burn in power stations; it would be needed for planes. Many people in Europe may find this an uncomfortable thought.

In June 2008 (*Daily Mail*, 9 June 2008), Mr O'Leary conceded the economic picture had changed dramatically in the past few months and that, if petrol prices increased, profits would vanish. He said that a no-profit situation could easily happen if the oil price reached $150 a barrel. O'Leary spoke about the possibility of the industry being hit by oil prices, a weak pound and falling demand. But then he added: 'There can only be one competitive response to any consumer uncertainty, and that is for Ryanair to slash fares and yields, stimulate traffic, encourage price-sensitive consumers, and promote new routes.'

Despite the turmoil surrounding the aviation industry, Mr O'Leary said he had no intention of getting out of the business. He had previously suggested he may go in 2009 but he said things were too interesting.

In June 2008 German carrier Air Berlin also abandoned its full-year profit goal and said it would scrap unprofitable routes as it tries to weather soaring fuel costs. British Airways said in May 2008 that it was braced for a turbulent year, with fuel costs set to rise to £1 billion.

The takeover attempts of Aer Lingus

The competition (and also relationship) between the two Irish airlines has always been intense. Ryanair CEO Michael O'Leary always thought that buying Aer Lingus would give Ryanair long-haul routes and create a company that would approach the size of Europe's leading airlines. On two occasions Ryanair announced specific plans to buy the rival Irish airline, but the efforts have been unsuccessful until now.

First attempt

On 5 October 2006, Ryanair launched a bid to buy Aer Lingus. Ryanair CEO Michael O'Leary said the move was a 'unique opportunity' to form an Irish airline. The 'new' airline would carry over 50 million passengers a year. Ryanair said it had bought a 16 per cent stake in Aer Lingus and was offering €2.80 for remaining shares. On the same day, Aer Lingus rejected Ryanair's takeover bid. Ryanair then confirmed it had raised its stake to 19 per cent, and said it had no problem with the Irish government keeping its 28 per cent. There were also reports in the *Irish Times* that the government would possibly seek judgement from the courts, and referral to competition authorities in Dublin – although this would be automatic under European regulation, as the combined group would control 78 per cent of the Dublin– London passenger air traffic.

On 29 November 2006, Ryanair confirmed it had taken its stake to 26 per cent of the airline.

On 21 December 2006, Ryanair announced it was withdrawing its current bid for Aer Lingus, with the intent of pursuing another bid in the near future after the European Commission finished investigating the current bid. The Commission had been concerned that the takeover would reduce consumer choice and increase fares.

On 27 June 2007, the European Commission announced their decision to block the bid on competition grounds, saying the two airlines controlled more than 80 per cent of all European flights to and from Dublin airport.

Second attempt

On 1 December 2008, Ryanair launched a second takeover bid of Aer Lingus, making an all-cash offer of €748 million (corresponding to €1.4 per share). Ryanair already owned 30 per cent of the former state carrier. Since Ryanair's previous bid, Aer Lingus's share price had fallen from a high of $3.80 in December 2006 to a low of $1.27 in November 2008. The offer of €1.4 per share was a 28 per cent premium on the value of Aer Lingus stock during the preceding 30 days.

Ryanair CEO Michael O'Leary thought that the proposed merger of Ryanair and Aer Lingus would form one Irish airline group with the financial strength to compete with Europe's three major airline groups – Air France, British Airways and Lufthansa.

The Irish government held about 25 per cent of Aer Lingus shares; the airline's management and representatives of Aer Lingus employees controlled another 14 per cent of the shares.

The Aer Lingus board rejected the offer and advised its shareholders to take no action. The offer was rejected by all shareholders. It was the second failed attempt by Michael O'Leary to take over the national flag carrier. Ryanair left the offer open to Aer Lingus until they withdrew their bid on 30 January 2009. The Irish government slammed O'Leary's offer as 'undervaluing the airline' and stated that a Ryanair takeover would have a 'significant negative impact' on competition in the industry and on the Irish consumer.

On 11 March 2009 Aer Lingus announced a loss of €108 million. Furthermore, Aer Lingus announced that it would experience a larger operating loss in 2009 than in 2008.

Michael O'Leary's comment was:

Irish taxpayers are entitled to ask the Department of Transport why they rejected Ryanair's €1.40 offer and claimed that 'The €1.40 offer for Ryanair greatly undervalues Aer Lingus', when just ten weeks later the taxpayer investment in Aer Lingus has collapsed by more than 50%. What does this say about the Department of Transport's financial judgement?

Also on 11 March 2008, *Ryanair News* reported thus:

Consumers can celebrate Aer Lingus's continuing losses and failure as Ryanair this morning released 108,000 free seats – 1,000 seats for every €1m after tax losses announced by Aer Lingus this morning – for travel in March and returning in the first week of April. These will be the last free flights on Ryanair from Ireland before the Government introduces its crazy €10 tourist tax in Ireland.

International competition

The concept of LCCs (low-cost carriers), also known as budget or 'no frills' airlines was first developed in the US, with the creation of Southwest Airlines as early as 1971 and remaining by far the leading airline in terms of passengers and revenue passenger kilometres (RPKs). The company took a no-frills approach to flying, eliminating meal service, in-flight entertainment and assigned seats, thus targeting travellers who might otherwise choose to drive. Thus prices were low, flights direct and departures frequent, echoing the economy, directness and flexibility of travel by private car. Distances flown were also short, with the average flight covering just 425 miles.

Over the years, however, the LCC concept has evolved because of an increasingly competitive environment and the need to constantly adapt corporate strategies to avoid losing market share. Not surprisingly, LCCs have diversified their product portfolios and ventured into new regions, e.g. Western Europe.

Globally, Ryanair (like easyJet) is a small player in air travel with a ranking of 41 and a world market share of 0.5% in 2005. However, the company is one of the longest established low-cost airlines in the world, with its geographical focus being Western Europe.

As a result of the company's limited geographical range and low-cost niche market, it does not compete with the global giants, such as Air France or British Airways, in the full-service aviation sector. However, Ryanair is one of the most profitable companies in air transportation despite this.

The low-cost aviation sector in Europe has been dominated by airlines, such as Ryanair and easyJet for a number of years. However, the future is set to change, as a number of new brands will expand during the forecast period, creating greater competition and heralding a period of gradual consolidation.

British Airways launched its own low-cost carrier called BA Connect in 2006 and will enter the sector at a very interesting time. If successful, the new service provided by British Airways will create an extra challenge to the existing players.

The European region offers other competition with the likes of Wizz Air and SkyEurope, both based in Eastern Europe, which also have growing ambitions.

The main competitors

British Airways

British Airways ranked sixth in air transportation in 2006. The airline has an extensive international scheduled route network comprising some 147 destinations in 75 countries. Including code-sharing and franchise arrangements, flights with British Airways serve some 345 destinations in 109 countries. Its main location is London Heathrow, which serves a large geographic area with a relatively high proportion of point-to-point business. Eastern Europe offers significant growth opportunities in the short term, with developing travel infrastructures, an expanding middle class and a rise in foreign tourism and international business boosting air travel sales. British Airways is in the process of expanding its presence in the region, launching new services to Tirana in Albania, Varna in Bulgaria and Sarajevo in Bosnia-Herzegovina.

British Airways is notably focused on developing the upper end of its operations. The company has refreshed its First Class offer. The new Club World offer, launched in November 2006, highlights the way in which the company is seeking to enhance the customer experience. Indeed, British Airways states that it provides 'a whole experience from the moment a customer decides to fly with British Airways to the moment they arrive at their destination'. This includes the provision to book tickets online, as well as choosing hotels, car hire and insurance; the opportunity to use a spa or business centre at the airport or pre-flight dining on the aircraft; an enhanced cabin, a new privacy screen in the seat; and the opportunity to use the arrivals lounge to take a shower, have a meal, have a spa treatment or catch up on work.

Table 8.2	Market share of airlines, 2007	

Rank	Airline	Market share (retail value) %
1	Air France-KLM Group SA	5.5
2	AMR Corp (American)	5.4
3	Deutsche Lufthansa AG	3.9
4	Delta Airlines Inc.	3.6
5	United Airlines Corp.	3.5
6	British Airways Plc	3.1
–		
40	easyGroup Ltd (easyJet)	0.5
41	Ryanair Holdings Plc	0.5

Sources: Different public sources; adapted from Euromonitor International (www.euromonitor.com).

easyJet

easyJet (owned by easyGroup Ltd.), based in the UK, also enhanced its services in order to attract a larger number of business travellers. The company has focused on key areas such as check-in, luggage allowances, booking hours, travel flexibility, flight frequency and security. The '10 reasons to fly easyJet for business' clearly states all benefits offered by the airline to business travellers, such as fast check-in for those carrying hand luggage only, no weight limit on hand baggage, 24-hour booking, changing and viewing of flights, sale of one-way fares, the ability to catch an earlier or a later flight depending on the time a customer arrives at the airport, ticketless boarding and free seating.

easyJet has been expanding its interests into Europe during the review period at an incredible pace, although Ryanair has also extended its operations but in a more gradual fashion.

Marketing strategy of Ryanair

The marketing angle that Ryanair has adopted is one of remaining very distinct from its rivals. Poster campaigns, which are characterised by colourful and sometimes humorous twists and are designed to capture the consumer's eye, feature highly in its brand support strategy. However, perhaps the most important avenue of advertising for the airline is through its website, which is the main booking platform for the company. Its main website, Ryanair.com, has 20 language-specific extensions that can be accessed.

Ryanair's website is the only means by which to book flights and associated travel products, such as hotel accommodation and car rental. It was one of the first airlines to push for all of its bookings to be made via the Internet.

By the nature of its business, Ryanair remains focused on ensuring its marketing budget is cost-effective and kept under tight control. The airline realises the importance of advertising its services but also recognises the need to maintain a strong focus on costs. Ryanair rarely spends more than 2 per cent of its total annual revenues on marketing activities and is heavily dependent on its exposure via the Internet.

Ryanair did cause some media controversy in early 2006, when a Channel 4 programme entitled *Ryanair Caught Napping* was broadcast in the UK. The report revealed various allegations, such as inadequate safety and security checks, dirty planes, exhausted cabin crew and pilots complaining about the number of hours they fly. However, the negative coverage, which Ryanair later dismissed as being untrue, did not tarnish the company brand and the airline remained relatively unscathed by the publicity.

Communication

After announcing a 27 per cent drop in profits for the last quarter of 2007, Ryanair decided to cut its marketing budget and focus primarily on using controversial one-off press ads (frequently banned by the Advertising Standards Authority) to promote its airfares. It was an attempt to get 'more bang for the buck' (*Marketing Week*, 7 February 2008).

Irish discount airline Ryanair has caused a stir in Europe with the publication of its Girls of Ryanair calendar, with feminist groups accusing the carrier of sexism.

The calendar, which features photographs of scantily clad flight attendants posing in front of jet engines, fuel pumps and tool kits, drew heated criticism from a number of groups, including the Women's Institute and a government-run rights organisation in Spain, where this year's calendar was shot, according to a report on Spiegel Online. 'It is significant that only women are used, in a sector in which there is a considerable percentage of men,' the group said in a statement quoted by Britain's *Daily Mail*. Spokesman María Jesús Ortiz told the *Daily Mail* that the images presented the women as 'sexual objects'.

According to the German news organisation, the Spanish group has complained to Irish and European authorities and is considering legal action against the airline. Ryanair apparently continues to differ. Stephen McNamara, a Ryanair spokesman, said that Ryanair will continue to defend the right of girls to take their clothes off, particularly when it is for charity. The carrier has also sent a copy to Swedish politician Birgitta Ohlsson, who recently launched an attack against a Ryanair ad, which used a model in a short top and mini skirt, and accused Ryanair of exploiting women.

More than 700 female workers reportedly applied to take part in the 2009 calendar.

On 20 January 2009 Ryanair presented Dublin Simon Community with a cheque for €100,000 after all 10,000 copies of its 2009 Ryanair Cabin Crew Charity Calendar sold out in just four weeks. Dublin Simon Community (which provides vital services for the homeless in Dublin) was chosen from over 100 charities throughout Europe to receive the entire sale proceeds from the 2009 calendar.

Future trends

The demand for LCCs is growing. Ticket price is the number one criterion for most passengers when selecting a flight, well ahead of the availability of a non-stop service.

Ryanair's Michael O'Leary with the girls of Ryanair calendar
Source: Janerik Henriksson/Press Association Images

In view of this growing trend, Ryanair is planning to expand its global fleet size and could be in a position to benefit from the growing airline industry.

Ryanair is charging its passengers for food, drink, blankets and pillows. Such a strategy may be too bold for most carriers, but some may move in this direction. This may result in a new business model for scheduled airlines, with careful cost models and fewer perks and benefits, and help prevent further revenue losses, although it is doubtful that consumers will wholly welcome this trend, particularly when accompanied by rising prices. According to a survey by Amadeus, consumers are ready to pay more for greater choice, amenities and options, if they deem these to be in line with their travel needs.

QUESTIONS

1   What is the customer value created by Ryanair?

2   Prepare a SWOT analysis for Ryanair.

3   What are the competitive advantages of Ryanair?

4   How would you characterise Ryanair's competitive strategy?

5   What are the motives behind Michael O'Leary's wish to take over Aer Lingus?

6   How do you consider Michael O'Leary's communication capabilities when he commented on the rejection by the Irish government?

7   What do you think about the communication effectiveness and the ethics of the 2009 Ryanair calender and its 'contents'?

SOURCES

Ryanair (www.ryanair.com); Euromonitor International (www.euromonitor.com); and various public media.

QUESTIONS FOR DISCUSSION

1 What benefits are to be gained from market segmentation, as opposed to treating the market as a single entity?

2 What stages are involved in identifying market segments?

3 Is market segmentation always a good idea? Under which conditions, if any, might segmentation be unnecessary or unwise?

4 Can market segmentation be taken too far? What are the potential disadvantages of over-segmenting a market? What strategy might a firm pursue when it believes that the market has been broken into too many small segments?

5 Which variables or descriptors might be most appropriate for segmenting the market for the following products and services? Explain your reasoning.
   (a) Breakfast cereals.
   (b) Personal computers (PCs).
   (c) Software, games for PCs.
   (d) Lawnmowers.
   (e) Photocopiers.
   (f) Wind turbines.

6 Explain the idea of positioning and why products are repositioned periodically.

REFERENCES

Adage Global (2000) BMW awards German shop global launch of new Mini, *Adage Global*, 30 September (www.adageglobal.com).

Advertising Age (2000) BMW puts $40 mil effort behind its revamped Mini, *Advertising Age*, Chicago, 71(42) (9 October): 34–6.

Ashton, J. E., Cook, F. X. Jr and Schmitz, P. (2003) Uncovering hidden value in a midsize manufacturing company, *Harvard Business Review*, June: 111–19.

Automotive Industries (2000) Risking brand image with new brand, *Automotive Industries*, 18(10) (October): 30–1.

Barron, J. and Hollingshead, J. (2002) Making segmentation work, *Marketing Management*, January/February: 24–8.

BBC (2001) A new life for the Mini, *BBC News*, 22 May (http://news.bbc.co.uk).

Beverage Industry (2000a) Bottled water comes of age, *Beverage Industry*, 91(9) (September): 26–9.

Beverage Industry (2000b) Bottled water soars, *Beverage Industry*, 91(9) (September): 22–6.

Beverage Industry (2000c) State of the industry, *Beverage Industry*, 91(7) (July): 38–40.

Bonoma, T. V. and Shapiro, B. P. (1983) *Segmenting the Industrial Market*, D.C. Heath and Co., Lexington.

Burns, D. J. and Warren, H. B. (2008) Consumer warfare: implications for marketing strategy, *Journal of Business Strategy*, 29(6): 44–52.

Busch, P. S. and Houston, M. J. (1985) *Marketing Strategic Foundations*, Richard D. Irwin, Burr Ridge, IL.

Business and Finance (1999) Ballygowan: the 'Hoover' of the Irish water industry in just fifteen years, *Business and Finance*, 23 September.

China Internet Information Center (2003) Battery giant Gillette obtains rival Nanfu, *www.china.org.cn*, 22 August (http://mdjnkj.china.com.cn/english/BAT/73007.htm).

CNN (2001) BMW rolls out new Mini, *CNN Financial News*, 22 May (http://cnnfn.cnn.com).

Crittenden, V. L., Crittenden, W. F. and Muzyka, D. F. (2002) Segmenting the business-to-business marketplace by product attributes and the decision process, *Journal of Strategic Marketing*, March: 3–20.

Der Market der Automoblie (1999) Fakten '99, *Focus* (www.focus.de/medialine).

Dyer, J. H., Cho, D. S. and Chu, W. (1998) Strategic supplier segmentation, *California Management Review*, 40(2) (Winter): 57–77.

Elliott, G. and Glynn, W. (2000) Segmenting industrial buyers by loyalty and value, IMP Conference, Bath, UK.

Elliott, S. (1998) Levi Strauss begins a far-reaching marketing campaign to reach gay men and lesbians, *New York Times*, 19 October: 11.

Fortune (1998) BMW – takes its own route, *Fortune*, 26 October: 103–8.

Freytag, P. V. and Clarke, A. H. (2001) Business to business market segmentation, *Industrial Marketing Management*, 30: 473–86.

Freytag, P. V. and Clarke, A. H. (2008) An intra- and inter-organizational perspective on industrial segmentation, *European Journal of Marketing*, 42(9/10): 1023–38.

Gadiesh, O., Leung, P. and Vestring, T. (2007) The battle for China's good-enough market, *Harvard Business Review*, September: 81–9.

Gibson, L. D. (2001) Is something rotten in segmentation? *Marketing Research*, Spring: 20–5.

Gilbert, X. and Strebel, P. (1988) Developing competitive advantage, in J. B. Quinn, H. Mintzberg and R. M. James (eds), *The Strategic Process*, Prentice Hall, Englewood Cliffs, NJ.

Goller, S., Hogg, A. and Kalafatis, P. (2002) A new research agenda for business segmentation, *European Journal of Marketing*, 36(1/2): 252–71.

Håkansson, H. and Snehota, I. (1995) *Developing Relationships in Business Networks*, Routledge, London.

Harrell, G. D. and Frazier, G. L. (1999) *Marketing: Connecting with Customers*, Prentice Hall, Englewood Cliffs, NJ.

Jonk, G., Handschuh, M. and Niewiem, S. (2008) The battle of the value chains: new specialized versus old hybrids, *Strategy & Leadership*, 36(2): 24–9.

Kalafatis, S. P., Tsogas, M. H. and Blankson, C. (2000) Positioning strategies in business markets, *Journal of Business & Industrial Marketing*, 15(6), 416–37.

Kotler, P. (2000) *Marketing Management: The Millennium Edition*, 10th edn, Pearson Education, Inc., Upper Saddle River, NJ.

Kotler, P. and Singh, R. (1981) Marketing warfare in the 1980s, *Journal of Business Strategy*, Winter: 30–41.

Kullin, H. (2006) The brand 'Björn Borg' sold for 18 MUSD, *www.kullin.net* (www.kullin.net/2006/12/brand-bjrn-borg-sold-for-18-musd.html).

Kumar, V. and Naspal, A. (2001) Segmenting global markets: look before you leap, *Marketing Research*, Spring: 8–13.

Marketing (2000) BMW picks Rover man to market new Mini, *Marketing*, 7 September: 5–6.

Millier, P. (2000) Intuition can help in segmenting industrial markets, *Industrial Marketing Management*, 29(2) (March): 147–55.

Mitchell, V.-W. and Wilson, D. F. (1998) Balancing theory and practice, *Industrial Marketing Management*, 27: 429–45.

Mittal, V. and Katrichis, J. M. (2000) Distinctions between new and loyal customers, *Marketing Research*, 12(1) (Spring): 26–32.

Morehouse, J., O'Meara, R., Hagen, C. and Huseby, T. (2008) Hitting back: strategic responses to low-cost rivals, *Strategy & Leadership*, 36(1): 4–13.

Motor (2000) The mini's back . . . after 30 years, *Motor*, 193(4) (April): 51–2.

O'Mahony, P. (2006) Björn Borg brand headed for stock exchange, *The Local: Swedish News in English*, 7 December (www.thelocal.se/5733/20061207/).

Peppers, D., Rogers, M. and Dorf, B. (1999) Is your company ready for one-to-one marketing? *Harvard Business Review*, January–February: 151–60.

Porter, M. E. (1980) *Competitive Strategy*, Free Press, New York.

Porter, M. E. (1985) *Competitive Advantage: Creating and Sustaining Superior Performance*, Free Press, New York.

Powers, T. L. and Sterling, J. U. (2008) Segmenting business-to-business markets: a micro–macro linking methodology, *Journal of Business & Industrial Marketing*, 23(3): 170–7.

Prince, G. W. (2001) Rock the boat, *Beverage World*, 15 April: 53–7.

Raynor, M. E. and Weinberg, H. S. (2004) Beyond segmentation, *Marketing Management*, 13(6): 22–8.

Ries, A. and Trout, J. (1986) *Positioning: The Battle for Your Mind*, 2nd edn, McGraw-Hill, New York, pp. 1–210.

Roper Starch Worldwide (2000) Re-mapping the world of consumers, *American Demographics*, October (www.demographics.com).

Schmid, K. L., Rivers, S., Latimer, A. E. and Salovey, P. (2008) Targeting or tailoring, *Marketing Health Services*, 28(1) (Spring): 32–7.

Smith, W. (1956) Product differentiation and market segmentation as alternative marketing strategies, *Journal of Marketing*, 21 (July): 3–8.

Townsend, M. (2001) Record demand as healthier lifestyles take off but the tap stuff is just as good, bottled water floods in, *The Express*, 6 March: 10.

Ward's Auto World (2000) BMW previews new mini, *Ward's Auto World*, 36(10) (October): 33–4.

Wind, Y. and Cardozo, R. N. (1974) Industrial market segmentation, *Industrial Marketing Management*, 7: 153–66.

Wyner, G. A. (2000) Customer selection, *Marketing Research*, 12(1) (Spring): 42–4.

CHAPTER 9
CSR strategy and the sustainable global value chain

LEARNING OBJECTIVES

After studying this chapter you should be able to:

- define CSR

- understand how value creation goes beyond profit maximisation, according to CSR

- identify the most important stakeholder in CSR

- identify different levels of CSR

- understand how social marketing is an integrative part of CSR

- explain the most important drivers of CSR

- understand how CSR can create international competitiveness

- explain how 'value added' may be created through CSR activities

- understand how 'poverty' and 'global warming' can create new business opportunities

9.1 INTRODUCTION

Corporate social responsibility (CSR) has become an important issue among marketers in the corporate world.

In the 1960s 'marketing' was defined as a transaction between the provider and the receiver of the product, where the provider satisfies the goals of the receiver and obtains some type of compensation in return. The definition emphasises the four components of the marketing mix (the four Ps).

Corporate social responsibility (CSR)
The continuing commitment by companies to behave ethically and contribute to worldwide economic development while improving the quality of life of the workforce and their families as well as of the local community and the international society at large.

The notion of societal marketing introduced in the 1980s saw that marketing should take society's interests into consideration as well.

In this chapter we will consider value creation which goes beyond profit maximisation and includes long-term business survival alongside the meeting of societal (and stakeholder) needs and expectations.

It started off as a fad, just like total quality management 15 years ago. However, today there is no doubt that corporate social responsibility (CSR) is an issue that all industries are taking very seriously (Czarnowski, 2009).

CSR is still at an early stage in its development as a new business discipline. One of the consequences of this is that, when managers are asked what CSR contributes to their company, there is little consistency in their responses. The general consensus, however, is that if CSR is not at the centre of the company's operations, there is a fundamental risk to the business (Szmigin *et al.*, 2007; Strategic Direction, 2009).

Definition of CSR

The concept of CSR captures the dynamics of the relationship between business and society. According to Greenberg and Baron (2008), corporate social responsibility describes:

> business practices that adhere to ethical values that comply with legal requirements, that demonstrate respect for individuals, and that promote the betterment of the community at large and the environment. It involves operating a business in a manner that meets or exceeds those ethical, legal and public expectations that society has of business.

Let us look into what the concept of CSR stands for. The core theme of CSR is to deal, interact and relate with stakeholders with an ethical approach that is not harming or hurting any stakeholder. CSR represents the voluntary (non-enforced) set of activities of a business organisation. At the bare minimum CSR stands for being legally compliant to the rules of the land. But the dominant theme and directive of CSR is to better the condition of various stakeholders such as the neighbouring local communities, broader society and the natural environment. In the present day debate, CSR has been seen as a continuous process of engagement with the stakeholders by a business firm (Rigby and Tager, 2008; Robinson and Tager, 2008).

As Archie Carroll put it more than a decade ago:

> for the better part of 30 years now, corporate executives have struggled with the issue of the firm's responsibility to its society . . . new governmental bodies established that national public policy now officially recognized the environment, employees and consumers to be significant and legitimate stakeholders of business . . . CSR, to be accepted as legitimate, had to address the entire spectrum of obligations business has to society, including the most fundamental – economic. (Carroll, 1991)

The result of integrating ethics and responsibility into the common discussion framework about competitiveness is the emergence of a new concept and practice: responsible competitiveness. Therefore, a relatively different approach to competitiveness (associated with an ethical dimension) is developed when the challenge and vision of responsible competitiveness is to embed social and environmental goals and outcomes in the very heart of competitiveness.

9.2 DIFFERENT LEVELS OF ETHICAL BEHAVIOUR

The ethical commitment of a company is illustrated in Figure 9.1 as a continuum from unacceptable ethical behaviour to the most ethical decision making.

At the first level of the acceptable ethical behaviour, marketing ethics refer to principles and standards that define acceptable conduct as determined by the public, government regulators, private

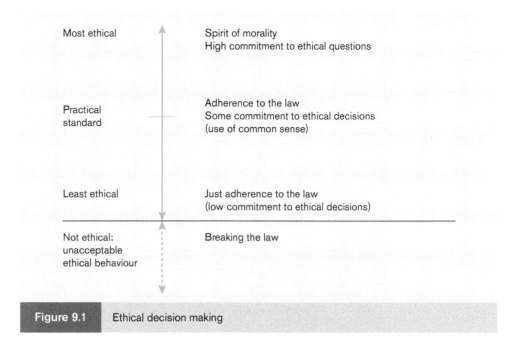

| **Figure 9.1** | Ethical decision making |

interest groups, competitors and the organisation itself. The most basic of these principles have been codified as laws and regulations to induce marketers to conform to society's expectations of conduct. However, it is important to understand that marketing ethics goes beyond legal issues: ethical marketing decisions foster trust, which helps build long-term marketing relationships.

Being ethical and responsible requires commitment. For this reason, many firms simply ignore these issues and focus instead on satisfying their economic and legal responsibilities, with the overall aim being profit maximisation. While the firm may do nothing wrong, it misses out on the long-term benefits that can be derived from satisfying ethical and philanthropic responsibilities. Firms that choose to take these extra steps are concerned with increasing their overall positive impact on society, their local communities and the environment, with the aim being increased goodwill towards the firm as well as increased profits.

A classification of a company as a highly ethical company requires that the firm's code of ethics should address the following six major issues:

- *organisational relations*: including competition, strategic alliances and local sourcing;
- *economic relations*: including financing, taxation, transfer prices, local reinvestment and equity participation;
- *employee relations*: including compensation, safety, human rights, non-discrimination, collective bargaining, training and the absence of sexual harassment;
- *customer relations*: including pricing, quality and advertising;
- *industrial relations*: including technology transfer, research and development, infrastructure development and organisational stability/longevity;
- *political relations*: including legal compliance, bribery and other corrupt activities, subsidies, tax incentives, environmental protection and political involvement.

It is easy to generalise about the ethics of political pay-offs and other types of payments; it is much more difficult to make the decision to withhold payment of money when the consequences of not making the payment may affect the company's ability to do business profitably or at all. With the variety of ethical standards and levels of morality that exist in different cultures, the dilemma of ethics and pragmatism that faces international business cannot be resolved until more countries decide to deal effectively with the issue.

Product issues
• Reducing package size while holding prices constant • Product quality dishonesty (shortcuts in design/manufacture) • Unsafe products (particularly for children) • Poor service or no service after the sale • Adding useless features to command higher prices
Promotion issues
• Bait-and-switch (comparitive) advertising • Overstated claims for product • Push-money paid to salespeople • Advertising to children • Sex or fear as an advertising appeal • Exaggerated product benefits • High-pressure or misleading salespeople • Bribery of salespeople or purchasing agents
Pricing issues
• Price fixing between competitors • Predatory pricing • Excessive pricing • Misleading credit/financing practices • Fraudulent warranty or refund policiesr
Distribution issues
• Opportunistic behaviour among channel members • Slotting allowances paid to retailers to gain shelf space • Extortion • Tying contracts • Distribution of counter feit products

Figure 9.2	Possible ethical issues in marketing
	Sources: Adapted from Peter and Donelly (1994), p. 274 and Pride and Ferrell (1997), p. 59.

It is imperative that marketers become familiar with many of the ethical and social issues that may occur in marketing so that these issues can be identified and resolved when they occur. Some of these issues are shown in Figure 9.2. Essentially, any time an activity causes marketing managers, or customers in their target market, to feel manipulated or cheated, an ethical issue exists, regardless of the legality of the activity. Many ethical issues can develop into legal problems if they are not addressed in the planning process. Once an issue has been identified, marketers must decide how to deal with it.

9.3 SOCIAL MARKETING AS PART OF CSR

Within the marketing literature, much fragmentation can be observed in terms of the unit of analysis considered and the dimensions of social responsibility investigated. When marketing scholars started expressing concern for corporate social responsibilities in the 1960s and 1970s, they focused on the social duties attached to the marketing function and not on the overall social role of the firm. As a result, the field of social marketing has emerged and has specialised in the contribution of marketing activities to socially desirable behaviours and goals (Maignan and Ferrell, 2004).

Social marketing
Planning, execution and evaluation of programmes to influence the voluntary behaviour of target audiences in order to improve their personal welfare (e.g. encouraging people to give up smoking).

Social marketing can be understood as the application of commercial marketing technologies to the analysis, planning, execution and evaluation of programmes designed to influence the voluntary behaviour of target audiences in order to improve their personal welfare and that of their society (Hastings, 2003).

So social marketing is about changing behaviour: encouraging people to give up smoking, take exercise or visit a sexual health clinic. These changes do not, for the most part, occur overnight. They involve a series of steps from initial contemplation through to reinforcement after the fact, a process that is both dynamic and precarious: the individual can regress or change heart at any point.

Social marketing is founded on trust, and therefore we have to start thinking in terms of long-term relationship building (Hollensen, 2007).

Social marketing has clear relations to commercial marketing. Still, social marketing is distinct from commercial marketing in that it focuses on resolving social problems, whereas commercial marketing focuses on producing various goods or services for a profit. The 'customer' of social marketing is normally not expected to pay a price equal to the cost of providing the service, whereas the customer of commercial marketing is expected to do so. Furthermore, social marketing should not be confused with socially responsible marketing, something in which all marketers should be engaged. Socially responsible marketing is commercial marketing that appropriately takes into account its social responsibilities in marketing ordinary products and services.

Social marketing focuses on influencing people's behaviour away from ways of acting or lifestyles that are designated as leading or contributing to a social problem and towards other ways of acting and lifestyles that will improve these people's well-being (or the well-being of others). This attempt to change people's behaviour may also involve modifications in their attitudes, values, norms and ideas. Indeed, it may also require behavioural and value changes in the communities or groups of people with whom they live and/or associate (Domegan, 2008).

The well-being of the individuals and/or society is not simply subjectively identified by the individuals involved but is subject to determination through processes of social argumentation and justification. This does not mean that everyone will agree with these processes.

Social marketers target people who may not believe, at least at the outset, that they suffer from a problem or any deficiency in their welfare. So social problems are identified independently of what any particular person or people may or may not believe. It is compatible with social marketing that the people social marketers address strongly believe that they do not have a problem. This might be the case of teenagers who abuse alcohol or drugs, fathers of Muslim girls in Bangladesh who do not really believe that their daughters should receive an education, or men in parts of Africa who wish to have their future wives undergo female circumcision. Case study 9.1 (YouthAIDS) illustrates some aspects of social marketing, by attempting to change sexual behaviour, especially among young people in developing countries.

9.4 CAUSE-RELATED MARKETING

Cause-related marketing
A combination of joint funding and a promotional strategy in which a firm's sales is linked (and a percentage of the sales revenue is donated) to a charity or another public cause. However, unlike philanthropy, money spent in cause-related marketing is considered an expense and is expected to show a return.

Cause-related marketing (also simply known as cause marketing) is an umbrella term that covers a rich range of marketing activity. Central to its definition is the idea of a marketing partnership between a business and a non-profit entity for mutual benefit. It is a strategic positioning and marketing tool that links a company or brand to a relevant social cause or issue. In that sense it is a commercial activity by which businesses and charities or causes form a partnership with each other to market an image, product or service for mutual benefit.

Cause-related marketing is a powerful marketing tool that business and non-profit organisations are increasingly leveraging. According to the Cone Millennial Cause Study in 2006, 89 per cent of Americans (aged 13 to 25) would switch from one brand to another brand of a comparable product (and price) if the latter brand was associated with a 'good cause'. The same study also indicated that a significant percentage surveyed would prefer to work for a company that was considered socially responsible.

See some examples of cause marketing campaigns in Exhibit 9.1 (see also Case study 9.1). The possible benefits of a cause marketing relationship for the non-profit organisation include an increased ability to promote the non-profit organisation's cause via the greater financial resources of a business, and an increased ability to reach possible supporters through a company's customer base. The possible benefits for the company include a positive public image, improved customer relations, additional marketing opportunities and growth in market share.

EXHIBIT 9.1
Examples of cause marketing campaigns

Campaign	Cause	Marketing strategy	Impact on cause/non-profit organisation	Impact on company
Dove soap	Self-esteem	Campaign for Real Beauty uses real women, not models, in its ads to energise Dove brands	Since 2004, has raised $13 million for Dove's Self Esteem Fund to help girls build confidence	Millions of dollars of free advertising and double-digit sales growth in US and European markets
M.A.C. Cosmetics	AIDS awareness	VIVA GLAM campaign donates 100% of sales of its $14 and $16 lipsticks to various AIDS charities	VIVA GLAM lipstick sales have raised $100 million for the M.A.C. AIDS Fund since 1994	M.A.C. is now the leading seller of make-up to minorities in the world
Aldo Shoes	AIDS awareness	Increased global awareness for shoe brand and boost youth market share with 'Hear No Evil, See No Evil' cause campaign	Raised $3.5 million for YouthAIDS since 2005	Foot traffic in stores increased by double digits, and same-store sales increased by far more than the industry average
Gibson Guitars	Music, New Orleans flood relief	Dusts off brand for youth market with special-issue Music Rising guitars	Donated profits from sales of 200 special guitars to musicians displaced by flooding	Increased global visibility for guitars and millions of dollars in free advertising
Select comfort mattresses	Children's health	Holds celebrity events to boost awareness of its Sleep Number bedding line	Since 2001, has donated 4,700 beds, and 11,500 mattresses to the Ronald McDonald House	Boosted brand awareness by 50%, won distinctive media coverage in14 of its 20 markets, sold 21,000 additional pillows
Jones Apparel Group	Children's education	Creates Jones New York in the Classroom initiative	Raised some $1.5 million to be split among four education non-profits	Employee retention; 90% of workers felt children's cause to be the most important

Source: Adapted from Sharn, L. (2009) Walking the talk: using emotion to make strides with young consumers, *Contribute* (www.contributemedia.com/trends_details.php?id=103).

9.5 IDENTIFICATION OF STAKEHOLDERS IN CSR

A business organisation is nothing but a web of relationships with various stakeholders. So, any attempt to develop a framework on strategic CSR will start from stakeholders. A firm's stakeholders are parties that can significantly affect or are significantly affected by firm activities.

Stakeholders have the power to influence the firm, and they face the consequences of a firm's decision to act, or not to act.

These are the most important stakeholders:

- owners/shareholders/investors
- top management
- employees (including employees abroad)
- customers
- suppliers/contractors
- competitors
- special interest groups (e.g. 'green' organisations)
- government.

Stakeholders can be classified either as primary stakeholders or as secondary stakeholders. Primary stakeholders are seen as stakeholders that impact or relate to the primary firm functions and thus are important for the survival of the organisation. Secondary stakeholders are concerned with the secondary (support) firm functions and thus are not of existential importance to the firm. Therefore, primary stakeholders consist of shareholders, employees, customers, suppliers, etc., while secondary stakeholders would typically be special-interest groups.

9.6 DRIVERS OF CSR

The factors driving this move towards corporate social responsibility include new concerns and expectations of stakeholders, citizens, consumers, public authorities and investors. For instance, consider the influence of social criteria in the investment decisions of individuals and institutions, both as consumers and as investors; the increased concern about the damage caused by economic activities to the environment; and the transparency of business activities brought about by the media and modern information and communication technologies. Generally, CSR is considered as a firm's obligation to protect and improve the welfare of society and its organisation, now as well as in the future, through various business and social actions, ensuring that it generates equitable and sustainable benefits for the various stakeholders.

Long-term benefit drivers of CSR

These five clusters of CSR business benefits are similar to the systematisation of value drivers of sustainability (Schaltegger and Wagner, 2006; Weber, 2008):

1 *Positive effects on company image and reputation*: Image represents 'the mental picture of the company held by its audiences', which is influenced by company communications. Reputation builds upon personal experiences and characteristics and includes a value judgement by a company's stakeholders. Whereas image can change quickly, reputation evolves over time and is influenced by consistent performance and communication over several years. Both image and reputation can influence company competitiveness.

2 *Revenue increases from higher sales and market share*: CSR can lead to revenue increases. These can be achieved indirectly through an improved brand image or directly, e.g. by CSR-driven product or market development.

3 *Positive effects on employee motivation, retention and recruitment*: On the one hand, effects in this area can result from an improved reputation. On the other hand, CSR can also directly influence employees as they might be more motivated through working in a better environment, or draw motivation from the participation in CSR activities such as volunteering programmes. Similarly, CSR activities can directly or indirectly affect the attractiveness of a company for potential employees.

4 *Cost savings*: Cost savings have been extensively discussed in sustainability research. For example, Epstein and Roy (2001: 598) argue that efficiency gains could result from a substitution of materials during the implementation of a sustainability strategy, improved contacts to certain stakeholders such as regulators (resulting in time savings), or improved access to capital due to a higher sensitivity of investors to sustainability issues.

5 *CSR-related risk reduction or management*: CSR can also be used as a means to reduce or manage CSR-related risks, such as the avoidance of negative press or customer/NGO boycotts.

9.7 THE SUSTAINABLE GLOBAL VALUE CHAIN (SGVC)

According to Cruz and Boehe (2008) following three factors may explain why the Sustainable Global Value Chain (SGVC) might achieve their objective of being internationally competitive:

1. *Bargaining power*: This topic refers to the type of relationship between suppliers and buyers all along the chain. Previous global value chain research assumed that chains are either buyer- or supplier-driven. Likewise, certification agencies have been considered as marginal players. In SGVCs, however, power relationships may change considerably, because the certification agency is simultaneously influencing several different stages of the chain keeping the entire chain working according to its parameters. Therefore, it is crucial to re-consider the role of the certification agency. By increasing end client demand for sustainable products, the certification agency strengthens the position of end clients vis-à-vis retailers and distributors.

2. *Product differentiation strategy*: In the case of conventional global commodity chains, differentiation strategies are rare, as commodity business is mainly dictated by prices. The dominant firm, often a global buyer, assumes international marketing and branding activities and may shape a possible differentiation strategy (if there is one). CSR-related product and process features a distinctive kind of differentiation. Accordingly, certification plays a key role as long as consumers are familiar with it and deem it trustworthy.

3. *Awareness building*: As mentioned, awareness building should not be confused with supplier development; rather, we are talking about creating a common consciousness, a shared vision regarding sustainability issues in the entire chain. In conventional global commodity chains, it is unlikely that there is any sort of awareness building regarding common goals, ethics or moral standards as the dominant chain player may use his power in an opportunistic fashion to impose his rules. In contrast, SGVCs rely on awareness building regarding sustainability standards all along the chain.

9.8 CSR AND INTERNATIONAL COMPETITIVENESS

Porter and Kramer (2006) advocated that, when a firm's CSR activities improve the competitiveness of the firm, the CSR activity becomes strategic in nature. The reinforcement of competitiveness by CSR initiatives would benefit the whole industry, so firms have to secure and capture the improvement so that the firm benefits. Thus, Porter and Kramer (2006) argue that strategic CSR activities should be so designed that they improve the context of competitiveness of a firm/industry and these benefits have to find a way into the firm's value chain. CSR activities could improve the input factors of production, such as skilled labour or necessary physical infrastructure required to compete. Demand conditions of products and services in a given industry could be influenced by CSR activities by setting higher standards for the quality of products and services in terms of product safety features, environment friendliness and socially responsible performance features. CSR initiatives could also make the local demand conditions more refined and of substantial size (Porter and Kramer, 2006).

When firms undertake such CSR initiatives, they can gain both tangible (physical resources such as raw materials, human resources, increased profits, etc.) and intangible resources (e.g. reputation, brand name, goodwill, know-how) which can be of strategic importance to the firm. If such resources are unique to the firm, valuable to the firm's customers, or are rare, inimitable or imperfectly substitutable, then such resources are strategic resources and can provide the firm with competitive advantage.

In the following we will analyse some specific conditions under which a sustainable global value chain (SGVC) might gain international competitiveness. Here, we use a bottom-line definition of international competitiveness: a global value chain is competitive internationally as long as its products can be sold profitably on export markets. In addition, we define SGVC as: the global value chains in which the products and the production process result from environmental, social and/or economic concerns and practices. Considering the growing number of contributions to sustainable development and CSR literature, we recognise that many different types of SGVC could be identified (related to specific social or environmental issues) with different specificities.

Value added from CSR activities can occur if revenues increase or costs decrease due to the CSR involvement of a company (see Figure 9.3).

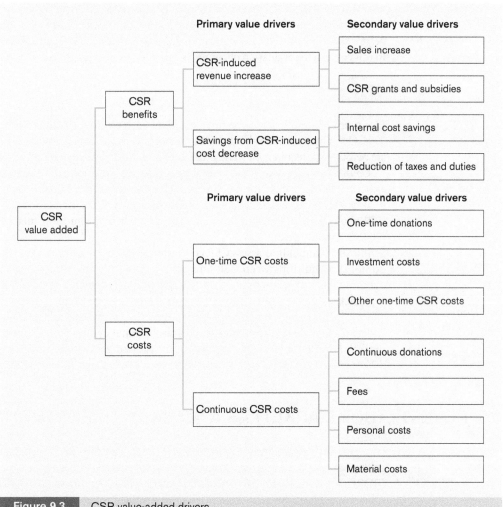

Figure 9.3	CSR value-added drivers

Source: Adapted from Weber, M. (2008) The business case for corporate social responsibility: a company-level measurement approach for CSR, *European Management Journal*, 26: 247–61. Copyright © 2008 Elsevier. Reproduced with permission.

CSR benefits

CSR-induced revenue increases can come from additional sales due to increases in sales quantities, prices or margins. These can be stimulated by cause-related marketing campaigns, CSR-specific product line changes or improved possibilities of winning public tenders (e.g. due to the use of environmentally friendly technologies). CSR-induced revenue increases can also refer to CSR grants and subsidies. Revenue may also increase as a result of:

- better branch value;
- better customer attraction and retention (higher repurchase rates, higher market shares);
- higher employee attraction (more applications per vacancy, better hiring rate);
- higher employee motivation and retention (lower fluctuation rate, lower absenteeism).

Savings from CSR-induced cost decreases can come from internal cost savings due to efficiency improvements or CSR-specific collaborations with, for example, NGOs that provide knowledge or contacts to critical stakeholders such as public authorities, reducing the costs for product or market development. Cost savings can also come from tax concessions or reductions of certain duties granted by governments to promote CSR activities, e.g. tax concessions for environmentally friendly technologies.

When evaluating CSR benefits, managers need to consider carefully the time period in scope. As CSR benefits often occur after a time lag, evaluations should focus on longer time periods. Remember, for some CSR benefits it is difficult to isolate the impact of CSR from other influencing factors. In this context, the evaluation of complementary figures as well as CSR KPIs can be helpful.

CSR costs

One-time CSR costs include one-time donations such as those to support the Tsunami victims in 2004. One-time CSR costs also include investment costs, e.g. for the installation of smoke filters that are beyond legal requirements, and other one-time costs related to the CSR activities in scope.

Continuous CSR costs include donations intended to support a certain cause and fees, such as licence fees to use certain labels or patents, which are paid on a continuous basis. They also include recurring personnel and material costs such as the costs for managers coordinating CSR projects or material costs for the production of promotion materials, e.g. for cause-related marketing campaigns.

It is often difficult to assess CSR costs using conventional cost accounting systems as these do not distinguish between CSR and non-CSR costs. Conventional cost accounting assigns overhead costs to products based on volume indicators, such as production volume.

Society is beset with a multitude of social and environmental problems varying in type and magnitude. Two major problems and, consequently, business market opportunities are widespread: poverty (section 9.9) and environmental degradation (section 9.10) – the 'green' market. Poverty threatens the survival of the present generation, while environmental degradation poses a threat to the healthy existence of present and future generations.

9.9 POVERTY (BOP MARKET) AS A 'MARKET' OPPORTUNITY

Poverty is a widespread reality in the modern world. The poor people's market has been seen as a golden opportunity for reaping business profits and it has been named the 'bottom of the pyramid' (BOP) market (Prahalad, 2004). According to Prahalad (2004), focus on the BOP market should be a part of core business and should not be viewed as just another CSR initiative: by catering to the BOP market (by satisfying unmet social needs and new consumer preferences), business organisations can create market opportunities of substantial value (e.g. the development of microfinance).

According to Prahalad (2004), marketers who believe that the BOP is a valuable unserved market also believe that even the poor can be good customers. Despite their low level of income, they are discerning consumers who want value and are well aware of the value brands favoured by more affluent consumers. This school of thought recognises the obstacle that low income creates. It postulates that if companies take the correct steps and devote sufficient resources to satisfying the needs of the BOP, they can overcome barriers to consumption.

Prahalad recognises that serving the low-income sector requires a commercial strategy in response to the needs of those people; to succeed, other players have to get involved – mainly local and central government, financial institutions and NGOs. He proposes four key elements to success in the low-income market:

1 creating buying power;

2 shaping aspirations through product innovation and consumer education;

3 improving access through better distribution and communication systems;

4 tailoring local solutions.

In the following we will divide the BOP market into two parts:

● the poor as consumers;

● the poor as marketers of products and services.

The poor as consumers

Poverty is a matter of degree and involves subjective judgements. Prahalad (2004) uses the criterion of $2 per day at purchasing power parity (PPP) rates at 1990 prices (equivalent to $3.50 at 2008 prices). At this level of poverty, the basic needs of survival are met, but only just.

Prahalad claims that the BOP potential market is $13 trillion at PPP. According to Karnani (2007) this grossly overestimates the BOP market size. The *average* consumption of poor people is $1.25 per day. Assuming there are 2.7 billion poor people, this implies a BOP market size of $1.2 trillion at PPP in 2002. According to Karnani (2007) this may also be an overestimated figure and he thinks that the global BOP market can be as little as $0.3 trillion compared to the $11 trillion economy in the USA alone.

According to Hammond *et al.* (2007), the BOP population is concentrated in four regional areas: Africa (12.3 per cent), Asia (72.2 per cent), Eastern Europe (6.4 per cent), and Latin America and the Caribbean (9.1 per cent). Rural areas dominate most BOP markets in Africa and Asia while urban areas dominate most in Eastern Europe and Latin America and the Caribbean.

Some researchers have been very critical towards Prahalad's (2004) BOP concept (e.g. Karnani, 2007; Pitta *et al.*, 2008). This group dismiss the published calculations about the size of the BOP and its wealth. They describe the economic size of the BOP as considerably smaller than Prahalad's estimate and cite the inherent subsistence problem: the poor spend 80 per cent of their income on food, clothing and fuel.

The critics of Prahalad also argue that it is very unlikely that companies will be able to attend to the BOP market profitably. In fact, the costs of serving this segment can be very high. BOP customers are usually much dispersed geographically; they are very heterogeneous, which reduces the opportunities for obtaining significant economies of scale; and their individual transactions usually represent a small amount of money. In addition, BOP consumers are very price sensitive, which again makes profitability a difficult goal to achieve.

According to Maslow, there are five core human motives that are satisfied in a hierarchical manner:

1 physiological needs

2 safety and security

3 belonging

4   self-esteem

5   self-actualisation.

According to this theory, unless lower-order needs are satisfied, higher-level ones remain dormant. However, the BOP market consumes more than mere survival needs. Indeed, the highest increase in the last decade has been in the category of communications and technology: a higher-order need (see also Exhibit 9.2). The need to communicate, improve social bonds, and attain greater knowledge and self-esteem are important too. So, while the Maslow framework is

EXHIBIT 9.2
Grameen Telecom

Professor Muhammad Yunus opens the International Telecommunication Union (ITU) Exhibition, 2006
Source: Samantha Sin/AFP/Getty Images

Grameen Telecom's heritage is striking: its roots go back to the Grameen family of enterprises, the brainchildren of Muhammad Yunus, the Chittagong-born economist who won the 2006 Nobel Peace Prize for inventing microfinance – the practice of lending tiny but life-transforming sums to the impoverished.

In 1996, Dr Yunus's Grameen Telecom, a non-profit group dedicated to rolling out a mobile network to Bangladesh's rural hinterland, teamed up with Telenor, the Norwegian group, to found Grameenphone. Today, Telenor owns 62 per cent, Grameen Telecom the remainder.

In some respects, Grameenphone has forged well ahead of its richer Western rivals: up to 4 million of its customers are using their Grameen Telecom mobile to access the Internet and, in a country with only 600,000 Web-connected fixed lines, this makes it the dominant Web provider. Groups such as Vodafone have spent billions on 3G licences in the West in an effort to attain the same status – but to no avail.

For the moment, however, Grameenphone must work at providing ultra-cheap services to a cash-strapped population. Nearly 40 per cent of Bangladeshis live on less than a dollar a day. The company's average revenues per mobile user (known in the industry as Arpu) per month languish at about $3 or $4, a fraction of those in the West.

Source: From Blakely, R. (2008) Grameen Telecom hears the call to take on poverty, *The Times*, 17 November: 410. Reproduced with permission from News International Syndication.

a useful way to categorise basic needs, motivation and priority for BOP's higher-order needs might perhaps be explained by other concepts such as social capital, family systems, cultural differences and compensatory consumption (Subrahmanyan and Gomez-Arias, 2008).

BOP consumers, like all other consumers, also look for goods and services to provide entertainment, sports, cultural and spiritual outlets. Traditional forms of entertainment such as religious festivals and fairs continue to be popular. For example, many poor Indian families spend beyond their means on weddings to save face and to confirm to social norms (Subrahmanyan and Gomez-Arias, 2008). Western firms attempting to reap profits from the BOP using current marketing techniques will probably fail. Failure will result because the products are too expensive or complicated, are not available in small enough quantities or sizes, or are simply not what the poor want. The BOP market is not low-hanging fruit. It is a market with potential, and achieving that potential will require costly effort and innovative strategies.

Entrepreneur
A risk-taking individual who sees an opportunity and is willing to undertake a venture to create a new product or service.

Rather than viewing the poor primarily as consumers, the following suggests a focus on the segment of producers and marketers of products and services, i.e. potential **entrepreneurs** that can improve their economic situation by increasing their income level.

The poor as marketers of products and services

In order for the BOP to develop successful entrepreneurs, there are three critical aspects that should be fulfilled in order to serve the BOP market (Pitta *et al.*, 2008):

- access to credit (microfinance);
- the establishment of alliances;
- adaptation of the marketing mix.

Access to credit (microfinance)

The concept that a poor consumer could gain a small loan and become a producer contributing to family income and independence is tantalising. There is evidence that microloans have succeeded in aiding the bottom of the pyramid. There is also evidence that many of the would-be entrepreneurs failed to capitalise on such credit (Karnani, 2007).

Formal commercial credit has been unavailable to this market and the cost of accessing financial services in the informal financial market is enormous.

The decision to award the 2006 Nobel Peace Prize to Muhammad Yunus and the Grameen Bank in Bangladesh underlined the potential of microfinance in developing countries. Microfinance banks have been set up in most African countries over the past decade but the sheer scale of the Grameen operations is staggering. Providing individuals or very small businesses with access to what are often very small sums of money may seem like a marginal contribution to economic growth but it can widen a nation's economic base and promote the kind of growth that leads to real increases in living standards.

Grameen Bank has now provided credit to over 7 million people, 97 per cent of them women. Most loans are very small and rarely exceed $100. In Bangladesh, the bank usually operates in local temples or village halls. Loans are often used to improve irrigation or to buy new tools to improve efficiency. As part of the Nobel Prize, Yunus was awarded 10 million Swedish kronor ($1.35 million), which will be used to find new ways of helping poor people set up their own businesses.

The establishment of alliances

BOP requires the involvement of multiple players, including private companies, governments, non-governmental organisations (NGOs), financial institutions and other organisations – e.g. communities.

By integrating the profit motive into value creation, the hope is that private companies will take the leading role in serving the BOP and, thus, the purpose of alleviating poverty will more likely succeed.

The public sector also has an important role in developing the BOP proposition. The focus is shifting from delivery of traditional governmental assistance to different ways of creating a sustainable environment for aiding the BOP. For example, the provision of funding and training to entrepreneurs is a way governments can support BOP consumers and producers.

Furthermore, alliances in the healthcare sector are very important. For example, the cost of a ten-day supply of a life-saving antibiotic cannot be reduced realistically by using the 'smaller package size' option. The implication would be either reduced daily doses or fewer full-strength doses. Both are likely to breed drug-resistant organisms and thereby threaten the life of the patient and society. To remedy this situation, other players such as governments and NGOs will be important. Marketers must realise that collaborating with them is important.

Adaptation of the marketing mix

It is no surprise that serving different market segments may require different marketing mixes. Therefore, for-profit firms need to understand how the BOP segment differs from upper tiers, and adapt the marketing approach to meet the characteristics of these consumers.

We use the familiar 4P framework to further examine marketing implications of approaching the BOP segment.

Product

Marketers face the challenge of designing relevant and practical products for the BOP market. Some successful strategies have been in redesigning and adapting existing products (for the top of the pyramid) in terms of features, shape, size and usage. For example, Haier washing machines were redesigned for washing vegetables or making cheese in China after observing how consumers use them.

Another answer to the challenge is to create a bare-bones product with fewer product features that the poor can afford. One example, Nirma detergent made in India, highlights a 'poorer' product that is affordable. A single entrepreneur created Nirma to compete with Hindustan Lever's market-leading detergent Surf. Surf gained market share because it is an excellent product. It has numerous additives that make it effective yet gentle to humans. Its cost was significant. In fact, Nirma does not contain many of the ingredients and safeguards of its rival. It works but can cause blisters on the skin (Ahmad and Mead, 2004). Despite its harshness, the poor embraced it because they could afford it. The implication is that 'research must also seek to adapt foreign solutions to local needs' (Prahalad and Hart, 2002). Low-income consumers prefer products in small sizes, even if the per unit cost is higher, because of their income and space constraints.

Price

BOP is defined on an income basis. So, not surprisingly, price does play a major role in purchase decisions. Not only are disposable incomes low and volatile, but many consumers in BOP receive daily wages and do not have opportunities to save.

Pricing for the bottom of the pyramid is, of course, very critical. In this regard, the concept of *'fair pricing'* is relevant. For example, flexibility in the price negotiation can lead to an increased sense of fairness (Diller, 2008; Maxwell, 2008). The challenge here is twofold. On the one hand, there is the issue of affordability: prices need to be affordable to BOP consumers. On the other hand, flexibility in payments is also very important. Providing options of how and when low-income consumers can pay for their products and services constitutes both a challenge and a source of competitive advantage to private companies. To do this, private companies may need the assistance of commercial banks and NGOs as key partners.

Place

Making products available to BOP consumers is one of the biggest challenges in serving this segment due to poor infrastructure and the fragmented nature of the market. Information and communication technologies have allowed marketers to leapfrog old world methods and enable distribution in certain product categories such as mobile communication, healthcare and banking. Still, the BOP market needs appropriate distribution systems both for its own consumption and for selling what it produces.

Marketers also need to revisit distribution channels in order to attend to the BOP market effectively.

EXHIBIT 9.3
Grameen Danone Foods opens plant in Bangladesh

Source: Sipa Press/Rex Features

Grameen Danone Foods Ltd, a joint venture between four Grameen companies and French Danone, has been set up to provide nutrition-rich yogurts for children in Bangladesh.

The company was officially introduced by French football star Zinedine Zidane at a function in Dhaka, marking the start of production at the company's first plant in Bogra, Bangladesh.

The yogurt, Shakti Doi, is made from full cream milk and contains protein, vitamins, iron, calcium and zinc to fulfil the nutritional needs of children. The initial price has been set with a view to being affordable to low-income groups.

Professor Muhammad Yunus, chairman of the Grameen Group, says: 'This represents a unique initiative in creating a social business enterprise with a declared mission to maximise benefits to the people served.'

Over 1,000 women will sell the products locally, generating additional income for their families. Also, by sourcing raw materials and marketing products locally, business opportunities will be created for local people.

It will also aim to reduce its ecological imprint by selling the yogurt in biodegradable cups and partly powering the plant by biogas and solar power.

The main objective of the company will not be profit maximisation but creating job opportunities for the poor. Indeed, it has been agreed not to take profits from the company.

Source: Adapted from Dairy Industries International (2006) Grameen Danone Foods opens plant in Bangladesh, *Dairy Industries International*, December (www.dairyindustries.com/story.asp?id=2024176)

The idea of closeness in distribution channels for consumers at the bottom of the pyramid is very important. This means, for example, having stores that are both geographically close and affectively close. In other words, emotional proximity is also very important. A good example is Banco Estado, a state-owned commercial bank, which consumers consider the 'closest' to the BOP segment. The reasons are its extensive distribution, its perception of being adaptive to people's needs, its flexibility, and its position as affectively close.

Undoubtedly, the high cost of distribution makes the poor poorer. Today, with escalating global fuel costs adding to the cost of transportation, the poor face an increasingly rigorous future. The lack of infrastructure serving rural areas also increases prices.

One way for firms to reach this fragmented market is to have tie-ups with existing forms of distribution reaching this market, such as postal services. In India, for example, the postal service has a very large reach with 155,000 post offices and several thousand more mobile (as in a van) post offices all over the country (www.indiapost.gov.in/). These post offices have for many decades offered financial services for low-income consumers. Better utilisation of this infrastructure to offer more efficient services with wider reach should be considered.

Promotion

Some of the challenges inherent in communicating with BOP consumers are lower literacy rates, no access to conventional advertising media such as TV, and very diverse markets in terms of culture and language. Billboard and word of mouth are effective forms of promotion for this market. SMART used such methods in the Philippines. Using local methods of entertainment such as street performances has been used by Hindustan Lever to promote soap and toothpaste. Local forms of theatre are commonly used for disseminating healthcare information in developing countries (Mbizwo, 2006). Rural radio could also be a viable way of creating awareness. Combining it with mobile phones can create an interactive form of communication.

9.10 THE 'GREEN' MARKET AS A BUSINESS OPPORTUNITY

Green marketing
Marketing ecologically sound products and promoting activities beneficial to the physical environment.

Despite some attention in the 1970s, it was really only in the late 1980s that the idea of **green marketing** emerged. Early academic treatments of green marketing spoke of the rapid increase in green consumerism at this time as heralding a dramatic and inevitable shift in consumption towards greener products. While the perspective of looking at social problems as business opportunities is a relatively new one, the win–win perspective between environmental initiatives and competitiveness has been a well accepted and popular view for firms for a long time now. Many studies have demonstrated the positive relationship between firm environmental initiatives and business performance (Bhattacharyya *et al.*, 2008; Ginsberg, 2004).

A green strategy for an enterprise – public or private, government or commercial – is one that complements the business, operational and asset strategies that are already well understood and often well articulated by the enterprise. A green strategy fundamentally helps an enterprise make decisions that have a positive impact on the environment. The principles that form the basis of a green strategy should lead an organisation to make decisions based on solid business logic and make good business sense (Gerson, 2007; Jones, 2006).

The growth in market research identifying consumer concern about the environment during the 1990s meant that it was taken for granted in many quarters that 'green would sell' and many firms responded by rapidly adjusting their promotional campaigns. This led to what we refer to as a 'green selling' approach, namely a post-hoc identification of environmental features in existing products, thus prompting a (usually short-term) hop on to the green bandwagon. This reflected a typical sales orientation, since interest in the environment tended to be limited to promotional activity, with little or no input into product development. The same products continued to be produced, but green themes were added to promotional campaigns in order to take advantage of any environmental concerns of consumers (Peattie and Crane, 2005).

Enviropreneur marketing

Another failed approach to green marketing has been enviropreneur marketing, whereby a committed individual, section or company seeks to bring innovative green products to market (Menon and Menon, 1997). Here we have seen the emergence of new green brands in a wide range of markets such as cleaning products, paper goods, cosmetics and food. Boutique enviropreneur marketing involved the marketing of innovative green products from a production orientation. All efforts were focused on producing the most environmentally benign products, rather than the products that consumers actually wanted. Thus, firms ended up with products that were perceived as under-performing, or over-priced, or just too worthy and 'unsexy'. The average consumer would not understand that the reason their green detergents did not get their clothes 'whiter that white' was that they lacked the optical brightener additives that conventional detergents deposit on clothes (which hardly qualifies as 'cleaning' them). Similarly, they would not understand that green washing-up liquids would not produce a big fluffy bowl of soap bubbles because they lacked polluting, cosmetic ingredients. So, the enviropreneur marketers may have meant well, but, while they had the right environmental goals, they were always destined to have problems establishing a significant market presence in the long term because they failed to successfully research, understand or educate their customers (Peattie and Crane, 2005).

Global warming (climate change)

During the past five years, society at large has awakened to the climate issue. Climate change and the environment are higher in the minds of consumers around the world than any other socio-political question. Executives across a broad range of sectors have started to recognise that this mindset is a business reality – whether they believe in the science or not (Lash and Wellington, 2007).

It was not until December 1997 that global warming began to assume a prominent position on business executives' agendas. That is when representatives of 160 nations, convened by the United Nations in Kyoto, Japan, adopted a plan that would limit the amounts of carbon dioxide and other so-called greenhouse gases being released into the atmosphere. If ratified, the Kyoto Protocol would require industrial nations to dramatically reduce emissions of those gases by not later than 2012.

Under the terms of the Protocol, signatory countries must reduce their emissions of GHG (greenhouse gas) by an average 5.2 per cent by 2008–2012 from their 1990 level. Developing countries such as China and India have no constraining obligation with respect to the Protocol. The absence of specific requirements for these developing countries that account for an increasing proportion of global GHG emissions has fuelled opposition to and criticism of the Kyoto Protocol, especially in the US.

During the next three to five years, most companies in energy, transportation and other heavy industries will need to act on climate change in a major way. Sectors that have so far featured less prominently in the debate, such as consumer goods, high tech and financial services, will have to get moving as well.

Although there is great uncertainty about how the shift to a low-carbon CO_2 economy will play out, the value at stake over the next two decades and beyond is going to be enormous. Some companies will be clear winners, others clear losers – in fact, the outcome may be as unambiguous as it was when the Industrial Revolution shifted business from manual labour to energy-intensive factories. To help companies benefit from the coming transition, their managers should carefully begin to reposition them for a low-carbon landscape. Three related developments provide the starting point for this analysis and for any strategic response:

1 There will be efforts to optimise the carbon efficiency of existing assets and products: infrastructure (e.g. buildings, power stations, data centres and factories), supply chains and finished goods (e.g. automobiles, flat-screen TVs, PCs). This optimisation will involve measures to improve energy efficiency, as well as a shift to less carbon-intensive sources of power, such as nuclear, wind, solar and geothermal.

2 Demand is growing for new low-carbon solutions that can meet the need for sustained, drastic emission reductions. Value chains that disrupt existing industries and create new ones will spring up – industries based, for instance, on the large-scale supply of biomass to power plants and on second-generation bio fuels. New business models that reward suppliers and end users in the power and transport sectors for consuming less energy will be as important as new technologies.

3 Public policy and the widespread belief that higher energy prices are here to stay are driven by both of these developments. The coming economy-wide discontinuity may be the first one driven largely by regulation.

Many companies tend to maintain the status quo and not react as long as they are not obliged to do so. This reactive response is more likely to occur in industries in which the renewal cycle for infrastructure and production facilities is slow.

In order to decide where, when and how far an organisation can adopt a proactive strategy, managers should undertake a stepping and progressive approach. This approach in developing and implementing a climate change policy should begin with preliminary measures based on three main actions (Enkvist *et al.*, 2008):

1 Organisations should implement an environmental intelligence programme or service intended to collect information on the main issues and impacts of global warming. Given the potential costs and complexity of such a programme, organisations can share human or financial resources to establish an alliance or an inter-organisational structure. Universities, external experts and consultants can also be involved in this environmental intelligence effort requiring interdisciplinary and team approaches.

2 Organisations should draw up as exact an inventory of their GHG emissions as possible. The inventory is needed to gain a better understanding of the main sources of emissions and to determine more precisely what environmental initiatives should be undertaken first. An inventory also helps to measure environmental performance, which is a requirement if companies are to participate in the GHG trading system. To ensure the credibility and reliability of these measurements, organisations can use the new ISO 14064 standard for GHG accounting and verification. Launched in 2006, this standard was developed by 175 experts from 45 countries to provide a set of reliable and verifiable specifications for quantification, reporting and verification of GHG emission reduction efforts.

3 Organisations should determine what options would be the most efficient in reducing GHG emissions, based on different objectives, regulations and environmental intelligence information. Investments in clean technologies are not the only option. Managers can also buy emission permits on international CO_2 markets or launch reforestation programmes to offset company emissions.

What will it take to utilise business opportunities through 'global warming'?

Making new low-carbon business models and value chains happen is fundamentally about orchestration. The solar-power value chain, for instance, includes competitors from the semiconductor industry, oil and gas, consumer electronics, and utilities. The big winners will have not only distinctive insights and proprietary technologies or capabilities but also the ability to integrate them with skills from a variety of industries to create entire value chains of new low-carbon businesses. Moreover, these winners will bring together public and private stakeholders and shape the regulatory environment so that socially efficient solutions are economically attractive as well. New companies in the electric car segment, for instance, are looking to build consortia that include power companies, high-tech suppliers of car batteries, municipalities and consumers.

9.11 SUMMARY

CSR (corporate social responsibility) goes beyond profit maximisation and includes long-term stakeholder needs and expectations. This also includes a different approach on competitiveness, associated with an ethical and socially responsible dimension.

The most important stakeholders in CSR are owners/shareholders, top management, employees, suppliers, customers, competitors, special interest groups and governmental organisations. CSR can increase the firm's international competiveness (bottom line) in two ways, by influencing CSR benefits or influencing CSR costs:

1 CSR benefits
   - CSR-induced revenue increase
   - savings from CSR-induced cost decrease.

2 CSR costs
   - one-time CSR costs
   - continuous CSR costs.

A CSR perspective may also imply that the company sees new market opportunities, for example:

1 *poverty market*: catering to the 'bottom of the pyramid' (BOP) market, where micro financing of new business in developing countries is one of the new business opportunities

2 *green market*: where e.g. global warming has brought new business opportunities.

The poverty market

The market of the economically marginalized (people earning less than $2 a day residing in developing countries) can throw up new business opportunities and emerging markets. Certain CSR initiatives can start off as micro enterprises or new business and can cater to satisfy certain needs of the society. Advances in information and communication technologies have enabled the BOP market to connect to the global economy. Providing 'marketplace' services and education are crucial services that enable greater sustainability of BOP marketing. Mobilising community efforts, creative pricing methods, innovative product designs and tapping into culturally and locally prevalent ways of communicating are some of the successful marketing strategies for this segment.

To be effective, any collaboration must be proactive. Marketers wishing to serve the BOP must recognise the importance of alliances with others, and should seek out relationships with both government agencies and NGOs. Early and persistent outreach will be valuable in alerting all of the players to each other's strengths and in creating an accurate picture of the challenges.

Given the economies of the BOP, it is likely that if profits come they will come later rather than sooner. Organisations need to choose a long-term involvement in order to avoid disappointment and a financially ruinous mid-term decision to exit.

The green market

Global warming (climate change) will have big implications for energy providers as demand gradually shifts from high- to low-carbon energy. Equipment suppliers using carbon-efficient technologies (such as car engines modified for bio fuels) become increasingly competitive. Most companies, in their role as energy users, will have to follow stricter technical rules and standards, as well as have access to energy-saving technologies. Corporate leaders should consider several ways to benefit from the shift.

CASE STUDY 9.1

YouthAIDS
Social marketing in a private non-profit organisation

As an education and prevention programme of PSI (Population Services International, www.psi.org), YouthAIDS is a social marketing organisation, that uses media, pop culture, music, theatre and sports to stop the spread of HIV/AIDS and reach 600 million young people in more than 60 countries with life-saving messages, products, services and care. The YouthAIDS approach stresses self-empowerment and healthy decision making among youth, including the use of effective health products and services such as HIV counselling and testing. Their approach targets and educates at-risk youth groups through a variety of social marketing activities, including the use of music and television, peer education and community mobilisation.

Some facts about HIV/AIDS

HIV: the human immunodeficiency virus is a retrovirus that attacks the cells of the immune system. HIV is transmitted through an exchange of bodily fluids (e.g. exposure to infected blood, during sexual activity with an infected individual, by sharing needles). It can also pass from an infected mother to her child. HIV is the virus that eventually causes AIDS.

AIDS: an acquired immune deficiency syndrome diagnosis is made when symptoms that indicate the disease (primarily a decrease in the number of immune system cells in a person's bloodstream) are identified by a doctor in an HIV-positive person.

About 33 million people worldwide are living with HIV/AIDS. In 2008, approximately 2.5 million people were infected with HIV. Approximately 2 million people died from AIDS in 2008. In India about 2.4 million people have HIV/AIDS, while in South Africa 5.7 million are infected, 11.8 per cent of the population (US State Department, March 2009). Most victims are infected through heterosexual sex, and women are at particular risk, because they have been raped, because they are sex workers or have multiple partners and/or because they have no power to demand that the men in their lives wear a condom. Women account for an increasing percentage of the HIV/AIDS victims – now they constitute 50 per cent of all HIV/AIDS victims.

- Every minute five people around the world between the ages of 10 and 24 are infected with HIV.
- There are 2 million children under the age of 15 living with the disease worldwide.
- Most children under 15 who have HIV/AIDS are infected through their infected mothers – that is, through mother–child transmission.
- Sexual activity (the main route of disease transmission) starts in adolescence for most people worldwide.
- Poverty, lack of education, lack of medical resources and the commercial sexual exploitation of children also help spread HIV/AIDS among children worldwide.
- Children with HIV/AIDS may be stigmatised and/or rejected by their families and communities. This discrimination fosters ignorance about HIV/AIDS and stigma against testing for and treating the disease. This in turn makes it difficult to prevent the spread of HIV/AIDS.
- Children are orphaned when their parents die from HIV/AIDS.

Background of YouthAIDS

YouthAIDS (www.youthaids.org) was founded in 2001 by Kate Roberts. Before Kate Roberts started up

YouthAIDS she was managing director of British advertising agency '141', which she helped start under the Saatchi & Saatchi umbrella. Mega-events were her strength. She brought all-night rave dance parties to Romania to promote Coca-Cola and other clients. Her focus was youth and how to market to them. With her designer clothes and edgy hairstyles, she developed a reputation as the ultimate party-giver, which she successfully employed in the promotion of cigarettes, soda, electronics and bubble gum to young people.

Her decision in 1997 to compete for an account developing the country's first national HIV/AIDS prevention campaign was part of the fun. Kate Roberts became determined to win it, not so much because it was a great public service but because she thought it would be cool to develop a campaign around condom use and youth.

In 1999 Kate Roberts had one of her rare holidays with her banker boyfriend. They went to South Africa. After some days there of witnessing the destruction of HIV/AIDS and the poverty people suffered, Kate said to herself:

Are these Gucci shoes what life is all about? . . . I have probably sold a billion sticks of cigarettes and encouraged kids to drink pop and eat all that rubbish that I have promoted. I now see kids in Africa with absolutely nothing but disease and death around them.

(Strauss, 2004)

Kate began thinking about what motivated her to get up every morning: fashion, travel, music, her work pitching companies . . . and realised it was a pretty empty and worthless existence.

This was the wake-up moment:

I suddenly realized that I was 30 years old and a third of the way through my life and had nothing to show for it. I wanted to be able to die and say that I had made some sort of difference, even if it was saying that I had saved one life.

(Strauss, 2004)

After she had declared 'I'm going to stop AIDS', she promoted her idea to officials at the Washington-based Population Services International (PSI), which provided her with the seed money and platform of programme to start YouthAIDS.

Roberts was approaching the fight against AIDS by doing what she knew best: selling something by making it trendy. The goal of YouthAIDS is to stop the

YouthAIDS Founder and Director Kate Roberts and PSI Board Member and Global Ambassador Ashley Judd enjoy a night of celebration and meaning at the 2007 annual YouthAIDS Gala: Faces of India.
Source: Courtesy of Darren Santos, 2007

spread of the disease by changing the behaviour of the people most likely to get infected: 15- to 24-year-olds. In today's celebrity-driven world, that requires the use of role models to encourage young men to put on a condom and to empower young women to insist on it.

She moved to Washington in 1999, with a strategy of developing HIV/AIDS funding and awareness as a business, not as a charity seeking a handout. YouthAIDS wants to develop campaigns that are a win–win for both the cause and for the company, foundation or person that donates money.

Since then Kate Roberts has turned YouthAIDS into a global effort, using theatre performances, media, concerts, fashion and sports to reach millions of young people. Justin Timberlake, Destiny's Child, Avril Lavigne, Christina Aguilera and other artists have recorded public service announcements for the group.

Since 2001 YouthAIDS has grown quickly to become a multi-million-dollar programme of PSI. The staff in Washington consists of about 150 employees, and the donated money for YouthAIDS in 2008 was about $10 million.

YouthAIDS ambassadors

The YouthAIDS global ambassador is Ashley Judd, who joined YouthAIDS in 2002. She has also been a PSI board member since 2004. Judd has visited AIDS programmes in slums, brothels, schools, hospices, drop-in centres and clinics in over 12 developing countries. As YouthAIDS global ambassador, Judd was the subject of three award-winning documentaries aired in more than 150 countries worldwide on VH1, the discovery Channel and the National Geographic Channel. In her role, Judd has graced the covers of countless magazines and been the subject of newspaper and television interviews, bringing vital awareness of YouthAIDS to those with potential financial funding and to those who have the power to create political change.

Other YouthAIDS models include Wynonna Judd (recording artist, Grammy Award winner), Seane Corn (yoga instructor), Josh Lucas (one of Hollywood's actor talents), Juanes (twelve-time Latin Grammy Winner), Emmy Rossum (actress and a fashion trend setter),

PSI Board Member and Global Ambassador Ashley Judd visits with two young sisters in India orphaned by AIDS. PSI and its YouthAIDS program provides young girls with the tools and resources necessary to make healthy decisions and lead productive lives.
Source: Courtesy of Marshall Stowell, 2007

Part of the 'Helping Each Other Act Responsibly Together' (HEART) campaign implemented by the Johns Hopkins University Center for Communication Programs in partnership with PSI/Zambia.

Source: Reprinted with the permission of Population Services International. All rights reserved, 2009.

Frederique Van der Wal (fashion model) and Anna Kournikova (professional tennis player and model).

YouthAIDS promotes sexual abstinence among young Africans

Young Africans often initiate sexual activity at an early age. In Zambia, the median age for first-time sex for women aged 25–49 is 16.8 and the median age for marriage is 17.8.

YouthAIDS/PSI and the Johns Hopkins University Center for Communication Programs, with the active participation of Zambian young adults, designed and implemented the HEART mass media campaign (Helping Each other Act Responsibly Together) to promote abstinence and condom use.

Building on research with Zambian girls that revealed they wanted reasons to remain virgins or return to abstinence, HEART sought to make abstinence 'cool' and to provide support for healthy sexual behaviour.

In Cameroon the campaign is being implemented in collaboration with government ministries, church and youth groups, volunteer agencies, United Nations agencies and legal advisers.

Through '100% Jeune', an adolescent reproductive health campaign, YouthAIDS/PSI encourages abstinence, fidelity, a reduction in sexual partners and correct and consistent condom use among 15- to 24-year-old youth. The key objectives are to break the silence, raise public awareness of the dangers involved and change societal views.

One of the main messages is 'No to Sugar Daddies, No to AIDS'. The phrase highlights the dangers of sugar daddy relationships and the society's complicity in this practice. The term 'sugar daddy' refers to a non-marital sexual relationship between partners with at least a ten-year age difference. Extreme poverty is one of the reasons young women become involved in these relationships: they are often financially supported in return for a sexual relationship and most of the older men seek status and prestige among their peers by having one or more younger girlfriends.

Strategic partnerships play a crucial role in YouthAIDS' success worldwide

The type and scope of strategic partnerships vary greatly – public and private, national and international – and the possibilities are almost endless.

Since 2001, PSI's YouthAIDS programme initiative has forged strategic partnerships with corporations and the media. YouthAIDS raises funds and awareness through the development of cause-related marketing campaigns, fundraising initiatives such as 'Kick Me!' and event sponsorships such as the annual YouthAIDS Gala.

The grass-roots, student-led campaign 'Kick Me!' (to increase awareness of HIV/AIDS among youth in the US) aims to reduce infection-related stigma and open a constructive dialogue among young people. The 'Kick Me!' campaign is based on the old prank of someone sticking a 'Kick Me' sign on another's back without their knowledge – just like 90 per cent of those infected with HIV/AIDS may not know they are carrying HIV.

The benefits of these strategic partnerships include:

- access to target demographics such as youth aged 15–24;
- celebrity endorsements;
- improved brand recognition and image.

YouthAIDS has developed successful cause-related marketing campaigns with corporations including Virgin Mobile, Roberto Coin, Cartier, Kiehl's, Levi's, H&M and Anthropologie.

YouthAIDS A non-profit organisation operating in more than 60 countries to stop the spread of HIV/AIDS	Provide awareness for Aldo Shoes by making the campaign/tag trendy among celebrities → ← US$3.5 million for the sale of nearly 1 million tags in Aldo stores	**Aldo Shoes** Canadian-owned shoe retail chain with 1,000 stores operating in 37 countries around the world

Figure 9.4   The 'Hear no evil' win–win YouthAIDS–Aldo marketing campaign
Source: Adapted from different public sources.

The YouthAIDS and Aldo Shoes partnership – a win–win alliance

In 2006, YouthAIDS achieved success with fashion footwear and accessories retailer Aldo Shoes through its second iteration of the 'Hear no evil, see no evil, speak no evil' global cause marketing campaign. Following the successful 2005 launch, this variation featured more than 20 celebrities in a series of black-and-white images that portrayed the celebrities and 'Empowerment Tags' in unexpected ways.

Empowerment Tags were sold at Aldo stores and on-line with the proceeds benefiting YouthAIDS programme. The result: more than $3,500,000 raised (up to April 2009) and nearly 2 billion editorial impressions since 2005.

Aldo's New York City ad agency, Kraft-Works, came up with the 'Hear no evil' theme and, in conjunction with that and a somewhat militant tone, metal tags were designed with the words 'See', 'Hear' or 'Speak'. Dubbed empowerment tags, to resonate with the activism that was obvious in youth marketing surveys, the tags sold for $4 each at Aldo stores and online for $5 each, with the entire net profit – about $4 per tag – going to YouthAIDS. YouthAIDS then leaned on its Hollywood and music industry connections to recruit celebrities who would resonate with young consumers in key markets. In all, eight megastars – including hip-hop artist LL Cool J and actress Salma Hayek – posed for photo shoots in Los Angeles and New York City. An additional 21 celebrities were featured in the spring 2006 campaign. A stand-alone website sold the tags, provided AIDS information, and triggered viral marketing for the cause and the company. People who went on to the site

(www.youthaids-aldo.org/) could e-mail campaign materials to others, and post campaign banners on personal websites with links back to the YouthAIDS–Aldo site.

For Aldo Shoes, the campaign launched for its fall 2005 fashion season could have been seen as risky. It did not show any of the new footwear styles in more than 1,000 Aldo stores around the world. Instead, ads showed black-and-white photographs of singer Christina Aguilera, model Cindy Crawford and other celebrities with tape over their mouths – to make the point that ignoring AIDS will elevate the pandemic into a global disaster. Since its 2005 launch, the company's high-profile 'Hear no evil, see no evil, speak no evil' campaign, about the dangers of keeping silent about AIDS, has raised some $3.5 million for Aldo's non-profit education partner, YouthAIDS, and has boosted Aldo shoe sales among many of the young consumers the shoe company has sought to reach. Close to 1 million 'Empowerment Tags' – 'dog' tags urging people to speak up about the virus – have been sold by Aldo, elevating YouthAIDS and Aldo's profile; many hundreds of thousands, if not millions, of people have seen the ads urging people to get tested for the virus.

As far as cause marketing campaigns go, the Aldo–YouthAIDS initiative did precisely what it was supposed to accomplish: it increased brand visibility, generated millions of dollars of free advertising for Aldo and boosted sales. 'Foot traffic' in Aldo stores increased by double digits, and same-store sales increased by 6.1 per cent, far more than the industry average. And Aldo sales remained strong for a long period. The boost is sustainable.

But is success sustainable? Aldo says that people have sent thousands of e-mails saying the 'See no evil' campaign has personally helped them to deal with the stigma of AIDS. Sales remain strong. The campaign has also helped Aldo attract attention from new potential employees; people have applied for jobs at Aldo who might not have otherwise.

For the new 2009 campaign the website (www. youthaids-aldo.org/) is now offering a bracelet (the AFA Cuff), where the principle is the same: 100 per cent of all net proceeds from the sale of each bracelet will help fund YouthAIDS programmes, worldwide. The price for the bracelet is US$5 and US$4 goes to the YouthAIDS programmes.

Other YouthAIDS activities

To further raise awareness among consumers and at-risk youth, YouthAIDS produces films, secures media interviews and places stories. In March 2007, YouthAIDS produced its third documentary in partnership with the National Geographic Channel.

The film followed Ashley Judd and Bollywood stars Sushmita Sen, Akshay Kumar and Shah Rukh Khan as they visited PSI programmes in India. The documentary was aired internationally on World AIDS Day 2007 on the National Geographic Channel.

QUESTIONS

1 What have been the key competences of YouthAIDS since it started in 2001?

2 How are these competences utilised in YouthAIDS' alliances?

3 What do you think about the YouthAIDS campaigns in Africa, including the message about sexual abstinence? Is that going to be successful? Discuss the pros and cons.

4 Which future alliance partners would it be relevant for YouthAIDS to cooperate with?

SOURCES

Aldo Fights AIDS (www.youthaids-aldo.org); Aldo Shoes (www. aldoshoes.com); Population Services International (PSI) Annual Reports 2007 and 2008; Sharn, L. (2009) Walking the talk: using emotion to make strides with young consumers, *Contribute* (www.contributemedia.com/trends_details.php?id=103); Strauss, V. (2004) A consuming cause: master marketer Kate Roberts, sold on the need for AIDS education, *Washington Post*, 7 September, C01 (style section); YouthAIDS (www.youthaids.org).

QUESTIONS FOR DISCUSSION

1 What role do you think cultural differences play in ethical standards?

2 List the most important ethical issues to consider in preparing a marketing strategy.

3 What aspects of ethical behaviour are important to consider in building marketing relationships?

REFERENCES

Bhattacharyya, S. S., Sahay, A., Arora, A. P. and Chaturvedi, A. (2008) A toolkit for designing firm level strategic corporate social responsibility (CSR) initiatives, *Social Responsibility Journal*, 4(3): 265–82.

Blakely, R. (2008) Grameen Telecom hears the call to take on poverty, *The Times*, 17 November, 41.

Boiral. O. (2006) Global warming: should companies adopt a proactive strategy, *Long Range Planning*, 39: 315–30.

Brett, G. (2007) CSR best practices, *China Business Review*, 35(3): 20–5.

Brugmann, J. and Prahalad, C. K. (2007) Co-creating business's new social compact, *Harvard Business Review*, 85(2): 80–90.

Carroll, A. B. (1991) The pyramid of corporate social responsibility: towards the moral management of organisational shareholders, *Business Horizons*, 34(4).

Czarnowski, A. (2009) Ethics still strong in a cold climate, *Brand Strategy*, February: 52–3.

Cruz, L. B. and Boehe, D. M. (2008) CSR in the global market place – towards sustainable global value chains, *Management Decision*, 46(8): 1182–209.

Dairy Industries International (2006) Grameen Danone Foods opens plant in Bangladesh, *Dairy Industries International*, December (www.dairyindustries.com/story.asp?id=2024176).

Diller, H. (2008) Price fairness, *Journal of Product & Brand Management*, 17(5): 353–5.

Domegan, C. T. (2008) Social marketing: implications for contemporary marketing practices classification scheme, *Journal of Business & Industrial Marketing*, 23(2): 135–41.

Enkvist, P. E., Navclér, T. and Oppenheim, J. (2008) Business strategies for climate change, *McKinsey Quarterly*, Issue 21.

Ginsberg, J. M. and Bloom, P. N. (2004) Choosing the right green marketing strategy, *MIT Sloan Management Review*, 46(1): 79–84.

Greenberg, J. and Baron, R. A. (2008) *Behavior in Organizations*, Pearson Prentice Hall, Upper Saddle River, NJ.

Hammond, A.L., Krammer, W. J., Katz, R. S., Tran, J. T. and Walker, C. (2007) *The Next 4 Billion Market Size and Business Strategy at the Base of the Pyramid*, World Resource Institute, International Finance Corporation.

Hollensen, S. (2007) *Global Marketing*, 4th edn, Pearson, Harlow, UK.

Jones, H. (2006) Nike: not just doing it for themselves, *Brand Strategy*, September: 48–9.

Karnani, A. (2007) The mirage of marketing to the bottom of the pyramid: how the private sector can help alleviate poverty, *California Management Review*, 49(4) (Summer): 90–111.

Lash, J. and Wellington, F. (2007) Competitive advantage on a warming planet, *Harvard Business Review*, March: 95–102.

Maignan, I. and Ferrell, O. C. (2004) Corporate social responsibility and marketing: an integrative framework, *Journal of the Academy of Marketing Science*, 32(1) (Winter): 3–19.

Maxwell, S. (2008) Fair price: research outside marketing, *Journal of Product & Brand Management*, 17(7): 497–503.

Peattie, K. and Crane, A. (2005) Green marketing: legend, myth, farce or prophesy? *Qualitative Market Research: An International Journal*, 8(4): 357–70.

Peter, J. P. and Donelly, Jr, J. H. (1994) *A Preface to Marketing Management*, 6th edition, Richard D. Irwin, Burr Ridge, IL.

Pitta, D. A., Guesalaga, R. and Marshall, P. (2008) The quest for the fortune and the bottom of the pyramid: potential and challenges, *Journal of Consumer Marketing*, 25(7): 393–401.

Porter, M. E. and Kramer, M. R. (2006) Strategy and society: the link between competitive advantage and corporated social responsibility, *Harvard Business Review*, 84(12): 56–68.

Prahalad, C. K. (2004) *The Fortune at the Bottom of the Pyramid: Eradicating Poverty through Profits*, Pearson Education, Delhi.

Pride, W. M. and Ferrell, O. C. (1994) *Marketing: Concepts and Strategies*, 10th edition, Houghton Mifflin, Boston, MA.

Rigby, D. and Tager, S. (2008) Learning the advantages of sustainable growth, *Strategy & Leadership*, 36(4): 24–8.

Roberts, J. (2008) Once more with feeling, *Brand Strategy*, April: 25–9.

Robinson, D. A. and Harvey, M. (2008) Global leadership in a culturally diverse world, *Management Decision*, 46(3): 466–80.

Sabrahmanyan, S. and Gomez-Arias (2008) Integrated approach to understand consumer behaviour at the bottom of the pyramid, *Journal of Consumer Marketing*, 25(7): 402–12.

Sharn, L. (2009) Walking the talk, *Contribute Media* (www.contributemedia.com/trends_details .php?id=103).

Strategic Direction (2009) Is CSR the kind face of capitalism? *Strategic Direction*, 25(1): 10–12.

Szmigin, I., Carrigan, M. and O'Loughlin, D. (2007) Integrating ethical brands into our consumption lives, *Brand Management*, 14(5): 396–409.

Weber, M. (2008) The business case for corporate social responsibility: a company-level measurement approach for CSR, *European Management Journal*, 26: 247–61.

Yip, G. S., Biscarri, J. G. and Monti, J. A. (2000) The role of the internationalization process in the performance of newly internationalizing firms, *Journal of International Marketing*, 8(3): 10–35.

PART IV

Developing marketing programmes

CASE STUDIES

Functional plans (e.g. production, R&D, financial, HR) are designed to transform the strategic plans of the corporate and divisional levels into tactical actions that govern the day-to-day operations of the various functional departments within each business unit. It is at this functional level of planning that each organisation finds out the degree to which the desired outcomes expressed in the mission statement and marketing goals can be realised and applied in practical terms.

In the typical organisation, each business function has a potential impact on customer satisfaction. Under the marketing concept, all departments should try to think of the customer and work together to satisfy customer needs and expectations.

This part will first explain the framework for executing the marketing mix, i.e. how to establish, develop and manage buyer–seller relationships (Chapter 10). This chapter will form the basis for the execution of the 4Ps of the marketing mix (Chapters 11–14). The diagram below shows the structure of Part IV. Chapter 10 tries to combine the

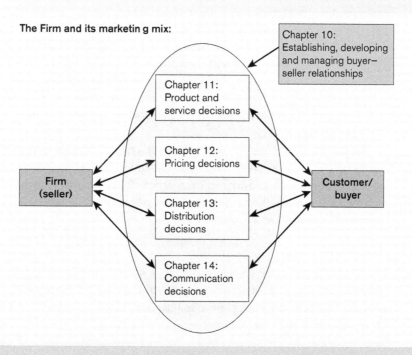

The structure of Part IV

more short-term marketing mix with the more holistic approach of establishing and retaining long-term relationships with customers.

Increasingly, goods and services will be treated as a way of creating value together with individual customers, and the customer's role in production will be more important. That is the reason why Chapter 10 is included as an attempt to expand the traditional '4P' thinking.

The original 4P marketing mix was primarily derived from research on manufacturing (B2C) companies, where the essence of the marketing mix concept is the idea of a set of controllable variables or a 'tool kit' (the 4Ps) at the disposal of marketing management which can be used to influence customers. However, especially in B2B marketing, the marketing mix is also influenced by the interaction process itself between buyer and seller, so that the influence process is negotiation and not persuasion as implied by the traditional 4P mix. Furthermore there has been concern that the classic 4Ps do not incorporate the characteristics of services – namely inherent intangibility, perishability, heterogeneity (variability), inseparability and ownership.

The extended marketing mix

The most influential of the alternative frameworks is, however, Booms and Bitner's (1981) 7P mix where they suggest that the traditional 4Ps need to be extended to include an additional three Ps: participants, physical evidence and process. Their framework is discussed below.

Participants

Any person coming into contact with customers can have an impact on overall satisfaction. Participants are all human actors who play a part in service delivery, namely the firm's personnel and customers. Because of the simultaneity of production and consumption, the firm's personnel occupy a key position in influencing customer perceptions of product quality. That is especially the case in 'high-contact' services, such as restaurants, airlines and professional consulting services. In fact, the firm employees are part of the product and hence product quality is inseparable from the quality of the service provider. It is important, therefore, to pay particular attention to the quality of employees and to monitor their performance. This is especially important in services because employees tend to be variable in their performance, which can lead to variable quality.

The participants' concept also includes the customer who buys the service and other customers in the service environment. Marketing managers therefore need to manage not only the service provider–customer interface but also the actions of other customers. For example, the number, type and behaviour of people will partly determine the enjoyment of a meal at a restaurant.

Process

This is the process involved in providing a service to the customers. It is procedures, mechanisms and flow of activities by which the service is acquired and delivered. The process of obtaining a meal at a self-service, fast-food outlet such as McDonald's is clearly different from that at a full-service restaurant. Furthermore, in a service situation customers are likely to have to queue before they can be served and the service delivery itself is likely to take a certain length of time. Marketers have to ensure that customers understand the process of acquiring a service and that the queuing and delivery times are acceptable to customers.

Physical evidence

Unlike a product, a service cannot be experienced before it is delivered, which makes it intangible. This therefore means that potential customers perceive greater risk when deciding whether or not to use a service. To reduce the feeling of risk, thus improving success, it is often vital to offer customers some tangible clues to assess the quality of the service provided. This is done by providing physical evidence, such as case studies or testimonials. The physical environment itself (i.e. the buildings, furnishings, layout, etc.) is instrumental in customers' assessment of the quality and level of service they can expect, for example in restaurants, hotels, retailing and many other services. In fact, the physical environment is part of the product itself.

It can be argued that there is no need to amend or extend the 4Ps, as the extensions suggested by Booms and Bitner can be incorporated into the existing framework. The argument is that consumers experience a bundle of satisfactions and dissatisfactions that derive from all dimensions of the product whether tangible or intangible. The process can be incorporated in the distribution. Buttle (1989), for example, argues that the product and/or promotion elements may incorporate participants (in the Booms and Bitner framework) and that physical evidence and processes may be thought of as being part of the product. In fact, Booms and Bitner (1981) themselves argue that product decisions should involve the three extended elements in their proposed mix.

Therefore Part IV of this text still uses the structure of the 4Ps, but at the same time the three extended Ps will be incorporated in Chapter 10 and the other chapters.

The Ministry of Tourism (Indian Tourist Board) is the govermental agency for the development and promotion of tourism in India. It has the following aims:

- formulating national policies and programmes;
- co-coordinating and supplementing the efforts and activities of various central government agencies, state/union territories governments;
- catalysing private investments;
- strengthening promotional and marketing efforts;
- providing trained manpower resources;

- developing infrastructure;
- conducting research and analysis.

The Indian Tourist Board provides executive directions for the implementation of various policies and programmes. It has a network of 20 offices within the country and 13 offices abroad. The overseas offices are primarily responsible for tourism promotion and marketing in their respective areas and the field offices in India are responsible for providing information services to tourists and monitoring the progress of field projects.

Incredible India website
Source: Courtesy of Ministry of Tourism

The Indian tourist industry (2007)

Number of Indian nationals going abroad (outbound)	9.78 million
Number of foreign tourist arrivals (FTAs) in India (inbound)	5.08 million
Number of foreign tourist arrivals for all countries in the world	903.00 million
India's share of world tourist arrivals	0.56%
India's ranking in world tourist arrivals	42nd

Competitors ranking	2007 (% of 903 million FTAs)
1 France	9.07
2 Spain	6.56
3 USA	6.20
4 China	6.06
5 Italy	4.84
6 UK	3.40
7 Germany	2.70
8 Ukraine	2.56
9 Turkey	2.46
10 Mexico	2.37
. . .	. . .
42 India	0.56

Source: Ministry of Tourism, India (www.incredibleindia.org).

The Indian tourist industry and international competition

See Table PIV.1 for data regarding the Indian tourist industry. Even though India is quite low in the ranking, the number of FTAs in India has doubled over the last 10 years. The most FTAs in India come from the UK and the USA. These two countries represent 30 per cent of FTAs in India.

Please watch the video before answering the questions.

QUESTIONS

1 What are the brand values of India?

2 How is the marketing of a country (e.g. India) different from the marketing of physical products or services, such as a hotel stay?

3 Which parts of the marketing mix would you primarily use in the marketing and promotion of India?

SOURCE

Ministry of Tourism India (www.incredibleindia.org).

CHAPTER 10
Establishing, developing and managing buyer–seller relationships

LEARNING OBJECTIVES

After studying this chapter you should be able to:

- understand the stages in the development of a dyadic buyer–seller relationship (acts, episodes, sequences and relationships)
- explain the importance of loyalty
- identify the different categories (segments) of loyalty
- describe the steps in building a loyalty-based, relationship-based strategy
- explain how to create e-loyalty
- understand the importance of customer lifetime value and how it is calculated
- develop ideas for creating customer loyalty programmes
- describe the stages in the KAM relationship development model
- explain the purpose of a customer complaint management system

10.1 INTRODUCTION

Relationships in marketing encompass a range of exchange phenomena, from relationships between firms (B2B relationships) to relationships between firms and individual consumers.

Managing relationships with customers, suppliers and competitors is now an integral part of a firm's strategic marketing agenda (Pass and Kuijlen, 2001; Thakur *et al.*, 2006). This criticality is reflected in the growth in the importance of relationships in the academic literature. Subject areas such as RM, networks, alliances, partnering and key account management encompass a growing set of theories and normative approaches to managing relationships. This chapter will concentrate on the relationship between the buyer (customer) and the seller (supplier).

Managing buyer–supplier relationships involves a consideration of a multiplicity of different relationship types. Webster (1992) conceived these types as representing a continuum from a price-based transaction to close interactive relationships. Whether relationship types can be thought of as a continuum, or as radically different approaches, is a matter for debate. However, the close and distant opposites are two types that can readily be understood and managed. Jackson (1985) examined the difference between close (lost-for-good) and transaction (always-a-share) accounts and developed a framework for managing this difference (Figure 6.9).

Marketing executives need a more advanced tool for examining loyalty, and creating enthusiastic customers who come back to buy their product again and again – and are happy about doing it. It is about turning customers into advocates (Blasberg *et al.*, 2008).

10.2 BUILDING BUYER–SELLER RELATIONSHIPS IN B2B MARKETS

Why build a relationship in the first place? Relationships enhance value in several ways. The pooling of partners' knowledge may improve market vision. Combining the partners' unique competences and matching them to the most promising value opportunities may enhance customer value (Xevelonakis, 2008; Jackson, 2007; Bhalla, 2004).

In most business-to-business situations, especially where the benefits exceed the risks, it is desirable for both the seller and the customer to maintain a long-term relationship. A relationship is warranted in a situation where there is congruence between goals of the the seller and the customer, meaning where the organisation and the customer realise that the potential gains from acting cooperatively will exceed the gains from acting opportunistically. From a strategic perspective, the seller wants to maintain a long-term relationship with a customer because it is generally much cheaper to keep an existing customer than to attract a new customer; a long-term customer can provide feedback on existing products and insights into new or re-engineered products; and a long-term customer almost becomes part of the selling team because it can provide recommendations and encourage new business. Also, as time passes and experience steps in, a long-term customer becomes easy to work with because communication channels will usually open and expand, the customer's needs and problems are known, and a comfortable working, and sometimes personal, relationship exists between personnel in both firms.

Before any vendor can develop a relationship with another company, the selling organisation must focus internally. The selling organisation must determine its marketing goals and strategy, analyse its current culture, ensure that the strategy and culture match, and, if necessary, activate a customer service-oriented culture.

There seem to be different phases in the development of a customer relationship, as illustrated in Figure 10.1.

Many salespeople waste a great deal of time cold-calling or trying to breathe life into old customer leads. That is because they cannot see clearly into prospective firms to know when the companies are getting ready to buy. The right screening process of finding new qualified opportunities and proposals can make the process of finding a new customer much easier (left side of Figure 10.1). A salesperson's network for finding new leads in the marketplace can be made up of contacts who know different people. In that way, each direct contact in the network can connect the salesperson to other contacts, creating a wider network (Üstüner and Godes, 2006; Rese, 2006; Mouzas *et al.*, 2008). Once the salesperson has identified a new customer, and this customer has actually bought something, the new challenge is to turn is this customer into a loyal customer by cross-selling and up-selling.

Cross-selling is defined as selling an additional product or service to an existing customer. In practice businesses define cross-selling in many different ways. Elements that might influence

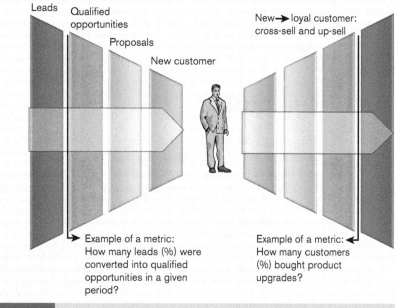

Figure 10.1 | CRM structure: gain and retain

the definition might include: the size of the business, the industry sector it operates within and the financial motivations of those required to define the term. The objectives of cross-selling can be either to increase the income derived from the client(s) or to protect the relationship with the client(s). The approach to the process of cross-selling can be varied. Unlike the acquiring of new business, cross-selling involves an element of risk that existing relationships with the client could be disrupted. For this reason it is important to ensure that the additional product or service being sold to the client(s) enhances the value the client(s) get from the organisation.

There are three forms of cross-selling:

1 *Additional needs*: the seller of product or service provider may hear of an additional need, unrelated to the first, that the customer has and offer to meet it. For example, in conducting an audit, an accountant is likely to learn about a range of needs for tax services, for valuation services and others. To the degree that regulations allow, the accounts may be able to sell services that meet these needs. This kind of cross-selling helped major accounting firms to expand their businesses considerably.

2 *Add-on services*: this is another form of cross-selling. This happens when a supplier shows a customer that it can enhance the value of its service by buying another product or service from a different part of the supplier's company. When you buy a product, the salesperson will offer to sell you insurance beyond the terms of the warranty. Though common, this kind of cross-selling can leave a customer feeling strange. The customer might well ask the salesperson why he needs insurance on a new product. Is it really likely to break in just 12 months?

3 *Solution selling*: in this case, the customer buying air conditioners is sold a package of both the air conditioners and installation services. The customer can be considered buying relief from the heat, contrary to just air conditioners.

Up-selling
A sales technique whereby a salesperson attempts to have the customer purchase more expensive items, upgrades or other add-ons in an attempt to make a more profitable sale.

Up-selling is a sales technique whereby a salesperson attempts to have the customer purchase more expensive items, upgrades or other add-ons in an attempt to make a more profitable sale. Up-selling usually involves marketing more profitable services or products, but up-selling can also be simply exposing the customer to other options he or she may not have considered previously.

As indicated here, in practice there is often an overlap between the two concepts of cross-selling and upselling.

10.3 RELATIONSHIP QUALITY

In any commercial relationship between two parties, interaction is the key concept. Interactions are the basic phenomena in quality and value creation. The perception of relationship quality occurs in ongoing interactions, which may be either continuous, such as in security and cleaning services, or discrete, such as in bank services or goods transportation. Holmlund (2000) has developed a framework for understanding and analysing ongoing interactions. These interactions may be very different depending on the type of marketing situation involved. Some contacts are between people, some between customers and machines and systems, and some between systems of the supplier and customer respectively. In every case interactions are involved. The framework is equally valid for describing and analysing relationships in consumer markets and relationships between organisations. Originally, the framework was developed for services, but it may also be used for suppliers of physical goods, but with some services involved.

The framework consists of a continuous flow of acts, episodes and sequences, which form the relationships. Figure 10.2 illustrates this relationship framework.

An act (A) is the smallest unit of analysis in the interaction process. Examples of acts include phone calls, plant visits, service calls and hotel registration. In service management literature they are often called *moments of truth*. Acts may be related to any kind of interaction elements, physical goods, services, information, financial aspects or social contacts.

Interrelated acts form a minor part of a relationship. These are called episodes (or service encounters, to use a concept frequently found in the service management literature) and examples of these include paying bills from a home computer, visiting a bank to withdraw money, a negotiation, a shipment of goods or dinner at a hotel restaurant during a stay at that hotel. Every episode includes a series of acts. For example, a shipment may include such acts as placing an order, assembling and packing the products, transporting the products, making a complaint and payment.

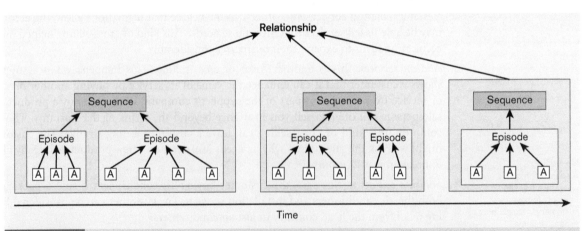

| Figure 10.2 | Interaction levels in a relationship: acts, episodes and sequences |

Source: Adapted from Holmlund, M. (2000) Perceived Quality in Business Relationships, Hanken, School of Economics, Helsinki/Helsingfros, Finland, CERS, p. 96. Reproduced with permission from Maria Holmlund–Rytkonen.

Interrelated episodes form the next level of analysis in the interaction process, a sequence. Sequences can be defined in terms of a time period, a product introduction, a campaign or a project, or a combination of these. The analysis of a sequence may contain all kind of interactions related to a particular project, which may take up to a year or even longer. As an example, in a hotel context a sequence comprises everything that takes place during one stay at a particular hotel, including episodes such as accommodation, eating in the hotel restaurant, etc. Sequences may naturally overlap, so that episodes belonging to one sequence may also be part of another sequence.

The final and most aggregated level of analysis is the relationship. Several sequences form a relationship. Sequences may follow each other directly, may overlap or may follow after longer or shorter intervals depending, for example, on the type of business or on whether the service is of a continuous or discrete nature. This way of dividing the interaction process into several layers on different levels of aggregation gives the marketer a detailed enough instrument to be used in the analysis of interactions between a supplier or service provider and the customers.

All different types of element in the interaction process – goods and service outcomes, service processes, information, social contacts, financial activities, etc. – can be identified and put into their correct perspective in the formation of a relationship over time.

The relationship between a customer and a salesperson is like a marriage. It starts with a courtship period, when both parties begin to know each other. Next a ceremony, or contract to do business, binds both parties to certain terms. The relationship is then maintained by developing high levels of trust and service norms that guide future interactions. If the relationship becomes unsatisfactory for either party, they divorce.

Developing strong relationships with customers gives a salesperson a sustainable competitive advantage in the marketplace. If a customer feels a certain level of commitment to the relationship, which has been fostered by the salesperson's attention to detail and willingness to do that bit extra in after-sales service, then, when a problem does occur, the customer will not immediately seek another supplier. Even though the marketplace may have many attractive potential partners, the customer will be loyal to a salesperson who has shown commitment and dedication over the long term.

To develop a long-term relationship, it is important for the salesperson to first understand the customer's needs and then to adapt selling techniques to those needs. However, the relationship has to be sustained, and it is sustained through attention to service, such as promptly returning calls, making special deliveries quickly and personally, seeking out answers to technical questions, and working with the customer to design the next generation of products and services.

10.4 BUILDING BUYER–SELLER RELATIONSHIPS IN B2C MARKETS

Firms that practise customer focus shift the power from the seller to the customer. Once the basic principle of shifting the power to customers is accepted, Internet technology makes it more achievable.

Customer focus promises to provide something that traditional strategies never could – increasing return. The value an organisation derives from products diminishes over time, but the value of locking customers in can increase (Vandermerwe, 2000).

When a customer is locked in, it has no choice. There may be only one supplier with a monopoly for as long as its particular technology wave lasts. Or customers may have invested in one product and then find that the switching costs are too high. The customers are locked in a continuous relationship life cycle until an alternative comes along.

In Figure 10.3 a customer relationship life cycle of an airline transportation service is shown.

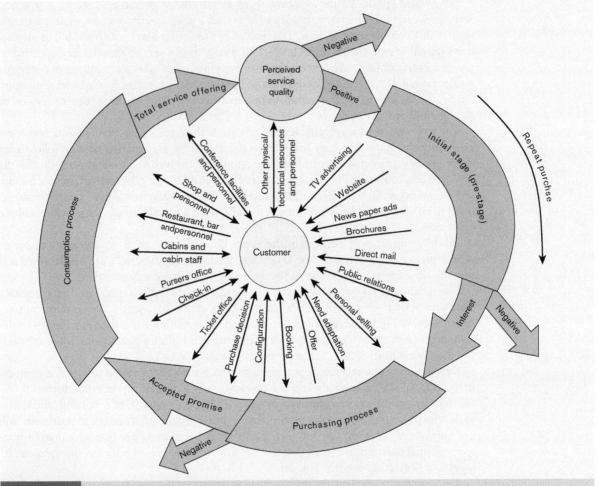

Figure 10.3	The customer relationship life cycle in the airline business

Source: Grönroos, C. (1983) *Strategic Marketing and Marketing in the Service Sector*, Marketing Science Institute, Cambridge, MA, p. 75. Reproduced with permission.

Market space
A virtual marketplace such as the Internet in which no direct contact occurs between buyers and sellers.

Vandermerwe (2000) has expanded the product or service space into a **market space**, which is an aggregation of all the customer-activity cycles in a particular segment. For example, in the air travel industry, the pre, during, and post phases of a customer-activity cycle might include: first deciding where to go and how, booking flights and getting to the airport; second, taking the trip, getting to and experiencing the destination; and, finally, leaving the destination, finding transport, coming home and paying the bills. Customer-activity cycle methodology can help managers assess opportunities for providing new kinds of value to customers at each critical experience.

Any interruption in the flow of the customer-activity cycle creates value gaps, or discontinuities, that open access to competitors, unless the company fills the gaps first with added value services.

In air travel, the British airline Virgin Atlantic challenged the diminishing returns, capacity-managing thinking of conventional airlines by merging travel and leisure into one integrated customer experience (see Figure 10.4).

Virgin Atlantic has succeeded in turning a value added service into a strong competitive element. Virgin is always exploring new ways of increasing passenger comfort and offers superior service and quality. The price of an upper-class ticket (comparable to business class on other airlines) includes a luxury limousine service that picks up passengers from their

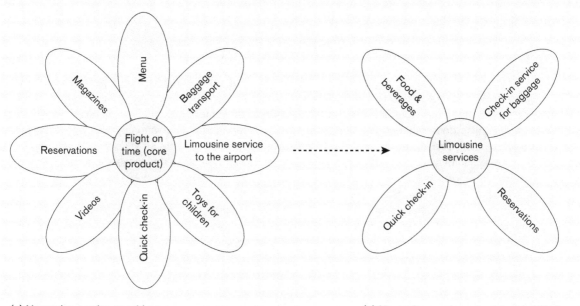

(a) Limousine service as add-on

(b) Limousine service as core product that encompasses different value added services

Figure 10.4	Virgin Atlantic's add-on service
	Source: Hennig-Thurau, T. and Hansen, U. (2000) *Relationship Marketing: Gaining Competitive Advantage Through Customer Satisfaction and Consumer Retention*, Springer Verlag, Berlin-Heidelberg, p. 121. Reproduced with permission from T. Hennig-Thurau and U. Hansen.

home, an on-board entertainment centre with a selection of videos, comfortable reclining seats, and masseurs who help passengers to relax on even the longest flights.

Other services are also incorporated, such as help with baggage at the check-in counter.

Virgin Atlantic creates value gaps in the customer-activity cycle and then fills them with added value services. Virgin's goal is to redistribute value for business-class and first-class customers over the whole activity cycle.

EXHIBIT 10.1
Employee commitment drives value at Southwest Airlines

A Southwest Airlines Boeing B737

Source: © David Osborn/Alamy

At Southwest Airlines, the seventh largest US domestic carrier, positions are designed so that employees can perform several jobs if necessary. Schedules, routes and company practices – such as open seating and the use of simple, colour-coded, reusable boarding passes – enable the boarding of three and four times more passengers per day than competing airlines. In fact, Southwest deplanes and reloads two-thirds of its flights in 15 minutes or less. Because of aircraft availability and short-haul routes that don't require long layovers for flight crews, Southwest has roughly 40 per cent more

pilot and aircraft utilisation than its major competitors: its pilots fly on average 70 hours per month versus 50 hours at other airlines. These factors explain how the company can charge fares from 60 per cent to 70 per cent lower than existing fares in markets it enters. At Southwest, customer perceptions of value are very high, even though the airline does not assign seats, offer meals or integrate its reservation system with other airlines. Customers place high value on Southwest's frequent departures, on-time service, friendly employees and very low fares. Southwest's management knows this because its 14,000 employees are in daily contact with customers and reports its findings back to management. In addition, the Federal Aviation Administration's performance measures show that Southwest, of all the major airlines, regularly achieves the highest level of on-time arrivals, the lowest number of complaints, and the fewest lost-baggage claims per 1,000 passengers. When combined with Southwest's low fares per seat-mile, these indicators show the higher value delivered by Southwest's employees compared with most domestic competitors. Southwest has been profitable for 23 consecutive years.

Source: Adapted from Heskett *et al.* (2008).

10.5 MANAGING LOYALTY

Managing loyalty means not only managing behaviour but also managing a state of mind. It means affecting the customer's attitude to doing business with the supplier over the long term – not merely until the next visit or the next purchase. This means that a properly managed approach to loyalty must make the customer want to do more business with the supplier over the long term or, at least, sustain its existing level of business.

Steps in a loyalty-based relationship strategy

Customer retention for all customers is key. There are six steps in a retention strategy, as illustrated in Figure 10.5.

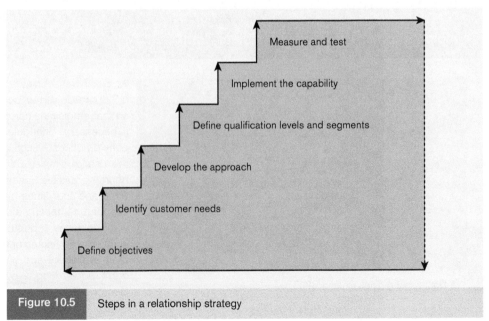

Measure and test

Implement the capability

Define qualification levels and segments

Develop the approach

Identify customer needs

Define objectives

| Figure 10.5 | Steps in a relationship strategy |

Define objectives

The need to develop a loyalty approach over and above existing marketing, sales and service approaches should be identified as part of an overall audit of customer management. Such an audit might reveal, for example:

- competitive attempts to target precisely your best customers;
- falling repurchase rate among your best customers;
- falling levels of state-of-mind loyalty;
- increasing numbers of customers switching away from your products and services.

Your objectives for the loyalty approach should be set in quantifiable terms or else the approach will be impossible to evaluate, whether by research or through business performance. These objectives should always contain some financial component or else the loyalty approach may be vulnerable to the criticism that it makes your customers feel good but has no effect on profits.

Identify your customers' needs (and their propensities to be loyal)

If you are considering introducing a loyalty approach, you must establish, usually through research and/or testing, the following:

- Which groups of customers are strategically important to you?
- What is the propensity of these groups to respond to different marketing, sales and service approaches?
- How, and by how much, do they respond and, in particular, how does their loyalty increase mentally (as measured by research, perhaps) and behaviourally?

Remember that the customer base of the firm is the greatest potential market research tool. It can provide market researchers with an excellent sampling frame, which is why the formal research process should be built into marketing contacts, involving where possible the use of questionnaires and structured telephone interviews. If executed properly, research will reinforce the brand and values you wish to transmit to customers.

Develop the approach

This involves the following. Find the best loyalty reinforcers. Identify those aspects of the marketing and service mix that can be deployed most effectively (taking into account the nature of your target customers for the loyalty approach) to reinforce and build loyalty.

There is a tendency to focus first on promotional incentives (discounts, free or low-cost promotional products and services, etc.), but these have the disadvantage of focusing on specific behaviours, as the qualification to receive the incentive is usually fixed in terms of those behaviours. A key area of focus should be the interface with the customer. Put simply, how you deal with your customers, in terms of managing their requirements and exchanging information with them, should hold the key to sustaining and building their loyalty.

You should find the most valued reinforcers. Find those elements of the product or service mix that have the highest perceived value to your customers, but relatively low costs of provision. This may seem a strange point, but it is the key to most schemes that work in the long term. The justification of loyalty schemes is that they reduce marketing costs because:

- less has to be spent on acquiring new customers;
- it costs less to sell more to existing customers, because we already know them and have access to them.

Loyalty schemes can also reduce service costs, partly because existing customers have learnt how to work with you. But these financial benefits may take some time to emerge.

Define qualification levels and segments

This is a detailed analysis of the profile of your best customers. We advise starting with a broad definition of best, rather than just the ones who buy the most.

A thorough profiling and tracking of purchase histories, transactional values, promotional responses and sources is vital here. It also helps identify the potential market size of similar customers for the acquisition programme. This is sometimes referred to as a relationship marketing audit. Many financial institutions, when they have undertaken this activity, have been surprised to learn how many customers are multiple purchasers of the products.

You must work out to which groups of customers you wish to provide the benefits of your loyalty approach, and the divisions between these groups of customers. Conventionally, this is done in terms of how much they buy from you, but there are many other approaches:

- how much they buy of a key product or service;
- how often they buy;
- the spread of their purchases;
- their potential future purchases;
- their actual or potential importance as a recommender of your services;
- how much you buy from them (for reciprocal approaches);
- how much information they give you.

It is common to set tiered qualification levels, with increasing loyalty commitment from customers matched by increasing service levels and bonuses from you.

This makes sense provided that the customer's movement between tiers is normally upwards. Being downgraded is not a pleasant experience for customers in any context, but particularly disappointing for those who have been 'nurtured upwards' for a long period. One demotion can destroy a relationship built up over years.

Also it is important not to let temporary reductions in purchasing (which may be totally uncorrelated with loyalty) lead to downgrading. For example, a member of a frequent flyer scheme may temporarily fly less overall, rather than fly more with another airline. Demotivating them by downgrading them immediately makes little sense.

Implement the capability

Capability is defined as the support infrastructure necessary to deliver relationship marketing. It includes:

- briefing marketing service suppliers such as advertising and direct marketing agencies, in-house magazine publishers, etc.;
- customer service definition;
- staff training and motivation approaches;
- acquisitions, adaptations and development of customer-facing information systems;
- setting pricing and terms of payment;
- policy and process development.

The workload involved in all these is, of course, significant, but the point is that if your approach is developed logically, starting with proper strategic evaluation and with the right analysis of customer needs, behaviour and experience, then the follow-through should be relatively straightforward, based on a phased approach.

Measure effectiveness

Loyalty approaches must in the end pay by producing better sales and profits than would have been yielded without the approach.

On a more detailed level, whatever stage of the life cycle a customer is at, it is always worth having a continued series of tests to establish optimum timing, frequency, offer and creative treatments.

Wansink and Seed (2001) researched the effectiveness of different loyalty programmes in the B2C market and found that marketers need to understand that for a loyalty programme to be successful, it must offer obvious benefits to the consumer.

EXHIBIT 10.2
Developing service loyalty at Volkswagen

Volkswagen AG is the largest car manufacturer in Europe. Worldwide, there are more than 36 million Volkswagen vehicles on the road. In an increasingly competitive market, direct contact with customers takes on vital importance. In recent years, therefore, Volkswagen has been developing and extending its relationship management activities, as part of a strategic customer bonding concept. So what does relationship marketing mean for a company like Volkswagen?

The development of service loyalty is shown in Figure 10.6. It shows that the older a vehicle, the greater the demand for related services. However, loyalty to Volkswagen dealerships decreases over the same time period. A car has US$160–210 a year spent on it (for vehicle-related services) in the first few years after purchase, and VW has a market share of about 85 per cent. Eleven years after purchase, annual spending rises to US$810, but VW's market share falls to only 25 per cent. This means that VW is losing contact with the car owner after the first change of ownership (after an average 3.7 years). In reality, this means VW has no real information on many of its customers.

What is VW doing to give customers reasons to stay loyal towards VW services? For many years, VW has been a trendsetter in terms of service development in the car industry. It has developed services that have not been offered by competitors, and these services have often been the reason why a customer has chosen to

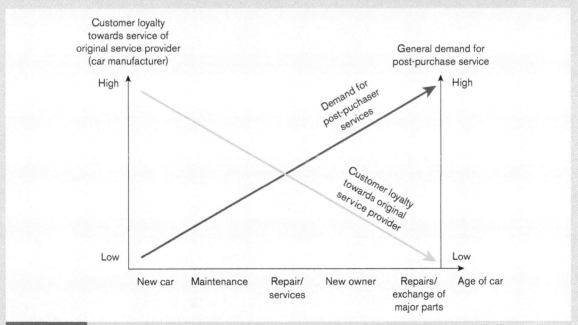

Figure 10.6	The development of service loyalty

Source: Hennig-Thurau, T. and Hansen, U. (2000) *Relationship Marketing: Gaining Competitive Advantage Through Customer Satisfaction and Consumer Retention*, Springer Verlag, Berlin-Heidelberg, p. 52. Reproduced with permission from T. Hennig-Thurau and U. Hansen.

EXHIBIT 10.2
Developing service loyalty at Volkswagen (*continued*)

purchase their products. The services include a service guarantee, an emergency plan, a mobility guarantee, a customer club and a toll-free service telephone.

Volkswagen has bundled some service options into a premium concept called the Volkswagen Exclusive Service. This special service concept includes a mobility guarantee, service telephone hotline, a pick-up and delivery service and finally a courtesy car. These kinds of activity will be well known to experienced service marketers, but Volkswagen has now decided to go one important step further by extending these measures into a comprehensive club card concept.

The club card is a membership card which gives the customer out-of-hours access to the reception area of a Volkswagen dealership. The card also carries the mobility guarantee seal and is the first stage toward receiving a service card.

The bonus programme rewards customer loyalty by letting him or her collect bonus points every time he or she purchases something from Volkswagen (e.g. a car, accessory or service) or from one of the partner organisations (e.g. Deutsche Bundesbahn). These bonus points can then only be exchanged for products and services from the Volkswagen organisation. Research has shown that customers have a very positive impression of the programme; it strengthens the contact between customer and dealer and is an excellent instrument for binding customers to the dealer organisation.

None of these programmes is able to help increase customer satisfaction and loyalty if customers are not aware that they exist. Database management is therefore the starting point for managing customer relations and is something which will grow in importance in the future. The only companies able to construct lasting relationships with their customers are those that properly process and maintain a customer database.

Key information for this database resource includes data on the customers themselves, the relevant dealer, the customer's present vehicle, the customer's use of the Volkswagen service card and the products that have already been offered to him or her.

VW also considers including information about the customer's hobbies. If VW knows that a customer's hobby is winter sports and it knows that the customer travels by car to his or her chosen winter resort, then VW can offer him or her snow tyres, snow chains, a roof rack (for skis) and more.

Source: Adapted from Hennig-Thurau and Hansen (2000), Chapter 3.

Creating e-loyalty

E-commerce companies care deeply about customer retention and consider it vital to the success of their online operations. They know that loyalty is an economic necessity: acquiring customers on the Internet is enormously expensive, and unless those customers remain loyal and make lots of repeat purchases over the years, profits will remain elusive. They also know it is a competitive necessity: in every industry some company will figure out how to harness the potential of the Web to create exceptional value for customers, and that company is going to lock in many profitable relationships at the expense of slow rivals. Without loyalty stickiness, even the best-designed e-business model will collapse.

Reichheld and Schefter (2000) and Hoffman and Lowitt (2008) studied e-loyalty and they found out that the Web is actually a very sticky space in both the business-to-consumer and the business-to-business spheres. Most of today's online customers exhibit a clear proclivity towards loyalty, and Web technologies, used correctly, reinforce that inherent loyalty. If executives do not quickly gain the loyalty of their most profitable existing customers and acquire the right new customers, they will face a dismal future left with only the most price-sensitive buyers.

It was shown that in e-industry after e-industry, the high cost of acquiring customers renders many customer relationships unprofitable during their early years. Only in later years, when the cost of serving loyal customers falls and the volume of their purchases rises, do relationships generate big returns.

At the beginning of a relationship, the outlays needed to acquire a customer are often considerably higher in e-commerce than in traditional retail channels. In clothing e-tailing, Reichheld and Schefter (2000) found that new customers cost 20–40 per cent more for pure Internet companies than for traditional retailers with both physical and online stores. That means that the losses in the early stages of relationships are larger.

However, Web customers tend to consolidate their purchases with one primary supplier, to the extent that purchasing from the supplier's site becomes part of their daily routine. This phenomenon is particularly apparent in the business-to-business sector.

In the end, loyalty is not won with Web technology. It is won through the delivery of a consistently superior customer experience. The Internet is a powerful tool for strengthening relationships, but the basic laws and rewards of building loyalty have not changed.

EXHIBIT 10.3
Best Buy's approach to loyalty, compared to competitor Circuit City

Central to the growth of Best Buy, the US electronics retail giant, has been its decision to embrace customer centricity. As part of the customer centricity strategy, Best Buy overhauled its customer loyalty programme, called Rewards Zone. After soliciting and receiving feedback from customers, the company realised that its loyalty programme wasn't aligned with what mattered most to its customers – savings and rewards. The customers told Best Buy that they wanted a rewards programme that was free. They were also looking to accelerate their reward potential. The changes that Best Buy made to the Reward Zone programme directly addressed their requests. So Best Buy eliminated its initiation fee to join Reward

Best Buy store, Ohio
Source: © Todd Muskopf/Alamy

Zone, added a Best Buy credit card to speed rewards accumulation and enabled customers to interact with their Reward Zone account online. As a result of these and other actions to make its offering more attractive, Reward Zone membership has nearly quadrupled from 7 million members at the time that Best Buy adjusted its loyalty programme (2003) to 25 million members by the end of 2008.

Compare Best Buy's actions with Circuit City's efforts to cultivate loyal customers. Whereas Best Buy has had a loyalty programme since 2001, Circuit City launched its loyalty campaign in 2006. While the benefits of the two programmes don't appear to differ greatly, consider this – in 2007 Circuit City replaced its most highly paid sales associates with lower paid associates. From the outside looking in, Circuit City hasn't embraced the concept of relying on service to retain loyal customers. And some of its recent actions are consistent with a defensive, not offensive, loyalty strategy posture.

Source: Adapted from Hoffman and Lowitt (2008).

10.6 THE CRM PATH TO LONG-TERM CUSTOMER LOYALTY

The customer relationship management (CRM) loyalty development process is illustrated in Figure 10.7.

Stage 1: Customer acquisition (the courtship)

Before acquiring a customer, the firm must first get to know the potential customer. In this phase, loyalty is considered very weak because it is not based on relationships, but solely on look and feel – products and prices. In fact, the customer may switch to a competitor if its products and prices are better. The attitude is summed up as, 'What have you done for me lately?' A good example of this is the fierce competition in the mobile telephone market.

In stage 1, a company's main focus is customer acquisition. Attention is directed towards building a customer base through the use of technology and initiative-specific training to increase the effectiveness of salespeople. Stage 1 companies also spend a significant amount of time on best-practice benchmarking, analysing customer care processes and conducting initial customer research.

Stage 2: Customer retention (the relationship)

At this stage affection grows and a solid relationship is created. The firm engages with customer attitudes both before and after the purchase. It listens to the customer who is gradually getting to know the enterprise. Loyalty is no longer based on price and product alone. The relationship is also becoming a factor, even though there is no guarantee the customer will not go elsewhere. But the relationship is solid enough for loyalty to no longer be seen as fleeting. A mutual desire exists, and both parties begin to see a benefit in continuing to grow the relationship (Laaksonen *et al.*, 2008).

When a company enters stage 2, the focus has shifted to maximising the customer relationships. A stage 2 company distinguishes itself from its stage 1 colleagues by beginning to segment its customers into groups with similar needs in order to serve each client group more effectively.

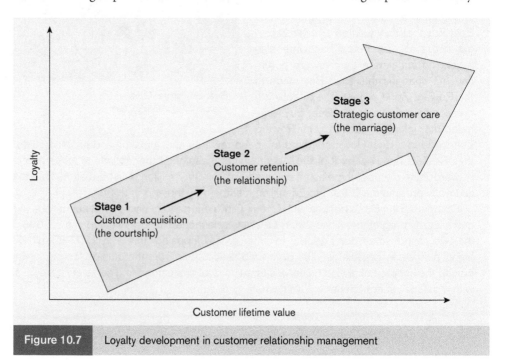

| Figure 10.7 | Loyalty development in customer relationship management |

Stage 3: Strategic customer care (the marriage)

At this stage a long-lasting relationship is mutually agreeable, and both parties become inextricably linked. At this stage, loyalty is based on a high degree of satisfaction and the customer will get personally involved with the enterprise. As the marriage continues, the bonds between customer and enterprise are gradually strengthened. Here the feeling of customer satisfaction increases and with it loyalty to the enterprise. On the basis of such a relationship, one can speak of true loyalty and the beginning of customer dependency.

For the marriage or relationship to continue both the enterprise and customer must receive a positive benefit even though both parties will inevitably experience disappointments on the way to their final goal.

Stage 3 organisations have realised that they cannot be all things to all people. While most customers are potentially profitable, some hold more long-term promise than others. The ability to predict who these customers are is a necessary skill on the upward path to strategic customer care. By wisely applying the right technology and information tools (technology is not a solution on its own), companies at the stage of strategic customer care deliver a core level of service for all their customers and a distinctive, optimised level for their best customers. Equally important, stage 3 businesses have orchestrated a winning situation for both their clients and for themselves: the clients are dependent on the business for their success and vice versa (Stace and Bhalla, 2008; Mascarenhas, 2006).

10.7 KEY ACCOUNT MANAGEMENT (KAM)

Key account management (KAM)
An approach to selling which focuses resources on major customers and uses a team selling approach in taking care of the total relationship with such an important customer.

KAM can be understood as a relationship-oriented marketing management approach focusing on dealing with major customers in the business-to-business market. Key accounts are customers in a business-to-business market identified by selling companies to be of strategic importance.

KAM is a management concept, including both organisational and selling strategies, to achieve long-lasting customer relationships. Key account manager is one of the most popular job titles today in the area of marketing management in companies operating in the business-to-business market. It has been used in several contexts, but the nature of this approach is very unclear and requires further conceptualisation.

A key account manager is the person in the selling organisation who represents the seller's capabilities to the buying company, the buyer's needs to the seller, and brings the two together. Successful KAM often requires an understanding of the logic of both product and service management. Moreover, excellent operational level capabilities are useless if strategic level management is inferior, and vice versa – the KAM approach combines strategic and operational level marketing management.

The starting point for the following is the firm that wishes to implement KAM. The development of KAM is examined from a dyadic perspective.

Implementation of KAM

The firm that wants to implement successful KAM with suitable key accounts may go through the following four steps (Ojasalo, 2001):

1   identifying the selling firm's key accounts;

2   analysing the key accounts;

3   selecting suitable strategies for the key accounts;

4   developing operational level capabilities to build, grow and maintain profitable and long-lasting relationships with key accounts.

1 Identifying the selling firm's key accounts

This means answering the following question: which existing or potential accounts are of strategic importance to us now and in the future?

The following criteria can be used to determine strategically important customers:

- sales volume;
- age of the relationship;
- the selling firm's share of customers' purchase: the new RM paradigm measures success in terms of long-term gains in its share of its customers' business, unlike mass marketing which counts wins or losses in terms of market share increases that may well be temporary (Peppers and Rogers, 1995);
- profitability of the customer to seller;
- use of strategic resources: extent of executive/management commitment.

There is a positive correlation between the criteria and the likelihood of customers being identified as key accounts (strategic customers).

2 Analysing the key accounts

This includes activities such as analysing:

- *Basic characteristics of a key account*: includes assessing the relevant economic and activity aspects of their internal and external environment. This, for example, includes the account's internal value chain inputs, markets, suppliers, products and economic situation.
- *Relationship history*: involves assessing the relevant economic and activity aspects of the relationship history. This includes volume of sales, profitability, key account's objectives, buying behaviour (the account's decision-making process), information exchange, special needs, buying frequency and complaints. Among these aspects, knowing or estimating relationship value plays a particularly important role. The revenues from each key account (customer lifetime value) should exceed the costs of establishing and maintaining the relationship within a certain time span.
- *Level and development of commitment to the relationship*: the account's present and anticipated commitment to the relationship is important, since the extent of the business with the account depends on that.
- *Goal congruence*: or commonality of interests between buyer and seller, greatly affects their cooperation both at the strategic and operational levels. Common interests and relationship value together determine whether two companies can be partners, friends or rivals. A seller that aims its sights lower than the sort of partnership relationship an account is looking for risks losing long-term share of that account's business.
- *Switching costs*: it is useful to estimate both the key account's and the selling company's **switching costs** in the event that the relationship dissolves. Switching costs are the costs of replacing an existing partner with another. These may be very different for the two parties and thus affect the power position in the relationship. Switching costs are also called transaction costs (Williamson, 1979), and they are affected by irretrievable investments in the relationship, the adaptations made, and the bonds that have developed. High switching costs may prevent a relationship from ending even though the key account's accumulated satisfaction with the selling company may be non-existent or negative.

Switching costs
The costs to a buying organisation of changing from one supplier to another.

3 Selecting suitable strategies for the key accounts

This depends greatly on the relative positions of the seller and the key account. The power structure within different accounts may vary significantly. Thus, the seller may typically not freely select the strategy – there is often only one strategic alternative to be chosen if there is a desire to retain the account.

Perhaps the seller might prefer to avoid very powerful accounts. Sometimes the seller realises that accounts which are less attractive today may become attractive in the future. Thus, with certain accounts, the objective of the strategy may be merely to keep the relationship alive for future opportunities.

4 Developing operational level capabilities

This refers to customisation and development of capabilities related to the following.

Product/service development and performance

Joint R&D projects are typical between a selling company and a key account in industrial and high-technology markets. In addition, information technology (IT) applied in just-in-time production and distribution channels increases the possibilities of customising the offering in consumer markets as well.

New products developed in a partnership are not automatically more successful than those developed in-house. However, R&D projects may bring other kinds of long-term benefits, such as access to account organisation and learning. Improving capabilities for providing services to key accounts is extremely important, because even when the core product is a tangible good, it is often the related services that differentiate the seller from its competitors and provide competitive advantage.

Organisational structure

The seller's organisational ability to meet the key account's needs can be developed, for example by adjusting the organisational structure to correspond to the key account's global and local needs and by increasing the number of interfaces between the seller and the account, and thus also the number of people interacting. Organisational capabilities can also be developed by organising teams, consisting of people with the necessary competences and authorities, to take care of key accounts.

Individuals (human resources)

A company's capabilities related to individuals can be developed by selecting the right people for key account managers and key account teams, and by developing the skills of these people. The key account manager's responsibilities are often complex and varied, and therefore require a large number of skills and qualifications, which should be taken into account in the selection and development of key account managers.

It is quite common to find that the current set of key account managers may be good at maintaining their own relationships with their existing contacts but lack the skills required to lead an account team through a transition in the account relationship.

Therefore, an assessment of the total desired interfaces between the seller and the customer needs to be considered. It may be that a change is required by moving the relationship from a dependency on a one-to-one relationship (between the key account manager and the chief buyer) to a network of organisational relationships spanning many different projects, functions and countries.

Information exchange

Information exchange between the seller and a key account is particularly important in KAM. An important relationship-specific task is to search, filter, judge and store information about the organisation, strategies, goals, potentials and problems of the partners. However, this mainly depends on the mutual trust and attitudes of the parties, and on the technical arrangements. A key account's trust is something that the seller has to earn over time by its performance, whereas the technical side can be developed, e.g. with IT.

Company and individual level benefits

Successful long-term KAM in a business-to-business context always requires the ability to offer both company and individual level benefits to key accounts.

Company level benefits are rational and may be either short or long term, direct or indirect, and typically contribute to the key account's turnover, profitability, cost savings, organisational efficiency and effectiveness, and image. Individual level benefits in turn may be rational or emotional. From the relationship management point of view, the key individuals are the ones with the power to continue or terminate the relationship. Rational individual level benefits contribute, for example, to the individual's own career, income and ease of job. Emotional individual level benefits include friendship, a sense of caring and ego enhancement.

Customer complaint management in KAM

Complaint management means satisfying the customer who has voiced the complaint and binding him or her to the company for the long term. Many firms have negative feelings about complaints. However, firms stand to benefit if the personnel in contact with the dissatisfied customer handle the process skilfully, achieve the desired outcome, and also derive personal satisfaction from the relevant tasks.

Customer complaints involve much more than just customers taking the initiative to articulate their dissatisfaction with products or services. They are complex psycho-sociological conflict management processes bounded by the relationship of the market partners. Within the framework of these processes, the qualifications required of contact personnel (in the form of appropriate interpersonal skills, for example) are of central importance.

Service personnel should be trained to handle complaints, so that they have consideration in the case of a service failure and allow customers to express frustration freely. Furthermore, service personnel should have the autonomy to help customers in real time. This means that service personnel must have the authority to offer a form of compensation without interference from management (Ruyter and Wetzels, 2000).

Therefore, internal marketing plays a key role here, creating the necessary psychological conditions for both the individual employee and the organisation, and thereby ensuring the successful implementation and acceptance of an effective complaint management system.

It is not always advisable to handle the customer complaint on the spot because it is relatively resource demanding. The specific situation determines the most appropriate structural and operating organisations for complaint management. Relevant factors could include the nature of the product, the frequency and manner of customer contacts, and the business form of the firm. From a structural standpoint, one can differentiate between centralised, decentralised and dual complaint management systems (Thurau and Hansen, 2000).

Centralised complaint management is advisable when a business has no personal contact with its customers, the complaint volume is relatively high, the types of complaints encountered are relatively simple and homogeneous, and changes in these conditions seldom occur. A key advantage is the routine nature of the work performed by the employees responsible for handling the complaints. Additionally, the employees are not subjected to those psychological pressure mechanisms associated with dealing with complaints, which they themselves have caused; the complaint handlers only deal with written or telephone complaints assigned to them by a centralised complaint management system.

Decentralised complaint management is advantageous when the relationships between the firm and customer are characterised by personal interactions distributed over a large number of customer contact points, and when the customer complaints are complex and less predictable. The biggest advantage of decentralisation is the direct, prompt, appropriate and on-the-spot resolution of the problem. The main disadvantage is that it requires more human resources. Furthermore, employees are directly confronted with mistakes they themselves have made or which were caused at an earlier stage in the value chain (e.g. delivery delays).

Decentralised complaint management also makes it difficult to motivate employees to take a proactive role in stimulating customers to lodge complaints.

In order to achieve a rapid resolution of complaints with a focus on pinpointing the underlying causes, employees have to be given wide-ranging authority in terms of decision-making responsibility, access to information and task assignment. This should ensure rapid and comprehensive solutions for the customers.

Dual complaint management combines the advantages of the centralised and decentralised approaches. It is appropriate for complex products and services, as well as for businesses featuring broad-based direct contact with customers (such as dealer networks).

Direct decentralised complaint management involves an interaction between employees and customers. It encompasses tasks related to the input, case handling and feedback functions. The quality and outcome of these processes is largely determined by the competences of the customer contact personnel. This is itself reflected in terms of how these staff perceive themselves and others, in their ability to engage in suitable interactions with customers, and in willingness to assume responsibility for complaints.

The effect of complaint management is at its greatest when management's existing external market orientation is expanded to include internal goals and, in particular, employee-related goals. In addition, internal marketing goes beyond the traditional goal-oriented interpretation of customer complaints to incorporate a relationship-oriented approach.

A lack of expertise and competence on the part of contact personnel can activate the latent potential for conflict and lead to an escalation of the complaint. This may not only lead to the termination of the relationship, but also to loss of sales and to damage to the company image through negative word of mouth spread by the dissatisfied customer.

The dyadic development of KAM

The model in Figure 10.8 describes and demonstrates the typical dyadic progression of a relationship between buyer and seller through five stages – pre-KAM, early KAM, mid-KAM, partnership KAM and synergistic KAM (Cheverton, 1999; McDonald *et al.*, 1997).

Pre-KAM stage

This describes preparation for KAM. A buyer is identified as having key account potential, and the seller starts to focus resources on winning some business with that prospect. Both seller and buyer are sending out signals (factual information) and exchanging messages (interactions) prior to the decision to engage in transactions.

Early KAM stage

At this stage, the seller is concerned with identifying the opportunities for account penetration once the account has been won. This is probably the most typical sales relationship, the classic bow-tie.

Adapted solutions are needed, and the key account manager will focus on understanding more about the customer and the market in which that customer is competing. The buyer will still be market testing other sellers. The seller must concentrate hard on product, service and intangibles – the buyer wants recognition that the product offering is the prime reason for the relationship – and expects it to work.

Mid-KAM stage

This is a transition stage between the classic bow-tie and the diamond of the partnership KAM stage.

At this stage the seller has established credibility with the buyer. Contacts between the two organisations increase at all levels and assume greater importance. Nevertheless, buyers still feel the need for alternative sources of supply. This may be driven by their own customers' desire for choice. The seller's offering is still periodically market tested, but is reliably perceived to be good value. The seller is now a preferred supplier.

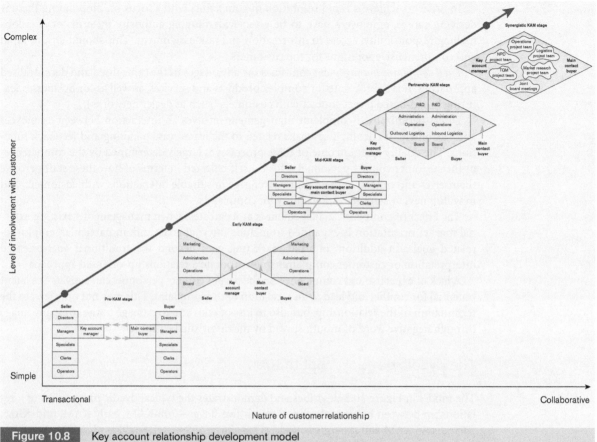

Figure 10.8	Key account relationship development model
	Sources: Adapted from Millman and Wilson (1994); and McDonald *et al.* (1996).

Partnership KAM stage

This is the stage where benefits should start to flow. When partnership KAM is reached, the seller is seen by the buyer as a strategic external resource. The two companies will be sharing sensitive information and solving problems jointly. Pricing will be long term and stable, but it will have been established that each side will allow the other to make a profit.

If a major disadvantage of the bow-tie of early relationship KAM was the denial of access to customers' internal processes and to their market, the main advantage of the diamond relationship is in seeing those barriers of understanding opening up (Leavy, 2004; McKenzie and Winkelen, 2006).

Key accounts will test all the seller's innovations so that they have first access to, and first benefit from, the latest technology. The buyer will expect to be guaranteed continuity of supply and access to the best material. Expertise will be shared. The buying company will also expect to gain from continuous improvement. There may be joint promotions, where appropriate.

Synergistic KAM stage

This stage is the ultimate stage in the relationship development model. The experience gained at the partnership stage – coordinating the team-sell, coaching the team on their interface roles – will be a good starting point for moving to synergistic KAM.

The seller understands that it still does not have an automatic right to the customer's business. Nevertheless, exit barriers have been built up. The buyer is confident that the relationship with the seller is delivering improved quality and reduced cost. Costing systems become transparent. Joint research and development will take place. There will be interfaces at every level and function between the organisations. Senior management commitment will be fulfilled through joint board meetings and reviews. There will be a joint business plan, joint strategies and joint market research. Information flow should be streamlined and information systems integration will be planned or in place as a consequence. Transaction costs will be reduced.

Though there are clear advantages for both partners in moving through the different KAM stages, there are also pitfalls. As the contacts proliferate through the stages, so does the speed of activity, and the risk of saying and doing the wrong things. Through the stages the key account manager changes from super salesperson to super-coach. In the last two stages the key account manager moves on to be a super-coordinator, who oversees everything.

If the key account manager does not move along, then the potential of losing control is great, resulting in well-meaning, but misdirected, individuals following their own quite separate courses.

Key account management requires process excellence and highly skilled professionals to manage relationships with strategic customers. For most companies, this represents a number of changes. A change is needed in the way activity is costed and costs are attributed, from product or geographical focus to customer focus. Currently, few financial or information systems in companies are sophisticated enough to support the higher levels of KAM. A transformation is needed in the way the person with responsibility for a customer relationship is developed, from an emphasis on selling skills to management skills, including cross-cultural management skills (McDonald *et al.*, 1997).

10.8 SUMMARY

The future cash flow of a firm is generated by purchases from existing customers and purchases from new customers. Hence, if a firm makes sound investments in acquiring only the right customers and in developing existing customers it should, over time, continually enhance its value. This chapter has shown that both acquisition and retention are important for survival, and that marketers who focus only on the former are ignoring exciting opportunities and essential information.

In order to achieve customer loyalty you must start with a holistic picture of the customer. Remember, the customer is a strategic asset, one that is in short supply, one that must be treated with care. Therefore, regard customer information as a strategic asset. Once you have a customer, surround him or her with care. Establish team-based selling as the rule rather than the exception, and use each customer contact as an opportunity to create loyalty.

A loyalty programme is a long-term proposition, not a short-term promotion. Management has to be committed to a programme that will last for years, not months. Such commitment will help develop and maintain a strong lifetime relationship with customers. The result of such a close connection will bring many rewards to both sides.

KAM is the development towards customer focus and RM in business-to-business markets. It offers critical benefits and opportunities for profit enhancement to both sides of the seller–buyer relationship.

The scope of KAM is widening and becoming more complex. The skills of professionals involved in it at strategic and operational levels need to be constantly updated and developed.

Customer complaints are latent conflicts between customers and employees. The psycho-sociological dimension of the customer complaint is determined through the personality structures of the partners and the relationship itself.

Internal marketing provides a wide range of instruments for supporting the customer complaint management process.

The basic task of internal marketing is to convince staff of the economic benefits to be derived from effective complaint management and to overcome preconceived notions of how to handle dissatisfied customers. The associated business principles can be conveyed through specific internal communications instruments such as the employee newsletter, intranet messages or staff meetings.

The goal of internal marketing is to positively influence internal relationships, thereby guaranteeing a positive external relationship experience for the employee and customer. One of the fundamental purposes of internal interactions between management and employees relates to the sensitivity of customer contact personnel to the important role they play in the interface between the firm and the customer.

CASE STUDY 10.1

Dassault Falcon
The private business jet, Falcon, is navigating in the global corporate business sector

Dassault Aviation is a French aircraft manufacturer of military, regional and business jets, a subsidiary of Dassault Group. Dassault Aviation is the only aircraft company that designs, manufactures and sells both combat aircraft, instruments of political independence, and executive jets, work and economic development tools. By the end of 2009, nearly 8,000 aircraft had been sold.

History of Dassault Aviation

It was founded in 1930 by Marcel Bloch as Société des Avions Marcel Bloch or 'MB'. During the occupation of France the country's aviation industry was virtually disbanded. Marcel Bloch was imprisoned by the Vichy government in October 1940. In 1944 Bloch (as a Jew) was deported to the Buchenwald concentration camp by the German occupiers, where he remained until it was liberated on 11 April 1945. After the Second World War, Marcel Bloch changed his name to Marcel Dassault. 'Dassault' was the pseudonym of his brother, General Darius Paul Bloch, in the French resistance and means 'for assault', originally from '*char d'assaut*', French for tank. Marcel Dassault converted to Catholicism in 1950. The name of the company was changed to Avions Marcel Dassault on 20 December 1947. In 1971, Dassault acquired Breguet, forming Avions Marcel Dassault-Breguet Aviation (AMD-BA). In 1990, the company was renamed Dassault Aviation.

Today's Falcon jets are designed and manufactured alongside Dassault Aviation's famous fighter aircraft, the Mirage and the Rafale. Dassault's military aircraft account for 40 per cent of Dassault Aviation's total yearly sales – the business jets account for the majority of the company's sales (60 per cent).

History of Falcon

The jet business of Dassault Aviation (Falcon) (www.dassaultfalcon.com) started in 1963, when Charles Lindbergh visited the Avions Marcel Dassault factory in Mérignac, France. He was part of a team sent by Pan American World Airways Inc. seeking a business aircraft to market in the United States. Lindbergh relayed his unequivocally positive impressions of the Mystère 20 directly to then-Pan Am Chairman Juan Trippe.

On that recommendation, Pan Am's newly created business jet division was established to market and support the Falcon 20, then known as the 'Fan Jet Falcon'. As sales grew and the number of Falcons in service increased, the need for closer coordination between the manufacturer and its marketing organisation soon became apparent. In 1972, Dassault and Pan Am formed a joint venture company, Falcon Jet Corporation, and assigned it the sales and support duties previously held by Pan Am. In October 1980, Dassault purchased Pan Am's interest in the joint venture, making Falcon Jet a wholly owned subsidiary.

On 1 January 1995, Dassault Aviation and Falcon Jet merged certain worldwide operations and renamed the US company Dassault Falcon Jet Corp. Today Dassault Falcon Jet is responsible for selling and supporting Falcon business jets in North, South and Central America as well as Asia and the Pacific Rim. It employs a total workforce of more than 2,300 persons in its three facilities, Teterboro, Wilmington and Little Rock. Little Rock facility is the biggest facility of the Dassault Group with 1,800 employees. It is also one of the biggest completion centres in the world.

The Dassault Falcon business today

Dassault Falcon is responsible for selling and supporting Falcon business jets throughout the world. It is part of Dassault Aviation, a leading aerospace company with a presence in over 70 countries across 5 continents. Dassault Aviation produces the renowned Mirage and Rafale fighter jets as well as a complete line of Falcon business jets. The company has assembly and production plants in both France and the United States and service facilities on both continents. It employs a total workforce of over 12,000.

Since the rollout of the first Falcon 20 in 1963, over 1,700 Falcon jets have been delivered to more than 65 countries worldwide. Since 1975, Falcon export sales exceed 90 per cent.

The Falcon family of jets encompasses distinct aircraft, all positioned at the top end of the business jet market. Currently in production are the tri-jets – the Falcon 50EX, 900DX, 900EX EASy and the new 7X – as well as the twin-engine Falcon 2000 and 2000EX EASy.

The founding Dassault family owns 50 per cent of the company; aerospace group EADS owns about 46 per cent. The rest is divided among some smaller investors.

Dassault had been hurt by the ailing commercial flight sector, but in 2006 sales of commercial aircraft rebounded back to levels not seen since 2002.

The company opened a new technological research centre, named the Jacques-Louis Lions Cooperation Center in 2003.

Dassault Aviation launched the Falconcare service in June 2005, which offered a transfer of the financial exposure of maintenance for all scheduled and unscheduled maintenance operations of new Falcons.

Seven major European aerospace manufacturers – Airbus, Dassault Aviation, Eurocopter, Liebherr-Aerospace Lindenberg, Rolls-Royce, Safran and Thales – signed a letter of intent on a Clean Sky Joint Technology Initiative in July 2006.

NetJets Europe signed an order with Dassault Aviation for 24 Falcon 7X jets valued at US$1.1 billion in September 2006. The company is looking to its new Falcon 7X corporate jets as a potential cash cow in the future.

Falcon 7X

The Dassault Falcon 7X is the large-cabin, long-range business jet manufactured by Dassault Aviation, the flagship offering of their business jet line. It was first presented to the public at the 2005 Paris Air Show.

As of 2009 the approximate unit price of the 7X is US$45 million, but still this is a little cheaper than its nearest competitors in the long-range, large-cabin market segment, e.g. the Gulfstream G550 and Bombardier Global Express.

The Falcon 7X in the air
Source: Courtesy of Dassault Aviation

Interior of Falcon 7X
Source: Courtesy of Dassault Aviation

General characteristics

- Necessary crew: 3 (pilot, co-pilot and 1 cabin crew)
- Capacity: up to 12 passengers (not including crew)
- Length: 23.19 m
- Empty weight: 15,456 kg
- Max take-off weight: 31,299 kg
- Maximum speed: 953 km/h
- Cruise speed: 900 km/h
- Range: 11,019 km 8 passengers – e.g. it will be able to fly directly from London to Los Angeles

Segmentation of the business jet market

The business jet market can be segmented according to the different criteria such as the flight performance, range in kilometres, characteristics such as avionics, cabin size and equipment, fuel consumption and maintenance costs, noise level and of course the price for the aircraft. In Table 10.1 the total market is divided into six categories.

Table 10.1   Different business jet segments (2008 figures)

Segment	Seats	Range km	Price US$m
Very light jet (VLJ)	4–7	2,400–4,000	3–5
Light	6–8	2,600–4,500	5–10
Light medium	7–9	3,500–5,000	10–15
Medium	8–12	3,700–6,300	15–25
Long range	5–19	5,700–8,300	25–35
Very long range	8–19	8,000–13,000	> 35

Source: Adapted from HSH Nordbank (2005) *Sector Report: Business Jets Market, Operator Models, Owners, Market Trends, Secondary Market*, March, p. 5.

The very light jet (VLJ) market

This segment is emerging at the lower end of the market, i.e. smaller planes and shorter range. This large market segment in terms of fleet numbers and number of units comprises affordable, tried-and-tested models that offer a flexibility advantage over larger models as they are able to take off on short runways. The leading manufacturers in this segment are Cessna and Raytheon. However, in market value, the VLJ market is only expected to be about US$250 million in 2008, less than 2 per cent of the total market size (in value) in Table 10.2.

Light market segment

The largest market segment in terms of fleet numbers comprises affordable, tried-and-tested models, which offer a flexibility advantage over larger models as they are able to take off on short runways. The leading manufactures in this segment are Cessna, Bombardier and Raytheon.

Light medium market segment

The light medium segment is the second largest in terms of fleet numbers and will see the addition of new models in the coming years. Cessna plans to launch the Citation XLS and Sovereign, while Gulfstream will launch the G150. This segment is considered to have a big growth potential.

Medium market segment

This segment of relatively small intercontinental jets costing between US$15 and 25 million is comparatively small. It is therefore surprising to see the host of new models that compete in this segment. If the market is weak, low sales figures represent a major risk for manufacturers in this segment. If the market develops positively, all models are expected to be produced in acceptable numbers.

Long range market segment

This segment is dominated by Dessault Falcon, Gulfstream and Bombardier. Bombardier and Gulfstream have launched their G350, G450 and Challenger 800 models and Dessault Falcon has launched its 7X. This segment has good growth potential thanks to the new models and growing demand for larger jets.

The world market for business jets

The business jet fleet (in the world market) has increased from around 5,000 aircraft in 1981 to about 14,000 in 2008 (see also Table 10.2), corresponding with a CAGR of approximately 6 per cent.

The yearly deliveries (units sold) have increased from 200 units in 1985 to approximately 900 in 2008 (see also Table 10.2) and 70 per cent of the whole fleet is located in United States.

The vast majority (95 per cent) of the business jet market is controlled by five competitors: Cessna (TXT), Dassault Falcon, Gulfstream (General Dynamics), Bombardier and the former Raytheon (Hawker/Premier), which was acquired by Goldman Sachs Capital Partners and Onex in late 2006, both private equity firms. We restrict our analysis here to these five competitors. There are other manufacturers serving the high-end including Boeing and Airbus.

In 2009 several of the business jet manufacturers had problems because of the global financial crisis. For

Table 10.2	The world market for business jets, 2008		
Manufacturer	Current business jet fleet	Unit sales	Value sales
Total	**14,000**	**900**	**US$16 billion**
	%	%	%
Cessna (Textron) (USA)	30	35	20
Bombardier (Canada)	15	15	30
Gulfstream (General Dynamics) (USA)	15	25	25
Dassault Falcon (France)	10	10	15
Raytheon (USA)	30	15	10
Total	100	100	100

Source: Different public sources.

example, in April 2009 Bombardier had a 40 per cent drop in deliveries compared to the same time in 2008.

According to *Aviation Week*, some 13,300 business jets are in operation throughout the world; 25 per cent of the total are older than 25 years. Assuming that they have a useful life of 25 to 30 years, one can expect substantial demand for replacements in the coming years. About one-third of yearly unit sales is attributable to replacements for business jets taken out of service and two-thirds to market growth.

The secondary market for used business jets is very well organised. If we regard the older jets as 'sediment', there is only a relatively limited number of young business jets for sale. These are marketed by a small number of dealers and brokers. Databases such as JetNet help bring buyers and sellers together and provide access to the specifications of nearly all jets available for sale worldwide, such as flight hours of the individual turbines, location of the jet, maintenance information and so on.

Nevertheless, the average number of years a used business jet stays in the market has reached a historical high.

Competition among manufacturers of business jets – Dassault Falcon's competitors

Cessna (Textron) is the clear leader on a unit basis followed by Bombardier and Raytheon. On a revenue basis, Bombardier and Gulfstream are the leaders.

Cessna (Textron) (USA)

Thanks to their ability to combine the fuselages, wings and engines in different ways, Cessna has traditionally had one of the largest product ranges behind Bombardier. Given that a large part of the range was launched in the past decade, Cessna is under no pressure to develop new models. Cessna's strengths also include the broad customer base and the established service network. Cessna models account for about one-third of the global business jet fleet.

One of the company's weaknesses is the fact that it has no high-end model and therefore no presence in the upper market segment.

Key models in production: CJ1, CJ2, CJ3, Citation Bravo, Encore, Excel, Citation X, Citation Mustang, Sovereign, XLS.

Bombardier (Canada)

Bombardier has the largest range of jets and mainly operates in the medium and upper market segment with the Learjet and Canadair (Challenger) series. According to industry experts Bombardier will have difficulties in keeping its market share. This is primarily attributable to the strategy of the new CEO, Paul Tellier, who attaches

greater importance to profits than to market share. Accordingly, the main focus is no longer on the variety of models in the medium price segment.

Key models in production: Learjet 31A, 40, 45/XR, 60, Challenger 300, 604, Global Express, Challenger 800, Global 5000.

Gulfstream (General Dynamics) (USA)

General Dynamics' acquisition of Galaxy Aerospace helped Gulfstream more or less catch up with Bombardier. Gulfstream had a market share of around 25 per cent in the last decade and may even expand this share in coming years. Good business jet sales are expected, especially in the government and defence sector.

Gulfstream's wide range of business jets are mainly positioned in the upper market segments. Besides the refinement of existing models, Gulfstream is also working on the design of a 'silent' supersonic jet.

Key models in production: G100, G200, G300, G400, G500, G550, G150, G350, G450.

Raytheon (USA)

The very small product range and a current market share of about 10 per cent makes Raytheon the smallest of the Big 5. While the Hawker Horizon was added to the product range in 2004, the company still lacks a business jet in the high-end segment. The company's future will largely depend on the success of the tried-and-tested models.

Key models in production: Premier I, Hawker 400 XP, 800 XP, Hawker Horizon.

Figure 10.9 illustrates the structuring of the main actors within the commercial jet industry, thus revealing the total value chain.

Commercial jet operators/intermediaries

As seen in Figure 10.9, the different operator models can generally be classified into four groups: charter/air taxi, fractional ownership, full ownership and jet membership programme/private jet cards. The choice of a concept mainly depends on the estimated annual flight volume (in hours). Another aspect is whether the number of passengers is the same for each flight or whether it varies strongly. If transport requirements vary strongly (passenger numbers, distance between destinations), usage concepts with a free choice of the business jet type are preferable (see Figure 10.10).

Charter/air taxi

Charter/air taxi is recommendable for companies travelling less than 100 flight hours per year. There should be

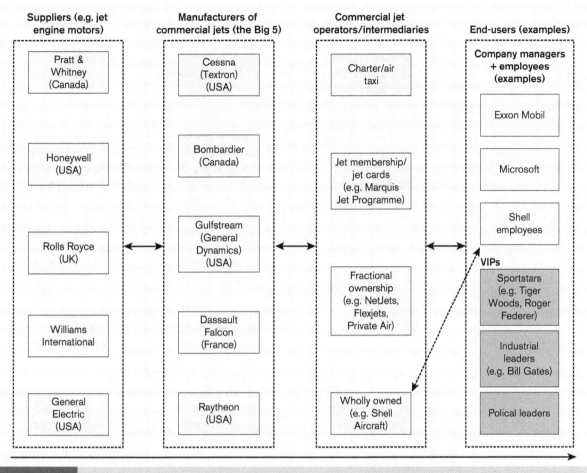

| Figure 10.9 | The value chain in the business jet industry |

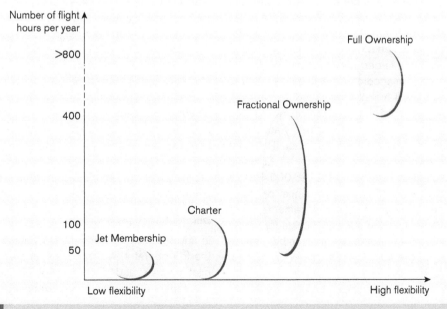

| Figure 10.10 | Different business jet operator models |

Source: HSH Nordbank (2005) *Sector Report: Business Jets Market, Operator Models, Owners, Market Trends, Secondary Market*, HSH Nordbank, March, p. 5.

at least four passengers per flight though. This relatively low travelling volume would make (fractional) ownership of a jet uneconomical.

Charter concepts comprise on-demand charters and contract charters. In the case of on-demand (ad hoc) charters, availability of the jets is not guaranteed and prices are somewhat higher than for contract (block) charters. Contract charters are based on a longer-term contract stipulating a defined flight volume (in hours) for the term of the contract. Charter customers are charged for positioning costs and empty flights.

Corporate shuttles are a special form of contract chartering and allow a company's employees to travel between different production plants or branches. The time savings and the productivity of employees during the flights more than offsets the costs of a corporate shuttle, making them an attractive alternative to scheduled flights. To make a corporate shuttle profitable, some companies share the flight services, which would otherwise be too costly for a single company.

Private jet membership/jet cards

Jet membership models are derived from fractional ownership schemes and ad hoc charter programmes. Such models typically allow customers to use a defined number of flight hours in a certain jet type within a defined period of time. Unused hours usually lapse at the end of the agreed utilisation period.

Jet membership cards enable customers to use several jets at the same time. Such systems are therefore recommendable for travellers who have several destinations at the same time or overlapping flight schedules. The total flight volume should not exceed 50 hours p.a. as otherwise other usage concepts would be more favourable. Should the aircraft 'booked' by jet card not be available, another jet will be provided. If required, a larger jet or an aircraft with a larger range can be used – the costs will be charged in accordance with the exact number of hours travelled; if higher-quality models are used, the hours on the jet card will be used up quicker (or slower if aircraft models of a smaller category are used). This is based on a defined translation factor. The flight hours must be paid in advance. Marquis Jet Europe's programme starts at 25 flight hours at €126,000. Private jet memberships avoid the disadvantages of other usage concepts such as capital requirements, non-availability of charter jets and additional costs for empty flights. The special aspect of private jet memberships is that the price is fixed in advance. Compared to charters, where the price for the same route may fluctuate over time, the price for jet memberships is always the same. Moreover, some jet membership programmes offer

bonuses in the form of free flight hours for each return route. DeltaAirElite offers bonuses of up to 40 per cent (in flight hours). Nevertheless, jet membership cards have a relatively high fixed price and are rather recommendable for high net worth individuals than for corporations.

Fractional ownership

Fractional ownership shares (FO) are usually acquired by corporate customers who either wish to extend their own corporate flight service or who do not have the critical size to justify the use of their own corporate business jet. Fractional ownership concepts are suitable for flight volumes between 50 and 400 hours per year. Fractional ownership means that the user acquires a fraction of a certain jet. The minimum fraction to be acquired is 1/16 or 50 flight hours per year. Travellers with an annual volume of approximately 100 flight hours should acquire 1/8. Fractional ownership allows users to benefit from the advantages offered by a business jet without having to organise charter services on the one hand or having to perform the management tasks of a jet owner on the other hand. This task is performed by the operator of the FO programme.

Should a user's own jet (fraction) not be available at the desired time, another jet from the FO operator's fleet will be made available. This is made possible by exchange agreements with other FO owners, which aim to increase or guarantee jet availability. Most FO agreements have a term of five years. Some FO programmes require the FO to be repurchased by the FO operator every five years, while others merely require the operator contract to be renewed to reflect current monthly and hourly rates. Unused flight hours can be carried forward to the following years and do not expire. However, the maximum total number of flight hours per five-year term is limited to 1,000. The number of flight hours acquired may be exceeded by a maximum of 50 per cent per year. However, in this case, users will incur additional costs.

Fractional ownership can be acquired by way of a one-time payment. NetJets offers a 1/16 fraction at a price starting at only US$200,000. Alternatively, this one-time payment can be refinanced via the FO company or the fraction can be leased. Monthly leasing fees are relatively high as they must compensate for the value impairment of the jet expected at the end of the term.

Different fractions available

In addition, the fractional owner pays a monthly fee to the FO operator, which covers all fixed costs such as pilot salaries and pilot training, hangar fees, regular maintenance, administrative expenses and insurance costs. The fixed costs are spread over the different owners in accordance with their respective ownership fractions. The FO is capitalised as an asset by the owner's balance sheet, which means that it is subject to annual depreciation. In addition to the one-time payment and the monthly fees, users incur variable costs for the number of flight hours used. Variable costs include costs for fuel, maintenance costs, cabin crews, food, general tax on consumption, and airport fees. Under applicable laws, fractional owners are responsible for the safety of the passengers and should therefore have sufficient insurance cover.

Should a user sell their FO, they will be charged a re-sale fee of 5–7 per cent of the current market value. Another disadvantage is the fact that, if the FO is returned or sold, the loss is higher than if the jet were fully owned due to the higher utilisation rate.

The important aspect is that the buyer of an FO does not acquire the right to fly but rather actual fractional ownership of the jet. Nevertheless, fractional owners cannot use the whole jet as collateral. On the other hand, the rights of a fractional owner are not affected by the financial liabilities of other fractional owners. Fractional owners can pledge only their own share in the jet, and the continued operation of a partially pledged jet is guaranteed in the case of the realisation of collateral by a creditor. At the bottom line, fractional ownership is almost always more expensive for the user than jet charters or full ownership and operation of a business jet. FO is an interesting option only for annual flight requirements of between 50 and 400 hours.

NetJets Inc. (www.netjets.com), a Berkshire Hathaway company, is the worldwide leader in private aviation and provides the safest and most secure private aviation solutions. NetJets fractional aircraft ownership allows individuals and companies to buy a share of a private business jet at a fraction of the cost of whole aircraft ownership, and guarantees availability 365 days a year with just a few hours' notice. The NetJets programmes worldwide offer the largest and most diversified fleet in private aviation, which includes 15 of the most popular business jets in the world. Access to the NetJets fleet is also available in the form of a short-term lease, sold on an all-inclusive, pre-paid basis in 25-hour increments, through an exclusive alliance with Marquis Jet Partners. NetJets Inc. also offers aircraft management, charter management and on-demand charter services through its subsidiary Executive Jet Management.

The market for fractional aircraft ownership is growing quickly. Over the past decade, the total number of owner shares has grown from approximately 1,500 to over 7,000 expected this year. On average, the market has grown by 8.5 per cent annually.

For the last two years, NetJets' market share has been around 70 per cent based on net value of aircraft sold and leased. NetJets has flown more flights than all of its competitors combined and manages more than 390,000 flights annually.

FlightSafety is a sister company of NetJets through Berkshire Hathaway and is the world's largest provider of aviation training, educating more than 75,000 pilots annually across 43 Learning Centers in the United States, Canada, France and the United Kingdom.

FlightSafety will more than double the number of its existing simulators, creating its largest concentration of simulators in the United States.

In 2007, NetJets worldwide flew over 390,000 flights, 237,000,000 miles to more than 173 countries, employing nearly 7,300 worldwide (3,957 pilots, 400 flight attendants). In the US NetJets fractional programme alone spent over $34 million on catering; arranged more than 100,000 cars and limos; landed at over 1,500 airports; spent $66 million on pilot training at FlightSafety International; and required over 1.8 million maintenance work hours.

Full ownership

Full ownership is suitable for companies with more than 400 flight hours per year. The owner of the jet is also the operator and is therefore responsible for jet management; this task may also be assigned to an external service provider. Full ownership costs comprise the acquisition costs, annual depreciation and current operating expenses. When the jet is not needed, it may be chartered to other users, so that income is generated.

The end-users

In terms of the number of business registered jets, North America leads the other continents by a wide margin. This means that North America is the world's best developed business jet market, with 70 per cent of all registrations. Canada only accounts for a small fraction (approximately 2 per cent) of the total number.

The share of business jets used for corporate purposes is relatively high, at around 90 per cent. The rest is represented by the VIP segment (sports stars, rock stars, political leaders, etc.)

Reasons for using business jets

There are many reasons for companies, private individuals or the government to use business jets. Above all, there is the special flexibility offered by a business jet. These jets have a lower weight than scheduled aircraft and can therefore land on much shorter runways. This allows the user to choose a destination airport that is closer to the final destination than the usual major airports. This results in a shorter ground transfer to the final destination, which, together with the shorter airport check-in times in dedicated business jet terminals, lead to substantial cost savings compared to scheduled flights. The departure time is determined by the passenger and not by the airline, and the passenger can fly straight to their desired destination, with no need to change flights and no risk of missing connecting flights. Moreover, as a result of the stricter safety standards introduced after the 9/11 terrorist attacks, more time is needed for scheduled flights. General safety concerns regarding scheduled flights have also increased demand for business jet transports. For business travellers, the greater productivity during the flight is also an important argument in favour of business jets. Business travellers can talk to their employees or read files without being watched or disturbed by other passengers. Some models feature a conference room, Internet connection and other communications facilities. Business jets also offer much greater travelling comfort than regular flights. In some cases, passengers can drive straight to the aircraft in their private cars and board it without having to wait – while their luggage is being safety checked. This way, they do not have to walk long distances as is the case in most major airports.

According to a Bombardier market study on European business jet customers, they attach importance to:

- time savings and convenience;
- direct access even to remote destinations;
- relatively new aircraft adapted to customers' personal tastes (colours, equipment);
- easy booking, payment and service provision;
- safety of the jets and quality of the operators;
- usage concepts that do not require users to own the jet;
- avoiding public attention or criticism for using business jets.

Future perspectives

Going forward, we will see a growing number of partnerships between jet operators and other service providers for effective marketing support. American Express is a pioneer in this area. Together with Le Bas International (a charter company that cooperates with over 5,000 jet operators and airlines), American Express offers a bonus programme to its Platinum Card or Centurion Card customers. These customers can charter business jets using their credit card and benefit from special advantages such as high jet availability and more bonus points for their credit card turnover.

Marquis Jet's partnerships go even one step further. Marquis Jet customers who buy a yacht from Sea Ray get a certain number of flight hours as an incentive, depending on the yacht model chosen. Marquis Jet has also entered partnerships to offer services such as private jet plus rental car and private jet plus holiday club. This shows that private jets are well suited for being marketed in combination with other high-end products.

QUESTIONS

1 Please explain which relationships in the total value chain would be most important for Dassault Falcon to focus on.

2 Please explain how Dassault Falcon can benefit from a collaboration with a complementor or (in)direct competitor.

3 Is key account management (KAM) relevant to use for Dassault Falcon? If yes, how?

SOURCES

Datamonitor (www.datamonitor.com); Euromonitor International (www.euromonitor.com); HSH Nordbank (2005) *Sector Report: Business Jets Market, Operator Models, Owners, Market Trends, Secondary Market*, March, p. 5.

QUESTIONS FOR DISCUSSION

1 Identify the measures that can be used to encourage long-term relationships with customers.

2 What specific segmentation criteria could be used to categorise different loyalty segments?

3 Evaluate the strengths and weaknesses of frequent user programmes.

4 What are the arguments for spending money to keep existing customers loyal (customer retention)?

5   Put the arguments for and against the statement that 'the customer is always right'.

6   What are the motives for entering KAM?

7   Describe the different stages in KAM.

8   What is the purpose of implementing a customer complaint management system?

REFERENCES

Adage Global (2001) Daily news, *Adage Global*, 19 February (www.adageglobal.com).

BBC (2000) Millionaire show earns owners a fortune, *BBC Business News*, 14 December (http://news.bbc.co.uk/).

BBC (2001a) Millionaire? Cleared of ratings 'fix', *BBC Business News*, 15 January (http://.bbc.co.uk/).

BBC (2001b) Boeing signs Russian space deal, *BBC Business News*, 13 April (http://news.bbc.co.uk).

BBC (2001c) Quiz show scoops business award, *BBC Business News*, 20 April (http://news.bbc.co.uk/).

BBC (2001d) Will ITC website capture the net? *BBC Business News*, 25 April (http://news.bbc.co.uk).

BBC (2002) TV's Millionaire misses the jackpot, *BBC Business News*, 7 March (http://news.bbc.co.uk).

Bhalla, G., Evgeniou, T. and Lerer, L. (2004) Customer relationship management and networked healthcare in the pharmaceutical industry, *International Journal of Medical Marketing*, 4(4): 370–79.

Blasberg, J., Vishwanath, V. and Allen, J. (2008) Tools for converting consumers into advocates, *Strategy & Leadership*, 36(2): 16–23.

Booms, B. H. and Bitner, M. J. (1981) Marketing strategies and organization structures for service firms, in J. H. Donnelly and W. R. George (eds) *Marketing of Services*, American Marketing Association, Chicago, IL, pp. 47–51.

Brown, P. J. (2000) Satellites: the next generation, *Broadcasting & Cable*, 31 July: 48–50.

Bullock, C. (2000) Alcatel Space cashes in on global joint ventures, *Interavia*, December: 45–7.

Buttle, F. (1989) Marketing services, in P. Jones (ed.) *Management in Service Industries*, Pitman, London, pp. 235–59.

Celador (2000) *Who Wants To Be A Millionaire?* format sold to Japan, Celador Productions press release, 25 February.

Cheverton, P. (1999) *Key Account Management: The Route to Profitable Supplier Status*, Kogan Page, London.

CNN (2000) 'Millionaire' quiz show import doesn't find success in Japan, *CNN Business News*, 9 August (www.cnn.com/2000/asianow).

Dick, A. S. and Basu, K. (1994) Customer loyalty: toward an integrated conceptual framework, *Journal of the Academy of Marketing Science*, 22(2): 99–113.

Grönroos, C. (2000) *Service Management and Marketing: A Customer Relationship Management Approach*, 2nd edn, John Wiley, Chichester.

Harbert, T. (2000) Beaming business abroad, *Electronic Business*, June: 76–84.

Hennig-Thurau, T. H. and Hansen, U. (2000) *Relationship Marketing: Gaining Competitive Advantage Through Customer Satisfaction and Consumer Retention*, Springer-Verlag, Berlin-Heidelberg.

Heskett, J. J., Jones, T. O., Loveman, G. W., Sasser, W. E., Jr, and Schlesinger, L. A. (2008) Putting the service-profit chain to work, *Harvard Business Review*, July/August: 118–29.

Hoffman, J. L. and Lowitt, E. M. (2008) A better way to design loyalty programs, *Strategy & Leadership*, 36(4): 44–7.

Holmlund, M. (2000) Perceived quality in business relationships, Hanken, Swedish School of Economics, Helsinki/Helsingfros, Finland, CERS.

HSH Nordbank (2005) *Sector Report: Business Jets Market, Operator Models, Owners, Market Trends, Secondary Market*, March.

Hutt, M. D. and Speh, T. W. (2001) *Business Marketing Management*, 7th edn, Harcourt College Publishers, Orlando, FL.

Jackson, B. B. (1985) Build customer relationships that last, *Harvard Business Review*, 63 (November/December): 120–8.

Jackson, T. W. (2007) Personalisation and CRM, *Database Marketing & Customer Strategy Management*, 15(1): 24–36.

Karantinou, K. M. and Hogg, M. K. (2007) Developing and managing relational market-based assets in professional services: client relationships in management consultancy, *The Marketing Management Journal*, 17(2): 16–39.

Keveney, B. (2001) ABC still placing bets on 'Millionaire': in 'good position' in event of strike, *USA Today*, 15 January.

Laaksonen, T., Pajunen, K. and Kulmala, H. I. (2008) Co-evolution of trust and dependence in customer–supplier relationships, *Industrial Marketing Management*, 37(8): 910–20.

Leavy, B. (2004) Partnering with the customer, *Strategy & Leadership*, 32(3): 10–13.

McDonald, M., Millman, T. and Rogers, B. (1996) Key account management: learning from supplier and customer perspectives, Cranfield School of Management in association with The Chartered Institute of Marketing.

McDonald, M., Millman, T. and Rogers, B. (1997) Key account management: theory, practice and challenges, *Journal of Marketing Management*, 13: 737–57.

McKenzie, J. and van Winkelen, C. (2006) Creating successful partnerships: the importance of sharing knowledge, *Journal of General Management*, 31(4) (Summer): 45–61.

Mascarenhas, O. A., Kesavan, R. and Bernacchi, M. (2006) Lasting customer loyalty: a total customer experience approach, *Journal of Consumer Marketing*, 23(7): 397–405.

Millman, T. and Wilson, K. (1994) From key account selling to key account management, Tenth Annual Conference on Industrial Marketing and Purchasing (IMP), University of Groningen, the Netherlands. Also published in the *Journal of Marketing Practice*, 1(1): 9–21.

Mouzas, S., Henneberg, S. and Naudè, P. (2008) Developing network insight, *Industrial Marketing Management*, 37(2): 167–80.

Ojasalo, J. (2001) Key account management at company and individual levels in business-to-business relationships, *Journal of Business and Industrial Marketing*, 16(3): 199–218.

Paas, L. and Kuijlen, T. (2001) Towards a general definition of customer relationship management, *Journal of Database Marketing*, 9(1): 51–60.

Peppers, D. and Rogers, M. (1995) A new marketing paradigm: share of customer, not market share, *Harvard Business Review*, July–August: 105–13.

Raymond, J. (2001) Home field advantage, *American Demographics*, April: 34–6.

Reichheld, F. F. (1994) Loyalty and the renaissance of marketing management, *Marketing Management*, 12(4): 17–25.

Reichheld, F. F. and Schefter, P. (2000) E-loyalty: your secret weapon on the web, *Harvard Business Review*, 7(1): 105–13.

Rese, M. (2006) Successful and sustainable business partnerships: how to select the right partners, *Industrial Marketing Management*, 35(1): 72–82.

Ruyter, K. and Wetzels, M. (2000) Customer considerations in service recovery: a cross-industry perspective, *International Journal of Service Industry Management*, 11(1): 91–108.

Smith, B. A. (1999) New launchers seek commercial market share, *Aviation Week & Space Technology*, 13 December: 50–2.

Stace, D. and Bhalla, A. (2008) Sustaining the 'connective tissue' of customer relationships, *Strategic Change*, 17(4): 57–68.

Tenneco Automotive (2000) Tenneco Automotive and Futaba Industrial Co. sign agreements to form a global strategic alliance and establish a joint venture in the UK, *Tenneco Automotive News*, 30 October.

Thakur, R., Summey, J. H. and Balasubramanian, S. K. (2006) CRM as strategy: avoiding the pitfall of tactics, *The Marketing Management Journal*, 16(2): 147–54.

Üstüner, T. and Godes, D. (2006) Better sales networks, *Harvard Business Review*, July/August: 102–12.

Vandermerwe, S. (2000) How increasing value to customers improves business results, *Sloan Management Review*, Fall: 27–37.

Wansink, B. and Seed, S. (2001) Making brand loyalty programs succeed, *Brand Management*, 8(3) (February): 211–22.

Webster, F. E. (1992) The changing role of marketing in the corporation, *Journal of Marketing*, 56 (October): 1–17.

Williamson, O. E. (1979) Transaction cost economics: the governance of contractual relations, *Journal of Law and Economics*, 22 (October): 232–62.

Xevelonakis, E. (2008) Managing event-driven customer relationships in telecommunications, *Database Marketing & Customer Strategy Management*, 15(3): 146–52.

Yip, G. S. and Bink, A. J. M. (2007) Managing global accounts, *Harvard Business Review*, September: 103–11.

CHAPTER 11
Product and service decisions

LEARNING OBJECTIVES

After studying this chapter you should be able to:

- explain the mix of product and service elements
- explore levels of a product offer
- define the categories of service
- determine the 'service quality gap'
- explore the stages in 'new product development'
- discuss different forms of the product life cycle
- discuss what it means to develop new products for foreign markets
- discuss the term 'brand equity'
- define and explain the different branding alternatives
- discuss how the Internet might be integrated in future product innovations
- discuss the implications of the 'long tail' concept

11.1 INTRODUCTION

The product decision is among the first decisions that a marketing manager makes in order to develop a marketing mix. This chapter examines product-related issues and suggests conceptual approaches for handling them. Also discussed are product development, brand (labelling) strategies, service policies and Internet product decisions (including 'long tail').

What is a product?

Products, or services, are the vital ingredients of the market offering and are the vehicles for providing customer satisfaction. The product is the object of the exchange process, the thing which the producer or supplier offers to a potential customer in exchange for something else which the supplier perceives as equivalent or greater value. Conventionally, this something else is money. In the absence of money, we must resort to barter or counter trade where goods are traded against other goods. It follows that for an exchange to occur someone must have a demand for the object in question and be willing to exchange money or other assets, which are seen as possessing value.

Two particularly important ideas have been introduced in the discussion of demand preference and substitutability. Preference defines the extent to which a consumer will favour one product over another, while substitutability reflects how well one product may take the place of another. The latter qualification is particularly important to marketers because it is similar to brand switching.

Importance of service

The value of global trade in services is growing by over 10 per cent per year and this trend is expected to continue. The traditional G-D (Goods dominant) logic suggests that the firm "produces" value and that the customers (consumers) are users of value. In this way customers are exogenous to the value creation process. According to the evolving Service Dominant (S-D) logic, customers are endogenous to value creation, because they constitute active co-creators of value, together with the firm (Vargo & Lusch, 2008; Merz et al., 2009).

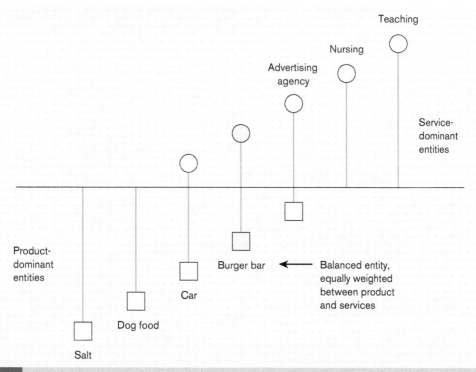

| Figure 11.1 | Combination of service and product for different products |

Source: From Shostack, G. L. (1981) How to design a service, in J. Donnelly and W. George (eds) *Marketing of Services*, American Marketing Association, Chicago, p. 22. Reproduced with permission.

11.2 THE COMPONENTS OF THE PRODUCT OFFER

In creating an acceptable product offer for international markets, it is necessary to examine first what contributes to the total product offer. Kotler (2000) suggests that there are five levels of the product offer which should be considered by marketers in order to make the product attractive to international markets. In the product components of Figure 11.2 we include not just the core physical properties, but also additional elements such as packaging, branding and after-sales service that make up the total package for the purchaser.

We can also see from Figure 11.2 that it is much easier to standardise the core product benefits (functional features, performance, etc.) across borders than it is to standardise the support services, which often have to be tailored to the business culture and sometimes to individual customers.

11.3 SERVICE STRATEGIES

Characteristics of services

Before considering possible international service strategies, it is important to consider the special nature of global service marketing. Services are characterised by the following features:

Intangibility
A characteristic of services, namely that they cannot be touched, seen, tasted or smelled.

- **Intangibility:** as services such as air transportation or education cannot be touched or tested, the buyers or services cannot claim ownership or anything tangible in the traditional sense. Payment is for use or performance. Tangible elements of the service, such as food or drink on airlines, are used as part of the service in order to confirm the benefit provided and to enhance its perceived value.

- *Perishability*: services cannot be stored for future usage – for example, unfilled airline seats are lost once the aircraft takes off. This characteristic causes considerable problems

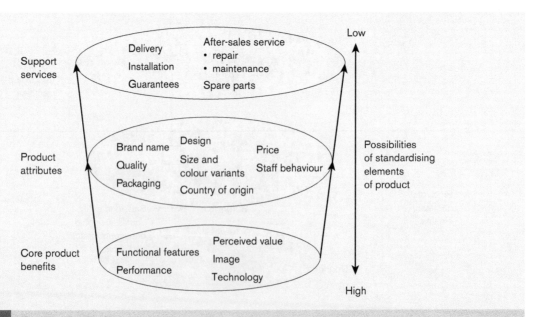

Figure 11.2	The three levels of a product

Source: Hollensen, S. (2001) *Global Marketing: A Market Responsive Approach*, 2nd ed., Financial Times-Prentice Hall, Harlow, p. 396. Reproduced with permission.

in planning and promotion in order to match supply and demand. To maintain service capacity constantly at levels necessary to satisfy peak demand will be very expensive. The marketer must therefore attempt to estimate demand levels in order to optimise the use of capacity.

- *Heterogeneity*: services are rarely the same because they involve interactions between people. Furthermore, there is high customer involvement in the production of services. This can cause problems of maintaining quality, particularly in international markets where there are quite different attitudes towards customer service.

- **Inseparability**: the time of production is very close to or even simultaneous with the time of consumption. The service is provided at the point of sale. This means that economies of scale and experience curve benefits are difficult to achieve, and supplying the service to scattered markets can be expensive, particularly in the initial setting-up phase.

Inseparability
A characteristic of services, namely that their production cannot be separated from their consumption.

Categories of service

All products, both goods and services, consist of a core element that is surrounded by a variety of optional elements. If we look first at the core service products, we can assign them to one of three broad categories depending on their tangibility and the extent to which customers need to be present during service production. These categories are presented in Table 11.1.

Determining the service quality gap

Quality is often considered to be one of the keys to success. The competitive advantage of the firm is said to depend on the quality and value of its goods and services.

Figure 11.3 illustrates how quality factors are connected to traditional marketing activities resulting in a perceived service quality. Good total quality is obtained when the gap between the customer's expected service quality and perceived service quality is zero or very small, meaning that perceived service quality meets the customer's expectations of the expected service quality. If expected service quality is much higher than the perceived service quality, the gap will be large and the total service quality will be low, even if the perceived service quality, measured in an objective way, is good.

As shown in Figure 11.3 the customer's expected service quality and perceived service quality is a function of a number of factors, most of which can be controlled by the company. The expected service quality is highly influenced by the firm's marketing and communication tools. The image and word of mouth factors, as well as public relations, are only indirectly controlled by the firm. The needs of the customers and their past experience with the company may also have an impact on their expectations.

On the other hand, what really counts is the quality as it is perceived by the customers (perceived service quality). Basically, the perceived service quality has two factors: a *technical* or outcome factor, and a *functional* or process-related factor. The hotel guest will be provided with a room and a bed to sleep in, the airline passenger will be transported from one place to another, a company may get its goods transported from its warehouse to a customer. These are examples of the technical quality factor. What the customers basically receive in their interaction with a firm is clearly important to them and their quality perception. It is what the customer is left with, when the service production process and its buyer–seller interactions are over. Sometimes this dimension can be measured relatively objectively by customers because of its characteristic as a technical solution to a problem. However, as there are a number of interactions between the service provider and the customer, the customer will also be influenced by the way in which the technical quality is transferred to him or her. This is called the functional quality of the process. It is easy to see that the functional quality cannot be evaluated as objectively as the technical factor; it is frequently perceived very subjectively. The

Table 11.1	Three categories of service		
Categories of service	Characteristics	Examples (service provider)	Possibilities of worldwide standardisation (hence utilising economies of scale, experience effects, lower costs)
People processing	Customers become part of the production process. The service firm needs to maintain local geographic presence.	Education (schools, universities). Passenger transportation (airlines, car rental). Healthcare (hospitals). Food service (fast food resturants). Lodging service (hotel).	No good possibilities: because of 'customer involvement in production', many local sites will be needed, making this type of service very difficult to operate globally.
Possession processing	Involve tangible actions to physical objects to improve their value to customers. The object needs to be involved in the production process, but the owner of the object (the customer) does not. A local geographic presence is required.	Car repair (garages). Freight transport (forwarding agent). Equipment installation (electrician). Laundry service (laundrette).	Better possibilities: compared to people-processing services, this involves a lower degree of contact between the customer and the service personnel. This type of service is not so culture-sensitive.
Information-based services	Collecting, manipulating, interpreting and transmitting data to create value. Minimal tangibility. Minimal customer involvement in the production process.	Telecommunication services (telephone companies). Banking. News. Market analysis. Internet services (producers of homepages on Web, database providers).	Very good possibilities: worldwide standardisation from one central location (single sourcing) because of the 'virtual' nature of these services.

Source: Hollensen, S. (2001) *Global Marketing: A Market Responsive Approach*, 2nd ed., Financial Times-Prentice Hall, Harlow, p. 399. Reproduced with permission.

Single sourcing
Purchasing a product on a regular basis from a single vendor.

two quality factors, what and how, are not only valid for services. The technical solution for a customer provided by, for example, a machine – in the production function – is part of the overall technical quality perceived by this customer. But attempts to tailor this machine to the specific demands of a customer is an additional value and therefore part of the overall functional quality which the customer experiences.

The technical quality of a service process is normally a prerequisite for good quality. It has to be at an acceptable level. The definition of an acceptable level depends on the firm's strategy and the needs and expectations of the customers. However, once the outcome is good enough, this becomes transparent, and should not be used as a way of differentiating the product or service.

The functional quality (how) perception is also influenced by elements of the physical environment. The where aspect is considered to be part of the how factor, which is logical

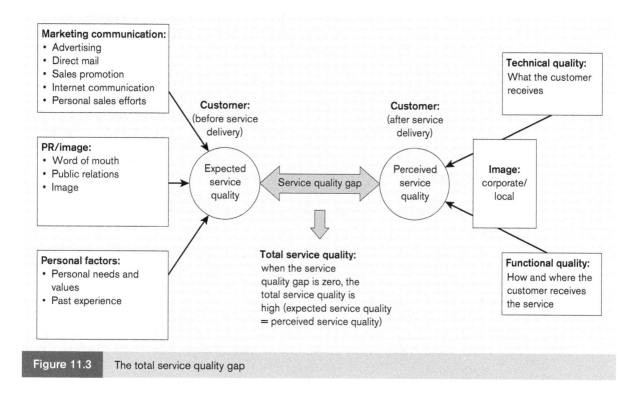

Figure 11.3 The total service quality gap

because the perception of the process clearly is dependent on the service process in, for example, a restaurant.

Usually the service provider cannot hide behind brand names or distributors. In most cases the firm, its resources and its operating methods are visible to the customers. The firm's corporate and/or local image is therefore of the utmost importance to most services. It can affect the perception of quality in various ways. If the provider has a favourable image in the minds of the customers, minor mistakes will probably be forgiven. However, if mistakes often occur, the image will be damaged.

As far as the perceived service quality is concerned, the image can be viewed as a filter, as illustrated in Figure 11.3 (Grönroos, 2000).

After-sales services (AS)

Customer service provides one important means by which a company can tailor its offerings to the needs and desires of its customers. By offering good service, a company assures consumers that it stands behind its products and projects a reliable and high-quality image. Customer services offered after the sales transaction is completed are of crucial importance in this respect. Here, AS is defined as those activities in which a firm engages after purchase of its product that minimise potential problems related to product use and maximise the value of the consumption experience. Researchers have suggested that AS consists of a number of elements. Here, AS is conceptualised as consisting of: the installation and start-up of the purchased product, the provision of spare parts for products, the provision of repair services, technical advice regarding the product, and the provision and support of warranties.

AS adds to the product's value and is often treated as an integral part of the product. Levitt (1983) suggests that because the provision of AS enhances product value in a manner similar to other intangible product components, these service elements should be regarded as part of the augmented product (Asugman *et al.*, 1997).

The potential financial importance of these services has been called to the attention of corporations. Herbig and Palumbo (1993) suggest that 'Profit margins for aftermarket services are typically about 15% to 25% before taxes, whereas those for products are only 7% to 11% . . . Often, up to 25% to 40% of corporate revenues and from 20% to 50% of corporate profits can be generated from the aftermarket service components of a business.'

Customer support in after-sales service

Goffin and New (2001) suggest that there are seven key elements of customer support in B2B after-sales service:

- *Installation*: for many products, the first element of product support following the sale is installation. For complex products, or where safety issues are involved, personnel from the manufacturing company or their representatives usually perform this.
- *User training*: the complexity of some types of equipment means that manufacturers must provide good training for users. For example, the successful implementation of new manufacturing equipment often depends on extensive training. Many products include functions that help users learn to use them more efficiently; these can range from simple help functions to full computer training packages.
- *Documentation*: most products require some form of documentation. Typical forms of documentation cover equipment operation, installation, maintenance and repair. Good documentation can reduce support costs (Miskie, 1989).
- *Maintenance and repair*: historically, this has always been an important element of customer support. Maintenance is necessary to clean, refurbish or replace parts or equipment which otherwise would be liable to fail. If equipment fails, fast and efficient repair is essential in many markets because down-time costs are very high – often many times the price of spare parts or service. Manufacturers need to have effective logistics for the management of customer support engineers and the movement of spares, the parts used in repairs.
- *Online support*: telephone advice on products is important in many industries. Product experts give online consultations to customers to help them use products more efficiently, or sometimes to trace the cause of faults.
- *Warranty*: manufacturers' warranties reduce the financial risk of owning products. Over the working lifetime of a product, support costs can be high and so many manufacturers offer customers the possibility to purchase an extended warranty.
- *Upgrades*: customers may be offered the opportunity to enhance the performance of existing products. For example, computer upgrades increase the working lifetimes of products.

Over the years there has been a change in the relative importance of different elements of customer support. In the past, when many products had high failure rates, the most important aspect of support was fast and reliable repair. New technologies have now typically led to more reliable products. However, increased product complexity (which is often software based) means that the importance of user training and online support has increased.

Full service contracts

Based on Stremersch *et al.* (2001), 'full service' can be defined as:

> a comprehensive bundle of products and/or services, that fully satisfies the needs and wants of a customer related to a specific event or problem.

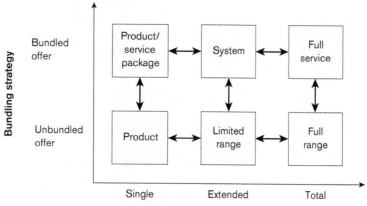

Figure 11.4 The full service concept

Source: From Stremersch, S., Wuyts, S. and Frambach, R. T. (2001) The purchasing of full-service contracts, *Industrial Marketing Management*, 30. Copyright © 2001 Elsevier Science. Reproduced with permission.

The concept of a full service strategy is clearly related to the concepts of 'bundling' and 'systems selling'. Bundling can be defined as 'the offering of groups of products and/or services as a package'.

Thus, the concept of full service is composed of two conceptually distinct components, that is, a bundling strategy (a bundle of products and/or services) and an extension in customer need fulfilment (that fully satisfies the needs and wants of a customer related to a specific event or problem).

In Figure 11.4 these components are examined in the following way:

- *Bundling strategy*: does the supplier firm bundle its products and/or services? Within this component three types are distinguished: pure components (unbundled offer), mixed bundling (components are available in a bundled as well as an unbundled offer) and pure bundling (components are only available in a bundled offer) (Smith, 2006).

- *Extension in need fulfilment*: this component comprises the extent to which customer needs are satisfied by the supplier firm; the three levels of customer need fulfilment are indicated in Figure 11.4, that is, single, extended and total.

Figure 11.4 positions full-service strategies relative to other (B2B) marketing strategies. It illustrates that firms pursuing a full-service strategy can be challenged on two factors. Competitive offerings may compete with full-service suppliers by focusing on satisfying specific customer needs, either by means of bundled or unbundled offers. Alternatively, competitors may choose to satisfy multiple needs by offering different unbundled solutions. This approach may appeal to customers seeking high levels of flexibility in their purchasing behaviour.

Therefore, it is clear that industrial customer firms will evaluate full service offerings differently from mere product or service offerings. These differences are likely to be related to both the purchasing criteria used as well as the purchasing process itself. The high degree of comprehensiveness and potential implications for full service contracts is likely to positively influence both more of the DMU (decision making unit) members and the DMU's heterogeneity.

In the research of service maintenance contracts, Stremersch *et al.* (2001) found that maintenance companies (and OEMs) will have to broaden their marketing and sales approach in a horizontal as well as a vertical way. Higher management levels are involved in the buying process as well as other departments. Furthermore, other buying motives will come into play through the involvement of different people. Maintenance firms will also have to be prepared for a longer decision-making process and develop specific tools, for instance to calculate the total cost of ownership, for specific phases throughout the extended buying process (Heskett *et al.*, 2008; Reinartz, 2008; Frei, 2008; Allmendinger and Lombreglia, 2005).

11.4 NEW PRODUCT DEVELOPMENT (NPD)

Long-term success is dependent on the ability to compete with others. One of the most important conditions for achieving this is to ensure that your firm's products are superior to the competition, by adding new competitive products to the product portfolio.

Idea generation stage
The stage in new product development in which a marketer engages in a continuing search for product ideas consistent with target market needs and the organisation's objectives.

The traditional NPD model involves the following stages in product development: **idea generation**, screening, concept development and testing, business analysis, product development and testing, **test marketing**, commercialisation or launch (Baker and Hart, 1999, pp. 154–7).

The multiple convergent process model

Test marketing
The stage of new product development where the product and marketing programme are tested in realistic market settings, such as a well-defined geographic area.

Baker and Hart (1999) have suggested the following multiple convergent process model (Figure 11.5) that has been derived from the idea of parallel processing (Smith *et al.*, 2007).

In the multiple convergent approach, there are tasks that must be carried out in different internal departments (research and development, marketing, engineering/design, manufacturing) and carried out in cooperation with external partners (suppliers and customers). Hence, the total number of different actors/departments involved in the NPD process is six, as illustrated in Figure 11.5. The tasks have to be carried out simultaneously and the results must converge at some point, which is likely to happen several times due to the iterations in the process.

Consequently, there are multiple convergent points that link the activity-stage model to the decision-stage models. The extent of involvement of internal and external groups will be determined by the firm's specific needs in the product development process.

One of the advantages of this model is that it recognises the involvment of external partners in the product development process. There is growing interest in the need for supplier and customer involvement in the NPD. From the customers, the firm can benefit from new product ideas and product adaptations to specific customer needs. The supplier can contribute with supplier innovation and just-in-time techniques.

Product platform/modularity in NPD

The modular approach to product development is an important success factor in many markets. By sharing components and production processes across a product platform, companies can develop differentiated products efficiently, increase the flexibility and responsiveness of their manufacturing processes, and take market share away from competitors that develop only one product at a time.

The modular approach is also a way to achieve successful mass customisation – the manufacture of products in high volumes that are tailored to meet the needs of individual customers. It allows highly differentiated products to be delivered to the market without consuming excessive resources.

Product modularity consists of designing a platform that is a collection of assets that are shared by a set of products. These assets can be divided into four categories (Robertson and Ulrich, 1998), as follows:

- *Components*: the part designs of a product, the fixtures and tools needed to make them, the circuit designs, and the programs burned into programmable chips or stored on disks.

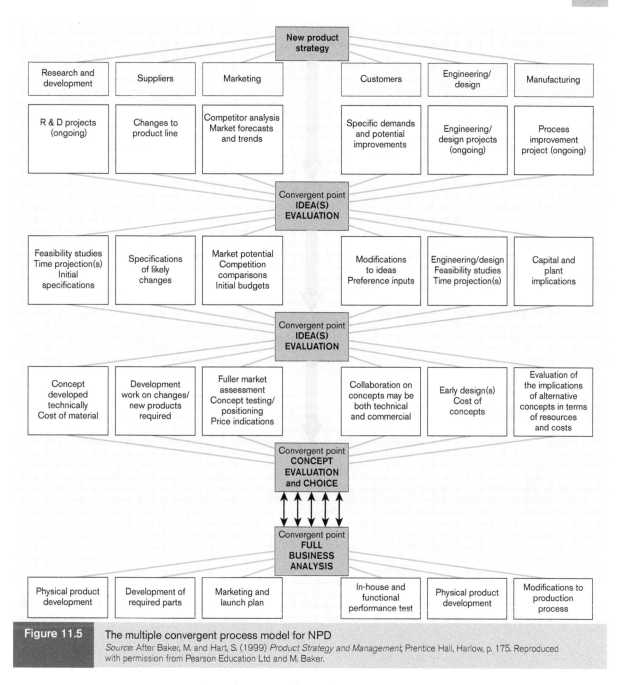

Figure 11.5	The multiple convergent process model for NPD

Source: After Baker, M. and Hart, S. (1999) *Product Strategy and Management*, Prentice Hall, Harlow, p. 175. Reproduced with permission from Pearson Education Ltd and M. Baker.

- *Processes*: the equipment used to make components or to assemble components into products and the design of the associated production process and supply chain.
- *Knowledge*: design know-how, technology applications and limitations, production techniques, mathematical models and testing methods.
- *People and relationships*: teams, relationships among team members, relationships between the team and the larger organisation, and relationships with a network of suppliers.

This general product platform should then be used for tailoring end products to the needs of different market segments or customers. The platform approach reduces the incremental cost of addressing the specific needs of a market segment or of an individual customer. See also Figure 11.6 for an example of the modular approach in new product development. For simplicity, only the interaction between two product modules is illustrated.

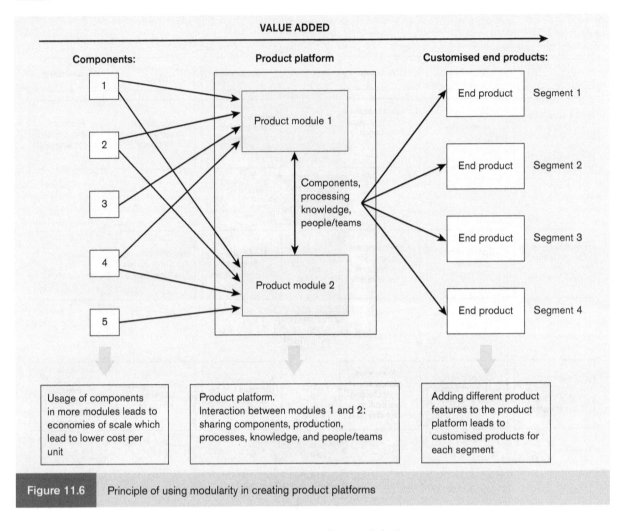

| Figure 11.6 | Principle of using modularity in creating product platforms |

The firm's advantages in using product modularity are:

- *reduction of development cost and time*: parts and assembly processes developed for one end product can be used for other products;
- *reduction of variable costs*: when producing larger volumes of common components, companies achieve economies of scale, which cuts costs in materials management, logistics, distribution, inventory management, sales and service, and purchasing;
- *reduction of production investments*: machinery, equipment and tooling, and the engineering time needed to create them, can be shared across higher production volumes;
- *reduction of risks*: the lower investment required for each product developed from a platform results in decreased risk for each new product. Sharing components across products allows companies to stock fewer parts in their production and service parts inventories, which translates into better service levels and/or lower service costs.

11.5 THE PRODUCT LIFECYCLE

The concept of the product lifecycle (PLC) provides useful inputs into making product decisions and formulating product strategies (Kvesic, 2008).

Products, like individuals, pass through a series of stages. Each stage is identified by its sales performance and characterised by different levels of profitability, various degrees of competition

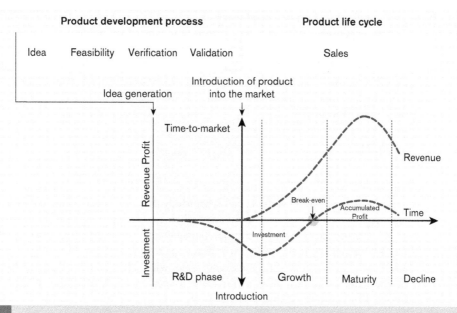

Figure 11.7 The PLC and time-to-market

and distinctive marketing programmes. The four stages of the product life cycle are introduction, growth, maturity and decline. The basic model of the PLC is shown in Figure 11.7, where also the stages prior to the actual sales are included. In total these stages represent the so-called time to market (TTM).

Time to market (TTM) is the length of time it takes from a product being conceived to its being available for sale. TTM is important in industries where products are outdated quickly, for example in the IT industry.

Rapid time-to-market is important for the competitive success of many companies for the following reasons:

- competitive advantage of getting to market sooner;
- premium prices early in life cycle;
- faster break-even on development investment and lower financial risk;
- greater overall profits and higher return on investment.

The key process requirements for rapid time-to-market are:

- clear understanding of customer needs at the start of the project and stability in product requirements or specifications;
- a characterised, optimised product development process;
- a realistic project plan based on this process;
- availability of needed resources to support the project and use of full-time, dedicated personnel;
- early involvement and rapid staffing build-up to support the parallel design of product and process;
- virtual product development including digital assembly modelling and early analysis and simulation to minimise time-consuming physical mock-ups and testing;
- design re-use and standardisation to minimise the design content of a project.

Pure speed, that is, bring the product to market as quickly as possible, is valuable in fast-moving industries, but it is not always the best objective. Many managers figure that the shorter the product development project, the less it will cost, so they attempt to use TTM as a means of cutting expenses. Unfortunately, a primary means of reducing TTM is to staff the project more heavily, so a faster project may actually be more expensive.

The PLC emphasises the need to review marketing objectives and strategies as products pass through various stages. It is helpful to think of marketing decisions during the lifetime of a product, but managers need to be aware of the limitations of the PLC so they are not misled by its prescriptions.

Limitations of the product life cycle

Misleading strategy prescriptions

The PLC is a dependent variable that is determined by the marketing mix; it is not an independent variable to which firms should adapt their marketing programmes (Dhalla and Yuspeh, 1976). If a product's sale is declining, management should not conclude that the brand is in the decline stage. If management withdraws marketing resources from the brand, it will create a self-fulfilling prophecy and the brand's sales will continue to decline. Instead, management might increase marketing support in order to create a new cycle. This could be realised by use of one or more of the following measures:

- product improvements (e.g. new product packaging);
- reposition perception of the product;
- reach new users of the product (via new distribution outlets);
- promote more frequent use of the product (fulfilling same need);
- promote new uses of the product (fulfilling new needs).

Fads

Fads
Fashions that enter quickly are adopted with great speed, peak early and decline very fast.

Not all products follow the classic PLC curve. **Fads** are fashions that are adopted very quickly by the public, peak early and decline very fast. It is difficult to predict whether something will be only a fad, or how long it will last. The amount of mass-media attention together with other factors will influence the fad's duration.

Unpredictability

The duration of the PLC stages is unpredictable. Critics charge that markets can seldom tell what stage the product is in. A product may appear to be mature when actually it has only reached a temporary plateau prior to another upsurge.

Levels of the product life cycle

The PLC concept can be examined at various levels, from the life cycle of a whole industry or product form (the technological life cycle or TLC) (Popper and Buskirk, 1992) to the life cycle of a single model of a specific product. It is probably most useful to think in terms of the life cycle of a product form such as photocopiers or video cassette recorders. Life cycles for product forms include definable groups of direct and close competitors and a core technology. These characteristics make life cycles for product forms easier to identify and analyse, and would seem to have more stable and general implications. In Figure 11.8 an example of different PLC levels is shown.

Another example of a TLC shift happened when the compact disc (CD) format was introduced as a result of a joint development between Philips and Sony. A key success factor of the CD format in displacing the old LP record format was the ownership by Sony of CBS in the USA, and by Philips of Polygram in Europe, which are two of the biggest music companies in the world. This contributed to the new CD format establishing itself as the industry standard.

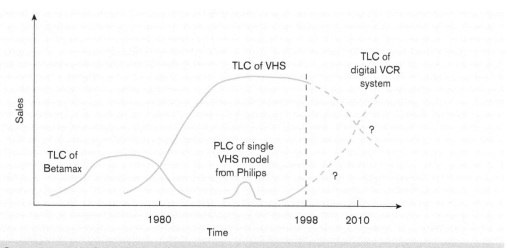

Figure 11.8	Comparisons of TLC for different VCR systems and PLC of a single VCR model

Source: Hollensen, S. (2001) *Global Marketing: A Market Responsive Approach*, 2nd ed., Financial Times-Prentice Hall, Harlow, p. 403. Reproduced with permission.

However, there were also a number of barriers to the adoption of the new format. The potential users had already invested in LP record collections and the prices of discs and players were relatively high at the beginning of the TLC.

11.6 NEW PRODUCTS FOR THE INTERNATIONAL MARKET

Customer needs are the starting point for product development, whether for domestic or global markets. In addition to customer needs, conditions of use and ability to buy the product form a framework for decisions on new product development for the international market.

Developing new products/cutting the time-to-market

As a consequence of increasing international competition, speed is becoming a key success factor for an increasing number of companies that manufacture technologically sophisticated products.

This speed of change in the environment is accelerating, leading to greater complexity and added 'turbulence', or discontinuity. Technological developments are combining to shorten product life cycles and speed up commercialisation times. The increasing turbulence in the market makes it particularly difficult to predict. As a result planning time scales have been shortened. Where long-term plans in relatively predictable markets could span 10–15 years, very few companies today are able to plan beyond the next few years in any but the most general terms.

In parallel to shorter PLCs, the product development times for new products are being greatly reduced. This applies not only to technical products in the field of office communication equipment, but also to cars and consumer electronics. In some cases there have been reductions in development times of more than half.

Similarly, the time for marketing and selling, and hence also to pay off R&D costs, has gone down from about four years to only two years and less for a number of products, such as printers and computers, over a period of ten years (Töpfer, 1995, p. 68).

For all types of technological products it holds true that the manufactured product must be as good as required by the customer (i.e. as good as necessary), but not as good as is technically feasible. Too frequently, technological products are over-optimised and therefore too expensive from the customer's point of view.

Traditionally, Japanese and European suppliers to the car industry have had different approaches to the product development process. Normally the Japanese have been able to develop a product in a shorter time using the newest technology.

The reason for the better time competition of the Japanese manufacturers is the intensive use of:

- early integration of customers and suppliers;
- multi-skilled project teams;
- interlinking of R&D, production and marketing activities;
- total quality management;
- parallel planning of new products and the required production facilities (simultaneous engineering);
- high degree of outsourcing (reduction of internal manufacturing content).

Today product quality is not enough to reach and to satisfy the customer. Quality of design and appearance play an increasingly important role. Highly qualified product support staff and high quality customer service are also required.

Degrees of product newness

A new product can have several degrees of newness. A product may be an entirely new invention (new to the world) or it may be a slight modification of an existing product (cost reductions). In Figure 11.9, newness has two factors: newness to the market (consumers, channels and public policy) and newness to the company.

Let us briefly discuss the main categories in Figure 11.9.

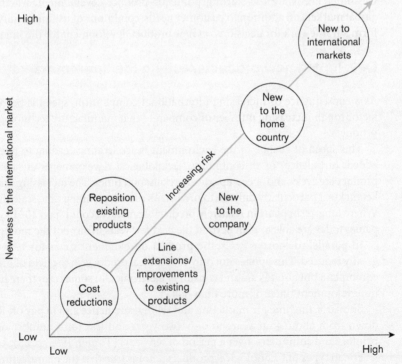

Figure 11.9   Different degrees of product newness

Source: Hollensen, S. (2001) *Global Marketing: A Market Responsive Approach*, 2nd ed., Financial Times-Prentice Hall, Harlow, p. 409. Reproduced with permission.

New to international markets

These represent a small proportion of all new products introduced. Most new products modify and improve a company's existing products. They are inventions that usually contain a significant development in technology such as a new discovery or manipulation of existing technology in a very different way leading to revolutionary new designs such as the Sony Discman. Other examples include Polaroid's instant camera and 3M's Post-its.

New to the company

Although not new to the marketplace, these products are new to the particular company. They provide an opportunity for the company to enter an established market for the first time. For example, Microsoft was able to enter the games console market when it launched X-Box, competing with Sony and Nintendo.

Line extensions

In this situation the company already has a line of products in the market. For example Virgin Soft Drink's Energy is an addition to its established line of cola brands.

Reposition existing products

This has more to do with new customer perception and branding than technical development. Therefore, this alternative may be new to the market (new perception) but not new to the company itself.

11.7 PRODUCT CANNIBALISATION

Cannibalisation
A situation where a new brand gains sales at the expense of another of the company's brands.

Introducing new brands that have a negative impact on the sales of existing products has often been regarded as a wrong product strategy. However, it is important that managers realise that proactive **cannibalisation** may be a sound strategy under certain conditions (Cravens *et al.*, 2000). This strategy ensures a continuing flow of new products, and recognises that products need to be replaced as they move through their life cycles. Managers of innovative firms often resist the instinct to preserve the value of part of the investment in products. Instead, these companies pursue a continuing strategy of investing in new products that will cannibalise existing products (Chandy and Tellis, 1998).

Conditions for successful cannibalisation

Successful cannibalisation strategies are more likely to occur in companies where:

- Effective market-sensing capabilities have been developed, enabling the firms to form accurate visions about their markets and how they are most likely to change.
- Some internal competition across business units is prevalent. Innovation is encouraged, and managers must compete for resources. Executives in these organisations accept cannibalisation threats, but by encouraging competition across business units, they focus their attention on the most promising product concepts. Senior management must coordinate these processes towards optimal performance for the product portfolio.
- New product champions are able to influence corporate decisions. For example, the chief executive may play a central leadership role in new product development.

A good example of successful proactive cannibalisation is as follows (Cravens *et al.*, 2000).

The German automobile group Volkswagen (VW) now holds more than 18 per cent of the European market, six points clear of its nearest rival, Fiat. This gain has been achieved by VW's multi-brand strategy. The VW group includes automobiles from the VW brand portfolio, but also the Audi, Seat and Skoda operations. There are several platforms across the group and shared R&D. The brands compete directly with each other in several car segments across Europe, but have different strengths in different national markets. Although the VW brand's sales have been cannibalised, the result has been overall market leadership.

11.8 PRODUCT POSITIONING

Product positioning is a key element in the successful marketing of any organisation in any market. The product or company that does not have a clear position in the customer's mind consequently stands for nothing and is rarely able to command more than a simple commodity or utility price. Premium pricing and competitive advantage are largely dependent upon the customer's perception that the product or service on offer is markedly different in some way from competitive offers (Devaney and Brown, 2008). How can we achieve a credible market position in international markets?

Since it is the buyer/user perception of benefit-generating attributes that is important, product positioning is the activity by which a desirable 'position' in the mind of the customer is created for the product. Positioning a product for international markets begins with describing specific products as comprising different attributes that are capable of generating a flow of benefits to buyers and users.

The global marketing planner puts these attributes into bundles so that the benefits generated match the special requirements of specific market segments. This product design problem involves not only the basic product components (physical, package, service and country of origin), but also brand name, styling and similar features.

Viewed in a multidimensional space (commonly denoted as 'perceptual mapping'), a product can be graphically represented at a point specified by its attributes. The location of a product's point in perceptual space is its 'position'. Competitors' products are similarly located (see also Johansson and Thorelli, 1985). If points representing other products are close to the point of the prototype then these other products are close competitors of the prototype. If the prototype is positioned away from its closest competitors in some international markets and its positioning implies important features for customers, then it is likely to have a significant competitive advantage.

11.9 BRAND EQUITY

A study by Citibank and Interbrand in 1997 found that companies basing their business on brands had outperformed the stock market for 15 years. The same study does, however, note the risky tendency of some brand owners to have reduced investments in brands in the mid-1990s with negative impacts on their performance (Hooley *et al.*, 1998, p. 120).

The following two examples show that brands add value for customers:

- The classic example is that in blind tests 51 per cent of consumers prefer Pepsi to Coca-Cola, but in open tests 65 per cent prefer Coca-Cola to Pepsi: soft drink preferences are based on brand image, not taste (Hooley *et al.*, 1998, p. 119).

- Skoda cars have been best known in the United Kingdom as the butt of bad jokes, reflecting a widespread belief that the cars are of very low quality. In 1995 Skoda was preparing to launch a new model in the United Kingdom, and did 'blind and seen' tests of the consumers' judgement of the vehicle. The vehicle was rated as better designed and worth more by those who did not know the make. With the Skoda name revealed, perceptions of the design were less favourable and estimated value was substantially lower. This leads us from the reputation of the company to branding (Hooley *et al.*, 1998, p. 117).

Definitions of 'brand equity'

Brand equity
The value of a brand, based on the extent to which it has high brand loyalty, name awareness, perceived quality, strong brand associations and other assets such as patents, trademarks and channel relationships.

Although the definition of **brand equity** is often debated (Raggio, 2009; Neal and Strauss, 2008), the term deals with the brand value, beyond the physical assets associated with its manufacture.

David Aaker of the University of California at Berkeley, one of the leading authorities on brand equity, has defined the term as 'a set of *brand assets and liabilities* linked to the brand, its name and symbol, that add to or subtract from the value provided by a product or service to a firm or to the firm's customers' (Aaker, 1991, p. 15).

Aaker has clustered those assets and liabilities into five categories:

1 *Brand loyalty*: encourages customers to buy a particular brand time after time and remain insensitive to competitors' offerings.

2 *Brand awareness*: brand names attract attention and convey images of familarity. May be translated to: how big a percentage of the customers know the brand name.

3 *Perceived quality*: 'perceived' means that the customers decide upon the level of quality, not the company (Wise and Zednickova, 2009).

4 *Brand associations*: the values and the personality that are linked to the brand.

5 *Other proprietary brand assets*: these include trademarks, patents and marketing channel relationships.

Brand equity can be thought of as the additional cash flow achieved by associating a brand with the underlying values of the product or service. In this connection it is useful (although incomplete) to think of a brand's equity as *the premium a customer/consumer would pay for the branded product or service compared to an identical unbranded version of the same product/service.*

Hence brand equity refers to the strength, depth and character of the consumer–brand relationship. A strong equity implies a positive force that keeps the consumer and the brand together, in the face of resistance and tension. The strength, depth and character of the customer–brand relationship is referred to as the *brand relationship quality* (Marketing Science Institute, 1995).

Closely linked to product positioning is the question of branding.

11.10 BRANDING

A brand signals to the customer the source of the product, and protects both the customer and the producer from competitors who would attempt to provide products that appear to be identical. From the customer's point of view, a brand can be defined as the total accumulation of his or her experiences, and is built at all points of contact with the customer (Ghodeswar, 2008).

The basic purposes of branding are the same everywhere in the world. In general, the functions of branding are as follows:

- to distinguish a company's offering and differentiate one particular product from its competitors;
- to create identification and brand awareness;
- to guarantee a certain level of quality and satisfaction;
- to help with promotion of the product.

All of these purposes have the same ultimate goals: to create new sales (market shares taken from competitors) or induce repeat sales (keep customers loyal).

Company name	What they stand for	Brand attributes	Brand theme
The Coca-Cola Company (www.coca-cola.com)	The spirit of refreshment. Only the original will do. Bringing people together.	Refreshing, exciting sociable, red	Always Coca-Cola
McDonald's Corporation (www.mcdonalds.com)	Affordable good food for the family.	Trust, convenience, value	To be the nations favourite family restaurant
British Airways (www.british-airways.com)	The world's leading provider of travel services.	Global, caring	The world's favourite airline
Intel Corporation (www.intel.com)	To do a great job for our customers, stockholders and employees by being the pre-eminent building block supplier to the computer industry worldwide.	Safety, technology, leader, intelligence, unexpected	Intel inside
Nike Inc. (www.nike.com)	Experiencing the emotion of competition, winning and crushing competitors.	Performance, achievement, individualism, attitude	Just do it
American Express Company (www.americanexpress.com)	Personal enablement. Heroic customer service. Worldwide reliability of services.	Respect, worldliness, trust, security, success	Do more
BMW Group (www.bmw.com)	The best car company in the world.	Quality, performance, technology	The ultimate driving machine

Figure 11.10 Some world-class brands

Source: First published in Allen, D. (2000) The ACID Test™: a communications tool for leadership teams who want to interact with the whole organisation, *The Journal of Brand Management*, 7(4). Reproduced with permission.

World-class brand
A product that is widely distributed around the world with a single brand name that is common to all countries and is recognised in all its markets.

Thus a brand name is more than a label employed to differentiate among the manufacturers of a product. It is a complex symbol that represents a variety of ideas and attributes. It tells the consumer many things – not only by the way it sounds (and its literal meaning if it has one), but more importantly by the body of associations it has built up and acquired as a public object over a period of time. The net result is the public image, character or personality that may be more important for the customers. Figure 11.10 shows the communication of some **world-class brands** and what they stand for.

The concept of the brand represents an acceptance of the fact that all purchasing decisions for both products and services involve a combination of rational and emotional criteria. The rational criteria are the physical components or factual elements of the product or service in question. The emotional criteria are the sum of the impressions, ideas, opinions and random associations that the potential purchaser has stored in his or her mind about the product or service. Rational and emotional elements combine to form a brand image. The word 'brand' is used to represent everything that people know, think or feel about anything. There are a number of implications of this definition.

Successful brand management necessitates the firm innovating to stay abreast of constantly changing market conditions, ideally anticipating evolving tastes, and telling their brand stories to each new generation of consumers. The notion of storytelling is key. Well-managed brands are continually telling stories about themselves, and updating these stories to take account of underlying changes in society, though their core values usually remain constant. Clever brand management also involves decisions about the service element that supports a brand and the extent to which a brand should embrace some higher-order universal value.

Nike is the most quoted example of this phenomenon. This hugely successful worldwide brand rarely talks about the product itself, which is understandable as all manufacturing is outsourced, but about core values such as achievement, competitiveness and winning. Nike stories are parables, a tried and trusted technique for communicating desired messages. John Scully, the well-known chief executive of Apple, is another proponent of this approach. He is on record as saying that he doesn't want Apple advertising to mention anything to do with megabytes or memory or any other technical terms that could be employed to create a superior brand store for Apple computers. Scully believes that Apple's core value is that it believes that people with passion can change the world for the better (Fanning, 1999).

Branding decisions

As Figure 11.11 shows, there are four levels of branding decisions. Each alternative at the four levels has a number of advantages and disadvantages, which are presented in Table 11.2. We will discuss these options in more detail.

Brand versus no brand

Branding is associated with added costs in the form of marking, labelling, packaging and promotion. Commodities are unbranded or undifferentiated products. Examples of products with no brand are milk, metals, salt, beef and other agricultural products.

Private label versus co-branding versus manufacturer's own brand

These three options can be graded, as shown in Figure 11.12.

The question of consumers having brand loyalty or shop loyalty is a crucial one. The competitive struggle between the manufacturer and the retailer emphasised the need for a better understanding of shopping behaviour (Herstein and Gamliel, 2006). Both players need to be aware of the determinants of shop choice, shopping frequency and in-store behaviour. Where manufacturers pay little attention to the shopping behaviour of consumers, this information helps to anticipate the increasing power of certain retail chains (Moss, 2008).

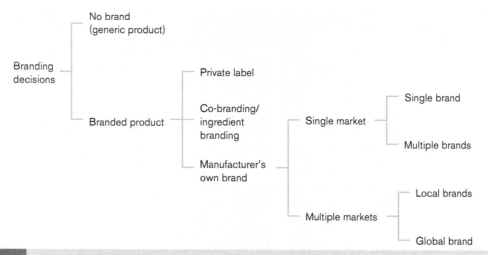

Figure 11.11	Branding decisions

Source: Onkvisit, S. and Shaw, J. J. (1993) *International Marketing: Analysis and Strategy*, 2nd ed., p. 534. Reproduced with permission from Sak Onkvisit and John J. Shaw.

Table 11.2	Advantages and disadvantages of branding alternatives

	Advantages	Disadvantages
No brand	Lower production cost. Lower marketing cost. Lower legal cost. Flexible quality control.	Severe price competition. Lack of market identity.
Branding	Better identification and awareness. Better chance for production differentiation. Possible brand loyalty. Possible premium pricing.	Higher production cost. Higher marketing cost. Higher legal cost.
Private label	Possibility of larger market share. No promotional problems.	Severe price competition. Lack of market identity.

**Co-branding/
ingredient branding**
	Adds more value to the brand.
	Sharing of production and
	   promotion costs.
	Increases manufacturer's power in gaining
	   access to retailer's shelves.
	Can develop into long-lasting relationships
	   based on mutual commitment.
		Consumers may become confused.
		Ingredient supplier is very dependent on
		   the success of the final product.
		Promotion cost for ingredient supplier.

Manufacturer's own brand	Better price due to higher price inelasticity. Retention of brand loyalty. Better bargaining power. Better control of distribution.	Difficult for small manufacturer with unknown brand. Requires brand promotion.

**Single market,
single brand**
	Marketing efficiency.
	Permits more focused marketing.
	Eliminates brand confusion.
	Good for product with good reputation
	   (halo effect).
		Assumes market homogeneity.
		Existing brand's image harmed when
		   trading up/down.
		Limited shelf space.

Single market/ multiple brands	Market segmented for varying needs. Creates competitive spirit. Avoids negative connotation of existing brand. Gains more retail shelf space. Does not harm existing brand's image.	Higher marketing cost. Higher inventory cost. Loss of economies of scale.
Multiple markets, local brand	Meaningful names. Local identification. Avoidance of taxation on international brand. Allows variations of quantity and quality across markets.	Higher marketing cost. Higher inventory cost. Loss of economies of scale. Diffused image.
Multiple markets, global brands	Maximum marketing efficiency. Reduction of advertising costs. Elimination of brand confusion. Good for culture-free product. Good for prestigious product. Easy identification/recognition for international travellers. Uniform worldwide image.	Assumes market homogeneity. Problems with black and grey markets. Possibility of negative connotation. Requires quality and quantity consistency. LDCs' opposition and resentment. Legal complications.

Source: Adapted from Onkvisit, S. and Shaw, J. J. (1993) *International Marketing: Analysis and Strategy*, 1st ed., Macmillan, Andover. Reproduced with permission.

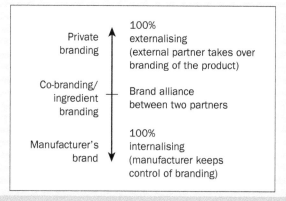

Figure 11.12   The three brand options

Source: Hollensen, S. (2001) *Global Marketing: A Market Responsive Approach*, 2nd ed., Financial Times-Prentice Hall, Harlow, p. 417. Reproduced with permission.

Private label

> **Private brand (or label)**
> A brand created and owned by a reseller (retailer) of a product or service.

Private labelling is most developed in the United Kingdom, where Marks & Spencer, for instance, only sells own-label (**private label**) products. At Sainsbury's own labels account for 60 per cent of the sales. Compared with the high share of private labelling in northern Europe, the share in southern Europe (e.g. Spain and Portugal) is no higher than 10 per cent.

The retailer's perspective

For the retailer there are two main advantages connected with own-label business:

- Own labels provide better profit margins. The cost of goods typically makes up 70–85 per cent of a retailer's total cost (*The Economist*, 1995). So if the retailer can buy a quality product from the manufacturer at a lower price, this will provide a better profit margin for the retailer. In fact, private labels have helped UK food retailers to achieve profit margins averaging 8 per cent of sales, which is high by international standards. The typical figure in France and the USA is 1–2 per cent.

- Own labels strengthen the retailer's image with its customers. Many retail chains try to establish loyalty to their particular chain of shops by offering their own quality products. In fact, premium private-label products (e.g. Marks & Spencer's St Michael) that compete in quality with manufacturers' top brands have seen a growth in market share, whereas the share of cheap generics is tiny and declining.

The manufacturer's perspective

Although private brands are normally regarded as threats for manufacturers, there may be situations where private branding is a preferable option:

- Since there are no promotional expenses associated with private branding for the producer, the strategy is especially suitable for SMEs with limited financial resources and limited competences in the downstream functions.

- The private brand manufacturer gains access to the shelves of the retail chains. With the increasing internationalisation of the big retail chains, this may also result in export business for the SME that has never been in international markets.

There are also a number of reasons why private branding is bad for the manufacturer:

- By not having its own identity, the manufacturer must compete mainly on price, because the retail chain can always switch supplier.

- The manufacturer loses control over how its products should be promoted. This may become critical if the retailer does not do a good job in pushing the product to the consumer.

- If the manufacturer is producing both its own brands and private brands, there is a danger that the private brands will cannibalise the manufacturer's brand name products.

Exhibit 11.1 shows an example with Kellogg, which has moved the other way, from a brand strategy to a private brand strategy.

Quelch and Harding (1996) argue that many manufacturers have overreacted to the threat of private brands. Increasing numbers of manufacturers are beginning to make private-label products to take up excess production capacity. According to Quelch and Harding (1996), more than 50 per cent of the US manufacturers of branded consumer goods already make private-label goods as well.

Managers typically examine private-label production opportunities on an incremental marginal cost basis. The fixed overhead costs associated with the excess capacity used to make the private-label products would be incurred anyway. But if private-label manufacturing were evaluated on a full-cost basis rather than on an incremental basis, it would, in many cases, appear much less profitable. The more private-label production grows as a percentage of total production, the more an analysis based on full costs becomes relevant (Quelch and Harding, 1996).

Manufacturer's own brand

From the Second World War until the 1960s the brand manufacturers managed to build a bridge over the heads of the retailers to the consumers. They created consumer loyalty for their particular brand by using sophisticated advertising (culminating in TV advertising) and other promotional techniques.

Since the 1960s various sociological changes (notably the car) have encouraged the rise of large, efficient retailers. Nowadays the distribution system is being turned upside down. The traditional supply chain, powered by manufacturer push, is becoming a demand chain, driven by consumer pull. Retailers have won control over distribution not just because they decide the price at which goods are sold but also because individual shops and retail companies have become much bigger and more efficient. They are able to buy in bulk and to gain economies of scale, mainly due to advances in transport and, more recently, in information technology. Most retail chains have not only set up computer links between each store and the distribution warehouses, they are also linked to the computers of the firm's main suppliers, through an EDI (electronic data interchange) system.

Generic product, or generic brand
A product that carries neither a manufacturer nor a distributor brand. The goods are plainly packaged with stark lettering that simply lists the contents.

After some decades of absence, private labels reappeared in the 1970s as **generic products** pioneered by Carrefour in France but were soon adopted by UK and US retailers. Some 15 years ago, there was a distinct gap in the level of quality between private-label and brand name products. In recent years the gap has narrowed: private-label quality levels are much higher

EXHIBIT 11.1
Kellogg is under pressure to produce Aldi's own-label goods

In February 2000 Kellogg (the cereal giant) made an own-label deal with German supermarket chain Aldi. It is the first time that Kellogg has supplied own-label goods.

A slogan on Kellogg's cereal packets claims: 'If you don't see Kellogg's on the box . . . it isn't Kellogg's in the box'. But now Kellogg has negotiated a deal with Aldi to supply products in Germany bearing a different brand name. Reports in Germany say that the deal was made after Aldi announced it would no longer pay brand suppliers' prices and threatened to cut top brands from its shelves.

Sources: Adapted from various public media.

than ever before, and they are more consistent, especially in categories historically characterised by little product innovation.

Co-branding/ingredient branding

This has already been discussed in Chapter 6.

Single brand versus multiple brands (single market)

A single brand or family brand (for a number of products) may be helpful in convincing consumers that each product is of the same quality or meets certain standards. In other words, when a single brand in a single market is marketed by the manufacturer, the brand is assured of receiving full attention for maximum impact.

The company may also choose to market several (multiple) brands on a single market. This is based on the assumption that the market is heterogeneous and consists of several segments.

Local brands versus a global brand (multiple markets)

A company has the option of using the same brand in most or all of its foreign markets, or using individual, local brands. A single, global brand is also known as an international or universal brand. A Eurobrand is a slight modification of this approach, as it is a single product for a single market of 12 or more European countries, with an emphasis on the search for inter-market similarities rather than differences.

A global brand is an appropriate approach when a product has a good reputation or is known for quality. If global brands have any power, it is when they provide better value for the customer (Pitta and Franzak, 2008). In such a case, a company would be wise to extend the brand name to other products in the product line. Examples of global brands are Coca-Cola, Shell and the Visa credit card. Although it is possible to find examples of global brands, local brands are probably more common among big multinational companies than people realise (Hollensen, 2001, pp. 424–5).

11.11 IMPLICATIONS OF THE INTERNET FOR PRODUCT DECISIONS

Firms are realising the importance of collaboration for creating and sustaining competitive advantage. Collaboration with partners and even competitors has become a strategic imperative for firms in the networked world of business. More recently, scholars in strategy and marketing have focused on collaboration with customers to co-create value (Prahalad and Ramaswamy, 2004).

The Internet is an open, cost-effective and ubiquitous network. These attributes make it a global medium with unprecedented reach, contributing to reduce constraints of geography and distance. The Internet enhances the ability of firms to engage customers in collaborative innovation in several ways. It allows firms to transform episodic and one-way customer interactions into a persistent dialogue with customers. Internet-based virtual environments allow the firm to engage in interaction with a much larger number of customers without significant compromises on the richness of the interaction (Evans and Wuster, 2000).

Customisation and closer relationships

The new business platform recognises the increased importance of customisation of products and services. Increased commoditisation of standard features can only be countered through customisation, which is most powerful when backed up by sophisticated analysis of customer data.

Mass-marketing experts such as Nike are experimenting with ways of using digital technology to enable customisation. Websites that can display three-dimensional images, for example, will certainly boost the attractiveness of custom tailoring.

The challenge is clear: to use IT to get closer to customers. There are already many examples of this. Dell is building a closer relationship with its end customers by letting them design their own PCs on the Internet. Customers who have ordered their computers from Dell can then follow their computers along the various stages of the production process in real time on their personalised website. Such experimentation is advisable because the success of 'build-to-order' models such as Dell's represents a challenge to current 'build-to-stock' business platforms, which Compaq generally uses. A comparison of the business models of Dell and HP shows that Dell's basic business principle is the close relationship between the PC manufacturer and the end customer, without further intermediaries in the distribution channel. This allows Dell to individualise the computers to customers' specific needs.

Computers can also be remotely diagnosed and fixed over the network today; this may soon be true of many other appliances. Airlines now communicate special fares to preferred customers through e-mails and special websites. Cars will soon have Internet protocol addresses, which will make possible a range of personal, in-vehicle information services.

Customers can also be involved in the early stages of product development so that their inputs can shape product features and functionality. Pharmaceutical companies are experimenting with the possibility of analysing patients' genes to determine precisely what drugs should be administered in what dosages.

The transformation in the business platform can be seen in university textbook publishing. This industry – which has seen little innovation since the advent of the printing press – is now in the midst of major changes. Publishers are creating supplementary website links to provide additional ways for students and lecturers to be connected during courses (e.g. www.pearsoneduc.com and www.wiley.com). The publisher's role, which traditionally was selling textbooks at the beginning of term, is becoming that of an educational consultant or value-adding partner throughout the term.

EXHIBIT 11.2
Ducati motorcycles – product development through Web communities

Founded in 1926, Italian Ducati builds racing-inspired motorcycles characterised by unique engine features, innovative design, advanced engineering and overall technical excellence. The company produces motorcycles in six market segments which vary in their technical and design features and intended customers: Superbike, Supersport, Monster, Sport Touring, Multistrada and the new SportClassic. The company's motorcycles are sold in more than 60 countries worldwide, with a primary focus in Western European, Japanese and North American markets. Ducati has won 13 of the last 15 World Superbike Championship titles and more individual victories than the competition put together.

A Ducati motorcycle club meeting
Source: © David Morgan/Alamy

Ducati was quick to realise the potential of using the Internet to engage customers in its new product development efforts. The company set up a Web division and a dedicated website, www.ducati.com. Ducati considers

→

the community of fans to be a major asset of the company and it strives to use the Internet to enhance the 'fan experience'. Ducati involves its fans on a systematic basis to reinforce the places, the events and the people that express the Ducati lifestyle and Ducati's desired brand image. The community function is tightly connected with the product development and the fan involvement in the community directly influences product development.

Virtual communities play a key role in helping Ducati to explore new product concepts. Ducati has promoted and managed ad hoc online forums and chat rooms for over three years to harness a strong sense of community among Ducati fans.

Modern and classic Ducati motorcycles
Source: © frank'n'focus/Alamy

Ducati has also realised that a significant number of its fans spend their leisure time not only riding their bikes, but also maintaining and personalising them. As a result, Ducati fans have deep technical knowledge that they are eager to share with other fans. To support such knowledge sharing, the company has created the 'Tech Café', a forum for exchanging technical knowledge. In this virtual environment, fans can share their projects for customising motorcycles, provide suggestions to improve Ducati's next generation products, and even post their own mechanical and technical designs, with suggestions for innovations in aesthetic attributes as well as mechanical functions.

While not all fans participate in the online forums, those who do participate provide rich inputs for exploring new product concepts and technical solutions. These forums also help Ducati to enhance customer loyalty, because its fans are more motivated to buy products they have helped to create.

Ducati managers also monitor vertical portals created for bikers, including Motorcyclist.com and Motoride.com; and Ducati monitors other virtual communities that have lifestyle associations with the Ducati brand. For instance, Ducati has entered into a partnership with the fashion company DKNY to tap into its community and interact with its members.

To validate its insights, Ducati uses online customer surveys to test product concepts and to quantify customer preferences. As a testimony to the ability of Ducati to create an ongoing customer dialogue and create a sense of engagement with its fans, Ducati gets extraordinary response rates, often in excess of 25 per cent when it surveys its customers. Ducati uses customer feedback for activities that go beyond product development.

Ducati also pursues Internet-based customer collaboration at the back end of its NPD process. Virtual communities play an important role at the product design and market testing stages. For instance, in early 2001, the community managers of Ducati.com identified a group of customers on its website that had particularly strong relationships with the company. They decided to transform such customers into active partners, involving them in virtual teams that cooperate with Ducati professionals from R&D, Product Management and Design. These virtual teams of customers work with the company's engineers to define attributes and technical features for the 'next bike'.

Within the virtual community, current and future Ducati bike owners discuss and review proposed product modifications that can be tested online in the form of virtual prototypes. They can even vote to reject proposed modifications, personalise products to their preferences, and ask Ducati technicians for suggestions on personalising their bikes to individual taste.

Sources: Adapted from Ducati Motor Holding S.p.A. (www.ducati.com) and Sawhney *et al.* (2005).

Dynamic customisation of product and services

The second stage of the customer interaction vector focuses on the opportunities and challenges in dynamically customising products and services. Competitive markets are rapidly eroding margins due to price-based competition, and companies are seeking to enhance margins through customised offerings. Dynamic customisation is based on three principles; modularity, intelligence and organisation:

1 *Modularity*: An approach for organising complex products and processes efficiently. Product or service modularity requires the partitioning of a task into independent modules that function as a whole within overall architecture.

2 *Intelligence*: Continuous information exchange with consumers allows companies to create products and processes using the best possible modules. Website operators can match buyer and seller profiles and make recommendations based on their shared interests. The result is intelligent sites that learn their visitors' (potential buyers') tastes and deliver dynamic, personalised information about products and services.

3 *Organisation*: Dynamic customisation of products and services requires a customer-oriented and flexible approach that is fundamentally committed to operating in this new way.

How can the Internet be integrated in the future product innovation?

Figure 11.13 shows some of the implications of the Internet on future product innovation. The Internet is seen as the medium through which each 'box' communicates with the R&D function in the company:

● *Design*: data is gathered directly from the product and is part of designing and developing the product. New product features (such as new versions of software programs) may be built into the product directly from the Internet.

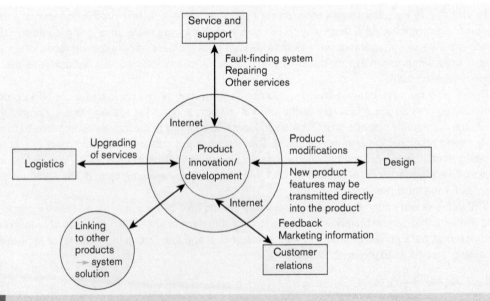

Figure 11.13   **Product innovation through the Internet**
Source: Hollensen, S. (2001) *Global Marketing: A Market Responsive Approach*, 2nd ed., Financial Times-Prentice Hall, Harlow, p. 428. Reproduced with permission.

- *Service and support*: the service department can perform troubleshooting and correction directly through the Internet set-up. For example, a Mercedes car driving on the highway may be directly connected to the Mercedes service department. It will monitor the main functions of the car and if necessary make online repairs of, for example, the software of the car.

- *Customer relations*: data gathered from the product may form part of statistics, comparisons between customers, etc. In this way the customer can compare the performance of their product (e.g. a car) with other customers' product (a kind of benchmarking). This may also strengthen an existing customer relationship.

- *Logistics*: concurrently with increasing demands for just-in-time deliveries, the Internet will automatically find the distribution and transport that will take the goods from the sub-supplier to the producer and then to the customers in the cheapest and most efficient way (and on time).

A fundamental shift in thinking is to replace the term 'supply chain' with 'demand chain'. The critical difference is that demand-chain thinking starts with the customers and works backwards. This breaks away from parochial approaches that focus solely on reducing transport costs. It supports a 'mass customisation' viewpoint, in which bundles of goods and services are offered in ways that support customers' individual objectives.

This does not necessarily imply product differentiation. In fact the service aspects often require differentiation. For example, a company such as Unilever will provide the same margarine to both Tesco and Sainsbury's. However, the ways in which the product is delivered, transactions are processed and other parts of the relationship are managed can and should be different, since these two competing supermarket chains each have their own ways of evaluating performance. The information systems required to coordinate companies along the demand chain require a new and different approach to that required within individual companies. Some managers believe that if they and their suppliers choose the same standard software package, such as SAP, they will be able to integrate their information systems.

Link to other products

Sometimes a product is used as a subcomponent in other products. Through links in the Internet such subcomponents may be essential inputs for more complex product solutions. The car industry is an example of an industry that already makes a targeted effort in this direction. New 'stylish' cars are linked together by the Internet. In the wake of this development a new industry is created, the purpose of which is to provide integrated transport. In this new industry developing and producing cars is only one of several important services. Instead systems are to be developed that can diagnose faults (and correct the error) while the car is running, systems for regulation of traffic, and interactive systems that enable drivers to have the desired transport at their disposal when and where they want it without tiresome rental agreements, etc.

The music industry is also undergoing a change. Today you can buy portable 'players' that can download music from the Internet using the MP3 format, and subsequently play the music that is stored in the 'player'. The CD is skipped – and so is the whole distribution facility. The music industry will become completely altered through the different economic conditions. The struggle will be about creating the best portal to the Internet, where the consumer can find the best information on music and the largest selection of music. The problems regarding rights are, however, still being discussed, and the lawyers and politicians have to find a final solution before the market can increase significantly.

Thus innovative product development of the future demands that a company possesses the following characteristics:

- *Innovative product development and strategic thinking*: product development will contain much technology and demand an interdisciplinary, strategic overview and knowledge in order to find out what new services are worth aiming at.

- *Management of alliances*: few companies have all the necessary qualifications themselves – innovative product development and the resulting services demand that companies enter into alliances very dynamically and yet in a structured way.

- *New customer relations*: the above-mentioned car industry example clearly shows that the customers are not car buyers any longer but *buyers of transport services*, and that is quite another matter. This means that companies have to focus on understanding the customers' needs in a quite different way.

Developing brands on the Internet

Clearly consumer product companies such as Procter & Gamble, Colgate and Kraft Foods and consumer durables and business-to-business companies such as General Motors, General Electric, Allied Signal and Caterpillar have crafted their business strategies by leveraging physical assets and developing powerful global brands supported by mass advertising and mass distribution. But remote links with customers apply equally well to these companies. Remote and continuous links with customers become critical as the concepts of brand identity and brand equity are redefined by the Internet.

Kraft Interactive Kitchen (www.kraftfoods.com) is an example of a consumer products company keeping in touch with its consumers by providing information-based services such as meal planners, recipes, tips and cooking techniques. Kraft's intention is to have remote connections and interactions with consumers in new ways.

However, some companies find it difficult to translate a strong offline brand (such as Nike and Levi's) to the Internet, because many of the well-known brands are based on an extensive 'physical' retail distribution system, and many of the retailers are reluctant to support online brands because of the fear of disintermediation (see section 11.6 for more discussion of this issue).

In fact many sites that are run by top brands register minimal online traffic, according to a report by Forrester Research. Forrester studied brand awareness and Web surfing behaviour among 16- to 22-year-olds, whom advertisers consider to be strongly brand conscious.

Companies are taking a broad approach to branding, integrating it with an overall advertising and marketing strategy. On the Net branding is more than logos and colour schemes; it is about creating experiences and understanding customers. Consequently Web brand building is not cheap. Building a brand requires a persistent online presence. For some brands, that entails a mass-appeal site; for others, brand building requires a combination of initiatives, from banner ads to sponsorships.

11.12 'LONG TAIL' STRATEGIES

Anderson's (2006) 'long tail' is basically a theory of selling that suggests that in the Internet era, selling fewer copies to more people is a new strategy that can be successfully pursued. In the past, all the interesting business was around a few hits, and many businesses focused entirely on producing the next hit. The group of people that buy the hard-to-find or 'non-hit' items is the customer demographic called the 'long tail'. Given a large enough availability of choice, a large population of customers, efficient search engines and negligible stocking and distribution costs, it becomes possible to profitably target the long tail in Chris Anderson's view.

Chris Anderson (2008) puts forth two distinct but related ideas:

1   Merchandise assortments are growing because when goods do not have to be displayed on store shelves, physical and cost constraints on selection disappear. Search and recommendation tools can keep a selection's vastness from overwhelming customers. In Figure 11.14, all possible offerings in an imagined product sector are ranked by their sales volume, with the

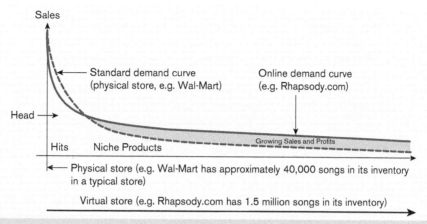

Figure 11.14	Long tail theory: online channels will fatten the Long Tail
	Source: Anderson, C. (2006) *The Long Tail: Why the Future of Business Is Selling Less of More*, New York: Hyperion. Reproduced with permission.

Long tail
Refers to a graph showing fewer products selling in large quantities versus many more products that sell in low quantities. The low-quantity items (the very broad product range) stretch out on the x-axis of the graph, creating a very long tail that generates more revenue overall. Even though a smaller quantity of each item is sold, there is a much greater variety of these items to sell and these 'rare' items are very easy to find via online search tools.

'green' part representing products that are unprofitable through brick-and-mortar channels. The long tail, in other words, reveals a previously untapped demand.

2 Online channels actually change the shape of the demand curve, because consumers value niche products geared to their particular interests more than they value products designed for mass appeal. As Internet retailing enables them to find more of the former, their purchasing will change accordingly. In other words, the tail will steadily grow not only longer, as more obscure products are made available, but also fatter (including the red part in Figure 11.14), as consumers discover products better suited to their tastes.

In Figure 11.14 the power of the long tail is illustrated by an example: the online download music company Rhapsody.com, which has an inventory of some 1.5 million tracks, receives 40 per cent of its revenue from songs that are simply not available in retail stores. In contrast, a typical Wal-Mart store has a maximum of 40,000 songs on their CDs on the shelves, and their top 200 CD albums account for 90 per cent of Wal-Mart's sales because they do not have the space to stock tracks that might sell only once a month. For online stores that use technology to cut their cost of inventory, the amount of total business for objects in the tail increases.

However, Elberse (2008) tries to prove that Anderson's 'long tail' concept is very problematic. It seems that Elberse (2008) is saying that consumers are not finding 'hidden gems' out in the long tail, and in fact that they are not even venturing into the tail that much. She gives evidence that the activity in the head is even more unusual. What happened? Elberse's (2008) research implies that anything good out on the long tail will quickly be elevated to the head if it has any broad appeal at all because of the way the Internet works. It will only be those products of an extremely limited appeal that do not make that jump. Suddenly, a perfectly legitimate long tail buying process has resulted in the 'discovery' of a blockbuster and in the process has ignored the fact that it started out in the long tail.

11.13 SUMMARY

All goods and services consist of a core element that is surrounded by a variety of optional elements. If we look first at the core service products, we can assign them to one of three broad categories depending on their tangibility and the extent to which customers need to be physically present during service production.

The perceived service quality has two factors: a technical or outcome factor and a functional or process-related factor. The technical quality of a service process is normally a prerequisite for good quality. It has to be at an acceptable level.

After-sales service adds to the product's value and is often treated as an integral part of the product.

The traditional new product development models involve the following stages in product development: idea generation, screening, concept development and testing, business analysis, product development and testing, test marketing, and commercialisation or launch.

Products pass through a series of stages. Each stage is identified by its sales performance and characterised by different levels of profitability, various degrees of competition and distinctive marketing programmes. The four stages of the product life cycle are introduction, growth, maturity and decline.

A new product can have several degrees of newness. A product may be an entirely new invention (new to the world) or it may be a slight modification of an existing product.

Brand equity can be defined as 'a set of brand assets and liabilities linked to the brand, its name and symbol, that add to or subtract from the value provided by a product or service to a firm or to the firm's customers'.

Branding is a very important issue and alternatives have been discussed. For example, because large (often transnational) retail chains have won control over distribution, they try to develop their own labels. For the retailer, private labels provide better profit margins and strengthen the retailer's image with its customers. Because of the power shift to retailers, the percentage of retail grocery sales derived from private brands has increased in recent years.

The basic purposes of branding are the same everywhere in the world. In general, the functions of branding are:

- to distinguish a company's offering and differentiate one particular product from its competitors;

- to create identification and brand awareness;

- to guarantee a certain level of quality and satisfaction;

- to help with promotion of the product.

The products sold over electronic markets and the Internet can be grouped into two categories: physical products and purely digital goods and services.

The 'long tail' is basically a theory of selling that suggests that in the Internet era, selling fewer copies to more people is a new strategy that can be successfully pursued.

CASE STUDY 11.1

Fisherman's Friend
Introducing chewing gum in some new markets

Lofthouse of Fleetwood Ltd, a family-owned company, first created Fisherman's Friend Original Extra Strong Lozenges in 1865 in Fleetwood, Lancashire. James Lofthouse, a Fleetwood pharmacist, devised a fluid made with liquorice, capsicum, eucalyptus and menthol to protect fishermen against the rigours of the North Atlantic fishing grounds.

Today the lozenges are available in 120 countries worldwide, and have grown to become a major international brand (www.fishermansfriend.com). The core proposition of Fisherman's Friend as a unique, strong-tasting medicinal sweet that comes wrapped in a paper bag remains constant globally (Fisherman's Friend Original Extra Strong Lozenges are still manufactured to exactly the same formulation as in 1865) but other elements of the marketing mix vary country by country. The lozenges are now available in many different versions including Original Extra Strong, Aniseed, Original Tooth-friendly, Mint Sugar Free, and Lemon Sugar Free.

Source: Courtesy of Lofthouse of Fleetwood Ltd

History

The Friend was unknown outside Fleetwood until 1963. In 1969 the Lofthouse family gave up the unequal struggle of hand packing their growing orders and turned an old tram shed into a packing and distribution warehouse. The company then employed 8; now it provides work for 250 as the town's second-largest private employer. It has a 300,000 sq ft plant with computer-controlled lines producing lozenges 21 hours a day.

By 1974 the Friend was being exported to Norway and was beginning to move into the European Community. A second flavour, aniseed, was introduced in 1976, a mere 111 years after the first. Fisherman's Friend is now one of Britain's greatest export successes, with annual sales of over 4.5 billion lozenges in a total of 107 countries.

Introduction of Fisherman's Friend chewing gum

All in all it has been a very profitable business during recent years, as indicated in Table 11.3. However, during the last three years the revenues have been stagnating, which also leads the Managing Director of Lofthouse of Fleetwood, J. A. Lofthouse, to conclude that it is necessary to supplement the famous lozenges with another confectionery product where the brand, Fisherman's Friend, can also be used. After some time, the management of the company chose chewing gum as the next product.

In 2006, Lofthouse introduced chewing gum into its product range. The chewing gum stays true to the brand's trademark of being the 'strongest there is' (in terms of a fresh taste). Available in the strong mint and eucalyptus menthol varieties, the gum, manufactured in Denmark, has a long-lasting cooling sensation, is sugar-free and does not cause tooth decay.

But what should the marketing plan for the new product look like? Managing Director J. A. Lofthouse thinks that it is important in the beginning to start penetrating the home market (UK) with the new product.

Table 11.3	Lofthouse of Fleetwood – key financial figures 2005–2007		
	2007	2006	2005
Total revenue (£m)	31.9	30.8	33.9
Pre-tax profit (£m)	7.2	2.8	3.9
Number of employees	305	310	312

Source: Adapted from LexisNexis.

Then afterwards the company may consider further international markets. In order to get some good input for the marketing mix decisions, J. A. Lofthouse has got hold of a short report about the global chewing gum industry, and a further report about the UK chewing gum market.

The global chewing gum industry

Chewing gum has benefited enormously from the rise in health consciousness that has affected sales of other confectionery products. The heightened interest in the dental benefits of sugar-free chewing gum and the introduction of a wide variety of functional chewing gums have reinvigorated a category that was stagnating just 10 years ago. Chewing gum is currently the most dynamic category.

One of the major factors driving high growth in the chewing gum industry is higher consumption of sugar-free gums that is growing 4 per cent above the overall growth of chewing gum markets globally. Another chewing gum category, the well-being category (based on functional items offering health and wellness benefits), is posting 15 per cent annual growth and is presently undergoing a round of innovation.

Two multinational companies, Wrigley and Cadbury, together account for some 60 per cent market share of the worldwide chewing gum market. The estimated global market shares for the top 5 chewing gum companies are shown in Table 11.4.

The worldwide chewing gum industry in 2007 is estimated to be worth $19 billion in sales or 1.3 million metric tonnes of gum, and has grown by more than 7 per cent in the last 3 year.

Chewing gum accounts for 85 per cent of global sales, and bubble gum the other 15 per cent.

What follows is a characterisation of the two main players in the global chewing gum industry, Mars-Wrigley and Cadbury-Schweppes.

Mars-Wrigley

Until recently Wrigley was the world's No. 1 maker of chewing and bubble gum. The company's products include such popular brands as Big Red, Doublemint, Eclipse, Extra, Freedent, Juicy Fruit, Orbit, Spearmint and Winterfresh, as well as novelty gums (Hubba Bubba Bubble Tape and other kid-friendly chews). It also offers non-gum products including Altoids, Creme Savers, Life Savers and Velamints. The Wrigley family controlled the company. In 2008 it agreed to be acquired by the candy company Mars.

Wrigley sells its products in more than 180 countries and has 22 manufacturing operations in 14 countries. The company derives nearly all its revenues from gum. Competition from mint makers and other candy companies (especially Cadbury) has hurt Wrigley's sales in North America; however, the company has grown in the non-North American sector, which now accounts for about 68 per cent of sales.

Table 11.4	The global chewing gum market, 2007	
Manufacturer (country)	Most popular brands	Value market share (%)
Mars-Wrigley (USA)	Extra, Airwaves, Freedent, Orbit, Hubba Bubba, Spearmint, Doublemint, Juicy Fruit	35
Cadbury Schweppes (UK)	Trident, Dentyne, Clorets, Hollywood, Stimorol, V6, Chiclets, Sportlife, Tonigum, Bubblicious, Bubbaloo	26
Lotte (South Korea/Japan)	Cool Mint, Eve, Free Zone, Fresh Mist, Freshmint, Enervic, Bub Up, Bupuro	14
Perfetti Van Melle (Italy/NL)	Chlormint, Happydent, Vigorsol, Big Babol, Brooklyn Chewing Gum	6
Hershey's (USA)	Ice Breakers, Bubble Yum	2
Others (approximately 200 smaller gum manufacturers – some will also produce private (store) brands		17
Total		100
Total world market (2006)		$19 billion in sales or 1.3 million metric tonnes

Sources: Adapted from Euromonitor International (www.euromonitor.com) and different public media.

Until May 2008 Mars had virtually no exposure to the chewing gum market. Then, in May 2008, Mars completed an £11.5 billion takeover of the chewing gum group Wrigley, making it the largest worldwide confectioner. The merged Mars-Wrigley dominates global confectionery with a 14.4 per cent market share, ahead of Cadbury with 10.1 per cent and Nestlé with 7.7 per cent, according to Euromonitor.

Warren Buffet's Berkshire Hathaway is helping finance the acquisition and upon closing the deal, which is contingent on regulatory approval, Buffett will own a 10 per cent interest in Wrigley.

Mars, which is family-owned and based close to Washington DC, is the world's largest chocolate seller. Adding Wrigley's worldwide gum and mints business to its operations will vault the company ahead of Britain's Cadbury Schweppes Plc as the world's largest confections maker.

After the buy-out is completed, in 6 to 12 months, Wrigley will become a Mars subsidiary and a private company. Wrigley will continue to be based in Chicago, where it has operated since it was founded by the Wrigley family in 1891.

The combined organisation will have a product portfolio containing some of the world's most recognisable and well-loved confectionery brands – including Orbit, Extra, Doublemint, M&M's, Snickers and Mars – as well as leading food, beverage and petcare brands, totalling over $27 billion in global sales. Combining the marketing and distribution operations of both companies will result in increased synergies, as well as cost savings, particularly in times of rising commodity prices.

The merger could spark a wave of further consolidation in the confectionery market. Competitors, most notably Cadbury, Hershey's and Nestlé, may feel pressure given the scale, scope and power of the Mars-Wrigley combination, which brings together a big stable of brands with worldwide distribution.

Cadbury Schweppes

Cadbury Schweppes Plc is the world's leading confectioner, and also has a diverse international business comprising a number of packaged food and beverages sectors. Its confectionery interests cover chocolate and sugar confectionery, as well as gum, and include tablets, bagged selflines/softlines, boxed assortments, seasonal chocolate, boiled sweets, mints and chewing gum. Among the company's best-known confectionery brands are Cadbury, Trident, Trebor, Halls, Dentyne and Hollywood.

The company operates 67 manufacturing plants for its confectionery throughout the world, of which the key centre is still Bournville, near Birmingham, England.

In 2006, the company's sales increased to £6.6 billion, from £6.4 billion in the previous year. Profit from operations fell by 9 per cent to £909 million, and margins were down to 11 per cent, compared to its competitors Wrigley and Hershey's, whose margins were over 18 per cent.

Cadbury's gum business has been successful in recent years, fuelled by several significant acquisitions of regional gum players. Cadbury's global gum sales witnessed growth of 11 per cent between 2005 and 2006. In gum, sugar-free gum was the most dynamic type with sales growth of 19 per cent between 2005 and 2006. The company's share in gum was boosted by the highly successful launch of centre-filled gum under local brand names such as Trident Splash in Greece, Hollywood Sweet Gum in France, and Stimorol Fusion in Sweden, Switzerland and Benelux. Cadbury is positioned well to benefit from the overall market growth as the majority of its chewing gum brands are sugar free and brand penetration is high in Latin America and Western Europe, with share in gum 65 per cent and 21 per cent respectively in 2006.

The UK market for chewing gum

In the UK chewing gum is still dominated by Mars-Wrigley, but it has seen a significant decline in value share, of 8 percentage points compared to 2006, due to the entrance of Cadbury Trebor Bassett's Trident brand. However, its value sales stand strong, at £285 million in 2008. Trident has experienced a substantial increase in its share of the gum sector, jumping by 10 percentage points to 13 per cent, although it is still a long way behind Wrigley's 72 per cent share. Trident's sales increased to £50 million in 2008, a massive rise from the £9 million achieved in 2006.

Cadbury has set a new standard, and its model is what other players should look to for inspiration. Trident has adopted a different strategy to Wrigley, and has steered clear of 'breath freshening' as its main objective. Trident's flavours, which have now expanded to include Trident Splash Apple and Apricot, Raspberry and Peach, and Strawberry Smoothie.

Private label has a very small share in UK gum. This is due to the increase in popularity of discounters and supermarket retailers, which have also expanded their chewing gum ranges. The high street pharmacist and beauty retailer Boots has its own brand of chewing gum, competing mainly with Wrigley's brand Extra.

Trends in UK chewing gum

Whitening is no longer a desired functionality of gum with British chewers having lost faith in the results and, consequently, the UK currently does not have any major

Table 11.5	The UK market for chewing gum, 2008	
Manufacturer (country)	Most popular brands	Value market share (%)
Mars-Wrigley (USA)	Extra, Airwaves, Orbit, Hubba Bubba, Juicy Fruit, Spearmint, Doublemint	72
Cadbury Schweppes (UK)	Trident, Clorets, Bubblicious, Bubbaloo, Trebor	13
Private labels	e.g. Boots	4
Others		11
Total		**100**
Total UK market (2007)		€700 million in sales or 31,000 tonnes

Sources: Adapted from Euromonitor International (www.euromonitor.com) and different public media.

teeth-whitening gums; for example, Orbit's focus is not on whitening but on oral care as a whole. For new trends, gum manufacturers could look abroad to Japan, where gum and flavour is used as an appetite suppressant and a way to help lose weight, as with a grapefruit-flavoured chewing gum. Other ideas to revive functional gum include gum products which contain vitamins and ingredients that are beneficial to the skin.

The German market for chewing gum

The key trend in gum over 2007–08 was the success of larger plastic tub formats, which hold around 45 pieces of chewing gum. Wrigley was the first company to adopt this packaging format, doing so in an effort to help its gum brands stand out from the plethora of other confectionery products on retail shelves. During the early part of the review period, the trend towards shopping less frequently and buying more in one go in Germany had a negative impact on chewing gum, where purchases tend to be made on impulse. The introduction of larger plastic tub packs helped manufacturers to get round this problem, as evidenced by healthy growth in chewing gum volume and current value sales over 2006–08.

Sugar-free products accounted for 80 per cent of total gum volume sales in 2008, with standard sugarised variants claiming the remaining 20 per cent. The share of sugar-free gum products rose steadily throughout the review period, thanks largely to rising awareness of the damage that sugarised products can do to teeth. This trend continued into 2008, with media reports and advertising campaigns leading more Germans to realise that sugar-free gum products can help to reduce the build up of plaque on teeth, particularly after meals.

Table 11.6	The German market for chewing gum, 2008	
Manufacturer (country)	Most popular brands	Value market share (%)
Mars-Wrigley (USA)	Extra, Airwaves, Orbit, Hubba Bubba, Juicy Fruit, Spearmint, Doublemint	73
Hitschler International (Germany)	Hitschler	4
Haribo (Germany)	Vademecum	2
Private labels		9
Others		12
Total		**100**
Total German market (2008)		€645 million in sales or 23,000 tonnes

Sources: Adapted from Euromonitor International (www.euromonitor.com) and different public media.

Table 11.7	The French market for chewing gum, 2008	
Manufacturer (country)	Most popular brands	Value market share (%)
Cadbury (UK)	Hollywood, Malabar, Stimorol, Tonigum	43
Mars-Wrigley (USA)	Freedent, Extra, Airwaves, X-cite, Hubba Bubba	42
Perfetti	Mentos	5
Private labels		2
Others		8
Total		**100**
Total French market (2008)		€815 million in sales or 23,000 tonnes

Sources: Adapted from Euromonitor International (www.euromonitor.com) and different public media.

Trends in German chewing gum

The success of functional gum, the most dynamic category in volume and current value growth terms in 2008, is mainly due to its comparatively healthy image. During recent years, the category has also benefited from the growing preoccupation with cosmetic surgery and image enhancement in Germany, which has fuelled demand for tooth-whitening gum products. For many Germans, such products provide a low-cost alternative to professional tooth-whitening services that they cannot afford.

The French market for chewing gum

A key influence on the gum sector has been the smoking ban in France, starting 1 January 2008. It represents a major development opportunity for gum. Manufacturers in the sector took advantage of this new legislation to create a communication buzz, which helped to increase sales. For example, Wrigley France SNC ran a campaign focusing on changing the former 'smoking area' in cafés and bars to a 'chewing area'. According to a study commissioned by Wrigley, 52 per cent of the French population consider gum as a good aid to stopping smoking.

Cadbury France SA remained the leader in the gum sector in 2007, with 43 per cent of value sales. Cadbury France SA increased its sales thanks to the success of its Hollywood range. However, Cadbury France is being strongly challenged by Wrigley France SNC. Advertising was once again key in the gum sector. The campaigns were quite similar, with a focus on the diverse new product development in the sector. New products tended to be backed by sample distribution in order to create awareness. Wrigley France SNC was particularly

active, with free sample distribution for Freedent Tabs and an online advertising campaign for Freedent White.

Trends in French chewing gum

The fastest growing subsector in 2008 was functional gum, with 14 per cent growth in volume terms and 16 per cent in value terms. This strong growth was due in part to the fact that the functional gum subsector remains underdeveloped compared to the main sugar-free gum subsector in France. The cosmetic promise of whiter teeth has proved to be extremely successful among French consumers. Manufacturers developed their offer further with products such as Freedent Expert and Mentos Cube with xylitol.

The US market for chewing gum

Gum sales in 2008 were characterised once again by a distinct shift from sugarised to sugar-free and functional gums. These gums are promoted as being beneficial to teeth and gum health, as well as being better alternatives than higher calorie snacks. One of the largest recent hits since its launch in 2007 was Wrigley's 5, a gum that claims to add sensations to the mouth when chewed: tingling for spearmint, warming for cinnamon, and cooling for peppermint. Such novelties continue to make sugar-free gums much more interesting to consumers than older, unhealthier sugarised brands.

Cadbury Adams, as a subsidiary of a large multinational corporation (Cadbury Schweppes UK), remains the only company with the resources, investment and distribution might to seriously challenge the lead of Wrigley in US gum sales. Distant third ranked Hershey's remains more focused on the development of its chocolate and sugar confectionery brands.

Table 11.8	The US market for chewing gum, 2008	
Manufacturer (country)	**Most popular brands**	**Value market share (%)**
Mars-Wrigley (USA)	Orbit, Extra, Eclipse, Wrigley's 5, Airwaves, Hubba Bubba, Juicy Fruit, Spearmint, Doublemint,	50
Cadbury Adams (US/UK)	Trident, Dentyne, Stride, Clorets, Bubblicious, Bubbaloo, Trebor	31
Hershey's	Ice Breakers, Bubble Yum	4
Others		15
Total		**100**
Total US market (2007)		€3,200 million in sales or 217,000 tonnes

Sources: Adapted from Euromonitor International (www.euromonitor.com) and different public media.

Private label does not play any role in the US gum market.

Trends in US chewing gum

Since sugar-free gums have now become the more common form of gum purchased, consumers do not have the same letdown in expectations when they buy these brands, making them more marketable as a food to be consumed instead of sweet snacks.

One possible threat to future gum sales is a wave of bad publicity surrounding sorbitol, an artificial sweetener used in several sugar-free gums, among other products. Sorbitol can act as a laxative when consumed in large quantities. This side-effect has been detailed in many other clinical studies over the years, and gum manufacturers typically have responded by pointing out the large amounts of gum that would need to be consumed to cause adverse effects, anywhere from 15 to 20 sticks to 60 pieces or more per day. Nevertheless, such negative media coverage could continue to make consumers worried, especially as it runs counter to the message of health and wellness behind most sugar-free gum marketing.

QUESTIONS

1 Is it a wise decision to launch a Fisherman's Friend chewing gum? Why / why not?

2 How should the Fisherman's Friend product strategy in chewing gum be differentiated from the two major global players' chewing gum?

3 Please prepare a ranking of the four most attractive markets for the Fisherman's Friend's chewing gum.

4 Would you suggest a standardised or differentiated product strategy across the target international markets?

QUESTIONS FOR DISCUSSION

1 How would you distinguish between services and products? What are the main implications of this difference for the marketing of services?

2 What implications does the product life cycle theory have for product development strategy?

3 Why is the international product policy likely to be given a higher priority in most firms than other elements of the global marketing mix?

4 What are the requirements that must be met so that a commodity can effectively be transformed into a branded product?

5 Discuss the factors that need to be taken into account when making packaging decisions for a firm's products.

6 When is it appropriate to use multiple brands in (a) a single market and (b) several markets/countries?

7 What is the importance of 'country of origin' in international product marketing?

8 What are the distinguishing characteristics of services? Explain why these characteristics make it difficult to sell services in foreign markets.

9 Identify the major barriers to developing brands.

10 Discuss the decision to add or drop products to or from the product line in existing markets.

11 Why should customer-service levels differ internationally? Is it, for example, ethical to offer a lower customer-service level in developing countries than in industrialised countries?

12 What are the characteristics of a good international brand name?

REFERENCES

Aaker, D. A. (1991) *Managing Brand Equity*, The Free Press, New York.

Aaker, D. A. (1996) Measuring brand equity across products and markets, *California Management Review*, 38(3): 102–20.

Allen, D. (2000) The ACID test: a communication tool for leadership teams who want to interact with the whole organisation, *Journal of Brand Management*, 7(4).

Allmendinger, G. and Lombreglia, R. (2005) Four strategies for the age of smart services, *Harvard Business Review*, October; 131–44.

Amine, L. S and Magnusson, P. (2007) Cost–benefit models of stakeholders in the global counter-feiting industry and marketing response strategies, *Multinational Business Review*, 15(2): 63–85.

Anderson, C. (2006) *The Long Tail: Why the Future of Business Is Selling Less of More*, New York: Hyperion.

Asugman, G., Johnson, J. L. and McCullough, J. L. (1997) The role of after sales service in international marketing, *Journal of International Marketing*, 5(4): 11–28.

Business Line (2001) Joyco to test-market 2 brands this year, *Yahoo Finance*, 6 September (http://in.biz.yahoo.com/010905/17/1472h.html).

Business Standard, The Strategist (2000) Double bubble, *Business Standard*, 18 April (www.bsstrategist.com/00apr18/1story.htm).

Chandy, R. K. and Tellis, G. J. (1998) Organizing for radical product innovation, Marketing Science Institute, report, no. 98–102.

Cravens, D. W., Piercy, N. G. and Prentice, A. (2000) Developing market-driven product strategies, *Journal of Product & Brand Management*, 9(6): 369–88.

Czinkota, M. R. and Ronkainen, L. A. (1995) *International Marketing*, 5th edn, Dryden Press, Fort Worth, TX.

Devaney, T. and Brown, J. (2008) The new brand landscape, *Marketing Health Services*, 28(1): 14–17.

Dhalla, N. K. and Yuspeh, S. (1976) Forget the product life cycle concept, *Harvard Business Review*, January–February: 102–12.

Driver, J. C. (2001) Airline marketing in regulatory context, *Marketing Intelligence Planning*, 19(2): 125–35.

Economist, The (1995) Retailers' own labels: a threat for manufacturers, *The Economist*, 4 March: 10.

Elberse, A. (2008) Should you invest in the Long Tail? *Harvard Business Review*, July–August: 88–96.

Enders, A., Hungenberg, H., Denker, H.-P. and Mauch, S. (2008) The long tail of social networking: revenue models of social networking sites, *European Management Journal*, 26(3): 199–211.

Evans, P. B. and Wuster, T. S. (2000) *Blown to Bits: How the New Economics of Information Transforms Strategy*, Harvard Business School Press, Boston, MA.

Fan, Y. (2007) Marque in the making, *Brand Strategy*, June: 52–4.

Fanning, J. (1999) Tell me a story: the future of branding, *Irish Marketing Review*, 12(2): 3–15.

Feldwick, P. (1996) What is brand equity anyway, and how do you measure it? *Journal of the Market Research Society*, 38(2): 85–104.

Frei, F. X. (2008) The four things a service business must get right, *Harvard Business Review*, April: 70–80.

Ghodeswar, B. M. (2008) Building brand identity in competitive markets: a conceptual model, *Journal of Product & Brand Management*, 4–12.

Goffin, K. and New, C. (2001) Customer support and new product development, *International Journal of Operations & Production Management*, 21(3): 275–301.

Grönroos, C. (2000) *Service Management and Marketing*, John Wiley & Sons, Chichester.

Herbig, P. A. and Palumbo, F. (1993) Serving the aftermarket in Japan and the United States, *Industrial Marketing Management*, 22: 339–46.

Herstein, R. and Gamliel, E. (2006) Striking a balance with private branding, *Business Strategy Review*, Autumn: 39–43.

Heskett, J. L., Jones, T. O., Loveman, G. W., Sasser, W. E. Jr and Schlesinger, L. A. (2008) Putting the service-profit chain to work, *Harvard Business Review*, July–August: 118–29.

Hollensen, S. (2001) *Global Marketing: A Market Responsive Approach*, 2nd ed., Financial Times/Prentice Hall, Harlow.

Hooley, G. J., Saunders, J. A. and Piercy, N. (1998) *Marketing Strategy and Competitive Positioning*, 2nd edn, Prentice-Hall Europe, Harlow.

India Infoline (2001) Joyco launches new milk candy, *India Infoline*, 18 July (http://www.indiainfoline.com/news/fmcg2001JUL18121114.html).

James, D. (2002) Skoda is taken from trash to treasure, *Marketing News*, 8 February: 4–5.

Jones, M. C. (2006) Secrets and lies, *Brand Strategy*, October: 25–9.

Keller, K. L. (1993) Conceptualizing, measuring, and managing customer-based brand equity, *Journal of Marketing*, 57(1): 1–22.

Kotler, P. (2000) *Marketing Management*, Prentice Hall, Englewood Cliffs, NJ.

Kvesic, D. Z. (2008) Product lifecycle management: marketing strategies for the pharmaceutical industry, *Journal of Medical Marketing*, 8(4): 293–301.

Lassar, W., Mittal, B. and Sharma, A. (1995) Measuring customer-based brand equity, *Journal of Consumer Marketing*, 12: 11–19.

Lauterborn, R. (1990) New marketing litany: 4Ps passé – C-words take over, *Advertising Age*, 1 October: 25–7.

Levitt, T. (1983) After the sale is over . . . , *Harvard Business Review*, 16: 87–93.

Mahnert, K. F. and Torres, A. M. (2007) The brand inside: the factors of failure and success in internal branding, *Irish Marketing Review*, 19(1/2), 54–63.

Marketing Science Institute (1995) Brand equity and marketing mix: creating customer value; conference summary, Marketing Science Institute, report 95–111, September: 14.

Mason, T. (2001) Mars evolves brands into biscuit variants, *Marketing*, 26 July: 19.

Melewar, T. C., Badal, E. and Small, J. (2006) Danone branding strategy in China, *Brand Management*, 13(6): 407–17.

Merz, M. A., He, Y. and Vargo, S. L. (2009), 'The evolving brand logic: a service-dominant logic perspective', *Journal of Academy Marketing Science*, Vol. 37, pp. 328–344.

Meyer, C. (2001) While customers wait, add value, *Harvard Business Review*, 79(7): 24–5.

Miskie, R. (1989) Documentation: not a 'necessary evil' but a valuable resource, *Network World*, 6(8): 35.

Moss, G. D. (2008) Brand domination vs. brand decline, *Journal of Medical Marketing*, 8(4): 287–92.

Neal, W. and Strauss, R. (2008) A framework for measuring and managing brand equity, *Marketing Research,* Summer: 6–12.

Onkvisit, S. and Shaw, J. J. (1993) *International Marketing: Analysis and Strategy,* 2nd edn, Macmillan, London.

Pardo, C., Henneberg, S. C., Moozas, S. and Naude, P. (2006) Unpicking the meaning of value in key account management, *European Journal of Marketing,* 40(11/12): 1360–74.

Pitta, D. A. and Franzak, F. J. (2008) Foundations for building share of heart in global brands, *Journal of Product & Brand Management,* 17(2): 64–72.

Popper, E. T. and Buskirk, B. D. (1992) Technology life cycles in industrial markets, *Industrial Marketing Management,* 21(1): 23–34.

Prahalad, C. K. and Ramaswamy, V. (2004) *The Future of Competition: Co-creating Unique Value with Customers,* Harvard Business School Press, Boston, MA.

Quelch, J. A. and Harding, D. (1996) Brands versus private labels: fighting to win, *Harvard Business Review,* January–February: 99–109.

Raggio, R. D. and Leone, R. P. (2009) Chasing brand value: fully leveraging brand equity to maximize brand value, *Brand Management,* 16(4): 248–63.

Reinartz, W. and Ulaga, W. (2008) How to sell services more profitability, *Harvard Business Review,* May: 90–6.

Roberts, J. (2008) Once more with feeling, *Brand Strategy,* April: 25–9.

Robertson, D. and Ulrich, K. (1998) Planning for product platforms, *Sloan Management Review,* 4 (Summer): 19–31.

Ruyter, K. and Wetzels, M. (2000) Customer considerations in service recovery: a cross-industry perspective, *International Journal of Service Industry Management,* 11(1): 91–108.

Samiee, S. (1999) The internationalisation of services: trends, obstacles and issues, *Journal of Services Marketing,* 13(4/5): 319–28.

Sawhney, M., Verona, G. and Prandelli, E. (2005) Collaborating to create: the Internet as a platform for customer engagement in product innovation, *Journal of Interactive Marketing,* 19(4): 4–17.

Shostack, G. L. (1981) How to design a service, in J. Donnelly and W. George (eds), *Marketing of Services,* American Marketing Association, Chicago, IL.

Simms, C. D. and Trott, P. (2006) The perceptions of the BMW Mini brand: the importance of historical associations and the development of a model, *Journal of Product & Brand Management,* 15(4): 228–38.

Simon, C. J. and Sullivan, M. W. (1990) The Measurement and determinants of brand equity: a financial approach, Graduate School of Business, University of Chicago, Chicago, II, working paper.

Smith, A., Fischbacher, M. and Wilson, F. A. (2007) New service development: from panoramas to precision, *European Management Journal,* 25(5): 370–83.

Smith, G. E. (2006) Leveraging profitability in low-margin markets, *Journal of Product & Brand Management,* 15(6): 358–66.

Stremersch, S., Wuyts, S. and Frambach, R. T. (2001) The purchasing of full-service contracts, *Industrial Marketing Management,* 30: 1–12.

Swait, J., Erdem, T., Louvriere, J. and Dubelaar, C. (1993) The equalization price: a measure of consumer-perceived brand equity, *International Journal of Research in Marketing,* 10: 23–45.

Töpfer, A. (1995) New products: cutting time to market, *Long Range Planning,* 28(2): 61–78.

Vargo, S. L. and Lusch, R. E. (2008), Service-dominant logic: continuing the evolution, *Journal of Academy Marketing Science,* Vol. 36, pp. 1–10.

Wilson, T. L. (1999) International after-sales services, *Journal of Global Marketing,* 13(1): 5–27.

Wise, R. and Zednickova, J. (2009) The rise and rise of the B2B brand, *Journal of Business Strategy,* 30(1): 4–13.

CHAPTER 12
Pricing decisions

LEARNING OBJECTIVES

After studying this chapter you should be able to:

- understand why an appropriate customer value proposition is a useful guide to pricing strategy
- explain how cost-based pricing methods work and what their primary drawbacks are
- formulate pricing decisions for services
- explain how internal and external variables influence pricing decisions
- explain why and how prices escalate in different distribution channels
- discuss the strategic options in determining the price level for a new product
- undertake a break-even analysis
- explain what is meant by experience curve pricing
- evaluate reasons why base prices change over time in both business and consumer markets
- understand the implications of the Internet for pricing behaviour in the market, particularly price 'customisation'

12.1 INTRODUCTION

Pricing is the only element of the marketing mix to generate revenue. However, price affects not only the profit through its impact on revenue, it also affects the quantity sold through its influence on demand. Price has an interactive effect on the other elements of the marketing mix, so pricing decisions must be integrated with the other three Ps of the marketing mix. Price is the only area of the global marketing mix where policy can be changed rapidly without large direct cost implications. In addition, overseas consumers are often sensitive to price changes made in other areas of the firm's marketing programme. It is thus important that management realises that constant fine tuning of prices in overseas markets should be avoided and that many problems are not best addressed by changing prices.

Generally, pricing policy is one of the most important yet often least recognised of all the elements in the marketing mix. The other elements in the marketing mix all lead to costs. The only source of profit to the firm comes from revenue, which in turn is dictated by pricing policy. In this chapter, we focus on a number of pricing issues of special interest to international marketers.

The objective of marketing is not simply to sell a product but to create value for the customer and the seller. Consequently, marketers should price products fairly, to reflect the value produced as well as received. Innovative marketers create value by offering, for example, a better product, faster delivery, better service, easier ordering, and more convenient locations. The greater the value perceived by customers, the more often they demand a company's products, and the higher the price they are willing to pay.

12.2 PRICING FROM AN ECONOMIST'S PERSPECTIVE

Market demand and market growth are often dependent on price level. With high prices at the beginning of the product life cycle, consumers simply cannot enter the market. As the price of mobile phones, CD players and computers decrease, more consumers enter these markets.

Ideally, the price maker would like information about the following two interrelated questions:

- What will be the quantity demanded at any given price?

- What will the effect of changes in price be on sales volume?

Figure 12.1 illustrates the principal issues with the help of a simple demand curve. It shows how market demand for a product varies as a function of price change. We normally refer to

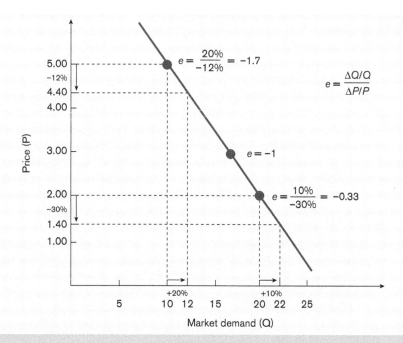

| Figure 12.1 | Price elasticity on the demand curve |

this as *price elasticity* of demand. It is important to distinguish between the demand curve for the industry as a whole and that faced by the individual company. In this chapter, the individual firm is analysed. Formally, price elasticity of demand can be calculated as follows:

$$\text{price elasticity of demand: } e = \frac{\text{percentage change in quantity demand}}{\text{percentage change in price}}$$

$$= \frac{\Delta Q/Q}{\Delta P/P}$$

Figure 12.1 shows that at each price along the diagonal demand curve, there is a different level of price elasticity.

Measures of price elasticity commonly range through:

$e < 1$ Relatively price-inelastic − quantity demanded rises (falls) by a smaller percentage than price falls (rises).

$e = 1$ Neutral price elasticity − quantity demanded rises (falls) by the same percentage that price falls (rises).

$e > 1$ Relatively price-elastic − quantity demanded rises (falls) at a greater rate than price falls (rises).

While, by definition, the ratio usually has a negative sign (this is because as prices rise, demand usually falls), it is customary, in illustrating elasticities, to drop the sign (only mentioning the numerical value).

A business might continue to lower prices to grow demand, but when the price elasticity reaches −1.0, the sales revenue will have reached its maximum. At this point, raising or lowering prices will result in lower overall sales revenue. This is the price point at which a not-for-profit organisation doing fund-raising events would be able to maximise the revenues received, if that is their objective. However, a business wanting to maximise profits may price above or below this price point, as we shall see in Section 12.3. Here, the optimum price change is dependent on the contribution margin.

The relationship between the price of one product and the quantity demanded of another is an important measure. It is known as the cross-price elasticity of demand (CPE). In this case:

- products are substitutes for one another if CPE > 0;
- products are complements to one another if CPE < 0.

Competitor price response

Many managers might ask, 'What will my competitors do in response to my price change?' If a business lowers prices to gain market share, and competitors follow, there is likely to be very little real gain. And at reduced margins, with a limited increase in volume, total contribution is likely to go down. On the other hand, if a business raises prices to improve margins and competitors do not follow, the business could lose market share and total contribution would be lower, even though margins are higher.

In any given market, competitor response to price change is going to depend on a variety of supply and demand forces, as outlined in Figure 12.2. As the forces shift from the left to the right, they will contribute to the likelihood of a full and fast competitor response to a price cut. Overall, there is generally a high degree of price interdependence among competing firms (Docters *et al.*, 2008).

Lambin (1976) showed that the average competitor price response elasticity was 0.71. This means that if a business lowered its prices by 10 per cent, it could expect competitors to lower prices by 7.1 per cent.

Probability of full and fast competitive
response to price cut

Competitor characteristics/internal forces:	Low		High
Variable cost structure	High	←——→	Low
Capacity utilisation	Full	←——→	Low
Product perishability	None	←——→	High
Product differentiation	High	←——→	None
Competitor financial position	Poor	←——→	Strong
Strategic importance	Low	←——→	High

Demand forces:

Price elasticity	Inelastic	←——→	Elastic
Efficiency in price shopping	Low	←——→	High
Customer loyalty	High	←——→	Low
Market growth rate	High	←——→	Low
Complementary products	None	←——→	Important
Substitute products	None	←——→	Many

Figure 12.2	Forces favouring competitive price response

Source: Adapted from Best, R. J. (2000) *Market-based Management*, 2nd ed., Prentice Hall, Upper Saddle River, NJ, p. 186. Reproduced with permission.

EXHIBIT 12.1
Johnny Walker whisky faced positive price elasticity in Japan

In Japanese markets, perceived value is a principal influence on product success. The images of quality significantly outweigh the actual value of the product, as quality is predominantly associated with high prices. This is demonstrated by the domination of Mercedes and BMW in the foreign import market. Johnny Walker whisky also represented images of high status. In an attempt to gain market share from its main rival Chivas, it reduced its price. Japanese consumers perceived the reduction in price to be a reduction in quality and status, resulting in a drastic decline in sales.

Source: Adapted from Marsh (2000), p. 200.

12.3 PRICING FROM AN ACCOUNTANT'S PERSPECTIVE

Break-even analysis
The calculation of the quantity needed to be sold to cover total costs.

Break-even pricing
Setting price to break even on the costs of making and marketing a product; or setting price to make a target profit.

In contrast to the economist's focus on demand, the accountant's approach to pricing is often based essentially on costs. **Break-even analysis** and **break-even pricing** are generally viewed as accounting concepts, but are extremely useful in evaluating the profit potential and risk associated with a pricing strategy, or any marketing strategy. The purpose of this section is to examine, from a marketing viewpoint, the usefulness of break-even volume.

For a given price strategy and marketing effort, it is useful to determine the number of units that need to be sold in order to break even, i.e. produce a net profit equal to zero. The break-even point is normally represented as that level of output where the total revenue from sales of a product or service matches exactly the total costs of its production and marketing (break-even quantity). Such an analysis of cost–revenue relationships can be very useful to the pricing decision maker.

One use of break-even analysis is to compare the break-even volumes associated with different prices for a product. A simplified example of this is shown in Figure 12.3.

The effect of charging a higher price is to steepen the total revenue curve and as a consequence lower the break-even volume. The pricing decision maker can then assess the effect of

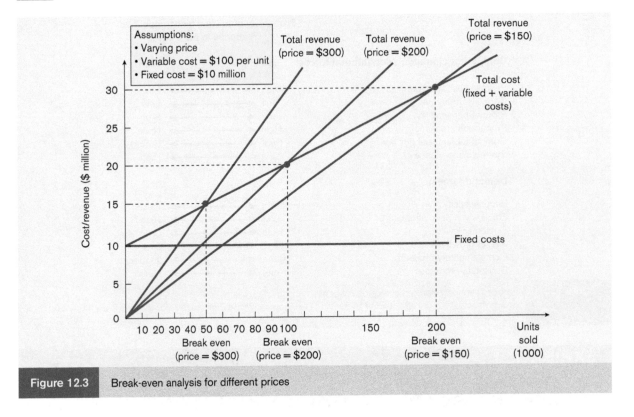

Figure 12.3 Break-even analysis for different prices

charging different prices in terms of what these different prices and break-even volumes mean to the company. Specifically, the information given by a break-even chart is:

- profit or losses at varying levels of output;
- break-even points at varying levels of price;
- effect on break-even point and profits or losses if costs change.

The break-even volume is the volume needed to cover the fixed costs on the basis of a particular contribution per unit. Although break-even volume can be estimated graphically, as illustrated in Figure 12.3, it can be computed more directly as follows:

$$\text{selling price} - \text{variable cost per unit} = \text{contribution per unit}$$

$$\text{break-even volume} = \frac{\text{fixed costs}}{\text{contribution per unit}}$$

The notion of contribution per unit is also a valuable addition to the price maker's armoury. It illustrates that, in the short term at least, it may pay a company to sell a product at a price that is less than the full cost of producing it. Remember that fixed costs are those that do not vary with the level of output. If a company produces and sells nothing, it will still incur these costs. At any price above the variable cost of producing each product, the company is receiving a contribution towards those fixed costs. In the long run, of course, a company must cover all its costs through the prices it sets on its products.

Break-even market share

Because break-even volume is an unconstrained number, the reasonableness of the break-even volume should be considered further. Because market share is constrained between 0 and 100 per cent, break-even market share provides a better framework from which to judge profit potential and risk. To compute break-even market share requires only that we divide the break-even volume by the size of the total market:

$$\text{break-even market share} = \frac{\text{break-even volume}}{\text{total market}} \times 100$$

If the total market for a product were 1 million units per year, then the break-even market share would be as follows using the three prices from Figure 12.3:

$$\text{Break-even market share (price} = \$300) = \frac{50{,}000}{1{,}000{,}000} \times 100 = 5\%$$

$$\text{Break-even market share (price} = \$200) = \frac{100{,}000}{1{,}000{,}000} \times 100 = 10\%$$

$$\text{Break-even market share (price} = \$150) = \frac{200{,}000}{1{,}000{,}000} \times 100 = 20\%$$

Of course management would feel much better if the break-even share was only 5 per cent instead of 20 per cent. In this example reducing the price by 50 per cent (from $300 to $150) would mean that the market share should be increased by 400 per cent.

It is clear that neither the economist's model of price setting (with help from the demand curve and price elasticity) nor the accountant's contribution of break-even analysis is in itself a sufficient basis on which to determine prices. Nevertheless, taken together, they do point to a clear-cut and universal assumption for delineating pricing decisions which can be incorporated into a more realistic and marketing-oriented approach to pricing. This more market-oriented approach to pricing will be discussed in the following sections.

12.4 A PRICING FRAMEWORK

An SME which markets its products for the first time, with little knowledge of the market that it is entering, is likely to set a price that will ensure that the sales revenue generated at least covers the cost incurred. It is important that firms recognise that the cost structures of a product are very significant, but they should not be regarded as the sole determinants when setting prices.

Pricing policy is an important strategic and tactical competitive weapon that, in contrast to the other elements of the global marketing mix, is highly controllable and inexpensive to change and implement. Therefore, pricing strategies and actions should be integrated with the other elements of the global marketing mix.

Figure 12.4 presents a general framework for international pricing decisions. According to this model, factors affecting international pricing can be broken down into two main groups (internal and external factors) and four sub-groups, which we will now consider in more detail.

Firm-level factors

International pricing is influenced by past and current corporate philosophy, organisation and managerial policies. The short-term tactical use of pricing in the form of discounts, product offers and reductions is often emphasised by managers at the expense of its strategic role. Yet pricing has played a very significant part in the restructuring of many industries, resulting in the growth of some businesses and the decline of others. In particular, Japanese firms have approached new markets with the intention of building market share over a period of years by reducing price levels, establishing the brand name, and setting up effective distribution and servicing networks. The market share objective of the Japanese firms has usually been accomplished at the expense of short-term profits, as international Japanese firms have

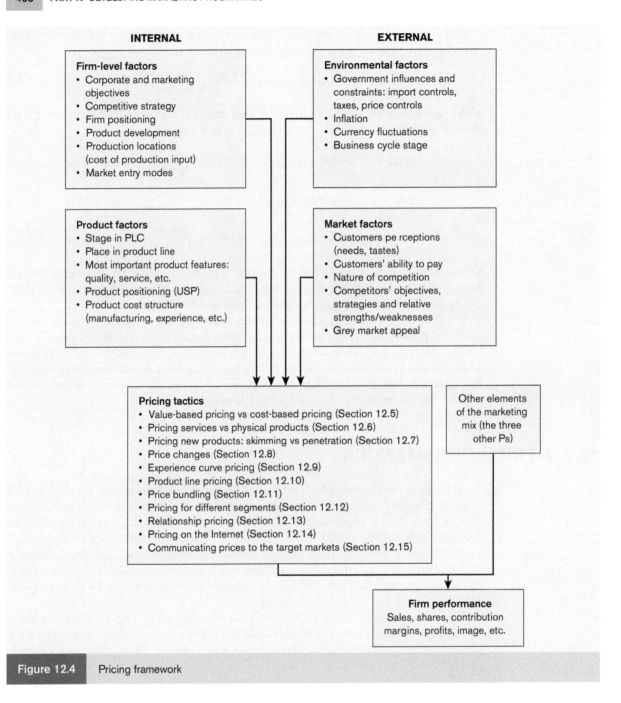

Figure 12.4   Pricing framework

consistently taken a long-term perspective on profit. They are usually prepared to wait much longer for returns on investment than some of their Western counterparts.

The choice of foreign market entry mode also affects the pricing policy. A manufacturer with a subsidiary in a foreign country has a high level of control over the pricing policy in that country.

Product factors

Key product factors include the unique and innovative features of the product and the availability of substitutes. These factors will have a major impact on the stage of the product lifecycle, which will also depend on the market environment in target markets. Whether the product is a service, a manufactured product or a commodity sold into consumer or industrial markets is also significant.

The extent to which the organisation has had to adapt or modify the product or service, and the level to which the market requires service around the core product, will also affect cost and thereby have some influence on pricing.

Costs are also helpful in estimating how rivals will react to the setting of a specific price, assuming that knowledge of one's own costs helps in the assessment of competitors' reactions. Added to the above is the intermediary cost, which depends on channel length, intermediary factors and logistical costs. All these factors add up and lead to **price escalation** through the distribution channel.

Price escalation
The tendency of prices to creep upwards when marketing products and services abroad through several middlemen.

The example in Figure 12.5 shows that, due to additional shipping, insurance and distribution charges, the exported product costs 21 per cent more in the export market than at home. If there is an additional distribution link (an importer), the product will cost 39 per cent more abroad than at home.

Many marketers are not aware of rapid price escalation; they are preoccupied with the price they charge to the importer. However, the final consumer price should be of vital concern because it is on this level that the consumer can compare prices of different competitive products and it is this price that plays a major role in determining the foreign demand.

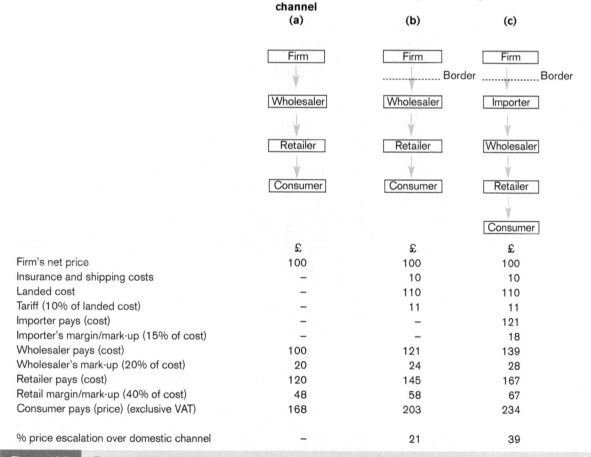

	Domestic channel (a) £	Foreign marketing channel (b) £	Foreign marketing channel (c) £
Firm's net price	100	100	100
Insurance and shipping costs	–	10	10
Landed cost	–	110	110
Tariff (10% of landed cost)	–	11	11
Importer pays (cost)	–	–	121
Importer's margin/mark-up (15% of cost)	–	–	18
Wholesaler pays (cost)	100	121	139
Wholesaler's mark-up (20% of cost)	20	24	28
Retailer pays (cost)	120	145	167
Retail margin/mark-up (40% of cost)	48	58	67
Consumer pays (price) (exclusive VAT)	168	203	234
% price escalation over domestic channel	–	21	39

Figure 12.5   Example of price escalation
Source: Hollensen, S. (2001) *Global Marketing: A Market Responsive Approach*, 2nd ed., Financial Times-Prentice Hall, Harlow, p. 450. Reproduced with permission.

Price escalation is not the only problem for marketers. It affects all firms involved in cross-border transactions. Companies that ship substantial amounts of goods and materials to subsidiaries in other countries are exposed to many of the additional charges that cause price escalation.

The following management options are available to counter price escalation:

- rationalising the distribution process by, e.g. reducing the number of links in the distribution process, either by doing more in-house or by circumventing some channel members;
- lowering the export price from the factory (firm's net price), thus reducing the multiplier effect of all the **mark-ups**;
- establishing local production of the product within the export market to eliminate some of the cost;
- pressuring channel members to accept lower profit margins. This may be appropriate if these intermediaries are dependent on the manufacturer for much of their turnover.

It may be dangerous to overlook traditional channel members. In Japan, for example, the complex nature of the distribution system, which often involves many different channel members, makes it tempting to consider radical change. However, existing intermediaries do not like to be overlooked, and their possible network with other channel members and the government may make it dangerous for a foreign firm to attempt to cut them out.

Environmental factors

The environmental factors are external to the firm and thus uncontrollable variables in the foreign market. The national government control of exports and imports is usually based on political and strategic considerations.

Generally, import controls are designed to limit imports in order to protect domestic producers or reduce the outflow of foreign exchange. Direct restrictions commonly take the form of **tariffs**, quotas and various **non-tariff trade barriers**. Tariffs directly increase the price of imports unless the exporter or importer is willing to absorb the tax and accept lower profit margins. Quotas have an indirect impact on prices. They restrict supply, thus causing the price of the import to increase.

Since tariff levels vary from country to country, there is an incentive for exporters to vary the price somewhat from country to country. In some countries with high customs duties and high price elasticity, the base price may have to be lower than in other countries if the product is to achieve a satisfactory volume in these markets. If demand is quite inelastic, the price may be set at a high level, with little loss of volume, unless competitors are selling at lower prices.

Government regulations on pricing can also affect the firm's pricing strategy. Many governments tend to have price controls on specific products related to health, education, food and other essential items. Another major environmental factor is fluctuations in the exchange rate. An increase (revaluation) or decrease (devaluation) in the relative value of a currency can affect the firm's pricing structure and profitability.

Market factors

One of the critical factors in the market is the purchasing power of the customers (the customer's ability to pay). The pressure of competitors may also affect international pricing. The firm has to offer a more competitive price if there are other sellers in the market. Thus, the nature of competition (e.g. **oligopoly** or **monopoly**) can influence the firm's pricing strategy.

Under conditions approximating pure competition, the price is set in the marketplace and tends to be just enough above costs to keep marginal producers in business. Thus, from the point of view of the price setter, the most important factor is costs. The more easily a product can be substituted, the closer prices must be, and the greater the influence of costs in determining prices (assuming that there is a large enough number of buyers and sellers).

Mark-up
A mark-up expressed as a percentage of the cost of an item.

Tariff
A tax levied by a government against certain imported products. Tariffs are designed to raise revenue or to protect domestic firms.

Non-tariff trade barriers
Non-monetary barriers to foreign products, such as biases against a foreign company's bids, or product standards that go against a foreign company's product features.

Oligopoly
A market structure characterised by a small number of sellers who control the market.

Monopoly
Exists if there is one seller in the market, such as a state-owned company, e.g. a local electricity supplier, postal service company or a gas company. The seller has the control over the market and can solely determine the price of its product.

Under a monopoly or imperfect competition, the seller has some discretion to vary the product quality, promotional efforts and channel politics in order to adapt the price of the total product to serve preselected market segments. Nevertheless, the freedom to set prices is still limited by what competitors charge, and any price differentials from competitors must be justified in the minds of customers on the basis of differential utility: that is, perceived value.

When considering how customers will respond to a given price strategy, Nagle (1987) has suggested nine factors which influence the sensitivity of customers to prices. Price sensitivity is reduced when:

- the product is more distinctive;
- there is greater perceived quality of products;
- consumers are less aware of substitutes in the market;
- there is difficulty in making comparisons (e.g. in the quality of services such as consultancy or accountancy);
- the price of a product represents a small proportion of total expenditure of the customer;
- the perceived benefit for the customer increases;
- the product is used in association with a product bought previously, so that, for example, components and replacements are usually extremely highly priced;
- costs are shared with other parties;
- the product or service cannot be stored.

In the following sections we discuss the different pricing strategies that are available.

12.5 MARKET VALUE-BASED PRICING VERSUS COST-BASED PRICING

To arrive at the proper balance between the needs of the market and the needs of the firm, it is important to understand value-based pricing. Value-based pricing recognises that price reflects value, not simply costs. Traditionally, firms assessed the costs of doing business, added a profit, and arrived at the price. Once it was set, the marketer's job was to convince customers that the product was worth it. If the marketer was not successful, then the price was lowered. If demand turned out to be higher than anticipated, then the price was raised. An important point is that the customer was the last person to be considered in this chain of events.

Value-based pricing begins by understanding customers and the competitive marketplace. The first step is to look at the value customers perceive in owning the product and to examine their options for acquiring similar products and brands.

Although cost-based pricing is easier, it ignores the customer and the competition. Marketers know that it is impossible to predict demand or competitors' actions simply by looking at their own costs. Consequently, cost-based pricing is becoming less popular.

Because prices send powerful messages, it is extremely important that they reflect the customer value the company delivers. Customer value is derived from the product itself, the services surrounding it, the company–customer interaction, and the image the customer associates with the product. Volvo, for example, has captured buyers at relatively high prices for years because of a reputation for durability and safety.

The firm is likely to incur higher costs when producing increased value. For example, it often costs more to make better products, create better distribution systems, or develop service facilities. The trick is to find a balance between what customers are willing to pay and the costs associated with the strategy.

It is not easy to establish precisely what price both buyers and seller agree is fair. We need to look at how customer value is derived, recognising that people place different values on the products they buy as well as the relationship they have with companies. Several pricing strategies may work. It all depends on how price is perceived, how competitors act, and how a strategy is designed and implemented.

12.6 PRICING SERVICES VERSUS PHYSICAL PRODUCTS

The intangibility of service performance and the invisibility of the necessary facilities and labour makes it harder for customers to see what they are getting for their money than when they purchase a physical product (Indounas, 2009; Hinterhuber, 2008).

Intangibles like services are inherently more difficult to price than goods, because it is harder to calculate the financial costs involved in serving a customer than it is to identify the labour, materials, machine time, storage and shipping costs associated with producing a physical product. The **variability** of both inputs and outputs means that units of service may not cost the same to produce, nor may they be of equal value to customers – especially if the variability extends to greater or lesser quality. Making matters even more complicated, it is not always easy to define a unit of service, raising questions as to what should be the basis of service pricing.

Variability
The characteristic of services referring to the fact that services are heterogeneous – that is, the quality of delivered services can vary widely.

A very important distinction between goods and services is that many services have a much higher ratio of fixed costs to variable costs than is found in manufacturing firms. Service businesses with high fixed costs include those with an expensive physical facility (such as a hotel, a hospital, a college or a theatre) or a network (such as a telecommunications company, an Internet provider, a railway). On the other hand, the variable costs of serving one extra customer may be minimal. Under these conditions, managers may feel that they have tremendous pricing flexibility and it is tempting to price very low in order to make an extra sale. However, there can be no profit at the end of the year unless all fixed costs have been recovered.

Another factor that influences service pricing concerns the importance of the time factor, since it may affect customer perceptions of value. In many instances, customers may be willing

EXHIBIT 12.2
Pricing in the airline business

As the marginal cost of carrying a passenger, rather than having the seat unfilled, is very low – meals, some extra fuel, and airport and over-flying charges – the price can be brought down to a sufficiently low level to sell those remaining seats as departure time approaches. However, experience also shows that associated with ticket flexibility there will be some passengers who do not turn up. The precise number is uncertain, but airlines typically overbook to allow for the passengers who do not turn up, though they run a risk of bumping passengers on to other flights at often relatively high prices if there are more passengers than available seats.

The pricing of scheduled airline tickets is complex, with features that are little appreciated by the traveller. For instance, irrespective of the product factors or service provision the price typically charged per kilometre is uniform neither for different passengers on a single flight nor in comparison with distance flown on other routes. The reason for this is that there are many categories of fare, which enables airlines to practise differential pricing by having special requirements or conditions. The principal methods are the amount of flexibility associated with the ticket, the period prior to flight when it was purchased and certain characteristics of the passenger, perhaps age or occupation.

Ticket flexibility on a scheduled flight enables the passenger to substitute another flight without notice or penalty and to book a flight virtually on demand. The desirability of doing this depends on the urgency of changing plans and the availability of alternative flights and it is possible to have reservations on many flights, where only one will be used. Arising from the airlines' responsibility to provide such flexibility, enough capacity must be provided, thereby increasing costs. Typically this degree of flexibility is intended for the business traveller whose fare is paid by an employer.

Source: Adapted from Driver (2001).

to pay more for a service delivered quickly than for one delivered more slowly. Sometimes greater speed increases operating costs, too – reflecting the need to pay overtime or use more expensive equipment.

12.7 PRICING NEW PRODUCTS

Skimming vs penetration pricing

The strategic decision of pricing new products can be best understood by examining the policies at the boundaries of the continuum – from *skimming* (high initial price) to *penetration* (low initial price).

Skimming

Skimming price
A relatively high price, often charged at the beginning of a product's life. The price is systematically lowered as time goes by.

Skimming pricing, which is appropriate for a distinctly new product, provides the firm with an opportunity to profitably reach market segments that are not sensitive to the high initial price. As a product ages, as competitors enter the market, and as organisational buyers become accustomed to evaluating and purchasing the product, demand becomes more price elastic. The policy of using skimming at the outset, followed by penetration pricing as the product matures, is termed *time segmentation*. A skimming policy enables the marketer to capture early profits, then reduce the price to reach segments that are more price sensitive. It also enables the innovator to recover high developmental costs quicker.

Problems with skimming are as follows:

- Having a small market share makes the firm vulnerable to aggressive local competition.

- Maintenance of a high-quality product requires a lot of resource (promotion, after-sales service) and a visible local presence, which may be difficult in distant markets.

Grey markets
The marketing of authentic, legally trademarked goods through unauthorised channels.

- If the product is sold more cheaply at home or in another country, a **grey market** (**parallel import**) is likely.

Penetration

Parallel importing
When importers buy products from distributors in one country and sell them in another to distributors who are not part of the manufacturer's normal distribution; caused by big price differences for the same product between different countries.

Penetration pricing is appropriate when there is high price elasticity of demand, strong threat of imminent competition, and opportunity for a substantial reduction in production costs as volume expands. Drawing upon the experience effect, a firm that can quickly gain substantial market share and experience can gain a strategic advantage over competitors. The viability of this strategy increases with the potential size of the future market. By taking a large share of new sales, experience can be gained when there is a large market growth rate. Of course, the value of additional market share differs markedly between industries and often among products, markets and competitors within a particular industry. Factors to be assessed in determining the value of additional market share include the investment requirements, potential benefits of experience, expected market trends, likely competitive reaction, and short- and long-term profit implications.

Penetration price
A low introductory price meant to quickly establish a product in the market.

Penetration pricing can be effective for fixed periods of time and in the right competitive situation, but many firms overuse this approach and end up creating a market situation where everyone is forced to lower prices continually, driving some competitors from the market and guaranteeing that no one realises a good return on investment. Managers can prevent the fruitless slide into kamikaze pricing by implementing a value-driven pricing strategy for the most profitable customers (Holden and Nayle, 1998).

Japanese companies have used penetration pricing intensively to gain market leadership in a number of markets, such as cars, home entertainment products and electronic components.

Figure 12.6 summarises the main features of skimming and penetration pricing. Because neither is likely to achieve strong buyer loyalty in competitive markets, most companies use pricing approaches that fall somewhere between these extremes.

	Skimming	Penetration pricing
Definition	Setting a relatively high price during the initial stage of a product's life. A strategy designed to obtain a relatively high price from relatively few consumers, who have the resources and desire to buy irrespective of price.	Setting a relatively low price during the initial stage of a product's life. A strategy that seeks the maximum number of buyers by charging low prices.
Objectives	To serve customers who are not price conscious while the market is at the upper end of the demand curve and competition has not yet entered the market. To recover a significant portion of promotional and research and development costs through a high margin.	To discourage competition from entering the market by quickly taking a large market share and by gaining a cost advantage through realising economies of scale.
Requirements	Heavy promotional expenditure to introduce product, educate consumers, and induce early buying. Relatively inelastic demand at the upper end of the demand curve. Lack of direct competition and substitutes. If companies perceive they can obtain a monopoly position for a short time, then they may skim to generate profits that provide investment capital for further innovations. To sustain skimming, companies must offer unusual products of the highest quality or artistic value.	Product must appeal to a market large enough to support the cost advantage. Demand must be highly elastic in order for the firm to guard its cost advantage.
Expected results	Market segmented by price-conscious and not so price-conscious customers. High margin on sales that will cover promotion and research and development costs. During the first stages in the PLC, the firm is able to create a price umbrella because the competition cannot match the firm's relative advantage, as shown here. *[Graph: Cost per unit vs Time, showing Price and Cost curves]* As the demand for a high-priced segment is saturated, price can be lowered to systematically attract more customers until prices reach a level affordable to most potential customers.	High sales volume and large market share. Low margin on sales. Lower unit costs relative to competition due to economies of scale. A cost leadership position can enable a business to use penetration pricing to build market share and discourage competition from either entering the market or staying in the market. In this situation, the market leader is simply further down the cost curve and is able to price at a lower level and still maintain a satisfying contribution. If costs are sensitive to volume, then these will drop dramatically as share increases relative to competitors. This is a way to keep rivals from entering the market. *[Graph: Cost per unit vs Time, showing Price and Cost curves]*
Illustrative examples/ problems	In the pharmaceutical industry many prescription drugs (like Pfizer's Viagra) are patented. Under this protection, the holder may create higher-than-normal prices. However, many times this strategy does not produce loyal customers, since subsequent entrants eventually offer better value at a lower price. In the past, IBM dominated personal computer sales, but as smaller companies entered the market it had to price more competitively.	Compaq Computer was an early entry in the personal computer market. Compaq priced aggresively to build market share in a market where all computer manufacturers could offer the same product. In these instances, product differentiation is minimal, customers are price-sensitive, there are many competitors or substitutes, and competitor entry is easy. The price leader can often both gain an early cost advantage with a large volume and charge lower prices, discouraging competitors from entering the market. The problem with penetration pricing is that losses are likely, especially in the short term. Because profit margins tend to be very small, demand must meet expectations in order to generate enough earnings. Furthermore, when customers buy only because of price, loyalty tends to be low. They are likely to switch to competition offering an even lower price or innovations of higher value at a higher price.

Figure 12.6   Two new product pricing strategies

Market pricing

If similar products already exist in the target market, market pricing may be used. The final customer price is based on competitive prices. This approach requires the exporter to have a thorough knowledge of product costs, as well as confidence that the product life cycle is long enough to warrant entry into the market. It is a reactive approach and may lead to problems if sales volumes never rise to sufficient levels to produce a satisfactory return. Although firms typically use pricing as a differentiation tool, the global marketing manager may have no choice but to accept the prevailing world market price.

From the price that customers are willing to pay, it is possible to make a so-called retrograde calculation where the firm uses a 'reversed' price escalation to calculate backwards (from market price) to the necessary (ex-factory) net price. If this net price can create a satisfactory contribution margin, then the firm can go ahead.

12.8 PRICE CHANGES

Price changes on existing products are called for when a new product has been launched or when changes occur in overall market conditions (such as fluctuating foreign exchange rates).

Table 12.1 shows the percentage sales volume increase or decrease required to maintain the level of profit. An example shows how the table functions. A firm has a product with a contribution margin of 20 per cent. The firm would like to know how much the sales volume should be increased as a consequence of a price reduction of 5 per cent, if it wishes to keep the same total profit contribution. The calculation is as follows:

Before price reduction

Per product	sales price	£100
	variable cost per unit	£80
	contribution margin	£20

Total contribution margin: 100 units @ £20 = £2000

After price reduction (5%)

Per product	sales price	£95
	variable cost per unit	£80
	contribution margin	£15

Total contribution margin: 133 units @ £15 = £2000

As a consequence of a price reduction of 5 per cent, a 33 per cent increase in sales is required. If a decision is made to change prices, related changes must also be considered. For example, if an increase in price is required, it may be accompanied, at least initially, by increased promotional effort.

When changing prices, the degree of flexibility enjoyed by decision makers will tend to be less for existing products than for new products. This follows from the high probability that the existing product is now less unique, faces stronger competition and is aimed at a broader segment of the market. In this situation, the decision maker will be forced to pay more attention to competitive and cost factors in the pricing process (Davidson and Simonetto, 2005).

The timing of price changes can be nearly as important as the changes themselves. For example, a simple tactic of announcing price increases after competitors can produce the perception among customers that you are the most customer-responsive supplier. The extent of the time lag can also be important (Matthyssens *et al.*, 2009).

Table 12.1	Sales volume increase or decrease (%) required to maintain total profit contribution

	Profit contribution margin (price – variable cost per unit as % of the price)								
Price reduction (%)	5	10	15	20	25	30	35	40	50
	Sales volume increase (%) required to maintain total profit contribution								
2.0	67	25	15	11	9	7	7	5	4
3.0	150	43	25	18	14	11	9	8	6
4.0	400	67	36	25	19	15	13	11	9
5.0		100	50	33	25	20	17	14	11
7.5		300	100	60	43	33	27	23	18
10.0			200	100	67	50	40	33	25
15.0				300	150	100	75	60	43
	Profit contribution margin (price – variable cost per unit as % of the price)								
Price increase (%)	5	10	15	20	25	30	35	40	50
	Sales volume reduction (%) accepted to maintain total profit contribution								
2.0	29	17	12	9	7	6	5	5	4
3.0	27	23	17	13	11	9	8	7	6
4.0	44	29	21	17	14	12	10	9	7
5.0	50	33	25	20	17	14	12	11	9
7.5	60	43	33	27	23	20	18	16	13
10.0	67	50	40	33	29	25	22	20	17
15.0	75	60	50	43	37	33	30	27	23

Source: Hollensen, S. (2001) *Global Marketing: A Market Responsive Approach*, 2nd ed., Financial Times-Prentice Hall, Harlow, p. 454. Reproduced with permission.

In one company, an independent survey of customers (Garda, 1995) showed that the perception of being the most customer-responsive supplier was generated just as effectively by a six-week lag in following a competitor's price increase as by a six-month lag. A considerable amount of money would have been lost during the unnecessary four-and-a-half-month delay in announcing a price increase.

12.9 EXPERIENCE CURVE PRICING

Price changes usually follow changes in the product's stage in the life cycle. As the product matures, more pressure will be put on the price to keep the product competitive despite increased competition and less possibility of differentiation.

Let us also bring the cost aspect into the discussion. The experience curve has its roots in a commonly observed phenomenon called the learning curve, which states that as people repeat a task they learn to do it better and faster. The learning curve applies to the labour portion of manufacturing cost. The Boston Consulting Group extended the learning effect to cover all the value-added costs related to a product – manufacturing plus marketing, sales, administration, etc.

The resulting experience curves, covering all value chain activities (see Figure 3.1 in Chapter 3), indicate that the total unit cost of a product in real terms can be reduced by a certain percentage with each doubling of cumulative production. The typical decline in cost is 30 per cent (termed a 70 per cent curve), although greater and lesser declines are observed.

If we combine the experience curve (average unit cost) with the typical market price development within an industry, we will have a relationship similar to that shown in Figure 12.7.

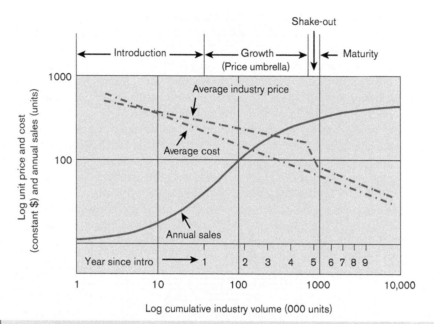

Figure 12.7   Product life cycle stages and the industry price experience curve

Source: Boston Consulting Group (1970) Perspectives on Experience, BCG. Copyright © 1970, The Boston Consulting Group. Reproduced with permission.

Figure 12.7 shows that, after the introduction stage (during part of which the price is below the total unit cost), profits begin to flow. Because supply is less than demand, prices do not fall as quickly as costs. Consequently, the gap between costs and prices widens, in effect creating a price umbrella, attracting new competitors. However, the competitive situation is not a stable one. At some point the umbrella will disappear as one or more competitors reduce prices in an attempt to gain market share. The result is that a shake-out phase will begin: inefficient producers will be shaken out by rapidly falling market prices, and only those with a competitive price/cost relationship will survive. Experience curve pricing is seen in many industries, e.g. in the pharmaceutical and medical area (Brown *et al.*, 2008; Rao, 2008; Brown *et al.*, 2007).

12.10 PRODUCT LINE PRICING

As a business adds more product to its product line, it enhances sales growth but also increases the chances of cannibalisation of existing product sales. It is necessary to know both a product's price elasticity and the degree to which there is a cross-elasticity with other products. Products that have a *positive* cross-elasticity are *substitutes;* lowering the price of one product will decrease the demand for the other product. Products that have a *negative* cross-elasticity are *complementary* products; lowering the price for one product will increase the demand for both products. Because the margins may be different for alternative products in a product line, one has to give careful consideration to any price change to ensure that the total profits are increased for the entire product line.

A firm may add to its product line – or even develop a new product line – to fit more precisely the needs of a particular market segment. If both the demand and the costs of individual product line items are interrelated, production and marketing decisions about one product line item inevitably influence both the revenues and costs of the others.

Are specific product line items substitutes or complements? Will a change in the price of one item enhance or retard the usage rate of this or other products in key market segments? Should a new product be priced high at the outset in order to protect other product line items (for example, potential substitutes) and in order to give the firm time to update other items in the line? Such decisions require knowledge of demand, costs, competition and strategic marketing objective.

With **product line pricing**, the various items in the line may be differentiated by pricing them appropriately to indicate, for example, an economy version, a standard version and a superior version. One of the products in the line may be priced to protect against competitors or to gain market share from existing competitors.

Products with less competition may be priced higher to subsidise other parts of the product line, so as to make up for the lost contribution of such fighting brands. Some items in the product line may be priced very low to serve as **loss leaders** and induce customers to try the product. A special variant of this is the so-called buy in, follow on strategy (Weigand, 1991). A classic example of this strategy is the razor blade link where Gillette, for example, uses penetration pricing on its razor (buy in) but skimming (relatively high price) on its razor blades (follow on). Thus, the linked product or service – the follow on – is sold at a significant contribution margin. This inevitably attracts others who try to sell follow on products without incurring the cost of the buy in.

Other examples of the strategy are as follows:

- Telephone companies sell mobile phones at a near giveaway price, hoping that the customer will be a heavy user of the profitable mobile telephone network.

- Nintendo often sells its game consoles at below cost but makes a handsome profit on the game software.

This kind of pricing is a particularly attractive strategy if it not only generates future sales but also creates an industry platform or standard to which all other rivals must use or conform (that is, a technological path dependency).

Product line pricing
Setting the price steps between various products in a product line based on cost differences between the products, customer evaluations of different features, and competitors' prices.

Loss leader
A product priced below cost to attract consumers, who may then make additional purchases.

12.11 PRICE BUNDLING

Price bundling
A strategy whereby the price of a group of products is lower than the total of the individual prices of the components. An example is selling a new car with an 'options package'.

Products can be **bundled** or unbundled for pricing purposes. The bundled approach gives a single price for the entire offering. Bundling can be defined as the sale of two or more separate products in one package at a discount. For example, the direct online seller of PCs, Dell, markets to consumers who may want to buy a portable computer system consisting of a basic laptop, a modem and a CD writer. It could sell these products as separate items, but they choose also to sell them as a price bundle by giving a discount to consumers if they buy all three products together (Arora, 2008; Stremersch and Tellis, 2002).

Many physical goods and services unite a core product with a variety of supplementary products at a set price. This has become a popular marketing strategy (Johnson *et al.*, 1999).

Manufacturers of industrial goods, such as machine tools, electronic components and chemical substances, frequently offer their products at a system price in conjunction with an assortment of services. In the service sector, travel companies bundle flights, rental cars, accommodation and events into one package. Strategically this bundling activity is designed to benefit the consumer by reducing administration costs and consequently transaction costs.

Should such service packages be priced as a whole (referred to as the bundle), or should each element be priced separately? To the extent that people dislike having to make many small payments, bundled pricing may be preferable. But if customers do not like being charged for product elements they may not use, itemised pricing may be preferable.

Many firms offer an array of choices. Telephone subscribers, for instance, can select from several service options, ranging from paying a small monthly fee for basic service and then extra for each phone call made, or paying a higher flat rate and getting a certain number of local, regional or long-distance calls free. At the top of the scale is the option that provides business users with unlimited access to long-distance calls over a prescribed area – even internationally. Bundled prices offer a service firm a certain guaranteed revenue from each customer, while giving the latter a clear idea in advance of how much the bill will be. Unbundled pricing provides customers with flexibility in what they choose to acquire and pay for, but may also cause problems. For instance, customers may be put off by discovering that the ultimate price of what they want is substantially higher than the advertised base price that attracted them in the first place.

12.12 PRICING FOR DIFFERENT SEGMENTS

Marketers very often have different marketing programmes for different consumer segments.

Geographic segments

It is possible that price sensitivity varies across geographic regions. For example, some grocery retailers have different price zones and prices are likely to vary across those zones. Competition and consumer profiles may differ between geographic segments. Products can be positioned with a high price in one country and a low price in another. This can be attributed to the pricing structure of international markets, viewed here as a major determinant of the product pricing policy.

Europe was a price differentiation paradise as long as markets were separated. But it is becoming increasingly difficult to retain the old price differentials. There are two developments which may force companies to standardise prices across European countries:

- international buying power of cross-European retail groups;
- parallel imports/grey markets. Because of differentiated prices across countries, buyers in one country are able to purchase at a lower price than in another country. As a result there will be an incentive for customers in lower-price markets to sell goods to higher-price markets in order to make a profit.

Simon and Kucher (1993) suggest a price 'corridor' (Figure 12.8). The prices in the individual countries may only vary within that range. Figure 12.8 is also interesting in the light of the

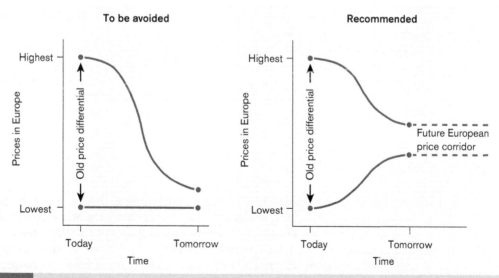

Figure 12.8   Development of prices in Europe
Source: Simon, H. and Kucher, E. (1993) The European pricing bomb: and how to cope with it, *Marketing and Research Today*, February: 25–36. Reproduced with permisssion from ESOMAR.

euro, which was fully implemented in January 2002, when new euro notes and coins were circulated. But this does not mean that a uniform price across Europe is required. Price differences which can be justified by transport costs, short-term exchange rate fluctuations, etc., may still be maintained.

They recommend that business in smaller countries should be sacrificed, if necessary, in order to retain acceptable pricing levels in the big markets such as France, Germany, the UK and Italy. For example, for a pharmaceutical manufacturer it is more profitable not to sell in the Portuguese pharmaceutical market than to accept a price reduction of 10 per cent in the German market due to parallel imports from Portugal.

Usage segments

It is common for marketers to recognise high-volume users and reward them with different prices. For example, regular customers at a particular store who carry the store's frequent shopper card will receive discounts at the checkout that other shoppers will not receive.

Time segments (off-peak pricing)

The most common form of usage segmentation pricing is based on the time of usage. Long-distance phone companies, electricity utilities, hotels, bars, restaurants, amusement parks and cinemas all use off-peak demand pricing. For firms like these, demand for their products and services fluctuates over time, and they cannot store their production. Consequently, they have periods of under-utilisation and often low incremental variable costs. At off-peak times, such companies welcome any additional revenue, as long as it makes some contribution toward their high fixed costs.

Off-peak pricing explains post-Christmas sales and end-of-season fashion sales. Unfortunately, some price sensitive shoppers learn when these sales occur and wait for them. This has the effect of reducing the overall average selling price and contribution margin.

Demographic segments

A concert hall might provide special prices for students or children to encourage attendance, or may give discounts to senior citizens. This is a common strategy used by museums, athletic events and amusement parks.

Family recreational air travel is much more price sensitive than business travel. Because of this, airlines charge less for children and offer early booking discounts that effectively exclude businesspeople from purchasing such tickets. As with all forms of price discrimination, segment pricing works best when buyers in the high-priced target segment cannot buy the product or service directly or indirectly (through resale) at the lower price.

12.13 RELATIONSHIP PRICING

When developing and maintaining long-term customer relationships, pricing strategy has an important role to play. Pricing low to win new business is not the best approach if a firm is seeking to attract customers who will remain loyal – those who are attracted by cut-price offers can easily be enticed away by another offer from a competitor. More creative pricing strategies focus on giving customers both price and non-price incentives to consolidate their business with a single supplier.

However, a strategy of discounting prices for large purchases can often be profitable for both parties, since the customer benefits from lower prices while the supplier may enjoy lower variable costs resulting from economies of scale. An alternative to volume discounting on a single service is for a firm to offer its customers discounts when two or more services are purchased together. The greater the number of different services a customer purchases from a single supplier, the closer the relationship is likely to be and the greater the exit barriers for the partners in the relationship. Both parties get to know each other better, and it is more inconvenient for the customer to shift its business.

Pricing is becoming more fluid. Even before the advent of the online medium, industrial markets and third-world bazaars have long followed a customised pricing mechanism based on bargaining and discount schedules. The online medium has made it feasible to apply flexible pricing more broadly. Online prices can be tailored to specific users and raised or lowered instantly for assessing price elasticity at different prices. The ability to create truly fluid pricing is only limited by customer acceptance. Technology is now available to vary pricing in ways that were not possible in the past. New in-store technology allows supermarkets to customise pricing based on specific times of the day through digital price labels or even to tailor discounts and coupons to individuals based on their past purchasing patterns.

Due to the influence of the online medium, we expect that all firms will be called upon to revamp their pricing strategies completely. The fixed one-price strategy of the past has been completely eroded over the past few years. In the years ahead, 'dynamic pricing' that takes advantage of instantaneous market conditions will become the norm. Interestingly, these developments do not necessarily mean that prices will decline. The convenience, time-saving aspects and product matching features of online markets can increase the price a customer is willing to pay.

When customers become familiar and comfortable with a retail website it reduces their incentive to shift to other sites for lower prices. Further, if a company understands the customer (e.g. by tracking and understanding what customers do while visiting its website) and facilitates the creation of a co-production process to produce a product and service tailored to the customer's need, there is relatively little opportunity or incentive for customers to compare other shops based on price. Customisation of the product or service adds so much value and strengthens the relationship that the price becomes a less important factor.

Establishing global pricing contracts (GPCs)

As globalisation increases, the following is heard frequently among global suppliers and global customers: 'Give me a global pricing contract (GPC) and I'll consolidate my worldwide purchase with you.' Increasingly, global customers are demanding such contracts from suppliers. For example, in 1998, General Motor's Powertrain Group told suppliers of components used in GM's engines, transmissions and subassemblies to charge GM the same for parts from one region as they did for parts from another region.

Suppliers do not need to lose out when customers globalise. The most attractive global pricing opportunities are those that involve suppliers and customers working together to identify and eliminate inefficiencies that harm both. Sometimes suppliers do not have a choice. They do not want to shut themselves out of business with their largest and fastest-growing customers.

Suppliers and customers have different advantages and disadvantages with global pricing contracts. Table 12.2 illustrates some of them.

One chemicals manufacturer concentrated on relationships with a few select customers. It found out that its strength lay in value-added services but that potential customers in emerging markets were more concerned with price. The select customers, however, were interested in money-saving supply and inventory management initiatives developed jointly with the supplier.

Global customers' demands for detailed cost information can also put suppliers at risk. Toyota, Honda, Xerox and others force suppliers to open their books for inspection. Their

Table 12.2	Global pricing contracts (GPCs): advantages and disadvantages

Customers	Suppliers
Advantages	• Easily gain access to new markets and grow the business.
• Lower prices worldwide coupled with higher levels of service.	• Consolidate operations and achieve economies of scale.
• Standardisation of products and services offered across markets.	• Work with industry leaders and influence market development by using them as showcase accounts.
• Efficiencies in all processes, including new product development, manufacturing, inventory, logistics and customer service.	• Collaborate with customers and develop strong relationships that are difficult for potential competitors to break into.
• Faster diffusion of innovations globally.	• Rectify price and service anomalies in a customer relationship across country markets.
Disadvantages	• Local managers sometimes resist change, and supplier may get caught in the crossfire between customer's HQ and country.
• Customer might be less adaptable to local market variance and changes over time.	• Supplier might lose the ability to serve other attractive customers.
• Supplier might not have capabilities to provide consistent quality and performance across markets.	• Customer might not be able to deliver on promises.
• Supplier might use customer's over-dependence to extract higher prices.	• Customer might take advantage of cost information shared in the relationship.
• Local managers might resist global contracts and prefer dealing with local suppliers.	• Supplier might become over-dependent on one customer, even when there are other more attractive customers to serve.
• Costs of monitoring global contracts might outstrip the benefits.	• Supplier might have a conflict with existing channels of distribution in the new markets.

Source: Narayandas, D., Quelch, J. and Swartz, G. (2000) Prepare your company for global pricing, *MIT Sloan Management Review*, Fall: 61–70. Copyright © 2000 by Massachusetts Institute of Technology. All rights reserved. Distributed by Tribune Media Services.

stated objectives are to help suppliers identify ways to improve processes and quality while re-ducing costs – and to build trust. But, in an economic downturn, the global customer might also seek price reductions and supplementary services.

12.14 PRICING ON THE INTERNET

The virtual value chain offers different options on products and services to customers. The extra value obtained by the customer can be billed at a different price option. With the sim-plest mass-produced products, a flat price may be appropriate. However, when customers can order from different sources to customise their choice, the Internet company, which is re-sponsible for assembling this choice, may charge different prices. In the case of digital prod-ucts, these options can also be extended with regard to time and place. For example, at peak times, when most of the customers are likely to log on to the site, the company may charge a premium price to minimise the Internet traffic. During off-peak hours the company may re-duce the price of the products or services to keep the optimum level of Internet traffic on the site. Similarly, customers may have the option to obtain the product through the regular mail at a different price from when they directly download the product/service. Price variations can also be employed based on the need for the product or the service. For example, a cus-tomer who wants to search for and read a particular piece of information is likely to pay less than a person who will download and print the information. Similarly, a customer who wants to review only the summary of the information is likely to pay less than a person who needs the complete information. A customer who needs immediate access to new pieces of information is likely to be charged a higher price than a customer who can accept some delay in accessing the information.

A virtual value chain makes it easier for customers to compare the prices of similar offerings by different companies. Not only can customers obtain the price of the offerings, but they can also understand the prices charged for add-on features. With this information, customers can quickly customise their selections in products and services. Consequently, the Internet will lead to increased price competition and the standardisation of prices across borders.

The ability to compare prices across all suppliers using the Internet and online shopping services will lead to increased price competition. Finally, the price of providing Internet-based services (especially information-based services) often contains little marginal costs. Thus, the ability of technology to offer services at a cheaper cost would make it difficult to determine the appropriate price for a consumer (Allen and Fjernestad, 2001).

Among the most popular applications of the Internet is the online auction in the consumer market. Online auctions attract thousands, sometimes millions, of bidders who compete with each other for items ranging from computer-related products to antiques. Companies such as eBay and Amazon.com have entered into the online auction business in a big way (Massad and Tucker, 2000).

In the B2B market many companies are likely to adopt online auctions as part of their ongoing purchasing process or perhaps even outsource the bulk of purchasing aided by new technology. It is an attractive technological solution for reducing costs, but it does not help uncover the root causes of poor cost management worked out by the buying firm (Emiliani, 2000).

12.15 COMMUNICATING PRICES TO THE TARGET MARKETS

Customers in the B2B market must be very price conscious. Each item they buy contributes to their costs and thus to their profits and competitiveness. Many of them keep extensive records using formalised purchasing systems designed to obtain the best value for the price. Consumers in the B2B market tend to be less aware of actual prices.

Consequently, the final task, once each of the other issues has been addressed, is to decide how the organisation's pricing policies can best be communicated to the target market(s). People need to know the price for some product offerings well in advance of purchase; they may also need to know how, where and when that price is payable. This information must be presented in ways that are intelligible and unambiguous, so that customers will not be misled and question the ethical standards of the firm.

Managers must decide whether or not to include information on pricing in advertising for the service. It may be appropriate to relate the price to the costs of competing products or to show alternative ways of spending one's money. Certainly, salespeople and customer service representatives should be able to give prompt, accurate responses to customer queries about pricing, payment and credit. Good signage at retail points of sale will save staff members from having to answer basic questions on prices.

12.16 SUMMARY

In this chapter we have considered the role of pricing decisions in overall company and marketing strategies. Price setting is a complex decision which involves many factors. To establish a price, the manager must identify the firm's objectives and analyse the behaviour of demand, costs and competition.

A good deal of basic microeconomic theory is devoted to the relationship between price and demand. While many of the principles that have been developed have relevance to what happens in the real world, there are nevertheless many factors (other than demand and cost) that have to be taken into account.

Pricing strategies must balance the needs of both the customer and the firm. Value-based pricing, which includes the concepts of value in use and value in exchange, is increasingly popular. Since customers seeking differing types of value and competition have a broad range of choices in how to price, other strategies are viable as well. In devising a pricing strategy, it is important to identify a customer value proposition that matches the capabilities of the organisation. Pricing new products offers a different set of challenges. In general, two main opposing strategies are seen:

Total quality management (TQM)
Programmes designed to constantly improve the quality of products services and marketing processes.

- *skimming*: high price, to skim off the short-term profit;
- *penetration*: low price, to maximise long-term market share.

Practical pricing tactics may include experience curve pricing, product line pricing, price bundling, pricing on the Internet, etc.

CASE STUDY 12.1

Harley-Davidson
Is the image justifying the price level in a time of recession?

Source: © Robert Convery/Alamy

Harley-Davidson's mission statement is: 'We fulfil dreams through the experience of motorcycling.'

History

The Harley-Davidson Motorcycle Company (www.harley-davidson.com) was founded in 1903. Harley-Davidson (H-D) soon became the world's leading manufacturer of motorcycles, based on a reputation of quality and reliability. After the Second World War, and the demise of the American Indian motorcycle, Harley-Davidson became

the sole US manufacturer of motorcycles. In 1969, Harley-Davidson was sold to American Machine and Foundry (AMF).

AMF almost tripled production to 75,000 units annually over a four-year period to meet the increase in demand. Unfortunately, product quality deteriorated significantly as over half the motorcycles that came off the assembly line had parts missing and dealers had to repair them in order to make sales. Little money was invested in improving design or engineering. The motorcycles leaked oil, vibrated and could not match the excellent performance of the Japanese products.

During this time, Honda was beginning to penetrate the American motorcycle market and gain a significant market share. Honda manufacturing plants incorporated the principles of total quality management (TQM). Honda began producing motorcycles with constantly improving quality at a time when the quality of Harley-Davidson was drastically decreasing. By the early 1980s Honda almost totally dominated the world motorcycle market.

Japanese manufacturers also moved into the heavyweight motorcycle market and began selling Harley look-alike motorcycles. Yamaha was the first company to do so and was soon followed by the three other major Japanese manufacturers, Honda, Suzuki and Kawasaki. Their products looked so similar to Harley-Davidson's that it was difficult to tell the difference without reading the name on the petrol tank. The Japanese companies also copied the style of the Harley-Davidson advertisements.

In order to stay in business while the necessary changes in design and production were being accomplished, the executives turned to William G. Davidson, Harley's styling vice president. Known as 'Willie G.' and a grandson of one of the company's founders, he designed a number of new models by combining components from existing models. These included the Super Glide, the Electra Glide the Wide Glide and the Low Rider. Each model was successful and other executives credit Davidson's skill with saving the company.

In 1982, Harley-Davidson faced new problems. Overall demand for motorcycles dropped dramatically and Harley-Davidson's share of this smaller market also continued to drop. The company had a large inventory of unsold products and could not continue in business with its level of production and expenses. Production was cut drastically, and more than 1,800 of the 4,000 employees were made redundant.

In 1983, President Reagan increased the tariffs on large Japanese motorcycles from 4.4 per cent to 49.4 per cent, but these would decline each year and be effective for only five years. While this did reduce the number of imports and gave Harley-Davidson some protection, Japanese manufacturers found ways to evade most of the tariffs, for example by assembling more of their heavyweight bikes in their US plants. In 1983, Harley-Davidson's share of the heavyweight motorcycle market slipped to 23 per cent, the lowest ever, although it did earn a slight profit.

In 1998 H-D moved to expand its presence within the motorcycle industry when it acquired the outstanding shares of the Buell Motorcycle Company. While sharing components and technology with H-D, the performance-oriented Buell is intended to attract younger and non-traditional riders to the H-D family.

Harley-Davidson today

The company now has a new direction. Harley-Davidson is now out of survival. H-D spent a lot of time putting together its business process, values, issues, mission statement . . . all those things H-D believes in. H-D wants to get everyone pointed in the same direction (Milligan and Carbone, 2000).

Much of the value of a Harley resides in its tradition – the look, sound and heritage that have made it an All-American symbol. The bikes represent something very basic – a desire for freedom, adventure and individualism.

Harley-Davidson Inc. is the parent company for the following three companies.

1　Harley-Davidson Motor Company, the only major US-based motorcycle manufacturer, produces heavyweight motorcycles and offers a complete line of motorcycle parts, accessories, clothing and general merchandise. Strategic licensing of the Harley-Davidson brand helps create future generations of Harley-Davidson enthusiasts. The US market launch of the Fisher-Price Power Wheels® Ride-On-Toy, a four-wheeled, battery-operated children's toy, became the most successful Power Wheels introduction in the last ten years.

2　Buell Motorcycle Company produces sport and sport-touring motorcycles.

3　Harley-Davidson Financial Services Inc. (HDFS) provides wholesale and retail financing, insurance and credit card programmes to Harley-Davidson dealers and customers. In the United States, HDFS financed 53.5 per cent of the new Harley-Davidson motorcycles retailed by independent dealers during 2008. The wholesale division of HDFS provides dealers with financing for motorcycles and related products, and store expansion or renovation.

The Buell does not appear to be cannibalising Harley-Davidson sales because it is a very different kind of bike. The rider's position is thrust forward to create a racing feeling, while the Harley-Davidson is designed more for riders who want to cruise. Nor is a Buell as big or as heavy as a Harley-Davidson, and it is easier to manoeuvre. Harley-Davidson faces the task of attracting younger customers, as its average customer's age increases and sales decrease. Part of reshaping their image includes releasing new Buell motorcycles designed for young professional men and women.

The average US retail purchaser of a new Harley-Davidson motorcycle is a married male in his mid to late forties (nearly two-thirds of US retail purchasers of new Harley-Davidson motorcycles are between the ages of 35 and 54) with a median household income of approximately $87,000. Nearly three-quarters of the US retail sales of new Harley-Davidson motorcycles are to buyers with at least one year of education beyond high school and 32 per cent of the buyers have college/graduate degrees. Approximately 12 per cent of US retail motorcycle sales of new Harley-Davidson motorcycles are to female buyers.

Formed in 1983, the company-sponsored Harley's Owner Group or HOG® has over 1 million members worldwide as of 2005. The Buell Riders Adventure Group or BRAG® is an 11,000-member-strong counterpart to HOG®. Both groups sponsor events including national rides and rallies. The company also sponsors racing activities. Harley's buyers aren't locked into any social class. You are just as likely to find a CEO on a Harley as a worker off the assembly line. Harley owners are loyal, with 90 per cent of buyers reporting the intention of purchasing another Harley bike. Clearly image sells to this demographic: Harley ranks near the 100th percentile on the Brand Asset Valuator scale for such qualities as authentic, rugged, daring, dynamic, distinctive and high performance. As one Harley owner put it: 'What Harley-Davidson appeals to me is that we all think we're cooler than we really are' (Bronson and Beaver, 2004).

Harley-Davidson is trying to soften its bad-guy image to make biking more mainstream. It is encouraging the spread of Harley-Davidson owner groups, supporting charities and taking toys to hospitals. But the company does not want to change its image too much. There are some upscale neurosurgeons and bankers who are riding Harleys because they want people to think there is a little bad in them. H-D does not want to completely squash that image (Holstein, 2000).

The motorcycle market in the three main regions of the world is shown in Table 12.3. For the fiscal year ended 2008, total Harley-Davidson motorcycle shipments were 303,500 units compared with 204,592 units in 2000, a 48 per cent increase. However, it was a decrease compared to 2007 when the number of sold units was 330,600. Of the total H-D shipments in 2008, 68 per cent went to USA and 16 per cent to Europe. Of the rest, Japan, Canada and Australia were the biggest H-D markets. Total Buell motorcycle shipments were 13,119 in 2008, compared to 10,189 units in 2000, a 29 per cent gain.

Harley-Davidson motorcycle net revenue in 2008 was US$5,594 million compared to US$2,250 million in 2000.

The total market in North America has fallen from 543,000 units in 2006 to 480,000 units in 2008. On the other hand, the European market has increased from 361,000 in 2006 to 397,000 in 2008. During the same period H-D's market share has decreased from 50 per cent to 46 per cent, whereas the European market share has remained stable around 10 per cent.

Distribution

In the United States, H-D distributes its motorcycles and related products to 686 independently owned full-service Harley-Davidson dealerships.

In the European region H-D distributes all products sold to 383 independent dealers or distributors through its European subsidiary located in Oxford, England, or through one of its sales offices in the United Kingdom, France, Germany, Italy, Netherlands, Spain, Switzerland or South Africa.

In the Asia-Pacific region, H-D distributes all products sold to 205 independent dealers in Japan and Australia through H-D owned subsidiaries in those countries, and all products sold to independent dealers for the remaining Asia-Pacific.

Dealerships can be found in 36 European/Middle Eastern/African countries, 8 Asian countries and 15 Latin America countries. Most dealerships sell only Harley-Davidson and Buell products.

Table 12.3	Registrations of heavyweight motorcycles (over 650cc), 2008		
	North America	Europe	Asia-Pacific
Total industry (1000s)	480	397	80
Market share	%	%	%
Harley-Davidson/Buell	46	10	25
Honda	15	14	19
Yamaha	9	14	13
Kawasaki	8	12	15
Suzuki	13	17	12
BMW	2	15	5
Ducati	1	6	4
Triumph	2	7	1
Others	4	5	6
Total	100	100	100

Source: Harley-Davidson Financial Report 2008, including 10-K report.

Competitors

All of Harley-Davidson's major competitors have their headquarters outside the US, most in Japan. Most of the major competitors are operating units of larger diversified companies, e.g. Honda, Yamaha, Kawasaki, Suzuki and BMW. At least one of H-D's major competitors, Honda, manufactures its largest motorcycles in the US. A major exception to the larger diversified company rule is Ducati, an Italian company that is a major in the European performance market.

The following characterises the most important competitors (Bronson and Beaver, 2005).

Honda

Honda is one of the leaders in the motorcycle industry with 15 per cent of the North American market, 14 per cent of the European market, and 19 per cent of the Asian-Pacific market. Honda combines excellent engineering and quality with highly automated manufacturing to achieve significant economies of scale. Honda has been able to leverage its low-cost advantage into global leadership.

Honda is a diversified company that at one time surpassed Chrysler and Toyota in sales to become the third largest automobile company in the US. In addition to motorcycles and automobiles Honda manufactures ATVs, outboard motors, generators, lawn care equipment and other power products. Honda has a presence in the financial services industry, providing financing options for motorcycle and automobile dealers and consumers. Honda's niche in the US motorcycle market is touring bikes. With up to 1500cc water-cooled engines, Honda's touring bikes are high quality, refined, comfortable and fuel-efficient.

Honda's corporate culture is egalitarian with all employees, including the president, wearing the same uniform and sharing the same facilities. Input is sought from all levels of the company. Honda encourages creativity and is widely regarded as being the leader in 4-cycle gasoline engine technology. The company goes to considerable lengths to structure its operations around the needs of local markets. Honda is committed to continuing its leadership position through attention to markets, continual improvement and the introduction of new models and technologies.

Yamaha

Yamaha has manufacturing facilities, distribution and R&D operations in many international markets. Yamaha focuses on tailoring its products to local market conditions. Yamaha Motor Company has a diverse product line including outboard motors, boats, personal watercraft, generators, golf cars, ATVs, snowmobiles, outdoor power equipment, race kart engines, accessories, apparel and motorcycles. Yamaha produces a full line of motorcycles ranging from scooters to heavyweights; however, their competitive advantage focuses on speed and high-performance racing bikes. Yamaha's motorcycle sales are strong globally. Their target market throughout the world is the young and thrill-seeking consumer who sees riding and speed as a sport.

Kawasaki

Kawasaki is a world leader in the transportation equipment and industrial goods industries with diverse product lines in each category. Kawasaki Motors is focused on motorcycles, all-terrain vehicles, jet ski watercraft, utility vehicles, rail cars, wheels, robots and engines for consumer products such as lawnmowers. Kawasaki is well known for providing a wide range of products that offer high-performance and low-maintenance attributes. Kawasaki offers multiple models of motorcycles, which makes them competitive in many different facets of the industry including touring bikes, sports bikes, off-road bikes, dual-purpose bikes, street bikes and police bikes.

Kawasaki has a large international presence with production facilities in South-East Asia, China, Europe and the United States. They have their strongest market position in Asia Pacific.

Suzuki

Suzuki manufactures automobiles, commercial vehicles, outboard motors and ATVs. Suzuki is the third largest manufacturer of motorcycles, lagging behind only Honda and Yamaha. Motorcycles comprise around 20 per cent of the company's total sales. Suzuki motorcycles have a significant international presence with sales in over 190 countries; 80 per cent of Suzuki's total motorcycle sales are in offshore markets. Suzuki began using joint manufacturing efforts in foreign countries in 1993 and uses direct sales subsidiaries to reach customers. Suzuki uses cost-reduction activities to achieve their ongoing goal of providing a low-cost product. Efficiency is the backbone of Suzuki's low-cost position in the industry.

BMW

BMW's focus is on putting their best efforts into a small range of products, which makes their products unique in quality, style and performance. Their motorcycle production concentrates on three different series stressing superior quality. BMW's strategy is based on premium pricing and building the best motorcycle that money can buy by setting the standard in technology, environment and safety in all of their product offerings. Each of their motorcycles portrays the traditional motorcycle image; however, the BMW brand also includes elements of sophistication and class in their products. All of BMW's motorcycles have high resale values; however, their high price level limits their market share.

BMW is the only manufacturer of cars and motorcycles worldwide that concentrates on premium standards and outstanding quality for all of its product lines. Throughout their quest and their commitment to enhancing their international presence, BMW has expanded with 23 car production and assembly plants located in seven countries and BMW has marketing subsidiaries in 33 countries. BMW is synonymous with high quality and performance, which is reinforced by strong brand recognition and customer loyalty, for those who can afford it.

Ducati

Ducati is representative of Harley-Davidson's European competition. Ducati has adopted a cyberspace model (www.ducati.com) selling motorcycles, accessories and clothing online. The company promotes its cyberspace model through participation in motorcycle racing where Ducati has dominated the world Superbike Championships for over ten years. Unlike Harley-Davidson, Ducati does not build bikes on the basis on nostalgia and comfort; rather Ducati sells style and performance based on technologically advanced designs. Ducatis are race-proven bikes, sold for use on the street – the ultimate café racer. Like Harley-Davidson, Ducati employs a premium pricing strategy. Ducati customers tend to be younger and somewhat less affluent; consequently, sales vary more with the economic cycle.

H-D lacks significant scale in comparison to its competitors in the market. Many of its competitors such as Bayerische Motoren Werke AG (BMW) and Honda Motor Company Limited are much larger in size, operation and coverage. BMW, for instance, recorded revenues of US$77 million during fiscal year 2007, and Honda Motor Company Limited recorded revenue of US$94 billion during the same period. Harley- Davidson, in contrast, recorded revenues of around $6 billion in 2007. Lack of scale limits the company's ability to compete effectively with larger players, which can also utilise synergies from other parts of their operations, e.g. from their automobile businesses.

Pricing

The price competition is getting tougher. Compared to similar models from Honda, Harley-Davidson still has about a 30 per cent price premium.

Harley-Davidson's premium pricing limits the number of younger buyers. Two-thirds of its customers are between the ages of 35 and 54. Recently H-D has redesigned some of its bikes to better accommodate female riders. The percentage of female buyers has reached 12 per cent and continues to move slowly upward. H-D also offers motorcycle rider education courses, where 40 per cent of the participants are women.

Harley-Davidson owners still wear T-shirts saying 'I'd rather push a Harley than drive a Honda.'

Today, Harley-Davidson's overseas business outside the USA is around 30 per cent of its annual total. Europeans like cruiser bikes, but maybe not the Harley-Davidson prices. In fact some Harley-Davidson bikes have recently been shipped back from Europe due to lack of demand.

QUESTIONS

1 What are the main reasons for Harley-Davidson's enormous success over the last 15 years?

2 Describe Harley-Davidson's general pricing strategy. What does the company's positioning have to do with its pricing strategy?

3 Should Harley-Davidson alter its price, given that there are strong price pressures from rivals?

4 What should Harley-Davidson do to improve its market share in Europe?

SOURCES

Bronson, J. W. and Beaver, G. (2004) Strategic change in the face of success? Harley-Davidson, Inc., *Strategic Change*, 13(4): 205–18; Bronson, J. W. and Beaver, G. (2005) Harley-Davidson and the international market for luxury goods, (http://road.uww.edu/road/bronsonj/788%20WEB/Web%20Cases%20&%20Readings/H-D&LuxuryGoods_080106.doc); Harley-Davidson Inc. (2009) *2008 Harley-Davidson Annual Report*, including Form 10-K; Holstein, W. (2000) Rebels with a cause: Harley revamps itself in a drive for new, young hog riders, *US News & World Report*, 19: 46–7; Klayman, B. (2005) Harley-Davidson CEO sees strong growth, *Reuters* (http://go.Reuters.co.uk/newsArticle.jhtml); Milligan, B. and Carbone, J. (2000) Harley-Davidson win by getting suppliers on board, *Purchasing*, 5 (21 September): 52–65.

QUESTIONS FOR DISCUSSION

1   What is value-based pricing? How does it differ from cost-based pricing?
2   a) What does the economist contribute to the pricing decision?
    b) What does the accountant contribute to the pricing decision?
3   What are skimming and penetration pricing?
4   What is umbrella pricing?
5   List three aspects of product line pricing.
6   Why is cost-based pricing particularly problematic in service industries?
7   How does competition affect a company's prices? Briefly describe a major competitor-based pricing approach.
8   Many firms enter a market as price leaders, but they end up dominating the bottom end of the market. What could be the reasons for this change?

REFERENCES

Allen, E. and Fjernestad, J. (2001) E-commerce marketing strategies: an integrated framework and case analysis, *Logistics Information Management*, 14(1): 14–33.

Arora, R. (2008) Price bundling and framing strategies for complementary products, *Journal of Product & Brand Management*, 17(7): 475–84.

BBC (1996) *Branded: Heinz Case*, BBC TV.

Best, R. J. (2000) *Market-based Management*, 2nd edn, Prentice Hall, Harlow.

Brennan, R., Canning, L. and McDowell, R. (2007) Price-setting in business-to-business markets, *The Marketing Review*, 7(3): 207–34.

Brown, A., Meenan, B. J. and Young, T. P. (2007) Medical device prices follow the experience curve, *Journal of Medical Marketing*, 7(3): 203–12.

Brown, A., Meenan, B. J., Dixon, D., Young, T. P. and Brennan, M. (2008) Application of the experience curve to price trends in medical devices: implications for product development and marketing strategies, *Journal of Medical Marketing*, 8(3): 241–55.

Curtis, J. (2001) Body Shop plans to scale down its political activity, *Marketing*, 26 July: 3.

Czepiel, J. A. (1992) *Competitive Marketing Strategy*, Prentice Hall, Englewood Cliffs, NJ.

Czinkota, M. R. and Kotabe, M. (1999) Bypassing Japan's marketing barriers, *Marketing Management*, 8 (Winter): 33–43.

Davidson, A. and Simonetto, M. (2005) Pricing strategy and execution: an overlooked way to increase revenues and profits, *Strategy & Leadership*, 33(6): 25–33.

Docters, R., Schefers, B., Korman, T. and Durman, C. (2008) The neglected demand curve: how to build one and how to benefit, *Journal of Business Strategy*, 29(5): 19–25.

Driver, J. C. (2001) Airline marketing in regulatory context, *Marketing Intelligence Planning*, 19(2): 125–35.

Emiliani, M. L. (2000) Business-to-business online auctions: key issues for purchasing process improvement, *Supply Chain Management: An International Journal*, 5(4): 176–86.

Freedonia Group (2000) *World Major Household Appliances Report*, Freedonia Press, Cleveland, OH.

Garda, R. A. (1995) Tactical pricing, in S. J. Paliwoda and J. K. Ryans (eds) *International Marketing Reader*, Routledge, London.

Hinterhuber, A. (2008) Customer value-based pricing strategies: why companies resist, *Journal of Business Strategy*, 41–50.

Holden, R. K. and Nayle, T. T. (1998) Kamikaze pricing, *Marketing Management*, 7(2): (Summer): 30–9.

Hollensen, S. (2001) *Global Marketing: A Market Responsive Approach*, 2nd edn, Financial Times/Prentice Hall, Harlow.

Holstein, W. (2000) Rebels with a cause: Harley revamps itself in a drive for new, young hog riders, *US News & World Report*, 19: 46–7.

Indounas, K. (2009) Successful industrial service pricing, *Journal of Business & Industrial Marketing*, 24(2): 86–97.

Johnson, M. D., Hermann, A. and Baner, H. H. (1999) The effects of price bundling on consumer evaluations of product offerings, *International Journal of Research in Marketing*, 16: 129–42.

Lambin, J. (1976) *Advertising, Competition and Market Conduct in Oligopoly Over Time*, North Holland-Elsevier, Amsterdam.

Marsh, G. (2000) International pricing: a market perspective, *Marketing Intelligence & Planning*, 18(4): 200–5.

Massad, V. J. and Tucker, J. M. (2000) Comparing bidding and pricing between in-person and on-line auction, *Journal of Product & Brand Management*, 9(5): 325–32.

Matthyssens, P., Vandenbempt, K. and Goubau, C. (2009) Value capturing as a balancing act, *Journal of Business & Industrial Marketing*, 24(1): 56–60.

Milligan, B. and Carbone, J. (2000) Harley-Davidson win by getting suppliers on board, *Purchasing*, 5 (21 September): 52–65.

Nagle, T. T. (1987) *The Strategies and Tactics of Pricing*, Prentice Hall, Englewood Cliffs, NJ.

Narayandas, D., Quelch, J. and Swartz, G. (2000) Prepare your company for global pricing, *Sloan Management Review*, Fall: 61–70.

Rao, S. K. (2008) An innovative approach to developing and managing biopharmaceutical pricing strategy, *Journal of Medical Marketing*, 8(2): 94–100.

Simon, H. and Kucher, E. (1993) The European pricing bomb: and how to cope with it, *Marketing and Research Today*, February: 25–36.

Stremersch, S. and Tellis, G. J. (2002) Strategic bundling of products and prices: a new synthesis for marketing, *Journal of Marketing*, 66 (January): 55–72.

Weigand, R. E. (1991) Buy in : follow on strategies for profit, *Sloan Management Review*, Spring: 29–38.

CHAPTER 13
Distribution decisions

LEARNING OBJECTIVES

After studying this chapter you should be able to:

- understand why relationships occur between manufacturer and distributor
- explore the determinants of channel decisions
- discuss the key points in putting together and managing marketing channels
- discuss the factors influencing channel width (intensive, selective or exclusive coverage)
- explain what is meant by integration of the marketing channel
- discuss the role of retailing in modern marketing

13.1 INTRODUCTION

A trading or distribution relationship is a relationship between a buyer and a seller who resells the goods and services. Trading relationships have been important since humans began to trade.

Access to international markets is a key decision area facing firms in the twenty-first century. After the firm has chosen a strategy to get its products into foreign markets, the next challenge is the distribution of products within national markets. The first part of this chapter concerns the structure and management of foreign distribution. The second part of the chapter is concerned with the management of logistics.

A *distribution channel* is a set of organisations that make a product or service available for purchase by consumers or businesses. The distribution channel serves to connect a manufacturer, or a service provider, with consumers or users. In simple terms, a distribution channel is a pipeline or pathway to the market (Morelli, 2006).

Distribution channels are needed because producers are separated from prospective customers.

A distribution channel consists of at least a producer and a customer. Most channels, however, use one or more intermediaries to help move products to the customer.

Intermediaries are independently owned organisations that act as links to move products between producers and the end user. The primary categories are brokers, wholesalers and distributors, and retailers. Agents do not purchase the goods they handle but instead negotiate the sale for the client. A familiar example is estate agents, who negotiate the sale of property for their customers. Companies have more control over the activities of brokers, including the final price to the customer, because brokers do not own the goods they sell. *Wholesalers* (also referred to as distributors) take title to products and resell them to retail, industrial, commercial, institutional, professional or agricultural firms, as well as to other wholesalers.

Most distribution channels flow from the manufacturer to the end user, but goods sometimes move in the opposite direction. A *reverse channel* flows from the end user to the wholesaler and/or the manufacturer. An example is recycling of bottles and cans.

Recycling services have become increasingly important, given the growth of waste materials and the high costs associated with their disposal. Volunteer groups have been important in the recycling process, particularly in the collection and transport of waste to recycling plants. But the problem of disposing waste materials is growing so fast that more commercial solutions must be found despite the fact that many cities are mandating that consumers sort their waste to facilitate pick-up and disposal. Some specialists have become more involved, including manufacturer-owned redemption centres and independent recycling centres, but on the whole current channels are not entirely satisfactory, and more cost-efficient ones are needed.

According to Bucklin *et al.* (1996), distribution channels typically account for 15–40 per cent of the retail price of goods and services in an industry.

Over the next few years, the challenges and opportunities for channel management will multiply, as technological developments accelerate channel evolution. Data networks are increasingly enabling end users to bypass traditional channels and deal directly with manufacturers and service providers.

Electronic data interchange (EDI) is now used for the exchange of orders and invoices between suppliers and their customers. By monitoring stock online, customers are also able to order directly from suppliers on a **just-in-time (JIT)** basis, and thereby to avoid holding stock altogether or to minimise the time it is held.

At the same time, new channels are continuing to emerge in one industry after another, opening up opportunities for companies to cut costs or improve their effectiveness in reaching specific market segments. Catalogue retailing, telephone ordering, cable TV shopping and Internet ordering are all becoming increasingly important to consumer goods manufacturers. Despite the scale and importance of these opportunities, however, few companies manage to take full advantage of them.

Electronic data interchange (EDI)
Electronic links between suppliers and retailers allowing purchase orders, packing lists, delivery.

Just-in-time (JIT)
Aims to minimise stocks by organising a supply system which provides materials and components as they are required.

13.2 THE BASIC FUNCTIONS OF CHANNEL PARTICIPANTS

Channel member
A layer of intermediaries that performs some work in bringing the product and its ownership closer to the final buyer.

Transaction
A trade of values between two parties.

The most common function of a marketing **channel member** is to resell the product into a market that could not be reached as efficiently or effectively by the original seller. Intermediaries have already established goodwill with their customers, and those customers trust the intermediary's buying judgements. Retailers often have multiple selling outlets that are both in prime geographical locations and have the right image. This gives the manufacturer both physical and psychological market positioning.

Figure 13.1 shows how the number of **transactions** (contact lines) between three manufacturers and three customers (using one intermediary) is reduced.

Intermediaries play a major role in bringing the product or service to the end user at the right time by transporting and storing it.

Many intermediaries also cooperate with the manufacturer to provide customer training, education and after-sales maintenance and repair services.

Sometimes merchants do take risks with, for example, seasonal products and are caught with stock at the end of a season that has to be sold at a loss or carried over to the next year.

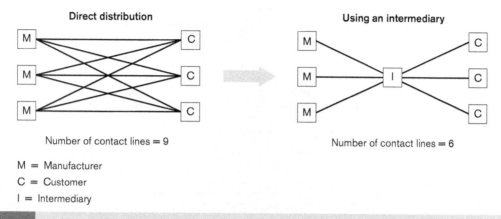

M = Manufacturer
C = Customer
I = Intermediary

Figure 13.1	How an intermediary increases distribution efficiency

However, the risk-taking and financing activities of channel intermediaries have been greatly reduced over the last hundred years. Nowadays, many new products are sold to retailers on consignment (retailers pay for what they sell and return the rest) or are purchased with buy-back deals in the contract. Some retailers are even demanding up-front cash payments to compensate for the cost and the risk of placing a new product on their shelves. With established products, the credit allowances given to the wholesaler or retailer are such that a high-turnover product is often sold by the retailer before the wholesaler or retailer pays the manufacturer for the product.

Channel members are able to provide valuable customer feedback, but often the manufacturer also provides information down the channel to retailers that creates interest and support for its product. Hence, market research and information flows both ways with findings and data often being interpreted in different ways by the various parties.

13.3 DISTRIBUTOR PORTFOLIO ANALYSIS

A distributor analysis can be undertaken by reviewing the information on a distributor's growth rate and the firm's percentage of the distributor's total sales. Using Table 13.1 as an input, Figure 13.2 is an example of a manufacturing firm, X, which, within an SBU, has four distributors each serving a different segment. The strategic recommendations in Figure 13.2 are only based on the variables included in the distributor portfolio (Table 13.1). Before making final recommendations, Firm X should also include its dependence on each distributor, e.g. by calculating how its total sales are distributed among its four distributors.

Table 13.1	A manufacturer's distributor portfolio analysis

Segment	Mainly served by	Percentage of Firm X in distributor's total purchases	Distributor annual growth rate within the segment
Segment A	Distributor A	60%	50%
Segment B	Distributor B	30%	30%
Segment C	Distributor C	75%	−25%
Segment D	Distributor D	20%	−40%

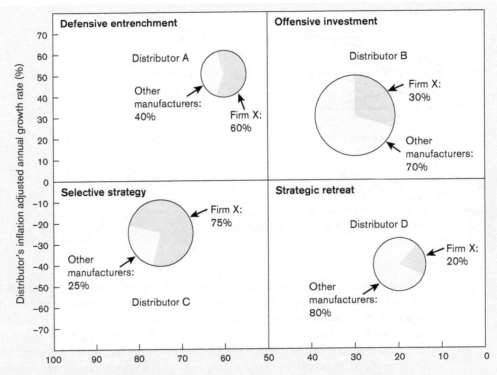

Penetration per cent: Firm X's share of distributor's product-line sales – the area of each circle is proportional
to the value of the distributor's total purchase, from Firm X and others

Figure 13.2	A manufacturer's distributor portfolio analysis

Source: Adapted from Dickson, P. R. (1982), Distributor portfolio analysis and channel dependence matrix, *Journal of Marketing*, 47 (Summer): 35–44. Reproduced with permission from the American Marketing Association.

13.4 DEVELOPING AND MANAGING RELATIONSHIPS BETWEEN MANUFACTURER AND DISTRIBUTOR

A relationship occurs when there is a fit between the marketing strategies and implementation skills of the manufacturer and distributor in the process of adding customer value. Customer value is created by what each party brings to the relationship and how they work together to add additional customer services and marketing campaigns.

In addition to trading relationships and processes that raise the perceived quality of the product and supporting services, a unique trading relationship advantage can come from both the manufacturer and distributor working together to reduce the costs of doing business. If the cost-reduction drives and efforts of both parties are synchronised and if this synchronisation between the manufacturer and distributor is better than any other trading relationship that manufacturers or distributors are in, then the trading relationship will have a unique competitive cost advantage towards customers.

It is always important to remember that the competitive advantage of a manufacturer–distributor relationship is managed by people at the manufacturer and the distributor.

Historically, the way firms viewed personal relationships depended on their size. Among small firms, relationships mainly existed among owners. Larger firms operated under the sales representative/purchasing agent model. This model assumes that a firm's trading relationship is funnelled primarily through single agents: the personal relationship between the selling firm's salesperson (agent) and the buying firm's purchasing manager (**agent**). Other agency relationships were expected to develop among engineers working on supply-chain

Agent
A marketing intermediary who does not take title to the products but develops a marketing strategy and establishes contacts abroad.

engineering specifications. But the salesperson acted as a gatekeeper to the buying organisation.

The modern RM approach to the supply chain argues that this funnelling is unnecessarily restrictive. It proposes that trading relationships in the supply chain should be among cross-functional teams.

The new RM approach emphasises that at the heart of the trading relationship is the set of relationship processes, such as decision making and learning, that integrate the operational and implementation processes between the two firms.

The reality of an important trading relationship is that it is held together by relationship processes and personal relationships among agents at several levels. At the strategic level, quality relationship processes have to enable senior management to initiate, agree on and invest in creating a unique competitive position for the relationship. In addition, if senior managers get on well together, it makes a big difference in obtaining subordinates' cooperation in managing operations. The development of such inter-firm personal relationships is particularly valuable in very competitive markets when trading relationships are stressed and have to adapt creatively to new competitive realities. Such personal relationships nurture the personal trust and commitment that enables the relationship to survive market crises through creative, cooperative improvisation.

What is personal trust and commitment? Personal trust is when what the individual representatives say is their bond, and they are prepared to help each other to solve problems. Commitment is commitment to the goal of developing and nurturing the competitiveness of the relationship, compared to other competitive trading relationships. Mutual trust and commitment are determined by a history of shared values, open communication, both parties giving more to the relationship than to alternative relationships, and, particularly, not taking advantage of (or exploiting) the trust. The long-term return from the relationship is perceived to be higher than the return from nurturing other relationships. The driver of this long-term return is relationship process innovation: innovations in reducing process costs, increasing process speed, and increasing process output. Personal relationship goodwill and trust are needed when conflict arises and when attempts are initiated to improve systems and processes.

New information technology helps strengthen long-term relationships between manufacturers and distributors.

Integrated channel information systems (channel intranets) enable a manufacturer to assess the performance of distributors, the profitability of doing business with them, and the success of promotional programmes and new, more efficient operating processes. Not being a part of such an information system may become a real barrier to entering some markets. On the other hand, being part of the system may also limit the managerial options of the participant by limiting the company's ability to switch to alternative distribution options.

We will now look at a systematic approach to the major decisions in distribution by discussing the main variables influencing the distribution channel decision.

13.5 EXTERNAL AND INTERNAL DETERMINANTS OF CHANNEL DECISIONS

Customer characteristics

The customer, or final consumer, is the keystone in any channel design. Thus the size, geographic distribution, shopping habits, outlet preferences and usage patterns of customer groups must be taken into account when making distribution decisions.

Consumer product channels tend to be longer than industrial product channels because the number of customers is greater, the customers are more geographically dispersed, and they buy in smaller quantities. Shopping habits, outlet preferences and usage patterns vary considerably from country to country and are strongly influenced by sociocultural factors.

Nature of the product

Convenience product
A relatively inexpensive, regularly purchased consumer product bought without much thought and with a minimum of shopping effort.

Product characteristics play a key role in determining distribution strategy. For low-priced, high-turnover **convenience products**, the requirement is an intensive distribution network. On the other hand, it is not necessary or even desirable for a prestigious product to have wide distribution. In this situation a manufacturer can shorten and narrow its distribution channel. Consumers are likely to do some comparison shopping and will actively seek information about all brands under consideration. In such cases limited product exposure is not an impediment to market success.

Transportation and warehousing costs of the product are also critical issues in the distribution and sale of industrial goods such as bulk chemicals, metals and cement. Direct selling, servicing and repair, and spare parts warehousing dominate the distribution of such industrial products as computers, machinery and aircraft. The product's durability, ease of adulteration, amount and type of customer service required, unit costs and special handling requirements (such as cold storage) are also significant factors.

Nature of demand/location

The perceptions that the target customers hold about particular products can force modification of distribution channels. Product perceptions are influenced by the customer's income and product experience, the product's end use, its life cycle position and the country's stage of economic development.

The geography of a country and the development of its transportation infrastructure can also affect the channel decision.

Competition

The channels used by competing products and close substitutes are important because channel arrangements that seek to serve the same market often compete with one another. Consumers generally expect to find particular products in particular outlets (e.g. speciality stores), or they have become accustomed to buying particular products from particular sources. In addition, local and global competitors may have agreements with the major wholesalers in a foreign country that effectively create barriers and exclude the company from key channels.

Sometimes the alternative is to use a distribution approach totally different from that of the competition and hope to develop a competitive advantage.

Legal regulations/local business practices

A country may have specific laws that rule out the use of particular channels or intermediaries. For example, until recently all alcoholic beverages in Sweden and Finland had to be distributed through state-owned outlets. Other countries prohibit the use of door-to-door selling. Channel coverage can also be affected by law. In general, exclusive representation may be viewed as a restraint of trade, especially if the product has a dominant market position. EU antitrust authorities have increased their scrutiny of exclusive sales agreements. The Treaty of Rome prohibits distribution agreements (e.g. grants of exclusivity) that affect trade or restrict competition.

Furthermore, local business practices can interfere with efficiency and productivity and may force a manufacturer to employ a channel of distribution that is longer and wider than

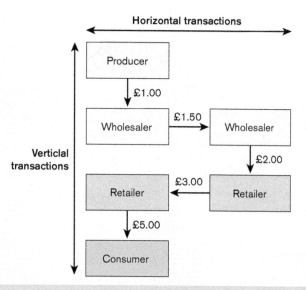

Horizontal transactions

Verticlal transactions

Producer			
£1.00			
Wholesaler	£1.50	Wholesaler	
		£2.00	
Retailer	£3.00	Retailer	
£5.00			
Consumer			

Figure 13.3	**A hypothetical channel sequence in the Japanese consumer market**
	Source: Adapted from Pirog, S. F. and Lancioni, R. (1997) US–Japan distribution channel cost structures: is there a significant difference? *International Journal of Physical Distribution and Logistics Management,* 27(1): 57. Copyright © 1997 Emerald Group Publishing Ltd. All rights reserved. Reproduced with permission through Rightslink.

Market coverage
Coverage can relate to geographical areas or number of retail outlets. Three approaches are available: intensive, selective or exclusive coverage.

desired. Because of Japan's multitiered distribution system, which relies on numerous layers of intermediaries, foreign companies have long considered the complex Japanese distribution system as the most effective non-tariff barrier to the Japanese market.

Figure 13.3 shows how the complex Japanese distribution system escalates prices by a factor of 5 through both vertical transactions and horizontal transactions (e.g. from one wholesaler to another wholesaler).

Let us now return to the major decisions concerning the structure of the distribution channel.

13.6 THE STRUCTURE OF THE CHANNEL

Market coverage

The amount of **market coverage** that a channel member provides is important. Coverage is a flexible term. It can refer to geographical areas of a country (such as cities and major towns) or the number of retail outlets (as a percentage of all retail outlets). Regardless of the market coverage measure(s) used the company has to create a distribution network (dealers, distributors and retailers) to meet its coverage goals.

As shown in Figure 13.4, three different approaches are available:

Intensive distribution
Stocking the product in as many outlets as possible.

Selective distribution
The use of a limited number of outlets in a geographical area to sell products of a supplier.

Exclusive distribution
An extreme form of selective distribution where only one wholesaler, retailer or industrial distributor is used in a geographical area to sell products of a supplier.

- *Intensive coverage*: this calls for distributing the product through the largest number of different types of intermediary and the largest number of individual intermediaries of each type.

- *Selective coverage*: this entails choosing a number of intermediaries for each area to be penetrated.

- *Exclusive coverage*: this involves choosing only one intermediary in a market.

Channel coverage (width) can be identified along a continuum ranging from wide channels (intensive distribution) to narrow channels (exclusive distribution). Figure 13.5 illustrates some factors favouring **intensive, selective** and **exclusive distribution**.

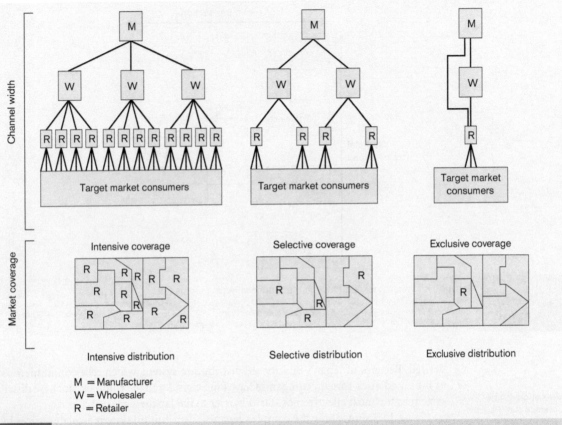

M = Manufacturer
W = Wholesaler
R = Retailer

Figure 13.4 Three strategies for market coverage
Source: From Lewison, D. M. (1996) *Marketing Management: An overview.* South-Western College Publishing, a division of Thomson Learning. Reproduced with permission from Dale M. Lewison.

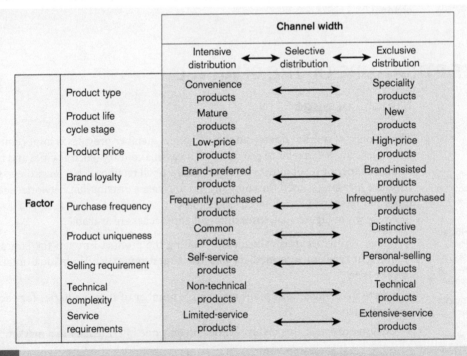

Figure 13.5 Factors influencing channel width
Source: From Lewison, D. M. (1996) *Marketing Management: An overview.* South-Western College Publishing, a division of Thomson Learning. Reproduced with permission from Dale M. Lewison.

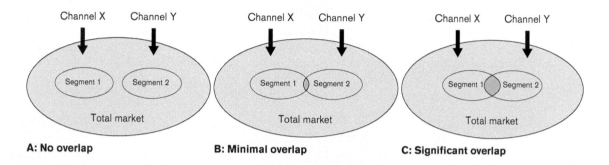

Figure 13.6   Channel overlap

When analysing a channel's market coverage it is relevant to distinguish between market coverage of current and of new channels. To ensure the best possible market coverage, it is essential to have a view of what customer segment the current channel structure covers. This is necessary in order to identify any overlap between the channels' coverage of the identified segments (Figure 13.6).

In situation A, there is no overlap at all. Channels X and Y each work with their unique market segments, and there is no subject of conflict. On the other hand, the problem is that the entire market is not covered, which means lost earnings and the possibility of competitors moving into the open areas and then maybe even encroaching on the areas covered as well.

In situation B, the scenario is close to optimal. The market coverage is complete and the overlap small with only minimal potential conflicts. In practice, the situation is seldom this simple. Often some of the channels will be more appropriate than others depending on the characteristics of the product and the strength of the intermediaries.

Finally, competitors can influence the market coverage. For example, in the consumer goods industry, leading brand name suppliers usually want to be represented by the same sales channel as other leading brand names. This ultimately results in excess coverage between the sales channels.

In situation C, both markets are covered, but there is significant overlap. This may result in conflict between the sales channels, and it is likely that the situation will not be the best possible based on the fundamental goal of creating profit. However, the situation may be tolerable, if this surplus supply acts as a shield against new competitors.

Channel length

Channel length
Number of levels
(middlemen) in the
distribution channel.

Channel length is determined by the number of levels or different types of intermediary. Longer channels, those with several intermediaries, tend to be associated with convenience goods and mass distribution. As seen in Figure 13.3, Japan has longer channels for convenience goods because of the historical development of its system. One implication is that prices increase considerably for the final consumer (price escalation: see section 12.3).

Control/cost

The 'control' of one member in the vertical distribution channel means its ability to influence the decisions and actions of other channel members. Channel control is of critical concern to international marketers wanting to establish international brands and a consistent image of quality and service worldwide.

The company must decide how much control it wants to have over how each of its products is marketed. The answer is partly determined by the strategic role assigned to each market. It is also a function of the types of channel member available, the regulations and rules governing distribution activity in each foreign market, and to some extent the roles traditionally assigned to channel members.

Normally a high degree of control is provided by the use of the firm's own salesforce in international markets. The use of intermediaries will automatically lead to loss of some control over the marketing of the firm's products.

An intermediary typically performs certain functions:

- carrying of inventory
- demand generation, or selling
- physical distribution
- after-sales service
- extending credit to customers.

In getting its products to end-user markets a manufacturer must either assume all of these functions or shift some or all of them to intermediaries. As the old saying goes, 'You can eliminate the intermediary, but not the functions of the intermediary.'

In most marketing situations there is a trade-off between a producer's ability to control important channel functions and the financial resources required to exercise that control. The more intermediaries involved in getting a supplier's product to user customers, the less control the supplier can generally exercise over the flow of its product through the channel and the way it is presented to customers. On the other hand, reducing the length and breadth of the distribution channel usually requires that the supplier perform more functions itself. In turn this requires the supplier to allocate more financial resources to activities such as warehousing, shipping, credit, field selling or field service.

In summary, the decision to use an intermediary or to distribute via a company-owned salesforce requires a major trade-off between the desire to control global marketing efforts and the desire to minimise resource commitment costs.

Degree of integration

Control can also be exercised through integration. Channel integration is the process of incorporating all channel members into one channel system and uniting them under one leadership and one set of goals. There are two different types of integration:

1 vertical integration: seeking control of channel members at different levels of the channel;

Horizontal integration
Seeking control of channel members at the same level of the channel, e.g. the manufacturer's acquisition of the competitor.

2 **horizontal integration**: seeking control of channel members at the same level of the channel (i.e. competitors).

Integration is achieved either through acquisitions (ownership) or through tight cooperative relationships. Getting channel members to work together for their own mutual benefit can be a difficult task. However, today cooperative relationships are essential for efficient and effective channel operation.

Figure 13.7 shows an example of vertical integration.

The starting point in Figure 13.7 is the conventional marketing channels, where the channel composition consists of isolated and autonomous participating channel members. Channel coordination is here achieved through arm's-length bargaining. At this point, the vertical integration can take two forms – forward and backward:

Vertical marketing system
A network of vertically aligned establishments that are managed professionally as a centrally administered distribution system.

- The manufacturer can make forward integration when it seeks control of businesses of the wholesale and retail levels of the channel.

- The retailer can make backward integration, seeking control of businesses at wholesale and manufacturer levels of the channel.

- The wholesaler has two possibilities: both forward and backward integration.

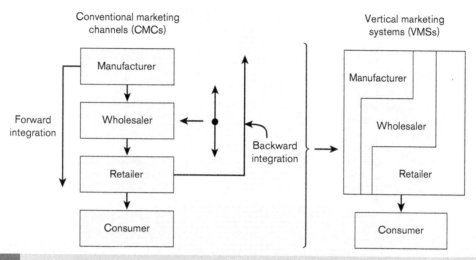

| Figure 13.7 | Vertical integration |

Source: Hollensen, S. (2001) *Global Marketing: A Market Responsive Approach*, 2nd edn, Financial Times-Prentice Hall, Harlow, p. 489. Reproduced with permission.

The result of these manoeuvres is the **vertical marketing system** (Figure 13.7). Here the channel composition consists of integrated participating members, where channel stability is high due to assured member loyalty and long-term commitments.

13.7 MULTIPLE DISTRIBUTION CHANNEL STRATEGY

Multiple channel strategy
A product/service is available to the market through two (dual distribution) or more channels of distribution. Multiple channels may include the Internet, sales force, distributors, call centres, retail stores and direct mail.

A **multiple channel strategy** is employed when a firm makes a product available to the market through two or more channels of distribution. Multiple channels include the Internet, salesforce, call centres, retail stores and direct mail.

This strategy has been a very popular channel design during the last decade (Valos, 2008). The increasing popularity of this strategy results from the potential advantages provided: extended market coverage and increased sales volume; lower absolute or relative costs; better accommodation of customers' evolving needs; and more and better information. This strategy, however, can also produce potentially disruptive problems: consumer confusion; conflicts with intermediaries and/or internal distribution units; increased costs; loss of distinctiveness; and, eventually, an increased organisational complexity.

A special case of 'multiple channel marketing' is often referred to as 'dual marketing' where the same product is sold to both the consumer and the business market at the same time

Different customers with different buying behaviours will seek channels that best serve their needs. With a multiple channel design it is also possible for marketers to match low-cost channels such as the Internet to the low-value customers, and to allocate more expensive channels, such as salesforce, to high-value customers.

In a hybrid multiple distribution channel, the marketing functions are often shared by the producer and the channel intermediaries. The former usually handles promotion and customer-generation activities, whereas the intermediary may be in charge of sales and distribution.

In Figure 13.8 both the supplier and its channel partners divide up the execution of the channel functions. The supplier performs some functions such as brochures and advertising material, while its channel partners deliver local sales negotiation, physical distribution and order fulfilment. Other channel members might specialise in functions such as after-sales service. The members work together with certain members specialising in certain functions.

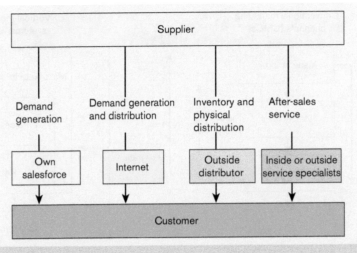

| Figure 13.8 | Multiple channel strategy |

13.8 MANAGING AND CONTROLLING DISTRIBUTION CHANNELS

In the beginning of a market entry, partnerships with local distributors make good sense: distributors know the distinctive characteristics of their market, and most customers prefer to do business with local partners. Arnold (2000) proposes the following guidelines to the international marketer (manufacturer) in order to anticipate and correct potential problems with international distributors:

- *Select distributors – do not let them select you*: typically, manufacturers are approached by potential distributors at international fairs and exhibitions, but the most eager potential distributors are often the wrong people to partner with.

- *Look for distributors capable of developing markets, rather than those with a few obvious contacts*: this means sometimes bypassing the most obvious choice – the distributor that has the right customers and can generate quick sales – in favour of a partner with a greater willingness to make long-term investments and an acceptance of an open relationship.

- *Treat the local distributors as long-term partners, not temporary market-entry vehicles*: many companies actively signal to distributors that their intentions are only for the short term, drawing up contracts that allow them to buy back distribution rights after a few years. Under such a short-term agreement the problem is that the local distributor does not have much incentive to invest in the necessary long-term marketing development.

- *Support market entry by committing money, managers and proven marketing ideas*: many manufacturers are reluctant to commit resources at the early stages of a market entry. However, to retain strategic control, the international marketer must commit adequate corporate resources. This is especially true during market entry, when companies are least certain about their prospect in new countries.

- *From the start, maintain control over marketing strategy*: an independent distributor should be allowed to adapt the manufacturer's strategy to local conditions. However, only companies providing solid leadership for marketing will be in a position to exploit the full potential of a global marketing network.

- *Make sure distributors provide you with detailed market and financial performance data*: most distributors regard data such as customer identification and local price levels as key sources of power in the relationship with the manufacturer. But the manufacturer's ability to exploit its competitive advantages in the international market depends heavily on the quality of information it obtains from the market. Therefore, a contract with the distributor must include the exchange of such information, e.g. detailed market and financial performance data.

- *Build links among national distributors at the earliest opportunity*: the links may take form of creating an independent national distributor council or a regional corporate office. The transfer of ideas within local markets can improve performance and result in greater consistency in the execution of international marketing strategies because links to other national distributor networks could be established. This could lead to a cross-national transfer of efficient marketing tools.

Once the basic design of the channel has been determined the international marketer must begin to fill it with the best available candidates, and must secure their cooperation.

Screening and selecting intermediaries

Figure 13.9 shows the most important criteria (qualifications) for selecting foreign distributors, grouped in five categories.

After listing all important criteria, some of these must then be chosen for a more specific evaluation, where the potential candidates are compared and contrasted against determining criteria.

The example in Table 13.2 uses the first two criteria in each of Figure 13.9's five categories for screening potential channel members, in total ten criteria. The specific criteria to be used

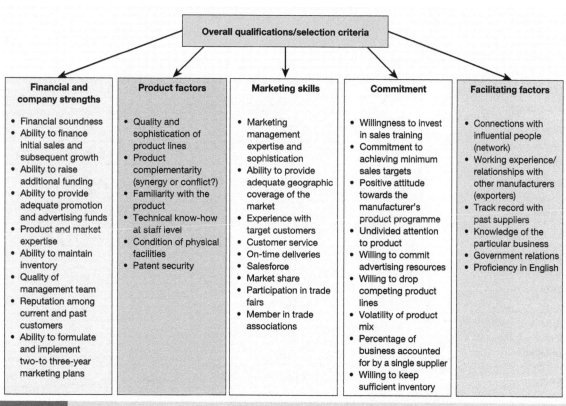

| **Figure 13.9** | Criteria for evaluating foreign distributors |

Source: Adapted from Cavusgil, S. T., Yeoh, P.-L. and Mitri, M. (1995) Selecting foreign distributors: an expert systems approach, *Industrial Marketing Management*, 24: 297–304. Copyright © 1995 Elsevier. Reproduced with permission.

Table 13.2	An example of distributor evaluation by the use of selection criteria from Figure 13.9

Criteria (no ranking implied)	Weight	Distributor 1		Distributor 2		Distributor 3	
		Rating	Score	Rating	Score	Rating	Score
Financial and company strengths:							
Financial soundness	4	5	20	4	16	3	12
Ability to finance initial sales and subsequent growth	3	4	12	4	12	3	9
Product factors:							
Quality and sophistication of product lines	3	5	15	4	12	3	9
Product complementarity (synergy or conflict?)	3	3	9	4	12	2	6
Marketing skills:							
Marketing management expertise and sophistication	5	4	20	3	15	2	10
Ability to provide adequate geographic coverage of the market	4	5	20	4	16	3	12
Commitment:							
Willingness to invest in sales training	4	3	12	3	12	3	12
Commitment to achieving minimum sales targets	3	4	12	3	9	3	9
Facilitating factors:							
Connections with influential people (network)	3	5	15	4	12	4	12
Working experience/ relationships with other manufacturers (exporters)	2	4	8	3	6	3	6
Score			**143**		**122**		**97**

Scales:

Rating
5 Outstanding
4 Above average
3 Average
2 Below average
1 Unsatisfactory

Weighting
5 Critical success factor
4 Prerequisite success factor
3 Important success factor
2 Of some importance
1 Standard

depend on the nature of a firm's business and its distribution objectives in given markets. The list of criteria should correspond closely to the marketer's own determinants of success – all the things that are important to beating the competition.

The hypothetical manufacturer (a consumer packaged goods company) used in Table 13.2 considered the distributor's marketing management expertise and financial soundness to be of greatest importance. These indicators will show whether the distributor is making money and is able to perform some of the necessary marketing functions such as extension of credit to customers and risk absorption. Financial reports are not always complete or reliable, or may lend themselves to differences of interpretation, pointing to the need for a third-party opinion. In order to make the weighting and grading in Table 13.2, the manufacturer must have had some personal interviews with the management of each potential distributor. In the example of Table 13.2, Distributor 1 would be selected by the manufacturer.

Alternatively, an industrial goods company may consider the distributor's product compatibility, technical know-how, technical facilities and service support of high importance, and the distributor's infrastructure, client performance and attitude towards its products of low importance. Quite often global marketers find that the most desirable distributors in a given market are already handling competitive products and are therefore unavailable.

A high-tech consumer goods company, on the other hand, may favour financial soundness, marketing management expertise, reputation, technical know-how, technical facilities, service support and government relations. In some countries religious or ethnic differences might make an agent suitable for one part of the market coverage but unsuitable for another. This can result in more channel members being required in order to give adequate market coverage.

Contracting (distributor agreements)

When the international marketer has found a suitable intermediary a foreign sales agreement is drawn up. Before final contractual arrangements are made it is wise to make personal visits to the prospective channel member. The agreement itself can be relatively simple but, given the numerous differences in the market environments, certain elements are essential. These are listed in Figure 13.10.

The long-term commitments involved in distribution channels can become particularly difficult if the contract between the company and the channel member is not carefully drafted. It is normal to prescribe a time limit and a minimum sales level to be achieved, in

- Names and addresses of both parties.
- Date when the agreement goes into effect.
- Duration of the agreement.
- Provisions for extending or terminating the agreement.
- Description of sales territory.
- Establishment of discount and/or commission schedules and determination of when and how paid.
- Provisions for revising the commission or discount schedules.
- Establishment of a policy governing resale prices.
- Maintenance of appropriate service facilities.
- Restrictions to prohibit the manufacture and sale of similar and competitive products.
- Designation of responsibility for patent and trade mark negotiations and/or pricing.
- The assignability or non-assignability of the agreement and any limiting factors.
- Designation of the country and state (if applicable) of contract jurisdiction in the case of dispute.

Figure 13.10 Items to include in an agreement with a foreign intermediary (distributor)
Source: From Jain, S. (1996) *International Marketing Management*, 5th ed., South-Western College Publishing, Cincinnati, OH. Reproduced with permission from Subhash C. Jain.

addition to the particular responsibilities of each party. If this is not carried out satisfactorily the company may be stuck with a weak performer that either cannot be removed or is very costly to buy out from the contract.

Contract duration is important, especially when an agreement is signed with a new distributor. In general, distribution agreements should be for a specified, relatively short period (one or two years). The initial contract with a new distributor should stipulate a trial period of either three or six months, possibly with minimum purchase requirements. Duration is also dependent on the local laws and their stipulations on distributor agreements.

Geographic boundaries for the distributor should be determined with care, especially by smaller firms. Future expansion of the product market might be complicated if a distributor claims rights to certain territories. The marketer should retain the right to distribute products independently, reserving the right to certain customers.

The *payment section* of the contract should stipulate the methods of payment as well as how the distributor or agent is to draw compensation. Distributors derive compensation from various discounts, such as the functional discount, whereas agents earn a specific commission percentage of net sales (typically 10–20 per cent). Given the volatility of currency markets the agreement should also state the currency to be used.

Product and conditions of sale need to be agreed on. The products or product lines included should be stipulated, as well as the functions and responsibilities of the intermediary in terms of carrying the goods in inventory, providing service in conjunction with them, and promoting them. Conditions of sale determine which party is to be responsible for some of the expenses (e.g. marketing expenses) involved, which will in turn have an effect on the price to the distributor. These conditions include credit and shipment terms.

Means of communication between the parties must be stipulated in the agreement if a marketer–distributor relationship is to succeed. The marketer should have access to all information concerning the marketing of its products in the distributor's territory, including past records, present situation assessments and marketing research.

Motivating

Geographic and cultural distance make the process of motivating channel members difficult. Motivating is also difficult because intermediaries are not owned by the company. Since intermediaries are independent firms they will seek to achieve their own objectives, which will not always match the objective of the manufacturer. The international marketer may offer both monetary and psychological rewards. Intermediaries will be strongly influenced by the earnings potential of the product. If the trade margin is poor and sales are difficult to achieve intermediaries will lose interest in the product. They will concentrate upon products with a more rewarding response to selling efforts, since they make their sales and profits from their own assortment of products and services from different companies.

It is important to keep in regular contact with agents and distributors. A consistent flow of all relevant types of communication will stimulate interest and sales performance. The international marketer may place one person in charge of distributor-related communications and put into effect an exchange of personnel so that both organisations gain further insight into the workings of the other.

Controlling

Control problems are reduced substantially if intermediaries are selected carefully. However, control should be sought through the common development of written performance objectives. These performance objectives might include some of the following: sales turnover per year, market share growth rate, introduction of new products, price charged and marketing communications support. Control should be exercised through periodic personal meetings.

Evaluation of performance has to be done against the changing environment. In some situations economic recession or fierce competition activity prevents the possibility of objectives being met. However, if poor performance is established, the contract between the company and the channel member will have to be reconsidered and perhaps terminated.

Termination

Typical reasons for the termination of a channel relationship are as follows:

- The international marketer has established a sales subsidiary in the country.
- The international marketer is unsatisfied with the performance of the intermediary.

Open communication is always needed to make the transition smooth. For example, the intermediary can be compensated for investments made, and major customers can be visited jointly to assure them that service will be uninterrupted.

Termination conditions are among the most important considerations in the distribution agreement. The causes of termination vary and the penalties for the international marketer may be substantial. It is especially important to find out what local laws say about termination and to check what type of experience other firms have had in the particular country.

In some countries terminating an ineffective intermediary can be time consuming and expensive. In the European Union one year's average commissions are typical for termination without justification. A notice of termination has to be given three to six months in advance. If the cause for termination is the manufacturer's establishment of a local sales subsidiary, then the international marketer may consider engaging good employees from the intermediary as, for example, managers in the new sales subsidiary. This can prevent a loss of product know-how that has been created at the intermediary's firm. The international marketer could also consider an acquisition of this firm if the intermediary is willing to sell.

13.9 IMPLICATIONS OF THE INTERNET FOR DISTRIBUTION DECISIONS

Disintermediation
The elimination of a layer of intermediaries from a marketing channel or the displacement of traditional resellers by radically new types of intermediaries.

Channel conflict
Disagreement among marketing channel members on goals and roles – who should do what and for what rewards. A significant threat arising from the introduction of an Internet channel is that, while disintermediation gives the opportunity for a company to sell direct and increase the profitability of products, it also threatens distribution arrangements with existing partners.

The Internet has the power to change drastically the balance of power among consumers, retailers, distributors, manufacturers and service providers. Some participants in the distribution chain may experience an increase in their power and profitability. Others will experience the reverse; some may even find that they have been bypassed and have lost their market share.

Physical distributors and dealers of goods and services that are more conveniently ordered and/or delivered online are indeed subject to increasing pressure from e-commerce. This **disintermediation** process, with increasing direct sales through the Internet, leads manufacturers to compete with their resellers, which may also result in **channel conflict**.

The reality is that the Internet may eliminate the traditional 'physical' distributors, but in the transformation process of the value chain new types of intermediaries may appear. So the disintermediation process has come to be balanced by a reintermediation force – the evolution of new intermediaries tailor-made for the online world (Figure 13.11).

The transformation of any industry structure in the Internet economy is likely to go through the intermediation–disintermediation–reintermediation (IDR) cycle. The IDR cycle will occur because new technologies are forcing change in the relationships among buyers, suppliers and middlemen. Intermediation occurs when a firm begins as a middleman between two industry players (e.g. buyer–supplier, buyer–established intermediary or established intermediary–supplier). Disintermediation occurs when an established middleman is pushed out of the value chain. Reintermediation occurs when a once disintermediated player is able to re-establish itself as an intermediary.

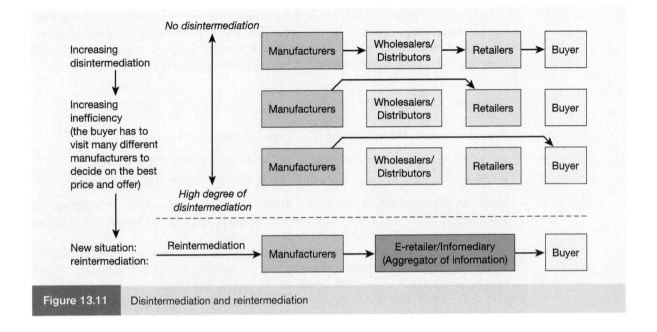

Figure 13.11 Disintermediation and reintermediation

Distinction between e-marketing and m-marketing

A key distinction between e-marketing and m-marketing (mobile marketing) lies in the different enabling technologies. Most notably, the facilitative mode for traditional e-marketing, the PC, is a relatively large and cumbersome device that is probably deskbound and equipped with a Web browser through standard connectivity. Even when configured as a laptop it is not easy to move.

M-marketing is faced with the challenge of developing capabilities in a much more diverse technical context, albeit within the single framework of mobility. Mobile devices currently vary in terms of the network to which they are connected – the 'European' standard or the North American standard.

Rapidly emerging innovations will deliver the possibility of smart phones able to use product bar codes to access product-related information and phones able to act as e-wallets, as either a prepaid card for small purchases or a fully functioning credit/debit card unit.

Benefits of m-marketing

The introduction of m-marketing should bring a series of benefits to consumers, merchants and telecommunication companies. As with all technologies, many benefits will arise in the future that are not yet even imagined. Some benefits that are apparent now, however, include the following.

For consumers

- *Comparison shopping*: Consumers can access on demand, at the point of purchase, the best prices in the marketplace. This can be done now without mobility, with services such as pricescan.com.
- *Bridge the gap between bricks and clicks*: Services permitting users to examine merchandise in a store and still shop electronically for the best price.
- *Opt-in searches*: Customers may receive alerts from merchants when products they are looking for become available.
- *Travel*: Ability to change and monitor scheduled travel any time, any place.

For merchants

- *Impulse buying*: Consumers may buy discounted products from a Web page promotion or a mobile alert, increasing their willingness to buy as they are near or even inside the store, and thus increasing merchants' sales.

- *Drive traffic*: Companies will guide their customers to where it is easier to carry out the transaction, to either online or offline stores, due to the time-sensitive, location-based and personalised characteristics of the mobile device.

- *Education of consumers*: Companies will send information to customers about product benefits or new products.

- *Perishable products*: This is especially important for products that do not retain their value when unused, such as service-based products. For example, the use of an aeroplane seat that, when unused, generates no revenue and is lost value. This will enable companies to better manage inventory.

- *Drive efficiency*: Companies will save time with their clients. Because information is readily available on the mobile device they will not have to talk about the benefits of the different products or about prices.

- *Target market*: Companies will be better able to target their products and promotions to those in a given geographic area at a specific time.

For telecommunication companies the advantages are primarily more airtime used by the consumers and higher fees charged to content providers for each m-commerce transaction.

M-marketing requires direct marketers to rethink their strategies to tap into already existing communities such as sports fans, surfers, music fans and time-context communities such as spectators at sports events and festivals, and location-sensitive communities such as gallery visitors and small shoppers, and develop ways to get them to opt in to m-marketing.

Applications must be responsive to location, customer needs and device capabilities. For example, time- and location-sensitive applications, such as travel reservations, cinema tickets and banking, will be excellent vehicles for young, busy and urban people.

Finally, as highlighted, mobile marketing enables distribution of information to the consumer at the most effective time, place and in the right context. This suggests that m-marketing, via mobile devices, will cement further the interactive marketing relationship.

13.10 RETAILING

In the continuing integration of the world economy, internationalisation not only concerns advertising, banking and manufacturing industries, it also affects the retailing business. The trend in all industrialised countries is towards larger units and more self-service. The number of retail outlets is dwindling, but the average size is increasing.

However, retailing still shows great differences between countries, reflecting different histories, geography, culture and economic development (Doherty, 2007).

Trade marketing

For too long manufacturers have viewed vertical marketing channels as closed systems, operating as separate, static entities. The most important factors creating long-term, integrated strategic plans and fostering productive channel relationships were largely ignored. Fortunately, a new philosophy about channel management has emerged, but to understand its potential we must first understand how power has developed at the retailer level.

Power in channel relationships can be defined as the ability of a channel member to control the marketing decision variables of any other member in a channel at a different level of distribution. A classic example of this is the amount of power wielded by retailers against the food and grocery manufacturers. As the balance of power has shifted, more merchandise is controlled by fewer and fewer retailers (Strategic Direction, 2009).

There is a worldwide tendency towards concentration in retailing. A consequence of this development is that there has been a worldwide shift from manufacturer to retailer dominance. Power has become concentrated in the hands of fewer and fewer retailers, and the manufacturers have been left with little choice but to accede to their demands. This often results in manufacturing the retailers' own brands (private labels) (Sorensen, 2008).

Therefore, we can see that traditional channel management, with its characteristics of power struggles, conflict and loose relationships, is no longer beneficial. New ideas are emerging to help channel relationships become more cooperative. This is what is known as **trade marketing**. Trade marketing is when the manufacturer (supplier) markets directly to the trade (retailers) to create a better fit between product and outlet. The objective is to create joint marketing and strategic plans for mutual profitability.

Trade marketing
Marketing to the retail trade.

For the manufacturer (supplier), it means creating twin marketing strategies: one to the consumer and another to the trade (retailers). However, as Figure 13.12 shows, potential channel conflicts exist because of differences in the objectives of the channel members.

Despite potential channel conflicts, what both parties share, but often forget, is their common goal of consumer satisfaction. If the desired result is to create joint marketing plans, a prerequisite must be an improved understanding of the other's perspective and objectives.

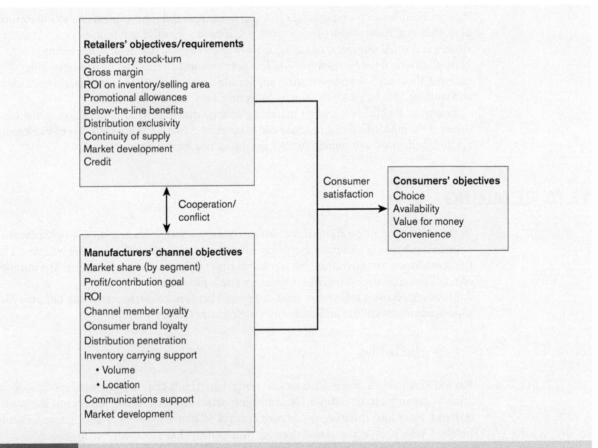

Figure 13.12 Channel relationships and the concept of trade marketing
Source: Hollensen, S. (2001) *Global Marketing: A Market Responsive Approach*, 2nd ed., Financial Times-Prentice Hall, Harlow, p. 507. Reproduced with permission.

Retailers are looking for potential sales, profitability, exclusivity in promotions and volume (Chakravarthy and Lorange, 2007). They are currently in the enviable position of being able to choose brands which fulfil those aims.

A private label manufacturer has to create different packages for different retailers. By carefully designing individual packages, the manufacturer gains a better chance of striking up a relationship with the best-matched retailer.

Manufacturers can offer retailers a total support package by stressing their own strengths. These include marketing knowledge and experience, market position, proven new product success, media support and exposure, and a high return on investment in shelf space.

If a joint strategy is going to be successful, manufacturers and retailers must work together at every level, perhaps by matching counterparts in each organisation. As a consequence of the increasing importance of the individual customer, the concept of the key account (key customer) was introduced. Key accounts are often large retail chains with a large turnover (in total as well as of the supplier's products), which are able to decide quantity and price on behalf of different outlets.

Segmentation of customers is therefore no longer based only on size and geographic position, but also on customers' (retailers') structure of decision making. This results in a gradual restructuring of sales from a geographic division to a customer division. This reorganisation is made visible by employing key account managers (managers responsible for customers).

ECR (efficient consumer response) in retailing

Twenty years ago, consumer goods manufacturers managed the distribution channel with advertising campaigns that pulled new products through the channel and with trade promotions used by a salesforce that pushed the product down the channel. Such a push/pull strategy often does not work today, and the reason has to do with not only faster and more accurate ordering processes and cycles, but also faster and more reliable quick-response delivery processes that now use tracking information to move bar-coded products down the distribution channel. The combination of these new computer-driven order and delivery processes is called efficient consumer response.

Efficient consumer response (ECR) programmes are designed to improve the efficiency of replenishing, delivering and stocking inventory while promoting customer value. Enhanced cooperation among channel members in order to eliminate activities that do not add value is a primary goal.

In the past, the presence of many slow-moving finished goods held in inventory by wholesalers and retailers helped manufacturers 'own' distribution channels because channel members had to move these mountains of manufacturers' goods to make a living. Now distribution channels carry small inventories of particular manufacturers' products, making the wholesalers and retailers less dependent on manufacturers. Conversely, with so little stock in distribution channels, what income manufacturers make next week almost literally depends on what they sell today. As a result, a problem with a major distribution channel has immediate effects on manufacturing and cash flow. A manufacturer has a short time to negotiate, to react and at worst to switch some of its business to another distribution channel.

13.11 MYSTERY SHOPPING IN RETAILING

Mystery shopping is a process for measuring service quality, with feedback, that is understandable to the front-line people in retailing. It is a form of participant observation, using researchers to act as customers or potential customers to monitor the quality of processes and procedures used in the delivery of a service. The need for specific performance information stems from the increasing emphasis being placed on service performance by service managers. While service standards are invariably set by head office staff and senior management, the task of delivering these standards falls to individual customer-facing personnel. Variations in service performance can have a major impact on customer satisfaction.

The stages in the mystery shopping process are now highlighted (Erstad, 1998; Wilson, 1998).

Step 1: The objectives

Know what you want to get out of the shopping programme. The objectives should be related to having satisfied customers as well as satisfied employees. Mystery shopping is meant to reinforce positive behaviour and modify improper behaviour, but not to punish.

Step 2: The evaluation form

Use employees to define and set the measurable standards to be met. Find out what customers value and incorporate these into the evaluation form.

Step 3: The mystery shopper

Select, inform and train the mystery shopper in line with the company's objectives. The shopper must match a customer profile that is appropriate for the scenario that is being enacted.

Step 4: Conducting the shop visit

Produce an unbiased, mainly objective evaluation (but include a limited amount of subjective information) of the shop.

Step 5: The analysis

Identify gaps in the service delivery and determine their origin. The information obtained from the shopping visit is matched to the pre-established objectives and standards to determine outstanding performance as well as any gaps that might exist. Identifying the reasons for the gaps is the challenge of management and employees participating in the programme.

Step 6: The action needed

Develop a reward and incentive scheme related to employee performance in mystery shopping programmes. Provide coaching to further develop employees' technical and behavioural skills. Work on the service delivery system if gaps exist because of poor design. Repeat the mystery shopper visit.

The results of individual shopping visits should not go to senior management, but to the people directly involved, including the front-line employees. Data have to be communicated positively and in a way that is relevant to those involved. Coaching is the key to dealing with service delivery problems arising from lack of training.

In general, mystery shopping tends to lead to improvements in quality of service. However, in the longer term, the novelty of being 'shopped' can wear off, leaving personnel complacent about their service and lacking motivation to take steps to improve it further. To overcome this, standards need to be constantly updated and staff need to see the ultimate consequences and rewards of mystery shopping.

13.12 SUMMARY

In this chapter we have examined the management of international distribution channels and logistics. From the discussion it is evident that the marketer has a broad range of alternatives for selecting and developing an economical, efficient and high-volume international distribution channel.

In many instances, the channel structure is affected by external factors and it may vary from country to country. Physical distribution (external logistics) concerns the flow of goods from the manufacturer to the customer. This is one area where cost savings through efficiency are feasible, provided the decision is made systematically. The changing nature of retailing influences distribution planning. During the last decade, the balance of power (between manufacturers and retailers) has shifted in favour of the retailers. The manufacturer often has no other choice than to cooperate with large and increasingly concentrated retailers in terms of the 'trade marketing' concept.

Mystery shopping is getting a customer's view of the retail business and is widely recognised as a valuable marketing and customer service tool. Mystery shoppers visit the business, posing as an average customer. They evaluate what they find based on criteria established by the company.

CASE STUDY 13.1

Lindt & Sprüngli
The Swiss premium chocolate maker is considering an international chocolate café chain

The beginnings of Lindt & Sprüngli (in the following sometimes abbreviated to Lindt) were in 1845, when father and son for the first time manufactured solid chocolate in their small confectionery Sprüngli & Son, at that time yet a partnership. Quickly growing, it was transformed into a joint stock company in 1898 and one year later the company acquired the Bern production facilities of Rodolphe Lindt with all the manufacturing secrets and trademark rights to the then already famous brand. At the same time, the company's name was changed to Chocoladefabriken Lindt & Sprüngli AG, which in 1994 has become the parent company's name. Since then, the enterprise has grown steadily, transforming itself into a multinational group through progressive integration of licensees and strategic acquisitions.

Lindt dark chocolate
Source: Courtesy of Lindt & Sprüngli International AG

Lindt & Sprüngli today

With six production sites in Europe, two in the USA and distribution and sales companies on four continents, Chocoladefabriken Lindt & Sprüngli AG is recognised as a leader in the market for premium quality chocolate, offering a large selection of products in more than 80 countries around the world. During the nearly 160 years of Lindt & Sprüngli's existence, it has become known as one of the most innovative and creative companies making premium chocolate. Lindt's strong focus on chocolate confectionery leaves it exposed to potential downturns in demand.

In 2008 Lindt & Sprüngli achieved total net sales of CHF2,937 million (€1,938 million), of which net income was CHF261 million (€172 million). By the end of 2008 the total number of employees in the Lindt & Sprüngli group was around 8,000. Overall Lindt & Sprüngli has a strong financial base – Lindt has developed a robust, debt-free financial base, placing it in a strong position to expand through future acquisition.

Lindt has established a wide-ranging international presence, ranking in the top 10 confectionery manufacturers in the three developed regional markets, Western Europe, North America and Australasia, as well as registering significant sales in every emerging region. Lindt & Sprüngli has production and sales subsidiaries in the following countries: Switzerland, Germany, Austria, France, Italy and the United States. Furthermore, Lindt & Sprüngli has sales subsidiaries in these countries: the UK, Spain, Czech Republic, Poland, Canada, Australia, Mexico, Sweden and Hong Kong.

Lindt is a major player in premium chocolate, which is driving chocolate confectionery growth around the world. Publicity surrounding studies claiming health benefits resulting from dark chocolate consumption is generating increased demand for dark chocolate and creating potential for Lindt to extend its dark chocolate offer. However, the company's premium focus means that it is sensitive to the negative impact of deteriorating macroeconomic conditions on consumer spending power.

The international chocolate markets

In 2007 the global chocolate confectionery market was worth US $50 billion (€37 billion). Europe accounted for 45 per cent, the United States for 31 per cent, Asia-Pacific for 18 per cent and the rest of the world accounted for 6 per cent.

The global market for chocolate confectionery is more consolidated in the Western regions, while the Asia-Pacific market, which is rapidly catching up with the West, is more fragmented. Product innovation and stable customer tastes have kept the market secure and mature in the West, while production is only just increasing in Asia-Pacific. The sheer size of the Asia-Pacific market shows great prospects for the industry if it continues to expand. Tastes in chocolate vary from region to region. Milk chocolate is the most popular choice in the US, the UK and Japan, while most of Europe prefers plain chocolate, and white chocolate is particularly popular in some parts of Asia. The most successful competitors in each region are those whose products most satisfy the regional tastes.

Within the European market there is a clear north/ south divide when it comes to chocolate consumption, reflecting among other things the difference in average temperatures in the two halves of the continent.

The top four countries in the rankings are all in the north. The British are the biggest consumers of chocolate in Europe, munching their way through more than 10 kg each every year. The Netherlands takes fourth place, with per capita consumption of 5 kg, while the main southern European countries covered by the report (Italy and Spain) are well down the list – Italians eat just 2.5 kg of chocolate each year while Spaniards consume just 1.7 kg.

Perhaps reflecting the fact that it straddles both the north and the south of the continent, France comes between these two groups with consumption of 4.9 kg per person.

While most Europeans eat chocolate on a regular basis, their tastes differ greatly, and not just in terms of the cocoa content.

For example, the most popular type of chocolate confectionery in the UK is countlines such as Kit Kat, Snickers or Crunchie, which account for 45 per cent of total volume sales, followed by moulded bars (solid chocolate bars, blocks or tablets shaped by pouring melted chocolate into moulds, with or without added ingredients such as fruit and/or nuts) at 22 per cent and boxed chocolate at 13 per cent.

German consumers prefer moulded bars, while the French prefer chocolate that offers simplicity and purity of taste, without additional flavours and with little sugar. Italian tastes are geared towards the more indulgent and sophisticated end of the market.

In Spain, chocolate manufacturers are trying to follow the rest of the confectionery market and increase their market share by introducing low-fat products, Datamonitor claims. But this strategy has not been particularly successful and some companies are now focusing on the high-quality, premium-price boxed chocolate sector of the market.

Generally, the Western European sales of chocolate confectionery have been affected by a rising sense of health consciousness, having a particular impact on the chocolate segment.

The focus for growth is consequently shifting towards Eastern and Central Europe. Russia is the largest in volume terms–it's a big market with very low prices. Low prices in Russia and across the East are serving to boost volume sales rates, especially as average incomes are rising, although there are still questions over the solidity of economic growth and reconstruction in some countries, including Russia.

Lindt & Sprüngli's international markets

Lindt's core regional market is Western Europe, which accounted for 73 per cent of the company's packaged food sales in 2008.

The company's second largest regional market, North America, which accounted for 22 per cent of Lindt's packaged food sales in 2008, is expected to register the second slowest growth in chocolate confectionery over the next years.

Lindt is expanding its presence in emerging regions such as Asia-Pacific and Eastern Europe: 2007 saw the company achieve strong growth in China and Hong Kong driven by the successful launch of dark Excellence and the increasing popularity of Lindor balls as a gift for the Chinese New Year. The development of modern retail formats played an important part in driving company growth in markets such as Poland and India. In Poland, for example, Lindt's market presence was boosted by consolidation in the retail trade and the increasing importance of the major multinational retail chains.

Lindt faces significant challenges in its core Western European markets, as an increasingly sophisticated private label category competes in terms of quality as well as price and the expansion of upper-mass products sees mass-market manufacturers seek to tap into the premium trend. In Germany, the increasing competition from private label has been driven by the development of hard discounters' offers in an upmarket direction. Lidl, for example, launched 'Fairglobe' chocolate, a private label Fair Trade line in 2006. Moreover, the discounter format is expanding aggressively in Western Europe, a process which is bolstering the strength of private label throughout the region.

The encroachment of private label and the upper-mass segment on the territory of premium brands is increasing the pressure on Lindt's efforts to differentiate its offer through product innovation and marketing. In response, the company has focused strongly on the development of new products tapping into emergent demand trends. Lindt has responded to consumers' growing willingness to experiment with new flavours with the introduction of products such as Creation 70 per cent tablets combining dark chocolate with exotic fillings such as fig and caramel, and cherry and chilli, for example.

Competitive situation

Overall, the regional market shares of Lindt & Sprüngli in chocolate confectionary can be seen in Table 13.3.

The competition in chocolate confectionary is intense. The leading multinational players with their main brands and market shares (in different markets) are illustrated in Table 13.4.

The global market is generally difficult for new players to penetrate, as it is dominated by a series of major international players with a long and established history of success in the chocolate market. These players include Nestlé, Mars, Ferrero and Kraft Foods, which have all experienced strong sales throughout the West. So far, Nestlé is the only one of these companies which has managed to achieve significant success in Asia-Pacific, but it still lacks a leading position in the region's market. The leading players in the US and the UK – Hershey

and Cadbury – have not expanded their businesses beyond their home markets, in spite of their success on the domestic level.

In the United States and Canada, Hershey Co (with brands like Reese's and Hershey's Milk Chocolate) is a market leader in chocolate confectionary, but is mainly a North American player. In 1988 Hershey purchased the Cadbury US operations, and since then Hershey holds the licence to manufacture and sell Cadbury chocolate products in the USA. This is the reason why Cadbury has no market shares in the United States (see Table 13.4), though Cadbury chocolates are being sold there.

The growth of the Asia-Pacific market offers great prospects for the competitive landscape, as it will allow an increase in international trade as Western companies attempt to break into the market and capitalise on regional tastes. If the Western industry leaders acquire successful positions in the Asia-Pacific market, further consolidation is likely to occur as they acquire the smaller domestic players in Asia-Pacific.

Lindt & Sprüngli distribution

In the mature Western European market, Lindt is also exploring new distribution channels with changing consumer lifestyles and demand trends. Impulse channels such as forecourt retailing and kiosks are a particular target, as consumers' busy lifestyles drive demand for indulgent on-the-go snacks. This has included the development of products tailored specifically to the requirements of such channels, with smaller servings of brands. For example, the company has introduced smaller, 35 g Excellence tablets tailored to the convenience-oriented demand of impulse channels, designed for on-the-go consumption. In addition, Lindt is expanding its Internet activity, with the Ghirardelli Chocolate Company subsidiary nearly doubling sales via its Internet platform in 2007.

Lindt is also expanding its distribution while seeking to maintain a focus on its premium image. Thus, while Lindt products are available in a number of mass retail channels, the company has also utilised branded outlets

| Table 13.3 | Lindt & Sprüngli AG: world and regional shares in packaged food by sector, 2008 |

% retail value rsp	Western Europe	Eastern Europe	North America	Latin America	Asia	Aus	Africa/ Middle East	Total world
Chocolate confectionery	3.8%	0.2%	1.8%	0.7%	0.2%	1.3%	0.4%	2.0%

Sources: Adapted from Euromonitor International (www.euromonitor.com) and own estimates.

Table 13.4	The competitive situation in the main international market and worldwide (2008)

Manufacturer	Main brands	United Kingdom (%)	Germany (%)	France (%)	United States (%)	Total world (%)
Mars (US)	Mars, Snickers, M&Ms, Bounty, Twix, Dove, Milky Way	23	12	6	32	7
Nestlé (CH)	Quality Street, Milky Bar, After Eight, Smarties, Rolo	18	6	13	5	15
Cadbury (UK)	Cadbury's Dairy Milk, Cadbury's Roses, Cadbury's Crème Egg	29	–	3	– (Sold under a Hersey licence	8
Kraft Foods (USA)	Terry's, Toblerone, Milka	5	12	10	1	8
Ferrero (Italy)	Kinder, Duplo, Hanuta, Mon Chéri, Ferrero Rocher	2	19	16	1	7
Hershey (USA)	Reese's, KitKat (under licence from Nestlé), Hershey's Kisses	–	–	–	34	8
Ritter GmbH (Germany)	Ritter Sport, Quadrago	–	7	1	–	1
Lindt & Sprüngli (CH)	Lindt, Lindor, Les Pyréneens, Excellence, Champs Elyssées, Créations 70%, Fioretto, Swiss Tradition	1	8	11	2	2
Private labels	–	7	12	10	2	10
Others	–	15	24	30	24	30
Total		100	100	100	100	100

Sources: Adapted from Euromonitor International (www.euromonitor.com); Datamonitor (www.datamonitor.com); and own estimates.

as flagships for brand development. In the US, for example, the company's 100 Lindt boutiques, which demonstrate the expertise of its maîtres chocolatiers, made a significant contribution to the development of Lindt's premium image. Similarly, Lindt Chocolate Cafés are proving popular and enhancing the company's image in the Australian market, where a new outlet was added to the network in 2007.

Duty free/travel retail plays an important part in Lindt's distribution strategy, with the company benefiting from a strong presence in airport shops. During 2007, the company strengthened its presence in the channel with the introduction of new recipes such as Lindor Cocoa 60 per cent, while Lindt Swiss Premium Napolitains also proved popular around the world.

Lindt & Sprüngli is closing down own boutiques in the US market

Lindt & Sprüngli is now to close nearly two-thirds of its retail boutiques in the US as people switch from its fancy chocolates to cheaper brands.

Lindt's gloomy forecast contrasts with more upbeat outlooks by mass-market chocolate manufacturers such as Nestlé and Cadbury, both of which have reported rising sales for mainstream brands such as Cadbury Dairy Milk and KitKat in 2009.

To save money, in 2009 Lindt & Sprüngli is shutting down 50 of its 80 US retail boutiques, concentrating on boutiques in shopping malls. It first started exporting chocolate to the US in 1987 and began opening its own stores in 1994 to raise awareness of its brand.

Lindt no longer feel the need for the boutiques because most of its US sales are now made through well-known retailers such as Wal-Mart, Costco, Target and Walgreens, and because shoppers are unwilling to pay the higher prices charged at its own stores.

Lindt plans to keep its own stores in upmarket downtown locations, as well as in outlet malls, where consumers can shop at discount stores.

Green & Blacks, the organic chocolate brand owned by Cadbury, has also suffered sales declines in 2009, with the group reporting flat sales growth last year in the UK after previously having recorded annual sales growth of as much as 30 per cent.

One of the new Lindt chocolate cafes in Sydney, Australia
Source: Lindt & Sprüngli International AG

Lindt Chocolat Cafés as a new distribution channel

Lindt has been inspired by the new successful coffee café chains, such as Starbucks. Therefore, in 2004 Lindt opened three chocolate cafés in Sydney, Australia. A fourth store opened in Miranda Westfield, in Sydney's Sutherland Shire in November 2008. A fifth store was established in Melbourne, Australia, in January 2009. There is also planning in the earliest of stages for the first United States chocolate café in Wrentham, MA.

The café is famous for its rich hot chocolates which are available in dark or milk. They also sell crafted chocolates, cakes and ice cream.

QUESTIONS

1 Please discuss Lindt's strategic distribution alternatives in order to gain further market shares in the world confectionery market

2 Lindt is now considering further international expansion of the chocolate cafés and turning them into a separate business unit as a café chain within the Lindt Group. Please discuss the pros and cons for such an international chocolate café chain (Lindt Chocolate Cafés).

3 Which markets would you consider the most attractive for Lindt Chocolate Cafés?

4 Explain the business model that should be used for such a chocolate chain.

SOURCES

Datamonitor (www.datamonitor.com); Euromonitor International (www.euromonitor.com); The Lindt and Sprüngli Group (www.lindt.com); and various public sources.

Lindt's Fifth Avenue store, New York
Source: Lindt & Sprüngli International AG

QUESTIONS FOR DISCUSSION

1 Discuss current distribution trends in world markets.

2 What are the factors that affect the length, width and number of marketing channels?

3 In attempting to optimise marketing channel performance, which of the following should a marketer emphasise: training, motivation or compensation? Why?

4 When would it be feasible and advisable for a company to centralise the coordination of its foreign market distribution systems? When would decentralisation be more appropriate?

5 What is the idea behind 'mystery shopping' in retailing?

6 Why is physical distribution important to the success of global marketing?

7 Discuss the reasons why many exporters make extensive use of the services of freight forwarders.

8 Discuss the implications for the international marketer of the trend towards cross-border retailing.

9 Many markets have relatively large numbers of small retailers. How does this constrain the international marketer?

10 What services would the manufacturer like to receive from the retailer?

REFERENCES

Adweek (2001) Absolut find alternate US entry: Fortune Brands unveils a $740m distribution deal with Swedish firm, *Adweek*, 20 March (www.adweek.com).

Albaum, G., Strandskov, J., Duerr, E. and Dowd, L. (1994) *International Marketing and Export Management*, Addison Wesley, Reading, MA.

Arnold, D. (2000) Seven rules of international distribution, *Harvard Business Review*, November–December: 131–7.

Barth, K., Karch, N. J., Mclaughlin, K. and Shi, C. S. (1996) Global retailing: tempting trouble, *The McKinsey Quarterly*, 1: 117–25.

Beverage Industry (2000) Big news is behind the scenes, *Beverage Industry*, 3 March: 24–32.

Brabbs, C. (2001) Red Bull soars into top three soft drinks, *Marketing*, 8 February: 2.

Bucklin, C. B., Defalco, S. P., DeVincentis, J. R. and Levis III, J. P. (1996) Are you tough enough to manage your channels? *The McKinsey Quarterly*, 1: 105–14.

Cateora, P. R. (1993) *International Marketing*, 8th edn, Irwin, Homewood, IL.

Cavusgil, S. T., Yeoh, P.-L. and Mitri, M. (1995) Selecting foreign distributors: An expert systems approach, *Industrial Marketing Management*, 24: 297–304.

Chakravarthy, B. and Lorange, P. (2007) Continuous renewal, and how Best Buy did it, *Strategy & Leadership*, 35(6): 4–11.

Chee, H. and Harris, R. (1994) *Marketing: A Global Perspective*, Pitman, London.

CNN (2001) Vin & Sprit inks Absolut deal, *CNN Financial News* (http://cnnfn.cnn.com).

Cohen, A. (2000) When channel conflict is good, *Sales and Marketing Management*, 15(4): 13–14.

Day, J. and Robinson, R. (2000) Drink responds to fluid needs, *Marketing Week*, 24 August: 25–6 (www.mad.co.uk).

Dickson, P. R. (1982) Distributor portfolio analysis and channel dependence matrix, *Journal of Marketing*, 47 (Summer): 35–44.

Doherty, A. M. (2007) The internationalization of retailing, *International Journal of Service Industry Management*, 18(2): 184–205.

EIU (1995) The EU50: corporate case studies in single market success, Economist Intelligence Unit, Research Report, pp. 77–8.

Erstad, M. (1998) Mystery shopping programmes and human resource management, *International Journal of Contemporary Hospitality Management*, 10(1): 34–8.

Fitzgerals, K. (2000) Red Bull charged up, *Advertising Age*, 22 August: 26–8.

Hollensen, S. (2001) *Global Marketing: A Market Responsive Approach*, 2nd edn, Financial Times/Prentice-Hall, Harlow.

Jain, S. (1996) *International Marketing Management*, 5th edn, South-Western College Publishing, Cincinnati, OH.

Kumar, N. (1999) Internet distribution strategies: dilemmas for the incumbent, in Mastering Information Management, Part 7: Electronic Commerce, *Financial Times*, 15 March.

Lewison, D. M. (1996) *Marketing Management: An Overview*, Dryden Press/Harcourt Brace College Publishers, Fort Worth, TX.

Liu, S. S. and Cheng, M. (2000) Toward a framework for entering China's pharmaceutical market, *Marketing Intelligence & Planning*, 18 May: 227–35.

McGoldrick, P. J. and Davies, G. (1995) *International Retailing: Trends and Strategies*, Pitman, London.

MarketingWeek (2001a) Bud branches into energy drinks, *MarketingWeek*, 11 January.

MarketingWeek (2001b) Drnec lashes out at rival energy drinks, *MarketingWeek*, 15 February.

MarketingWeek (2001c) Scottish Courage to enter energy drinks market with Red Snapper, *Marketing Week*, 22 March.

Morelli, G. (2006) The right channel to reach your market, *Industrial Management*, July–August: 26–30.

Morrall, K. (1994) Mystery shopping tests service and compliance, *Bank Marketing*, 26(2): 13–15.

Onkvisit, S. and Shaw, J. J. (1993) *International Marketing: Analysis and Strategy*, 2nd edn, Macmillan, London.

Paliwoda, S. (1993) *International Marketing*, Heinemann, Oxford.

Pirog III, S. F. and Lancioni, R. (1997) US–Japan distribution channel cost structures: is there a significant difference? *International Journal of Physical Distribution and Logistics Management*, 27(1): 53–66.

Rosa, J. (1999) Forming an alliance, *Computer Reseller News*, 21 June: 49–50.

Rydholm, J. (1998) *Quirk's Marketing Research Review*, January, article no. 297.

Sletmo, G. K. and Picard, J. (1984) International distribution policies and the role of air freight, *Journal of Business Logistics*, 6: 35–52.

Sorensen, H. (2008) Retailing without frontiers, *Brand Strategy*, February: 40–1.

Spegel, R. (2000) Sony shocks Japanese dealers with direct sales web site, *E-Commerce Times*, 1 February.

Strategic Direction (2009) Winning the Wal-Mart way, *Strategic Direction*, 25(4): 5–8.

Toyne, B. and Walters, P. G. P. (1993) *Global Marketing Management: A Strategic Perspective*, 2nd edn, Allyn & Bacon, Needham Heights, MA.

Valos, M. J. (2008) A qualitative study of multi-channel marketing performance measurement issues, *Journal of Database Marketing & Customer Strategy Management*, 15(4): 239–48.

Varley, M. (2009) Can Hello Kitty continue to rule the world? *Brand Strategy*, February: 32–6.

Wall Street Journal (2000) Condomi in alliance with MCM Klosterfrau, *Wall Street Journal*, interactive section, press release, 27 July.

Wilson, A. M. (1998) The role of mystery shopping in the measurement of service performance, *Managing Service Quality*, 8(6): 414–20.

CHAPTER 14
Communication decisions

LEARNING OBJECTIVES

After studying this chapter you should be able to:

- define and classify the different types of communication tool
- explain what is meant by 'mass customisation' and one-to-one marketing
- describe and explain the major steps in advertising decisions
- describe the techniques available and appropriate for setting the advertising budget in foreign markets
- discuss the possibilities of marketing via the Internet
- discuss which points should be considered when creating a website on the Internet
- explain how important personal selling and salesforce management are in the international marketplace
- discuss how standardised international advertising has both benefits and drawbacks

14.1 INTRODUCTION

Communication is the fourth part of the global marketing programme. The role of communication in global marketing is similar to that in domestic operations: to communicate with customers so as to provide the information that buyers need to make purchasing decisions. Although the communication mix carries information of interest to the customer, in the end it is designed to persuade the customer to buy a product, at the present time or in the future.

Marketers need to ensure that all elements of the marketing mix – product, price, promotion (communication) and place – are working together. This chapter deals with communication, which is broader than promotion but includes it within its scope.

Communication is the exchange of information between or among parties. It involves sharing points of view and is at the heart of forming relationships. You simply cannot connect with

Integrated marketing communications (IMC)
A system of management and integration of marketing communication elements – advertising, publicity, sales promotion, internet marketing sponsorship marketing and point-of-sale communications – with the result that all elements adhere to the same message.

Share of voice (SOV)
The communication expenditures (advertising, PR, sales force, etc.) for the firm's band in percentage of the total communication expenditures for all brands in a product category.

customers unless you communicate with them. Promotion is the process whereby marketers inform, educate, persuade, remind and reinforce consumers through communication. It is designed to influence buyers and other groups. Although most marketing communications are aimed at consumers, a significant number also address shareholders, employees, channel members, suppliers and society. In addition, we will see that effective communication works in two directions: receiving messages is often as important as sending them. **Integrated marketing communication (IMC)** is the coordination of advertising, sales promotion, personal selling, public relations and sponsorship to reach consumers with a powerful unified effect. These five elements should not be considered as separate entities. In fact, each element of the communication plan often has an effect on the other.

The total amount of communication activities in the market is the so-called '**Share of voice**' **(SOV)**. How to measure SOV more precisely? Secondary market research may be used to accumulate measured media expenditures and estimated costs for other communications activities. Information should be gathered for all competitors on an annual basis. Each competitor's percentage of the aggregate total is its share of voice.

For example, if five different brand names advertise in one product category and the percentage of advertising for one of them is 60 per cent of the total volume of advertising in that product category, that brand will have the greatest SOV (in that product category). A recession can provide opportunities for marketers, partly because of likely reduced marketing communication activity by rivals – which enables a brand to increase its share of voice, and consequently gain market share, if it simply maintains its marketing spending (see also Figure 14.1).

Clearly the Internet offers exciting new targeting opportunities that will increasingly affect the way marketers combine and orchestrate various communication activities to create the most effective IMC mix.

To communicate with and influence customers, several tools are available. Advertising is usually the most visible component of the promotion mix, but personal selling, exhibitions, sales promotions, publicity (PR) and direct marketing (including the Internet) are also part of a viable international promotion mix.

One important strategic consideration is whether to standardise the promotion mix worldwide or to adapt it to the environment of each country. Another consideration is the availability of media, which varies around the world.

For many years there has been considerable debate about how advertising works. Researchers agree that there can be no single all-embracing theory that explains how all advertising works.

AIDA
Awareness, interest, desire, action – the stages through which a consumer is believed to pass before purchasing a product.

One of the models is the frequently advocated **AIDA** model, where a person passes through the stages of awareness, interest, desire and action. According to this model, advertising is strong enough to increase people's knowledge and change people's attitudes and as a

If the companys 'share of voice' in the market (compared to competitors') is bigger than the company's current market share, then it will lead to a gain in market share (all other things being equal).

This is a particularly relevant point in times of economic recession, when competitors are decreasing their promotion and communication budgets. Then the company should consider doing the opposite of its competitors, because even with a constant marketing budget, it might gain market share.

Figure 14.1   Share of voice compared to share of market

consequence is capable of persuading people who have not previously bought a brand. It is therefore a conversion theory of advertising: non-buyers are converted to buyers. Advertising is assumed to have a powerful influence on consumers.

Other hierarchy of effects models tend to describe the same processes from different viewpoints. After AIDA, the most quoted model within the advertising industry is DAGMAR (defining advertising goals for measuring advertising results) which splits the process into four steps of awareness, comprehension, conviction and action.

These models are all limited by certain forces. Although they may work in a cold sales call, in other complex marketing situations they do not take into account time and experience. One major weakness is that they fail to take into account the history of the brand. Buying decisions are rarely made in isolation. They are an accumulation of months, even years, of experience on the part of the buyer.

14.2 THE COMMUNICATION PROCESS

Opinion leadership

Opinion leader
Person within a reference group, who, because of special skills, knowledge, personality or other characteristics, exerts influence on others.

Marketing communications reach customers directly and indirectly. Figure 14.2 illustrates both paths. In *one-step communication*, all members of the target audience are simultaneously exposed to the same message. *Multiple-step communication* uses influential members of the target audience, known as **opinion leaders**, to filter a message before it reaches other group members, modifying its effect positively or negatively for the rest of the group.

Because of their important role, opinion leaders have often been called gatekeepers to indicate the control they have over ideas flowing into the group. Marketers interested in maximising communication effectiveness nearly always attempt to identify opinion leaders. Opinion leaders are open to communication from all sources. They are more inclined to be aware of information regarding a broad range of subjects. They read a lot, talk with salespeople and other people who have information on products. Opinion leaders can intensify the strength of the message if they respond positively and pass it on to others, especially if it is

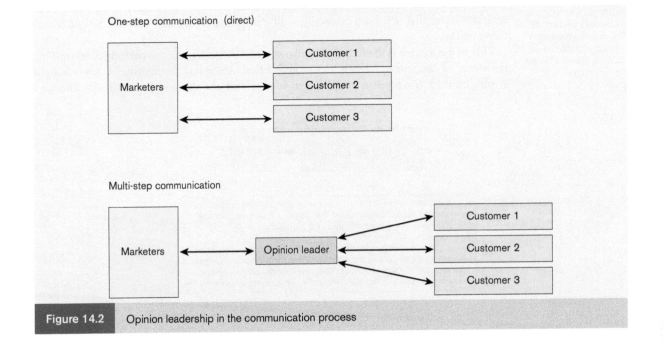

Figure 14.2   Opinion leadership in the communication process

going on through the mass media. Consequently, the resources used to gain support from opinion leaders are probably well spent.

Public figures are often opinion leaders. Consider the sales boost after Oprah Winfrey introduced her book of the month club feature. She has influenced so many consumers with her highly regarded opinion that her selections have become bestsellers.

Buyer initiative in the communication process

In considering the communication process we normally think about a manufacturer (sender) transmitting a message through any form of media to an identifiable target segment audience. Here the seller is the initiator of the communication process. However, if the seller and the buyer have already established a relationship, it is likely that the initiative for the communication process will come from the buyer. If the buyer has a positive post-purchase experience with a given offering in one period of time, this may dispose the buyer to buy again on later occasions; that is, take initiatives in the form of making enquiries or placing orders (so-called reverse marketing).

The likely development of the split between total sales volume attributable to buyer and seller initiatives is shown in Figure 14.3. The relative share of sales volume attributable to buyer initiative will tend to increase over time. Present and future buyer initiatives are a function of all aspects of a firm's past market performance; that is, the extent, nature and timing of seller initiative, the competitiveness of offerings, post-purchase experience and the relationships developed with buyers, as well as the way in which buyer initiative has been dealt with (Ottesen, 1995).

Key attributes of effective communication

All effective marketing communication has four elements: a sender, a message, a communication channel and a receiver (audience).

To communicate in an effective way, the sender needs to have a clear understanding of the purpose of the message, the audience to be reached and how this audience will interpret and

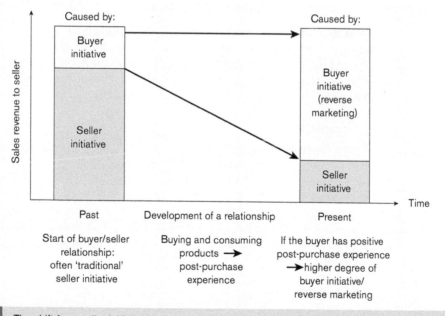

Figure 14.3	The shift from seller initiative to buyer initiative in buyer–seller relationships

Source: Hollensen, S. (2001) *Global Marketing: A Market Responsive Approach*, 2nd ed., Financial Times-Prentice Hall, Harlow, p. 516. Reproduced with permission.

respond to the message. However, sometimes the audience cannot hear clearly what the sender is trying to say about its product because of the 'noise' of rival manufacturers making similar and often contradictory claims about their products.

Another important point to consider is the degree of fit between medium and message. For example, a complex and wordy message would be better for the press than for a visual medium such as television or cinema.

Other factors affecting communication

Language differences

A slogan or advertising copy that is effective in one language may mean something different in another language. Thus, the trade names, sales presentation materials and advertisements used by firms in their domestic markets may have to be adapted and translated when used in other markets.

There are many examples of unfortunate translations of brand names and slogans. One of General Motors' models in the UK was called the Vauxhall Nova – in Spanish it means 'it does not go'. In Latin America, 'Avoid embarrassment – use Parker pens' was translated as 'Avoid pregnancy – use Parker pens'.

A Danish company made the following translation for its cat litter in the UK: 'Sand for cat piss'. Unsurprisingly, sales of the firm's cat litter did not increase! Another Danish company translated 'teats for baby bottles' as 'loose tits'. In Copenhagen Airport the following poster could be seen until recently: 'We take your baggage and send it in all directions'. A slogan thus used to express a wish of giving good service might give rise to some concern as to where the baggage might end up (Joensen, 1997).

Economic differences

In contrast to industrialised countries, developing countries may have radios but not television sets. In countries with low levels of literacy, written communication may not be as effective as visual or oral communication.

Socio-cultural differences

Cultural factors (religion, attitudes, social conditions and education) affect how individuals perceive their environment and interpret signals and symbols. For example, the use of colour in advertising must be sensitive to cultural norms. In many Asian countries, white is associated with grief; hence an advertisement for a detergent where whiteness is emphasised would have to be altered for promotional activities in, say, India.

Legal and regulatory conditions

Local advertising regulations and industry codes directly influence the selection of media and content of promotional materials. Many governments maintain tight regulations on content, language and sexism in advertising. The type of product that can be advertised is also regulated. Tobacco products and alcoholic beverages are the most heavily regulated products in terms of promotion. However, the manufacturers of these products have not abandoned their promotional efforts. Philip Morris engages in corporate-image advertising using its Marlboro man. Regulations are found more in industrialised economies than in developing economies, where the advertising industry is not yet as highly developed.

Competitive differences

As competitors vary from country to country in terms of number, size, type and promotional strategies used, a firm may have to adapt its promotional strategy and the timing of its efforts to the local environment.

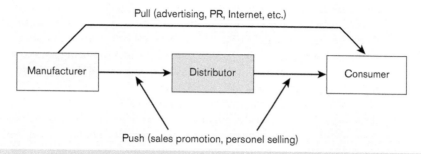

Figure 14.4	Push versus pull strategies

Push versus pull strategies

Push strategy
A promotional strategy whereby a supplier promotes a product to marketing intermediaries, with the aim of pushing the product through the channel of distribution.

Pull strategy
Involves a relatively heavy emphasis on consumer-oriented advertising to encourage consumer demand for a new brand and thereby obtain retail distribution. The brand is pulled through the channel system in the sense that there is a backward tug from the consumer to the retailer.

Where a marketer uses any form of distribution channel, he or she is faced with two extremes in terms of promotion. Marketers attempt to influence the market through either a **push strategy** or a **pull strategy**, as illustrated in Figure 14.4. In many cases they use both strategies.

Pull strategy

A pull strategy attempts to influence consumers directly. Communication is designed to build demand so consumers will pull the product through the channel of distribution. In other words, consumers ask retailers for the product, who in turn ask wholesalers, who in turn contact the manufacturer. When pursuing this strategy, a manufacturer focuses primarily on building selective demand and brand loyalty among potential customers through media advertising, consumer promotion, extended warranties and customer service, product improvements, line extensions and other actions aimed at winning customer preference. Thus, by building strong consumer demand, the manufacturer increases its ability to promote economic rewards in the form of large sales volumes to its channel members in return for their cooperation.

Push strategy

The push strategy involves communicating to distribution channel members, who in turn promote to the end user. This is particularly common in industrial or business-to-business marketing. Marketers often train distribution channel members on the sales techniques they believe are most suited to their products. The push technique is also used in retail marketing.

Smaller firms with limited resources, those without established reputations as good marketers, and those attempting to gain better channel support for existing products with relatively small shares and volumes often have difficulty achieving relationships with end customers.

In such situations firms usually adopt a push strategy in which much of the product's marketing budget is devoted to direct inducements to gain the cooperation of wholesalers and/or retailers. Typically, a manufacturer offers channel members a number of rewards, each aimed at motivating them to perform a specific function or activity on the product's behalf. The rationale is that by motivating more wholesalers or retailers to carry and aggressively sell the product, more customers are exposed and persuaded to buy it.

It thus tends to revolve around sales promotion and is sometimes referred to as '**below the line**'. This term is derived from the days when advertising agencies managed all promotional activity, and the items on the accounts that did not relate to advertising were put below the line that divided the agency's main activity on the expenditure reports. This technique is particularly favoured by organisations without strong brands that are involved in price competition.

Often, a combined push-pull strategy is appropriate. The combination approach sells to the channel and to the end user. This can speed product adoption and strengthen market share. As we learned in Chapter 13, conflicts often occur between the marketing organisation and its distributors. For example, in the food industry, retailers want to carry products that yield the greatest profitability. Since these may not be brands with the strongest pull, retailers may charge marketers for shelf space. Essentially, they are being paid to push the product to the end user. Using a pull strategy to create strong demand at the consumer level makes channel members more willing to handle the product.

With a pull strategy the marketer aims promotional effort (typically advertising) at the end customer in the belief that he or she will be motivated to 'pull' the product through the channel (by demanding it from retailers, for example). Due to its association with advertising, it is sometimes referred to as '**above the line**'. This technique is usually favoured by the owners of strong, differentiated brands, such as Procter & Gamble or Nestlé.

Above-the-line advertising
Advertising in the mass media, including press, radio, television and posters.

Mass customisation, one-to-one marketing and the push-pull strategy

As shown in the following, new trends in product manufacturing have a great impact on the way that firms communicate more and more directly to the customer.

The phrase mass customisation is striking, for it seems a contradiction in terms. Mass production implies uniform products, whereas customisation connotes small-scale crafts. Combining the best of both promises exciting choices for consumers and new opportunities for business.

The concept of mass customisation is about allowing companies to produce products tailored to customers' requirements. It is really an extension of product differentiation. The traditional form of product differentiation involves changing the product characteristics to differentiate one firm's product from another firm's. Differentiation can also assume the role of distinguishing several of a single firm's products from each other. The goal is to fit the product to the customer's needs better. The ultimate goal of mass customisation is to fit the product and communication to the customer's needs perfectly. This one-to-one marketing relationship is difficult to achieve because of its nature and complexity.

Pitta (1998) proposed four basic steps companies must go through to practise one-to-one principles.

Identify customers

Companies must know their customers. It is vital to learn which are the heavy, medium, light and non-users of your products. When companies identify consumers who will never purchase their products at all, they can stop spending money and effort trying to win them over. They simply will not purchase. More important, it is vital to learn who are the loyal customers. They represent the best prospects for company success and are the company's most valued asset. It is important for companies to take the right actions to ensure they keep their business, forever.

Differentiate each customer

Identifying the most valuable customers, recognising their unique preferences and needs, and treating them differently is the essence of one-to-one marketing. Customers have different needs from the firm, and from each other. Moreover, they have different values to the organisation. The value of a customer determines how much time and investment should be allocated to that customer, and a customer's needs represent the key to keeping and to growing that customer's business. This applies both to individual consumers and to industrial customers.

Interact with each customer

Interacting with your customers is another one-to-one marketing fundamental. Every contact with a customer represents the opportunity to learn more about his needs and his value to the organisation. In some cases, direct contact will be possible and considerable thought should go into how maximum learning can take place. In some cases, direct questions will be possible. In others, consumers will make choices and the firm can infer customer preferences.

Customise products for each customer

This seems logical and apparent, but producing and delivering a product customised to an individual customer is the most difficult principle to put into practice. It is difficult. If it were not, everyone would already be doing it. The difficulty depends in part on successful completion of the previous three steps.

Customisation may create competitive advantages, but it is also a big challenge to implement it. It is only made possible by integrating the production process with the firm's customer feedback. A company that has been able to implement successful mass customisation is Dell Computer. Dell's story is by now a familiar one. Over the Web, customers select what they want from hundreds of different components to configure the computer of their choice, which Dell builds only when it has the money for it. The company has become the envy of manufacturers of all kinds.

But mass customisation is not necessarily feasible for all goods. Assembling cars, for example, is more complex and difficult than building computers. Still, car companies such as BMW, Ford and General Motors have high hopes for the build-to-order (BTO) approach (equivalent to one-to-one marketing), a variant of mass customisation.

Agrawal *et al.* (2001) are very doubtful about the benefits of BTO in the car industry. Moving from a mass manufacturing (or push) system of production, which car makers have continually refined over the years, to a BTO (or pull) system would require numerous operational and organisational changes throughout the car industry value chain (see Figure 14.5).

The pay-off of a BTO strategy is unclear. Luxury-car buyers seem eager to specify their preferences in great detail. But it is still too early to tell whether mainstream customers want their vehicles built to order.

Yet, a true pull system would mean a massive reduction in finished goods (for both the manufacturers and the dealers) and in component inventories (for both the manufacturers

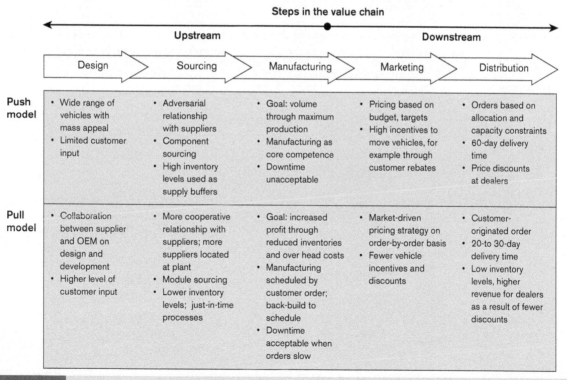

Figure 14.5 Push and pull strategies in the car industry value chain
Source: Agrawal, M., Kumaresh, T. V. and Mercer, G. A. (2001) The false promise of mass customization, *McKinsey Quarterly*, 3: 62–71. Reproduced with permission from McKinsey and Company.

and the suppliers). Industry analysts estimate that, if a majority of customers bought cars built to order, the industry could capture as much as 70 per cent of the capital lost or locked up in the present push system – lost when inventory becomes obsolete following a change in models, production processes and assembly structures, or locked up in components stored to meet unanticipated demand.

Already today some degree of BTO is a reality. At the lowest level, customers (or sometimes dealers) can (via the Internet) check the inventories of various dealers within a given area to see whether a car being sought already exists. Customers can also ask their dealers to order cars from the manufacturer.

Also car makers are trying to achieve BTO by modularising – that is, by fabricating individual cars not from thousands of distinct parts, but from mere dozens of larger mix-and-match modules. But car makers might have to carry a range of modules, some of which may vary slightly in colour, choice of fabric or even an individual part.

Thus it seems that a balanced selection would not be BTO, but rather locate-to-order. Customers should not care whether the car they purchased was built expressly for them or found for them somewhere in the supply chain, as long as it had the features they wanted and they got it in a reasonable amount of time. Certainly, Dell's customers do not know whether their PCs were actually made for them or pulled from an order queue. For car makers, this is a low-cost solution that is easier to implement than BTO yet likely to provide high customer satisfaction (Agrawal *et al.*, 2001).

14.3 COMMUNICATION TOOLS

Earlier in this chapter we mentioned the major forms of promotion. In this section the different communication tools, listed in Table 14.1, will be further examined.

Advertising

Advertising is one of the most visible forms of communication. Because of its wide use and its limitations as a one-way method of communication, advertising in international markets

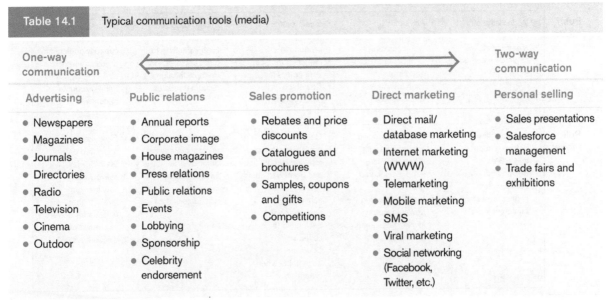

| Table 14.1 | Typical communication tools (media) |

One-way communication	← →			Two-way communication
Advertising	Public relations	Sales promotion	Direct marketing	Personal selling
• Newspapers	• Annual reports	• Rebates and price discounts	• Direct mail/ database marketing	• Sales presentations
• Magazines	• Corporate image	• Catalogues and brochures	• Internet marketing (WWW)	• Salesforce management
• Journals	• House magazines	• Samples, coupons and gifts	• Telemarketing	• Trade fairs and exhibitions
• Directories	• Press relations	• Competitions	• Mobile marketing	
• Radio	• Public relations		• SMS	
• Television	• Events		• Viral marketing	
• Cinema	• Lobbying		• Social networking (Facebook, Twitter, etc.)	
• Outdoor	• Sponsorship			
	• Celebrity endorsement			

Source: Hollensen, S. (2001) *Global Marketing: A Market Responsive Approach*, 2nd ed., Financial Times-Prentice Hall, Harlow, p. 519. Reproduced with permission.

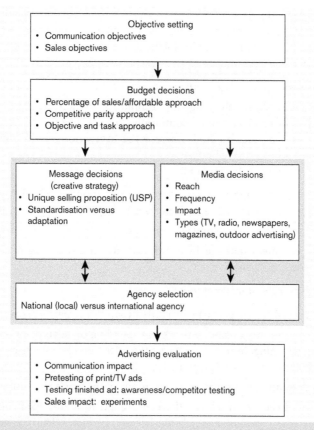

Figure 14.6	The major advertising decisions
	Source: Hollensen, S. (2001) *Global Marketing: A Market Responsive Approach*, 2nd ed., Financial Times-Prentice Hall, Harlow, p. 520. Reproduced with permission.

is subject to a number of difficulties. Advertising is often the most important part of the communications mix for consumer goods, where there are a large number of small-volume customers who can be reached through mass media. For most business-to-business markets, advertising is less important than the personal selling function.

The major decisions in advertising are shown in Figure 14.6. We will now discuss these different phases.

Objective setting

Advertising objective
A specific communication task to be accomplished with a specific target audience during a specific period of time.

Although advertising methods may vary from country to country, the major **advertising objectives** remain the same. Major advertising objectives (and means) might include:

● increasing sales from existing customers by encouraging them to increase the frequency of their purchases; maintaining brand loyalty via a strategy that reminds customers of the key advantages of the product; stimulating impulse purchases;

● obtaining new customers by increasing consumer awareness of the firm's products and improving the firm's corporate image among a new target customer group.

Budget decisions

Controversial aspects of advertising include determining a proper method for deciding the size of the promotional budget, and its allocation across markets and over time.

In theory, the firm (in each of its markets) should continue to put more money into advertising, as money spent on advertising returns more money than money spent on anything else. In practice, it is not possible to set an optimum advertising budget. Therefore, firms have developed more practical guidelines. The manager must also remember that the advertising budget cannot be regarded in isolation, but has to be seen as one element of the overall marketing mix.

Affordable approach/percentage of sales

Affordable approach
Setting the promotion budget at the level management thinks the company can afford.

Affordable approach budgeting techniques link advertising expenditure directly to some measure of profits or, more commonly, to sales. The most popular of these methods is the percentage of sales method, whereby the firm automatically allocates a fixed percentage of sales to the advertising budget.

Advantages of this method:

- For firms selling in many countries, this simple method appears to guarantee equality among the markets. Each market seems to get the advertising it deserves.
- It is easy to justify in budget meetings.
- It guarantees that the firm only spends on advertising as much as it can afford. The method prevents wastage.

Disadvantages of this method:

- It uses historical performance rather than future performance.
- It ignores the possibility that extra spending on advertising may be necessary when sales are declining, in order to reverse the sales trend by establishing a 'recycle' on the product life cycle curve (see Chapter 11).
- It does not take into account variations in the firm's marketing goals across countries.
- The percentage of sales method encourages local management to maximise sales by using the easiest and most flexible marketing tool: price (that is, lowering the price).
- The method's convenience and simplicity encourage management not to bother investigating the relationships between advertising and sales or analysing critically the overall effectiveness of advertising campaigns.
- The method cannot be used to launch new products or enter new markets (zero sales = zero advertising).

Competitive parity approach

Competitive parity approach
Setting the promotion budget to match competitors' outlays.

The **competitive parity approach** involves estimating and duplicating the amounts spent on advertising by major rivals. Unfortunately, determining the marketing expenditures of foreign-based competitors is far more difficult than monitoring home country businesses, whose financial accounts (if they are limited companies) are open to public inspection and whose promotional activities are obvious the moment they occur. Another danger in following the practice of competitors is that they are not necessarily right.

Furthermore, the method does not recognise that the firm is in different situations in different markets. If the firm is new to a market, its relationships with customers are different from those of existing companies. This should also be reflected in its promotion budget.

Objective and task approach

Objective and task approach
Developing the promotion budget by defining specific objectives, determining the tasks that must be performed to achieve these objectives, and estimating the costs of performing these tasks. The sum of these costs is the proposed promotion budget.

The weaknesses of the above approaches have led some firms to follow the **objective and task approach**, which begins by determining the advertising objectives and then ascertaining the tasks needed to attain these objectives. This approach also includes a cost–benefit analysis, relating objectives to the cost of achieving them. To use this method, the firm must have good knowledge of the local market.

Hung and West (1991) showed that only 20 per cent of companies in the USA, Canada and the UK used the objective and task approach. Although it is the theoretically correct way of determining the promotion budget, it is sometimes more important to be operational and to use a percentage of sales approach. This is not necessarily a bad method if company experience shows it to be reasonably successful. If the percentage is flexible, it allows different percentages to be used in different markets.

Message decisions (creative strategy)

Unique selling proposition (USP)
A unique characteristic of a product or brand identified by the marketer as the one on which to base a promotional campaign. It is often used in a product-differentiation approach to promotion.

This concerns decisions about what **unique selling proposition (USP)** needs to be communicated, and what the communication is intended to achieve in terms of consumer behaviour in the country concerned. These decisions have important implications for the choice of advertising medium, since certain media can better accommodate specific creative requirements (use of colour, written description, high definition, demonstration of the product, etc.) than others.

An important decision for international marketers is whether an advertising campaign developed in the domestic market can be transferred to foreign markets with only minor modifications, such as translation into appropriate languages. Complete standardisation of all aspects of a campaign over several foreign markets is rarely attainable. Standardisation implies a common message, creative idea, media and strategy, but it also requires that the firm's product has a USP that is clearly understood by customers in a cross-cultural environment.

Standardising international advertising can lead to a number of advantages for the firm. For example, advertising costs will be reduced by centralising the advertising campaign in the head office and transferring the same campaign from market to market, as opposed to running campaigns from different local offices.

However, running an advertising campaign in multiple markets requires a balance between conveying the message and allowing for local nuances. The adaptation of global ideas can be achieved by various tactics, such as adopting a modular approach, adapting international symbols and using international advertising agencies.

Media decisions

The selection of the media to be used for advertising campaigns needs to be done simultaneously with the development of the message. A key question in media selection is whether to use mass media or a targeted approach. The mass media (television, radio and newsprint) are effective when a significant percentage of the general public are potential customers. This percentage varies considerably by country for most products, depending on, for example, the distribution of incomes in different countries.

The selection of the media to be used in a particular campaign typically starts with some idea of the target market's demographic and psychological characteristics, regional strengths of the product, seasonality of sales, and so on. The media selected should be the result of a careful fit of local advertising objectives, media attributes and target market characteristics.

Furthermore, media selection can be based on the following criteria:

Reach
The number of people exposed to an advertisement carried by a given medium.

Frequency
Average number of times within a given timeframe that each potential customer is exposed to the same ad.

Impact
Depends on the compatibility between the medium used and the message (the 'impact' on the consumer's brain).

Gross rating points (GRPs)
Reach multiplied by frequency. GRPs may be estimated for individual media vehicles. Media planning is often based on 'cost per 1000 GRPs'.

- **reach**: total number of people in a target market exposed to at least one advertisement in a given time period ('opportunity to see', or **OTS**);
- **frequency**: average number of times within a given time period that each potential customer is exposed to the same advertisement;
- **impact**: depends on compatibility between the medium used and the message. *Penthouse* magazine continues to attract advertisers for high-value-added consumer durables, such as cars, hi-fi equipment and clothes, which are geared primarily to a high-income male segment.

High reach is necessary when the firm enters a new market or introduces a new product so that information about, for example, the new product's availability is spread to the widest possible audience. A high level of frequency is appropriate when brand awareness already exists and the message is about informing the consumer that a campaign is under way. Sometimes a campaign should have both a high frequency and extensive reach, but limits on the advertising budget often create the need to trade off frequency against reach.

A media's **gross rating points (GRPs)** are the result of multiplying its reach by the frequency with which an advertisement appears within the media over a certain period. Hence it contains duplicated exposure, but indicates the 'critical mass' of a media effort. GRPs may be estimated for individual vehicles, for entire classes of media or for a total campaign.

Hence it contains duplicated exposure, but indicates the critical mass of a media effort. GRPs may be estimated for individual vehicles, for entire classes of media or for a total campaign.

The cost of running a media campaign also has to be taken into consideration. Traditionally, media planning is based on a single measure, such as **cost per thousand (CPM)** GRPs. When dealing with two or more national markets, the selection of media also has to take into account differences in:

- the firm's market objectives across countries;
- media effectiveness across countries.

Since media availability and relative importance will not be the same in all countries, plans may require adjustment in cross-border campaigns.

As a way of distributing advertising messages through new communication channels, co-promotion now has a strong foothold.

Let us now take a closer look at the main media types.

Television

Television is an expensive but commonly used medium in attempting to reach broad national markets. In most developed countries, coverage is no problem. However, television is one of the most regulated communications media. Many countries have prohibited the advertising of cigarettes and alcohol other than beer. In other countries (e.g. Scandinavia, the UK) there are limits on the number of minutes that TV advertising is permitted to be shown. Some countries also prohibit commercial breaks in TV programmes.

Radio

Radio is a lower-cost broadcasting activity than television. Commercial radio started several decades before commercial television in many countries. Radio is often transmitted locally and therefore national campaigns have to be built up area by area.

Newspapers

In virtually all urban areas of the world, the population has access to daily newspapers. In fact, the problem for the advertiser is not having too few newspapers, but rather having too many of them. Most countries have one or more newspapers that can be said to have a truly national circulation. However, in many countries newspapers tend to be predominantly local or regional and, as such, serve as the primary medium for local advertisers. Attempting to use a series of local papers to reach a national market is considerably more complex and costly.

Many countries have English-language newspapers in addition to local-language newspapers. For example, the aim of the *Asian Wall Street Journal* is to supply economic information in English to influential Asian business people, politicians, senior government officials and intellectuals.

Magazines

In general, magazines have a narrower readership than newspapers. In most countries, magazines serve to reach specific segments of the population. For technical and industrial products, magazines can be quite effective. Technical business publications tend to be international in their coverage. These publications range from individual businesses (e.g. beverages, construction, textiles) to worldwide industrial magazines covering many industries.

Marketers of international products have the option of using international magazines that have regional editions (e.g. *Newsweek*, *Time* and *Business Week*). In the case of *Reader's Digest*, local-language editions are distributed.

Cinema

In countries where it is common to subsidise the cost of showing films by running commercials prior to the feature film, cinema advertising has become an important medium. India, for

Cost per thousand (CPM)
Calculated by dividing the cost of an ad placed in a particular advertising vehicle (e.g. certain magazine) by the number of people (expressed in thousands) who are exposed to that vehicle.

example, has a relatively high level of cinema attendance per capita (few have television at home). Therefore cinema advertisements play a much greater role in India than in, for example, the USA.

Cinema advertising has other advantages, one of the most important being that it has a truly captive audience (no channel hopping!).

Outdoor advertising

Outdoor advertising includes posters/billboards, shop signs and transit advertising. This medium shows the creative way in which space can be sold to customers. In the case of transit advertising, for example, a bus can be sold as an advertising medium. In Romania transit advertising is very effective. According to a survey by Mueller (1996), in Bucharest 91 per cent of all consumers surveyed said they remembered the content of transit advertisements, compared with 82 per cent who remembered the content of print adverts. The use of transit media is expanding rapidly in China as well. Outdoor posters/billboards can be used to develop the visual impact of advertising. France is a country associated with the effective use of poster and billboard advertising. In some countries, legal restrictions limit the amount of poster space available.

Public relations

Word-of-mouth advertising is not only cheap, but it is also very effective. Public relations (PR) seeks to enhance corporate image building and influence favourable media treatment. PR (or publicity) is the marketing communications function that carries out programmes which are designed to earn public understanding and acceptance. It should be viewed as an integral part of the global marketing effort.

PR activities involve both internal and external communication. Internal communication is important to create an appropriate corporate culture. The target groups for public relations are shown in Table 14.2.

The range of target groups is far wider in public relations than it is for the other communications tools. Target groups are likely to include the main stakeholder groups of employees,

Table 14.2	Target groups for public relations

Public or target groups: domestic markets	Extra factors: international markets
Directly connected with the organisation • Employees • Shareholders	• Wider range of cultural issues • The degree of remoteness of the corporate headquarters
Suppliers of raw materials and components • Providers of financial services • Providers of marketing services (e.g. marketing research, advertising, media)	• Is this to be handled on a country-by-country basis, or is some overall standardisation desirable?
Customers of the organisation • Existing customers • Past customers • Those capable of becoming customers	• May have less knowledge of the company • The country-of-origin effect will influence communications
Environment • The general public • Government: local, regional, national • Financial markets generally	• Wide range of general publics • Host governments • Regional grouping (e.g. EU), world groupings

Source: Adapted from Phillips, C., Poole, I. and Lowe, R. (1994) *International Marketing Strategy: Analysis, Development and Implementation*, Routledge, Andover. Reproduced with permission from Cengage Learning.

customers, distribution channel members and shareholders. For companies operating in international markets, this gives a very wide range of communication tasks. Internal communications in different country subsidiaries, employing people from a number of different countries, with different cultural values, will be particularly challenging.

In a more market-oriented sense, the PR activity is directed towards an influential, though relatively small, target audience of editors and journalists who work for newspapers/magazines, or towards broadcasting aimed at the firm's customers and stakeholders.

Since the target audience is small, it is relatively inexpensive to reach. Several methods can be used to gain PR. Such methods include the following:

Sponsorship
A business relationship between a provider of funds, resources or services and an individual, event or organisation which offers in return some rights and association that may be used for commercial advantage.

- contribution of prizes at different events;

- **sponsorship**: according to Meenaghan (1996), one of the fastest growing aspects of marketing and marketing communications is the practice of corporate sponsorship. Sponsorship takes two forms: event sponsorship (such as athletic and entertainment events) and cause-oriented sponsorship. Event marketing is growing rapidly because it provides companies alternatives to the cluttered mass media, an ability to segment on a local or regional basis, and opportunities for reaching narrow lifestyle groups whose consumption behaviour can be linked with the local event (Milliman *et al.*, 2007). Cause-related marketing, a form of corporate philanthropy with benefits accruing to the sponsoring company, is based on the idea that a company will contribute to a cause every time the customer undertakes some action. In addition to helping worthy causes, corporations satisfy their own tactical and strategic objectives when undertaking cause-related efforts. By supporting a deserving cause, a company can enhance its corporate or brand image, generate incremental sales, increase brand awareness, broaden its customer base and reach new market segments;

- press releases of news about the firm's products, plant and personnel;

- announcements of the firm's promotional campaign;

- lobbying (government);

Celebrity endorsement
The use of famous spokespersons or celebrities in marketing communications.

- **celebrity endorsement**: a recent estimate indicates that approximately 25 per cent of American commercials use celebrity endorsers (Silvera and Austad, 2004). In support of this practice, research indicates that celebrity endorsements can result in more favourable advertisement ratings and product evaluations and can have a substantial positive impact on financial returns for the companies that use them. One possible explanation for the effectiveness of celebrity endorsers is that consumers tend to believe that major stars are motivated by genuine affection for the product rather than by endorsement fees. Celebrities are particularly effective endorsers because they are viewed as highly trustworthy, believable, persuasive and likeable. Although these results unequivocally support the use of celebrity endorsers, other research suggests that celebrity endorsements might vary in effectiveness depending on other factors such as the 'fit' between the celebrity and the advertised product (Seno and Lukas, 2007; Hosea, 2007). Case studies 9.1 (YouthAIDS) and 14.1 (TAG Heuer) describe further examples of celebrity endorsements.

The degree of control of the PR message is quite different. Journalists can use PR material to craft an article of so many words, or an interview of so many seconds. How material is used will depend on the journalist and the desired storyline. On occasions a thoroughly negative story can result from a press release that was designed to enhance the company image.

Hence, PR activity includes anticipating criticism. Criticisms may range from general ones against all multinational corporations to more specific ones. They may also be based on a market; for example, doing business with prison factories in China.

Sales promotion

Sales promotion is defined as those selling activities that do not fall directly into the advertising or personal selling category. Sales promotion also relates to so-called below-the-line

EXHIBIT 14.1
American Express uses celebrity endorsement

Source: © Carlsson Inc./Alamy

Since 2004, American Express has used the tagline 'My Life, My Card' with a group of celebrities including Robert De Niro, Tiger Woods and Kate Winslet, aiming to show that high-achievers of all types choose American Express. Director Martin Scorsese and photographer Annie Leibowitz worked on the campaign to achieve the brand's desired look and feel.

Source: Adapted from Mortimer (2007).

Advertising agency
A marketing services firm that assists companies in planning, preparing, implementing and evaluating all or portions of their advertising programmes.

Point-of-sale displays
Includes all signage – posters, signs, shelf cards and a variety of other visual materials – that are designed to influence buying decisions at the point of sale.

Cross-selling
Selling an additional product or service to an existing customer.

activities such as point-of-sale displays and demonstrations, leaflets, free trials, competitions and premiums such as 'two for the price of one'. Unlike media advertising which is above the line and earns a commission, below-the-line sales promotion does not. To an **advertising agency**, above the line means traditional media for which they are recognised by the media owners, entitling them to commission.

Sales promotion is a short-term effort directed primarily to the consumer and/or retailer, in order to achieve specific objectives such as:

- consumer product trial and/or immediate purchase;
- consumer introduction to the shop;
- encouraging retailers to use **point-of-sale displays** for the product;
- encouraging shops to stock the product.

When a manufacturer owns two or more brands, current loyal customers are excellent candidates for **cross-selling**, promoting another of the brands or using one product to boost sales of another, often an unrelated product. Different companies also may work together to cross-sell.

In the USA, the sales promotion budgets for fast-moving consumer goods (FMCG) manufacturers are larger than the advertising budgets. In Europe, the European Commission estimates that the rate of spending growth on sales promotions was double that for conventional advertising throughout the period 1991–4 (Bennett, 1995, p. 321). Factors contributing to the expansion of sales promotion activities include:

- greater competition among retailers, combined with increasingly sophisticated retailing methods;
- higher levels of brand awareness among consumers, leading to the need for manufacturers to defend brand market shares;
- improved retail technology (e.g. electronic scanning devices that enable coupon redemptions, etc., to be monitored instantly);
- greater integration of sales promotion, public relations and conventional media campaigns.

In markets where the consumer is hard to reach because of media limitations, the percentage of the total communication budget allocated to sales promotions is also relatively high. Some of the different types of sales promotion are as follows:

- *price discounts*: very widely used. A variety of different price reduction techniques is available, such as cash-back deals;
- *catalogues/brochures*: the buyer in a foreign market may be located at quite a distance from the closest sales office. In this situation, a foreign catalogue can be very effective. It must be able to close the gap between buyer and seller such that the potential buyer is supplied with all the necessary information, from prices, sizes, colours and quantities to packing, shipping time and acceptable forms of payment. In addition to catalogues, brochures of various types are useful for salespeople, distributors and agents. Translations should be done in cooperation with overseas agents and/or distributors;
- *coupons*: a classic tool for FMCG brands, especially in the USA. A variety of coupon distribution methods exists: door-to-door, on packs, in newspapers. Coupons are not allowed in all European countries;
- *samples*: gives the potential foreign buyer an idea of the quality that cannot be attained by even the best picture. Samples may prevent misunderstandings over style, sizes, models and so on;
- *gifts*: most European countries have a limit on the value of the premium or gift given. Furthermore, in some countries it is illegal to offer premiums that are conditional on the purchase of another product. The USA does not allow beer to be offered as a free sample;
- *competitions*: this type of sales promotion needs to be communicated to the potential customers. This can be done on the pack, in stores via leaflets or through media advertising (Friel, 2008).

The success of sales promotion depends on local adaptation. Major constraints are imposed by local laws which may not permit premiums or free gifts to be given. Some countries' laws control the amount of discount given at the retail level; others require permits for all sales promotions. Since it is impossible to know the specific laws of each and every country, international marketers should consult local lawyers and authorities before launching a promotional campaign.

Direct marketing

According to Onkvisit and Shaw (1993, p. 717), direct marketing is all the activities by which products and services are offered to market segments in one or more media for informational purposes or to solicit a direct response from a present or prospective customer or contributor by mail, telephone or personal visit.

Direct marketing covers direct mail (marketing database), telephone selling and marketing via the Internet. A number of factors have encouraged the rapid expansion of the international direct marketing industry (Bennett, 1995, p. 318):

- developments in mailing technology which have reduced the costs of distributing direct-mail literature;
- escalating costs of other forms of advertising and sales promotion;
- the increasing availability of good-quality lists of prospective customers;
- developments in information technology (especially database technology and desktop publishing) which enable smaller companies to produce high-quality direct marketing materials in-house;
- the increasing availability throughout the developed world of interactive television facilities, whereby consumers may order goods through a teletext system.

Direct mail

Direct mail is a viable medium in many countries. It is especially important when other media are not available. Direct mail offers a flexible, selective and potentially highly cost-effective means of reaching foreign consumers. Messages can be addressed exclusively to the target market, advertising budgets may be concentrated on the most promising market segments, and it will be some time before competitors realise that the firm has launched a campaign. In addition, the size, content, timing and geographical coverage of mailshots can be varied at will: the firm can spend as much or as little as necessary to achieve its objectives. There are no media space or airtime restrictions, and no copy or insertion deadlines to be met. All aspects of the direct-mail process are subject to the firm's immediate control, and it can experiment by varying the approach used in different countries. Direct mail can take many forms – letters, catalogues, technical literature – and it can serve as a vehicle for the distribution of samples. A major problem in the effective use of direct mail is the preparation of a suitable mailing list (marketing database).

European marketers are still far behind the United States in exploiting the medium and also with regard to the response to direct mail in the form of mail order. Per capita mail-order sales in the USA are more than double those of any European country (Desmet and Xardel, 1996, p. 58).

The use of direct mail in Japan is also below that in the USA. One reason for this discrepancy is that the Japanese feel printed material is too impersonal and insufficiently sincere.

Direct mail is not only relevant for the consumer market. However, effective use of direct mail for business-to-business purposes requires the preparation of an accurate customer profile (marketing database), including industry classification, size of target company (measured, for example, by turnover, number of employees or market share), the people to approach in each business (purchasing officer, project development engineer, product manager, etc.), industry purchasing procedures and (where known) supplier selection criteria and the buying motives of prospective customers (Lester, 2008; Brand Strategy, 2006).

Telemarketing

Telemarketing is today used for both consumer and business-to-business campaigns throughout the industrialised world. The telephone can be used both to obtain orders and to conduct fast, low-cost market research. Telemarketing covers cold calling (unsolicited calls) by salespeople, market surveys conducted by telephone, calls designed to compile databases of possible sales prospects, and follow-ups to customer requests for further information, resulting from print and broadcast advertisements. Currently, the majority of cross-border telemarketing campaigns focus on business-to-business contacts, essentially because of the combined telephone/database facilities that an increasing number of companies possess and, in consequence, the greater reliability of business-to-business communications.

The administration of international telemarketing normally requires the use of a commercial telemarketing agency. Language skills are required, plus considerable skills and experience in identifying decision makers in target firms.

In some European countries, cold calling consumers is receiving close scrutiny in the name of consumer protection and respect for privacy. For example, Germany has prohibited calls on the grounds of privacy invasion, and this ban even applies to an insurance salesperson's announcement of a visit.

Mobile marketing

Mobile marketing or M-marketing is defined as the application of marketing to the mobile environment of smart phones, mobile phones, personal digital assistants (PDA) and telematics. M-marketing is characterised by both the interaction with the World Wide Web and the location-specific context which enhances communication and delivery of information.

M-commerce combines the power and speed of the Internet with the geographic freedom of mobile telephony in terms of receiving and transmitting data and, importantly, the ability to conduct transactions. The emerging capacity to communicate with any individual, from any place, over any network, and to any device, regardless of time or geographical location, provides enormous potential for marketers. For this reason, the impact on marketing strategies for direct marketers needs to be addressed (Ranchhod, 2007; Karjaluoto *et al.*, 2007).

In the light of the development within Internet technologies it is very relevant to consider the Web as a direct marketing tool.

14.4 PERSONAL SELLING

Because personal selling is relatively costly, a firm should devote a major portion of its promotional budget to the salesforce only when its communications objectives can be accomplished more effectively by face-to-face communication than by any other method. As Table 14.3 summarises, there are a number of strategic circumstances where personal selling is likely to play a major role in a business's promotional mix, circumstances which favour the unique advantages of one-to-one communication.

The steps in personal selling

Personal selling can be divided into four main stages, as follows.

Pre-approach and planning

Pre-approach refers to preparing and planning for the initial meeting by learning about the potential customer. In this stage, territory management is extremely important. Salespeople must determine how the company's target marketing and positioning can best be applied in their territory. Because each area is different, it is important to make adjustments based on local conditions. Exceptional sales skills are of little use if calls are not made to the appropriate accounts with the right frequency and intensity. *Territory planning* determines the pool of customers, their sales potential and the frequency with which they will be contacted about various products. The fundamental objective is to allocate sales time and use company resources to obtain the best results. *Account planning* establishes sales goals and objectives for each major customer, such as the sales volume and profitability to be obtained. Increasingly, account objectives include customer satisfaction, often measured by loyalty (repeat business). Account plans are based on an understanding of the customer's business and how the seller's products contribute to it.

Approach

The approach is the first formal contact with the customer. The objective is to secure an initial meeting and gain customer interest. It is usually a good idea to schedule an appointment; that will save time and puts the prospect in the frame of mind for a sales call. Many times, a letter of introduction before calling will help in obtaining the first appointment.

Many techniques have been developed for the initial approach. The most successful ones focus on the potential customer's business, such as a brief explanation of how or why the seller's product can help. It is also important to determine not just when the meeting will take place but how long it will last and its objective. Organisations with a strong reputation generally have an advantage in the approach stage.

In the initial approach to a prospective customer, a sales representative should accomplish three things: develop a thorough understanding of the client's situation and the needs that the representative's products or services might help satisfy, determine who within

Table 14.3	Personal selling functions	
Functions	**Activities involved**	**Conditions where appropriate**
Winning acceptance for new products	Sales representatives build awareness and stimulate demand for new products or services among existing or potential customers.	Business pursuing prospector strategy; potential customers many or few; company's promotional resources limited; firm pursuing push distribution strategy.
Developing new customers	Sales representatives find and cultivate new customers and/or expanded distribution for business's products or services.	Target market in growth stage or firm wishes to increase share of mature market; potential customers many or few; company's promotional resources limited; firm pursuing push distribution strategy.
Maintaining customer loyalty	Sales representatives work to increase value delivered to customers by providing advice or training on product use, expediting orders and facilitating product service.	Business pursuing differentiated defender strategy, firm has large share of mature market and wants to maintain loyalty of existing customers; product technically complex and/or competition for distribution support is strong.
Technical service to facilitate sales	Sales representatives work to increase value to customers by helping integrate product or service with customer's other equipment or operations and by providing design, installation, and/or training.	Product technically complex; customers (or dealers) relatively few or many; product or service can be customised to fit needs of individual customers; products sold as parts of larger systems.
Communicating product information	Sales representatives work to increase understanding of product's features and applications as basis for possible future sales and to educate people who may influence final purchase.	Product technically complex and/or in introductory or at growth stage of life cycle; lengthy purchase decision process; multiple influences on purchase decision.
Gathering information	Sales representatives provide reports on competitors' actions, customers' requests or problems, and other market conditions, and conduct market research or intelligence activities.	Appropriate under all circumstances, but especially useful in industry introductory or growth stage, or when product technology or other factors are unstable; business implementing a prospector strategy.

Source: Adapted from Boyd, H. W., Walker, Jr, O. C., Mullins, J. W. and Larreche, J.-C. (1998) *Marketing Management*, 3rd ed., McGraw-Hill, New York. Reproduced with permission from the McGraw-Hill Companies.

the organisation is likely to have the greatest influence and/or authority to make a purchase, and obtain the information needed to qualify the prospect as a worthwhile potential customer.

Building the relationship

The importance of a problem-solving sales approach as a basis for establishing an enduring relationship with a potential customer should be obvious. But, as we have seen, organisational buying centres often consist of multiple individuals who have somewhat different concerns and play different roles in shaping the company's purchase decisions. Thus, it is important for salespeople to identify the key decision makers, their desires and their relative influence.

The sales presentation is a two-way process: the salesperson listens in order to identify customer needs and then describes how the product will fulfil them. The most important part of any good presentation is listening. In fact, it is often said that successful selling is 90 per cent listening and 10 per cent talking. Unfortunately, many salespeople believe their role is to tell prospects about products. Instead, by asking questions, they should put the customer first and demonstrate that they have the customer's best interests in mind. The first contact is the first opportunity to connect with a customer.

Organisations generally have to train their salesforce to be good listeners. This is a trait few people possess naturally. The training identifies ways to learn about the prospect's situation. It also teaches how to communicate that the salesperson is listening and is concerned about the customer's needs and wants. Empathy occurs when salespeople know precisely how prospects feel. Only when prospects know that the seller understands their wants and needs are they receptive to solutions the salesperson offers.

Closing the deal and building loyalty

Closing
The step in the selling process in which the salesperson asks the customer for an order.

One of the most important sales skills is the ability to overcome a buyer's objections. Assertive salespeople do not let the first objection stop the dialogue; they use it to advance the discussion. Most organisations have training programmes to teach salespeople how to manage objections. **Closing** means getting the first order. In many cases this is simple, such as asking directly if someone wants to buy the product or whether they will use cash or credit. In other cases, it involves elaborate contracts. Good salespeople know how important it is to help the buyer towards the final decision. In business-to-business situations, the salespeople may ask if the purchaser is ready to make a decision or would like to discuss the issue more thoroughly. A caution is in order regarding closing. If a buyer is not ready to make the commitment, then asking for an order prematurely can make the salesperson appear pushy and unconcerned with the buyer's needs. A great deal of sensitivity is required for an accurate reading of the buyer's state of mind.

There is a big difference between making a sale and gaining customer loyalty. In order to maintain relationships and gain customer loyalty, salespeople have to spend significant time servicing customers. They make sure products are delivered on schedule and operate to the buyer's liking. When there is a problem, the salesperson makes sure that it is resolved quickly and satisfactorily.

Follow-up occurs when a salesperson ensures that there is after-sale satisfaction in order to obtain repeat business. Follow-up also offers a way to identify additional sales opportunities. After the first sale is made, the second is easier. The salesperson who continues to work closely with the buying organisation can uncover other needs to supply. Good service builds strong customer loyalty, which is the goal of relationship selling.

Team selling
Using teams of people from sales, marketing, engineering, finance, technical support and even upper management to service large, complex accounts.

When the purchase decision is likely to be very complex, involving many people within the customer's organisation, the seller might adopt a policy of multi-level selling or **team selling**. Team selling involves people from most parts of the organisation, including senior executives, who work together to create relationships with the buying organisation. In a high-technology business such as aircraft manufacturing nearly every function is involved in the sales process. At Boeing it is the salesperson's job to coordinate contact between the company and the technical, financial and planning personnel from the airline. Even if the CEO is brought in, it is not unusual for the salesperson to remain in charge of the sale using the CEO where appropriate. The salespeople perform the leadership function because they know all aspects of their customers' business. They must also be thoroughly familiar with Boeing's services.

There are some differences between advertising and personal selling. Advertising is a one-way communication process, whereas personal selling is a two-way communication process with immediate feedback and less 'noise'. Personal selling is an effective way to sell products, but it is expensive. It is used mainly to sell to distribution channel members and in business-to-business markets. However, personal selling is also used in some consumer markets – for example for cars and for consumer durable products. In some countries, labour costs are very low. In these instances, personal selling will be used to a greater extent than in high-cost countries.

If personal selling costs in business-to-business markets are relatively high, it is relevant to economise with personal selling resources and use personal selling only at the end of the potential customer's buying process. Computerised database marketing (direct mail, etc.) is used in a customer screening process, to point out possible customers for the salesforce. Their job is to turn good customer candidates into real customers.

New technologies – particularly telemarketing systems – can help salespeople identify and qualify potential new customer leads.

The Internet is also proving to be a useful technology for providing leads for potential new customers. While increasing numbers of firms are soliciting orders directly via a home page on the Internet, many – particularly those selling relatively complex goods or services – use their Internet sites primarily to provide technical product information to customers or potential customers. These firms can then have their salespeople follow up technical enquiries from potential new accounts with a more traditional sales call.

Assessing salesforce effectiveness

There are five essential questions to ask in assessing salesforce effectiveness:

- *Is the selling effort structured for effective market coverage?* You should think about organisation, size of salesforce and territory deployment.

- *Is the salesforce staffed with the right people?* You should think about the type of international salesforce: expatriates/host country/third country, age/tenure/education profile, interpersonal skills, technical capabilities and selling technique.

- *Is strong guidance provided?* You should think about written guidelines, key tasks/mission definition, call frequency, time allocation, people to be seen, market/account focus, territory planning and control tools, and on-the-job coaching.

- *Is adequate sales support in place?* You should think about training, technical back-up, in-house sales staff, and product and applications literature.

- *Does the sales compensation plan provide the proper motivation?* You should think about total compensation, split of **straight salary/straight commission**, incentive design/fit with management objectives and non-cash incentives.

Straight salary
Compensation at a regular rate, not immediately tied to sales performance.

Straight commission
Remuneration based strictly on sales performance.

In the following we will go into further detail with the first two questions.

Own or outsourced salesforce?

One important aspect involved in 'getting the salesforce right' is the crucial decision of whether to outsource it. In the language of outsourcing, firms can choose to 'own' their own sales force; that is, use a salesforce comprised of employees as salespeople, which is also known as going direct. On the other hand, firms can choose to 'rent' a salesforce by contracting with an independent sales organisation, also known as a manufacturers' representative, to act as its salesforce. At first glance, it might seem strange for a firm to rent a function as important as its salesforce, but both research and practical experience have shown that, in many cases, opting for manufacturers' representatives is an appropriate way to organise the salesforce, although this is not to suggest that all firms should choose to do so. There are many reasons to go with one's own salesforce, and those reasons may sometimes outweigh the reasons for going with rep agencies (see Figure 14.7).

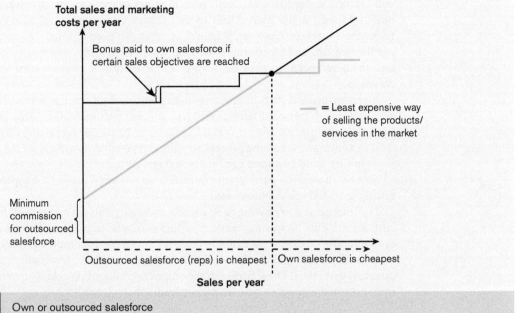

Figure 14.7 Own or outsourced salesforce

One of the most interesting decisions for a firm to make is when to switch from an outsourced salesforce to having its own salesforce. Figure 14.7 shows the total sales and marketing costs associated with using the two different distribution ways:

● *Outsourced salesforce (sales reps)*: This curve is based on a contract where the salesperson gets a minimum annual commission independent of annual sales. The salesforce will get the same percentage in commission independent of how much they will generate in annual sales.

● *Own salesforce*: This curve is based on the assumption that the salesforce will get a fixed salary per annum (independent of the annual sales), but will be paid an extra bonus if they fulfil certain sales objectives.

Under these circumstances there will be a certain break-even point from where it is most advantageous (from a financial standpoint) to switch from sales reps to own salesforce.

In reality, the most appropriate system often combines own salesforce and sales reps, with the choice being determined by other issues such as control, flexibility, territory, product class or even particular tasks that the salesforce must perform (Ross *et al.*, 2005; Crittenden and Crittenden, 2004).

Organisation of the international salesforce

In international markets, firms often organise their salesforces in a similar way to their domestic salesforce, regardless of differences from one country to another. This means that the salesforce is organised by geography, product, customer or some combination of these (Table 14.4).

A number of firms organise their international salesforce along simple geographical territories within a given country or region. Firms that have broad product lines and a large sales volume, and/or operate in large, developed markets may prefer more specialised organisations, such as product or customer assignment. The firm may also organise the salesforce based on other factors such as culture or languages spoken in the targeted foreign markets. For example, firms often divide Switzerland into different regions reflecting French, Italian and German language usage.

Table 14.4	Salesforce organisational structure		

Structure	Factors favouring choice of organisational structure	Advantages	Disadvantages
Geographic	• Distinct languages/cultures • Single product line • Underdeveloped markets	• Clear, simple • Incentive to cultivate local business and personal ties • Travel expenses	• Breadth of customers • Breadth of products
Product	• Established market • Broad product lines	• Product knowledge	• Travel expenses • Overlapping territories/ customers • Local business and personal ties
Customer*	• Broad product lines	• Market/customer knowledge	• Overlapping territories/products • Local business and personal ties • Travel expenses
Combination	• Large sales volume • Large/developed markets • Distinct language/cultures	• Maximum flexibility • Travel expenses	• Complexity • Sales management • Product/market/ geography overlap

*By type of industry, size of account, channel of distribution, individual company.

Source: Hollensen, S. (2001) *Global Marketing: A Market Responsive Approach*, 2nd ed., Financial Times-Prentice Hall, Harlow, p. 538. Reproduced with permission.

14.5 TRADE FAIRS AND EXHIBITIONS

Trade fairs, exhibitions or trade shows are major communication tools for marketers today. They account for about 20 per cent of the total communication budget for US industrial firms and about 25 per cent of the budget for European firms (Shoham, 1999).

A trade fair or exhibition is an event at which manufacturers, distributors and other vendors display their products and/or describe their services to current and prospective customers, suppliers, other business associates and the press. Figure 14.8 shows that trade fairs (TFs) are multi-purpose events involving many interactions between the TF exhibitor and numerous parties.

As TFs are very often annual affairs and have a mix of business and quasi-social events, buyers can maintain their contacts with sellers and other users. This is a long-term motive for a current buyer to attend and exhibit. Although they will not be repeating their purchase in the near term, it is important for them to maintain a relationship with sellers and others whom they may call upon for solutions to future problems.

TFs can enable a company to reach a group of interested prospects in a few days which might otherwise take several months to contact. Potential buyers can examine and compare the products of competing firms in a short period at the same place. They can see the latest developments and establish immediate contact with suppliers (Fowdar, 2004).

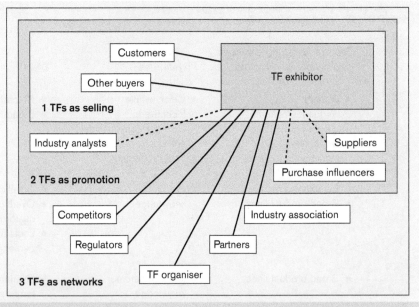

Figure 14.8	Three concepts of trade fairs: major interactions for a local exhibitor

Source: Adapted from Rosson, P. J. and Seringhaus, F. H. R. (1995), Visitor and exhibitor interaction at industrial trade fairs, *Journal of Business Research*, 32(1): 81–90. Reproduced with permission from Elsevier and P. J. Rosson.

Traditionally, TFs have been regarded as a personal selling tool, but Sharland and Balogh (1996) conclude that TFs are an excellent environment for non-selling activities such as information exchange, relationship building and channel partner assessment. TFs offer international firms the opportunity to gather vital information quickly, easily and cheaply. For example, within a short period a firm can learn a considerable amount about its competitive environment, which would take much longer and cost much more to get through other sources (e.g. secondary information).

Attendance at TFs is often viewed by a company as a reward to its employees. This motivation is consistent with the motive ascribed to selling companies in prior research: the use of exhibitions as a tool to build the morale of the salesforce (Godar and O'Connor, 2001).

We conclude this section by listing the arguments for and against participation in TFs.

Arguments for participation in TFs

- Marketers are able to reach a sizeable number of potential customers in a brief time period at a reasonable cost per contact. Orders may be obtained on the spot.

- Some products, by their very nature, are difficult to market without providing the potential customer with a chance to examine them or see them in action. TFs provide an excellent opportunity to introduce, promote and demonstrate new products.

- SMEs without extensive salesforces have the opportunity to present their products to large buying companies on the same face-to-face basis as large local rivals.

- Finding an intermediary may be one of the best reasons to attend a TF. A show is a cost-effective way to solicit and screen candidates to represent the firm, especially in a new market.

- Although many technical specialists and company executives refuse to see or take telephone calls from outsiders who try to sell them things at their places of work, these same managers often attend trade exhibitions. The customer goes to the exhibition in order to see the seller. This is also an important aspect in the concept of reverse marketing or buyer initiative (see, for example, Figure 14.3).

- An appearance also produces goodwill and improves the corporate image. Beyond the impact of displaying specific products, many firms place strong emphasis on 'waving the company flag' against competition. This facet also includes supporting the morale of the firm's sales personnel and intermediaries.

- TFs provide an excellent chance for market research and collecting competitive intelligence. The marketer is able to view most rivals at the same time and to test comparative buyer reactions.

- Visitors' names and addresses may be used for subsequent mailshots.

Arguments against participation in TFs

- There is a high cost in terms of the time and administrative effort needed to prepare an exhibition stand in a foreign country. However, a marketer can lower costs by sharing expenses with distributors or representatives. Furthermore, the costs of closing a sale through TFs are estimated to be much lower than those for a sale closed through personal representation.

- It is difficult to choose the appropriate TFs to attend. This is a critical decision. Because of scarce resources, many firms rely on suggestions from their foreign distributors on which TFs to attend and what specifically to exhibit.

- Coordination problems may arise. In LSEs with multiple divisions, more divisions may be required to participate in the same TF under the company banner. In SMEs coordination is required with distributors and agents if joint participation is desired, and this necessitates joint planning.

- Furthermore, the firm faces a lot of practical problems. For example, most people visit exhibitions to browse rather than to buy. How does the exhibiting firm obtain the names and addresses of the visitors who influence major buying decisions within their companies? Second, gimmicks may be highly effective in attracting visitors to a stand, but they can attract the wrong people. An audience may be greatly impressed by the music, dancing, demonstration or whatever is provided, yet not be remotely interested in the product. Third, how can the employees who staff a stand be prevented from treating the exercise as a holiday, paying more attention to the social aspects of their involvement with the exhibition than to finding customers? What specific targets can the staff be given and how can the attainment of targets be measured?

Whether a marketer should participate in a trade fair depends largely on the type of business relationship it wants to develop with a particular country. A company looking only for one-off or short-term sales might find the expense prohibitive, but a firm looking to build long-term relationships may find the investment worthwhile.

Trade fairs enable exhibitors to deliver their selling message to a large number of people at one time, thus providing an opportunity for face-to-face contact that is lacking in most other promotions and advertising media. This advantage is more important for internationally active firms, given the prohibitive costs of sales visits to foreign markets.

14.6 IMPLICATIONS OF THE INTERNET FOR COMMUNICATION DECISIONS

In the physical marketplace different communication tools are used in the buying process of customers (see Figure 14.9). Traditional mass communication tools (print advertising, TV and radio) can create awareness and this can result in consumers' identification of new needs. From then on other elements of the communication mix take over, such as direct marketing (direct marketing, personal selling) and in-store promotion. Unlike marketing in the physical

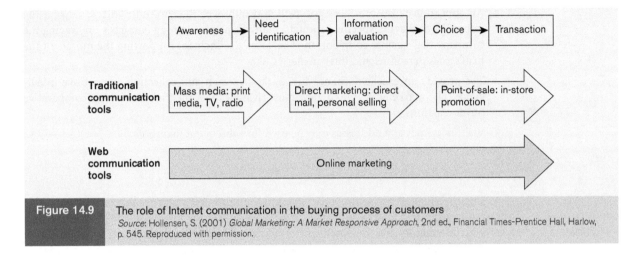

Figure 14.9 The role of Internet communication in the buying process of customers
Source: Hollensen, S. (2001) *Global Marketing: A Market Responsive Approach*, 2nd ed., Financial Times-Prentice Hall, Harlow, p. 545. Reproduced with permission.

marketplace the Internet/e-commerce encompasses the entire 'buying' process. Of course, the online markets also make use of traditional mass advertising in order to get potential customers into the online buying process (from the left in Figure 14.9)

Market communication strategies change dramatically in the online world. On the Internet it is easier than ever to actually *communicate* a message to large numbers of people. However, in many cases it is much harder for your message to be heard above the noise by your target audience. Various strategies for conducting online marketing have been developed in the past several years – from the most common (website linking) to the most expensive (banner advertising) to the most offensive (e-mail spamming), and everything in between. It is almost certain that a continual stream of new market communication strategies will emerge as the Internet medium evolves.

How, then, can a Web audience be created? One of the new possibilities in this field is viral marketing.

Viral marketing

Global selling and buying is part of a social process. It involves not only a one-to-one interaction between the company and the customer but also many exchanges of information and influence among the people who surround the customer.

For example, diffusion occurs when an innovation is communicated through certain channels among members of a social system. An innovation is an idea, practice or object that an individual or unit of adoption perceives as new (Rogers, 1995). According to Rogers, mass media channels are relatively more important for learning about an innovation, whereas interpersonal communication is especially important for persuasion. Thus, consumers communicating via e-mail may be persuaded more readily than those via mass media advertising.

Passing along e-mail is even easier than writing comments. Beyond this, pass-along e-mail seems particularly well suited for the spread of images and/or verbal content that is too detailed to be disseminated via word of mouth (Chiarelli, 2006).

The Internet has radically changed the concept of word-of-mouth, so much so that the term **viral marketing** was coined by venture capitalist Steve Jurvetson in 1997. The term was used to describe Hotmail's e-mail practice of appending advertising for itself to outgoing mail from its users. In the Hotmail case each e-mail sent arrived with the appended message, 'Get your private, free e-mail from Hotmail at http://www.hotmail.com.'

The assumption is that if such an advertisement reaches a 'susceptible' user, that user will become 'infected' (i.e. sign up for an account) and can then go on to infect other susceptible users.

Viral marketing
Online word-of-mouth is a marketing technique that seeks to exploit existing social networks to produce exponential increases in brand awareness.

Definition

Viral marketing can be defined as a marketing technique that seeks to exploit pre-existing social networks to produce exponential increases in brand awareness through viral processes similar to the spread of an epidemic. It is word-of-mouth delivered and enhanced online; it harnesses the network effect of the Internet and can be very useful in reaching a large number of people rapidly. From a marketing perspective, it is the process of encouraging individuals to pass along favourable or compelling marketing information they receive in a hypermedia environment: information that is favourable or compelling either by design or by accident.

Motives for viral marketing

The creation of technologies such as SMS technology (Johar, 2008), satellite radio and Internet ad blocking software are driving a fundamental shift in the way the public consumes media and the advertising often tied to it. Television ads, radio spots, online ads and even e-mails are facing increasing competition for effectively capturing the viewer's attention and provide positive ROI for the marketer. Additionally, consumers are becoming increasingly immune to mass marketing and advertising, so this form of marketing offers something that does not feel like they are being sold to, making them more receptive to the offer (Koppelmann and Groeger, 2009).

This competition, coupled with the rising cost of media buys, has caused marketers to search for an alternative means to reach the customer. Viral marketing is an attractive solution because it utilises the free endorsement of the individual rather than purchasing mass media to spread the word. Because the distribution model is free, viral can potentially be lower cost and more effective than traditional media (Esch *et al.*, 2009).

Advantages of viral marketing

- It incurs very little expense since the individual passing on the referral carries the cost of forwarding the brand message. Viral marketing offers SMEs the opportunity to target a whole new set of customers while keeping distribution costs to a minimum.

- Unlike traditional advertising, viral is not an interruptive technique. Instead, viral campaigns work the Internet to deliver exposure via peer-to-peer endorsement. Viral campaigns, whether ultimately liked or disliked, are often welcomed by the receiver. The act of forwarding electronic messages containing advertising is voluntary rather than a paid **testimonial** or a mass ad campaign and thus may be viewed more favourably by the recipient. The focus is on campaigns containing material that consumers want to spend time interacting with and spreading proactively.

- Those forwarding the messages will be more likely to know which of their friends, family members and work colleagues have similar interests and are thus more likely to read the message: hence, more effective targeting. Here, the term 'interests' refers not only to the narrow sense of just the product or service but also includes the way the message is presented, such as the humour, the artwork or the medium itself.

Testimonial
A type of advertising in which a person, usually a well-known or public figure, states that he or she owns, uses or supports the product being advertised.

Disadvantages of viral marketing

Viral marketing, like all marketing, is hit or miss. However, viral marketing by nature is often more risky or controversial than traditional marketing. If done improperly viral marketing can backfire and create negative buzz:

- If particular software is needed that is not widely used, then people will not be able to open or view the message.

- Many people receive viral marketing messages while at the office, and company anti-virus software or firewalls can prevent people from receiving or viewing any attachments.

- For a viral marketing campaign to be successful, it must be easy to use. For example, if the promotion is some sort of game or contest, then asking for referrals should be an option immediately after the game, not as a condition to play.

Developing a viral marketing campaign

Viral marketing is by no means a substitute for a comprehensive and diversified marketing strategy. In employing viral marketing to generate peer-to-peer endorsement, the technique should not be considered as a standalone miracle worker.

While the messaging and strategy ranges radically from campaign to campaign, most successful campaigns contain some commonly used approaches. These approaches are often used in combination to maximise the viral effect of a campaign.

Successful viral campaigns are easily spread. The key is to get your customers to do the hard work for you by recommending your company or its promotional offers to friends and colleagues, who in turn will recommend it to their friends and so on. An effective viral marketing campaign can get your marketing message out to thousands of potential customers at phenomenal speeds.

When creating a campaign marketers should evaluate how people will communicate the message or campaign to others.

Creating compelling content

Creating quality content can often be more expensive than simply offering a free product, but the results are often better. Fun is often a vital part of any viral marketing campaign. The general rule of thumb is that the content must be compelling, it must evoke a response on an emotional level from the person viewing it. This fact alone has allowed many smaller brands to capitalise on content-based viral campaigns. Traditionally, larger brands are more reserved and risk averse to the possibility of negative reaction. Central to the success of these campaigns is one or more of the following: their entry timing (early), their visibility or the simplicity of the idea.

Targeting the right audience

If a campaign is skewed towards a certain audience or certain regions (countries), marketers should make sure they seed (see below) towards that audience. Failure to do so may kill a campaign before it ever gets off the ground.

The influence and, in some cases, the power of reference groups or opinion leaders in individual decision making is significant.

Campaign seeding

'Seeding' the original message is a key component of a viral campaign. Seeding is the act of planting the campaign with the initial group who will then go on to spread the campaign to others. The Internet provides a wide array of options for seeding, including:

- e-mail/SMS
- online forums (e.g. Google groups)
- social networks (e.g. Facebook.com, MySpace.com)
- chatroom environment (e.g. MSN Messenger)
- blogs
- podcasts.

When determining where to seed it is important that marketers consider the audience they are aiming for. Is the target audience using the above-mentioned media (technologies) and to what degree?

Companies often use a combination of technologies to 'spread the virus'. Many use SMS. An example of an SMS campaign is that of Heineken, which linked an SMS promotion with the British pub tradition of playing quiz games. Heineken combined both online and offline promotions through point-of-sale signs in pubs, inviting customers to call from their mobile phones, type in the wordplay and receive a series of multiple-choice questions to answer. Food and beverage prizes were awarded for correct answers. From a promotional perspective, the idea was successful as customers told others what they were doing, prompting them to call in too.

Control/measuring results

The goal of a viral campaign is explosive reach and participation. To measure the success of a viral marketing campaign, establish specific and obtainable goals within a timeframe. For example, you would like to see a 20 per cent increase in traffic to a website within three months or to double your subscriber rate to an e-mail newsletter in one year.

Marketers should also be adequately prepared to meet the needs of participants in the event that the campaign is successful. Server space, bandwidth, support staff, fulfilment and stocking should be taken into consideration well in advance of campaign launch. The marketer should have the ability to capitalise on the full success of the campaign.

EXHIBIT 14.2
Philips 'Quintippio' viral ad campaign (created by advertising agency Tribal DDB)

In November 2005 a viral website with a fictional 15-bladed razor was developed in order to create some buzz and make fun of the real-life introduction of the four-bladed Schick Quattro and the five-bladed Fusion by Gillette in October 2005.

On the website it was possible to download an ad that had also run on TV. The script of the commercial proclaimed: 'Looking for a close shave? Then you're looking for the new Quintippio Mega Shave, now with 15 extra large blades!' A new product, 'Quintippio Multi-Shave', opens the spot and we find out that it has 15 blades. Then a puzzled man looks at it, wondering how he is going to shave his face with it. A voiceover says, 'Everyone's talking more blades – we're talking less irritation.' The selling point is an electric shaver that has a pump for dispensing Nivea skin cream as a shaving lubricant and moisturiser. The spot ends with the claim, 'As close as a blade with less irritation.'

The commercial is genuinely funny – it uses humour to serve the advertising strategy and reinforce the brand positioning. Philips makes fun of both Gillette and Schick for their multi-blade obsession.

Here is what works:

- *Norelco makes the category leader look out of touch*: although the end-benefit of 'multi-blade' is supposed to be 'close shave', it is not clear that either Gillette or Schick remembers this. Gillette's macho, tech-oriented advertising is so obsessed with the product that it seems to forget the consumer in the process.

- *Cool Shave focuses on a relevant, ownable end-benefit*: 'We're talking about less irritation', which presumably is a secondary benefit for many users but not owned by any male shaving system. This spot does a good job of using humour, voiceover, visuals and co-branding (with Nivea) to reinforce this end-benefit. The humour is used to reinforce the brand positioning.

- *Humour reinforces the brand positioning*: showing that Gillette and Schick don't 'get it' with their blade-spawning razors, and focusing on a different benefit, is worlds more effective than trying to argue that rotary shavers have more blades than multi-blade razors, for example.

That the issue raised in the commercial is relevant is underlined by the 'serious' magazine *The Economist*, which took up the 'Blade running' issue.

→

EXHIBIT 14.2
Philips 'Quintippio' viral ad campaign (created by
advertising agency Tribal DDB) (*continued*)

The article discusses whether Moore's law can be transferred from computer chips to a number of razor blades. The article concludes that the most likely projection is that if the so-called power-law curve is followed then the 14-bladed razor should arrive in year 2100. But, as we have seen, the fictional Philips 15-blade razor is already here, and so are the discussions in the media and among Internet users – so Philips has reached its goals for its viral marketing campaign.

Sources: Adapted from WorldNet Daily (2005) Razor wars: 15-blade fever, *WorldNet Daily* (www.wnd.com), 26 November; Economist, The (2006) The cutting edge: Moore's law for razor blades, *The Economist*, 16 March.

14.7 SUMMARY

Mass customisation is the capability, realised by a few companies, to offer individually tailored products or services on a large scale. One-to-one marketing aims to customise a product offering so carefully that it fits the customer perfectly. Both trends mean that the firm has to communicate more and more directly to customers.

Five aspects of communication have been presented in this chapter:

- Advertising
- Public relations
- Sales promotion
- Direct marketing
- Personal selling.

As marketers manage the various elements of the promotional mix in differing environmental conditions, decisions must be made about what channels are to be used in the communication, the message, who is to execute or help execute the programme, and how the results of the communication plan are to be measured.

Personal selling is the marketing task involving face-to-face contact with the customer. Unlike advertising, promotion, sponsorship and other forms of non-personal communication, personal selling permits direct interaction between buyer and seller. This two-way communication means that the seller can identify the specific needs and problems of the buyer and tailor the sales presentation to provide this background information.

Some communication tools, especially personal selling, have to be localised to fit the conditions of individual markets. Another reason for localisation of the personal selling tool is that distribution channel members are normally located firmly within a country. Consequently, decisions concerning recruitment, training, motivation and evaluation of salespeople have to be made at the local level.

A very important communication tool for the future is the Internet. Any company eager to take advantage of the Internet on a global scale must select a business model for its Internet ventures and estimate how information and transactions delivered through this new direct marketing medium will influence its existing distribution and communication system.

Viral marketing is by no means a substitute for a comprehensive and diversified marketing strategy. Viral marketing is a credible marketing tactic that can deliver positive ROI when properly executed as a component of an overarching strategic plan. Marketers should utilise viral marketing when the messaging can coincide with and support a measurable business goal.

CASE STUDY 14.1

TAG Heuer
The famous Swiss watch maker is using celebrity endorsement as a worldwide communication strategy

The world luxury watch market

At present, Swiss-made watches are completely dominating the worldwide luxury watch market, contributing almost 100 per cent share. These watches are exported to most of the developed countries. However, rising incomes in emerging markets have led to a new category of affluent young professionals with high purchasing power. These countries have become a potential opportunity for ultra expensive watch manufacturers.

Generally, the total watch market can be divided into the following price segments:

- mass price market: under €50
- middle price market: €50–299
- upper price market: €300–999
- luxury price market: €1,000 and above.

Furthermore, there is the 'horlogerie' market, with high complications and jewellery. Watches are priced €10,000 and above. Examples of brands are Patek Philippe, Zenith and Jaeger-LeCoultre.

Traditionally considered a male domain, women are also driving up sales now. Women are more fashion oriented. Luxury watch makers are trying their best to design the female equivalent of their most popular watch models. Women change watches more frequently – they seem to be attracted to quartz instead of mechanic, because then they do not need to set the time before wearing it. Women are also attracted by jewellery pieces (diamonds, etc.). Another notable trend is the integration of new technology and the use of unconventional materials in luxury watches. Also, all major brands are trying to raise their price levels by repositioning their products.

The world demand for luxury watches by region is shown in Table 14.5.

Rolex dominates the world luxury watch market (approximately €20 billion in manufacturers' selling prices) with around 40 per cent market share, followed by Omega (15–20 per cent MS), TAG Heuer (15–20 per cent MS), Breitling, Cartier, Bulgari, Chopard, Ebel, Girard-Perregaux, Jaeger-LeCoultre Longines and Patek Philippe.

Counterfeit products remain a problem in the industry. The lost value of this part represents 5–10 per cent of the total world market for luxury products. The main market for counterfeit goods is still the United States, representing over 66 per cent of global demand, and 80 per cent of demand for counterfeit products is for Rolex only. The remaining 20 per cent is divided up between the other 24 brands analysed. Japan is the only country in which there are more searches for counterfeit goods on Omega than Rolex.

Background of TAG Heuer

Founded by Edouard Heuer in 1860 at Saint-Imier in the Swiss Jura, TAG Heuer has now been in the vanguard of Swiss watchmaking for nearly 150 years. Soon after Edouard Heuer set up the company's first workshop in Switzerland, it patented the first chronograph mechanism and followed that up with a series of inventions that shaped the future of watches.

From the first patent for a chronograph mechanism in 1882, Heuer has written some of the finest chapters in watchmaking history. By 1966 Heuer had developed

Table 14.5	World demand of luxury watches by region	
Region	**Regional market share (%)**	**Main countries**
Europe	44	UK (14%), Germany (12%), Italy (10%), France (8%)
USA	43	
Asia	13	China (6%), Japan (5%), India (2%)
Total	100	

Source: Adapted from *World Watch Report 2009: Industry Report of Watches and Watchmakers* (WWR).

the Microtimer, the first one-1,000th of a second chronograph. And the company is still pioneering today. This has made TAG Heuer the inescapable reference brand in motor sports.

TAG Heuer's first ambassador of the brand was Jo Siffert and the first sponsoring contract was also signed with this Swiss driver, who became friends with Steve McQueen while teaching him driving skills on the set of the movie *Le Mans*. McQueen wore the Heuer Monaco chronograph in the movie, which made the timepiece an icon of the brand.

After the Swiss-based Techniques d'Avant Garde group took over TAG Heuer from the Heuer family in 1984, Christian Viros was hired as CEO to save the company from financial difficulties. The company had been hit by the recession in the early 1980s and the TAG Heuer brand was seen more as associated with scientific and timing instruments than a luxury brand. CEO Christian Viros transformed TAG Heuer into a lifestyle brand by concentrating on design and marketing. But his masterstroke was focusing on an association with sports. The sports-watch market was a new niche and Viros cornered it with advertisements featuring stars such as French skiing champion Luc Alphand and Formula 1 racing driver Ayrton Senna.

This strategy remains to this day. In addition to celebrities such as Uma Thurman and Brad Pitt (only from 2005 to 2008), its 'faces' include Tiger Woods, Maria Sharapova, Formula 1 world champions Kimi Räikkönen and Lewis Hamilton, and more recently Leonardo DiCaprio. The firm further exploits these associations when Formula 1 drivers test new prototypes during races, submitting them to extreme G-forces, vibration and shock.

In 1985, TAG Heuer became the chronograph of the McLaren team and won several Formula 1 world championships on the wrists of Niki Lauda, Alain Prost, Ayrton Senna and Lewis Hamilton. At the same time, it became the official timer of the Formula 1 World Championship, timing to the thousandth of a second, before becoming the official timer of the Indy 500 in 2004, timing to the ten-thousandth of a second – a feature that today remains unequalled.

Venture capital firm Doughty Hanson bought the business in the mid-1990s and later cashed out in a public flotation before luxury goods conglomerate Louis Vuitton Moët Hennesy (LVMH) bought the company for around $800 million in 1999.

In 2000 Jean-Christophe Babin was appointed CEO. He has reduced the product range from 800 to 200 lines in the past four years and is looking more closely at women's watches. Babin has also segmented the watch models into 'families'. Babin is also behind other successes, such as Heuer models brimming with nostalgia and images.

Today TAG Heuer is still an independent division under LVMH and considered a star brand of the group.

TAG Heuer employs 350 staff in the headquarters and factory in Switzerland and another 2,000 (inluding LVMH watch and jewellery staff) worldwide, organised in subsidiaries located in the most dynamic markets.

TAG Heuer's marketing strategy

By sponsoring sports where technology and accuracy are paramount, TAG has polished its reputation for precision while positioning itself as a luxury brand appealing to early achievers. Until now TAG's target market has been college-educated 30- to 40-year-olds: every year approximately 3 per cent of them buy a new luxury watch costing €1,000 or more.

The female sector is a potential growth market for TAG Heuer. Historically, TAG Heuer only sold 20 per cent of their watches to ladies, but they are now on their way to 40 per cent. Ladies buy more watches for themselves than men. 'If we want to double our female buyers, we need strong female communication and lady endorsers.' This is why Maria Sharapova and Uma Thurman have been integrated. Their determination, talent, success and strong characters fit well with the brand values of TAG Heuer, so they can help with gaining market share for TAG Heuer in a segment where they are under-represented. In 2008, Uma Thurman's contract came to an end and was not renewed due to the economic crisis, which has also been the main reason why TAG Heuer, from 2009, has decided to concentrate on core business. Even if the 'Women Strategy' remains in place, the choice was made to concentrate on acquired market shares. The existence of a second female ambassador was set '*entre parenthèses*' until the world economy shows signs of growth again.

TAG's average watch price is now approaching €1,500. As a result of its brand positioning TAG Heuer's revenues steadily increased from just €25 million in 1988 to over €1 billion in 2008.

With over 8,000 retailers globally stocking TAG, its annual sales of around 900,000 watches (2008) give it a 15–20 per cent share of the world luxury watch market.

Perhaps the best proof of TAG's success is that, having homed in on the lower end of the luxury market, it opened this sector up to watches from fashion brands such as Diesel, Fossil and Calvin Klein. TAG's greatest challenge to come could be differentiating itself from these newcomers as well as the upper end of connoisseur's timepieces. This recent strategy of the brand is also reinforced with the launch of the luxury line Grand Carrera in 2007 (priced €3,000–€5,000), which increases the average retail price and further differentiates from 'fashion' watches, supported by an intensive communication of know-how and heritage.

One of the main challenges for TAG Heuer's communication strategy is to be well represented on the Internet. However, brand advertising on official websites is no longer enough. The social networks are gaining marketing power: Facebook has now nearly 200 million members and, according to the World Watch Report 2009, Cartier is dominating Facebook with 30,000 fans, followed by TAG Heuer (18,500), Rolex (17,500), Bulgari (14,300) and Breitling (13,600). On YouTube 100 million videos are viewed monthly. Videos uploaded by fans are now taking up 38 per cent of brand visibility.

TAG Heuer's celebrity endorsement strategy

Since becoming CEO and president of Swiss watch firm TAG Heuer 10 years ago, Jean-Christophe Babin has put together a portfolio of global and local brand ambassadors and endorsers.

According to the Global Watch Report 2009, the top luxury watch ambassador in the industry represents Omega, accounting for 17 per cent of total Internet searches. Omega uses the 'Michael Phelps effect' (the American swimmer beat the Gold Medal record in a single Olympics, winning 8 in the 2008 Beijing Olympic Games).

Six of TAG Heuer's ambassadors are ranked in the top 20. At the top of the line is golfer Tiger Woods, who garners 15 per cent of Internet searches, followed by Bollywood star Shah Rukh Khan (7 per cent), Formula 1 racing driver Lewis Hamilton (4 per cent), actor Leonardo DiCaprio (3 per cent), tennis star Maria Sharapova (3 per cent) and deceased actor Steve McQueen (2 per cent).

TAG Heuer has enjoyed success through creating bespoke products for local markets, endorsed by local ambassadors such as Bollywood star Shah Rukh Khan, who is the main reason for the TAG Heuer growth in India. Yao Ming (the US-based Chinese basketball player) helped TAG Heuer to grow the brand in China (contract from 2005 to 2006) and it enabled the company to catch up with competitors that have been in this market much longer than TAG Heuer.

TAG Heuer's ambassadors are encouraged to participate in product development and this is what makes TAG Heuer ambassadors different from those of any other brand (see also the following examples of celebrity endorsements).

Examples

In 2008 tennis star Maria Sharapova launched her new TAG Heuer Formula 1 glamour diamonds watch with 120 diamonds. The price of this watch is around €2,000 in retail stores (see also YouTube video regarding Sharapova's launch of the watch: www.youtube.com/watch?v=z8gtDG97q-Q; www.youtube.com/watch?v= fmYuHQkSyTw).

The rare square case of the original TAG Heuer Monaco reshaped the way people look at watches and of watch making. The TAG Heuer Monaco was launched in 1969 (by Jack Heuer, today Honorary Chairman of TAG Heuer) and it was the world's first chronograph equipped with a microrotor for automatic rewinding.

At the prestigious 2009 World Watch Fair in Basel, TAG Heuer celebrated the 40th anniversary of the first introduction of the TAG Heuer Monaco by unveiling two special watches just for this occasion: the Monaco Twenty-Four Concept Chronograph and the Monaco Calibre 12 Chronograph Gulf Limited Edition.

The Monaco was the world's first square-cased chronograph, designed to match Steve McQueen's suit in the movie *Le Mans* (which itself was a replica of that worn by Jo Siffert, the first driver sponsored by TAG Heuer). His legendary Porsche Gulf 917 K, one of the most celebrated automobiles in motor racing, was only

The 40th Anniversary Monaco watch
Source: Courtesy of TAG Heuer SA

Steve McQueen in the movie *Le Mans*
Source: Collection CSFF/© Rue des Archives

The TAG Heuer Meridiist mobile
Source: Courtesy of TAG Heuer SA

produced from 1969 to 1973. Equipped with a 600+ horsepower, 5-litre engine and capable of speeds up to 362 km/h, its success surpassed all expectations, winning Le Mans in 1970 and 1971.

For his driving scenes in *Le Mans*, Steve McQueen insisted he was equipped with the complete driving suit of his friend Jo Siffert, which, of course, included the Monaco chronograph. The presence of the Monaco on the actor's wrist helped contribute to its legend, but it was above all its avant-garde style and its complete break with tradition that enabled it to become one of TAG Heuer's most sought-after icons.

The limited edition numbers 5,000 watches and the price is around €2,900 (see also YouTube video regarding launch of the watch: www.youtube.com/watch?v= j3iLvLpn-KY).

TAG Heuer's diversification strategy

Besides introducing eyewear, with a range of sunglasses and frames for prescription glasses, TAG Heuer has also introduced a mobile phone. In 2008 TAG Heuer's luxurious first handset was introduced, the TAG Heuer Meridiist handset.

The handset itself was developed in partnership with Modelabs and the mobile phone features a 2-megapixel camera, all-metal casing, 1.9-inch QVGA display, Bluetooth, multimedia player, sapphire crystal screen and a battery that will last around the seven-hour mark. Since TAG Heur has been a long-time timepiece maker, the first cell phone designed by them will have a more outstanding way to display the time. This is a new mobile phone with luxury and elegance in mind. The TAG Heuer Meridiist costs €3,400 to €3,900 depending on what customisations are requested.

Also in 2008, TAG Heuer launched a line of lifestyle accessories selling in TAG Heuer boutiques worldwide.

QUESTIONS

1 What is the target group for the Tag Heuer Meridiist mobile phone?

2 How are these TAG Heuer endorsers communicating to different end customer groups:

 - Maria Sharapova?
 - Kimi Räikkönen?
 - Leonardo DiCaprio?

3 Are multi-product brands better positioned to grasp the opportunity presented by social networks on the Internet?

4 Is uploading of videos on YouTube an opportunity for TAG Heuer to support these fans who often have a high power of persuasion on watch buyers' choice of watch brand?

5 Please propose a future communication strategy for TAG Heuer.

SOURCES

Davies, D. (2005) TAG Heuer: famous faces for watches, - *Independent*, 12 September; IC Agency/Europa Star (2009) *World Watch Report 2009: Industry Report of Watches and Watchmakers (WWR)*, IC Agency, Geneva; Sylt, C. (2007) Perfect timing: TAG Heuer chief executive Jean-Christophe Babin on maintaining the brand's reputation for brilliance, *bmiVoyager*, March (www.bmivoyager.com/2007/03/01/perfect-timing/); TAG Heuer (www.tagheuer.com).

QUESTIONS FOR DISCUSSION

1 What is the difference between 'mass customisation' and one-to-one marketing?

2 What are the implications of one-to-one marketing for the communications strategy of a firm?

3 Identify and discuss problems associated with assessing advertising effectiveness in foreign markets.

4 Compare domestic communication with international communication. Explain why 'noise' is more likely to occur in the case of international communication processes.

5 Why do more companies not standardise advertising messages worldwide? Identify the environmental constraints that act as barriers to the development and implementation of standardised global advertising campaigns.

6 Explain how personal selling may differ overseas from how it is used in the home market.

7 What is meant by saying that advertising regulations vary around the world?

8 Evaluate the percentage of sales approach to setting advertising budgets in foreign markets.

9 Explain how the multinational firm may have an advantage over local firms in training the sales force and evaluating its performance.

10 Identify and discuss problems associated with allocating the company's promotion budget across several foreign markets.

REFERENCES

Adage Global (2001) International campaign to reduce birth rate among cats, *Adage Global*, 5 April (www.adageglobal.com).

Agrawal, M., Kumaresh, T. V. and Mercer, G. A. (2001) The false promise of mass customisation, *McKinsey Quarterly*, 3: 62–71.

Autoliv (2000) Autoliv and Volvo launch new safety system, Autoliv press release, 4 September.

Baird, R. (1997) Patent place, *Marketing Week*, 14 March.

Balfour, F. (1993) Alcohol industry: companies in high spirits, *China Trade Report*, June: 4–5.

BBC (2000a) Analysis: Europe's car industry, *BBC Business News*, 12 May (http://news.bbc.co.uk).

BBC (2000b) Automotives empire, *BBC Business News*, 3 June (http://news.bbc.co.uk).

BBC (2001) Ferrari fuelled by new deal, *BBC Business News*, 25 May (http://news.bbc.co.uk).

Bennett, R. (1995) *International Marketing: Strategy, Planning, Market Entry and Implementation*, Kogan Page, London.

Beverage Industry (1999) Beer is Dutch, *Beverage Industry*, 90(9): 9.

Beverage Industry (2000) Europeans attack American brewers, *Beverage Industry*, 91(1): 10.

Biegel, B. A. (2007) The megatrends: what to expect in direct and interactive marketing in 2010, *Journal of Direct, Data and Digital Marketing Practice*, 9(2): 122–33.

Billing, C. (1994) No to Joe Camel, *China Trade Report*, December: 9.

Boddewyn, J. J., Soehl, R. and Picard, J. (1986) Standardisation in international marketing: is Ted Levitt in fact right? *Business Horizons*, 69–75.

Boyd, H. W., Walker, Jr, O. C. and Larréché, J.-C. (1998) *Marketing Management: A Strategic Approach with a Global Orientation*, Irwin McGraw-Hill.

Brand Strategy (2006) When B2B is hard to be, *Brand Strategy*, July/August: 48–9.

BusinessWeek (1984) Advertising Europe's new common market, *BusinessWeek*, July: 62–5.

Chiarelli, N. (2006) The global rise of word of mouth, *Brand Strategy*, October: 42–3.

Clef, U. (2001) Marketing verleiht Flüüügel, *Absatzwirtschaft, Sonderausgabe*, October: 22–30.

Crittenden, V. L. and Crittenden, W. F. (2004) Developing the sales force, growing the business: the direct selling experience, *Business Horizons*, 47(5): 39–44.

CSM Worldwide (2002) Automotive market forecast 2002, CSM Worldwide, Northville, MI (www.csmauto.com/forecastsummary.html).

Desmet, P. and Xardel, D. (1996) Challenges and pitfalls for direct mail across borders: the European example, *Journal of Direct Marketing*, 10(3): 48–60.

Dobele, A., Toleman, D. and Beverland, M. (2005) Controlled infection! Spreading the brand message through viral marketing, *Business Horizons*, 48(1): 143–9.

Economist, The (2006) The cutting edge: Moore's law for razor blades, *The Economist*, 16 March.

Esch, F.-R., Kritger, K. H. and Stenger, D. (2009) Virales Markenkommunikation: Wirksame Interaktion statt 'Trial and Error', *Marketing Review St. Gallen*, 1: 11–16.

Ferguson, D. (2000) Nike braces for earthquake if Woods switches golf balls, *Golfweek*, 18 May (www.golfweek.com).

Fowdar, R. R. R. (2004) Industrial trade shows: a study of related activities, *IIMB Management Review*, September: 44–55.

Friel, A. L. (2008) No purchase necessary, *Marketing Management*, March/April: 48–51.

Godar, S. H. and O'Connor (2001) Same time next year: buyer trade show motives, *Industrial Marketing Management*, 30: 77–86.

Griffin, T. (1993) *International Marketing Communications*, Butterworth Heinemann, Oxford.

Gunn, E. (2001) Product placement prize, *Advertising Age*, Chicago, 12 February: 72.

Harper, T. (1986) Polaroid clicks instantly in Moslem markets, *Advertising Age*, 30 January: 12 (special report on Marketing to the Arab world).

Hite, R. E. and Frazer, C. (1988) International advertising strategies of multinational corporations, *Journal of Advertising Research*, 28 (August–September): 9–17.

Hollensen, S. (2001) *Global Marketing: A Market Responsive Approach*, 2nd edn, Financial Times-Prentice Hall, Harlow.

Honeycutt, E. D. and Ford, J. B. (1995) Guidelines for managing an international sales force, *Industrial Marketing Management*, 24: 135–44.

Hosea, M. (2007) Bigger bucks, *Brand Strategy*, February: 12–13.

Hung, C. L. and West, D. C. (1991) Advertising budgeting methods in Canada, the UK and the USA, *International Journal of Advertising*, 10: 239–50.

Irish Times (2000) Barbie goes to Hollywood, *Irish Times*, 26 January: 11–12.

Joensen, S. (1997) What hedder it now on engelsk? *Politikken* (Danish newspaper) 24 April.

Johar, P. (2008) Moving beyond the SMS, *Brand Strategy*, April: 36–7.

Kaufman, L. (2000) And now a few more words about breasts, *New York Times*, 17 September: 43.

Karjaluoto, H., Lehto, H., Leppäniemi, M. and Mustonen, T. (2007) Insights into the implementation of mobile marketing campaigns, *International Journal of Mobile Marketing*, 2(2): 10–20.

Koppelmann, U. and Groeger, L. (2009) Virale Informationsverarbeitung: mit System den Faktor Zufall minimieren, *Marketing Review St. Gallen*, 1: 6–10.

Lester, R. (2008) Is direct mail dead? *Marketing Week*, 6 March: 20–1.

Lynch, R. (1994) *European Marketing*, Irwin, Homewood, IL.

MacNamee, B. and McDonnell, R. (1995) *The Marketing Casebook*, Routledge, London.

Meenaghan, T. (1996) Ambush marketing: a threat to corporate sponsorship, *Sloan Management Review*, Fall: 103–13.

Milliman, J. F., Olson, E. M. and Slater, S. F. (2007) Courting excellence, *Marketing Management*, March–April: 14–17.

Mortimer, R. (2007) Card of conscience, *Brand Strategy*, February: 20–3.

Mueller, B. (1996) *International Advertising: Communicating Across Cultures*, Wadsworth, Belmont, CA.

National Post (1999) Tilbury airbag plant to add 'curtains', *National Post*, 15 October.

Nørmark, P. (1994) Co-promotion in growth, *Markedsføring* (Danish marketing magazine), 14: 14.

Onkvisit, S. and Shaw, J. J. (1993) *International Marketing: Analysis and Strategy*, 2nd edn, Macmillan, London.

Ottesen, O. (1995) Buyer initiative: ignored, but imperative for marketing management – towards a new view of market communication, *Tidsvise Skrifter*, no. 15, avdeling for Ákonomi, Kultur og Samfunnsfag ved Høgskolen i Stavanger.

Paul, P. (1996) Marketing on the Internet, *Journal of Consumer Marketing*, 13(4): 27–39.

Phillips, C., Poole, I. and Lowe, R. (1994) *International Marketing Strategy: Analysis, Development and Implementation*, Routledge, London and New York.

Pitta, D. A. (1998) Marketing one-to-one and its dependence on knowledge discovery in databases, *Journal of Consumer Marketing*, 15(5): 468–80.

Ranchhod, A. (2007) Developing mobile marketing strategies, *International Journal of Mobile Marketing*, 2(1): 76–83.

Ross Jr, W. T., Dalsace, F. and Anderson, E. (2005) Should you set up your own sales force or should you outsource it? Pitfalls in the standard analysis, *Business Horizons*, 48(1): 23–36.

Rosson, P. J. and Seringhaus, F. H. R. (1995) Visitor and exhibitor interaction at industrial trade fairs, *Journal of Business Research*, 32(1): 81–90.

Rowland, S. (2006) Are you missing a B2B opportunity? *Brand Strategy*, October: 44–6.

Sargent, J. D., Tickle, J. J., Beach, M. L., Dalton, M. A. and Ahrens, M. B. (2001) Brand appearances in contemporary cinema films and contributions to global marketing of cigarettes, *The Lancet*, 6 January: 29–32.

Seno, D. and Lukas, B. A. (2007) The equity effect of product endorsement by celebrities, *European Journal of Marketing*, 41(1/2): 121–34.

Schlosser, J. (2001) Plugging in the TV, *Broadcasting & Cable*, 29 January: 34.

Schmidt, K. V. (2000) Why SFA is a tough sell in Latin America, *Marketing News*, 34(1): 4–5.

Sharland, A. and Balogh, D. (1996) The value of non-selling activities at international trade shows, *Industrial Marketing Management*, 25: 59–66.

Shelly, B. (1995) Cool customer, *Unilever Magazine*, 2: 13–17.

Shoham, A. (1999) Performance in trade shows and exhibitions: a synthesis and directions for future research, *Journal of Global Marketing*, 12(3): 41–57.

Silvera, D. H. and Austad, B. (2004) Factors predicting the effectiveness of celebrity endorsement advertisements. *European Journal of Marketing*, 38(11/12): 1509–27.

Sorenson, R. Z. and Weichman, V. E. (1975) How multinationals view marketing standardization, *Harvard Business Review*, May–June: 38–56.

Steinbreder, J. (2000) Nike deal is Woods' latest ace, *Golfweek*, 23 September (www.golfweek.com).

Teather, D. (2002) 'Bloated' Ford sacks 35,000, *Guardian*, 12 January: 23.

USWeb/CKS (1999) Audience development: a comprehensive process for building a profitable customer base on the Internet, White Paper, Washington, DC.

Willram, J. (2000) Miller takes a back seat in battle for global domination, *Financial Times, Companies and Finance: International*, 8–9 April: 9.

WorldNet Daily (2005) Razor wars: 15-blade fever, *WorldNet Daily* (www.wnd.com), 26 November.

Writer, S. and McLaughlin, M. (2001) Nike, Titleist wage ball battle, *CNN Financial News*, 4 April (http://cnnfn.cnn.com).

PART V

Organising, implementing and controlling the marketing effort

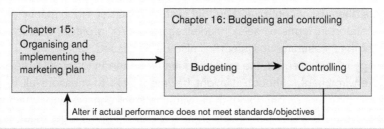

Organising, implementing and controlling the marketing effort

Chapter 15: Organising and implementing the marketing plan

Chapter 16: Budgeting and controlling

Budgeting → Controlling

Alter if actual performance does not meet standards/objectives

Structure of Part V

Designing marketing strategies and programmes that meet current and future market requirements is a necessary but not a sufficient condition for corporate success. They need to be translated into action through effective implementation.

The purpose of Part V is to introduce the marketing plan, which is a mechanism for integrating and coordinating marketing programmes in the midst of uncertainty about the future.

A marketing plan (Chapter 15) is a detailed and systematic formulation of actions to take place, including the resources to be used. An action plan is a key step in ensuring that the marketing strategy has been executed effectively.

It is also a set of specific decision or marketing activities designed to carry out marketing strategies and accomplish a company's stated objectives and goals.

The structure of Part V is shown in the diagram above.

A good plan will address the product and customer relationships and employee/employer cooperation plan (internal marketing). The plan should also address the cooperative effort needed among engineering, manufacturing, research, sales, transportation, channel distribution, dealer and retailer relations, price, packaging, competition, sales, advertising, feedback and promotion. This marketing plan reflects on past experience, assesses current trends and conditions, and forecasts future events.

The plan should incorporate all the assumptions, judgements, strategic options and contingencies developed during the planning process.

Building a marketing plan (Chapter 15) is a creative effort to provide direction for marketing implementation. An action plan, as related to developing marketing activities, encompasses the information needed to complete marketing planning and includes answers to the following questions:

- What activities are to be completed in implementing the variables of the marketing mix?
- Who will be responsible for each of these activities?
- When will the activities be initiated and completed?
- How will the activities be coordinated with each other?
- What resources are needed to carry out the activities?

The implementation of strategy decisions is further examined to address key issues as part of the marketing plan. Marketing managers have learned that strategy by itself is not enough; implementation is just as important.

A plan is not complete until it has been evaluated. In evaluating the marketing plan, the company's analysis of the past, present and future, and adoption of marketing strategy, will guide the marketing manager in formulating a specific plan. Also, a basic tool for evaluation could include a break-even analysis.

Marketing managers often use a control and budget system (Chapter 16) in monitoring the performance of marketing operations stated in terms of sales, market share and/or profitability (see diagram). Information requirements as part of the measurement system will also be discussed.

As marketing strategy is implemented, the marketing manager needs to track the results and monitor new developments in the environment, although it might be impossible to measure all relevant environmental changes. The company can count on one thing: the environment will change, and, when it does, the company will need to review and revise its strategies accordingly. The marketing manager must be aware of the nature of the changes taking place, and how the company and programme must be modified in order to adapt to these changes.

Pret A Manger Holdings (based in London) operates a quick-service restaurant chain with about 200 sandwich retaurants in the UK, the US and Hong Kong. All the restaurants are owned by Pret A Manger Holdings, and the company is not using the franchise concept. Its menu features handmade sandwiches (including baguettes and wraps), salads, sushi and desserts, along with teas and coffees. Fresh ingredients are delivered each morning to the shops, and leftovers are donated to local charities in the evenings. Co-founders, former surveyor Julian Metcalfe and his friend Sinclair Beecham, opened their first sandwich shop in 1986. An investment group led by Bridgepoint Capital owns the company.

Source: © Cobie Martin/Alamy

Company revenues (€ m)	2008	2007	2005
Revenue	299	256	199
Net income	35	18	9
Net profit	12%	7%	5%
Employees	2,778	3,062	2,895

Pret has become a popular chain in the UK, where it continues to build out locations to expand into new markets. However, the company had a more difficult time when it penetrated the US market (starting up in New York), where the sandwich market has become crowded by fast-food players such as Subway and Quiznos. Pret A Manger continues to operate more than a dozen locations in New York City.

Around 2007, Pret A Manger was looking for an infusion of cash from a new investor. In a €500 million deal Pret A Manger was taken over by the private equity firm Bridgepoint in 2008. US-based fast-food giant McDonald's cashed out its one-third stake in the business in the buy-out. It had acquired the interest in the company for about €30 million in 2001. Goldman Sachs also took a minority holding as part of the buy-out.

Pret A Manger is now planning for further international expansion.

QUESTIONS

1 How would you define the target market of Pret A Manger?

2 Pret A Manger is using very little on advertising and promotion (under 5 per cent of the sales). What is the reason for that?

3 How is Pret A Manger using 'mystery shopping' as a way of controlling the marketing effort?

4 How would you characterise the international marketing strategy of Pret A Manger? Standardisation or localisation?

5 Explain some of the problems that Pret A Manger experienced when they established the first restaurant in New York?

SOURCES

Pret A Manger website (www.pret.com); Hoover company records; other public sources.

CHAPTER 15
Organising and implementing the marketing plan

LEARNING OBJECTIVES

After studying this chapter you should be able to:

- understand the need for an integrated approach to marketing and the role of marketing planning in that process
- explain the background to preparing a marketing plan
- explain the stages in the marketing planning process
- outline and explain the structure and contents of a marketing plan
- understand the important issues in implementing the marketing plan
- understand the various ways of organising the marketing department

15.1 INTRODUCTION

This chapter introduces the structure and outline of a marketing plan. The implementation of the marketing plan requires an organisational structure, form and culture that is conducive to the firm's marketing effort. Within a marketing context, organising consists of designing the internal and external relationships and establishing the policies and procedures, as well as creating the means and methods by which various participants in the marketing function can carry out their responsibilities in an effective and efficient manner.

Marketing implementation is that part of the marketing management process concerned with translating marketing plans into action.

15.2 MARKETING AUDIT

As the first formal step in marketing planning, the marketing audit should only involve bringing together the source material, which has already been collected throughout the year as part of the normal work of the marketing department.

A marketing audit is a comprehensive, systematic, independent and periodic examination of a company's – or business unit's – marketing environment, objectives, strategies and activities with a view to determining problem areas and opportunities and recommending a plan of action to improve the company's marketing performance (Kotler, 2000). An *internal marketing audit* covers aspects such as the company's mission statement, goals and objectives; its structure, corporate culture, systems, operations and processes; product development and pricing; profitability and efficiency; advertising; and deployment of the salesforce. An *external marketing audit* covers issues such as economic, political, infrastructure, technological and consumer perspectives; market size and structure; and competitors, suppliers and distributors.

Although some organisations have successfully employed external consultants to conduct marketing audits, they are generally best undertaken by management who 'own' the marketing process. This is partly because they are the best people to understand the company, and how the marketing plan has been made.

Even more important, though, the audit is the best possible learning process for these managers because it introduces them to the factors that are most important to their management of marketing. Finally, and most important of all, it ensures that those who will have to implement the results of the planning process understand, and are committed to, the assumptions that lie behind it.

It is apparent that a marketing audit can be a complex process, but the aim is simple: it is only to identify those existing (external and internal) factors that will have a significant impact on the future plans of the company.

It is clear that the basic input material for the marketing audit should be comprehensive. As suggested earlier, the best approach is to continuously accumulate this material as it becomes available. This method avoids the otherwise heavy workload involved in collecting it as part of the regular, typically annual, planning process itself – when time is usually at a premium.

There is much evidence to show that many highly successful companies also start their planning cycle each year with a formal review, through an audit-type process, of everything that has had an important influence on marketing activities. Certainly in many leading consumer goods companies, the annual self-audit is a tried and tested discipline integrated into the management process.

15.3 BUILDING THE MARKETING PLAN

Basically, the major functions of the marketing plan are to determine where the firm is, where it wants to go, and how it can get there.

Marketing planning is linked to planning in other functional areas and to overall corporate strategy. It takes place within the larger strategic marketing management process of the corporation. To survive and prosper, the business marketer must properly balance the firm's resources with the objectives and opportunities of the environment. Marketing planning is a continuous process that involves the active participation of other functional areas.

The marketing plan is responsive to both corporate and business unit strategy, and formally describes all the components of the marketing strategy – markets to be served, products or services to be marketed, price schedules, distribution methods, and so on. The key components of the marketing planning process are situational analysis, marketing objectives and goal, marketing strategies and programmes, budgets, and implementation and control. Note that the planning process format centres on clearly defined market segments, a thorough

Market potential
The upper limit of industry demand. That is, the expected sales volume for all brands of a particular product during a given period.

assessment of internal and external problems and opportunities, specific goals and courses of action. Business market intelligence, **market potential** and sales forecasting (see Appendix) are fundamental in the planning process.

At a fundamental level, the marketing plan establishes specific objectives by market segment, defines marketing strategy and actions required to accomplish these objectives, and pinpoints responsibility for the implementation of these programmes. Ultimately, the marketing plan translates objectives and strategies into forecasts and budgets that provide a basis for planning by other functional areas of the firm.

A good marketing plan requires a great deal of information gathered from many sources. It is used to develop marketing strategy and tactics to reach a specific set of objectives and goals. The process is not necessarily difficult, but it does require organisation, especially if the marketer is not developing this plan by himself and is depending on others to assist or to accomplish parts of the plan.

Every marketing plan should have a planned structure or outline before it is started. This ensures that no important information is omitted and that the material is presented in a logical manner. One outline to recommend is this:

1 Title page
2 Table of contents
3 Executive summary
4 Introduction
5 Situational analysis
6 Marketing objectives and goals
7 Marketing strategies and programmes
8 Budgets
9 Implementation and control
10 Conclusion.

However, there are other ways to organise a marketing plan that are equally good.

Let us examine each section of the marketing plan structure in further detail.

Title page

The title page provides the reader with the following essential information:

- the business unit for which the plan was prepared;
- the individual or group of individuals for whom the plan was developed;
- the names and addresses of the individuals or agencies who authored the plan;
- the time period covered by the plan;
- the date on which the plan was submitted.

Table of contents

The table of contents lists the subject matter of the plan, identifies where various topics are to be found within the report, and shows how the plan is organised and presented. The table of contents is usually a listing of titles and subtitles used within the text of the report together with the various types of illustration – tables, graphs and photos.

A table of contents sounds rather superfluous, and the marketer may feel that it is unnecessary. The marketer might be especially inclined to discard the idea if the marketing plan is short. But a table of contents is absolutely necessary. It makes no difference whether the marketing plan is only a few pages or a hundred pages in length. It is required, never optional, because of a psychological factor that affects those who will evaluate the marketing plan for approval or rejection.

The need for a table of contents is especially critical when the plan is being submitted to venture capitalists, who put up large sums of money to businesses that already have a track record and a marketing plan for future growth.

You may have heard that venture capitalists look only at business plans. Marketing and business plans are very similar, especially in smaller companies and with start-ups and new products. When the marketer is trying to obtain resources from a venture capitalist, or any investor, the two plans are synonymous. Either the business plan must have a heavy marketing emphasis or the marketing plan must include complete financial, manufacturing and technical data.

Executive summary

This is an overview of the entire plan, including a description of the product or service, the differential advantage, the required investment, and anticipated sales and profits.

The executive summary is a short (about one page) and concise summary of the key points of the marketing plan. It is designed to give busy executives a quick overview of the report and to inform them of key provisions of the organisation's marketing effort with regard to a particular product or business unit. The executive summary centres on a brief description of the objectives to be achieved, the situations to be considered, and the programmes to be launched. Special issues that impact the marketing plan might also be reviewed.

Introduction

This includes the background and purpose of the project and a description of the product or service and how it fits into the market.

The introduction is the explanation of the details of your project. Unlike the executive summary, it is not an overview of the project. Its purpose is to give the background of the project and to describe the product or service so that any reader will understand exactly what is being proposed. The introduction can be a fairly large section.

Situational analysis

Situational analysis
The interpretation of environmental attributes and changes in light of an organisation's ability to capitalise on potential opportunities.

The **situational analysis** attempts to address the question, 'Where is the organisation now?' The situational analysis contains a vast amount of information and, as the term indicates, is an analysis of the situation that you are facing with the proposed product or service.

The situational analysis is divided into four categories based on the SWOT analysis (see Chapter 7).

Internal assessment

This should describe strengths and weaknesses with regard to company resources (key personnel, skills and capabilities, and resources):

- identify the organisation's cultures and values – shared beliefs that will act as a catalyst for consistent actions by its members;
- detail the marketing organisation, i.e. structure and purpose; lines of authority; functions and responsibilities;
- identify critical factors and skills for success in future activities of the organisation.

Describe the current products, experience and know-how, financial, human, capital resources, and suppliers. Do you enjoy favour with your customers or potential customers and, if so, why? Summarise the strengths and weaknesses as they apply to the project. In many respects this section includes the same items as the competitor section (see later).

External assessment

This should describe opportunities and threats with regard to the following factors:

- Demand and demand trends: what is the forecast demand for the product? Is it growing or declining? Who is the decision maker? The purchase agent? How, when, where, what and why do they buy?

- The target market: describe the target market segment in detail by using demographics, psychographics, geography, lifestyle or whatever segmentation is appropriate. Why is this your target market? How large is it?

- Economic and business conditions for this product at this time and the geographical area selected including a description of trends in the **macroenvironment**.

- State of technology for this class of product: is it high-technology and state of the art? Are newer products succeeding older ones frequently (short life cycle)? In short, how is technology affecting this product or service?

- Are politics (current or otherwise) in any way affecting the situation for marketing this product?

- What laws or regulations are applicable here?

- How does the availability or scarcity of funds affect the situation?

- Is current legislation in state, federal or local government likely to affect marketing of this product or service?

- Media: what is happening in the media? Does current publicity favour this project?

- Special interests: aside from direct competitors, are any influential groups likely to affect the marketing plan?

- Describe your main competitors, their products, plans, experience, know-how, financial, human and capital resources, suppliers, and strategy. Do they enjoy favour with their customers? If so, why? What marketing channels do the competitors use? What are their strengths and weaknesses?

Summarise your internal and external assessment in a SWOT matrix with the key points from the situational analysis.

Marketing objectives and goals

Macroenvironment
Broad societal forces that shape the activities of every business and non-profit marketer. The physical environment, sociocultural forces, demographic factors, economic factors, technical knowledge, and political and legal factors are components of the macroenvironment.

Marketing objective
A statement of the level of performance that an organisation, strategic business unit (SBU) or operating unit intends to achieve. Objectives define results in measurable terms.

Societal objectives
Organisational philosophy that stresses the importance of considering the collective needs of society as well as individual consumers' desires and organisational profits.

The **marketing objectives** and goals section of the marketing plan should answer the question, 'Where does the organisation want to go?' State precisely the marketing objectives and goals in terms of sales volume, market share, return on investment (ROI) or other objectives or goals for the marketing plan and the time needed to achieve each of them.

What is the difference between a goal and an objective? An objective is an overall goal. It is more general and may not be quantified. 'To establish a product in the marketplace' is an objective. So is 'to become the market leader' or 'to dominate the market'. Goals are quantified. 'To sell 100,000 units a year' is a goal. Goals are also quantified in terms of sales, profits, market share, return on investment or other measurements. There is one major cautionary note here: do not get trapped into setting objectives or goals that conflict. For example, your ability to capture a stated market share may require lower profits. Make sure that all the goals and objectives fit together. This is done by adjusting and reconfirming the goals and objectives after completing the financial portions of the plan.

Objectives may also include **societal objectives**. Societal objectives support the organisation's philosophy that its marketing efforts should satisfy not only the market and financial

Social responsibility
The collection of marketing philosophies, policies, procedures and actions intended primarily to enhance society's welfare.

objectives but also serve the best interests of society. Societal objectives can be classified as those related to **social responsibility** (e.g. specific standards regarding minimum age of employees, overtime pay, plant safety and healthy working conditions) or ethical business practices (e.g. eliminate problems associated with job discrimination, unfair labour practices, operating violations, misleading warranties, false advertising claims, counterfeit products, price discrimination, price fixing, deceptive sales promotions or practices, and illegal distribution arrangements).

Marketing strategies and programmes

This section will describe what is to be done to reach the objectives and goals. Marketing strategy is a what-to-do section. Marketing programmes are sets of activities organised around the four general marketing functions of creating, distributing, pricing and promoting products (the traditional marketing mix) plus how to establish and manage relationships with customers. All this was described in Part IV of this book. These marketing programmes are designed to satisfy the needs and tastes of a particular group of ultimate consumers or organisational buyers. It is at this point in the planning process that specific tactical actions are identified in sufficient detail to implement the annual marketing plan as well as plans that preceded it.

Marketing programmes are the means of achieving desired ends. They outline what needs to be done, how it will be done, when it will be done, and who will do it. The nature of the marketing programme suggests its decision-making character. That is, the development of the marketing programme is a series of decisions directed at the achievement of specific performance standards outlined by measurable objectives in the annual marketing plan.

Budgets

Having completed the major planning tasks, it is normal in this section to show the feasibility of the objectives and strategies in terms of the resulting market share, sales, costs and other financial figures. In most cases there would be a marketing budget for the first two to three years of the strategic marketing plan, but there would also be a very detailed budget for the first year of the plan, which would be included in the one-year operational plan.

Remember to include all required resources and costs to reach the planned sales in the marketing budget. Budgeting is discussed further in Chapter 16.

Assessments of sales projections, cash flows, start-up costs and break-even points are required in this section.

Implementation and control

Include procedures for measuring and controlling the progress of planned actions as well as financial analyses. After implementing the marketing programme the marketer has to monitor the marketing plan. Thus, if the budget is exceeded you will know where to cut back or to reallocate resources. If sales are not what they should be, you will know where to focus your attention to improve them.

Conclusion

The conclusion is not a summary (you have the executive summary), but here you conclude with the main contents of your marketing strategy, and why your plan will succeed.

It clearly states once again the differential advantage that the plan for this product or service has over the competition. The differential or competitive advantage is what you have that your competitors lack. The conclusion completes your marketing plan outline.

15.4 ORGANISING THE MARKETING RESOURCES

Organisation involves a coordinated effort, a resource allocation plan, and a system of checks and balances. Figure 15.1 outlines the three principal areas of concern when organising the marketing effort.

Organisational structure

Lines of authority and areas of responsibility need to be carefully identified within the marketing organisation. To accomplish this task, the marketing manager creates an organisational chart, which shows the formal relationships among various parts of the marketing organisation and defines the roles and the decision-making authority of each team member. As identified in Figure 15.1, the organisational structure needs to answer three important questions:

1 Should the organisation be vertical or horizontal?
2 Should the organisation be centralised or decentralised?
3 Should the organisation be bureaucratic or adaptive?

Vertical or horizontal organisation?

How many organisational levels are needed for the effective and efficient operation of the firm's marketing activities? The hierarchical structure of the marketing organisation ranges from a vertical organisation, in which there are several levels separating the chief marketing officer from junior marketing employees, to a horizontal organisation, which restricts the number of line managers.

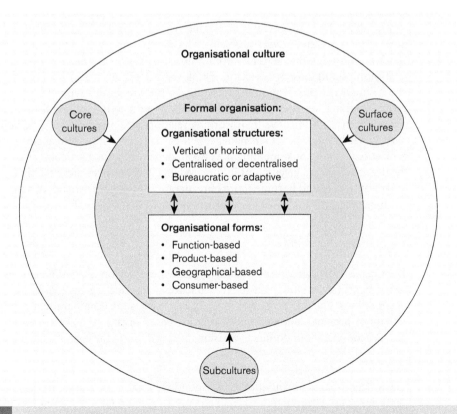

| Figure 15.1 | Organising the marketing effort |

These lines of responsibility, areas of authority and reporting relationships should be more clearly defined and established. On the other hand, horizontal organisations promote closer relationships and more adaptive personal interactions and lend themselves to team efforts and project management.

Centralised or decentralised organisation?

What magnitude of managerial focus is needed to operate effectively and efficiently? In a centralised organisation, decision-making authority is concentrated at the corporate or divisional level. Marketing managers who operate out of one centralised organisation are responsible for most of the important operational and marketing decisions. Organisational structures in which the decision-making authority is delegated to marketing managers at the local operational level are classified as decentralised organisations. Greater control, better coordination, more consistency and clearer direction are commonly cited strengths of the centralised marketing organisation. A decentralised organisation offers greater participation from all marketing personnel, which promotes higher morale, better understanding of customer needs (which results in closer relationships with the firm's customers), and quicker identification of operational and marketing problems (which allows faster response times to needed changes).

Bureaucratic or adaptive organisation?

What degree of structural rigidity is needed to control the organisation? From the perspective of structural design, marketing organisations can be classified along a continuum ranging from bureaucratic to adaptive organisations. Bureaucratic organisations are highly structured marketing organisations that tend to be characterised by high levels of centralised control, formal lines of authority, close supervision and a less personal approach to work relationships. The bureaucratic marketing organisation relies on rules and procedures for making decisions and solving problems. The adaptive organisation is a loosely structured organisational design that features decentralised control, team problem solving, informal work relationships and loose supervision. Employee participation and worker empowerment are two hallmarks of this form of organisational structure. In this type of learning organisation, people working together with integrity, honesty and collective intelligence are profoundly more effective as a business than working relationships based on politics, game playing and narrow self-interest. Whether management elects to go with a bureaucratic or adaptive organisational design or something in between depends on the particular circumstances facing the organisation at a given point in time. When circumstances dictate a high level of control, organisations tend to become more bureaucratic. On the other hand, dynamic environmental changes require highly adaptive organisations.

Organisational forms

The organisational structure of marketing activities takes on many different forms. Marketing departments can be loosely classified as functional-, product-, geographical- or customer-based organisations. The organisational form usually reflects the dominant nature of the marketing activity or problem. For example, a product-based organisational structure is needed when product considerations dominate decision making or are at the core of customers' problems.

Function-based organisations

The function-based organisation is one founded on the basic marketing functions performed. Tasks are grouped and jobs are classified by such functional areas as marketing research, promotions, sales, and product and distribution management. Figure 15.2 illustrates one common function-based marketing organisation. A high level of functional specialisation, a more

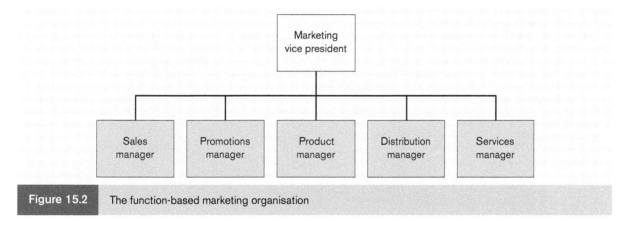

Figure 15.2   The function-based marketing organisation

focused approach to task responsibilities, and relatively simple administration are the most relevant advantages of this form of organisation. Safeguards must be initiated to overcome resistance to cross-functional activities. The function-based organisation tends to be more effective in small companies and loses some of its effectiveness as the firm becomes larger.

Product-based organisations

In a product-based organisation, many of the marketing functions are organised along product and brand lines. In this form of organisation, each product line, product category or brand often has its own marketing organisation. This organisational format is shown in Figure 15.3. For marketing organisations that must manage an extensive and linked set of

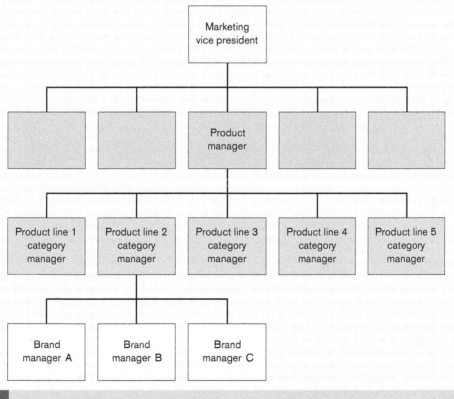

Figure 15.3   The product-based marketing organisation

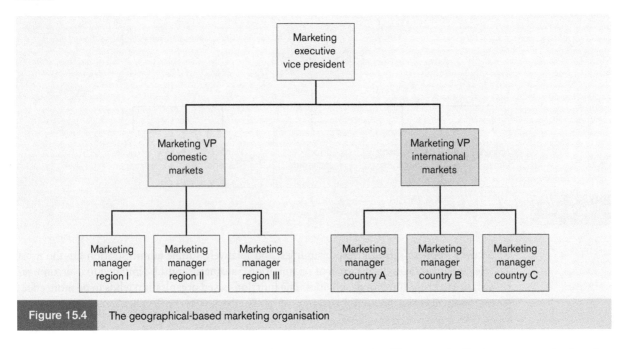

Figure 15.4	The geographical-based marketing organisation

product lines, this form of organisation is both efficient and effective. An organisation that focuses on product specialisation offers considerable benefits in attempting to tailor specific marketing programmes to targeted consumer groups. It is, however, an expensive approach to organising the marketing effort.

Geographical-based organisations

When the firm must market its products in diverse market areas under different market conditions a geographical-based organisation is appropriate. The vastly different demographic structures of market areas and the resulting differences in buying behaviour sometimes require that the organisation adapt its marketing programmes from one region to another. These adaptive requirements are pronounced when moving from domestic to international markets. Geographic diversity is an operational reality that must be accommodated in some fashion. Many firms have elected to meet these realities by assigning a marketing manager and creating a marketing organisation on the basis of geographical considerations. Figure 15.4 demonstrates this form or organisational structure.

Customer-based organisations

The customer-based organisation recognizes that different customer segments have different needs; hence, the firm is organised around the type of customer being served. By structuring and tailoring the firm's marketing effort to take into account the specific needs of certain customer groups, the organisation is better able to accommodate those differences and meet those needs. In reorganising its international operations, IBM is organising its marketing and sales staffs into 14 industry groups, rather than by country. Perhaps the most common form of a customer-based marketing organisation involves dividing the firm into two customer divisions – business-to-business marketing and consumer-products marketing.

Transition from a product-focused to a customer-focused structure

The main aspects of this transition are illustrated in Figure 15.5. The shift towards a more customer-focused organisation can be explained by the following factors:

- Production technologies allow 'mass customisation', which results in a greater ability to target smaller customer segments with product features that are more appropriate for their needs.

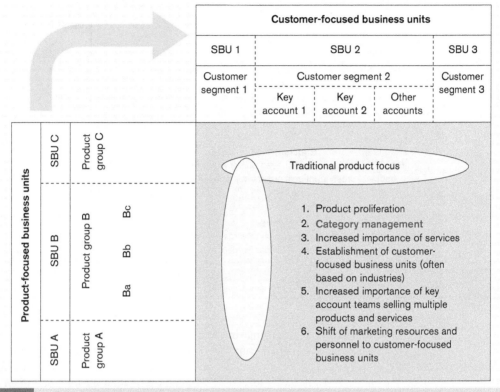

		Customer-focused business units			
		SBU 1	**SBU 2**		**SBU 3**
		Customer segment 1	Customer segment 2		Customer segment 3
			Key account 1	Key account 2	Other accounts	

Figure 15.5   Evolution from product-focused to customer-focused business units

Source: Homburg, C., Workman Jr, J. P. and Jensen, O. (2000) Fundamental changes in marketing organization: the movement toward a customer-focused organisational structure, *Journal of the Academy of Marketing Science*, 28(4): 459–79. Reprinted by permission from Springer Science + Business Media.

Category management
The management of brands in a group, portfolio or category with specific emphasis on the retail trade's requirements.

Organisational culture
Manifests in (1) the ways the organisation conducts its business, treats its employees, customers and the wider community, (2) the extent to which autonomy and freedom is allowed in decision making, developing new ideas and personal expression, (3) how power and information flow through its hierarchy, and (4) the strength of employee commitment towards collective objectives. It is termed 'strong' or 'weak' to the extent it is diffused through the organization.

- Customer data warehouse and data mining techniques (see Appendix) make it possible to uncover previously unknown patterns of customer behaviour. These IT-based tools ultimately help marketers to make better decisions regarding relationships with customers.

- The increased number of products available often results in resellers wanting assistance at the overall category level, not the product level. Thus, firms have increasingly established managers responsible for entire product categories.

- There is an increased importance of services with many major firms receiving more profits from services than from products.

- Many firms reorganise their salesforce around customer groups (often industry based) to develop coherent solutions out of the products and services from multiple divisions.

- Following on from such an industry segmentation, many firms then assign key account managers to be the single point of contact with major accounts, selling the entire range of products and services produced by their firm.

Organisational culture

All organisations have a culture which strongly impacts on how that organisation implements its marketing programmes. An **organisational culture** is created by accepting and sharing a set of values.

As companies attempt to reorient themselves around customers, individual employees will have to come to terms with changing cultural norms, organisational structures and the way their performance is measured and rewarded. This requires an organisational culture that is adaptive and responsive to change, and the quality of communication within an organisation

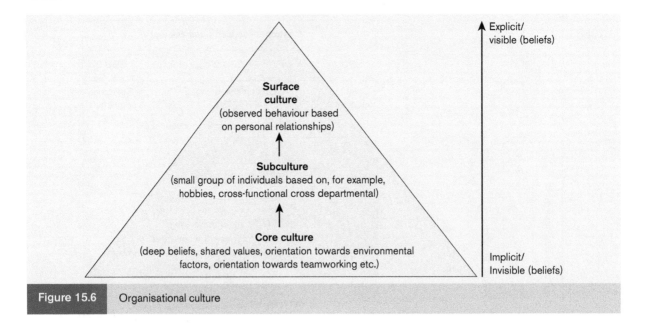

| Figure 15.6 | Organisational culture |

is an important aspect of any change initiative. Failure to successfully communicate a change initiative and its implications for employees can lead to failure; an effective internal communication strategy needs to be in place so that there is buy-in to the initiative led by the senior management team (Ryals and Knox, 2001). When most or all of the members of an organisation embrace a group of values, a prevailing set of traditions is created and passed on from older employees to new employees. The behaviour of managers and employees toward one another often reflects the type of culture that prevails within an organisation.

An organisation's culture exists at three levels. As shown in Figure 15.6 the core culture is the basic value system (the deep beliefs and understanding that shape and guide attitudes and actions) that serves as an invisible foundation for the observable behaviour within the surface culture. The surface culture manifests itself in the form of behavioural and personal relationships that can be observed or heard by walking around the organisation. It is how members of the marketing organisation relate. Given the high level of interpersonal relationships that surround most marketing activities, core and surface cultures are vital to the successful completion of the marketing mission. Pleasant working relationships, supportive working environments, amiable motivational pressure and strong marketing traditions are all benefits that organisational members hope to find within a well-established and tested cultural environment.

Under the surface culture of an organisation, a number of subcultures exist in which small groups of individuals hold to the core value system, but have slightly different perspectives that usually reflect their particular set of circumstances. Subcultures are based on gender and racial differences, age and educational variations, and occupational and managerial positions. Creating the comfortable and productive organisational culture is one of the toughest challenges facing the marketing manager and crucial to the effective execution of the marketing effort.

15.5 IMPLEMENTATION OF THE MARKETING PLAN

Simply put, implementation refers to the 'how' part of the marketing plan. Because marketing implementation is a very broad term, it is often used but frequently misunderstood.

Some of this misunderstanding may stem from the fact that marketing strategies almost always turn out differently than anticipated because of the difference between intended marketing strategies and realised marketing strategy. Intended marketing strategy is what the organisation wants to happen; it is the organisation's planned strategic choice. The realised marketing strategy, on the other hand, is the strategy that actually takes place. More often than not, the difference between the intended and realised strategy is the result of the way the intended marketing strategy is implemented. This is not to say that an organisation's realised marketing strategy is necessarily better or worse than the intended marketing strategy, just that it is different in some way. Such differences are often the result of internal and external environmental factors that change during implementation. As a result, when it comes to marketing implementation, Murphy's law usually applies: if anything can possibly go wrong, it will. This serves as a warning to all managers that the implementation of the marketing strategy should not be taken lightly.

Issues in marketing implementation

Marketing implementation is critical to the overall success of any organisation because it is responsible for putting the marketing strategy into action. Unfortunately, many organisations repeatedly experience failures in marketing implementation. We often encounter examples of these failures in our daily lives – out-of-stock items at the local supermarket, overly aggressive salespeople at car dealerships, long checkout queues at the local department store, and unfriendly or inattentive employees at a hotel. Such examples illustrate that even the best planned marketing strategies are a waste of time without effective implementation to ensure their success. In short, a good marketing plan combined with bad marketing implementation is a guaranteed recipe for disaster.

One of the most interesting aspects of marketing implementation is its relationship to the strategic planning process. Many managers assume that planning and implementation are interdependent, but separate issues. In reality, planning and implementation are intertwined within the marketing planning process. Many of the problems of marketing implementation occur because of this relationship to strategic planning (Dibb *et al.*, 2008; Kotler *et al.*, 2006). In the following we will look at one of the most common issues.

Planning and implementation are interdependent processes

Many marketing managers assume that the planning and implementation process is sequential. That is, strategic planning comes first, followed by marketing implementation. Although it is true that the content of the marketing plan determines how it will be implemented, it is also true that how a marketing strategy is to be implemented determines the content of the marketing plan. This two-way relationship between marketing strategy and marketing implementation is depicted in Figure 15.7.

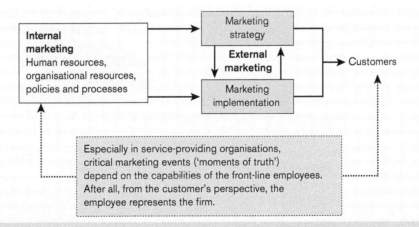

| Figure 15.7 | Two-way relationship between marketing strategy and implementation |

Certain marketing strategies will dictate some parts of their implementation. For example, a company such as Southwest Airlines with a strategy of improving customer service levels may turn to employee training programmes as an important part of that strategy's implementation. Through profit sharing, many Southwest Airlines employees are also shareholders with a vested interest in the firm's success. Employee training and profit-sharing programmes are commonly used in many companies to improve customer service. However, employee training, as a tool of implementation, can also dictate the content of the company's strategy. This leads us also to discuss the role of internal marketing.

15.6 THE ROLE OF INTERNAL MARKETING

As more companies come to appreciate the importance of people in the implementation process, they are becoming disappointed with traditional approaches to marketing implementation. These forces for change have been caused by several factors: high rates of employee turnover and its associated costs, and continuing problems in the implementation of marketing strategy. These problems have led many organisations to adopt alternative approaches to marketing implementation. One of these alternatives is internal marketing.

The internal marketing approach

Internal marketing
Involves treating employees as internal customers with the goal of increasing employees' motivation and customer focus.

The concept of **internal marketing** comes primarily from service organisations where it was first practiced as a tactic for making all employees aware of the need for customer satisfaction. Generally speaking, internal marketing refers to the managerial actions necessary to make all members of the organisation understand and accept their respective roles in implementing marketing strategy (Bowers *et al.*, 2007). This means that all employees, from the chief executive officer to front-line marketing personnel, must realise how each individual job assists in implementing the marketing strategy (Nowak *et al.*, 2008).

Under the internal marketing approach, every employee has two sets of customers: external and internal. For department store managers, for example, the people who shop in the store are called external customers, while the employees who work in the store are the manager's internal customers. In order for implementation to be successful, the store manager must serve the needs of both 'customer' groups. If the internal customers are not dealt with properly, then it is unlikely that the external customers will be completely satisfied.

This same pattern of internal and external customers is repeated throughout all levels of the organisation. Even the CEO is responsible for serving the needs of his or her internal and external customers. Thus, unlike traditional approaches where the responsibility for implementation rests with lower levels of the organisation, the internal marketing approach places this responsibility on all employees, regardless of organisational level. In the end, successful marketing implementation comes from an accumulation of individual actions where all employees are responsible for implementing the marketing strategy.

The internal marketing process

The process of internal marketing is straightforward and rests on many of the same principles used in external marketing. The overall internal marketing framework is presented in Figure 15.8. In this framework, internal marketing is seen as an output of and input to both marketing implementation and the external marketing programme. That is, neither the marketing strategy nor its implementation can be designed without some consideration for the internal marketing programme.

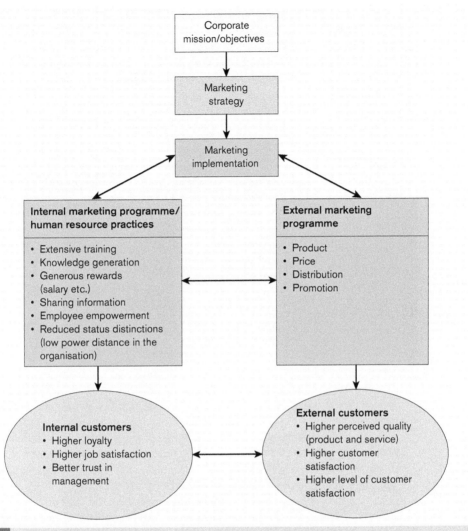

Figure 15.8   Internal marketing framework
Source: Adapted from Piercy, N. F. (1992) *Market-led Strategic Change*, Butterworth-Heinemann, Stoneham, MA, p. 371.
Copyright © 1992 Elsevier. Reproduced with permission.

The product, price, distribution and promotion elements of the internal marketing pro-gramme are similar, yet different from the elements of the external marketing programme. Internal products refer generally to marketing strategies that must be sold internally. More specifically, however, internal products refer to those employee tasks, behaviours, attitudes and values necessary to ensure implementation of the marketing strategy. The implementa-tion of any marketing strategy requires certain changes on the part of employees. They may have to work harder, change job assignments, or even change their attitudes and expand their abilities. The changes that employees must undergo in implementing the marketing strategy are called internal prices. Employees pay these prices through what they must do, change or give up when implementing a new marketing strategy.

Internal distribution refers to how the marketing strategy is communicated internally. Planning sessions, workshops, formal reports and personal conversations are all examples of internal distribution. Internal distribution also refers to employee training and education programmes designed to assist in the transition to a new marketing strategy. Finally, all com-munication aimed at informing and persuading employees about the merits of the marketing strategy comprise internal promotion. Internal promotion can take the form of speeches, video presentations, audiotapes and/or internal company newsletters. With the vast age disparity of today's employees, it is unlikely that any one medium will communicate successfully with all employees. Managers must realise that telling employees important information once in a single format is not communicating. Until employees understand it, communication has not taken place.

Implementing an internal marketing approach

Successfully using an internal marketing approach requires the integration of many factors already discussed in this chapter. First, the recruitment, selection and training of employees must be considered an important component of marketing implementation, with marketing having an input into the personnel function as necessary. This ensures that employees will be matched to the marketing tasks to be performed. Second, senior managers must be completely committed to the marketing strategy and overall marketing plan. It is naive to expect employees to be committed when senior managers are not. Simply put, the best planned strategy in the world cannot successfully proceed if the employees responsible for its implementation do not believe in it and are not committed to it.

Third, employee reward programmes must be linked to the implementation of the marketing strategy. This generally means that employees should be rewarded on the basis of their behaviours rather than on their work outcomes. In an organisation guided by a strong culture and a shared marketing plan, outcome-based control systems may not adequately capture the effort put in by employees. Fourth, the organisation should be characterised by open communication among all employees, regardless of organisational level. Through open, interactive communication, employees come to understand the support and commitment of senior managers, and how their jobs fit into the overall marketing implementation process (Aaker, 2008).

Finally, organisational structures, policies and processes should match the marketing strategy effectively. Although eliminating these constraints may mean that employees should be empowered to creatively fine-tune the marketing strategy or its implementation, empowerment should be used only if the organisation's culture can support it. However, if used correctly as a part of the internal marketing approach, the organisation can gain more motivated, satisfied and committed employees as well as enhanced customer satisfaction and improved business performance.

EXHIBIT 15.1
Merger of Mars' European food, pet care and confectionery divisions

Mars Inc. is a diversified multi-functional company whose primary products include foods, pet care, confectionery, electronics and drinks. Owned and controlled by the Mars family, this US giant is one of the world's biggest private companies, but also one of the most secretive.

Mars' decision in January 2000 to merge its food, pet care and confectionery divisions across Europe – and eventually with headquarters in the UK – has split the marketing industry.

The most well-known brands within the three divisions are:

- *Foods*: Uncle Ben's Rice, Uncle Ben's sauces
- *Pet care*: Whiskas, Pedigree
- *Confectionery*: M&Ms, Snickers, Milky Way, Mars Bar.

Mars UK says the decision to pool the businesses was taken to strike at the company's international competitors in food and confectionery, such as Nestlé and Unilever. The move also coincides with plans to create a

→

single European market and highlights the company's belief that its consumers' needs are the same across Europe.

But the combination of food and confectionery with pet care is not clear to all industry observers. One industry analyst made the comment: 'Generally speaking, Mars is doing the right thing by merging divisions to squeeze profits out of them. Before the advent of the euro it was acceptable to run separate companies in different European countries but not any more.'

Another analyst had this opinion:

I can't imagine it marketing all three sides of the business together. They're too different. The only visible benefit appears to be an improvement in distribution. Tastes across European markets are very different, whether you're selling products for animals or people.

It's all very well Mars saying it will tackle competitors such as Nestlé and Unilever, but they are only rivals in food and confectionery.

If Mars starts laying down too many controls by merging all its businesses – and therefore also its marketing and management strategies – it may streamline communications, but could lose the creativity available in different regions.

Source: Adapted from McCawley (2000).

15.7 SUMMARY

A marketing plan is like a map. It outlines where the business is, its desired destination (objectives), and the conditions it will face in its efforts to reach that destination. The plan helps to integrate activities, schedule resources, specify responsibilities and provide a means of measuring progress. Understanding the market situation reveals a set of key issues that need to be addressed in order to reach the desired destination. Situational analysis and identification of key performance issues are key inputs to the marketing plan.

In order to construct a realistic plan, managers need to estimate what total market demand might be. The marketing plan should have the following framework:

- Title page
- Table of contents
- Executive summary
- Introduction
- Situational analysis
- Marketing objectives and goals
- Marketing strategies and programmes
- Budgets
- Implementation and control
- Conclusion.

The marketing plan may be implemented around one of the following organisational forms: function-based, product-based, geographical-based or customer-based.

The development of a marketing plan involves process and structure, creativity and form.

If the marketing plan fails to produce the desired levels of performance, the marketing strategy needs to be re-examined.

Neither the marketing strategy nor its implementation can be designed without consideration for the internal marketing programme. Successful implementation of this can result in more motivated, satisfied and committed employees. In the end it can also improve business performance.

CASE STUDY 15.1

Triumph

How to manoeuvre as a modern brand in the global underwear market

In autumn 2009, Jan Rosenberg, corporate head of sales and marketing Triumph International packs his suitcase for his world trip to the fashion centres in London, Paris, New York and Mumbai. While packing, he thinks about the Triumph brand as one of the global brands leaders in the world lingerie industry. However, he also realises that Triumph is under attack in different places by smaller brands that can totally adjust to local and regional market needs. While thinking about this challenge, another thought pops up in Jan's mind: until now Triumph has not played any leading role in men's underwear, but at least Triumph is somehow active in this market with the sloggi brand. Should Triumph use more marketing resources in men's underwear and will such a change in strategy limit the focus in the women's underwear (lingerie) market?

Source: Courtesy of Triumph International

Background of Triumph

Triumph International is one of the world's leading manufacturers of lingerie, sleepwear and swimwear and was founded as a family business in Germany in 1886. Still a family business (privately owned by the Spiesshofer and Braun families), Triumph International has grown to more than 40,000 employees and an annual turnover of CHF2.37 billion (€1.7 billion).

Bad Zurzach in Switzerland has been the headquarters of the company, Triumph International, for more than 30 years. Triumph enjoys presence in over 120 countries encompassing the globe and is one of the leading underwear producers in the world. The company has about 50 subsidiaries around the world. Its topselling markets are Japan, Germany, Italy and the UK.

In 2007 women's underwear accounted for most of the revenues. Its main brands are Triumph, sloggi, Valisére and HOM.

History

In 1886, founders Braun and Spiesshoffer started operations in a barn in Heubach, Germany. It started as a classic corset factory with six sewing machines and six employees in the Württemberg region of southern Germany. The name 'Triumph' was registered as a trademark in 1902. The trademark idea came to Johann Gottfried Spiesshofer when he saw the Arc de Triomphe in Paris. During the 1930s Triumph became Europe's largest corsetry manufacturer. In 1933, the company opened its first international branch in Zurzach, Switzerland, where the global headquarters is based today. After the Second World War, the expansion continued in northern Europe, and on to southern Europe, Asia and the Middle East during the 1960s.

The 1950s marked Triumph's first very stylish lingerie fashion shows – for the first time the models did not wear leotards under the garments but marched past with the lingerie on their bare skin. 'More fashion for underwear' was the message in 1957 at the first Triumph Show in London's Royal Albert Hall. The next show followed at the international cotton fair in Cairo in 1958, and in 1959 the Berlin Hilton hosted the largest lingerie fashion show ever held up to that time: a presentation to 200 journalists from 16 countries.

The corporate structure was decentralised, a business strategy that enabled customers in each country to be served by locally based designers and business partners with particularly strong commitments to regional fashion trends and cultural conditions. During the 1970s, the company entered the Brazilian markets, took over 'House of Jenyns' in Australia and launched licensing production in South Africa. Production, sales and export subsidiaries were founded in the Philippines and Thailand, together with licensed sales operations in Indonesia and a subsidiary in Chile; production works in China followed in 1980. In the last 15 years, the company has added countries including Uruguay, Canada, New Zealand, Korea, Sri Lanka and Vietnam, and in Eastern Europe, Hungary, Poland, the Czech Republic, Slovenia and Russia. It has established production plants with ultra-modern technology in Bangkok and Morocco, and after the opening of the Chinese market it opened branches there.

Triumph 'Nostalgic Emotion' (approximate retail price: €68)

Source: Triumph International/Photographer: Olaf Wippefürth

Triumph today

Triumph International operates numerous brands and distinct subsidiaries in many of the countries in which it does business, with over 1650 retail locations/distribution centres. Triumph's products span women's intimates, swimwear, homewear and accessories though women's underwear accounted for most of the company's revenue in 2008.

The company's expansion has historically been based on geographical decentralisation. For example, the Asia operations are coordinated by Triumph International Overseas, headquartered in Hong Kong. As of the mid-1990s, the company's decentralization was considered unique: 'Triumph is the only international brand to be marketed and manufactured locally.'

Triumph's principal activities are the manufacturing and distribution of women's (and men's) underwear, as well as clothing worn for in-house and leisure purposes. The company distributes its products through its sole subsidiary Triumph International Vertriebs-GmbH, while product marketing is coordinated by other companies.

Among the most well-known brands in the Triumph portfolio are: Triumph, sloggi, BeeDees (a brand available only in Germany), Valisére and HOM. Sold individually and in multi-packs, sloggi's unique packaging and branding performed strongly on the shelves of leading department stores during the nineties. sloggi's success had turned briefs into a fast-moving-consumer-goods (FMCG) market. By late 2009, Triumph International had sold over 1.1 billion pieces of sloggi around the world.

The Triumph supply chain (value chain) is illustrated in Figure 15.9

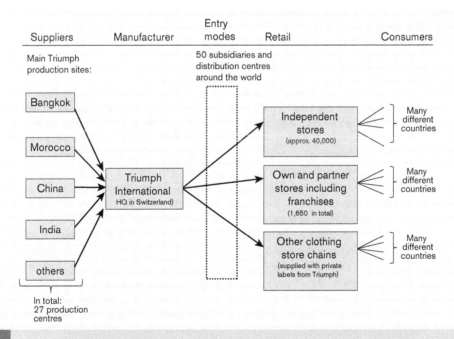

| Figure 15.9 | Triumph's supply and value chain |

Triumph's global design and marketing strategy

Triumph works with its design teams in Europe and Asia in order to ensure that the latest trends in lifestyle and fashion are reflected by its collections. Textile engineers ensure that their materials and the production is always state of the art.

Triumph is constantly balancing between fashionable design, sex appeal and function. However, this delicate balance is less an issue for women today than in the past. Women see their sexuality differently than they did a decade or more ago. Women are sexy for themselves, not to impress someone else.

In some markets Triumph is being challenged by smaller players, such as Agent Provocateur in UK. This brand has been most influential in terms of sexiness. It has commercialised British kinkiness by mixing it with a touch of French coquettishness. Triumph is aiming for what could be called the 'fashion feel'. Triumph's corporate size and the need to appeal to a wide variety of women across borders means it is unlikely to attain the sexiness of niche players like Agent Provocateur. Hosea (2009) claims, that 'Triumph is the Dove of underwear, where all women are naturally beautiful and all curves and busts are equally catered for.'

Triumph distribution

The products have always been designed and crafted with consumers in mind, but, until recent times, the distribution focus of underwear manufacturers was mostly oriented towards their wholesale customers. Today, many more activities revolve around consumers themselves as we have moved from a seller's to a consumer's market. Triumph today does not only produce fashionable, enchanting lingerie but also creates retail environments through the Triumph stores that make lingerie shopping entertaining, comfortable and relaxing.

Today's market is a consumer's market. Consumers rightly do not only expect fashionable products in excellent quality for their money, but they also expect a pleasant shopping experience to go with it.

Triumph is working together with approximately 40,000 retail trade customers across the world. Triumph's own retail stores including franchise and partner stores (altogether 1,650 stores worldwide to date) offer the opportunity to really showcase different Triumph brands, present its product in the way it should be and create an emotional experience for consumers. They provides the opportunity for Triumph to present its entire collections under one roof in selected locations.

CSR and the Triumph environmental policy

The greening of the apparel industry is a significant and evolving trend that is likely to affect every facet of this enormous global industry. Under both internal and external pressure to reduce the environmental impact of growing, processing, treating and dyeing fibres, and to eliminate exploitation and inequities in labour practices, textile and apparel companies are eager to show consumers a new, sustainable approach to fashion without sacrificing style or profit.

At the consumer and retail level, this trend is evident in a growing number of designers, manufacturers and marketers making sustainable claims. 'Sustainable apparel' is an umbrella concept that includes some or all of these practices:

- use of certified organic natural fibres (wool, cotton, linen);
- use of highly renewable fibres (bamboo, soy);
- use of low-impact synthetic or recycled fibres;
- use of non-toxic or reduced-toxicity fibre processes and treatments;
- use of low-impact or natural dyes;
- design and colour choices aimed at longevity rather than planned obsolescence;
- fair trade, ethical labour practices, and elimination of child labour and other exploitation;
- reduced energy use throughout the product life cycle;
- minimal or environmentally appropriate packaging.

For Triumph the application of ecological standards often turns out to be a source of innovation, both in the products themselves and in the manufacturing process. This is why it is constantly testing its environmental protection measures and rapidly implementing any new findings it makes. Numerous programmes integrate studies of environmental compatibility as well as the separation and recycling of waste, and Triumph is also constantly looking into how it can make do with less packaging material. The company also implements energy-saving concepts at all Triumph International locations in order to reduce carbon emissions.

Triumph also tries to involve the customers to integrate their environmental awareness on their skin. It uses the latest, ecologically certified materials for its collections. In addition, the Triumph brand has presented the first lingerie collection in biodegradable elastane. There is also a Sloggi range in which the fabric has not only been medically tested for body compatibility and freedom from pollutants, but is also manufactured from certified organic cotton.

General trends in the international underwear for women (lingerie) market

Generally American women buy more lingerie than European women. One of the reasons is that Americans have a tendency to throw everything in the washing machine, so the wear-out is quicker. Furthermore, lingerie in the United States is not sold through specialist shops (multi-brand shops) like in Europe, but through mass distribution channels such as Wal-Mart, which is estimated to have 20 per cent of the overall market. The US market is also much more price driven, and lingerie (e.g. bras) costs a lot less.

In Europe there seems to be a difference between northern and southern countries. In southern Europe they buy more lingerie than in northern Europe. One of the reasons could be that women in southern Europe place more emphasis on feeling romantic and sexy. Also, the more intensive sweating in these countries may lead to more purchase of lingerie. Another explanation could be that the northern countries are colder and women wear thicker clothes, so they are not so worried about how their underwear looks.

In order to make the right approach to the lingerie market, it is vital to analyse and interpret attitudes around sex and body image correctly across international markets. In general the US lingerie market is very conservative compared to Europe, though brands such as Victoria's Secret have moved the needle in the United States. While Scandinavia may have liberal attitudes to bodies and sexuality, other markets, such as India and Japan, are more demure.

As in other apparel designs, the trends in lingerie have been dictated by fabric developments. This has meant that glamour, the art of seduction and feminine charm are all ingredients in current vogue. In addition, many bras are designed for women who partake in jogging, aerobics, tennis, etc., to gain maximum benefit from their active lifestyles.

Regarding the distribution of the lingerie, more and more of the textile turnover is now going to branches other than lingerie itself. For instance, Tesco in England is offering fashion brands, mainly sourced from third countries, to its customers despite this practice being declared illegal by fashion brands. In Germany, for example, food retailers, drugstores and even coffee shops are also selling a significant amount of textile products. Thus, in the annual list of the largest textile retailers in Germany, the food discounter Aldi is ranked at number 9, and Tchibo – a chain of coffee – shops, at number 13. In Germany, these non-textile retailers already have a market share of 12 per cent of the total textile market. They do not normally have a full assortment and only sell offers and special items, which they buy in huge quantities and sell at extremely low prices. Also, the idea of concept assortments is being used by some of them. Thus, the coffee chain Tchibo is selling a completely different theme every week, wherein textile products are just a part of the overall offer.

Only companies with a sharp profile are successful in the market. Here are some examples of successful speciality stores:

- French group Orsay is increasing its business with their speciality concept for girls' fashion.
- German teen specialist New Yorker.
- Swedish H&M, with its concept of top fashion products at discounted prices, has been growing in almost all countries where it is present.
- Spanish Zara has also been opening stores worldwide in a remarkably short time frame for a similar target group.

Other speciality stores are also registering remarkable successes. Best examples of this can be seen in the sports and sports-fashion business, where speciality stores such as Runners Point (Germany), Foot Locker (USA), Sports Expert (Austria), Decathlon (France), Sketcher (USA) and The Sports Authority (USA) are gathering more and more market share and expanding worldwide.

The lingerie segment, earlier a fixed part of normal textile and fashion stores, is also witnessing a fast growth. For instance, Oysho (Zara, Spain), Women's Secret (Cortefield, Spain) and even Marks & Spencer are starting their own chains of lingerie outside their traditional shops.

Generally, a polarisation is taking place in the European lingerie market. The distribution of the lower-priced brands is being taken over by the huge retail chains, whereas the higher-priced brands are gaining market share by using their own concept shops, where personal service plays a much higher role. At present, the losers in the industry are the 'in-between' brands, which are 'stuck in the middle'.

Vertical integration

More and more manufacturers are opening their own stores and more and more fashion retailers are selling their own retail brands.

The vertical integration is a result of increasing efficiency between production and distribution given the assumption that organisation of production is best made from the POS (point of sale). Middlemen and wholesalers, as well as middle activities such as exhibitions, are cut out of the distribution channel to ensure that there are fewer costs and no losses of communication in the process. Success is more likely in cases where one company owns or controls the complete process from production to distribution. All fast-expanding fashion companies are working vertically. Wal-Mart, Zara, Uniglo, Mango, H&M, C&A, Esprit – all these successful international retailers fall into this category. Frequently, they work on a completely vertical system, while at other times they use a mixed system – selling their own brands as well as manufacturer brands.

The world market for underwear

Over the last few decades, there has been an increasing number of women worldwide participating in the workforce. Women's average disposable incomes are rising and the gender gap is closing, albeit at different rates in different parts of the world.

With their rising incomes, women are enjoying greater spending power and they now have the ability to decide (or co-decide) how resources will be distributed within the family. Higher levels of education for women and their higher salaries will ultimately increase their purchasing power. The traditional guilt that many women carried when spending on themselves is also expected to decline, leading to greater spending on women's products. This rising purchasing power and greater decision-making authority has made women, especially those in employment and aged 24–54, a large and powerful segment of the consumer market.

Price development

Average unit prices for clothing have declined worldwide over the last decades, as marketers sourced clothes from low-cost production locations. This situation gave customers more product choice at better prices, but the increased competition also forced manufacturers and retailers to keep their prices and margins down. The more intensive use of private label products is expected to drive average unit prices down even further, as retailers source products from low-cost locations to give themselves a competitive edge. To combat declining prices, manufacturers and retailers will seek new, more innovative products that are more insulated from price deflation.

Value of world market

The total world market for underwear (men and women) is estimated at €35.7 billion (see Table 15.1). The women's underwear (lingerie) market accounts for around 80 per cent of the total global underwear market, and the rest (20 per cent) is for the men.

The biggest total market is still the United States, followed by Germany and the UK.

Triumph is estimated to have its best market share in Germany, followed by the UK and markets in the Far East. In China and India, Triumph has a relatively good market position, though these markets are mainly dominated by domestic underwear manufacturers.

In the category 'Other global markets', the underwear markets in the developing economies of Asia, Eastern

---

Table 15.1   The total market for underwear (men and women) in main international markets and estimate for total world market

Country	Total market (€ billion) in manufacturers selling prices, 2008	Triumph: estimated market shares (%)
USA	11.0	<1.0*
Germany	4.2	10.0
United Kingdom	3.8	8.0
France	3.4	2.0
Italy	3.2	3.0
Russia	2.1	1.5
Other global markets (Australia, Japan, China, South America, etc.)	10.0	5.0
Total world market	**37.7**	4.5%

Sources: Hosea (2009); different public sources and own estimates.
*Triumph is not available in the US market with own brands.

Europe and Latin America are characterised by extreme fragmentation, with countless independent private label products dominating the competitive landscape. These products have strong price advantages and are still preferred by consumers in the mass market. At the same time, they also copy the latest fashion trends and are thus able to keep their customers satisfied.

For example, in Eastern Europe, the retail clothing market remains fragmented, lacking the presence of leading companies and brands. Open-air markets and family-owned clothing stores dominate the retail landscape. However, the distribution of underwear in the region is beginning to change as the share of specialist stores and retail chains is rising. The share of open-air markets is declining but it remains relatively high. Several retail chains, such as Peek & Cloppenburg, Stockmann, Debenhams, Marks & Spencer, Top Shop and C&A, have all entered this region over the past two years.

The number of shopping malls in the region is growing, particularly in major central and regional cities, and this is increasing the penetration of organised retail, especially for chains; for example, in Poland, the Spanish company Inditex (Zara) is developing its brand portfolio, introducing new clothing brands such as Bershka, Pull and Bear, Oysho and Stradivarius. The British chain Next has just opened its first store in Poland, while the Russian retailer Sela is due to open its first store in Warsaw.

In the future, the distribution share of big retailers will increase and the distribution share of less formal formats, such as open-air markets, will decrease, although open-air markets still maintain a share of about 35–45 per cent, depending on the specific clothing subsector being considered.

Furthermore, multinational underwear brands are not in the top ten brands in countries such as China, India and Russia, as domestic players are preferred for their price and style.

Retailing

The four biggest multinational clothing retailers in the world are GAP Inc., H&M, and Inditex/Zara.

US-based GAP is the largest clothing and underwear retailer, but with 90 per cent of its sales coming from the large US market. GAP brand stores are so popular in the United States that a shopping centre without a GAP or its subsidiaries, Banana Republic and Old Navy, is a rare sight. The retail chain offers own-brand men's and women's underwear, and women's and children's clothing, etc. Total GAP sales amount to US$17 billion, with 154,000 employees.

The largest European clothing retailers are Hennes & Mauritz (H&M), Inditex/Zara (Industria de Diseño Textil)

and C&A Mode Brenninkmeijer & Co. and all enjoyed sales growth during the last decade.

H&M, the Swedish-based clothing retailer, followed a strategy of setting the pace of style and making couture affordable. The chain saw its retail clothing sales grow, in the markets under study, from US$12.6 billion in 2004 to US$15 billion in 2008. The brand is the leader in the clothing markets in Sweden, Germany and the Netherlands.

Spanish company Inditex/Zara followed a strategy of selling multiple bands aimed at different target segments. The company has seven brands, the most popular being Zara, which is gaining share all across Europe. In Poland, Zara is gaining market share despite being perceived as very expensive. Inditex reported retail sales of US$13 billion in 2008, up from US$8.8 billion in 2004.

C&A has a strong presence in several clothing subsectors in Europe. It leads the market in Belgium and is a close second in Germany, where it has gained brand salience through sustained innerwear advertising on billboards, bus stops, etc. The company has also enjoyed success in the Latin American markets of Brazil and Mexico, where it has experienced high sales growth. In 2008, C&A retail sales in the countries under study stood at US$11 billion.

In the following section the US market and three major European markets for women's underwear (lingerie) are described (UK, Germany and France). At the end, one of the emerging markets (India) is also characterised.

The US market

The US market for men's and women's underwear is estimated at €11 billion in 2008. In the past 20 years, lingerie has blossomed from a commodity into a huge money-making segment of apparel retailing, thanks partly to lingerie retailing pioneer and marketing machine Victoria's Secret. Many merchants at major department stores are now cashing in on the lingerie market.

Even speciality stores that have never done lingerie in the past are developing strong lingerie alliances, whether branded or private label. Other retailers, recognising that the lingerie market has higher profit margins than regular apparel, are launching new lingerie lines and giving their older products a makeover. Lingerie manufacturers are focusing more on their alliances with lingerie speciality stores as compared to department stores.

The breakdown of 'physical' distribution channels remained fairly constant over recent years, with half of the underwear distributed via mixed retailers (including department stores and mass merchants) and the rest via clothing retailers.

Though a small part of the overall distribution picture, Internet sales of underwear (home shopping) continued to grow. The number of pure e-tailers is fairly small, but most major US clothing companies have a presence on the Internet. Many e-tailers began to offer free shipping and returns, facilitating purchases.

Manufacturers of underwear and their retailers are expected to focus their efforts on meeting the needs of women aged 35+ who have large disposable incomes but are increasingly unhappy with the fashions available to them.

This segment of the population is attractive to clothing manufacturers and retailers because they do not have qualms about spending money on clothing and do not always go for the cheapest items. These women also criticise designers and retailers for focusing too much on the youth market and are clamouring for clothing that, while still fashionable, is built to fit more mature bodies.

As a result, manufacturers and retailers at all price points will work to try to meet the needs of these consumers over the forecast period. K-mart chose to attack the problem by offering similar colour choices across their junior lines and those targeted at older women. Gap recently launched Forth & Towne, a new brand aimed at this age group. Saks Fifth Avenue, which was criticised for dropping its private label line to focus on designer wear for younger consumers, also announced it would relaunch this line, targeted at women with an average age of 48. As these efforts take hold, sales of women's underwear will also see growth.

The underwear industry in North America continues to show a high level of mergers and acquisitions. In 2006, Sara Lee spun off Hanesbrands into its own publicly traded company and, in January 2007, VF Corp announced it would sell its intimate clothing brands to Fruit of the Loom. Also in 2007 Victoria's Secret completed its acquisition of La Senza Corporation. La Senza is a Canadian speciality retailer offering lingerie and sleepwear.

The UK market

It is estimated that 2009 will be challenging for underwear retailers – for the first time since our records began in 1988, underwear expenditure growth will be negative, as the recession forces consumers to be more frugal.

The underwear market is becoming more competitive than ever as non-specialists aim to supplement their clothing sales with underwear, giving consumers a wider choice of retailers to buy from. Moreover, value retailers are growing their share of the market, exerting downward pressure on prices and posing a greater threat to midmarket players.

Expanding into underwear provides an opportunity for clothing specialists to boost sales, and offers added convenience for the customers. Underwear sales through clothing specialists increased between 2003 and 2008. However, their proportion of the market declined between 2003 and 2008 due to Marks & Spencer's loss of market share.

But while the product is good at M&S, there is increasing price competition. Key competitors, including Next and Debenhams, have been enhancing and expanding their ranges as well as sharpening price points.

The growth of grocery retailers looks to be as unstoppable in underwear as it does in outerwear (see below).

UK distribution: the threat of the grocery retailers

As grocers look to enhance their non-food offer through opening more space and the launch of new non-food-only fascias, clothing and lingerie are areas they are likely to expand in. This poses a series of threats to lingerie specialists. Range expansion and enhancement, product/own-brand innovation, department upgrades and strong advertising and marketing, as well as massive footfall, indicate that they will take an increasingly big share of the market.

A key development will be if these new players decide to stock name brands as well as their own labels, adding to competition for the mainstream retailers.

Grocers, in particular Asda and Tesco, pose a real threat to underwear specialists with their expanding ranges and growing store footprints. First, they continue to devote more space to clothing and underwear in-store as both retailers expand existing branches through extensions – including mezzanines, which facilitate shop-in-shop departments. With more space added to stores, clothing departments have grown larger, giving more space to underwear and lingerie.

The development of non-food-only stores under the Asda Living and Tesco Homeplus fascias has further expanded the retailers' clothing offers and, more importantly, given new growth opportunities as both chains find it increasingly tough to expand their grocery store footprints. These stores, still in their infancy, are set to pose a greater threat to underwear specialists going forward. However, located in retail parks they compete less directly with specialists and more with department stores and clothing specialists such as Next.

Sainsbury is enjoying strong growth with its TU collection and it is set to pose a greater threat going into 2009. From a smaller base than its two key rivals, with the range available in just 283 stores (in October 2008) and the full offer available in just 24 branches, TU has considerable expansion opportunity. With Sainsbury set to increase its focus on non-food, TU is likely to form the cornerstone of its growth and, with the brand reaching new heights of recognition as it expands into homewares, it is set to become a more pronounced authority in the market. Sainsbury aims to expand its clothing offer into 300 stores by 2010.

Besides just location and physical expansion, grocers have been enhancing their clothing offers, with Asda, for example, relaunching the George label in late 2008. With the aim of appealing more directly to its core shoppers through simplified ranges, improved quality and better in-store graphics, George has ambitious aims of regaining its position as the number one volume clothing brand from Primark by 2011.

Tesco also has ambitious targets for its F&F and Cherokee brands.

Underwear specialists are insulated to an extent from the value-based offer of grocers because they are largely midmarket to high-end market. Specialists' higher positioning has more direct appeal to affluent customers and their competitive strengths lie in range, quality and service. However, midmarket players are arguably the most exposed to strained consumer finances and are at the greatest risk of losing shoppers seeking value-based alternatives.

In general, consumers, inspired by celebrity style, are buying more bras and pants and showing a tendency to trade up. The total underwear market in the UK is estimated at €3.8 billion (2008) with sales of bras accounting for around a fourth of that value.

The sources of competition to traditional main street chains include supermarkets, mail order and online shopping. Because of this, retail prices have become aggressively competitive. The big corporate chains are claiming growing market share with fewer, but bigger, outlets. According to the Department of Trade and Industry (DTI), the largest shops and chains control about 75 per cent of the clothing market. The growing involvement of the grocery multiples is certainly adding low-price capacity.

Major retailers, especially Marks & Spencer, have improved their segmentation of bras and pants with more premium ranges under sub-brands, adding to the overall choice for consumers. At the same time, prices are dropping. This is due to cheaper imports, especially influenced by bras and pants coming in from Eastern Europe and the Far East. This has helped the discounters to serve an even wider range of bras and pants at low prices. These two factors have been influential in helping to stimulate demand.

Bras and pants have become a self-treat item for many women and are even a gift item at certain times of the year. The branded houses have all worked hard at improving their styling, bringing in new fabrics, new construction techniques (especially for bras) and plenty of fashionable ideas.

Consumer research carried out by Mintel highlights just how an evolving interest in fashion is creating numerous opportunities for manufacturers and retailers. Women are more likely to have a 'wardrobe' of underwear, buying different styles and types for different occasions. Necessity may well drive the market but fashion influences are creating a 'must-have culture' and stimulating demand. When Mintel asked UK consumers what made them buy a bra and pants in the last 12 months, 62 and 60 per cent respectively indicated replacement reasons. However, 29 and 26 per cent of respondents indicated that they bought bras and then pants 'to treat' themselves. This is an important factor that both suppliers and retailers can take into their marketing.

Table 15.2 shows the development in the lingerie (bra) market from 2000 to 2008.

Table 15.2	Brand share in the UK bra market 2000–08	
Brand	2000 market share (%)	2008 market share (%)
Marks & Spencer	34	30
Triumph	7	6
Gossard	6	5
Playtex	5	5
Calvin Klein	2	5
La Senza	2	4
Grocery stores' brands (Asda, Sainsbury, Tesco, etc.)	20	25
Others (Agent Provocateur, Primark, Debenhams, etc.)	24	20
Total	100	100

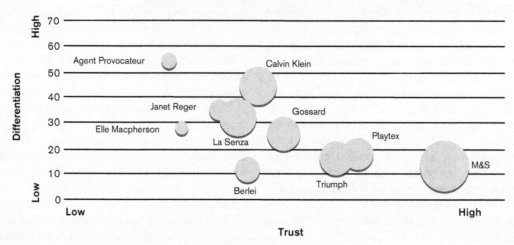

Bubble size: % of people who have ever used the brand.

Figure 15.10	Lingerie brand positioning in the UK market (2007 consumer survey)
	Source: Adapted from Hosea, M. (2009) Selling supportive strategies, *Brand Strategy*, December 2008–January 2009, p. 37. Reproduced with permission.

Overall, the leading British main street chain Marks & Spencer lost market share to the discounters (grocery retailers) and accounted for 30 per cent of UK bra sales, and similar market shares of briefs and hosiery. This has changed in a downward direction since consumer appetite for all things branded has encouraged newcomers on to the lingerie scene. In the past, most female consumers have thought of lingerie as a necessity or a commodity, and not fashion led. Even though much of the expensive and glamorous lingerie is imported from France and other European countries, US producers of upmarket and fashionable lingerie will most certainly also find a receptive audience in United Kingdom. The likes of GAP, Benetton and Calvin Klein have already spotted a niche in this market and are opening standalone lingerie formats.

German market

With a total market value of €4.2 billion (2008), Germany continues to be one of the largest European markets for underwear. Despite economic crises German women are spending more on lingerie than ever before. In addition to new fashion lingerie styles, individualism, decorative femininity and a new ethnic styling emphasise the new sleekness for the coming seasons. Fashion styles are rejuvenated by new colours and novel shapes. A surge in colour is found in the mixture of deep red with pink, green and intense yellow. Warm colours also add more life to the fashion. Manufacturers have recognised that their lingerie collections must include innovative colours and interesting shapes.

Successful penetration of the German market depends on a continuity of effort, regular participation in trade fairs, and the establishment of a sales office with warehousing, either in Germany or another European country. Appointment of sales agents is usually the first step.

The major countries of origin for imported lingerie to Germany in 2008 were: (1) China, (2) Turkey, (3) Poland, (4) India, (5) Romania, (6) Hong Kong, (7) Tunisia, (8) Italy, (9) Czech Republic, (10) Hungary.

The absolute brand market leader in the German lingerie market is Triumph, which has also got some German roots.

The big fashion chains worldwide are grabbing more and more market share in the lingerie market from the smaller traditional fashion retailers. For example, in Germany, a quarter of the market is covered by the four largest fashion retailers (Arcandor, Metro-Group, C&A and Otto). The 84 large fashion retailers in Germany have over 60 per cent of the total market share. According to official numbers, in Germany, every fifth small and medium-sized fashion retailer has been closing down in the past decade. This trend is also reflected in other countries. Even between the big ones, the competition is growing steadily and some of them, such as Gap, Marks & Spencer and C&A, are facing problems. In the current scenario, if a retailer does not have a proper and tight concept, the market would react adversely very fast. It is only the big ones that have been able to defend themselves better with larger power and resources at their command.

French market

In 2008 French underwear sales were estimated at €3.4 billion. Although the economic recession of the past three years has been particularly difficult for the textile industry, the lingerie market segment has proven itself relatively impervious to the downward economic trends.

On average, a French woman purchases approximately five briefs and two bras per year. She renews her nightwear every year. Women aged 15–34 purchase more lingerie items than other age categories; however, they buy less expensive lingerie. The most important element for consumers is comfort.

The following lingerie trends were noted:

- *romantic lingerie*: importance of second-skin bras for an invisible look with more microfibre lace with tulle. This romantic lingerie is made with fabrics that are smooth and is often accentuated with little touches of sophistication (pearl and embroidery);
- *beautiful lingerie*: sophisticated shapes with lace, floral embroidery and cut-away effects. Necklines are back, due to the cutaway effects, strappy looks and pretty, braided trim;
- *sporty lingerie*: a ready-to-wear product with bright colours (red, blue, pink, yellow).

According to recent statistics, the average annual budget for lingerie per woman in France is €100.

A key factor in establishing a brand in France is to have an adequate advertising budget. The foreign company should be able to promote its image and reinforce its position. New products should be aggressively marketed to appeal to French women's inherent 'passion for living' which influences their fashion preferences, expressing both their sensuality and femininity. For example, Calvin Klein recently undertook a large advertising campaign on the Parisian metro system.

Together with French companies, American companies dominate the lingerie market. Market leaders in France are Sara Lee (Dim, Cacharel, Playtex, Rosy), Warnaco (Warner's, Calvin Klein), Chantelle (Ava, Essensia Tulle, Mon Amour) and Vanity Fair Corporation (Bolero, Variance, Carina, Siltex, Lou).

The Indian market

The potential to expand international Triumph sales is particularly large in emerging countries such as India.

India holds immense growth potential for the lingerie industry, which is evident from the entry of large international brands in the Indian market in the last few years. A key factor characterising the blooming Indian lingerie market is the increasing size of the organised market and the declining share of the unorganised market, resulting in growing independent brands taking charge of the market. In addition, growing income levels of Indians and their changing lifestyles has rechristened lingerie

from just an undergarment to a fashion clothing item, at least in the urban centres.

Times have changed for the better for the Indian women like never before in terms of fashion, style and statement coupled with growing wealth that is helping the growth of the organised lingerie industry. From being a market worth €130 million in 2003, the organised lingerie market more than doubled to €276 million in 2008.

Trade analysts and industry insiders believe that this is because the whole scale of the Indian market has improved beyond recognition during the last five years following the advent of multinational brands in the marketplace and the growth of organised retail. This, perhaps, is the reason why the premium and super-premium segment of the lingerie industry, with bras priced above €4 and mostly characterised by the presence of international brands, are witnessing higher growth compared to midmarket and economy segments.

In view of the current situation, the premium and super-premium segments of the industry are advancing following a consumer shift from economy and midmarket segments to the premium segment, while the low and economy segment is gaining from the industry being more organised.

Characterising the premium segment are either international brands or joint ventures of Indian manufacturers with international companies. Lovable, Enamor and Triumph have successfully established themselves as premium lingerie brands and brands that are in expansion mode include Etam, Benetton, La Perla and About U.

The midmarket segment is characterised by the presence of domestic players such as Maxwell Industries (with Daisy Dee brand), BodyCare, Groversons, Vajolet, Underlines, Chic, Red Rose, Juliet, Jockey and Libertina.

Factors such as growth in income level, preference for recognisable brands and rapid growth of organised retail is anticipated to increase the current share of the organised lingerie market of 28 per cent in the next three years.

Triumph opened its first standalone store in Mumbai in September 2008 and at the end of 2009 it has eight stores – four in Mumbai, two in Delhi and one each in Ahmedabad and Hyderabad. There are more stores in the pipeline for Bangalore, Ludhiana and Chennai.

Men's underwear

Consisting of men's briefs, boxers, boxer-briefs and thermal underwear, purchases are largely driven by necessity – as opposed to the luxury that frequently characterises the women's underwear market.

However, men's underwear, which was considered as trivial and unimportant pieces of cloth for centuries, has suddenly received a boost in the market. Men have started showing much more interest in the innerwear segment. Now men can choose from various styles for their indoor and outdoor activities.

Boxers came into existence in 1944; they were originally called boxer shorts. They gained popularity in 1985 when English model and musician Nick Kamen appeared in a Levi's jeans ad wearing only a pair of white boxers.

Boxer rebellion among teenage boys began around 1990. Boxers are very fashionable and are available in various colours, prints and patterns. Men's boxer underwear is available in various fabrics but cotton is very popular because it is known for absorbing moisture. Men's underwear made of cotton is a breathable and comfortable choice.

Many women regard men's boxers as more sexy and appealing than briefs. Men aged 18–34 have a lot of purchasing power, and this segment tends to drive the fashion market.

Some of the famous brands are Joe Boxer, Calvin Klein, Hanes, Fruit of the Loom, Björn Borg, Perry Ellis, Tommy Hilfiger, 2xist and Puma.

The total picture masks a polarisation in the market performance between different types of men's underwear.

Retailers' own-brands (private labels) dominate the men's underwear sector and have further increased market share. However, there has also been growth in the premium/designer sector. The middle market has been more challenged, especially for less differentiated brands.

High-profile marketing and advertising can help sales: the men's underwear market shot into the spotlight at the end of 2007 with the David Beckham advertising images for Giorgio Armani. Sales of this brand, and of quality/premium underwear generally, were reported to have enjoyed a pre-Christmas boom as a result. So high-profile advertising and marketing using celebrities drives sales of men's underwear. Recently Cristiano Ronaldo took over as Beckham's successor in the Armani campaign.

In general, men are driven more by comfort than style, and so quality and the tangible benefits of the products are increasingly important. This should help drive the middle and premium brands.

Men are increasingly into keeping fit and doing sport. They are also more fashion-conscious and brand-aware. The two can go hand-in-hand to drive underwear sales of brands that marry attractive design/fashionability with quality/comfort.

Global competitors in men's and women's underwear (lingerie)

Hanesbrands, Inc., USA (Playtex)

The group's principal activities are to design, manufacture, source and sell a range of apparel essentials such

sloggi men – 'Fun' (approximate retail price: €16.95)
Source: Triumph International/Photographer: Stefan Noll

as T-shirts, bras, panties, men's underwear, kids' underwear, socks, hosiery, casualwear and activewear. It operates in four segments: innerwear, outerwear, international and hosiery. The group's brands include Hanes, Champion, C9 by Champion, Playtex, Bali, L Eggs, Just My Size and Wonderbra. The innerwear segment sells basic branded products such as women's intimate underwear, men's underwear, kids' underwear, sleepwear and socks. The outerwear segment sells products that are seasonal in nature such as casual wear and active wear. The international segment sells products in Asia, Canada and Latin America. The hosiery segment sells legwear products such as panty hose and knee highs.

In 2008 Hanesbrands' total net sales were down by 5 per cent to $4.25 billion, compared with $4.47 billion in 2007; 56 per cent of total sales is innerwear. Its biggest customer is Wal-Mart, which accounts for around 40 per cent of its total sales. The biggest sales areas for Hanesbrands are North America, Latin America and Asia. Europe only accounts for around 20 per cent of its international sales.

Fruit of the Loom, Inc.,

Fruit of the Loom is a global manufacturer and marketer of family apparel, and is America's biggest seller of men's underwear. The company's products also include underwear for women and children, as well as T-shirts, activewear, casualwear and clothing for children. During the late 1990s, the company's brands, which include BVD, Munsingwear and Gitano, were among the best known in the world. In addition to these popular brands, the company licensed characters for children's apparel – such as Winnie the Pooh and Batman – and the names, logos and trademarks of colleges, universities and professional sports teams. With more than 60 manufacturing and distribution facilities, the company had operations in ten states and in various countries around the world, including Canada, Mexico and Germany. Fruit of the Loom employs approximately 31,000 people.

Victoria's Secret

Victoria's Secret sells women's intimate and other apparel, personal care and beauty products, and accessories under the Victoria's Secret and La Senza brand names. Victoria's Secret merchandise is sold through retail stores, its website (www.victoriassecret.com) and its catalogue. Through its website and catalogue, certain of Victoria's Secret's merchandise may be purchased worldwide. La Senza products may also be purchased through its website (www.lasenza.com).

In January 2007, Victoria's Secret completed its acquisition of La Senza Corporation. La Senza is a Canadian speciality retailer offering lingerie and sleepwear as well as apparel for girls in the 7–14 age group. In addition, La Senza licensees operate independently owned stores in 45 other countries. The results of La Senza are included in the Victoria's Secret segment.

Victoria's Secret had net sales of US$5.6 billion in 2008 and operated 1,043 stores in the United States and 322 stores in Canada. At the moment it is not possible to buy Victoria's Secret merchandise in European stores, except in London.

In the following, two of Triumph's more regional and smaller competitors are described.

Marie Jo

Textile producer Van de Velde developed from a family enterprise in Belgium to an important player in the European field of lingerie for women. Van de Velde SA designs and manufactures luxury lingerie items under three brand names: Marie Jo (feminine and fashionable lingerie), Marie Jo L'Aventure (individualistic lingerie) and Prima Donna (luxurious and comfortable lingerie for large sizes).

Van de Velde's most famous brand, Marie Jo, was introduced in 1981.

In the 1990s Van de Velde introduced two new, high-quality brands: Prima Donna and Marie Jo L'Aventure. They were an overwhelming success. The Van de Velde image is nowadays one of creative, fashionable and stylish design combined with good quality and major emotional value. Today Van de Velde has more than 1,000 employees in five different countries.

In 2001 Van de Velde NV acquired a controlling share in the Hong Kong lingerie producer Top Form. The strategic advantages of this move for the Belgians are easy to see – integrated management at lower costs, and an opening to the Chinese mainland market.

Van de Velde, whose turnover amounted to €80 million in 2008, has production operations in Belgium, Hungary and Tunisia. However, 51 per cent of all products designed and sold by Van de Velde were assembled by Top Form, out of Hong Kong and mainland China.

Chantelle

Chantelle lingerie is a family-owned company established over 120 years ago. Chantelle has maintained its dedication to creating bras, panties, thongs and lingerie with the finest European laces and fabrics. Chantelle's commitment to fit, comfort, exquisite European styling and detail has allowed Chantelle to establish itself in over 70 countries worldwide. Its sales in 2008 amounted to €300 million.

The Chantelle brand is known throughout the world for its collections of fashionable and feminine lingerie. Delicate materials such as decorative lace and embroideries, high-end fabrics, support and comfortable cuts reflect the focus of Chantelle. Other brands of Le Groupe Chantelle include Latin-inspired Passionata and Darjeeling, for women who prefer the natural look.

The positioning of Triumph compared to some of the major competitors is illustrated in Figure 15.11

Celebrity branding – an idea for branding and communication in the lingerie market

Launching lingerie with celebrity status is the latest weapon in the battle for gaining market share in the industry. Common to all international markets, although used in varying degrees, is the interest in celebrities. Almost every lingerie manufacturer uses famous faces – and figures – to sell their products. It helps to make lingerie aspirational and remind people to buy what is often only an occasional purchase.

In 2003, Australian rock star Kylie Minogue came out with a line of lingerie called Love Kylie for European

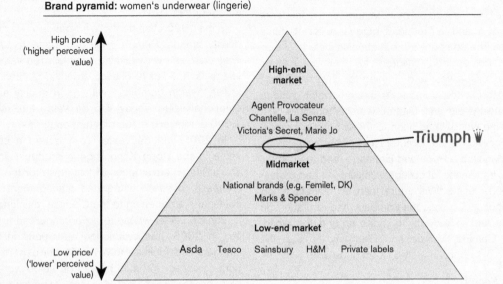

Brand pyramid: women's underwear (lingerie)

Figure 15.11	Positioning of the Triumph brand
	Source: Inspiration from Triumph.

distribution (under the Agent Provocateur brand), and supermodel Elle MacPherson expanded her EMI lingerie collection to the United Kingdom in 2002 from her native Australia. Since then a number of Hollywood sex kittens and wannabe superstars from TV, motion picture and music videos (e.g. Paris Hilton) have reached lucrative lingerie deals in the volume arena. Christina Aguilera also followed the celebrity fashion bandwagon – the petite rockstar, who is as comfortable in a satin bustier as she is in leather chaps, wants to bring her ideal of sexy to innerwear.

In November 2007 David Beckham signed a three-year royalty-based $40 million deal to be Giorgio Armanis global face for the brand's Emporio underwear collection. The contract gives the 34-year-old footballer an annual fee plus royalties and is unprecedented for any sportsman. The personal relationship between Beckham and Armani was definitely instrumental in this deal, but Armani also sees this as a sound business decision – few individuals have a truly global reach that can match David Beckham's.

In spring 2009 Armani chose Beckham's wife, Victoria, to launch its new global Emporio Armani women's underwear campaign, because she is a stylish and intriguing woman. Armani wanted to work with someone who would make a real impression. In 2010 Victoria Beckham's role has been taken over by Megan Fox.

In celebrity endorsement, Triumph has been using Louise Redknapp in its UK market. Louise Redknapp is a British singer and television presenter, known as a member of the girl group Eternal and subsequently as a

solo singer. She is also known as being married to former UK footballer Jamie Redknapp (a football commentator at Sky Sports).

At 35 years old, Louise Redknapp was chosen because she is perceived as beautiful but in a more attainable, girl-next-door way than some of the more aggressively fashionable celebrities. For Triumph it has been important that the personality fits with the brand.

The nature of celebrity collaborations differs from market to market. In Germany, the Triumph brand ambassador is Franziska Knuppe (model). For the Italian market, another model, Alena Seredova, is used. In India, the label was able to link itself with celebrities such as Priyanka Chopra (famous Bollywood star in India) by getting famous people to attend a glitzy Mumbai fashion show in November 2008.

At the Triumph Chinese launch of the new 2009 worldwide lingerie collection 'Zero to Sexy', supermodel Xiong Dailin (who had a performance in the popular movie *Ye Wen*) was invited to share her feeling of wearing 'Zero to Sexy' lingerie and her tips for choosing lingerie with the audience. Xiong Dailin has also been invited to be the judge of the Triumph Inspiration Award (TIA) China final 2009. In 2009 the TIA attracted 2,400 students from 28 countries to attend and explore the fashion industry.

In summary, in keeping with its global scale and attempt to appeal to all women, Triumph is unlikely to start releasing short online films featuring its models in various saucy acts like Agent Provocateur – it has to push its boundaries a little more slowly and carefully.

QUESTIONS

1 Evaluate the strengths and weaknesses of Triumph's global branding strategy.

2 Which of the described international markets would it be most relevant for Triumph to penetrate more in order to secure future growth?

3 Prepare a marketing plan for capturing more Triumph market share for women's underwear (lingerie) in the UK market.

4 Which marketing tools would be most effective in the attempt to capture more market share for the Triumph brand (sloggi men/HOM) in the men's underwear market?

5 Would it be relevant to sell underwear on the Internet? Evaluate the pros and cons, and make a conclusion.

SOURCES

Anderson, I. (2004) Lingerie brand to follow Kylie work with digital blitz, *Marketing (UK)*, 22 February; Bainbridge, J. (2004) Women's underwear: beyond the basics, *Marketing Journal*, 8 December; Fibre2Fashion (2008) Interview with Mr Jan Rosenberg, head of global marketing & sales, Triumph International Ltd, 7 July (www.fibre2fashion.com/face2face/jan-rosenberg/triumph-international-ltd.asp); Hanson, G. (2006) 'Bustin' out', *Scanorama: The SAS Group Magazine*, July/August: 39–45; Horne, J. (2003) King of bras, *Finance Asia*, 6 May (www.financeasia.com); Hosea, M. (2009) Selling supportive strategies, *Brand Strategy*, December 2008–January 2009: 34–9; InfoMat, fashion industry search engine (www.infomat.com); Monget, K. (2004) Lingerie liaisons pick up steam, *Women's Wear Daily*, 12 July, 188(7): 18–19; Parry, C. (2008) The boost it's been waiting for, *Marketing Week*, 3 June; and various other public sources.

QUESTIONS FOR DISCUSSION

1 Discuss the considerations involved in deciding marketing objectives.

2 What is a marketing audit and what is the purpose of it?

3 What are the principal decisions to be made when preparing the marketing plan?

4 What are the main criteria for the successful implementiation of a marketing plan?

5 Discuss the pros and cons of standardising the marketing management process. Is a standardised process of more benefit to a company pursuing a national market strategy or a global market strategy?

REFERENCES

Aaker, D. A. (2008) Marketing in a silo world: the new CMO challenge, *California Management Review*, 51(1): 144–56.

Adage Global (2000) German tea marketer enlists James Bond for mission, *Adage Global*, 20 September.

Beverage Industry (2000) Coffee and tea run hot and cold, *Beverage Industry*, September, 24–5.

Bowers, M. R. and Martin, C. L. (2007) Trading places redux: employees as customers, customers as employees, *Journal of Services Marketing*, 21(2): 88–98.

Candy Industry (2000) Wrigley launches new division, *Candy Industry*, 11 (November): 13.

Challener, C. (2001) Customer-focused approach key for Ciba Speciality Chemicals, *Chemical Market Reporter*, 13: 10–14.

Cosgrove, J. (2000) Coffee and tea: two hot segments poised for increased growth, *Beverage Industry*, December, 14–17.

Dibb, S., Simkin, L. and Wilson, D. (2008) Diagnosing and treating operational and implementation barriers in synoptic marketing planning, *Industrial Marketing Management*, 37(5): 539–53.

Fisher, M. G. (2000) A picture-perfect reorganization, *Sales and Marketing Management*, 21 November: 5–6 (www.salesandmarketing.com).

Homburg, C., Workman Jr, J. P., Jensen, O. (2000) Fundamental changes in marketing organization: the movement toward a customer-focused organizational structure, *Academy of Marketing Science Journal*, Greenvale, 28(4): 459–79.

Kotler, P. (2000) *Marketing Management*, Prentice Hall Inc., Englewood Cliffs, NJ.

Kotler, P., Rackham, N. and Krishnaswamy, S. (2006) Ending the war between sales and marketing, *Harvard Business Review*, July–August: 68–78.

Levere, J. L. (2000) A new campaign will try to differentiate Lipton's Iced Tea from its main competitors, *New York Times*, 4 May: C7.

McCawley, I. (2000) Can Mars bridge gaps in merger? *Marketing Week*, 13 January.

McDonald, M. (1999) *Marketing Plans: How to Prepare Them, How to Use Them*, 4th edn, Butterworth-Heinemann, Oxford,

Marber, A. and Wellen, P. M. (2007) Developing products with soul: the marketing strategy of Chanel in Japan, *The Marketing Management Journal*, 17(1): 198–207.

Medway, D. and Warnaby, G. (2008) Alternative perspectives on marketing and the place brand, *European Journal of Marketing*, 42(5/6): 641–53.

Nowak, P. and Murrow, J. (2008) Meet your new customers, *Marketing Health Services*, Spring: 27–31.

Piercy, N. F. (1992) *Market-led Strategic Change*, Butterworth-Heinemann, Stoneham, MA.

Ryals, L. and Knox, S. (2001) Cross-functional issues in the implementation of relationship marketing through customer relationship management, *European Management Journal*, 19(5): 534–42.

Sharma, A. (2006) Success factors in key accounts, *Journal of Business & Industrial Marketing*, 21(3): 141–50.

Simkin, L. (2002) Barriers impeding effective implementation of marketing plans: a training agenda, *Journal of Business & Industrial Marketing*, 17(1): 8–24.

Thompson, S. (1999) Lipton sets solid summer support for test of quick-iced-tea bag, *Brandweek*, 24 May 24: 14.

Welham, D. (1999) Back in black, *Supermarket Business*, 15 December: 41–3.

Witteman, B. (2001) Infused in the industry, *New York Times*, 11 February: CT1.

Yip, G. S. and Bink, A. J.-M. (2007) Managing global accounts, *Harvard Business Review*, September: 103–11.

CHAPTER 16
Budgeting and controlling

LEARNING OBJECTIVES

After studying this chapter you should be able to:

- understand why customer profitability is important
- define the concept of customer lifetime value (CLTV)
- understand why CLTV is important
- describe the key elements of the marketing control system
- list the most important measures for marketing performance
- understand the need for evaluation and control of marketing plans and their implementation
- explain how a marketing budget is established

16.1 INTRODUCTION

An organisation needs to budget in order to ensure that its expenditure does not exceed its planned revenue. Therefore, this chapter discusses how to use rational processes for developing budgets and allocating resources. Furthermore, the chapter will outline the need for a control system to oversee the marketing operations of the company.

16.2 BUDGETING

The classic quantification of a marketing plan appears in the form of budgets. Because these are so rigorously quantified, they are particularly important. They should represent a projection of actions and expected results, and they should be capable of accurate monitoring. Indeed, performance against budget is the main (regular) management review process.

The purpose of a marketing budget is to pull all the revenues and costs involved in marketing together into one comprehensive document. It is a managerial tool that balances what needs to be spent against what can be afforded and helps make choices about priorities. It is then used to monitor the performance. The marketing budget is usually the most powerful tool with which you think through the relationship between desired results and available means. Its starting point should be the marketing strategies and plans that have already been formulated in the marketing plan itself. In practice, the two will run in parallel and will interact. At the very least, the rigorous, highly quantified budgets may cause some of the more optimistic elements of the plans to be reconsidered.

Budgeting is also an organisational process that involves making forecasts based on the proposed marketing strategy and programmes. The forecasts are then used to construct a budgeted **profit-and-loss statement.** An important aspect of budgeting is deciding how to allocate all of the available money across all of the proposed programmes within the marketing plan.

Profit-and-loss statement (operating statement, income statement)
A financial statement that shows company sales, cost of goods sold, expenses and profits during a given period of time.

Profitability analysis
The calculation of sales revenues and costs for the purpose of calculating the profit performance of products, customers and/or distribution channels.

Profitability analysis

Regardless of the organisational level, control involves some form of profitability analysis. In brief, **profitability analysis** requires that analysts determine the costs associated with specific marketing activities to find out the profitability of such units in different market segments, products, customer accounts and distribution channels (intermediaries).

Profitability is probably the single most important measure of performance, but it has limitations. These are that many objectives can best be measured in non-financial terms (maintaining market share); profit is a short-term measure and can be manipulated by taking actions that may prove counter-productive in the longer term (e.g. reducing R&D expenses); and profits can be affected by factors over which management has no control (the weather).

Analysts can use direct or full costing in determining the profitability of a product or market segment. In full costing, analysts assign both direct, or variable, and indirect costs to the unit of analysis. Indirect costs involve certain fixed joint costs that cannot be linked directly to a single unit of analysis. For example, office costs, general management and the management of the sales force are all indirect costs for a multi-product company. Those who use full costing argue that only by allocating all costs to a product or a market can they obtain an accurate picture of its value.

Direct costing involves the use of contribution accounting. Those favouring the contribution margin approach argue there is really no accurate way to assign indirect costs. Further, because indirect costs are mostly fixed, a product or market may make a contribution to profits even if it shows a loss. Thus, even though the company must eventually absorb its overhead costs, the contribution method clearly indicates what is gained by adding or dropping a product or a customer.

Contribution analysis is helpful in determining the yield derived from the application of additional resources (for instance, to certain sales territories). Contribution analysis attempts to determine the amount of output (revenues) that can be expected from a given set of inputs (costs). You should be familiar with break-even analysis, which is a type of contribution analysis, used to determine the amount of revenue necessary to cover both variable and fixed costs (see Chapter 12).

There are three ways of building a marketing budget that is based on a specific strategic market plan and the tactical marketing strategy designed to achieve the target level of performance:

- *Top-down budget*: a new marketing budget based on projected sales objectives is determined, using past marketing expenses as a percentage of sales.
- *Customer mix budget*: the cost of customer acquisition and retention and the combination of new and retained customers are used to derive a new marketing budget.
- *Bottom-up budget*: each element of the marketing effort is budgeted for specific tasks identified in the marketing plan.

As this book has a customer-oriented approach the customer mix budget will be discussed in the following.

Customer mix budgets

Recognising the customer as the primary unit of focus, a market-based business will expand its focus to customers and markets, not just products or units sold. This is an important strategic distinction because there is a finite number of potential customers, but a larger range of products and services can be sold to each customer. And, as shown in Figure 16.1, a business's volume is its customer share in a market with a finite number of customers at any point in time, not the number of units sold:

customer volume = market demand (from customers) × market share (percentage).

Figure 16.1 presents an overall flow chart of how market-based net profits are derived. Customer volume, at the top of this diagram, is derived from a certain level of customer market demand and a business's share of that customer demand. Without a sufficient volume of customers, net profit will be impossible to obtain. Marketing strategies that affect customer volume include marketing strategies that:

- attract new customers to grow market share;
- grow the market demand by bringing more customers into a market;
- enter new markets to create new sources of customer volume.

Each of these customer-focused marketing strategies affects net profits, invested assets, cash flow and, as we will show later, shareholder value. Thus, a key component of profitability and financial performance is customer purchases and the collective customer volume produced.

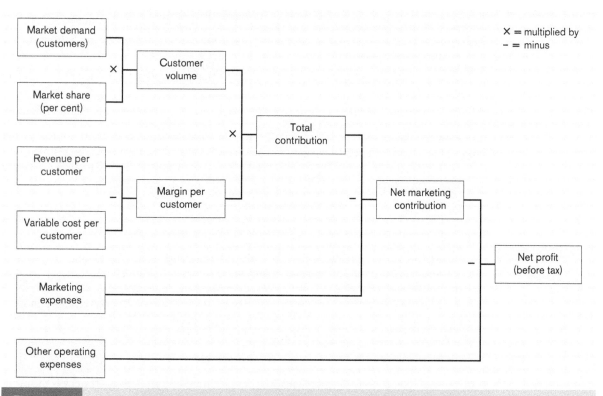

| **Figure 16.1** | A customer-based model of marketing contribution and net profits (before tax) |

Without customer purchases, there is no positive cash flow or potential for net profits or shareholder value.

In the following, the different components of Figure 16.1 will be discussed (Best, 2000). Customer-based budgeting recognises that companies are increasingly turning from traditional accounting methods, which identify costs according to various expense categories, to activity-based costing (ABC), which bases costs on the different tasks involved in performing a given activity.

Margin per customer

When customers decide to purchase an assortment of products and services from a business, the result is a certain revenue per customer. And, of course, a corresponding set of variable costs that go into each purchase and sales transaction must be taken into account to determine the margin per customer:

$$\text{customer contribution margin} = \text{revenue per customer} - \text{variable cost per customer}.$$

This measure of customer profitability could be computed on a transaction basis (monthly or annually), or based on customer lifetime value (CLTV), which is discussed further in Section 16.3. The bottom line is that a business has to make a positive margin per customer or it will produce no profits and, therefore, no shareholder value. In many instances, new customers may produce a small or negative customer margin. Over time, we would expect a business to manage its marketing strategies so as to increase customer margin. If it does not, it has several alternatives to consider, one of which is to not continue to serve that customer as part of the business's marketing strategy. In general, marketing strategies designed to improve margin per customer can include marketing strategies that:

- grow revenue per customer by product line extensions;
- grow revenue per customer by adding services that enhance customer value;
- improve margin per customer with improved products and services for which the customer is willing to pay a premium price;
- develop more cost-efficient marketing systems that lower variable sales and transaction costs;
- eliminate customers that are not able to produce an acceptable level of customer margin.

As shown in Figure 16.1, revenue per customer and variable cost per customer come together to produce a certain level of margin per customer. Because the customer is the primary unit of focus of market-based management, it is the business's responsibility to develop marketing strategies that systematically build customer volume and customer margin.

Total contribution

Ultimately, whether tracking product revenues and variable product costs or tracking customer volume and margin per customer, the end result will be a total contribution produced by the marketing strategies that have been developed and implemented. Once again, both approaches are needed in managing different aspects of a business. However, those in marketing should be more concerned with a customer perspective and how to develop marketing strategies that affect both customers and the total contribution of the business:

$$\text{total contribution} = \text{customer volume} \times \text{customer margin}.$$

As shown in Figure 16.1, the total contribution produced by a marketing strategy is the product of the customer volume it produces and customer margin derived from customer purchases. The total contribution produced by a marketing strategy is an important component in the profitability equation because from this point forward only expenses are introduced. Hence, building market-based strategies that increase total contribution is an important priority in developing marketing strategies that deliver profitable growth.

Net marketing contribution

All marketing strategies require some level of marketing effort to achieve a certain level of market share. Expenses associated with sales effort, market communications, customer service and market management are required to implement a marketing strategy designed to obtain a certain customer volume. The cost of this marketing effort is shown in Figure 16.1 as marketing expenses and must be deducted from the total contribution to produce a *net marketing contribution*. This is the net contribution produced after the marketing expenses are deducted from the total contribution produced:

net marketing contribution = total contribution − marketing expenses.

In effect, this is how the marketing function contributes to the business's profits. If the marketing team develops a marketing strategy that fails and, therefore, produces a lower net marketing contribution, then that marketing strategy has, in effect, lowered the net profits of the business.

Marketing strategies are generally designed to affect total contribution, whether by increasing market demand, market share or revenue per customer, or by decreasing the variable cost per customer. The net marketing contribution equation should make it clear that such strategies are profitable only if the increase in total contribution exceeds the increase in marketing expenses required to produce that increase in total contribution. That is, for a marketing strategy to improve profits for the business, it has to improve net marketing contribution.

Net profit (before tax)

Although marketing strategies contribute to net profits through net marketing contribution, net profit (before tax) is generally beyond the control of the marketing function or the marketing management team. Marketing strategies produce a certain level of net marketing contribution from which all other business expenses must be deducted before a net profit is realised, as illustrated in Figure 16.1. These operating expenses include fixed expenses, such as human resources management, research and development, and administrative expenses, and other operating expenses, such as utilities, rent and fees. In most instances, corporate overheads would also be allocated, which includes company expenses such as legal fees, corporate advertising and executive salaries:

net profit (before tax) = net marketing expenses − other operating expenses.

However, there are instances when a marketing strategy can affect other operating expenses. For example, a strategy to improve a product to attract more customers and build market share could involve research and development expenses to develop the new product.

Figure 16.1 is an illustration of the different budget element. Figure 16.2 illustrates the traditional marketing budget (per customer group) and its underlying determinants.

From Figure 16.2 the most important measures of marketing profitability may be defined as:

$$\text{contribution margin: } \% = \frac{\text{total contribution}}{\text{total revenue}} \times 100$$

$$\text{marketing contribution margin } \% = \frac{\text{total marketing contribution}}{\text{total revenue}} \times 100$$

$$\text{profit margin } \% = \frac{\text{net profit (before tax)}}{\text{total revenue}} \times 100$$

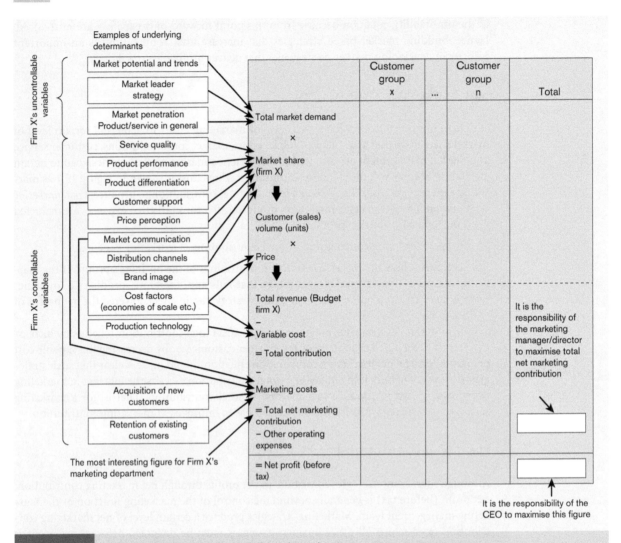

Figure 16.2 A marketing budget and its underlying determinants

If we had information about the size of assets (accounts receivable + inventory + cash + plant + equipment) we could also define:

$$\text{return on assets (ROA)} = \frac{\text{net profit (before tax)}}{\text{assets}}$$

ROA is similar to the well-known measure ROI (return on investment).

16.3 CUSTOMER PROFITABILITY AND CUSTOMER LIFETIME VALUE

Net present value (NVP)
Represents total present value (PV) of a time series of future cash flows

Traditional accounting systems have viewed customers as sources of revenue. More and more firms, however, are beginning to use their accounting systems to view customers as assets, basing their decisions on customers as much as they would base their decisions on investments. Therefore we propose customer lifetime value (CLTV) to be the central unit of measurement for customer profitability. We define CLTV as the **net present value (NPV)** of the profit a firm stands to realise on the average new customer during a given number of years.

The transition from market share to customer share (share of disposable income) is a prevalent theme in the CRM debate about customer loyalty and lifetime value. One result of the debate is a growing understanding that a large market share is not equivalent to having loyal customers. What you have today can be gone tomorrow, if the customer is not locked in or dependent (Gupta and Mela, 2008).

Loyal customers should be viewed as an asset by the firm, and it should work to create relationships that will maintain their loyalty (Forbes, 2007).

Long-term contracts and repeat sales produce predictable sources of revenue. In fact, the worth of many businesses can be calculated by the size of the customer base, such as the number of subscribers of a mobile phone company. Customers are not viewed as prospects for a single sale or as targets for problem solving. Rather, they are partners in a relationship that produces long-term cash flows for the seller (Turner *et al.*, 2007).

Ask yourself this question: What is the overall length of the relationship (retention) and how much will the customer buy in his or her lifetime?

Retention rate is used to measure customer turnover. It shows how large a percentage of its customer portfolio the enterprise retains yearly. The **churn rate**, on the other hand, shows how large a percentage of its customer portfolio the enterprise loses every year.

When an enterprise operates with a churn rate of 20 per cent – retention rate of 80 per cent – it means that it replaces one customer in five each year. In other words, it completely replaces all of its customers over a five-year period. In this case, the period over which the enterprise can generate income from the customer will be only five years – the so-called CLTV.

Retention rate has great significance for the creation of value. Research has shown that when the enterprise increases the retention rate from e.g. 80 to 90 per cent, it can double CLTV. Longevity creates value.

Realising the full profit potential of a customer relationship

How much is a loyal customer worth in terms of profits? Reichheld (1994) analysed the profit per customer in different service businesses, categorised by the number of years that a customer had been with the firm. Reichheld found that the longer the customer remained with a firm in each of these industries, the more profitable they became to serve. Annual profits per customer, which have been indexed over a seven-year period for easier comparison, are summarised in Table 16.1. As shown in Table 16.1, it is more profitable to keep existing customers than acquire new ones. During the normal development of a customer relationship, the cost to market and sell to these customers gradually declines, and the potential for **gross margin** improvement increases.

The loyal customer rarely focuses on price alone but instead sees customer relationships in terms of value for money. In this way, the customer acts as an advocate for the enterprise and thus helps attract new customers.

Churn rate
Refers to the proportion (%) of contractual customers or subscribers who leave a supplier during a given time period. A churn rate of 20% means that a company's customers on average stay with the supplier for 5 years.

Retention rate
The percentage of customers who continue to purchase from the supplier in a subsequent year. Retention rate = 100% − churn rate (%). If churn rate is 20%, the retention rate is 80%.

Gross margin
The difference between net sales and cost of goods sold.

Table 16.1	Calculation of CLTV for one mobile telephone customer		
Period	Cash flow ($)	Present value of $1 (discount rate = 10%)	Net present value (NPV) of cash flow ($)
0	−50	1.000	−50
1	15	0.909	+13.6
2	40	0.826	+33.0
3	50	0.751	+37.6
4	60	0.683	+41.0
5	70	0.621	+43.5
6	80	0.564	+45.1
7	90	0.513	+46.2
CLTV			+210

Let us assume that Table 16.1 illustrates an example with average profit per mobile telephone customer generated over a seven-year period. Acquiring a new customer produces a loss of US$50 the first year. Consequently, the break-even of this customer is at the beginning of year 3. In this example, the average customer life is seven years, meaning that the churn rate is 14 per cent ($1/7 \times 100\%$). Working backward, we can estimate the customer retention rate to be 86 per cent as in Table 16.1.

Customer retention

To estimate the lifetime value of the customer at this rate of customer retention, we need to compute the net present value of the customer cash flow in Table 16.1. In this example we assume that the yearly cash flow is equal to the yearly net profit. The calculation of present value is shown in Table 16.1 using a discount rate of 10 per cent.

The payback time of the investment ($50) in customer acquisition is a little more than two years. The CLTV per customer is $210. If the firm has 10,000 mobile telephone customers, the total CLTV would be $2.1 million.

If customer lifetime were only, say, four years, the customer value (net present value) would be considerably smaller. Thus, the higher rate of customer retention, the longer the average customer life expectancy and the greater the CLTV.

In Table 16.2 the CLTV calculation is a little more complex than in Table 16.1. Table 16.2 is based on an average of 1000 customers.

Table 16.2	Calculating CLTV for an average of 1000 customers				
	Year 1	Year 2	Year 3	Year 4	Year 5
Revenue					
Number of customers (left)	1,000	400	180	90	50
Retention rate	40%	45%	50%	55%	60%
Average annual sales per customer	$150	$150	$150	$150	$150
Total revenue	$150,000	$60,000	$27,000	$13,500	$7,425
Costs					
Cost percentage	50%	50%	50%	50%	50%
Total costs	$75,000	$30,000	$13,500	$6,750	$3,713
Profits					
Gross profit	$75,000	$30,000	$13,500	$6,750	$3,713
Discount rate	1.00	1.20	1.44	1.73	2.07
NPV profit	$75,000	$25,000	$9,375	$3,906	$1,790
Cumulative NPV profit	$75,000	$100,000	$109,375	$113,28	$115,072
CLTV (per customer)	$75.00	$100.00	$109.38	$113.28	$115.07

This spreadsheet might be typical of a firm marketing a magazine subscription. If we assume that the firm sells 1,000 new subscriptions in year 1 at $150 each, then the calculation of net revenue and net costs at 50 per cent of revenue are both simple procedures. A further important issue is retention – in simple terms, how many customers at the beginning of a year are still subscribers at the year's end. Table 16.2 assumes a retention rate of 40 per cent at the end of year 1, then increases this gradually over the five-year period. Thus, 400 customers are still subscribers at the beginning of year 2, 180 at the beginning of year 3, and so forth. Naturally, the revenues and costs for a year are functions of the number of customers in the beginning of that year. Calculating gross profit is then a simple subtraction procedure.

As in all investments, the NPV for a customer five years from now is not worth what it is today. The discount rate we have chosen in Table 16.1 is 20 per cent – a discretionary figure, the choice of which will vary from firm to firm. Some may choose a premium bank rate, others an internal rate of return, still others some minimum rate of investment acceptability. The final calculation is a simple one: what is the CLTV of a customer who became a customer in year 1? The answer is the NPV of the cumulative gross profit for the year divided by the number of customers (1,000) in year 1. Thus, the CLTV of one of these customers in year 4 would be $113.28; $115.07 in year 5, and so on.

An obvious application of this spreadsheet is its use in calculating what can be done to increase CLTV. The decision maker can change variables such as price, costs, the discount rate, the number of years an individual will be a customer, and the retention rate to determine the effects these will have on CLTV. In more general terms, however, it is worth considering what can be done from a marketing strategy perspective to maximise CLTV.

In summary we can increase CLTV by increasing the lifetime, increasing sales to customers and cutting the costs of serving a customer.

Increasing CLTV

Increasing customer life

There have been some excellent recent examples of firms extending the life of a customer by adapting the marketing strategy. Kimberly-Clark, manufacturer of Huggies disposable diapers, was subject to the limitations imposed by the fact that the 'life' of a Huggie customer (the baby) averaged only 18 months, until the child became toilet-trained. Market research also revealed a considerable degree of guilt among parents. Mothers and fathers felt guilty that little Johnny or Mary was still in 'nappies', while simultaneously feeling guilty at pushing a small child who might not be ready for pants. So Kimberly-Clark introduced 'trainer-pants', which fit like real pants but are disposable and have all the absorbency of the conventional nappy. No more guilt for parents. More important, Huggies have increased customer life by about six months. Though this might not seem much in real terms, it is effectively a 33 per cent average increase in customer life.

While the Huggies strategy has extended customer life, an alternative strategy would be to ask how a customer's life could start earlier. The Danish toy company Lego made building blocks that were played with by children between the ages of four and eight, on average. But this was a customer life of only about four years. So the company embarked on strategies that both began the customer life earlier and extended it for longer. In 1969 it launched Duplo – essentially, bigger Lego blocks that can be played with by children as young as two – thus adding two years to customer life. In 1977 it launched Lego Technic, an intricate set of construction blocks and fittings for older children (Pitt *et al.*, 2000).

Increasing retention rate

Current industry retention rates have a direct impact on long-term customer value. Where retention rates are 50 per cent or below, the average customer stays with the firm for two years or less. If a firm improves its retention rates from 50 per cent to 55 per cent, the average retention increases to 2.2 years from 2.0 years. In contrast, if average retention rates in an industry are relatively high, of the order of 75 per cent or greater, then an increase of 5 per cent in customer retention has a far greater impact. For example, improving retention rates from 75 per cent to 80 per cent improves customer retention from four years to five years. Here, long-term customer value is substantially greater and the leverage effect is more significant. The key to estimating and increasing average retention rates is to examine switching costs in the industry. To the extent that 'natural' or inherent switching costs exist, firms can retain their customer base with relatively less effort. These situations include monopolies, long-term contracts, warranties tied to service and buying arrangements (e.g. a business has preferred rates with a hotel chain). Generally, higher switching costs will be related to higher retention rates. Industries that have higher switching costs will tend to have some or all of the following characteristics (Butcher *et al.*, 2001).

Membership-based programmes

Membership services, such as banks, telephone firms and credit card companies, have a formal tie or link with the customer. The customer must make an explicit decision to break the link and some effort is required to move to another firm. Further, from the provider's viewpoint, the formal link offers valuable customer information that may be used to enhance loyalty.

Loyalty-based programmes

Loyalty card
Usually a plastic card which is issued by a company to a customer and is used to record the frequency of the customer's purchases and calculate resulting discounts, rewards or allowances.

A vast range of industries focus on customer retention and loyalty nowadays, from airline frequent flyer schemes to supermarket **loyalty card** programmes. Even Coca-Cola now has an established loyalty programme. Many companies reward customers simply by discounting or offering free products or services (airlines offering free flights, telephone companies discounting regular and frequent calls to friends and families). More and more firms are realising that all customers are not the same, and that more individualised strategies will be more effective at retaining them.

Loyalty is a function of both the customer's unwillingness to exit and his or her ability to exert a voice, so managers should focus on loyalty by reducing the tendency to exit and providing opportunities to voice any concerns or complaints.

Some practical illustrations of these issues in recent times can be seen in the airline industry. Most frequent flyer schemes attempt to reduce exit by offering air miles to customers, who are then presumably unwilling to leave because they do not wish to lose those miles (we might refer to this as the economies of loyalty). But for customers this is a false loyalty, as they might endure poor quality of service (normally a reason for exiting) merely to avoid losing the miles. Besides, frequent flyers who put in hundreds of thousands of miles annually are not likely to be motivated by the reward of even more flying.

High degree of customer contact

The opportunity to establish a relationship with the customer through personal knowledge and customisation to individual preferences will reduce risk and increase customer confidence in the firm. Professional service firms, hair stylists and financial services typically have either frequent contact and/or a long encounter when they meet their customers. The customer information gained during these encounters allows the firm to both meet and anticipate customer expectations.

Ability to differentiate

Services that are experience and/or credence based have a higher perceived risk (i.e. the cost of failure is high), and it is important to have a greater opportunity to be differentiated. Again, professional service firms, car repair services, delivery services and digital phone services can add customer value through offering various arrays of bundled services and/or better delivery of the core offering. Through effective differentiation these firms can improve retention rates.

Increasing sales to customers

This is done by raising either the firm's share of the customer's purchases or the customer's referral rate (the number of times the customer refers others to the firm's products and services).

If the firm can segment and target high volume or usage customers, the revenue generated is substantial. In a number of industries, including financial services, the revenue generated from the high volume customers accounts for 70 per cent or more of the firm's business. Increasing the retention rates among these customers, or increasing their expenditure will be profitable. The key point is that the customer base must have varying spending rates and the high volume customers need to be identified. That is, the firm must be able to determine the average profitability per year by customer or segment.

Cutting the costs of serving a customer

The more the costs of serving customers can be reduced, the greater the profit margin on those customers that can be realised in the future. In many environments, it is also possible to cut costs by getting the customer to perform some of the work involved in service delivery – what Downes and Mui (1998) call 'outsourcing to the customer'. Surprisingly, customers often prefer this because it gives them greater control over the delivery process. When firms can develop systems to process customer transactions efficiently and effectively, servicing costs are also lower. This occurs with many financial services and business markets where large volumes of transactions are a characteristic of the industry.

The reasons why the profit per customer increases over time are schematically illustrated in Figure 16.3. The economic effect of customer loyalty can be attributed to the following factors: acquisition costs, revenue growth, reduced cost, **referrals** and price premiums.

Referrals
Usually obtained by the salesperson asking current customers if they know of someone else, or another company, who might have a need for the salesperson's product.

The vertical axis in the figure is only an example (a mobile telephone customer), because the effects on profits of the various factors differ from industry to industry, firm to firm, and even customer to customer. However, the height of the sections gives some general indications of the relative importance of these factors. Every firm should, however, take the time and trouble to study its accounting and reporting system in order to make the necessary calculations of the influence on total profits per customer of these and possibly other profit

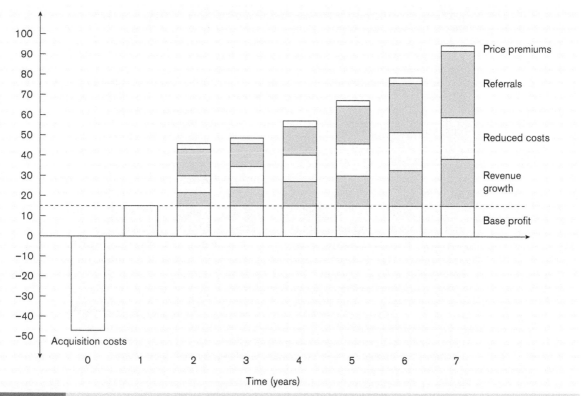

Figure 16.3	Illustration of customer lifetime value

Source: Adapted from Reichheld, F. F. (1994), Loyalty and the renaissance of marketing management, *Marketing Management*, 12(4): 17–25. Reproduced with permission from the American Marketing Association.

drivers. It is a time-consuming task, because in most firms the figures needed are not readily available – revenues and costs are usually registered on a per product basis and not usually on a per customer basis. These factors are discussed below.

Acquisition costs

The active acquisition of new customers using sales and external marketing efforts is required in most businesses. As a rule of thumb, getting a new customer costs five to six times as much as the costs of normal service operations (sales calls, providing information about new goods or services, etc.) to keep an existing satisfied customer. In other words, it costs only 15–20 per cent of what has to be invested in getting a new customer to keep an existing customer. The economics of customer loyalty are very apparent. These figures of course vary from industry to industry, and situation to situation, but are nevertheless remarkable. In Figure 16.3 the acquisition cost per customer appears as a negative profit effect in the year before the customer relationship starts.

Base profit

In many service industries the price paid by customers during the first year or even the first few years does not cover the costs of producing the service. This is the base profit in the figure. After some years, depending on the industry and other factors, the accumulated base profits have covered the initial marketing costs of getting the customer.

Revenue growth

In most situations a long-standing customer will bring more business to the same service provider. Customers may decide to consolidate their purchases with a single supplier who provides high quality service.

This means that, on average, customers can be expected to contribute more to a firm's profit as the relationship grows. The annual revenue per customer increases over the years, thus contributing to growing profits.

Reduced costs

As the service provider and the customer learn about each other, and they get experience with what to expect and how to perform, service processes will be smoother and take less time, and fewer mistakes that have to be corrected will be made. Thus, the average operating costs per customer will decrease, which in turn has a positive impact on profits.

Referrals

Positive word-of-mouth recommendations are like free advertising, saving the firm from having to invest as much money in these activities.

Long-standing and satisfied customers will create positive word-of-mouth communication and recommend the supplier or service provider to friends, neighbours, business associates and others. The customer takes over the role of marketer without any additional costs to the firm. A large number of businesses, especially smaller ones, thrive on good referrals by satisfied customers. In this way new customers are brought in with lower than normal acquisition costs, which has an extra positive effect on profits.

With many services, particularly those that are primarily experience based (e.g. restaurants) or credence based (e.g. professional services, technical services such as car tuning), word of mouth may be quite important in generating new business. Services that are high risk, which would include professional services, would also tend to have high impact from word of mouth.

Price premiums

New customers often benefit from introductory promotional discounts whereas long-term customers are more likely to pay regular (higher) prices. Moreover, when customers trust suppliers they may be more willing to pay higher prices at peak periods or for express work.

The argument is that the customer trusts the firm, values the relationship, and is therefore less sensitive to price increases.

Of course, it is not always the case that old customers pay a premium price. Sometimes, long-lasting relationships have given the customer a bargaining position based on power or social relationships, which keeps prices down. If this happens, a negative profit-eroding effect occurs.

EXHIBIT 16.1
Simulation of firm Xs customer value (cumulative sales for firm X over periods 1 to 10) with different retention rates

The assumptions for Table 16.3 are:

- Customer value is defined as accumulated sales for 100 customers of firm X from periods 1 to 10.
- Every customer makes one transaction per period.
- Every transaction is €100.
- The costs of the transaction are not considered.
- Firm X's ability to attract new customers is not considered.

Table 16.3 shows that if firm X can increase its retention rate from 50 per cent to 60 per cent the customer value (here defined as cumulative sales from periods 1 to 10) will increase 24 per cent, whereas an increase from 80 per cent to 90 per cent will increase cumulative sales by 46 per cent. Hence, the higher the retention rate, the higher the increase in customer value.

| Table 16.3 | Firm X's customer value under varying retention rates |

| Retention rate (repeat buying rate) | Number of customers left in each buying period | | | | | | | | | | Number of transactions | Customer value: cumulative sales from periods 1 to 10 | Growth of cumulative sales (%) |
	1	2	3	4	5	6	7	8	9	10			
50%	100	50	25	13	7	4	2	1	0	0	202	20,200	
													24%
60%	100	60	36	22	13	8	5	3	2	1	250	25,000	
													30%
70%	100	70	49	34	24	17	12	8	6	4	324	32,400	
													38%
80%	100	80	64	51	41	33	26	21	17	14	447	44,700	
													46%
90%	100	90	81	73	66	59	53	48	43	39	652	65,200	

16.4 CONTROLLING THE MARKETING PROGRAMME

The final, but often neglected, stage of marketing planning is the control process. Not only is control important to evaluate how we have performed, but it completes the circle of planning by providing the feedback necessary for the start of the next planning cycle. Unfortunately, control is often viewed by the people of an organisation as being negative. If individuals fear that the control process will be used not only to judge their performance, but as a basis for punishing them, then it will be feared and reviled.

The evaluation and control of marketing probably represents one of the weakest areas of marketing practice in many companies. Even the organisations that are otherwise strong in their strategic marketing planning have poor control and evaluation procedures for their global marketing. There are a number of possible reasons for this. First of all, there is no such thing as a standard system of **marketing control**.

Marketing control
A system of methods, procedures and devices used to ensure compliance with marketing policies and strategies.

The function of the organisational structure is to provide a framework in which objectives can be met. However, a set of instruments and processes is needed to influence the behaviour and performance of organisation members to meet the goals. The critical issue is the same as with organisational structures: what is the ideal amount of control? On the one hand, headquarters needs information to ensure that marketing activities contribute maximum benefit to the overall organisation. On the other hand, controls should not be construed as a code of law.

The key question is to determine how to establish a control mechanism capable of early identification of emerging problems. Considered here are various criteria appropriate for the evaluation process, control styles, feedback and corrective action. These concepts are important for all businesses, but in the international arena they are vital.

Design of a control system

In designing a control system, management must consider the costs of establishing and maintaining it and trade them off against the benefits to be gained. Any control system will require investment in a management structure and in systems design.

The design of the control system can be divided into two groups which depend on the object of control:

● output control (typically based on financial measures);
● behavioural controls (typically based on non-financial measures).

Output control may consist of expenditure control, which involves regular monitoring of expenditure figures, comparison of these with budget targets, and taking decisions to cut or increase expenditure where any variance is believed to be harmful. Measures of output are accumulated at regular intervals and typically forwarded from the foreign subsidiary to headquarters, where they are evaluated and criticised based on comparison with the plan or budget.

Behavioural controls require the exercise of influence over behaviour. This influence can be achieved, for example, by providing sales manuals to subsidiary personnel or by fitting new employees into the corporate culture. Behavioural controls often require an extensive **socialisation process**, and informal, personal interaction is central to the process. Substantial resources must be spent to train the individual to share the corporate culture; that is, the way things are done at the company.

Socialisation process
The process by which a society transmits its values, norms and roles to its members.

To build a common vision and values, managers at the Japanese company Matsushita spend a substantial amount of their first months in what the company calls cultural and spiritual training. They study the company credo, the 'Seven Spirits of Matsushita', and the philosophy of the founder, Kanosuke Matsushita.

However, there remains a strong tradition of using output (financial) criteria. A fixation with output criteria leads companies to ignore the less tangible behavioural (non-financial) measures, although these are the real drivers of corporate success. However, there is a weakness in the behavioural performance measures. To date there has been little success in developing explicit links from behaviour to output criteria. Furthermore, companies and managers are still judged on financial criteria (profit contribution). Until a clear link is established, it is likely that behavioural criteria will continue to be treated with a degree of scepticism.

We will now develop a marketing control system based primarily on output controls. Marketing control is an essential element of the marketing planning process because it provides a review of how well marketing objectives have been achieved. A framework for controlling marketing activities is given in Figure 16.4.

The marketing control system begins with the company setting some marketing activities in motion (plans for implementation). This may be the result of certain objectives and strategies, each of which must be achieved within a given budget. Hence budgetary control is essential.

The next step in the control process is to establish specific performance standards which will need to be achieved for each area of activity if overall and sub-objectives are to be achieved. For example, in order to achieve a specified sales objective, a specific target of performance for each sales area may be required. In turn, this may require a specific standard of performance from each of the salespeople in the region with respect to, for example, number of calls, conversion rates and, of course, order value.

The next step is to locate responsibility. In some cases responsibility ultimately falls on one person (e.g. the brand manager); in others it is shared (e.g. the sales manager and the sales force). It is important to consider this issue, since corrective or supportive action may need to focus on those responsible for the success of the marketing activity.

In order to be successful, the people involved and affected by the control process should be consulted in both the design and implementation stages of marketing control. Above all, they

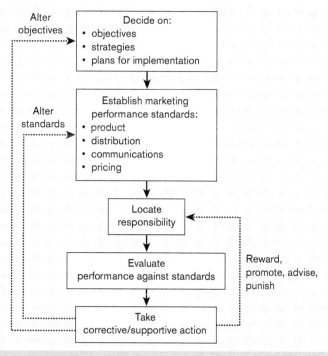

| **Figure 16.4** | The marketing control system |

Source: Hollensen, S. (2001) *Global Marketing: A Market Responsive Approach*, 2nd edn, Financial Times-Prentice Hall, Harlow, p. 600. Reproduced with permission.

will need to be convinced that the purpose of control is to improve their own levels of success and that of the company. Subordinates need to be involved in setting and agreeing their own standards of performance, preferably through a system of management by objectives.

Performance is then evaluated against these standards, which relies on an efficient information system. A judgement has to be made about the degree of success and failure achieved and what corrective or supportive action is to be taken. This can take various forms:

- Failure which is attributed to the poor performance of individuals may result in the giving of advice regarding future attitudes and actions, training and/or punishment (e.g. criticism, lower pay, demotion, termination of employment). Success, on the other hand, should be rewarded with praise, promotion and/or higher pay.

- Failure which is attributed to unrealistic marketing objectives and performance may cause management to lower objectives or lower marketing standards (Figure 16.4). Success which is thought to reflect unambitious objectives and standards may cause them to be raised in the next period.

Many firms assume that corrective action needs to be taken only when results are less than those required or when budgets and costs are being exceeded. In fact, both negative (underachievement) and positive (overachievement) deviations may require corrective action. For example, failure to spend the amount budgeted for, say, salesforce expenses may indicate that the initial sum allocated was excessive and needs to be reassessed, and/or that the salesforce is not as active as it might be.

It is also necessary to determine such things as the frequency of measurement (e.g. daily, weekly, monthly or annually). More frequent and more detailed measurement usually means more cost. We need to be careful to ensure that the costs of measurement and the control process itself do not exceed the value of such measurements and do not overly interfere with the activities of those being measured.

The impact of the environment must also be taken into account when designing a control system. The control system should measure only factors over which the organisation has control. Rewards make little sense if they are based on factors that may be relevant for overall corporate performance, but over which no influence can be exerted (e.g. price controls). Neglecting the factor of individual performance capability would send the wrong signals and severely impair the motivation of personnel.

Control systems should harmonise with local regulations and customs. In some cases, however, corporate behavioural controls have to be exercised against local customs even though overall operations may be affected negatively. This type of situation occurs, for example, when a subsidiary operates in markets where unauthorised facilitating payments are a common business practice.

Feedforward control

Much of the information provided by the firm's marketing control system is feedback on what has been accomplished in both financial (profits) and non-financial (customer satisfaction, market share) terms. As such, the control process is remedial in its outlook. It can be argued that control systems should be forward looking and preventive, and that the control process should start at the same time as the planning process. Such a form of control is feedforward control (Figure 16.5).

Feedforward control
The active anticipation and prevention of problems, rather than passive reaction.

Feedforward control continuously evaluates plans, monitoring the environment to detect changes that would call for objectives and strategies to be revised. Feedforward control monitors variables other than performance; variables that may change before performance itself changes. The result is that deviations can be controlled before their full impact has been felt. Such a system is proactive in that it anticipates environmental change, whereas other control systems are more reactive in that they deal with changes after they occur. Examples of early symptoms (early performance indicators) are presented in Table 16.4.

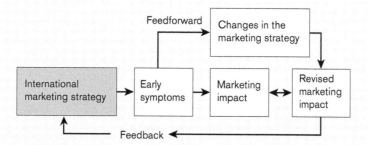

Figure 16.5	Adjustment of the marketing strategy

Source: Samli, A. C., Still, R. and Hill, J. S. (1993) *International Marketing: Planning and Practice*, Macmillan, London, p. 425. Reproduced with permission from A. Coskun Samli, the estate of Richard R. Still and John S. Hill.

Feedforward control focuses on information that is prognostic: it tries to discover problems waiting to occur. Formal processes of feedforward control can be incorporated into the business marketer's total control programme to enhance its effectiveness considerably. Utilisation of a feedforward approach would help ensure that planning and control are treated as concurrent activities.

Key areas for control in marketing

Kotler (2000) distinguishes four types of marketing control, each involving different approaches, different purposes and a different allocation of responsibilities. These are shown in Table 16.5. Here we will focus on annual plan control and profit control, since they are the most obvious areas of concern to firms with limited resources (e.g. SMEs).

Annual plan control

The purpose of annual plan control is to determine the extent to which marketing efforts over the year have been successful. This control will centre on measuring and evaluating sales in relation to sales goals, market share analysis and expense analysis.

Sales performance is a key element in the annual plan control. Sales control consists of a hierarchy of standards on different organisational control levels. These are interlinked, as shown in Figure 16.6.

We can see from the diagram that any variances in achieving sales targets at the corporate level are the result of variances in the performance of individual salespeople at the operational level. At every level of sales control, variances must be studied with a view to determining their causes. In general, variances may be due to a combination of variances in volume and/or price.

Table 16.4	Some key early performance indicators

Early performance indicators	Market implication
Sudden drop in quantities demanded.	Problem in marketing strategy or its implementation.
Sharp increase or decrease in sales volume.	Product gaining acceptance or being rejected quickly.
Customer complaints.	Product not debugged properly.
A notable decrease in competitors' business.	Product gaining acceptance quickly or market conditions deteriorating.
Large volumes of returned merchandise.	Problems in basic product design.
Excessive requests for parts or reported repairs.	Problems in basic product design, low standards.

Source: Samli, A. C., Still, R. and Hill, J. S. (1993) *International Marketing: Planning and Practice*, Macmillan, New York. Reproduced with permission of A. Coskun Samli, the estate of Richard R. Still and John S. Hill.

Table 16.5	Types of marketing control		
Type of control	Prime responsibility	Purpose of control	Examples of techniques/approaches
Strategic control	• Senior management • Middle management	• To see if planned results are being achieved	• Marketing effectiveness ratings • Marketing audit
Efficiency control	• Line and staff management • Marketing controller	• To examine ways of improving the efficiency of marketing	• Salesforce efficiency • Advertising efficiency • Distribution efficiency
Annual plan control	• Senior management • Middle management	• To see if planned results are being achieved.	• Sales analysis • Market share analysis • Marketing expenses to sales ratio • Customer tracking
Profit control (budget control)	• Marketing controller	• To examine where the company is making and losing money	• Profitability by e.g. product, customer group or trade channel

Source: Kotler, P. (2000) *Marketing Management: Millennium Edition*, 10th ed., Prentice Hall, Upper Saddle River, NJ. Copyright © 2000 Pearson Education, Inc. Reproduced with permission.

Global profit control

In addition to the previously discussed control elements, all international marketers must be concerned to control their profit. The budgetary period is normally one year because budgets are tied to the accounting systems of the company.

Table 16.6 presents an example of a global marketing budget for a manufacturer of consumer goods. Included in the budget are those marketing variables which can be controlled and changed by the sales and marketing functions (departments) in the home country and in

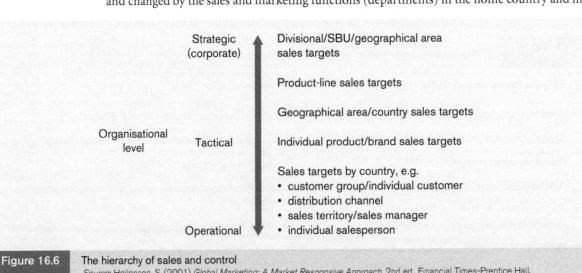

Figure 16.6	The hierarchy of sales and control

Source: Hollensen, S. (2001) *Global Marketing: A Market Responsive Approach*, 2nd ed., Financial Times-Prentice Hall, Harlow, p. 605. Reproduced with permission.

the export market. In Table 16.6 the only variable that cannot be controlled by the international sales and marketing departments is variable costs.

The global marketing budget system (as presented in Table 16.6) is used for the following (main) purposes:

- allocation of marketing resources among countries/markets to maximise profits. In Table 16.6 it is the responsibility of the global marketing director to maximise the total contribution 2 for the whole world;

- evaluation of country/market performance. In Table 16.6 it is the responsibility of export managers or country managers to maximise contribution 2 for each of their countries.

Please note that besides the marketing variables presented in Table 16.6, the global marketing budget normally contains inventory costs for finished goods. As the production

| Table 16.6 | An example of an international marketing budget |

		Europe			America		Asia/Pacific			Other markets		Total world Σ	
	UK		Germany	France	USA		Japan	Korea					
	B	A	B	A	B	A	B	A	B	A	B	A	B	A	B	A
International marketing	B	A	B	A	B	A	B	A	B	A	B	A	B	A	B	A

Budget year = _____

Net sales (gross sales less trade discounts, allowances, etc.)

÷ **Variable costs**

= **Contribution1**

÷ **Marketing costs**

Sales costs (salaries commissions for agents, incentives, travelling, training, conferences)

Consumer marketing costs (TV commercials, radio, print, sales promotion)

Trade marketing costs (fairs, exhibitions, in-store promotions, contributions for retailer campaigns)

= **Total contribution 2** (marketing contribution)

B = budget figures; A = actual.

Note: On a short-term (one-year) basis, the export managers or country managers are responsible for maximising the actual figures for each country and minimising their deviation from budget figures. The international marketing manager/director is responsible for maximising the actual figure for the total world and minimising its deviation from the budget figure. Cooperation is required between the country managers and the international marketing manager/director to coordinate and allocate the total marketing resources in an optimum way. Sometimes certain inventory costs and product development costs may also be included in the total marketing budget (see main text).

Source: Adapted from Hollensen, S. (2001) *Global Marketing: A Market Responsive Approach*, 2nd ed., Financial Times-Prentice Hall, Harlow, p. 605. Reproduced with permission.

runs of these goods are normally based on input from the sales and marketing department, the inventory of unsold goods will also be the responsibility of the international marketing manager or director.

Furthermore, the global marketing budget may also contain customer-specific or country-specific product development costs, if certain new products are preconditions for selling in certain markets.

In contrast to budgets, long-range plans extend over periods from two years up to ten years, and their content is more qualitative and judgemental in nature than that of budgets. For SMEs shorter periods (such as two years) are the norm because of the perceived uncertainty of diverse foreign environments.

Overall economic value with successful implementation of CRM

The CRM process creates value by working with the customer to improve performance and business processes (see Figure 16.7). For example, the firm may negotiate with the customer's team to implement a new inventory system. If the relationship reduces costs and can yield a price reduction for the customer, revenues may increase as a result of increasing market share for the firm. Revenues may also increase as a result of better in-stock availability at the end of

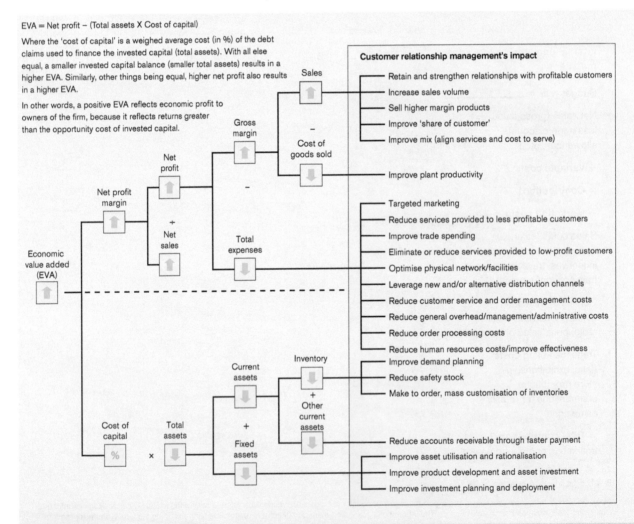

Figure 16.7   How customer relationship management affects economic value added (EVA)

Source: Adapted from Lambert, D. M. and Pohlen, T. L. (2001) Supply chain metrics, *The International Journal of Logistics Management*, 12(1): 10. Reproduced with permission from The Supply Chain Management Institute (www.scm-institute.org).

the supply chain. The cost of goods sold may decrease through better scheduling of material requirements and more efficient utilisation of plant capacity and labour.

The cost-of-goods sold may be reduced through the leveraging of larger buys with a smaller group of suppliers. Other costs may increase due to reduced order processing and forecasting costs. Inventory carrying costs decrease as point-of-sale data are used to schedule shipments instead of forecasting requirements and maintaining safety stock. Better capacity utilisation and collaborative planning and forecasting of requirements may reduce the need for customer-specific assets. In the end, the process improvements obtained through successful implementation of CRM can be translated into increased shareholder value through the use of an **economic value added (EVA)** model (Figure 16.7). By comparing net profit margin with cost of capital in Figure 16.7 the result would be a higher EVA.

EVA (economic value added) was popularised by the consulting firm of Stern and Steward (see further description in Steward, 1990).

EVA may be defined in the following way:

$$EVA = \text{Net profit} - (\text{Total assets} \times \text{Cost of capital}).$$

'Cost of capital' is a weighted average cost (in percentage terms) of the debt claims used to finance the invested capital (total assets). With all else equal, a smaller invested capital balance (smaller total assets) results in a higher EVA. Similarly, other things being equal, higher net profit also results in a higher EVA.

In other words, a positive EVA reflects economic profit to owners of the firm, because it reflects returns greater than the opportunity cost of invested capital.

> **Economic value added (EVA)**
> EVA = Net profit − (Total assets × Cost of capital). A smaller invested capital balance (smaller total assets) results in a higher EVA. Similarly, higher net profit also results in a higher EVA.

16.5 SUMMARY

Marketing strategies directly affect customers and sales revenue. However, they also affect margins, total contribution and marketing costs. These effects, in turn, lead to the total net marketing contribution. Because operating (manufacturing) costs and overhead costs are beyond the control of marketing managers, net marketing contribution plays the most important role for the marketing department, to determine the profit impact of a marketing strategy.

Traditional accounting systems have viewed customers as sources of revenue. More and more firms are beginning to use their accounting systems to view customers as assets, basing their decisions on customers as much as they would base their decisions on investments. Therefore, we propose *customer lifetime value* (CLTV) to be the central unit of measurement for customer equity. We define CLTV as the net present value (NPV) of the profit a firm stands to realise on the average new customer during a given number of years.

As marketing plans are being implemented, they have to be monitored and controlled. Control is the process of ensuring that global marketing activities are carried out as intended. It involves monitoring aspects of performance and taking corrective action where necessary. The global marketing control system consists of deciding marketing objectives, setting performance standards, locating responsibility, evaluating performance against standards, and taking corrective or supportive action.

In a conventional control system, managers wait until the end of the planning period to take corrective action. In a feedforward control system, corrective action is taken during the planning period by tracking early performance indicators and steering the organisation back to its desired objectives if they are not being achieved.

The most obvious areas of control relate to the control of the annual marketing plan and the control of profitability. The purpose of the global marketing budget is mainly to allocate marketing resources across countries to maximise the worldwide total marketing contribution. The process improvements obtained through successful implementation of CRM can be translated into increased shareholder value through the use of an economic value added (EVA) model.

CASE STUDY 16.1

Jordan
Developing an international marketing control and budget system for toothbrushes

Jordan is a family-owned international manufacturer of manual and mechanical oral hygiene products, household and painting tools, based in Oslo, Norway.

Jordan is among the 10 largest manufacturers of toothbrushes in the world, employing 780 people, including 180 in Norway. In 2007 the Jordan Group had net sales of €130 million, of which 45 per cent originated from toothbrushes. Net profit (EBIT) was €5 million.

Jordan-branded toothbrushes can be found in more than 100 countries on 5 continents. Jordan is the leading toothbrush in more European countries than any other brand.

The group's operations comprise the Norwegian parent company Jordan AS and four foreign subsidiaries. Jordan AS manufactures and sells oral care and household cleaning products. In addition, the company markets and distributes painting tools manufactured by its subsidiary, Anza AB.

- **Anza AB** produces and markets painting tools, and has become even more significant to the group after the acquisition of Britain's Hamilton Acorn in 2001. The company's head office is in Sweden.

- **Jordan (Far East) Ltd** is responsible for group sales in the Asia-Pacific region, with its head office in Malaysia.

- **Wisdom Toothbrushes Ltd** manufactures and markets toothbrushes in the UK, and has its head office in England.

- **Peri-dent Ltd** is one of the world's leading developers and manufacturers of dental floss, with its head office in Scotland.

History

1837: Wilhelm Jordan, Danish combmaker moved to Christiania (Oslo) and opened his workshop in the city centre. Soon afterwards he discovered that the town needed a brush factory. He hired the best local and foreign craftsmen, and the brushmaking business started to prosper.

1879: Wilhelm's son Fredrik Jordan took over the enterprise. The factory was modernised, and the variety of brushes became wider and wider.

1911–16: The founder's grandson Hjalmar Jordan, after taking the lead of the company, discovered the

Jordan manual toothbrushes
Source: Courtesy of Jordan AS

necessity of corporate changes. He bought two local competitors and moved the factory to bigger premises. At that time the product catalogue contained several thousand articles.

1927: Hjalmar Jordan, during his travels, found a new business opportunity: the toothbrush. Jordan became the first toothbrush manufacturer in Norway, by building a new factory only for toothbrush production. One thing was clear from the very beginning: Jordan's commitment to the best quality produced in the most sanitary conditions. The toothbrushes were sold under the 'Pronto' brand name.

1937: On its 100th anniversary, the company employed 144 people, produced 225,000 toothbrushes per year and had a turnover of NOK13 million. Jordan controlled the major part of the Norwegian market.

1940–50: Jordan remained stable after the war, and made further investments in new production technologies.

1958: Jordan entered the first export markets: Denmark, England, West Germany, Sweden and Finland. At the same time new methods of product presentation were introduced: toothbrushes were packed individually in a transparent plastic container.

1960–68: The product assortment was rationalised, and focus was put on toothbrushes and oral care products. Manufacturing of dental sticks started. Exports expanded, partnerships were formed, and by the end of the 1960s Jordan sold 25 million toothbrushes per year.

1969: Since this year, just like the export label, the domestic toothbrushes have been named 'Jordan'. New production site opened in Flisa, Norway.

1970: Jordan entered the paintbrush market by acquiring Anza in Sweden. In 1976 total turnover exceeded NOK100 million. The company moved to today's location. In 1973 the revolutionary spoon-shaped toothbrush was developed in association with dental experts. This brush (predecessor of today's Jordan Classic) set the direction for Jordan for the coming decades.

1983: The Colgate-Palmolive Company introduced a new type of toothbrush, which Jordan was asked to produce. A long-lasting relationship started based on the acknowledgement of Jordan's expertise.

1987: Freshly elected as 'Company of the Year 1986' in Norway, Jordan celebrated its 150th anniversary.

1988: Jordan opened its factory in Holland; Sanodent specialised in private label products. Peri-dent in Scotland was created as a joint venture and started to produce the total volume of Jordan dental flosses.

1992: Launch of Jordan Magic, the world's first colour-changing toothbrush.

1993: Launch of Jordan ActiveTip.

1995: Launch of Jordan Sport and Jordan Amigo.

1997: Launch of the Philips-Jordan electrical toothbrush.

1998: Jordan acquired Wisdom, England's leading toothbrush manufacturer (total sales in 1997: $16 million)

2000: Jordan consolidates its Norwegian toothbrush production at Flisa and discontinues production in Oslo.

2003: All toothbrush production is moved out of Norway to Wisdom in England.

2006: Jordan's interdental product programme is extended with a range of plastic dental sticks.

In addition to the Jordan-owned subsidiaries in Sweden, England, Scotland and Malaysia, Jordan toothbrushes are produced under licence in five countries: India, Nigeria, Syria, Malaysia and Indonesia.

The global toothbrush market

Table 16.7 shows the three general toothbrush market segments.

The main impetus to global growth was the phenomenal development of low-priced, mass-market

The Dental Floss Miracle (from the interdental programme)
Source: Courtesy of Jordan AS

Table 16.7	Toothbrush market segments, 2006	
Three toothbrush segments in the world market	**Examples of brands**	**Typical retail consumer prices (€)**
1 Manual toothbrushes	Jordan	3
2 Power toothbrush market, which can be divided into two sub-segments:		
(a) Battery-powered toothbrushes	P&G SpinBrush	7–8
(b) Electric toothbrushes (with rechargeable batteries)	Braun Oral-B	20

battery-operated toothbrushes, particularly in the US but also worldwide. This was triggered in the US by the acquisition of Dr John's Spinbrush by consumer products giant Procter & Gamble in late 2000. The global market for power toothbrushes amounted to just 55 million units in 2007, but this was a significant improvement on the level of 12.5 million units recorded in 1998.

Definitely the biggest buzz in the oral care category these days has been generated by battery-powered toothbrushes. According to Colgate-Palmolive, battery-powered brushes accounted for just 4 per cent of the toothbrush segment in 1999. Yet by the end of 2006, sales of these products accounted for 40 per cent of toothbrush sales in the EU-countries. The increasing popularity of power toothbrushes can also be seen in increasing sales figures for replaceable heads. All this means that manual toothbrushes have experienced a fallen market share in the total toothbrush market, whereas power toothbrushes have increased their market share.

The German toothbrush market

Although 99 per cent of Germans over 14 years already brush their teeth at least once a day, there is still scope for growth in toothbrushes. Dentists still tend to claim that more people could replace their toothbrush more often, with replacement being recommended at least once every three months.

Table 16.8 shows the general development in the German toothbrush market. As illustrated the power toothbrushes segment is divided into two sub-segments: battery and electric toothbrushes. Each of these segments is then divided into two segments.

German market for manual toothbrushes

Despite a negative attitude towards private label toothpaste, the share of private label toothbrushes is relatively high. Private label brands have adapted to consumer preferences and are now offering products with flexible

Table 16.8	Retail sales of toothbrushes by type: value (€m) 2003–2006			
	2003	2004	2005	2006
Manual toothbrushes	199.9	187.5	177.8	175.0
Power toothbrushes	53.1	103.1	120.5	124.4
● Battery toothbrushes	15.7	34.1	43.0	47.0
– Battery toothbrush units	5.4	11.9	15.8	17.2
– Battery toothbrush replacement heads	10.3	22.2	27.2	29.8
● Electric toothbrushes	37.5	69.0	77.5	77.4
– Electric toothbrush units	18.1	35.8	41.7	39.5
– Electric toothbrush replacement heads	19.4	33.2	35.8	37.9
Manual and power toothbrushes	253.1	290.6	298.3	299.4

Sources: Adapted from trade press (Lebensmittelzeitung, Lebensmittel Report), company research and reports, trade interviews, Euromonitor International (www.euromonitor.com) estimates.

Table 16.9	Replacement of manual toothbrushes 2006 (Germany)

Per cent of users changing their manual toothbrush	2006
Once a week	1.2
Once a month	27.4
Every three months	48.3
Every six months	16.8
Less than every six months	4.4
Never (don't need a manual toothbrush)	1.5
No reply	0.4
Total	100.0

Sources: Adapted from trade press and Euromonitor International (www.euromonitor.com) estimates.

toothbrush heads, X-shaped bristles or coloured indicators. As a result private label share has increased from 19 per cent in 2004 to 23 per cent in 2006.

While consumers at the high end of the market are still willing to pay up to €3.50 per brush, users of mid-range priced brushes are increasingly turning to private label products. Most of the main mass outlets, such as Schlecker, Aldi and DM, now include private label toothbrushes in their product ranges. As a result of growth in private labels and increased competition among brands, the average unit price of manual toothbrushes is stable at €3.0 in 2006.

The size of the market is determined by how often people are changing their toothbrush. Table 16.9 shows how often they do it.

Falling sales of child-specific manual toothbrushes

Value sales of children's brushes have decreased in line with the general decline of manual brushes. Parents hoping to improve their children's dental care are more likely to spend money on power brushes specifically designed for children, such as Colgate Motion Bzzz. For children, the shape, packaging and marketing of the toothbrushes is more important than the function. Consequently, children's brushes have become very colourful, often in the shape of popular cartoon characters or toys. Manufacturers of manual brushes are trying to attract children and their parents with features such as anti-slip grips or special toothbrushes for the different stages of dental development. This has led to higher average prices for child-specific brushes.

Competition in manual toothbrushes

Together, the four largest companies accounted for 70 per cent of value sales of manual toothbrushes in 2006. GlaxoSmithKline leads the way, with a 32 per cent share, due to the success of its Dr Best brand. Dr Best brushes are associated with a high level of expertise,

Toothbrushing – a family event
Source: Courtesy of Jordan AS

captured in a wide range of specialised toothbrushes. Oral-B, Procter & Gamble and Gaba follow, with 14 per cent, 12 per cent and 11 per cent shares in 2006. Gaba managed to increase its value share between 2004 and 2006, while other company shares remained stable or fell during the same time period. Elmex, Aronal and Meridol, the main Gaba brands, have a high level of recognition among German consumers, and are known as a forerunners in medical research.

Private label products are very successful, with a 23 per cent value share in 2006, up by 4.5 percentage points compared to 2003. The success of private label products in this sub-sector lies in the consumer perception of toothbrushes as secondary to toothpaste in terms of importance. While German consumers are likely to spend money on a 'quality' toothpaste, a private label toothbrush is perceived to do the same job as a similar branded product. This is especially the case with new private label brands, which keep up with branded labels in terms of new product development and innovations.

Power brushes change oral care

As early as the 1970s, Oral-B produced and sold electrical toothbrushes in Germany and other European countries, but it was not until 1998/9 that power brushes really took off. In 2000, the introduction of the first battery-operated toothbrushes gave the market new impetus, and their lower prices made them more affordable.

From 2000 onwards, power brushes made a real impact on oral hygiene, influencing other sub-sectors such as manual toothbrushes and toothpaste. In 2006, sales of power brushes and replacement heads amounted to €124.4 million.

Some models of battery brushes have to be replaced at regular intervals, while electric brushes have to be recharged. This means the number of replacement heads per sold unit is higher for electric brushes as new battery brushes come with a new head.

Switching between models

Consumers are expected to switch between brands and makes. Apart from the regular replacement of disposable battery toothbrushes, consumers are expected to switch from battery brushes to electric brushes. According to industry sources, many consumers use the cheaper battery brushes as an initial 'trial brush' before committing to the price of a more expensive electrical brush that might display additional benefits, such as different speed settings or gum protection against too much pressure. Likewise, users of electric toothbrushes are likely to upgrade their toothbrushes in line with new product developments.

QUESTIONS

Until now Jordan's market share in the total German toothbrush market was below 2 per cent, with high regional differences. In Norway the market share is around 60 per cent, in Denmark 25 per cent, in Sweden 20 per cent and in Poland it has risen to about 15 per cent.

Jordan's management in Norway is not satisfied with this market share in such a non-distant market as Germany. Therefore, you are contacted by the marketing director to help her with some suggestions for developing the marketing plan for Germany.

1 Discuss if it would be a good idea for Jordan to enter the German power toothbrush market with a new product? If yes, how should such a decision be implemented?

2 Outline a marketing plan for Jordan's existing product line (manual toothbrushes) in Germany.

3 Make a proposal for Jordan's marketing control and budget system – if possible, outline the specific Jordan marketing budget for the German market. Use the following for your marketing budget:

Financial calculation for a typical Jordan manual toothbrush (per unit):

Retail price	€4
Ex works price	€1.5
Variable costs	€1.0
Contribution margin	€0.5
Contribution margin	33%

(Please note that these figures are not official Jordan figures.)

SOURCES

Jordan AS (www.jordan.no); Euromonitor International (www.euromonitor.com); and various public sources: trade press, company research and reports, interviews

QUESTIONS FOR DISCUSSION

1 Why is customer profitability sometimes a better unit of measurement than market profitability?

2 Why is it important to consider customer lifetime value (CLTV)?

3   How can a firm increase CLTV?

4   Discuss why firms need marketing controls.

5   What is meant by performance indicators? What are they? Why does a firm need them?

6   Discuss the benefits gained by adopting a matrix organisational structure.

7   Discuss the problems involved in setting up and implementing a marketing control system.

8   To what general criteria should 'good' marketing objectives conform?

REFERENCES

Bartlett, C. and Ghoshal, S. (1989) *Managing Across Borders: The Transnational Solution*, Harvard University Press, Boston, MA.

Best, R. J. (2000) *Market-based Management*, Prentice Hall, Englewood Cliffs, NJ.

Butcher, K., Sparks, B. and O'Callaghan, F. (2001) Evaluative and relational influences on service loyalty, *International Journal of Service Industry Management*, 12(4): 310–27.

Downes, L. and Mui, C. (1998) *Unleashing the Killer Approach: Digital strategies for market dominance*, Harvard Business School Press, Boston, MA.

Forbes, T. (2007) Valuing customers, *Journal of Database Marketing & Customer Strategy Management*, 15(1): 4–10.

Gupta, S. and Mela, C. F. (2008) What is a free customer worth? *Harvard Business Review*, November: 102–9.

Hollensen, S. (2001) *Global Marketing: A Market Responsive Approach*, 2nd edn, Financial Times/Prentice Hall, Harlow.

Jobber, D. (1995) *Principles and Practice of Marketing*, McGraw-Hill, New York.

Katayama, O. (1994) Not toying around, *Look Japan*, November: 2–3.

Kotler, P. (2000) *Marketing Management: Analysis, Planning, Implementation and Control*, 10th edn, Prentice Hall, Englewood Cliffs, NJ.

Lambert, D. M. and Pohlen, T. L. (2001) Supply chain metrics, *The International Journal of Logistics Management*, 12(1): 1–12.

Lindström, O. (2001) US acquisitions, *Pulp and Paper International*, San Francisco, 43 (January): 15–20.

Lusch, R. F. (2000) Creating long-term marketing health, *Marketing Management*, 9(1) (Spring): 18–22.

Ortman, R. F. and Bucklmann D. M. (1998) Estimating marketing costs using activity-based cost drivers, *Journal of Cost Management*, July–August: 5–15.

Pitt, L. F., Ewing, M. T. and Berthon, P. (2000) Turning competitive advantages into customer equity, *Business Horizons*, September–October: 11–18.

Quelch, J. A. (1992) The new country managers, *The McKinsey Quarterly*, 4: 155–65.

Quelch, J. A. and Bloom, H. (1996) The return of the country manager, *The McKinsey Quarterly*, 2: 30–43.

Reichheld, F. F. (1994) Loyalty and the renaissance of marketing management, *Marketing Management*, 12(4): 17–25.

Samli, A. C., Still, R. and Hill, J. S. (1993) *International Marketing: Planning and Practice*, Macmillan, London.

Shelly, B. (1995) Cool customer, *Unilever Magazine*, 2: 12–17.

Steward, G. B. (1990) *The Quest for Value*, New York: Harper Business.

Turner, R., Lasserre, C. and Beauchet, P. (2007) Innovation in field force bonuses: enhancing motivation through a structured process-based approach, *Journal of Medical Marketing*, 7(2): 126–35.

Unilever (1996) *Introducing Unilever*, Unilever, Rotterdam.

APPENDIX
Market research and decision support system

LEARNING OBJECTIVES

After studying this appendix you should be able to:

- explain the concepts of data warehouses and data mining
- explain the main contents of a B2B customer file
- explain the importance of having a carefully designed international information system
- link global market research to the decision-making process
- discuss the key problems in gathering and using international market data
- distinguish between different research approaches, data sources and data types
- understand the relevance of the Web as an important data source in global marketing research

A.1 INTRODUCTION

The term market research refers to gathering, analysing and presenting information that is related to a well-defined problem. Hence the focus of market research is a specific problem or project with a beginning and an end.

Market research differs from a decision support system (DSS), which is information gathered and analysed on a continual basis. In practice, market research and DSS are often hard to differentiate, so they will be used interchangeably in this context.

Marketers have the idea that different customers should be treated differently to maximise the relationship with the best ones and minimise the involvement with the worst ones. Information technology helps to realise that desire. The reality comes at a cost, however, as relationship marketing presents a new set of challenges both to marketers and information systems managers. To succeed, an effective cross-functional team of information systems and marketing specialists must work harmoniously. In the past, the two groups barely understood or tolerated each other. On a positive note, a new breed of cross-disciplinary executives exists. They understand both marketing and technology. Overall, the most successful implementation will require true collaboration (Crie and Micheaux, 2006).

To be useful to organisations, knowledge tools must be accessible to mainstream users. They must be understandable and useful to marketing managers, not just statistical experts and information systems managers. To overcome potential problems in applicability, marketers must insist that several key goals be achieved. They include:

- putting the problem in the marketer's terms, including viewing the data from a marketing model perspective. Often the job of knowledge discovery is performed by analysts whose primary training is in statistics and data analysis. It is likely that these analysts do not have the same perspective as marketers. To be useful to marketing, the findings must be in a form that marketers can understand;

- presenting results in a manner that is useful for the business problem at hand. The foremost benefit of the analysis and the job of the analyst is to help solve business problems and increase or diminish the value of the analysis;

- providing support for specific key business analyses, marketers need to know about segmentation, market response, segment reachability. Knowledge discovery tools must support these analyses from the beginning;

- providing support for an extensive and iterative exploratory process. Realistic knowledge discovery is not simple and not linear. It is an interactive and iterative learning process. Initial results are fed back into the process to increase accuracy. The process takes time and can have a long lifespan.

The heart of RM (both for B2B and B2C marketing) is the database. The next section considers selected issues concerning data warehousing.

A.2 DATA WAREHOUSING

Data warehousing (or mining)
The storage and analysis of customer data gathered from their visits to websites for classification and modelling purposes so that products, promotions and price can be tailored to the specific needs of individual customers. The use of powerful computers to work through large volumes of data to discover purchasing patterns among an organisation's customers.

A customer data warehouse can be defined as large amounts of information about the customer, from sources both internal to the company and from the customer and third sources, such as the government, credit bureaus and market research firms. Data can include behaviours, preferences, lifestyle information, transactional data and data about communications with the firm before, during and after the sale. It may include information about customer profitability, satisfaction, retention, loyalty and referrals.

More generally, data warehouses can be described in terms of the processes and layers needed to automate and add value to communications with the customer and to facilitate mass customisation.

Data warehousing enables companies to extract information from the underlying data to develop a better understanding of the most profitable relationships, for example. Data mining relies on statistical modelling and the other tools discussed below to spot rules and patterns in customer information from the data warehouse.

A.3 DATA MINING

Data mining is a process that employs information technology – both hardware and software – to uncover previously unknown patterns of behaviour, trends and issues from the assessment of warehoused data.

The focus is on finding, for example, buying patterns that help marketers make better decisions. These data mining techniques may depend on a series of interactive, structured databases (data warehouse).

With the explosion in supermarket scanner data, techniques were developed to analyse supermarket sales data. The results portrayed the most important changes in a particular product's volume and market share. The reports often broke the results down by location, product type, price level or other factor. The most important element was the clear understandable business language used to write the reports. They offer real value to marketing managers. Since the initial efforts, factors such as distribution channels, price changes, promotional levels and competitive initiatives have been related to changes in volume, profits and share.

Still other knowledge tools have concentrated on the movement of retail stock at a point of sale. Such information can support decisions about shelf-space allocation, store layout, promotional effectiveness, product location and product turnover.

Databases can be centralised for common usage, distributed locally or widely for access by multiple users, and can apply to a single user.

A.4 THE CUSTOMER INFORMATION FILE

The benefits of a customer information file in RM are as follows (Gordon, 1998):

- Marketing effort becomes more efficient and more effective because the marketer is able to identify the most important customers and then present them with the right offer, product or service at the right time.
- Computer technology is harnessed to manage the vast amounts of data the marketer requires to interact with the customers in a truly personalised manner.
- A true 'dialogue' can be maintained with consumers by tracking interactions over time, identifying changes in purchasing, and allowing the marketer to anticipate future changes.
- New product development is facilitated by knowing who has purchased a product, how satisfied he or she is and whether any changes would enhance the performance of the product.

An example of a customer information file (from the B2B market) is presented in Table A.1 (only the most important data are shown).

Table A.1	An example of a B2B customer file
Identification	• Account or identification number • Company name • Main telephone number/fax/e-mail • Website address
Background	• Business demography – industry classification code (SIC) • History of company • Geography • Financial data, e.g. sales, growth rate and profitability, both overall and for relevant products; cash flow; return on investment; operating profit on net sales • Market position: market size for customer's products; market segment participation; market share; major customers. • Suppliers: major suppliers to this company and duration of relationships • Overall business strategies

→

Table A.1	An example of a B2B customer file (*continued*)
Pre-sale contact	<ul><li>Number of contacts prior to purchases</li><li>Types of information sought</li><li>Channels of communication initiated by customer (telephone, Internet, interactive voice response, etc.), by type of information sought</li><li>Call history – personal sales calls, by date, by audience</li></ul>
Purchases	<ul><li>Purchase behaviour</li><li>Frequency with which purchases are made (per day, week, month, year)</li><li>Amount spent on purchases</li><li>Average margin on customer's purchase</li></ul>
Decision makers	<ul><li>Names, titles</li><li>Staff who have relationships with these people</li></ul>
Decision making	<ul><li>Process (buying centre)</li><li>Decision initiators</li><li>Decision influencers</li><li>Decision makers</li><li>Executors of decision</li><li>Gatekeepers</li></ul>
Purchase cycle	<ul><li>Time required to make decision, by type of decision: new buy, modified rebuy and rebuy</li></ul>
Customer's buying criteria	<ul><li>Supplier selection criteria</li><li>Product selection criteria</li><li>Key selection and patronage criteria, overall company</li><li>Perceptions of company in respect of criteria</li><li>Perceptions of competitors in respect of criteria</li></ul>
Post-purchase behaviour	<ul><li>Services required</li><li>Items returned</li><li>Condition in which returned</li><li>Purchase amounts of returned product</li><li>Tone and manner of return, customer</li><li>Customer complaint frequency, recency</li><li>Customer satisfaction: overall and specific product/service</li></ul>
Distribution channels used by customers	<ul><li>Intermediaries used for product/service, type and name</li><li>Customer satisfaction with channel intermediaries</li></ul>
Pricing	<ul><li>Pricing history</li><li>Pricing expectations</li><li>Win/loss assessments: prices of winning vendors</li></ul>
Creditworthiness	<ul><li>Debt history</li><li>Receivables on account</li><li>Payment schedule</li><li>Credit scoring and rating</li></ul>

A.5 LINKING MARKET RESEARCH TO THE DECISION-MAKING PROCESS

Market research should be linked to the decision-making process within the firm. The recognition that a situation requires action is the initiating factor in the decision-making process.

Even though most firms recognise the need for domestic market research, this need is not fully understood for global marketing activities. Most SMEs conduct no international market research before they enter a foreign market. Often, decisions concerning entry and expansion in overseas markets and the selection and appointment of distributors are made after a subjective assessment of the situation. The research done is usually less rigorous, less formal and less quantitative than in LSEs. Furthermore, once an SME has entered a foreign market, it is likely to discontinue any research of that market. Many business executives therefore appear to view foreign market research as relatively unimportant.

A major reason that firms are reluctant to engage in global market research is the lack of sensitivity to cross-cultural customer tastes and preferences. What information should the global market research/DSS provide?

Table A.2 summarises the principal tasks of global market research, according to the major decision phases of the global marketing process. As can be seen, both internal (firm-specific) and external (market) data are needed. The role of a firm's internal information system in providing data for marketing decisions is often forgotten.

How the different types of information affect the major decisions have been thoroughly discussed in the different parts and chapters of this book. Besides the split between internal and external data, the two major sources of information are primary data and secondary data:

1 *Primary data*: These can be defined as information that is collected first-hand, generated by original research tailor-made to answer specific current research questions. The major advantage of primary data is that the information is specific ('fine grained'), relevant and

Table A.2	Information needed for major global marketing decisions
Global marketing decision	**Information needed**
Deciding whether to internationalise	● Assessment of global market opportunities (global demand) for the firm's products ● Commitment of the management to internationalise ● Competences and competitiveness of the firm compared to local and international competitors ● Domestic versus international market opportunities
Deciding which markets to enter	● Ranking of world markets according to market potential of countries/regions ● Local competition ● Political risks ● Trade barriers (tariff and non-tariff barriers) ● Cultural/psychic 'distance' to potential market
Deciding how to enter foreign markets	● Desired control, flexibility and risks ● Nature of the product (standard versus complex product) ● Size of markets/segments ● Behaviour of potential intermediaries ● Behaviour of local competition ● Transport costs ● Government requirements
Designing the global marketing programme	● Buyer behaviour (consumers and intermediaries) ● Competitive practice ● Available distribution channels ● Media and promotional channels
Implementing and controlling the global marketing programme	● Negotiation styles in different cultures ● Sales by product line, salesforce, customer type and country/region ● Contribution margins, financial metrics ● Marketing expenses per market

up to date. The disadvantages of primary data are, however, the high costs and amount of time associated with its collection.

2 *Secondary data*: These can be defined as information that has already been collected for other purposes and is thus readily available. The major disadvantage is that the data are often more general and 'coarse grained' in nature. The advantages of secondary data are the low costs and amount of time associated with its collection. For those who are unclear on the terminology, secondary research is frequently referred to as 'desk research'.

The two basic forms of research (primary and secondary research) will be discussed in further detail later in this appendix.

If we combine the split of internal/external data with primary/secondary data, it is possible to place data in four categories. In Figure A.1 this approach is used to categorise indicator variables for answering the following marketing questions. Is there a market for the firm's product A in country B? If yes, how large is it and what is the possible market share for the firm to obtain? Note that in Figure A.1 only a limited number of indicator variables are shown.

As a rule, no primary research should be done without first searching for relevant secondary information, and secondary data should be used whenever available and appropriate. Besides, secondary data often help to define problems and research objectives. In most cases, however, secondary sources cannot provide all the information needed and the company must collect primary data.

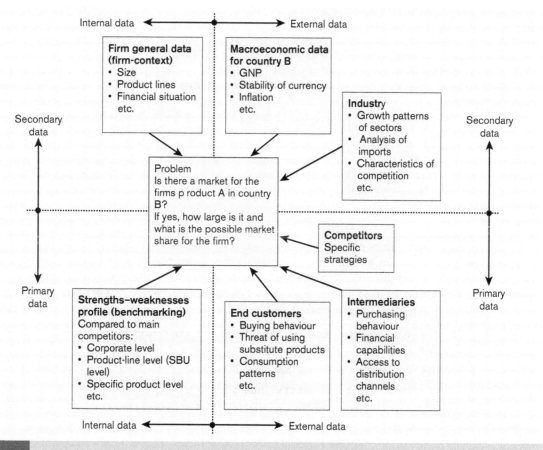

Figure A.1	Categorisation of data for assessment of market potential in a country

Source: Hollensen, S. (2001) *Global Marketing: A Market Responsive Approach*, 2nd ed., Financial Times-Prentice Hall, Harlow, p. 629. Reproduced with permission.

In Figure A.1 the most difficult and costly kind of data to obtain is probably the strengths and weaknesses of the firm (internal and primary data). However, because it compares the profile of the firm with those of its main competitors, this quadrant is a very important indicator of the firm's international competitiveness. The following two sections discuss different forms of secondary research and primary research.

A.6 SECONDARY RESEARCH

With many international markets to consider, it is essential that firms begin their market research by seeking and utilising secondary data.

Advantages of secondary research

Secondary research conducted from the home base is less expensive and less time consuming than research conducted abroad. No contacts have to be made outside the home country, thus keeping commitment to possible future projects at a low level. Research undertaken in the home country about the foreign environment also has the benefit of objectivity. The researcher is not constrained by overseas customs. As a preliminary stage of a market-screening process, secondary research can quickly generate background information to eliminate many countries from the scope of enquiries.

Disadvantages of secondary research

Problems with secondary research are as follows.

Non-availability of data

In many developing countries, secondary data are very scarce. Weak economies have poor statistical services – many do not even carry out a population census. Information on retail and wholesale trade is especially difficult to obtain. In such cases, primary data collection becomes vital.

Reliability of data

Sometimes political considerations may affect the reliability of data. In some developing countries, governments may enhance the information to paint a rosy picture of the economic life in the country. In addition, due to the data collection procedures used, or the personnel who gathered the data, many data lack statistical accuracy. As a practical matter, the following questions should be asked to judge the reliability of data sources (Cateora, 1993, p. 346):

- Who collected the data? Would there be any reason for purposely misrepresenting the facts?
- For what purpose was the data collected?
- How was the data collected (methodology)?
- Are the data internally consistent and logical in the light of known data sources or market factors?

Data classification

In many countries, the data reported are too broadly classified for use at the micro level.

Comparability of data

International marketers often like to compare data from different countries. Unfortunately, the secondary data obtainable from different countries are not readily comparable because national definitions of statistical phenomena differ from one country to another.

Although the possibility of obtaining secondary data has increased dramatically, the international community has grown increasingly sensitive to the issue of data privacy. Readily accessible large-scale databases contain information valuable to marketers but they are considered sensitive by the individuals who have provided the data. The international marketer must therefore also pay careful attention to the privacy laws in different nations and to the possible consumer response to using such data. Neglecting these concerns may result in research backfiring and the corporate position being weakened.

In doing secondary research or building a decision support system, there are many information sources available. Generally, these secondary data sources can be divided into internal and external sources (Figure A.1). The latter can be classified as either international/global or regional/country-based sources.

Internal data sources

Internal company data can be a most fruitful source of information. However, it is often not utilised as fully as it should be.

The global marketing and sales departments are the main points of commercial interaction between an organisation and its foreign customers. Consequently, a great deal of information should be available, including the following:

- *Total sales*: Every company keeps a record of its total sales over a defined time period; for example, weekly records, monthly records and so on.
- *Sales by countries*: Sales statistics should be split up by countries. This is partly to measure the progress and competence of the export manager or the salesperson (sometimes to influence earnings because commission may be paid on sales) and partly to measure the degree of market penetration in a particular country.
- *Sales by products*: Very few companies sell only one product. Most companies sell a range of products and keep records for each kind of product or, if the range is large, each product group.
- *Sales volume by market segment*: Such segmentation may be geographical or by type of industry. This will give an indication of segment trends in terms of whether they are static, declining or expanding.
- *Sales volume by type of channel distribution*: Where a company uses several different distribution channels, it is possible to calculate the effectiveness and profitability of each type of channel. Such information allows marketing management to identify and develop promising channel opportunities, and results in more effective channel marketing.
- *Pricing information*: Historical information relating to price adjustments by product allows the organisation to establish the effect of price changes on demand.
- *Communication mix information*: This includes historical data on the effects of advertising campaigns, sponsorship and direct mail on sales. Such information can act as a guide to the likely effectiveness of future communication expenditure plans.
- *Sales representatives' records and reports*: Sales representatives should keep a record card or file on every 'live' customer. In addition, sales representatives often send reports to head office on such matters as orders lost to competitors and possible reasons why, as well as on firms that are planning future purchasing decisions. Such information could help to bring improvements in marketing strategy.

External data sources

A very basic method of finding international business information is to begin with a public library or a university library. The Internet can help in the search for data sources. The Internet has made available thousands of databases for intelligence research (i.e. research on competitors). In addition, electronic databases carry marketing information ranging from the latest news on product development to new thoughts in the academic and trade press and updates in international trade statistics. However, the Internet will not totally replace other sources of secondary data. Cost compared to data quality will still be a factor influencing a company's choice of secondary data sources.

Links to some relevant international data sources may be reached at www.pearsoned .co.uk/hollensen.

Secondary data used for estimation of foreign market potential

Secondary data are often used to estimate the size of potential foreign markets. In assessing current product demand and forecasting future demand reliable historical data are required. As previously mentioned, the quality and availability of secondary data are frequently inadequate. Nevertheless, estimates of market size must be attempted in order to plan effectively. Despite limitations there are approaches to forecasting future demand in a market with a minimum of information. A number of techniques are available (see Craig and Douglas, 2000), but here only two are further explained: lead–lag analysis and estimation by analogy.

Lead–lag analysis

This technique is based on the use of time-series data from one country to project sales in other countries. It assumes that the determinants of demand in the two countries are the same, and that only time separates them. This requires that the diffusion process and specifically the rate of diffusion is the same in all countries. Of course this is not always the case, and it seems that products introduced more recently diffuse more quickly (Craig and Douglas, 2000).

Lead–lag analysis
Determinants of demand and the rate of diffusion are the same in two countries, but time separates the two.

Figure A.2 shows the principle behind the **lead–lag analysis** with an illustrative example in the DVD player market. By the end of 2003 it was assumed that 55 per cent of the US

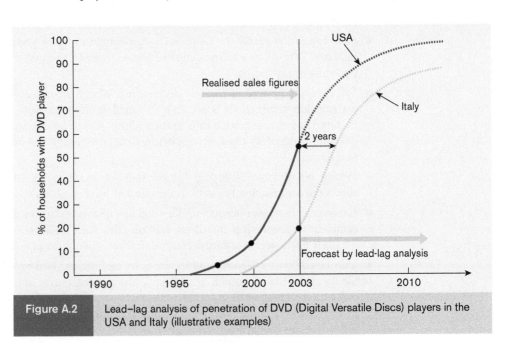

| Figure A.2 | Lead–lag analysis of penetration of DVD (Digital Versatile Discs) players in the USA and Italy (illustrative examples) |

households would have at least one DVD player in their home, whereas it was assumed that 'only' 20 per cent of Italian households would have one. We define the time lag between the American and the Italian DVD market as two years. To estimate the future penetration of DVD players in Italian households (and as a consequence also demand) we could make a parallel displacement of the S-formed US penetration curve by two years, as illustrated in Figure A.2. This also shows how rapidly new products today are diffused from market to market. The difficulty in using the lead–lag analysis includes the problem of identifying the relevant time lag and factors that impact future demand. However, the technique has considerable intuitive appeal to managers and is likely to guide some of their thinking.

When data are not available for a regular lead–lag analysis, estimation by analogy can be used.

Estimation by analogy

Estimation by analogy
A correlation value (between a factor and the demand for the product) for one market is used in another international market.

Estimation by analogy is essentially a single-factor index with a correlation value (between a factor and demand for a product) obtained in one country applied to a target international market. First a relationship (correlation) must be established between the demand to be estimated and the factor, which is to serve as the basis for the analogy. Once the known relationship is established the correlation value then attempts to draw an analogy between the known situation and the market demand in question.

Example

We want to estimate the market demand for refrigerators in Germany. We know the market size in the United Kingdom but we do not know it in Germany.

As nearly all households in the two countries already have a refrigerator, a good correlation could be number of households or population size in the two countries. In this situation we choose to use population size as the basis for the analogy:

- Population size in the United Kingdom: 60 million
- Population size in Germany: 82 million.

Furthermore we know that the number of refrigerators sold in the United Kingdom in 2002 was 1.1 million units.

Then by analogy we estimate the sales to be the following in Germany:

$$(82/60) \times 1.1 \text{ million units} = 1.5 \text{ million units.}$$

A note of caution

Generally caution must be used with 'estimation by analogy' because the method assumes that factors other than the correlation factor used (in this example population size) are similar in both countries, such as the same culture, buying power of consumers, tastes, taxes, prices, selling methods, availability of products, consumption patterns and so forth. Despite the apparent drawbacks to analogy it is useful where international data are limited.

A.7 PRIMARY RESEARCH

Qualitative and quantitative research

If a marketer's research questions are not adequately answered by secondary research it may be necessary to search for additional information in primary data. These data can be collected by **quantitative research** and **qualitative research**. Quantitative and qualitative techniques can be distinguished by the fact that quantitative techniques involve getting data from a large, representative group of respondents.

Quantitative research
Data analysis based on questionnaires from a large group of respondents.

The objective of qualitative research techniques is to give a holistic view of the research problem, and therefore these techniques must have a large number of variables and few

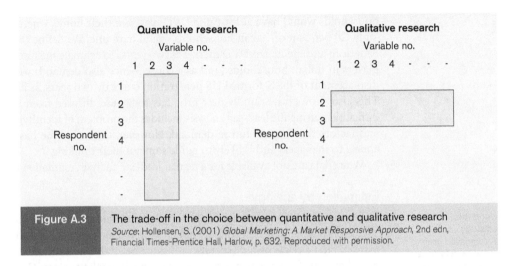

Figure A.3	The trade-off in the choice between quantitative and qualitative research
	Source: Hollensen, S. (2001) *Global Marketing: A Market Responsive Approach*, 2nd edn, Financial Times-Prentice Hall, Harlow, p. 632. Reproduced with permission.

Qualitative research
Provides a holistic view of a research problem by integrating a larger number of variables, but asking only a few respondents.

respondents (illustrated in Figure A.3). Choosing between quantitative and qualitative techniques is a question of trading off breadth and depth in the results of the analysis.

Other differences between the two research methodologies are summarised in Table A.3. Data retrieval and analysis of quantitative respondent data are based on a comparison of data between all respondents. This places heavy demands on the measuring instrument (the questionnaire), which must be well structured (with different answering categories) and tested before the survey takes place. All respondents are given identical stimuli, that is, the same questions. This approach will not usually give any problems, as long as the respondent group is homogeneous. However, if it is a heterogeneous group of respondents it is possible that the same question will be understood in different ways. This problem becomes especially intensified in cross-cultural surveys.

Data retrieval and analysis of qualitative data, however, are characterised by a high degree of flexibility and adaptation to the individual respondent and his or her special background. Another considerable difference between qualitative and quantitative surveys is the source of data:

- Quantitative techniques are characterised by a certain degree of distance as the construction of the questionnaire, data retrieval and data analysis take place in separate phases. Data retrieval is often done by people who have not had anything to do with the construction of the questionnaire. Here the measuring instrument (the questionnaire) is the critical element in the research process.

- Qualitative techniques are characterised by proximity to the source of data, where data retrieval and analysis are done by the same person, namely, the interviewer. Data retrieval is characterised by interaction between the interviewer and the respondent, where each new question is to a certain degree dependent on the previous question. Here it is the interviewer and his or her competence (or lack of the same) which is the critical element in the research process.

Qualitative techniques imply a less sharp separation between data retrieval and analysis/interpretation, since data retrieval (e.g. the next question in a personal interview) will be dependent on the interviewer's interpretation of the previous answer. The researcher's personal experience from fieldwork (data retrieval) is generally a considerable input into the analysis phase.

Triangulation: mixing qualitative and quantitative research methods

Quantitative and qualitative research methods often complement each other. Combined use of quantitative and qualitative research methods in the study of the same phenomenon is termed triangulation (Denzin, 1978; Jick, 1979). The triangulation metaphor is from navigation and

Table A.3	Quantitative versus qualitative research	
Comparison dimension	Quantitative research (e.g. a postal questionnaire)	Qualitative research (e.g. a focus group interview or the case method)
Objective	To quantify the data and generalise the results from the sample to the population of interest	To gain an initial and qualitative understanding of the underlying reasons and motives
Type of research	Descriptive and/or casual	Exploratory
Flexibility in research design	Low (as a result of a standardised and structured questionnaire: one-way communication)	High (as a result of the personal interview, where the interviewer can change questions during the interview: two-way communication)
Sample size	Large	Small
Choice of respondents	Representative sample of the population	Persons with considerable knowledge of the problem (key informants)
Information per respondent	Low	High
Data analysis	Statistical summary	Subjective, interpretative
Ability to replicate with same result	High	Low
Interviewer requirements	No special skills required	Special skills required (an understanding of the interaction between interviewer and respondent)
Time consumption during the research	*Design phase*: high (formulation of questions must be correct) *Analysis phase*: low (the answers to the questions can be coded)	*Design phase*: low (no 'exact' questions are required before the interview) *Analysis phase*: high (as a result of many 'soft' data)

military strategy, which use multiple reference points to locate an object's exact position. Similarly, market researchers can improve the accuracy and validity of their judgements by collecting both quantitative and qualitative data. Sometimes qualitative research methods explain or reinforce quantitative findings and even reveal new information.

Sometimes it is relevant to use qualitative data collected by, for example, in-depth interview of a few key informants as exploratory input to the construction of the best possible questionnaire for the collection of quantitative data. In this way triangulation can enrich our understanding of a research question before a structured and formalised questionnaire is designed.

Research design

Figure A.4 shows that designing research for primary data collection calls for a number of decisions on research approaches, contact methods, sampling plan and research instruments. The following pages will look at the various elements of Figure A.4 in further detail.

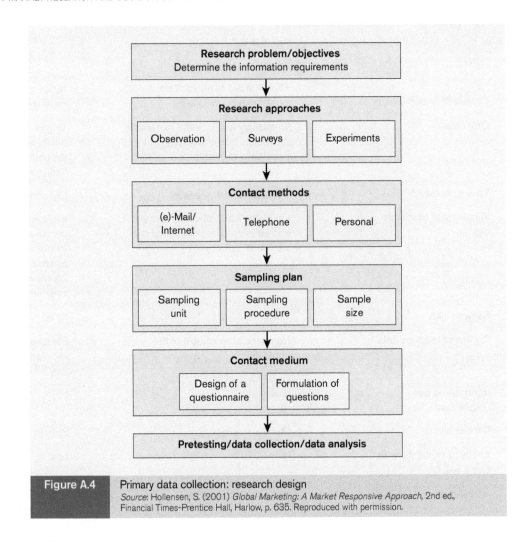

Figure A.4	Primary data collection: research design

Source: Hollensen, S. (2001) *Global Marketing: A Market Responsive Approach*, 2nd ed., Financial Times-Prentice Hall, Harlow, p. 635. Reproduced with permission.

Research problem/objectives

Companies are increasingly recognising the need for primary international research. As the extent of a firm's international involvement increases, so does the importance and complexity of its international research. The primary research process should begin with a definition of the research problem and the establishment of specific objectives. The major difficulty here is translating the business problem into a research problem with a set of specific researchable objectives. In this initial stage researchers often embark on the research process with only a vague grasp of the total problem. Symptoms are often mistaken for causes, and action determined by symptoms may be oriented in the wrong direction.

Research objectives may include obtaining detailed information for better penetrating the market, for designing and fine-tuning the marketing mix, or for monitoring the political climate of a country so that the firm can expand its operations successfully. The better defined the research objective is, the better the researcher will be able to determine the information requirement.

Research approaches

In Figure A.4 three possible research approaches are indicated: observation, surveys and experiments.

Observation

This approach to the generation of primary data is based on watching and sometimes recording market-related behaviour. Observational techniques are more suited to investigating what people do than why they do it. Here are some examples of this approach:

- *Store checks*: a food products manufacturer sends researchers into supermarkets to find out the prices of competing brands or how much shelf space and display support retailers give its brands. To conduct in-store research in Europe, for example, store checks, photo audits of shelves and store interviews must be scheduled well in advance and need to be preceded by a full round of introductions of the researchers to store management and personnel.
- *Mechanical observations*: these are often used to measure TV viewership.
- *Cash register scanners*: these can be used to keep track of customer purchases and inventories.

Observational research can obtain information that people are unwilling or unable to provide. In some countries individuals may be reluctant to discuss personal habits or consumption. In such cases observation is the only way to obtain the necessary information. In contrast, some things are simply not observable, such as feelings, attitudes and motives, or private behaviour. Long-term or infrequent behaviour is also difficult to observe. Because of these limitations, researchers often use observation along with other data collection methods.

Experiments

Experiments gather casual information. They involve selecting matched groups of subjects, giving them different treatments, controlling unrelated factors and checking for differences in group responses. Thus experimental research tries to explain cause-and-effect relationships.

The most used marketing research application of experiments is in test marketing. This is a research technique in which a product under study is placed on sale in one or more selected localities or areas, and its reception by consumers and the trade is observed, recorded and analysed. In order to isolate, for example, the sales effects of advertising campaigns, it is necessary to use relatively self-contained marketing areas as test markets.

Performance in these test markets gives some indication of the performance to be expected when the product goes into general distribution. However, experiments are difficult to implement in global marketing research. The researcher faces the task of designing an experiment in which most variables are held constant or are comparable across cultures. To do so represents a major challenge. For example, an experiment that intends to determine a casual effect within the distribution system of one country may be difficult to transfer to another country where the distribution system is different. As a result experiments are used only rarely, even though their potential value to the international market researcher is recognised.

Surveys

The survey research method is based on the questioning of respondents and represents, both in volume and in value terms, perhaps the most important method of collecting data. Typically the questioning is structured: a formal questionnaire is prepared and the questions are asked in a prearranged order. The questions may be asked verbally, in writing or via a computer.

Survey research is used for a variety of marketing issues, including the following:

- Customer attitudes
- Customer buying habits
- Potential market size
- Market trends.

Unlike experimental research, survey research is usually aimed at generating descriptive rather than casual data. Unlike observational research, survey research usually involves the respondent.

Because of the importance and diversity of survey research in global marketing, it is on this particular aspect that we now concentrate.

Contact methods

The method of contact chosen is usually a balance between speed, degree of accuracy and costs. In principle there are four possibilities when choosing a contact method: mail, internet/e-mail, telephone interviews and personal (face-to-face) interviews. Each method has its own strengths and weaknesses. Table A.4 gives an overview of these.

Mail

Mail surveys are among the least expensive. The questionnaire can include pictures – something that is not possible over the phone. Mail surveys allow the respondent to answer at their leisure, rather than at the often inconvenient moment they are contacted for a phone or personal interview. For this reason, they are not considered as intrusive as other kinds of interviews. However, mail surveys take longer than other kinds. You will need to wait several weeks after mailing out questionnaires before you can be sure that you have obtained most of the responses. In countries of lower educational and literacy levels, response rates to mail surveys are often too small to be useful.

Internet/e-mail surveys

These can collect a large amount of data that can be quantified and coded into a computer. A low research budget combined with a widely dispersed population may mean that there is no alternative to the mail/Internet survey. E-mail surveys are both very economical and very fast. It is possible to attach pictures and sound files. However, many people dislike unsolicited e-mail even more than unsolicited regular mail. Furthermore, it is difficult to generalise findings from an e-mail survey to the whole population. People who have e-mail are different from those who do not, even when matched on demographic characteristics, such as age and gender. In section A.8 the online research method will be further discussed.

Telephone interviews

In some ways these are somewhere between personal and mail surveys. They generally have a response rate higher than mail questionnaires but lower than face-to-face interviews, their cost is usually less than with personal interviews, and they allow a degree of flexibility when interviewing. However, the use of visual aids is not possible and there are limits to the number of questions that can be asked before respondents either terminate the interview or give quick (invalid) answers to speed up the process. With computer-aided telephone interviewing

Table A.4	Strengths and weaknesses of the four contact methods			
Questions/questionnaire	Mail	Internet/e-mail	Telephone	Personal
Flexibility (ability to clarify problems)	Poor	Fair	Good	Excellent
Possibility of in-depth information (use of open-ended questions)	Fair	Poor	Fair	Excellent
Use of visual aids	Good	Excellent	Poor	Good
Possibility of a widely dispersed sample	Excellent	Excellent	Excellent	Fair
Response rates	Poor	Fair	Good	Fair
Asking sensitive questions	Good	Poor	Poor	Fair
Control of interviewer effects (no interviewer bias)	Excellent	Fair	Fair	Poor
Speed of data collection	Poor	Excellent	Excellent	Good
Costs	Good	Excellent	Excellent	Poor

(CATI), centrally located interviewers read questions from a computer monitor and input answers via the keyboard. Routing through the questionnaire is computer controlled, helping the process of interviewing. Some research firms set up terminals in shopping centres, where respondents sit down at a terminal, read questions from a screen and type their answers into the computer.

Personal interviews

Personal interviews take two forms – individual and group interviewing. *Individual interviewing* involves talking with people in their homes or offices, in the street or in shopping arcades. The interviewer must gain the cooperation of the respondents. *Group interviewing* (*focus-group interviewing*) consists of inviting six to ten people to gather for a few hours with a trained moderator to talk about a product, service or organisation. The moderator needs objectivity, knowledge of the subject and industry, and some understanding of group and consumer behaviour. The participants are normally paid a small sum for attending.

Personal interviewing is quite flexible and can collect large amounts of information. Trained interviewers can hold a respondent's attention for a long time and can explain difficult questions. They can guide interviews, explore issues and probe as the situation requires. Interviewers can show subjects actual products, advertisements or packages, and observe reactions and behaviour.

The main drawbacks of personal interviewing are the high costs and sampling problems. Group interview studies usually employ small sample sizes to keep time and costs down, but it may be hard to generalise from the results. Because interviewers have more freedom in personal interviews the problem of interviewer bias is greater.

Thus there is no 'best' contact method – it all depends on the situation. Sometimes it may even be appropriate to combine the methods.

Sampling plan

Sampling unit

Except in very restricted markets it is both impractical and too expensive for a researcher to contact all the people who could have some relevance to the research problem. This total number is known statistically as the 'universe' or 'population'. In marketing terms, it comprises the total number of actual and potential users/customers of a particular product or service.

The population can also be defined in terms of elements and sampling units. Suppose that a lipstick manufacturer has a **sampling plan** to assess consumer response to a new line of lipsticks and wants to sample females over 15 years of age. It may be possible to sample females of this age directly, in which case a sampling unit would be the same as an element. Alternatively, households might be sampled and all females over 15 in each selected household interviewed. Here the sampling unit is the household, and the element is a female over 15 years old.

What is usually done in practice is to contact a selected group of consumers/customers to be representative of the entire population. The total number of consumers who could be interviewed is known as the 'sample frame', while the number of people who are actually interviewed is known as the 'sample'.

Sampling procedure

There are several kinds of sampling procedure, with probability and non-probability sampling being the two major categories:

- *Probability sampling*: here it is possible to specify in advance the chance that each element in the population will have of being included in a sample, although there is not necessarily an equal probability for each element. Examples are simple random sampling, systematic sampling, stratified sampling and cluster sampling (see Malhotra (1993) for more information).

Sampling plan
A scheme outlining the group (or groups) to be surveyed in a marketing research study, how many individuals are to be chosen for the survey, and on what basis this choice is made.

- *Non-probability sampling*: here it is not possible to determine the above-mentioned probability or to estimate the sampling error. These procedures rely on the personal judgement of the researcher. Examples are convenience sampling, quota sampling and snowball sampling (see Malhotra (1993) for more information).

Given the disadvantages of non-probability samples (results are not projectable to the total population, and sampling error cannot be computed) one may wonder why they are used so frequently by marketing researchers. The reasons relate to the inherent advantages of non-probability sampling:

- Non-probability samples cost less than probability samples.
- If accuracy is not critical non-probability sampling may have considerable appeal.
- Non-probability sampling can be conducted quicker than probability sampling.
- Non-probability sampling, if executed properly, can produce samples of the population that are reasonably representative (e.g. by use of quota sampling) (Malhotra, 1993, p. 359).

Sample size

Once we have chosen the sampling procedure the next step is to determine the appropriate sample size. Determining the sample size is a complex decision and involves financial, statistical and managerial considerations. Other things being equal the larger the sample, the less the sampling error. However, larger samples cost more money, and the resources (money and time) available for a particular research project are always limited.

In addition the cost of larger samples tends to increase on a linear basis, whereas the level of sampling error decreases at a rate only equal to the square root of the relative increase in sample size. For example, if sample size is quadrupled data collection costs will be quadrupled too, but the level of sampling error will be reduced by only one-half. Among the methods for determining the sample size are the following:

- *Traditional statistical techniques* (assuming the standard normal distribution).
- *Budget available*: although seemingly unscientific this is a fact of life in a business environment, based on the budgeting of financial resources. This approach forces the researcher to consider carefully the value of information in relation to its cost.
- *Rules of thumb*: the justification for a specified sample size may boil down to a 'gut feeling' that this is an appropriate sample size, or it may be a result of common practice in the particular industry.
- *Number of subgroups to be analysed*: generally speaking the more subgroups that need to be analysed, the larger the required total sample size.

In transnational market research, sampling procedures become a rather complicated matter. Ideally a researcher wants to use the same sampling method for all countries in order to maintain consistency. Sampling desirability, however, often gives way to practicality and flexibility. Sampling procedures may have to vary across countries in order to ensure reasonable comparability of national groups. Thus the relevance of a sampling method depends on whether it will yield a sample that is representative of a target group in a certain country, and on whether comparable samples can be obtained from similar groups in different countries.

Contact medium/measurement instrument

Designing the questionnaire

A good questionnaire cannot be designed until the precise information requirements are known. It is the vehicle whereby the research objectives are translated into specific questions. The types of information sought, and the types of respondent to be researched, will have a bearing upon the contact method to be used, and this in turn will influence whether the questionnaire is relatively unstructured (with open-ended questions), aimed at depth interviewing, or relatively structured (with closed-ended questions) for 'on the street' interviews.

In cross-cultural studies open-ended questions appear useful because they may help to identify the frame of reference of the respondents. Another issue is the choice between direct and indirect questions. Societies have different degrees of sensitivity to certain questions. Questions related to the income or age of the respondent may be accepted differently in different countries. Thus the researcher must be sure that the questions are culturally acceptable. This may mean that questions, which can be asked directly in some societies, will have to be asked indirectly in others.

Formulation (wording) of questions

Once the researcher has decided on specific types of questions the next task is the actual writing of the questions. Four general guidelines are useful to bear in mind during the wording and sequencing of each question:

- *The wording must be clear*: for example, try to avoid two questions in one.
- *Select words so as to avoid biasing the respondent*: for example, try to avoid leading questions.
- *Consider the ability of the respondent to answer the question*: for example, asking respondents about a brand or store that they have never encountered creates a problem. Since respondents may be forgetful, time periods should be relatively short. For example: 'Did you purchase one or more cola(s) within the last week?'
- *Consider the willingness of the respondent to answer the question*: 'embarrassing' topics that deal with things such as borrowing money, sexual activities and criminal records must be dealt with carefully. One technique is to ask the question in the third person or to state that the behaviour or attitude is not unusual prior to asking the question. For example: 'Millions of people suffer from haemorrhoids. Do you or does any member of your family suffer from this problem?' It is also a feasible solution to ask about 'embarrassing' topics at the end of the interview.

The impact of language and culture is of particular importance when wording questions. The goal for the global marketing researcher should be to ensure that the potential for misunderstandings and misinterpretations of spoken or written words is minimised. Both language and cultural differences make this issue an extremely sensitive one in the global marketing research process.

In many countries different languages are spoken in different areas. In Switzerland, German is used in some areas and French and Italian in others. And the meaning of words often differs from country to country. For example, in the United States the concept of 'family' generally refers only to the parents and children. In the southern part of Europe, the Middle East and many Latin countries it may also include grandparents, uncles, aunts, cousins and so forth.

When finally evaluating the questionnaire, the following items should be considered:

- Is a certain question necessary? The phrase 'It would be nice to know' is often heard, but each question should either serve a purpose or be omitted.
- Is the questionnaire too long?
- Will the questions achieve the survey objectives?

Pretesting

Pretesting
Conducting limited trials of a questionnaire or some other aspect of a study to determine its suitability for the planned research project. In the context of advertising, research carried out beforehand on the effectiveness of an advertisement. It begins at the earliest stages of development and continues until the advertisement is ready for use.

No matter how comfortable and experienced the researcher is in international research activities, an instrument should always be pretested. Ideally such a **pretest** is carried out with a subset of the population under study, but a pretest should at least be conducted with knowledgeable experts and/or individuals. The pretest should also be conducted in the same mode as the final interview. If the study is to be 'on the street' or in the shopping arcade, then the pretest should be the same. Even though a pretest may mean time delays and additional cost the risks of poor research are simply too great for this process to be omitted.

Data collection

The global marketing researcher must check that the data are gathered correctly, efficiently and at a reasonable cost. The market researcher has to establish the parameters under which the research is conducted. Without clear instructions the interviews may be conducted in different ways by different interviewers. Therefore the interviewers have to be instructed about the nature of the study, start and completion time, and sampling methodology. Sometimes a sample interview is included with detailed information on probing and quotas. Spot checks on these administration procedures are vital to ensure reasonable data quality.

Data analysis and interpretation

Once data have been collected the final steps are the analysis and interpretation of findings in the light of the stated problem. Analysing data from cross-country studies calls for substantial creativity as well as scepticism. Not only are data often limited, but frequently results are significantly influenced by cultural differences. This suggests that there is a need for properly trained local personnel to function as supervisors and interviewers; alternatively international market researchers require substantial advice from knowledgeable local research firms that can also take care of the actual collection of data. Although data in cross-country analyses are often of a qualitative nature the researcher should, of course, use the best and most appropriate tools available for analysis. On the other hand, international researchers should be cautioned against using overly sophisticated tools for unsophisticated data. Even the best of tools will not improve data quality. The quality of data must be matched with the quality of the research tools.

Problems with using primary research

Most problems in collecting primary data in international marketing research stem from cultural differences among countries, and range from the inability of respondents to communicate their opinions to inadequacies in questionnaire translation (Cateora *et al.*, 2000).

Sampling in field surveys

The greatest problem of sampling stems from the lack of adequate demographic data and available lists from which to draw meaningful samples. For example, in many South American and Asian cities street maps are unavailable, and streets are neither identified nor houses numbered. In Saudi Arabia, the difficulties with probability sampling is so acute that non-probabilistic sampling becomes a necessary evil. Some of the problems in drawing a random sample include:

- no officially recognised census of population;
- incomplete and out-of-date telephone directories;
- no accurate maps of population centres, therefore no area samples can be made.

Furthermore, door-to-door interviewing in Saudi Arabia is illegal.

Non-response

Non-response is the inability to reach selected elements in the sample frame. As a result, opinions of some sample elements are not obtained or properly represented. A good sampling method can only identify elements that should be selected; there is no guarantee that such elements will ever be included.

The two main reasons for non-response errors are as follows:

1 *Not being at home*: in countries where males are still dominant in the labour force it may be difficult to contact a head of household at home during working hours. Frequently only housewives or servants are at home during the day.

2 *Refusal to respond*: cultural habits in many countries virtually prohibit communication with a stranger, particularly for women. This is the case in the Middle East, much of the Mediterranean area and throughout most of South-East Asia – in fact wherever strong traditional societies persist. Moreover, in many societies such matters as preferences for hygienic products and food products are too personal to be shared with an outsider. For example, in many Latin American countries a woman may feel ashamed to talk with a researcher about her choice of brand of sanitary towel, or even hair shampoo or perfume. Respondents may also suspect that the interviewers are agents of the government, seeking information for the imposition of additional taxes. Finally, privacy is becoming a big issue in many countries: for example, in Japan the middle class is showing increasing concern about the protection of personal information.

Language barriers

This problem area includes the difficulty of exact translation that creates problems in eliciting the specific information desired and in interpreting the respondents' answers.

In some developing countries with low literacy rates written questionnaires are completely useless. Within some countries the problem of dialects and different languages can make a national questionnaire survey impractical – this is the case in India, which has 25 official languages.

The obvious solution of having questionnaires prepared or reviewed by someone fluent in the language of the country is frequently overlooked. In order to find possible translation errors marketers can use the technique of *back translation*, where the questionnaire is translated from one language to another, and then back again into the original language (Douglas and Craig, 2007). For example, if a questionnaire survey is going to be made in France, the English version is translated into French and then translated back to English by a different translator. The two English versions are then compared and, where there are differences, the translation is checked thoroughly.

Measurement

The best research design is useless without proper measurements. A measurement method that works satisfactorily in one culture may fail to achieve the intended purpose in another country. Special care must therefore be taken to ensure the reliability and **validity** of the measurement method.

In general, 'how' you measure refers to reliability and 'what' you measure refers to validity.

If we measure the same phenomenon over and over again with the same measurement device and we get similar results then the method is reliable. There are three types of validity, construct, internal and external:

Validity
If the measurement method measures what it is supposed to measure, then it has high validity (the 'what' dimension). There are three types of validity: construct, internal and external.

- *Construct validity*: this establishes correct operational measures for the concepts being studied. If a measurement method lacks construct validity it is not measuring what it is supposed to.
- *Internal validity*: this establishes a causal relationship, whereby certain conditions are shown to lead to other conditions.
- *External validity*: this is concerned with the possible generalisation of research results to other populations. For example, high external validity exists if research results obtained for a marketing problem in one country will be applicable to a similar marketing problem in another country. If such a relationship exists it may be relevant to use the analogy method for estimating market demand in different countries. Estimating by analogy assumes, for example, that the demand for a product develops in much the same way in countries that are similar.

The concepts of reliability and validity are illustrated in Figure A.5. In the figure, the bull's eye is what the measurement device is supposed to 'hit'.

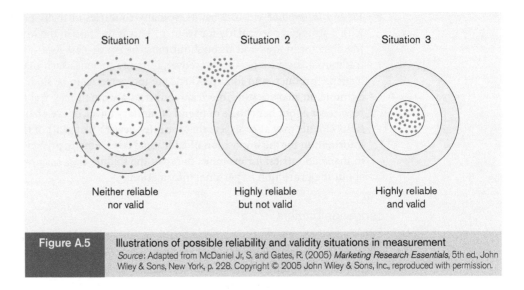

Figure A.5	Illustrations of possible reliability and validity situations in measurement

Source: Adapted from McDaniel Jr, S. and Gates, R. (2005) *Marketing Research Essentials*, 5th ed., John Wiley & Sons, New York, p. 228. Copyright © 2005 John Wiley & Sons, Inc., reproduced with permission.

Situation 1 shows holes all over the target, which could be due to the use of a bad measurement device. If a measurement instrument is not reliable there are no circumstances under which it can be valid. However, just because an instrument is reliable, the instrument is not automatically valid. We see this in *situation 2*, where the instrument is reliable but is not measuring what it is supposed to measure. The shooter has a steady eye, but the sights are not adjusted properly. *Situation 3* is the ideal situation for the researcher to be in. The measurement method is both reliable and valid.

An instrument proven to be reliable and valid in one country may not be so in another culture (Craig and Douglas, 2006). The same measurement scales may have different reliabilities in different cultures because of various levels of consumers' product knowledge. Therefore it may be dangerous simply to compare results in cross-country research. One way to minimise the problem is to adapt measurement scales to local cultures by pretesting measures in each market of interest until they show similar and satisfactory levels of reliability.

However, as different methods may have varying reliabilities in different countries, it is essential that these differences can be taken into account in the design of a multicultural survey. Thus, a mail survey could be most appropriate to use in country A and personal interviews in country B. In collecting data from different countries it is more important to use techniques with equivalent levels of reliability than to use the same techniques across countries.

A.8 ONLINE (INTERNET) PRIMARY RESEARCH METHODS

Although the Internet is still confined to the boundaries of the personal computer screen this will soon be a thing of the past; it is now clear that the Internet is definitely going to be a medium for the masses. Many researchers are amazed at how efficiently surveys can be conducted, tabulated and analysed on the Web. Additionally, online data collection lets marketers use complex study designs once considered either too expensive or too cumbersome to execute via traditional means. While initial forays were fraught with technical difficulties and methodological hurdles recent developments have begun to expose the medium's immense potential.

The earliest online tools offered little more than the ability to deploy paper-based questionnaires to Internet users. Today, however, online tools and services are available with a wide range of features at a wide range of prices.

For the international market researcher the major advantages and disadvantages of online surveys are the following (Grossnickle and Raskin, 2001).

Advantages of online surveys

- *Low financial resource implications*: the scale of the online survey is not associated with finance, i.e. large-scale surveys do not require greater financial resources than small surveys. Expenses related to self-administered postal surveys are usually in the form of outward and return postage, photocopying, etc., none of which is associated with online surveys.
- *Short response time*: online surveys allow questionnaires to be delivered instantly to their recipients, irrespective of their geographical location. Fast survey execution allows for most interviews to be completed within a week or so.
- *Saving time with data collection and analysis*: the respective questionnaire can be programmed so that responses can feed automatically into the data analysis software (SPSS, SAS, Excel, etc.), thus saving time and resources associated with the data entry process. Furthermore, this avoids associated data transcription errors.
- *Visual stimuli*: this can be evaluated, unlike CATI.

Disadvantages of online surveys

- *Respondents have no physical addresses*: the major advantage of postal over online surveys is that respondents have physical addresses, whereas not everyone has an electronic address. This is a particular international marketing research problem in geographical areas where the penetration of the Internet is not as high as in Europe and North America. For cross-country surveys the multimode approach (i.e. a combination of online and postal survey) compensates for the misrepresentation of the general population.
- *Guarding respondents' anonymity*: traditional mail surveys have advantages in guarding respondents' anonymity. Sensitive issues, which may prevent respondents from giving sincere answers, should be addressed via the post rather than online.
- *Time necessary to download pages*: problems may arise with older browsers that fail to display HTML questionnaires properly, and also with the appearance of the questionnaires in different browsers (Internet Explorer, Netscape).

Response rates to e-mail questionnaires vary according to the study context. Various factors have been found to inhibit response to e-mail or Internet data collection. These factors include poor design of e-mail questionnaires, lack of anonymity and completion incentives. By addressing these factors in the context of specific research objectives it may provide a way to tackle non-response to e-mail questionnaires. Incentives should be used to encourage response rates, especially if the e-mail questionnaires are lengthy. Potential respondents are likely to trade off their anonymity if incentives are used. The researcher can easily negotiate completion incentives if the sampling frame derives from a company's database (Michaelidou and Dibb, 2006).

Online quantitative market research (e-mail and Web-based surveys)

Online surveys can be conducted through e-mail or they can be posted on the Web and the URL provided (a password is optional depending on the nature of the research) to the respondents who have already been approached. When a wide audience is targeted the survey can be designed as a pop-up survey, which would appear as a Web-based questionnaire in a browser window while users are browsing the respective websites. Such a Web-based survey is appropriate for a wide audience, where all the visitors to certain websites have an equal chance to enter the survey.

However, the researcher's control over respondents entering the Web-based surveys is lower than for e-mail surveys. One advantage of Web-based surveys is the better display of the questionnaire, whereas e-mail software still suffers from certain limitations in terms of design tools and offering interactive and clear presentation. However, these two modes of survey may be mixed, combining the advantages of each (Ilieva *et al.*, 2002):

Online qualitative market research

There are many interesting opportunities to conduct international qualitative market research quickly and at relatively low cost, without too much travelling involved (Scholl *et al.*, 2002):

- *Saving money on travelling costs, etc*: many qualitative researchers often have to travel to countries in which research is conducted, briefing local moderators and viewing some groups or holding interviews to get a grasp of the local habits and attitudes. This leads to high travelling costs and increases the time needed to execute the fieldwork. It usually takes one or two weeks to recruit the respondents, and one or two weeks before the analysis can start. In online research the respondents can be recruited and interviewed from any computer anywhere in the world. Nearly everyone who is connected to the Internet knows how to use chat rooms. Fieldwork may start two days after briefing, and the analysis may start straight after the last interview on the basis of complete and accurate transcripts, with each comment linked to the respective respondent.

- *Cross-country qualitative research*: international online research is particularly interesting for multinational companies that sell their products on a global scale and are afraid to build the global marketing strategy on research which has been conducted in only a few of these countries. Online qualitative research could serve as an additional multicountry check. This is not intended to give insight into the psychology of customers but rather to check whether other countries or cultures may add to the general picture, which has been made on the basis of qualitative face-to-face research.

One of the limitations with, for example, online focus groups is that they seem to generate less interaction between members than the face-to-face groups. Discussions between respondents occur, but they are less clear and coherent.

A.9 OTHER TYPES OF MARKET RESEARCH

A distinction is made between ad-hoc and continuous research.

Ad-hoc research

An ad hoc study focuses on a specific marketing problem and collects data at one point in time from one sample of respondents. Examples of ad hoc studies are usage and attitude surveys, and product and concept tests via custom-designed or multiclient studies. More general marketing problems (e.g. total market estimates for product groups) may be examined by using Delphi studies (see below).

Custom-designed studies

These are based on the specific needs of the client. The research design is based on the research brief given to the marketing research agency or internal marketing researcher. Because they are tailor-made such surveys can be expensive.

Multiclient studies

These are a relatively low-cost way for a company to answer specific questions without embarking on its own primary research. There are two types of multiclient study:

1 *Independent research studies*: these are carried out totally independently by research companies (e.g. Frost and Sullivan) and then offered for sale.

2 **Omnibus studies**: here a research agency will target specified segments in a particular foreign market and companies will buy questions in the survey. Consequently interviews (usually face to face or by telephone) may cover many topics. Clients will then receive an analysis of the questions purchased. For omnibus studies to be of use the researcher must have clearly defined research needs and a corresponding target segment in order to obtain meaningful information.

Delphi studies

This type of research approach clearly aims at qualitative rather than quantitative measures by aggregating the information of a group of experts. It seeks to obtain answers from those who possess particular in-depth expertise instead of seeking the average responses of many with only limited knowledge.

The area of concern may be future developments in the international trading environment or long-term forecasts for market penetration of new products. Typically 10–30 key informants are selected and asked to identify the major issues in the area of concern. They are also requested to rank their statements according to importance and explain the rationale behind the ranking. Next the aggregated information is returned to all participants, who are encouraged to state clearly their agreements or disagreements with the various rank orders and comments. Statements can be challenged and then, in another round, participants can respond to the challenges. After several rounds of challenge and response a reasonably coherent consensus is developed.

One drawback of the technique is that it requires several steps, and therefore months may elapse before the information is obtained. However, the emergence of e-mail may accelerate the process. If done properly the Delphi method can provide insightful forecast data for the international information system of the firm.

Continuous research (longitudinal designs)

A longitudinal design differs from ad hoc research in that the sample or panel remains the same over time. In this way a longitudinal study provides a series of pictures that give an in-depth view of developments taking place. The panel consists of a sample of respondents who have agreed to provide information at specified intervals over an extended period.

There are two major types of panel:

● *Consumer panels*: these provide information on their purchases over time. For example, a grocery panel would record the brands, pack sizes, prices and stores used for a wide range of supermarket brands. By using the same households over a period of time, measures of brand loyalty and switching can be achieved, together with a demographic profile of the type of person or household who buys particular brands.

● *Retailer panels*: by gaining the cooperation of retail outlets (e.g. supermarkets) sales of brands can be measured by laser scanning the bar codes on goods as they pass through the checkout. Although brand loyalty and switching cannot be measured in this way retail audits can provide accurate assessments of sales achieved by store. A major provider of retail data is the A. C. Nielsen Company.

Sales forecasting

A company can forecast its sales either by forecasting the market sales (called *market forecasting*) and then determining what share of this will accrue to the company or by forecasting the company's sales directly. The point is that planners are only interested in forecasts when the forecast comes down to individual products in the company.

We shall now examine the applicability and usefulness of the short-, medium- and long-term forecasts in so far as company planners are concerned and shall then look at each from individual company departmental viewpoints:

- *Short-term forecasts*: these are usually for periods up to three months ahead, and as such are really of use for tactical matters such as production planning. The general trend of sales is less important here than short-term fluctuations.

- *Medium-term forecasts*: these have direct implications for planners. They are of most importance in the area of business budgeting, the starting point for which is the sales forecast. Thus if the sales forecast is incorrect the entire budget is incorrect. If the forecast is over-optimistic then the company will have unsold stocks, which must be financed out of working capital. If the forecast is pessimistic then the firm may miss out on marketing opportunities because it is not geared up to produce the extra goods required by the market. More to the point is that when forecasting is left to accountants they will tend to err on the conservative side and will produce a forecast that is less than actual sales, the implications of which have just been described. This serves to re-emphasise the point that sales forecasting is the responsibility of the sales manager. Such medium-term forecasts are normally for one year ahead.

- *Long-term forecasts*: these are usually for periods of three years or more depending on the type of industry being considered. In industries such as computers three years is considered long term, whereas for steel manufacture ten years is a long-term horizon. Long-term forecasts are worked out from macroenvironmental factors such as government policy, economic trends, etc. Such forecasts are needed mainly by financial accountants for long-term resource implications, but such matters of course are boards of directors' concerns. The board must decide what its policy is to be in establishing the levels of production needed to meet the forecast demand; such decisions might mean the construction of a new factory and the training of a workforce. Forecasts can be produced for different horizons, starting at an international level and then ranging down to national levels, by industry and then by company levels until we reach individual product-by-product forecasts. This is then broken down seasonally over the time span of the forecasting period, and geographically right down to individual salesperson areas. It is these latter levels that are of specific interest to sales management, or it is from this level of forecasting that the sales budgeting and remuneration system stems. Figure A.6 shows an example of trend forecasting.

The unit sales and trend are drawn in as in Figure A.6. The trend line is extended by sight (and it is here that the forecaster's skill and intuition must come in). The deviations from trend are then applied to the trend line, and this provides the sales forecast.

In this particular example it can be seen that the trend line has been extended slowly upwards, similar to previous years. The technique, as with many similar techniques, suffers from the fact that downturns and upturns cannot be predicted, and such data must be subjectively entered by the forecaster through manipulation of the extension to the trend line.

Scenario planning

Scenarios are stories about plausible alternative futures (Wright, 2005). They differ from forecasts in that they explore possible futures rather than predict a single future point. Figure A.7 shows two different scenarios – A and B – where the outcome – measured on two dimensions – is influenced by both **convergent** and **divergent forces**.

Scenarios
Stories about plausible alternative futures.

Convergent forces
Factors driving developments in the same direction.

Divergent forces
Forces driving developments apart from each other.

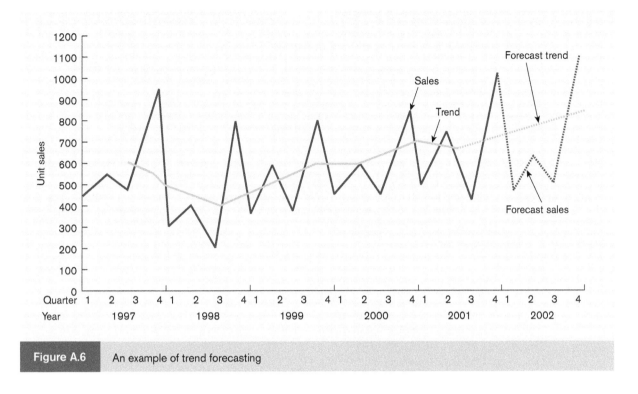

| **Figure A.6** | An example of trend forecasting |

Figure A.7 shows that the diverging and converging factors have to be balanced. Time flows from the left to right. The courses of the scenarios pass through a number of time windows, each made up of the key dimensions the scenario writers want to highlight. In Figure A.7 two 'time windows' are shown: one in two years from now and another one in five years from now. The two dimensions could be e.g. 'worldwide market share' and 'worldwide market growth' for one of the company's main products. The 'convergent forces' would mean

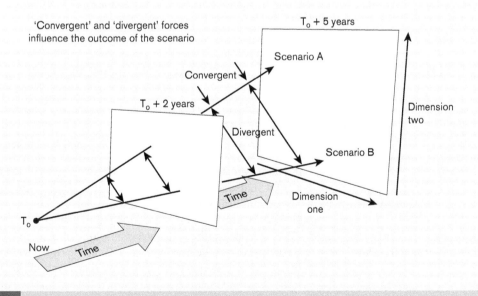

| **Figure A.7** | Development of scenarios A and B over time |

that Scenarios A and B would come nearer to each other over time. The 'divergent forces' would have the opposite effect.

Examples of *convergent* forces would be:

- high degree of macroeconomic stability in key international markets;
- increasing standardisation of products across borders.

An example of a *divergent* force would be 'cultural diversity' among target markets.

Scenario planning allows us to consider a range of 'alternative futures', each of which is dramatically different from the other and from the current operating environment. Rather than rely on a single 'most likely' forecast it is possible to compare and contrast alternative opinions on how your industry may evolve (Culver, 2006; Ringland, 2005).

Since it is externally oriented, scenario planning is very effective at identifying growth strategies for the company as well as potential threats to its market position. Scenarios can also help to identify the specific external industry changes that are causing falling market share or margins.

Guidelines for scenario planning

- *Establish a core planning team*: analysing the strategic implications of scenarios is best done in teams. The creative dynamics of an effective group are likely to provide the types of breakthrough that will make the scenario process worthwhile. What seems obvious to one person will be surprising to another. A good rule of thumb is to have five to eight people in the planning group.
- *Get a cross-section of expertise*: include the heads of all functional areas – sales, marketing, operations, purchasing, information technology, personnel, etc. We also recommend including individuals beyond the top executives. This injects new perspectives on your company or your line of trade. This is a great time to involve the rising stars and innovative thinkers in the organisation.
- *Include outside information and outside people*: focus on injecting interesting and challenging perspectives into the discussion. In a group composed solely of insiders it will be hard to achieve breakthrough insights. Outsiders may be customers, suppliers or consultants. If possible, involve an executive from another line of trade. However, many executives feel uncomfortable letting outsiders participate in the planning process of their companies.

A.10 SETTING UP A MARKETING INFORMATION SYSTEM (MIS)

Once research has been conducted, the data collected and analysed, the next step is to incorporate this information into management decision making. More and more businesses are now concerned with increasing the productivity of their marketing efforts, especially in their marketing research departments.

A massive amount of data is available from a wide variety of sources. The trick is to transform that data, ranging from statistics and facts to opinions and predictions, into information that is useful to the organisation's marketing decision makers. The importance of a timely and comprehensive information system is becoming more evident with the increased need to develop closer customer relationships, the increasing costs of making wrong marketing decisions, the greater complexity of the marketplace, and the elevated level of competitor aggressiveness. The need for current and relevant knowledge may result in the development and implementation of information systems that incorporate data management procedures involving generating new data or gathering existing data, storing and retrieving data, processing data into useful information, and disseminating information to those individuals who

International marketing information system
An interacting organisation of people, systems and processes devised to create a regular, continuous flow in information essential to the international marketer's problem-solving and decision-making activities around the world.

need it. The **international marketing information system** is an interacting organisation of people, systems and processes devised to create a regular, continuous and orderly flow of information essential to the marketer's problem-solving and decision-making activities. As a planned, sequential flow of information tailored to the needs of a particular marketing manager, the international MIS can be conceptualised as a four-stage process consisting of locating, gathering, processing and utilising information.

In this rather complete international MIS model, input data flow into the system from three major sources: the microenvironment, the macroenvironment and functional areas of the firm. The output information will then be made available to management for analysis, planning, implementation and control purposes. The proposed model meets the exigencies of the ever-expanding role of the MIS professional that has to provide timely, accurate and objective information for management to be able to navigate its way through the complex and fast-changing world of business globalisation. Against the backdrop of a dynamic business environment, companies are increasingly developing their marketing information systems to provide managers with real-time market information. Likewise, they are expanding from local to national to global operations while consumers are becoming ever more selective in their product choices.

A.11 SUMMARY

The basic objective of the global marketing research function is to provide management with relevant information for more accurate decision making. The objective is the same for both domestic and global marketing. However, global marketing is more complex because of the difficulty of gathering information about multiple and different foreign environments.

In this chapter, special attention has been given to the information collection process and the use of marketing information. This coverage is far from being exhaustive, and the reader should consult marketing research textbooks for specific details related to particular research topics.

An international marketer should initiate research by searching first for any relevant secondary data. Typically a great deal of information is already available, and the researcher needs to know how to identify and locate the international sources of secondary data.

If it is necessary to gather primary data the international marketer should be aware that it is simply not possible to replicate elsewhere the methodology used in one country. Some adaptation of the research method to different countries is usually necessary.

The firm should set up a decision support system or an international market information system (MIS) to handle the gathered information efficiently. This system should integrate all information inputs, both internal and external. In addition, an international MIS can support managers in their marketing decision making by providing interlinkage and integration between functional departments or international divisions. However, in the final analysis, every international marketer should keep in mind that an information system is no substitute for sound judgement.

QUESTIONS FOR DISCUSSION

1 Explore the reasons for using a marketing information system in the international market. What are the main types of information you would expect to use?

2 What are some of the problems that a global marketing manager can expect to encounter when creating a centralised marketing information system? How can these problems be solved?

3   What are the dangers of translating questionnaires that have been designed for one country for use in a multicountry study? How would you avoid these dangers?

4   Identify and classify the major groups of factors that must be taken into account when conducting a foreign market assessment.

5   What is the difference between 'data warehousing' and 'data mining'?

6   Identify and discuss the major considerations in deciding whether research should be centralised or decentralised.

7   Distinguish between internal and external validity. What are the implications of external validity for international marketers?

8   Would Tokyo be a good test market for a new brand planned to be marketed worldwide? Explain your reasoning.

9   If you had a contract to do market research in Saudi Arabia, what problems would you expect in obtaining primary data?

10   Do demographic variables have universal meanings? Is there a chance that they may be interpreted differently in different cultures?

11   In forecasting sales in international markets, to what extent can the past be used to predict the future?

12   How should the firm decide whether to gather its own intelligence or to buy it from outside?

REFERENCES

Cateora, P. R. (1993) *International Marketing*, 8th edn, Irwin, Homewood, IL.

Craig, S. C. and Douglas, S. P. (2000) *International Marketing Research*, 2nd edn, John Wiley & Sons, England.

Craig, C. S. and Douglas, S. P. (2006) Beyond national culture: implications of cultural dynamics for consumer research, *International Marketing Review*, 23(3): 322–42.

Criè, D. and Micheaux, A. (2006) From customer data to value: what is lacking in the information chain? *Database Marketing & Customer Strategy Management*, 13(4): 282–99.

Culver, M. (2006) Using tactical intelligence to help inform strategy, *Strategy & Leadership*, 34(6): 17–23.

Curry, A., Ringland, G. and Young, L. (2006) Using scenarios to improve marketing, *Strategy & Leadership*, 34(6): 30–7.

Dang, T. and Speece, M. (1996) Marketing research in Vietnam, *Journal of International Marketing and Marketing Research*, 21(3): 145–61.

Denzin, N. K. (1978) *The Research Act*, 2nd edn, McGraw-Hill, New York.

Douglas, S. P. and Craig, C. S. (2006) Collaborative and iterative translation: an alternative approach to back translation, *Journal of International Marketing*, 15(1): 30–43.

Gordon, I. (1998) *Relationship Marketing: New Strategies, Technologies and Techniques to Win Customers You Want and Keep Them Forever*, John Wiley & Sons, Etobicoke, Ontario.

Grossnickle, J. and Raskin, O. (2001) What's ahead on the Internet: new tools, sampling methods, and applications help simplify Web research, *Market Research*, Summer: 9–13.

Hollensen, S. (2001) *Global Marketing: A Market Responsive Approach*, 2nd edn, Financial Times/Prentice Hall, Harlow.

Ilieva, J., Baron, S. and Healey, N.M. (2002) Online surveys in marketing research: pros and cons, *International Journal of Market Research*, 44(3): 361–76.

Jick, T. D. (1979) Mixing qualitative and quantitative methods: triangulation in action, *Administrative Science Quarterly*, 24 (December): 602–11.

Lasserre, P. (1993) Gathering and interpreting strategic intelligence in Asia Pacific, *Long Range Planning*, 26(3): 55–66.

McDaniel, Jr, S. and Gates, R. (1993) *Contemporary Market Research: An Applied Orientation*, Prentice Hall, Englewood Cliffs, NJ.

Malhotra, N. K. (1993) *Marketing Research: An Applied Orientation*, Prentice Hall, Englewood Cliffs, NJ.

Malhotra, N. K. and Miller, G. L. (1999) Social responsibility and the marketing educator: a focus on stakeholders, ethical theories, and related codes of ethics, *Journal of Business Ethics*, 19(2): 211–24.

Michaelidou, N. and Dibb, S. (2006) Using email questionnaires for research: Good practice in tackling non-response, *Journal of Targeting, Measurement and Analysis for Marketing*, 14(4): 289–96.

Ringland, G. (2005) Using scenarios to create common understanding across different cultures, *Strategy & Leadership*, 33(6): 34–8.

Schmidt, M. and Hollensen, S. (2006) *Marketing Research: An International Approach*, Financial Times/Prentice Hall, Harlow.

Shariat, M. and Hightower, R. (2007) Conceptualizing business intelligence architecture, *The Marketing Management Journal*, 17(2): 40–6.

Wade, K. (2002) Focus groups' research role is shifting, *Marketing News*, 4 March: 47.

Wright, L. T. and Crimp, M. (2000) *The Marketing Research Process*, 5th edn, Financial Times/Prentice Hall, Harlow.

GLOSSARY

4 Ps The basic elements of the marketing mix: product, place (distribution), price and promotion; also called the controllable variables of marketing, because they can be controlled and manipulated by the marketer.

above-the-line advertising Advertising in the mass media, including press, radio, television and posters.

adoption process The mental and behavioural stages through which a consumer passes before making a purchase or placing an order. The stages are awareness, interest, evaluation, trial and adoption.

advertising Non-personal communication that is paid for by an identified sponsor, and involves either mass communication via newspapers, magazines, radio, television, and other media (e.g. billboards, bus stop signage) or direct-to-consumer communication via direct mail.

advertising agency A marketing services firm that assists companies in planning, preparing, implementing and evaluating all or portions of their advertising programmes.

advertising objective A specific communication task to be accomplished with a specific target audience during a specific period of time.

affordable approach Setting the promotion budget at the level management thinks the company can afford.

agent A marketing intermediary who does not take title to the products but develops a marketing strategy and establishes contacts abroad.

AIDA Awareness, interest, desire, action – the stages through which a consumer is believed to pass before purchasing a product.

allowance Promotional money paid by manufacturers to retailers in return for an agreement to feature the manufacturer's products in some way.

always-a-share customers Customers who have low switching costs and do not value long-term relationships with suppliers, making them more suited to transaction marketing.

baby boom The major increase in the annual birth rate following the Second World War and lasting until the early 1960s. The 'baby boomers', now moving into middle age, are a prime target for marketers.

below-the-line promotion Point-of-sale material, direct mail, exhibitions, i.e. any promotion which does not involve paid-for media channels.

benchmarking The process of comparing the company's products and processes to those of competitors or leading firms in other industries to find ways to improve quality and performance.

benefit segments Dividing the market into groups according to the different benefits that consumers seek from the product.

blue oceans The unserved market, where competitors are not yet structured and the market is relatively unknown. Here it is about avoiding head-to-head competition. See also *red oceans*.

bottom-up method A sales forecasting method that starts with small-scale estimates (e.g. product estimates) and works up to larger-scale ones. See also *top-down method*.

brand An identifying feature that distinguishes one product from another; more specifically, any name, term, symbol, sign or design, or a unifying combination of these.

brand equity The value of a brand, based on the extent to which it has high brand loyalty, name awareness, perceived quality, strong brand associations and other assets such as patents, trademarks and channel relationships.

brand extension Using a successful brand name to launch a new or modified product in a new category.

break-even analysis The calculation of the quantity needed to be sold to cover total costs.

break-even pricing Setting price to break even on the costs of making and marketing a product; or setting price to make a target profit.

bricks and mortar Physical retail stores.

broker A wholesaler who does not take title to goods and whose function is to bring buyers and sellers together and assist in negotiation.

business cycle Recurrent fluctuations in general economic activity. The four phases of the business cycle are prosperity, recession, depression and recovery.

business model The fundamental strategy underlying the way a business unit operates.

business-to-business (B2B) Marketing which involves exchange relationships between two or more business customers and suppliers.

business-to-consumer (B2C) Marketing which involves exchange relationships between a firm and its end customers, perhaps via retailers.

buy grid model   The organisational buying process – consisting of eight buying stages – can be mapped like a grid, where the other dimension is the complexity of the buying (new task, modified rebuy and straight rebuy).

buying centre   A group involved in the buying decision for purchasing an item or system solution for a company. Also known as a decision-making unit (DMU). Members of such a group are normally: initiator, influencer, decider, purchaser, user and gatekeeper.

bypass attack   Circumventing the defender's position, usually through technological leap-frogging or diversification.

cannibalisation   A situation where a new brand gains sales at the expense of another of the company's brands.

cash cow   A high market share product in a low-growth market.

cause-related marketing   A combination of joint funding and a promotional strategy in which a firm's sales are linked (and a percentage of the sales revenue is donated) to a charity or another public cause. However, unlike philanthropy, money spent in cause-related marketing is considered an expense and is expected to show a return.

category management   The management of brands in a group, portfolio or category with specific emphasis on the retail trade's requirements.

celebrity endorsement   The use of famous spokespersons or celebrities in marketing communications. The companies hire celebrities from a particular field to feature in its advertisement campaigns. The promotional features and images of the product are matched with the celebrity image, which tends to persuade a consumer to fix up their choice from a plethora of brands. The design of such campaigns and the subsequent success in achieving the desired result calls for an in-depth understanding of the product, the brand objective, choice of a celebrity, associating the celebrity with the brand, and a framework for measuring the effectiveness.

chain store   One of a group of two or more stores of a similar type, centrally owned and operated.

channel conflict   Disagreement among marketing channel members on goals and roles – who should do what and for what rewards. A significant threat arising from the introduction of an Internet channel is that, while disintermediation gives the opportunity for a company to sell direct and increase the profitability of products, it also threatens distribution arrangements with existing partners.

channel length   Number of levels (middlemen) in the distribution channel.

channel member   A layer of intermediaries that performs some work in bringing the product and its ownership closer to the final buyer.

churn rate   Refers to the proportion (%) of contractual customers or subscribers who leave a supplier during a given time period. A churn rate of 20% means that a company's customers on average stay with the supplier for 5 years.

clicks and mortar   Online retailers who also have physical retail stores.

closing   The step in the selling process in which the salesperson asks the customer for an order.

co-branding   The practice of using the established brand of two different companies on the same product with a common marketing message.

cognitive dissonance   Buyer discomfort caused by post-purchase conflict.

competitive benchmarking   A technique for assessing relative marketplace performance compared with main competitors.

competitive intelligence   Gathering, analysing and distributing information about products, customers, competitors and any aspect of the environment needed to support executives and managers in making strategic marketing decisions for an organisation

competitive parity approach   Setting the promotion budget to match competitors' outlays.

competitive triangle   Consists of a customer, the firm and a competitor (the 'triangle'). The firm or competitor 'winning' the competition depends on perceived value offered to the customer compared to the relative costs between the firm and the competitor.

competitor analysis   The process of identifying key competitors; assessing their objectives, strategies, strengths and weaknesses, and reaction patterns; and selecting which competitors to attack or avoid. This analysis provides both an offensive and defensive strategic context through which to identify opportunities and threats.

competitor intelligence (CI)   The process of identifying key competitors; assessing their objectives, strategies, strengths and weaknesses, and reaction patterns; and selecting which competitors to attack or avoid. This analysis provides both an offensive and defensive strategic context through which to identify opportunities and threats.

contract manufacturing   An agreement by which a domestic company allows a foreign producer to manufacture its product according to its specifications. Typically, the domestic company then handles foreign sales of the product.

control   The process by which managers ensure that planned activities are completely and properly executed.

convenience product   A relatively inexpensive, regularly purchased consumer product bought without much thought and with a minimum of shopping effort.

convenience store A small grocery store stressing convenient location and quick service and typically charging higher prices than other retailers selling similar products.

convergent forces Factors driving developments in the same direction.

cookies Bits of information about website visitors created by websites and stored on client computers.

core competences The principal distinctive capabilities possessed by a company – what it is really good at.

corporate social responsibility (CSR) The continuing commitment by companies to behave ethically and contribute to worldwide economic development while improving the quality of life of the workforce and their families as well as of the local community and the international society at large.

cost leadership The achievement of the lowest cost position in an industry, serving many segments

cost per thousand (CPM) Calculated by dividing the cost of an ad placed in a particular advertising vehicle (e.g. certain magazine) by the number of people (expressed in thousands) who are exposed to that vehicle.

criteria for successful segmentation Includes target markets that are heterogeneous, substantial, actionable and accessible.

CRM Customer relationship management.

cross-functional team A team made up of individuals from various organisational departments who share a common purpose.

cross-selling Selling an additional product or service to an existing customer

customer lifetime value (CLTV) It is the present value of the future cash flows attributed to the customer relationship or the amount by which revenue from a given customer over time will exceed the company's costs of attracting, selling and servicing that customer. Use of customer lifetime value as a marketing metric tends to place greater emphasis on customer service and long-term customer satisfaction, rather than on maximising short-term sales.

customer value The difference relation between the values the customer gains from owning and using a product and the costs of obtaining the product.

customisation Making something (product/service) according to a customer's individual requirements.

database marketing An interactive approach to marketing which uses individually addressable marketing media and channels to provide information to a target audience, stimulate demand and stay close to customers.

data warehousing (or mining) The storage and analysis of customer data gathered from their visits to websites for classification and modelling purposes so that products, promotions and price can be tailored to the specific needs of individual customers. The use of powerful computers to work through large volumes of data to discover purchasing patterns among an organisation's customers.

decider The buying-centre role played by the organisational member who makes the actual purchasing decision.

decision-making unit (DMU) The initiator, the decider, the influencers, the purchaser, the gatekeeper and the users. Often identical with the buying centre in B2B.

decision support system A computer system that stores custom data and transforms them into accessible information. It includes databases and software.

demographics Measures such as age, gender, race, occupation and income that are often used as a basis for selecting focus group members and market segments.

derived demand Demand for a product that depends on demand for another product.

diffusion The spread of a new product through society.

disintermediation The elimination of a layer of intermediaries from a marketing channel or the displacement of traditional resellers by radically new types of intermediaries.

dissolution phase 'Divorce' is the termination of the relationship. It can make the assets dedicated to the relationship obsolete

divergent forces Forces driving developments apart from each other.

diversification The market and product development strategy that involves expansion to a relatively large number of markets and products.

divest To improve short-term cash yield by dropping or selling off the product.

early adopter A member of the group of consumers who purchase a product soon after it has been introduced, but after the innovators have purchased it.

early majority A group of consumers, usually solid, middle-class people, who purchase more deliberately and cautiously than early adopters.

e-commerce Electronic commerce or business dealings using electronic media, such as the Internet.

economic value added (EVA) EVA = Net profit – (Total assets X Cost of capital). A smaller invested capital balance (smaller total assets) results in a higher EVA. Similarly, higher net profit also results in a higher EVA.

economies of scale and economies of scope Obtained by spreading the costs of distribution over a large quantity of products (scale) or over a wide variety of products (scope).

effectiveness Doing the right thing, making the correct strategic choice.

efficiency A way of managing business processes to a high standard, usually concerned with cost reduction.

electronic commerce (e-commerce) The general term for a buying and selling process that is supported by electronic means.

electronic data interchange (EDI) Electronic links between suppliers and retailers allowing purchase orders, packing lists, delivery.

entrepreneur A risk-taking individual who sees an opportunity and is willing to undertake a venture to create a new product or service.

estimation by analogy A correlation value (between a factor and the demand for the product) for one market is used in another international market.

e-tailers Online retailers.

exclusive distribution An extreme form of selective distribution where only one wholesaler, retailer or industrial distributor is used in a geographical area to sell products of a supplier.

exhibition An event which brings buyers and sellers together in a commercial setting.

exit barrier The barriers to leaving an industry, e.g. cost of closing down plant.

experience curve (learning curve) The drop in the average per-unit production cost that comes with accumulated production experience.

extranet Connects computers outside the firm with the intranet at the firm. The portions of an organisation's intranet that are shared by external collaborators, such as suppliers or customers.

fads Fashions that enter quickly are adopted with great speed, peak early and decline very fast.

family lifecycle A series of time stages through which most families pass.

feedforward control The active anticipation and prevention of problems, rather than passive reaction.

five sources model Corresponding to Porter's five competitive forces, there are also five potential sources for building collaborative advantages together with the firm's surrounding actors.

franchise A contractual association between a manufacturer, wholesaler or service organisation (a franchiser) and independent businesspeople (franchisees) who buy the right to own and operate one or more units in the franchise system.

frequency Average number of times within a given timeframe that each potential customer is exposed to the same ad.

gap analysis A technique which compares future likely company performance against desired performance outcomes in order to identify any gaps.

gatekeeper Those who control the flow of information, e.g. secretaries who may allow or prevent access to a DMU member, or a buyer whose agreement must be sought before a supplier can contact other members of the DMU.

generic The term generic means that the strategy can be applied to any organisation, regardless of size, industry sector, or product or service.

generic product, or generic brand A product that carries neither a manufacturer nor a distributor brand. The goods are plainly packaged with stark lettering that simply lists the contents.

global firm A firm that by operating in more than one country gains marketing, production, R&D and financial advantages in its costs and reputation that are not available to purely domestic competitors.

glocalisation The development and selling of products or services intended for the global market, but adapted to suit local culture and behaviour. (Think globally, act locally.)

green marketing Marketing ecologically sound products and promoting activities beneficial to the physical environment.

grey markets The marketing of authentic, legally trademarked goods through unauthorised channels.

gross margin The difference between net sales and cost of goods sold.

gross national product (GNP) The total value of all the goods and services produced by a nation's residents or corporations, regardless of their location.

gross rating points (GRPs) Reach multiplied by frequency. GRPs may be estimated for individual media vehicles. Media planning is often based on 'cost per 1000 GRPs'.

gross sales The total amount that a company charges during a given period of time for merchandise (before any discounts).

guanxi Describes a personal connection between two people in which one is able to prevail upon another to perform a favour or service, or be prevailed upon. It is based on a complex nature of personalised networks of influence and social relationships, and is a central concept in Chinese society.

horizontal integration Seeking control of channel members at the same level of the channel, e.g. the manufacturer's acquisition of the competitor.

idea generation stage The stage in new product development in which a marketer engages in a continuing search for product ideas consistent with target market needs and the organisation's objectives.

idiosyncratic investment Specific investment in a single relationship.

impact Depends on the compatibility between the medium used and the message (the 'impact' on the consumer's brain).

influencer The buying-centre role played by organisational members (or outsiders) who affect the purchase decision by supplying advice or information.

inseparability A characteristic of services, namely that their production cannot be separated from their consumption.

intangibility A characteristic of services, namely that they cannot be touched, seen, tasted or smelled.

integrated marketing communications (IMC) A system of management and integration of marketing communication elements – advertising, publicity, sales promotion, internet marketing, sponsorship marketing and point-of-sale communications – with the result that all elements adhere to the same message.

intensive distribution Stocking the product in as many outlets as possible.

internal marketing Involves treating employees as internal customers with the goal of increasing employees' motivation and customer focus.

international marketing information system An interacting organisation of people, systems and processes devised to create a regular, continuous flow in information essential to the international marketer's problem-solving and decision-making activities around the world.

Internet A worldwide network of interconnected computer networks that carry data and make information exchange possible.

intranets Connects the computers within a business together.

joint decisions Decisions made that are shared by all or some members of a group. Often, one decision maker dominates the process.

joint ventures The participation of two or more companies in an enterprise in which each party contributes assets, owns the new entity to some degree, and shares risk.

just-in-time (JIT) Aims to minimise stocks by organising a supply system which provides materials and components as they are required.

key account management (KAM) An approach to selling which focuses resources on major customers and uses a team selling approach in taking care of the total relationship with such an important customer.

key account manager A manager who is responsible for taking care of the total relationship with a special group of customers, or sometimes only one important customer.

key success factors (KSF) Those factors in a market which determine competitive success or failure in that market.

lead-lag analysis Determinants of demand and the rate of diffusion are the same in two countries, but time separates the two.

lead time The time from the moment the customer places an order to the moment it is received by the customer.

learning A change in the content of long-term memory. As humans, we learn because what we learn helps us respond better to our environment.

learning curves Track the decreasing cost of production and distribution of products or services over time as a result of learning by doing, innovation and imitation.

licensing agreement An agreement in which one firm permits another to use its intellectual property in exchange for compensation, typically a royalty.

lifestyle An individual's activities, interests, opinions and values as they affect his or her mode of living.

limited problem solving An intermediate level of decision making between routine response behaviour and extensive problem solving, in which the consumer has some purchasing experience, but is unfamiliar with stores, brands or price options.

line extension Using a successful brand name to introduce additional items in a given product category under the same brand name, such as new flavours, forms, colours, added ingredients or package sizes.

logistics The activities involved in moving raw materials and parts into a firm, moving in-process inventory through the firm, and moving finished goods out of the firm.

long tail Refers to a graph showing fewer products selling in large quantities versus many more products that sell in low quantities. The low-quantity items (the very broad product range) stretch out on the x-axis of the graph, creating a very long tail that generates more revenue overall. Even though a smaller quantity of each item is sold, there is a much greater variety of these items to sell and these 'rare' items are very easy to find via online search tools.

loss leader A product priced below cost to attract consumers, who may then make additional purchases.

lost-for-good customers Customers who have high switching costs and long-term horizons making them suitable for relationship marketing (RM).

loyalty card Usually a plastic card which is issued by a company to a customer and is used to record the frequency of the customer's purchases and calculate resulting discounts, rewards or allowances.

LSEs Large-scale enterprises. See also *SMEs*.

macroenvironment Broad societal forces that shape the activities of every business and non-profit marketer. The physical environment, sociocultural forces, demographic factors, economic factors, technical knowledge, and political and legal factors are components of the macroenvironment.

market coverage   Coverage can relate to geographical areas or number of retail outlets. Three approaches are available: intensive, selective or exclusive coverage.

market development   A strategy by which an organisation attempts to draw new customers to an existing product, most commonly by introducing the product in a new geographical area.

market growth rate   The theory behind the BCG model assumes that a higher growth rate is indicative of accompanying demands on investment. Inflation and/or gross national product have some impact on the range and thus the vertical axis can be modified to represent an index where the dividing horizontal line between low and high growth is at e.g. 5%. Industries expanding faster than inflation or GNP would show above the line and those growing at less than inflation or GNP would be classed as low growth and show below the line. The theory behind the BCG model assumes that a higher growth rate is indicative of accompanying demands on investment.

market orientation view (MOV)   Outside-in perspective. Adapting the firm's resources to market conditions and the competitive environment.

market penetration   A strategy for company growth by increasing sales of current products to current market segments without changing the product.

market potential   The upper limit of industry demand. That is, the expected sales volume for all brands of a particular product during a given period.

market space   A virtual marketplace such as the Internet in which no direct contact occurs between buyers and sellers.

marketing audit   An analysis and evaluation of the internal and external marketing environment of the company.

marketing control   A system of methods, procedures and devices used to ensure compliance with marketing policies and strategies.

marketing information system (MIS)   A system in which marketing information is formally gathered, stored, analysed and distributed to managers in accord with their informational needs on a regular, planned basis.

marketing management   The process of planning, executing and controlling marketing activities to attain marketing goals and objectives effectively and efficiently.

marketing myopia   The failure of a company to define its organisational purpose from a broad consumer orientation.

marketing objective   A statement of the level of performance that an organisation, strategic business unit (SBU) or operating unit intends to achieve. Objectives define results in measurable terms.

marketing plan   A marketing plan is a written document that details the necessary actions to achieve the company's marketing objectives. It can be for a product or service, a brand or a product line. Basically a marketing plan describes the marketing activities of a company in order to produce sales at the customer level. Marketing plans cover between one and five years. A marketing plan may be part of an overall business plan.

marketing planning   The process by which businesses analyse the environment and their capabilities, decide upon courses of marketing action and implement those decisions.

mark-up   A mark-up expressed as a percentage of the cost of an item.

marriage metaphor   The process of reducing the psychic distance + increasing dependence between buyer and seller = shared values and joint investments in the relationship.

mass customisation   The ability to create tailored marketing messages or products for an individual customer or a group of similar customers yet retain the economies of scale and the capacity of mass marketing of production.

mass marketing   One-to-many communications between a company and potential customers with limited tailoring of the message.

microenvironment   A company, its customers and the other economic actors that directly and regularly influence it marketing practices.

micro-segmentation   Segmentation according to choice criteria, decision-making unit structure, decision-making process, buying class, purchasing structure and organisational innovativeness.

modified rebuy   A purchase where the buyers have experience in satisfying the need, but feel the situation warrants re-evaluation of a limited set of alternatives before making a decision.

moments of truth   A critical or decisive time on which much depends; a crucial moment when seller's staff meets the customer.

monopoly   Exists if there is one seller in the market, such as a state-owned company, e.g. a local electricity supplier, postal service company or a gas company. The seller has the control over the market and can solely determine the price of its product.

multiple channel strategy   A product/service is available to the market through two (dual distribution) or more channels of distribution. Multiple channels may include the Internet, sales force, distributors, call centres, retail stores and direct mail.

nano-relationships Relations between internal customers, internal markets, divisions and business areas within organisations.

national account Large and important customers who may have centralised purchasing departments that buy or coordinate buying for decentralised, geographically dispersed business units.

net present value (NVP) Represents total present value (PV) of a time series of future cash flows

new task buying An organisational buying situation in which a buyer is seeking to fill a need never before addressed. Uncertainty and lack of information about products and suppliers characterise this situation.

niche marketing The process of targeting a relatively small market segment with a specific, specialised marketing mix.

non-tariff trade barriers Non-monetary barriers to foreign products, such as biases against a foreign company's bids, or product standards that go against a foreign company's product features.

not-for-profit organisation An organisation which attempts to achieve an objective other than profit, for example relief of famine, animal rights or public service.

objective and task approach Developing the promotion budget by defining specific objectives, determining the tasks that must be performed to achieve these objectives, and estimating the costs of performing these tasks. The sum of these costs is the proposed promotion budget.

OEM Original equipment manufacturer. In the OEM contract the customer is called the OEM or 'sourcer' whereas the parts suppliers are called manufacturers of OEM products.

oligopoly A market structure characterised by a small number of sellers who control the market.

omnibus study A regular survey usually operated by a market research specialist company which asks questions of respondents.

open-ended questions Allow respondents to determine the direction of the answer without being led by the question. They also prevent 'yes' or 'no' answers.

opinion leader Person within a reference group, who, because of special skills, knowledge, personality or other characteristics, exerts influence on others.

order point The level of inventory at which re-ordering is advisable to avoid out-of-stocks caused by the leadtime to resupply.

organisational buying behaviour The decision-making activities of organisational buyers that lead to purchases of products.

organisational culture Manifests in (1) the ways the organisation conducts its business, treats its employees, customers and the wider community, (2) the extent to which autonomy and freedom is allowed in decision making, developing new ideas and personal expression, (3) how power and information flow through its hierarchy, and (4) the strength of employee commitment towards collective objectives. It is termed 'strong' or 'weak' to the extent it is diffused through the organisation.

OTS Opportunity to see – total number of people in the target market exposed to at least one ad in a given time period ('reach').

outsourcing Using another firm for the manufacture of needed components or products or delivery of a service.

packaging An auxiliary product component that includes labels, inserts, instructions, graphic design, shipping cartons, and sizes and types of containers.

paradigm A shared way of thinking, or meta-theory that provides a framework for theory.

parallel importing When importers buy products from distributors in one country and sell them in another to distributors who are not part of the manufacturer's normal distribution; caused by big price differences for the same product between different countries.

penetration Entering a new market of customers.

penetration price A low introductory price meant to quickly establish a product in the market.

perceived risk Consumers' uncertainty about the consequences of their purchase decisions; the consumer's perception that a product may not do what it is expected to do.

perceived value The customer's overall evaluation of the product/service offered by a firm compared to a price paid.

percentage of sales Setting the promotion budget at a certain percentage of current or forecasted sales or as a percentage of the unit sales price.

perception The process by which people select, organise and interpret sensory stimulation into a meaningful picture of the world.

personal selling Person-to-person interaction between a buyer and a seller wherein the seller's purpose is to persuade the buyer to accept a point of view, to convince the buyer to take a course of action, or to develop a customer relationship.

point-of-sale displays Includes all signage – posters, signs, shelf cards and a variety of other visual materials – that are designed to influence buying decisions at the point of sale.

portal   A website that acts as a gateway to the information on the Internet by providing search engines, directories and other services such as personalised news or free e-mail.

Porter's diamond   The characteristics of the 'home base' play a central role in explaining the international competitiveness of the firm – the explaining elements consist of factor conditions, demand conditions, related and supporting industries, firm strategy, structure and rivalry, chance and government.

Porter's five forces model   The state of competition and profit potential in an industry depends on five basic competitive forces: new entrants, suppliers, buyers, substitutes and market competitors.

portfolio planning   Managing groups of brands and product lines.

positioning   How a product/service is perceived in the mind of the consumers in relation to other products in the market.

post-testing   In the context of advertising, testing that takes place after an advertisement has been run, to determine whether it has met the objectives set for it by management.

pretesting   Conducting limited trials of a questionnaire or some other aspect of a study to determine its suitability for the planned research project. In the context of advertising, research carried out beforehand on the effectiveness of an advertisement. It begins at the earliest stages of development and continues until the advertisement is ready for use.

price bundling   A strategy whereby the price of a group of products is lower than the total of the individual prices of the components. An example is selling a new car with an 'options package'.

price escalation   The tendency of prices to creep upwards when marketing products and services abroad through several middlemen.

primary data   Data collected for the first time for the specific purpose of a particular market research study.

private brand (or label)   A brand created and owned by a reseller (retailer) of a product or service.

product concept   The end result of the marketing strategist's selection and blending of a product's primary and auxiliary components into a basic idea emphasising a particular set of consumer benefits; also called the product positioning concept.

product lifecycle (PLC)   The course of a product's sales and profits over its lifetime. It involves five distinct stages: product development, introduction, growth, maturity and decline.

product line pricing   Setting the price steps between various products in a product line based on cost differences between the products, customer evaluations of different features, and competitors' prices.

product portfolio   A collection of products balanced as a group. Product portfolio analysis focuses on the interrelationships of products within a product mix. The performance of the mix is emphasised rather than the performance of individual products.

profit-and-loss statement (operating statement, income statement)   A financial statement that shows company sales, cost of goods sold, expenses and profits during a given period of time.

profitability analysis   The calculation of sales revenues and costs for the purpose of calculating the profit performance of products, customers and/or distribution channels.

Profit Impact of Marketing Strategy (PIMS)   An empirical study, which seeks to identify the key factors underlying profitability and strategic success in an industry.

prospect   An individual or organisation that is a possible buyer of a product.

prosumer   A contraction of *pro*ducer and con*sumer*. Prosumers are half consumers and half proactive producers of the value creation.

psychic distance   Refers to the *perceived* degree of similarity or difference between the business partners in two different markets. Psychic distance is operationalised in terms of both cultural and business distance.

psychographics   The characteristics of individuals that describe them in terms of their psychological and behavioural make-up.

pull strategy   Involves a relatively heavy emphasis on consumer-oriented advertising to encourage consumer demand for a new brand and thereby obtain retail distribution. The brand is pulled through the channel system in the sense that there is a backward tug from the consumer to the retailer.

push strategy   A promotional strategy whereby a supplier promotes a product to marketing intermediaries, with the aim of pushing the product through the channel of distribution.

qualitative research   Provides a holistic view of a research problem by integrating a larger number of variables, but asking only a few respondents.

quantitative research   Data analysis based on questionnaires from a large group of respondents.

reach   The number of people exposed to an advertisement carried by a given medium.

red oceans Tough head-to-head competition in mature industries often results in nothing but a bloody red ocean of rivals fighting over a shrinking profit pool. See also *blue oceans*.

reference group A group of people that influences an individual's attitude or behaviour.

referrals Usually obtained by the salesperson asking current customers if they know of someone else, or another company, who might have a need for the salesperson's product.

relationship marketing (RM) The process of creating, maintaining and enhancing strong long-term relationships with customers and other stakeholders through mutual exchange and trust. RM seeks to build a chain of relationships between the firm and its main stakeholders.

relative cost advantage A firm's cost position depends on the configuration of the activities in its value chain versus that of the competitors.

relative market share Comparing your market share with that of your biggest competitor. Having a relative market share of >1 means you are the market leader that outperforms the next biggest by this factor. A relative market share <1 shows how far away you are from being the market leader.

reliability If the same phenomenon is measured repeatedly with the same measurement device and the results are similar then the method is reliable (the 'how' dimension).

repositioning A product strategy that involves changing the product design, formulation, brand image or brand name so as to alter the product's competitive position.

resource-based view (RBV) Inside-out perspective. Proactive quest for markets that allows exploitation of the firm's resources.

retention rate The percentage of customers who continue to purchase from the supplier in a subsequent year. Retention rate = 100% − churn rate (%). If churn rate is 20%, the retention rate is 80%.

return on investment (ROI) A common measure of managerial effectiveness – the ratio of net profit to investment.

reverse auction A type of auction in which sellers bid prices for which they are willing to sell items or services.

reverse marketing The buyer (and not the seller as in traditional marketing) takes the initiative of searching for a supplier that is able to fulfil the buyer's needs.

reverse segmentation The buyer (and not the seller, as in traditional marketing) takes the initiative for searching out a supplier that is able to fulfil the buyer's needs.

royalty The remuneration paid by one firm to another under licensing and franchising agreements.

sampling plan A scheme outlining the group (or groups) to be surveyed in a marketing research study, how many individuals are to be chosen for the survey, and on what basis this choice is made.

scenarios Stories about plausible alternative futures.

screening The stage in new product or market development in which a marketer analyses ideas to determine their appropriateness and reasonableness in relation to the organisation's goals and objectives.

secondary data Data which already exist but were collected in the first instance for another purpose.

selective distribution The use of a limited number of outlets in a geographical area to sell products of a supplier.

share of voice (SOV) The communication expenditures (advertising, PR, sales force, etc.) for the firm's band in percentage of the total communication expenditures for all brands in a product category.

single sourcing Purchasing a product on a regular basis from a single vendor.

situational analysis The interpretation of environmental attributes and changes in light of an organisation's ability to capitalise on potential opportunities.

skimming price A relatively high price, often charged at the beginning of a product's life. The price is systematically lowered as time goes by.

SMEs Small and medium-sized enterprises. In the EU, SMEs are characterised as having 250 employees or less. They comprise approximately 99 per cent of all firms.

social marketing Planning, execution and evaluation of programmes to influence the voluntary behaviour of target audiences in order to improve their personal welfare (e.g. encouraging people to give up smoking).

social responsibility The collection of marketing philosophies, policies, procedures and actions intended primarily to enhance society's welfare.

socialisation process The process by which a society transmits its values, norms and roles to its members.

societal objectives Organisational philosophy that stresses the importance of considering the collective needs of society as well as individual consumers' desires and organisational profits.

sponsorship A business relationship between a provider of funds, resources or services and an individual, event or organisation which offers in return some rights and association that may be used for commercial advantage.

stakeholders Individuals or groups having a stake in the organisation's well-being, e.g. shareholders, employees.

standardised concept The approach to international marketing in which the 4 Ps are marketed with little or no modification.

star   A high market share product in a high-growth market.

STP-approach   Principle of segmentation, targeting and positioning in order to select a distinct group of consumers who require a special marketing mix.

straight commission   Remuneration based strictly on sales performance.

straight rebuy   A type of organisational buying characterised by automatic and regular purchases of familiar products from regular suppliers.

straight salary   Compensation at a regular rate, not immediately tied to sales performance.

strategic alliances   Informal or formal arrangements between two or more companies with a common business objective.

strategic business unit (SBU)   A unit of the company that has a separate mission, strategy and objectives and that can be planned independently from other company businesses. An SBU can be a company division, a product line within a division, or sometimes a single product or brand.

subculture   A group within a dominant culture that is distinct from the culture. Members of a subculture typically display some values or norms that differ from those of the overall culture.

subsidiary   A company which is owned by another.

supply chain management   How products are moved from the producer to the ultimate consumer with a view to achieving the most effective and efficient delivery system.

switching costs   The costs to a buying organisation of changing from one supplier to another.

tacit knowledge   Consists of things customers know, but which are difficult or nearly impossible to articulate. This intuitive information, while frequently critical to product success in the marketplace, is the most difficult to provide to the NPD team during product development.

tariff   A tax levied by a government against certain imported products. Tariffs are designed to raise revenue or to protect domestic firms.

team selling   Using teams of people from sales, marketing, engineering, finance, technical support and even upper management to service large, complex accounts.

telemarketing   Using the telephone as the primary means of communicating with prospective customers. Telemarketers often use computers for order taking.

test marketing   The stage of new product development where the product and marketing programme are tested in realistic market settings, such as a well-defined geographic area.

testimonial   A type of advertising in which a person, usually a well-known or public figure, states that he or she owns, uses or supports the product being advertised.

third-party logistics provider   An independent logistics provider that performs any or all of the functions required to get its client's product to market.

time-based competition   Competition based on providing time utility by delivering a product when the consumer wants it.

time to market   The time it takes for a company to develop a new product and turn it into a product which people can buy.

top-down method   A forecasting/planning approach based on objectives and works down to product/market estimates. See also *bottom-up method*.

total cost   Fixed costs plus variable costs.

total quality management (TQM)   Programmes designed to constantly improve the quality of products services and marketing processes.

trade marketing   Marketing to the retail trade.

trade-off   Balancing of two different options. If you have chosen a certain option, with certain advantages you also have to live with some disadvantages.

trade show   A meeting or convention of members of a particular industry where business-to-business contacts are routinely made.

transaction   A trade of values between two parties.

transaction costs   The total of all costs incurred by a buyer and seller as they gather information and negotiate a transaction.

transactional marketing (TM)   The major focus of the marketing programme (the 4 Ps) is to make customers buy. Independence among marketing actors ('arm's length') is considered vital for marketing efficiency.

undifferentiated marketing   A marketing effort not targeted at a specific market segment, but designed to appeal to a broad range of customers. The approach is appropriate in a market that lacks diversity of interest.

unique selling proposition (USP)   A unique characteristic of a product or brand identified by the marketer as the one on which to base a promotional campaign. It is often used in a product-differentiation approach to promotion.

up-selling   A sales technique whereby a salesperson attempts to have the customer purchase more expensive items, upgrades or other add-ons in an attempt to make a more profitable sale.

user   The buying-centre role played by the organisational member who will actually use the product.

validity   If the measurement method measures what it is supposed to measure, then it has high validity (the 'what' dimension). There are three types of validity: construct, internal and external.

value chain Chain of activities by which a company brings in materials, creates a good or service, markets it and provides service after a sale is made. Each step creates more value for the consumer.

value chain based view (VBV) Building sustainable competitive advantages based on the firm's positioning in the value chain.

value innovation A strategic approach to business growth involving a shift away from a focus on the existing competition to one of trying to create entirely new markets. Value innovation can be achieved by implementing a focus on innovation and creation of new marketspace.

value network The formation of several firms' value chains into a network, where each company contributes a small part to the total value chain.

value shop A model for solving problems in a service environment. Similar to workshops. Value is created by mobilising resources and deploying them to solve a specific customer problem.

variability The characteristic of services referring to the fact that services are heterogeneous – that is, the quality of delivered services can vary widely.

variable cost A cost that varies directly with an organisation's production or sales. Variable costs are a function of volume.

vertical integration Seeking control of channel members at different levels of the channel, e.g. the manufacturer's acqution of the distributor (= forward integration).

vertical marketing system A network of vertically aligned establishments that are managed professionally as a centrally administered distribution system.

viral marketing Online word-of-mouth is a marketing technique that seeks to exploit existing social networks to produce exponential increases in brand awareness.

web browser Computer program such as Microsoft Internet Explorer, Mozilla Firefox, Google Chrome and Apple Safari that enables users to view web pages.

wholesaler An organisation or individual that serves as a marketing intermediary by facilitating transfer of products and title to them. Wholesalers do not produce the product, consume it or sell it to ultimate consumers.

world-class brand A product that is widely distributed around the world with a single brand name that is common to all countries and is recognised in all its markets.

World Wide Web A portion of the Internet; a system of Internet servers – computers that support specially formatted documents.

INDEX

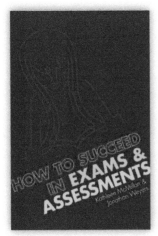